IUS CO

FOR THE CO

CASES, MATERIALS AND TEXT ON

CONSUMER LAW

IUS COMMUNE CASEBOOKS
FOR THE COMMON LAW OF EUROPE

Series General Editor
Walter van Gerven

Cases, Materials and Text on
Consumer Law

General Editors
Hans-W Micklitz, Jules Stuyck and Evelyne Terryn

Coordinating Editor
Dimitri Droshout

Chapter Authors

Jean-Sébastien Borghetti
Sergio Cámara Lapuente
Veerle Colaert
Geraint Howells
Hans-W Micklitz
Elise Poillot
Peter Rott
Jules Stuyck
Evelyne Terryn
Lubos Tichý
Christian Twigg-Flesner
Tom Van Dyck

·HART·
PUBLISHING
OXFORD AND PORTLAND, OREGON
2010

Published in North America (US and Canada) by

Hart Publishing
c/o International Specialized Book Services
920 NE 58th Avenue, Suite 300
Portland, OR 97213-3786
USA
Tel: +1-503-287-3093 or toll-free: (1)-800-944-6190
Fax: +1 503 280 8832
E-mail: orders@isbs.com
Website: www.isbs.com

Hart Publishing, 16C Worcester Place, Oxford, OX1 2JW
Telephone: +44 (0)1865 517530 Fax: +44(0)1865 510710
E-mail: mail@hartpub.co.uk
Website: http://www.hartpub.co.uk

British Library Cataloguing in Publication Data

Data Available

ISBN: 978-1-84113-749-0

Typeset by Forewords, Oxford

Printed and bound in Great Britain by
TJ International Ltd, Padstow

Companion Website

The reader's attention is drawn to a companion website, where additional information about the Ius Commune Casebook series as well as original language versions of and hyperlinks to full text versions of the excerpts reproduced in this casebook are available. The website also allows users to comment on excerpts or upload materials to supplement the Casebook.

www.casebooks.eu/consumerlaw/

IUS COMMUNE CASEBOOKS
FOR THE COMMON LAW OF EUROPE

www.casebooks.eu

JHM van Erp and B Akkermans (eds), *Cases, Materials and Text on National, Supranational and International Property Law* (Oxford, Hart Publishing) (forthcoming)

H Beale, B Fauvarque-Cosson, J Rutgers and S Vogenauer (eds), *Cases, Materials and Text on Contract Law* (2nd revised edition) (Oxford, Hart Publishing) (forthcoming)

HW Micklitz, J Stuyck, E Terryn and D Droshout (eds), *Cases, Materials and Text on Consumer Law* (Oxford, Hart Publishing, 2010)

D Schiek, L Waddington and M Bell (eds), *Cases, Materials and Text on National, Supranational and International Non-Discrimination Law* (Oxford, Hart Publishing, 2007)

J Beatson and E Schrage (eds), *Cases, Materials and Text on Unjustified Enrichment* (Oxford, Hart Publishing, 2003)

H Beale, H Kötz, A Hartkamp and D Tallon (eds), *Cases, Materials and Text on Contract Law* (Oxford, Hart Publishing, 2002)

W van Gerven, P Larouche and J Lever, *Cases, Materials and Text on National, Supranational and International Tort Law* (Oxford, Hart Publishing, 2000)

W van Gerven (ed), *Tort Law – Scope of Protection* (Oxford, Hart Publishing, 1998)

Note to the Reader

This book was written and prepared for publication prior to the entry into force of the Treaty of Lisbon. It retains the classic numbering of the provisions of the Treaty Establishing the European Community (the EC Treaty). Although the Treaty of Lisbon amends and renames the EC Treaty—now the Treaty on the Functioning of the European Union (TFEU)—the legal analysis in this book is not affected in any material way by the entry into force of the new Treaty.

As a matter of terminology, the Treaty amendments now require references to the Community to be read as Union, references to the common market as the internal market and references to the Court of First Instance (CFI) as the General Court.[1]

For the convenience of the reader, a table of equivalence for the provisions discussed or referred to in this book is provided below.[2]

Treaty on the Functioning of the European Union

Old numbering of the Treaty Establishing the European Community	**New numbering of the Treaty on the Functioning of the European Union**
Article 3, paragraph 1 (repealed)[3]	
Article 28	Article 34
Article 29	Article 35
Article 30	Article 36
Article 45	Article 51
Article 46	Article 52
Article 47	Article 53
Article 49	Article 56
Article 55	Article 62
Article 57	Article 64
Article 65	Article 81
Article 66 (replaced)	Article 74
Article 67 (repealed)	

[1] See Art 2(2) of the Treaty of Lisbon amending the Treaty on European Union and the Treaty establishing the European Community, signed at Lisbon, 13 December 2007.

[2] For the complete table of equivalence, see [2008] OJ C 115/361.

[3] Replaced, in substance, by Arts 3–6 TFEU.

Article 81	Article 101
Article 82	Article 102
Article 94 (moved)	Article 115
Article 95 (moved)	Article 114
Article 153,paragraphs 1, 3, 4 and 5	Article 169
Article 153, paragraph 2 (moved)	Article 12
Article 220 (repealed)[4]	
Article 226	Article 258
Article 234	Article 267

4 Replaced, in substance, by Art 19 TEU.

Preface

This book is the fifth volume in the series of *Casebooks on the Common Law of Europe* under the general editorship of Professor Walter van Gerven.

This Casebook fits within the broader objectives of the Ius Commune Casebook Project, which is a joint undertaking of the universities of Leuven (Belgium) and Maastricht (the Netherlands). The Casebook Project fosters co-operation among legal scholars from all over Europe, allowing them to join forces to develop teaching materials for use in comparative law courses. One of its main aims is to enable students across Europe and beyond to discuss the same leading cases and materials.

Like the other books in the series, the present volume follows a bottom-up approach to explore the extent to which, despite differences in approach, concepts and terminology, common principles underlie the laws of the EU Member States on consumer protection. Compared to the other volumes, this Casebook has a rather strong focus on European Community law, since, in consumer law, the *acquis communautaire* is more developed than in many other fields of the law.

This volume therefore contains quite a number of judgments of the European Court of Justice and extracts from directives and regulations. National case-law and legislation are primarily drawn from the English common law, French law and German law. Extracts from other legal families have been included, either because the solutions found were original, or – probably more often – because a legal system was accessible for one of the authors. In this sense, the choice is to a certain extent arbitrary. The authors believe that this is inevitable but hope that they have succeeded in presenting a relevant range of solutions. However, the readers and users of this Casebook are invited to draw the authors' attention to other relevant sources and are welcome to submit suggestions via the accompanying website (www.casebooks.eu/consumerlaw) where they can be made available as part of the digital 'supplement' to the Casebook which will be expanded at regular intervals. Needless to say, this interactive effort should enable us to strike a better balance in the next edition of this Casebook.

Consumer law is not a separate branch of the law *à part entière*. Consumer law is both private law and public law and, following the Casebook on Non-Discrimination Law, this Casebook is the second Casebook in the series also to deal with public law. A number of substantive private law rules discussed in this Casebook might overlap with the casebooks on contract law (eg with regard to the formation of contracts and unfair terms) and tort law (especially in the field of product liability). Nevertheless, this Casebook has its own focus and discusses the grand questions of consumer law, including enforcement questions which are increasingly at the heart of the debate (injunctions, class actions, public enforcement by agencies, etc).

Like its predecessors in the series, the Casebook builds on 'primary' texts, which not only include judgments and legislation, but also soft law and scholarly writings. The extracts are followed by notes and questions. The aim of these is to raise discussion. As Hugh Beale did in his preface to the *Casebook on Contract Law*, we would like to quote Walter van Gerven's foreword to *Tort Law:*

> It is not the intention of this book, or, of the series as a whole, to unify the existing laws of tort or of the other areas of law that are to be covered. That would not be possible, nor would it be desirable. For indeed, the diversity of European legal systems reflects not only a variety of legal cultures—which are bound to converge in step with European integration—but also and perhaps mostly a variety of value judgments or policy choices which find their expression in the legal systems. In their effort to uncover common roots, the authors do not wish to express any preference for the solutions embodied in one or the other legal system, where that would imply endorsing the underlying value judgment over alternative judgments. In the absence of a common European legislature (outside the limited areas for which national competences have been transferred to the European Union), there is indeed no authoritative source, other than national legislation or case law, from which a common understanding as to the fundamental value judgments underlying national law can be derived. Although that should not prevent legal writers from expressing their own personal preferences, we would prefer not to do that, or to do it only exceptionally, in a book like the present one which is intended to inquire into the common core of principles in the national and supranational legal orders existing within the European Union.

Our research for this Casebook confirmed an important finding: while many parts of consumer law are harmonised at the European level, there still remain quite a number of divergences between the laws in the Member States due to a multitude of factors, such as the—recently more or less abandoned—minimum character of the harmonisation, cultural differences, differences in the legal context in which directives have to be implemented, differences in enforcement, etc. Thus, some case-law dating from before the relevant Directives has also been included, especially where these cases addressed questions which may not (yet) have been (properly) tackled by European legislation.

Overall, like the other Casebooks, this volume will show that, irrespective of the differences in legal technicalities of the solution given to a particular problem, in effect the solution is very often the same in the different jurisdictions.

This Casebook goes to press amidst ongoing developments concerning the European Commission's review of the consumer *acquis* and the recent proposal of a consolidated Directive on consumer rights. This proposal, which came just before the manuscript was finalised (August 2009), could only partly be taken into account. Some time before, the Study Group on a European Civil Code and the Acquis Group had published the Draft Common Frame of Reference comprising Principles, Definitions and Model Rules of European Private Law (DCFR). This was another important element for reflection in several of the chapters of this Casebook.

The book is primarily intended for law students in European universities and elsewhere. In some countries, students are already familiar with the Casebook method. In others, it may be different. Be that as it may, we strongly believe that the format of the Casebooks will encourage students to look for the rationale behind the given rule or decision (and the underlying value judgments) and to put the legal rules into context. The comparison between solutions given to a certain problem in different jurisdictions and, as the case may be, in different Community instruments, will certainly improve the students' understanding of the law as it is and will help them to have a creative attitude in their professional careers.

This book is the result of real teamwork, although one or more authors are responsible for the separate chapters. Most of the chapters have been discussed at length during various group meetings in Bamberg, Leuven, Utrecht, London, Edinburg and Florence. These meetings were used to establish a common perspective, but it was decided not to strive for a complete uniformity. The variation between chapters reflects to some extent the different national background of the authors, as well as the varying influence of EC law. Whereas certain aspects of consumer law have been heavily influenced by EC law, such influence is less obvious—for the time being—for other aspects. The structure of certain chapters will therefore only at times come close to the structure of the relevant EC instruments.

These meetings were also used to make difficult decisions on what aspects to include in this Casebook. Some areas of the law mostly concern consumers, but often consumers are not the only ones affected. As this Casebook is in the first place intended as a teaching tool for students, our guiding principle was the likeliness that the materials included would actually be used for that purpose. This Casebook does not claim to be comprehensive, and some chapters should rather be read as a thorough introduction into new fields of law, though always from the perspective of the consumer.

All of the chapters have been reviewed by at least one member of our advisory board. We are very grateful to Ewoud Hondius (University of Utrecht), Norbert Reich (emeritus University of Bremen), Stephen Weatherill (University of Oxford) and Thomas Wilhelmsson (University of Helsinki) for making the time to provide critical comments and to review the final texts of several chapters. It goes without saying that responsibility for any mistakes remains with the authors of the chapters. The main authors for the different chapters are as follows:

- Chapter 1: Setting the Scene: Jules Stuyck (University of Leuven)
- Chapter 2: Trade Practices and Advertising: Hans-Wolfgang Micklitz (European University Institute Florence, University of Bamberg) and Geraint Howells (University of Manchester)
- Chapter 3: Consumer Contract Law: Sergio Cámara Lapuente (University of La Rioja) and Evelyne Terryn (University of Leuven)
- Chapter 4: The Right of Withdrawal and Standard Terms: Peter Rott (University of Bremen) and Evelyne Terryn
- Chapter 5: Sale of Goods: Christian Twigg-Flesner (University of Hull) and Elise Poillot (Université du Luxembourg)
- Chapter 6: Financial Services: Veerle Colaert (University of Leuven) and Tom Van Dyck (University of Leuven)

— Chapter 7: Product Liability: Geraint Howells and Jean-Sébastien Borghetti (Université de Nantes)
— Chapter 8: Litigation, Redress and Enforcement: Hans-Wolfgang Micklitz, Jules Stuyck, Evelyne Terryn and Lubos Tichý (Charles University Prague).

Chapter 1 focuses on the rationale for consumer law and on its actual object: the consumer. It provides an introduction into the main models of consumer law and discusses how consumer interests are affected by European competition policy and the European internal market programme. Chapter 2 deals with unfair commercial practices and advertising, an area recently harmonised by EC law, but the chapter illustrates that national law still has an important role to play. Chapters 3 and 4 treat protection mechanisms in contract law. This includes both general contract law mechanisms (Chapter 3) and more consumer-specific contract law mechanisms such as the right of withdrawal (Chapter 4). Sales contracts are probably one of the most common types of consumer contracts and hence Chapter 5 analyses the main national regimes and the influence of the Consumer Sales Directive. Chapter 6 considers the various methods of consumer protection in the field of financial services, ie credit services, investment services and payment services. The protection of consumers in the field of financial services builds further upon the protection mechanisms that also exist for consumers of general services, but two elements make the protection of consumers in the field of financial services stand out. First, financial services typically involve complicated products and transactions, which are often difficult to understand for the 'average' consumer and have important financial consequences. Second, there is a growing awareness that certain financial products and services enable individuals to participate fully in society and should therefore generally be accessible to everyone. The chapter focuses on those two themes. Chapter 7 discusses the liability of manufacturers and other suppliers for damage caused by their products. As such, product liability is not just a matter of consumer law, as damage caused by products can be inflicted on persons who do not act as consumers at the time of the accident. However, it is the development of a consumer society and the increase in the number of accidents caused by consumer goods, such as cars, pharmaceuticals, beauty products or domestic appliances, which led to the emergence of product liability as a distinct branch of law, and thus, it could not be omitted in this Casebook. Chapter 8 deals with the following simple but crucial question: how can consumers ensure that the rights conferred on them pursuant to the rules described in the preceding chapters are enforced. The chapter gives an overview of the existing mix of individual and collective redress mechanisms based on national and European legislation.

For this Casebook, a wide range of national material needed translation, and we are very conscious of the enormous challenge that translating legal texts involves. Sincere thanks are due to our translators, Philip Nelson, Kai Purnhagen, Rory Steven Brown, Roger and Kristof Terryn and Tessa Jones. The translations were reviewed by the authors of the chapters. The original texts will be made available on the above-mentioned website. Sincere thanks are also due to Anne Looijestijn-Cleary (senior lector at the University of Nijmegen, Netherlands) who has been so kind to check those parts of the manuscript written by non-native speakers, to Dorothy Gruyaert and Martina Oldani who were our student assistants and, finally, to Majo Werrebrouck who supplied logistic support at the Study Centre of Consumer Law of the University of Leuven.

Last but not least, it should be recognized that we would never have come to the end of this project had Dimitri Droshout, with his immense experience in the making of Casebooks, not guided us in a friendly but firm manner along the long and winding road to the finish.

Hans-W Micklitz
Jules Stuyck
Evelyne Terryn

Florence and Leuven, 1 October 2009

Contents

CHAPTER TWO
COMMERCIAL PRACTICES AND ADVERTISING

CHAPTER THREE
CONSUMER CONTRACT LAW

CHAPTER FOUR
RIGHT OF WITHDRAWAL AND STANDARD TERMS

CHAPTER FIVE
SALE OF GOODS

CHAPTER 6
FINANCIAL SERVICES

CHAPTER SEVEN
PRODUCT LIABILITY

CHAPTER EIGHT
LITIGATION, REDRESS AND ENFORCEMENT

Table of Abbreviations

Abs	Absatz (paragraph) (Germany)
AC	Appeal Cases (UK)
ACQP	Acquis Principles
AcP	Archiv für die civilistische Praxis (Germany)
ADR	Alternative Dispute Resolution
ADRs	Alternative Dispute Resolution Schemes
ASA	Advertising Standards Authority (UK)
AEADE	European Association of Law and Equity Arbitration
AFM	Autoriteit Financiële Markten (Financial Markets Authority) (Netherlands)
AG	Amtsgericht (Court of First Instance) (Germany)
AGBG	Gesetz fur Regelung des Rechts der Allgemeinen Geschäftsbedingungen (Standard Terms Act) (Germany)
AGCM	Italian Competition Authority
All ER	All England Reports (UK)
AMF	Autorité des Marchés Financiers (Financial Markets Authority)
App Cas	Law Reports Appeal Cases, House of Lords (UK)
APR	annual percentage rate
Arr Cass	Arresten van het Hof van Cassatie (Court of Cassation cases) (Belgium)
Art	Article
ASA	Advertising Standards Authority
Ass plén	Plenary Assembly (since 1967)
ATS	Austrian Schilling
B&S	Best & Smith's Queen's Bench Reports (UK)
B2B	Business to Business
B2C	Business to Consumer
BGB	Bürgerliches Gesetzbuch (Civil Code) (Germany)
BGB Info-V	Verordnung über Informations- und Nachweispflichten nach bürgerlichem Recht (Regulation on Information Duties Obligations to Produce Supporting Documents according to Civil law) (Germany)
BGBl	Bundesgesetzblatt (Germany)
BGH	Bundesgerichtshof (Germany)
BGHZ	Entscheidungen des Bundesgerichtshofes in Zivilsachen (Cases of the BGH in civil matters) (Germany)
Bull Ch mixte	Bulletin des arrêts de la Cour de cassation, chambre mixte (France), with reference to part of reporter and sequential number of cases

Bull civ	Bulletin des arrêts de la Cour de cassation, chambres civiles (France), with reference to part of reporter and sequential number of cases
Bull crim	Bulletin des arrêts de la Cour de cassation, chambres criminelles (France), with reference to sequential number of case
CAP	Code of Advertising Practice (UK)
Cass	Cour de cassation (France), as the case may be
Ch mixte	Mixed Chambers
civ	Civil Chamber (with chamber number after 1952)
comm	Commercial Chamber
crim	Criminal Chamber
CCC	Contrats Concurrence Consommation (France)
C civ	Code civil (Civil Code) France, Belgium)
CESR	Committee of European Securities Regulators
CFI	Court of First Instance of the Court of Justice of the European Communities
CFR	Common Frame of Reference
Ch	Law Reports, Chancery (UK)
Chron	Chroniques
CIA	Central Intelligence Agency (United States of America)
CISG	United Nations Convention on the International Sale of Goods
CLEF	Consumer Law Enforcement Forum
CML Rev	Common Market Law Review
CO	Consumer Ombudsman
COM	Document of the European Commission
CR	Computer und Recht (Germany)
D	Receuil Dalloz et Sirey (France)
DAR	Deutsches Autorecht (Germany)
DB	Der Betrieb (Germany)
DCCR	Droit de la consommation/Consumentenrecht (Belgium)
DCFR	Draft Common Frame of Reference
DEM	Deutschmark
DG	Directorate General
DKK	Danish Kroner
DP	Recueil Dalloz Périodique (France)
DTI	Department of Trade and Industry
ea	*et alii*
EBLR	European Business Law Review
EBS	Educational Business Service
EC	European Community
ECC-net	European Consumer Centres Network
ECHR	European Convention on Human Rights
ECJ	Court of Justice of the European Communities
ECR	Reports of cases before the Court of Justice of the European Communities and the Court of First Instance

ECtHR	European Court of Human Rights
Ed	editor
Edn	edition
Eds	editors
EEC	European Economic Community
EEJ-net	European Extra-Judicial Network
eg	example given
ELJ	European Law Journal
ELRev	European Law Review
EP	European Parliament
ERCL	European Review of Contract Law
ERPL	European Review of Private Law
EU	European Union
EuZW	Europäische Zeitschrift für Wirtschaftsrecht (Germany)
EWCA	England and Wales Court of Appeal
FernUSG	Fernunterrichtsgesetz (Distance Learning Act) (Germany)
FIN-Net	Network for financial services
FRF	French Franc
FSA	Financial Services Authority (UK)
FSR	Fleet Street Reports (UK)
Gaz Pal	Gazette du Palais (France)
GPR	Zeitschrift für Gemeinschaftsprivatrecht (Germany)
GRUR	Gewerblicher Rechtsschutz und Urheberrecht (Germany)
GWB	Gesetz gegen Wettbewerbsbeschraenkungen (Law on Restraints of Competition), (Germany)
HR	Hoge Raad (Supreme Court) (Netherlands)
HwiG	Haustürwiderrufsgesetz (Doorstep Selling Act)(Germany)
IPO	Initial public offering
ICT	Information and Communication Technology
ICO	Information Commission Office
IIC	International Review of Intellectual Property and Competition Law Review
J Bus Law	Journal of Business Law
JCB	Jurisprudence commercial de Belgique (Belgium)
JCP	Semaine Juridique or Juris-classeur périodique, General Edition (France)
JCP(E)	Juris-classeur périodique, Edition Entreprise (France)
JCP(G)	Juris-classeur périodique, Edition générale (France)
JORF	Journal Officiel de la République française
JTDE	Journal des Tribunaux – Droit Européen
JZ	Juristenzeitung (Germany)
KB	King's Bench (UK)
Kh	Rechtbank van koophandel (Commercial Court)(Belgium)
KO	Consumer Ombudsman (Sweden)
KSL	Konsumentskyddslagen (Consumer Protection Act) (Finland)

KschG	Konsumentenschutzgesetz (Consumer Protection Act) (Austria)
LG	Landesgericht (Court of first instance) (Germany)
LGDCU	Ley general defensa consumidores y usuarios (General Consumer Protection Act)(Spain)
LJ	Lord Justice (UK)
Lloyd's Rep	Lloyd's List Law Reports (UK)
LR	Law Reports (UK)
LQR	Law Quarterly Review (UK)
MB	Moniteur Belge (Belgium)
MDR	Monatschrift für Deutsches Recht (Germany)
MiFID	Markets in Financial Instruments Directive (2004/39/EC)
MMR	MultiMedia und Recht (Germany)
Mod LR	Modern Law Review
NJ	Nederlandse Jurisprudentie (The Netherlands)
NJOZ	Neue Juristische Online- Zeitschrift (Germany)
NjW	Nieuw Juridisch Weekblad (Belgium)
NJW	Neue Juristische Wochenschrift (Germany)
NJW-RR	Neue Juristische Wochenschrift—Rechtsprechungs-Report (Germany)
nyr	not yet reported
NTBR	Kwartaalbericht Nieuw BW (Netherlands)
OBG NW	Ordnungsbehördengesetz Nordrhein-Westfalen (Law governing the North Rhine –Westphalia Police authorities)
OECD	Organisation for Economic Co-operation and Development
OFT	Office of Fair Trading
OGH	Oberster Gerichtshof (Supreme Court) (Austria)
OHIM	Office of Harmonization for the Internal Market
OJ C	Official Journal of the European Communities, Information and Notices
OJ L	Official Journal of the European Communities, Legislation
OLG	Oberlandesgericht (Court of Appeal) (Germany)
OLGR	OLG- Report (Germany)
OUP	Oxford University Press (UK)
Para	Paragraph(s)
Pas	Pasicrisie (Belgium)
PEL	Principles of European Law
PEL S	Principles of European Law, Sales
PECL	Principles of European Contract Law
Prg	Praktijkgids (Netherlands)
ProdHaftG	Gesetz über die Haftung für fehlerhafte Produkte (Product Liability Act) (Germany)
Publ Eur Court HR Series A	Publications of the European Court of Human Rights Series A: Judgements and decisions
QB	Queen's Bench Reports (UK)

QBD	Queen's Bench Division of the High Court (UK)
QC	Queen's Counsel
Rb	Rechtbank van eerste aanleg (Court of first instance) (Belgium)
RCJB	Revue critique de jurisprudence belge (Belgium)
RDC/TBH	Revue de droit commercial belge/Tijdschrift voor Belgisch Handelsrecht (Belgium)
RDC	Revue de droit comptable (France)
RdW	Recht der Wirtschaft (Austria)
RGAR	Revue générale des assurances et des responsabilités (Belgium)
RGZ	Entscheidungen des Reichsgerichtes (Germany)
RIW	Recht der internationalen Wirtschaft (Germany)
RJ	Repertorio de Jurisprudencia Aranzadi (Spain)
RTDciv	Revue trimestrielle de droit civil (France)
RTDcom	Revue trimestrielle de droit commercial (France)
RTR	Road Traffic Reports (UK)
RW	Rechtskundig Weekblad
s	section(s)
SAP	Sentencia de la Audiencia Provincial (Spain)
SEPA	Single Euro Payments Area
SEW	Sociaal-economische wetgeving: tijdschrift voor Europees en economisch recht (Netherlands)
SLT Rep	Scottish Law Times Reports (UK)
SMEs	Small and medium-sized enterprises
STS	Spanish Supreme Court
TBBR	Tijdschrift voor Belgisch Burgerlijk Recht (Belgium)
TDA	Trade Descriptions Act (UK)
TGI	Tribunal de grande instance (France)
TI	Tribunal d'instance (France)
TMA	Tijdschrift voor Milieuaansprakelijkheid (The Netherlands)
TPR	Tijdschrift voor Privaatrecht (Belgium)
TPS	Telephone Practice Service
T Verz	Tijdschrift voor verzekeringen (Belgium)
UCPD	Unfair Commercial Practices Directive (2005/29/EC)
UNHCR	United Nation High Commissioner for Refugees
UWG	Gesetz über unlauteren Wettbewerb (Austrian/German Law on Unfair Competition)
VAT	Value Added Tax
VerbrKrG	Verbraucherkreditgesetz (Consumer Credit Act) (Germany)
VersR	Versicherungsrecht (Germany)
VVG	Versicherungsvertagsgesetz (Insurance Contract Act) (Germany)
VuR	Verbraucher und Recht (Germany)
WfT	Wet Financieel Toezicht (The Netherlands)
WLR	Weekly Law Reports (UK)
WPNR	Weekblad voor privaatrecht, notariaat en registratie (Netherlands)
WRP	Wettbewerb in Recht und Praxis (Germany)

ZAW	Zentralausschuss der Werbewirtschaft (Germany)
ZEuP	Zeitschrift für Europäisches Privatrecht (Germany)
ZIP	Zeitschrift für Wirtschaftsrecht (Germany)
ZVglRWiss	Zeitschrift für vergleichende Rechtswissenschaft

Country Codes

AT	Austria
BE	Belgium
BG	Bulgaria
CH	Switzerland
CZ	Czech Republic
DE	Germany
ES	Spain
EU	European Union
FI	Finland
FR	France
IT	Italy
NL	The Netherlands
SW	Sweden
UK	United Kingdom
US	United States of America

Table of Cases

National Cases

Germany (in chronological order)

European Jurisdiction (in alphabetical order)

Court of First Instance

European Court of Justice

Table of Legislative Instruments and Preparatory Documents

National Instruments/Documents

European Instruments/Documents (in chronological order)

International Instruments (in chronological order)

CHAPTER ONE
SETTING THE SCENE

I. CONSUMER LAW

I.A INTRODUCTION

'Consumer law': does it exist? Obviously. Here is a book on it and it is not the first one. But if it exists, what is it? That question is harder to answer.

Under a simple phenomenological approach consumer law can be described as the body of law protecting consumers—but even then a major problem arises. In many legal systems there is a *summa divisio* between public law and private law. Does consumer law belong to public law or private law? It belongs to both. This Casebook will reveal the existence of public law (including criminal law and administrative law enforcement) and private law tools (including private collective actions) for the protection of consumers. But how far does consumer law stretch? This also raises the question who the consumer is? The private end consumer only? Or the non-professional user in general? Is the consumer only the person who 'consumes'? Or does consumer law also encompass investor protection? These questions will be addressed in this and the following chapters.

But even the initial definition given is problematic: consumer protection? Should markets not take care of the consumer interest, rather than the state? In simplistic terms: on the one hand you have the 'free marketers' who believe in the market (the 'invisible hand' of Adam Smith) and find state intervention inefficient or even counterproductive; on the other you find the 'paternalists' who believe that the, by definition, weak consumer should be protected not only against 'rough traders' but against businesses in general because all of these only look at their own interest which does not coincide with the consumer interest. In between these extremes, some writers accept that some but not all markets may work efficiently, while others accept that some but not all consumers may need protection.

Why do legislatures intervene to protect consumers? Contemporary economists (including behavioural economists) have studied this question. They and scholars in law and economics have also addressed the question whether these interventions are appropriate, efficient, desirable and so on.[1]

A brief and accurate description of the rationale of consumer law can be found in a recent paper by Martijn Hesselink:[2]

> The economic analysis of law has produced a powerful theory of consumer protection. According to this theory the rationale for consumer protection is the existence of market failures. Just as the market may not be working perfectly because of power concentration on the supply side (which can be remedied by competition law), there may also be market failures as a result of lack of information on the demand-side, which can be remedied by consumer law, in particular pre-contractual information duties. In addition to this neo-classical analysis, more recently behavioural law & economics has added, as an additional failure, the limited rationality of consumers (ie when fully informed consumers do not always take the decisions that are in their own best interest) which may justify further-reaching intervention by the legislator.
>
> Much of the Community's consumer contract law seems to be inspired, or at least can be explained, by this economic rationale. The question is whether this rationale merely justifies the protection of consumers. [references omitted]

In the introduction to their book *Consumer Protection Law*, Geraint Howells and Stephen Weatherill write:[3]

> The Law of the market economy has a wide scope. It covers law which sustains, promotes, curtails and adjusts the structure of a free market. In many cases it is based on political perceptions of the nature of the market economy. Within an overall political acceptance of the desirability of a market economy, there are many nuances of approach towards the way that market should be permitted to operate, with law used to achieve such adjustments. However, an accumulation of legal rules introduced by governments of different political complexions in the UK over many years has left the law of the economy in a patchwork state.

These observations on the UK seem largely to apply to most if not all EU Member States, although it must be conceded that the overall political perception of the desirability of a market economy may be less pronounced in many Member States than in the UK.

The reasons why the state, including the European Union, intervenes for the protection of consumers are generally described as the lack of equilibrium between producers and consumers, especially in the field of information. The consumer is

[1] On the reasons for consumer law and policy and the different approaches to regulation of the price, quality and terms of consumer products and services, see I Ramsay, *Consumer Law and Policy. Texts and Materials on Regulating Consumer Markets*, 2nd edn (Oxford/Portland, Hart Publishing, 2007).

[2] M Hesselink, 'SMEs in European Contract Law' in K Boele-Woelki and W Grosheide (eds), *The Future of European Contract Law, Essays in honour of Ewoud Hondius* (Alphen aan den Rijn, Kluwer, 2007) 359.

[3] G Howells and S Weatherill, *Consumer Protection Law* (Aldershot, Ashgate, 2005).

often seen as the weaker party. Some consumers are seen as particularly vulnerable and in need of specific protection. Very often the question arises whether the need to protect some consumers justifies measures that protect all consumers (including those who do not need it but do not suffer from it).

Today consumer interests in Europe are greatly affected by competition policy (at the EU level) and the internal market programme, through harmonisation of national consumer laws. The 'consumer acquis' (the body of EC legislation in the consumer field) is becoming impressive and is presently the subject of a general review by the European institutions.

In the introductory part of this chapter the next subsection will be devoted to the consumer and competition policy and a last subsection to harmonisation of consumer laws and the review of the consumer acquis.

In the debate on European contract law (and the common frame of reference)[4] the review of the consumer acquis plays an important role. While consumer contract law is an important component of this Casebook, contract law issues will only be dealt with in this casebook to the extent that they are specific for business-to-consumer (B2C) relations. Nevertheless a certain overlap with the *Ius Commune Casebook on Contract Law* is inevitable.

I.B THE CONSUMER AND COMPETITION LAW

Articles 81 and 82 EC (prohibition of collusion and abuses of a dominant position) undoubtedly serve the consumer interest. However, normally the consumer interest in the application of these provisions is left inexplicit. Consumers can be seen as the ultimate beneficiaries of effective competition, even in case where their interests are not represented or even mentioned.[5]

Consumer protection can also justify arrangements which, according to competition law orthodoxy, are prima facie illegal.

[4] See Communication from the Commission to the European Parliament and the Council 'European contract law and the review of the acquis: the way forward' COM [2004] 651 and recently C von Bar, E Clive and H Schulte-Nölke (eds), *Draft Common Frame of Reference (DCRF) 'Principles, Definitions and Model Rules of European Private Law'* (München, Sellier, 2008), prepared by the Study Group on a European Civil Code and the Research Group of EC Private Law (Acquis Group).

[5] See J Stuyck, 'EC Competition Law after Modernisation: More than Ever in the Interest of Consumers' (2005) *Journal of Consumer Policy* 1; S Weatherill, 'The Links between Competition Policy and Consumer Protection' in G Howells, A Nordhausen, D Parry and C Twigg-Flesner (eds), *The Yearbook of Consumer Law 2007* (Aldershot, Ashgate, 2007) 193.

ECJ Joined Cases C-94/04 and C-202/04, 5 December 2006[6] **1.1 (EU)**
Federico Cipolla v Rosaria Fazari et al

RESTRICTIONS OF PRICE COMPETITION JUSTIFIED IN THE INTEREST OF CONSUMERS

Italian lawyers' fees

Restrictions of price competition between lawyers can be justified in the interest of consumers.

Facts: An Italian law provides that the criteria for determining lawyers fees will be set by the Consiglio Nazionale Forense (CNF, the National Lawyers' Council) established under the auspices of the Minister of Justice and composed of lawyers elected by their fellow members, with one representative for each appeal court district. The CNF sets the fees for two years. When the CNF has decided upon the scale of lawyers' fees, such fees must be approved under Italian legislation by the Minister of Justice. Parties are generally not allowed to derogate from the scale. Mr Cipolla, an Italian lawyer was instructed by three private clients to bring an action against a municipality in an expropriation matter. The clients contested his fees. The Corte d'appello di Torino referred preliminary questions to the ECJ on the compatibility of the Italian regime for lawyers fees with the EC competition rules and the rules on the free provision of services.

Judgment: 61. ... such a prohibition may be justified where it serves overriding requirements relating to the public interest, is suitable for securing the attainment of the objective which it pursues and does not go beyond what is necessary in order to attain it (see, inter alia, Case C-398/95 *SETTG* [1997] ECR I-3091, paragraph 21, and *Servizi Ausiliari Dottori Commercialisti*, paragraph 37). ...

64. In that respect, it must be pointed out that, first, the protection of consumers, in particular recipients of the legal services provided by persons concerned in the administration of justice and, secondly, the safeguarding of the proper administration of justice, are objectives to be included among those which may be regarded as overriding requirements relating to the public interest capable of justifying a restriction on freedom to provide services (see, to that effect, Case C-3/95 Reisebüro Broede [1996] ECR I-6511, paragraph 31, and the case-law cited, and Case C-124/97 Läärä and Others [1999] ECR I-6067, paragraph 33), on condition, first, that the national measure at issue in the main proceedings is suitable for securing the attainment of the objective pursued and, secondly, it does not go beyond what is necessary in order to attain that objective. ...

67. Although it is true that a scale imposing minimum fees cannot prevent members of the profession from offering services of mediocre quality, it is conceivable that such a scale does serve to prevent lawyers, in a context such as that of the Italian market which, as indicated in the decision making the reference, is characterised by an extremely large number of lawyers who are enrolled and practising, from being encouraged to compete against each other by possibly offering services at a discount, with the risk of deterioration in the quality of the services provided.

68. Account must also be taken of the specific features both of the market in question, as noted in the preceding paragraph, and the services in question and, in particular, of the fact that, in the field of lawyers' services, there is usually an asymmetry of information between 'client-consumers' and lawyers. Lawyers display a high level of technical knowledge which consumers may not have and the latter therefore find it difficult to judge the quality of the services provided to them (see, in particular, the

[6] [2006] ECR I-11421.

Report on Competition in Professional Services in Communication from the Commission of 9 February 2004 (COM(2004)83 final, p 10)).

69. However, the national court will have to determine whether professional rules in respect of lawyers, in particular rules relating to organisation, qualifications, professional ethics, supervision and liability, suffice in themselves to attain the objectives of the protection of consumers and the proper administration of justice.

Notes

(1) The judgment is not innovative in that it finds the competition rules not applicable. The judgment follows the earlier judgment in *Arduino*[7] and a whole line of cases: where a tariff is actually fixed by the state and not by a professional body Article 81 EC (restrictive practices by undertakings) does not apply.

(2) In a case where a professional body of lawyers, the Dutch Bar Council, had taken a decision falling within the scope of Article 81 EC, the *Wouters* case,[8] the Court ruled that not every agreement between undertakings or every decision of an association of undertakings which restricts the freedom of action of the parties or of one of them necessarily falls within the prohibition laid down in Article 81(1) EC. Account must be taken of its objectives, which are here connected with the need to make rules relating to organisation, qualifications, professional ethics, supervision and liability, in order to ensure that the ultimate consumers of legal services and the sound administration of justice are provided with the necessary guarantees in relation to integrity and experience. It has then to be considered whether the consequential effects restrictive of competition are inherent in the pursuit of those objectives. This approach by the Court deviates from its mainstream case-law, because it takes into account the interest of consumers in determining whether Article 81(1) EC applies in the first place, while the consumer interest is mentioned in Article 81(3) EC, meaning that generally a restrictive practice even when it serves the consumer interest, will be caught by Article 81(1) EC, but the prohibition of Article 81(1) EC will be declared inapplicable if the practice fulfils the conditions of Article 81(3) EC (efficiency, a fair share of the resulting benefit is passed to consumers, proportionality and no elimination of competition). *Wouters* has been seen as the application of a 'rule of reason' in EC competition law.

(3) What is new in *Cipolla* is that, while denying applicability of Article 81 EC, the ECJ examines an arrangement on lawyers' fees under Article 49 EC (free provision of services), and recalls that the protection of consumers, in particular recipients of the legal services, and the safeguarding of the proper administration of justice, are objectives to be included among those which may be regarded as overriding requirements relating to the public interest capable of justifying a restriction on freedom to provide services (following a well-established 'rule of reason' as regards the free provision of services).

(4) Somewhat surprisingly the ECJ accepts, as a matter of principle, the collective fixing (by the authorities) of lawyers' fees. Indeed minimum prices or fees

[7] Case C-35/99 [2002] ECR I-1529.
[8] Case C-309/99 [2002] ECR I-1577.

within a trade or profession are the prototype of anticompetitive arrangements (see for a recent example Commission Decision, 23 June 2004, *Belgian Architects*, OJ L 2005, 4/10; the Commission condemned the recommendation by the national council of Belgian architects of minimum fees for architects). This decision rests on the conviction that the consumer is deemed to be better off if there is price competition (between members of a liberal profession). In *Cipolla* the Court considers that although it is true that a scale imposing minimum fees cannot prevent members of the profession from offering services of mediocre quality, it is conceivable that such a scale does serve to prevent lawyers, in a context such as that of the Italian market which, as indicated in the decision making the reference, is characterised by an extremely large number of lawyers who are enrolled and practising, from being encouraged to compete against each other by possibly offering services at a discount, with the risk of deterioration in the quality of the services provided.

(5) The Court also stresses that in the field of lawyers' fees there is usually an asymmetry of information between 'client-consumers' and lawyers.

(6) The question thus arises whether the legal profession is so different from other economic activities that consumers need to be protected against the dangers of excessive competition on prices and whether imposing minimum fees is an efficient tool to avoid harmful competition leading to mediocre quality.

(7) In this respect it can first be remembered that the information asymmetry that is typical for the B2C relationship is probably even bigger in sectors such as those of the liberal professions by reason of the sophisticated nature of the service and the fact that most consumers do not regularly buy such services.

(8) Moreover recent empirical studies (eg concerning notaries in the Netherlands) have shown that liberalisation of fees for liberal professions can lead to higher prices.[9]

(9) Finally the judgment can be understood in the light of the ongoing debate about the relationship between quality and the regulation of professions and prices and the kind of competition that best serves the consumer interest. Nevertheless it seems at variance with the orthodoxy of competition law as it has been developed so far. The Commission has always held (see also the Belgian Architects case mentioned above) that minimum price fixing is not in the public interest and the Community Courts have never censured that point of view. It is still to be seen whether the Court will accept minimum price fixing for other goods or services than legal services.

[9] Y Montangie and R Van den Bergh, 'Competition in Professional Services Markets: Are Latin Notaries Different?' (2005) 2 *Siena Memos and Papers on Law and Economics* 189–214.

ECJ Joined Cases C-295/04 to 298/04, 13 July 2006[10] **1.2 (EU)**
Manfredi et al v Lloyd Adriatico et al

REMEDIES FOR CONSUMERS WHO ARE THE VICTIMS OF COMPETITION INFRINGEMENTS

Fixed Italian insurance premiums

Consumers can claim damages for loss caused to them by a contract or by conduct liable to restrict or distort competition.

Facts: In a decision of 8 July 2000 the Autoritá garante per la concorrenza e del mercato (AGCM, the Italian Competition Authority) declared that Italian insurance companies had implemented an unlawful agreement for the purpose of exchanging information in the insurance sector. That agreement enabled those undertakings to coordinate and fix the prices of civil liability motor insurance premiums so as to charge users large increases in premiums which were not justified by market conditions and which they could not escape. The decision was finally upheld by the Consiglio di Stato (Council of State). Manfredi and others brought their respective actions before the giudice di pace di Bitonto (Judge of the Peace of Bitonto) to obtain damages against each insurance company concerned for the increase in the cost of premiums paid by reason of the agreement declared unlawful by the AGCM. The giudice di pace raised preliminary questions before the ECJ. The main (third) question was whether Article 81 EC (prohibiting restrictive agreements) has to be interpreted as meaning that it entitles third parties who have a relevant legal interest to rely on the invalidity of an agreement or practice prohibited by that Community provision and claim damages for the harm suffered. In its fourth question the referring judge asked whether Article 81 EC is to be interpreted as meaning that for the purposes of the limitation period for bringing an action for damages based thereon, time begins to run from the day on which the agreement or concerted practice was adopted or the day on which the agreement or concerted practice came to an end.

Judgment: 90. As was pointed out in paragraph 60 of this judgment, the full effectiveness of Article 81 EC and, in particular, the practical effect of the prohibition laid down in Article 81(1) EC would be put at risk if it were not open to any individual to claim damages for loss caused to him by a contract or by conduct liable to restrict or distort competition.

91. Indeed, the existence of such a right strengthens the working of the Community competition rules and discourages agreements or practices, frequently covert, which are liable to restrict or distort competition. From that point of view, actions for damages before the national courts can make a significant contribution to the maintenance of effective competition in the Community (*Courage and Crehan*, cited above, paragraph 27). ...

94. However, it is settled case-law that Community law does not prevent national courts from taking steps to ensure that the protection of the rights guaranteed by Community law does not entail the unjust enrichment of those who enjoy them (see, in particular, Case 238/78 *Ireks-Arkady v Council and Commission* [1979] ECR 2955, paragraph 14, Joined Cases C-441/98 and C-442/98 *Micha Vlidis* [2000] ECR I-7145, paragraph 31, and *Courage and Crehan*, cited above, paragraph 30).

95. Secondly, it follows from the principle of effectiveness and the right of any individual to seek compensation for loss caused by a contract or by conduct liable to restrict or distort competition that injured persons must be able to seek compensation not only for actual loss (damnum emergens) but also for loss of profit (lucrum cessans) plus interest.

[10] [2006] ECR I-6619.

96. Total exclusion of loss of profit as a head of damage for which compensation may be awarded cannot be accepted in the case of a breach of Community law since, especially in the context of economic or commercial litigation, such a total exclusion of loss of profit would be such as to make reparation of damage practically impossible (see *Brasserie du pêcheur and Factortame*, cited above, paragraph 87, and Joined Cases C-397/98 and C-410/98 *Metallgesellschaft and Others* [2001] ECR I-1727, paragraph 91).

97. As to the payment of interest, the Court pointed out in paragraph 31 of Case C-271/91 *Marshall* [1993] ECR I-4367 that an award made in accordance with the applicable national rules constitutes an essential component of compensation.

98. It follows that the answer to the fourth question in Cases C-295/04 to C-297/04 and the fifth question in Case C-298/04 must be that, in the absence of Community rules governing that field, it is for the domestic legal system of each Member State to set the criteria for determining the extent of the damages for harm caused by an agreement or practice prohibited under Article 81 EC, provided that the principles of equivalence and effectiveness are observed.

99. Therefore, first, in accordance with the principle of equivalence, if it is possible to award specific damages, such as exemplary or punitive damages, in domestic actions similar to actions founded on the Community competition rules, it must also be possible to award such damages in actions founded on Community rules. However, Community law does not prevent national courts from taking steps to ensure that the protection of the rights guaranteed by Community law does not entail the unjust enrichment of those who enjoy them.

100. Secondly, it follows from the principle of effectiveness and the right of individuals to seek compensation for loss caused by a contract or by conduct liable to restrict or distort competition that injured persons must be able to seek compensation not only for actual loss (damnum emergens) but also for loss of profit (lucrum cessans) plus interest.

Notes

(1) In *Courage* (Case C-453/99, *Courage Ltd v Bernard Crehan and Bernard Crehan v Courage Ltd et al*)[11] the European Court of Justice (ECJ) recognised that any individual—including a party to a restrictive contract—can claim compensation for loss caused by a violation of Article 81 or 82 EC. The *Courage* judgment builds on the *Francovich* case-law on state liability for violations of Community law (Joined Cases C-6/90 and C-9/90, *Francovich et al* [1991] ECR I-5357). *Courage* does not expressly state that the right, for an individual, to claim damages in case of antitrust violations has a Community law basis. Be that as it may, the right is also vested in an individual who suffers from an antitrust violation by the conclusion of a contract to which he or she is a party. The ECJ rejected a limitation that existed in that regard under English contract law. In *Courage* the ECJ also recalled the procedural autonomy of the Member States, ie the right to lay down the procedural rules for bringing such actions, subject to the respect of the principles of equivalence (ie these rules should not be less favourable than those governing similar domestic actions) and effectiveness (ie these rules should not render impossible or excessively difficult the

[11] [2001] ECR I-6297.

exercise of the rights conferred by Community law) as well as the right for Member States not to allow unjust enrichment and the right to deny a party who has significant responsibility for the distortion of competition the right to obtain damages from the other contracting party. *Courage* gave little guidance as to the nature of the loss in the case of competition infringements and the problem of causation.[12]

(2) *Manfredi* clarifies that it follows from the principle of effectiveness and the right of individuals to seek compensation for loss caused by a contract or by conduct liable to restrict or distort competition that injured persons must be able to seek compensation not only for actual loss (*damnum emergens*) but also for loss of profit (*lucrum cessans*) plus interest. For consumers the right to damages in the case of violations of Articles 81–82 EC opens important perspectives. The consumer will often be the last link in the chain of damage and will effectively suffer prejudice without being able to pass it on someone else. On the other hand the prejudice of an individual consumer will often be very low (eg a price cartel that has led to a small price increase) and hence does not justify an individual legal action. In this respect class actions or other forms of group actions may offer a solution (see chapter 8 below).

Since the *Courage* judgment, the European Commission, DG Competition, has strongly advocated the necessity of improving private enforcement of antitrust law. In December 2005 the Commission published its Green Paper and Commission Staff Working Document on Damages Actions for Breach of the EC antitrust rules.[13] Following the comments made on the Green Paper, the Commission published a White Paper in the spring of 2008.

White Paper on Damage Actions for Breach of EC Antitrust Rules[14] **1.3 (EU)**

With respect to *collective redress*, the Commission considers that there is a clear need for mechanisms allowing aggregation of the individual claims of victims of antitrust infringements. Individual consumers, but also small businesses, especially those who have suffered *scattered and relatively low-value damage*, are often deterred from bringing an individual action for damages by the costs, delays, uncertainties, risks and burdens involved.

As a result, many of these victims currently *remain uncompensated*. On the rare occasions where a multitude of individual actions are brought in relation to the same infringement, *procedural inefficiencies* arise, for claimants, defendants and the judicial system alike.

The Commission therefore suggests a combination of two complementary mechanisms of collective redress to address effectively those issues in the field of antitrust:

—*representative actions*, which are brought *by qualified entities*, such as consumer associations, state bodies or trade associations, on behalf of identified or, in rather

[12] See J Stuyck, annotation of *Courage* in (2005) ERCL 235–37.
[13] COM [2005] 672.
[14] COM [2008] 165 final.

restricted cases, identifiable victims. These entities are either (i) officially designated in advance or (ii) certified on an *ad hoc* basis by a Member State for a particular antitrust infringement to bring an action on behalf of some or all of their members; and

—*opt-in collective actions*, in which victims *expressly decide* to combine their individual claims for harm they have suffered into one single action. ...

Difficulties also arise, on the other hand, if an *indirect purchaser* invokes the passing-on of overcharges as a basis *to show the harm suffered*. Purchasers at, or near the end of the distribution chain are often those most harmed by antitrust infringements, but given their *distance from the infringement* they find it particularly difficult to produce sufficient proof of the existence and extent of passing-on of the illegal overcharge along the distribution chain. If such claimants are unable to produce this proof, they will *not be compensated* and the infringer, who may have successfully used the passing-on defence against another claimant upstream, would retain an *unjust enrichment*. [Footnote omitted]

To avoid such scenario, the Commission therefore proposes to lighten the victim's burden and suggests that:

—indirect purchasers should be able to rely on the rebuttable presumption that the illegal overcharge was passed on to them in its entirety.

In the case of joint, parallel or consecutive actions brought by purchasers at different points in the distribution chain, national courts are encouraged to make full use of all mechanisms at their disposal under national, Community and international law in order to avoid under- and over-compensation of the harm caused by an infringement of competition law. [emphasis added]

I.C THE CONSUMER IN THE INTERNAL MARKET

ECJ Case C-470/93, 6 July 1995[15] **1.4 (EU)**
Verein gegen Unwesen in Handel und Gewerbe v Mars

THE CIRCUMSPECT AND WELL-INFORMED CONSUMER

+10% Mars ice-cream

The consumer in the internal market is reasonably circumspect.

Facts: Mars imported ice-cream bars from France where they were lawfully produced and packaged by an undertaking belonging to the US group, Mars Inc, Mc Lean, in a uniform presentation for distribution throughout Europe. The ice-cream bars were presented in wrappers marked '+10 per cent'. That presentation had been chosen as part of a short publicity campaign covering the whole of Europe during which the quantity of each product was increased by 10 per cent. The Verein gegen Unwesen in Handel und Gewerbe Köln eV (a trade association whose aim is to combat acts of unfair competition) brought an action in the Landgericht Köln (the district court of Cologne) against Mars and its German subsidiary Mars GmbH (hereafter 'Mars') contending that the campaign is misleading and thus violates paragraph 3 of the Unfair Competition Act (UWG). It contended first of all that the consumer is bound to assume that the advantage indicated by the '+10 per cent' marking is granted without any price increase, since a product whose composition is only slightly changed and which is sold at a higher price offers no advantage. So, in order not to mislead the consumer, the retailer should maintain the final price previously charged. Secondly, the plaintiff contended that the way in which the '+10 per cent' marking was incorporated in the presen-

[15] [1995] ECR I-1923.

tation gave the consumer the impression that the product had been increased by a quantity corresponding to the coloured part of the new wrapping. The coloured part occupied considerably more than 10 per cent of the total surface area of the wrapping and this, in the plaintiff's view, was misleading. The district court decided to refer the following question to the Court:

'Is it compatible with the principles of the free movement of goods to prohibit the marketing in a Member State of ice-cream snacks in a particular presentation which are produced in another Member State and lawfully marketed there in that same presentation, which is described in the application, (1) on the ground that the (new) presentation is liable to give consumers the impression that the goods are offered for the same price as under the old presentation, (2) on the ground that the visual presentation of the new feature '+ 10 per cent ice-cream' gives consumers the impression that either the volume or the weight of the product has been considerably increased?'

Judgment: 12. According to the case-law of the Court, Article [28] is designed to prohibit any trading rules of Member States which are capable of hindering, directly or indirectly, actually or potentially, intra-Community trade (see the judgment in Case 8/74 *Procureur du Roi v Dassonville* [1974] ECR 837, paragraph 5). The Court has held that, in the absence of harmonization of legislation, obstacles to the free movement of goods that are the consequence of applying, to goods coming from other Member States where they are lawfully manufactured and marketed, rules that lay down requirements to be met by such goods, such as those relating, for example, to their presentation, labelling and packaging, are prohibited by Article [28] even if those rules apply without distinction to national products and to imported products (judgment in Joined Cases C-267/91 and C-268/91 *Keck and Mithouard* [1993] ECR I-6097, paragraph 15).

13. Although it applies to all products without distinction, a prohibition such as that in question in the main proceedings, which relates to the marketing in a Member State of products bearing the same publicity markings as those lawfully used in other Member States, is by nature such to hinder intra-Community trade. It may compel the importer to adjust the presentation of his products according to the place where they are to be marketed and consequently to incur additional packaging and advertising costs.

14. Such a prohibition therefore falls within the scope of Article [28 EC].

The grounds of justification relied on

15. It is settled law that obstacles to intra-Community trade resulting from disparities between provisions of national law must be accepted in so far as such provisions may be justified as being necessary in order to satisfy overriding requirements relating, inter alia, to consumer protection and fair trading. However, in order to be permissible, such provisions must be proportionate to the objective pursued and that objective must be incapable of being achieved by measures which are less restrictive of intra-Community trade (see the judgments in Case 120/78 *Rewe-Zentral* [1979] ECR 649; Case C-238/89 *Pall* [1990] ECR I-4827, paragraph 12; and Case C-126/91 *Yves Rocher* [1993] ECR I-2361, paragraph 12).

16. It is contended in the main proceedings that the prohibition is justified on two legal grounds, which are indicated in the first and second parts of the preliminary question.

The consumer's expectation that the price previously charged is being maintained

17. It is argued that the '+10 per cent' marking may lead the consumer to think that the 'new' product is being offered at a price identical to that at which the 'old' product was sold.

18. As the Advocate General points out in Paragraphs 39 to 42 of his Opinion, on the assumption that the consumer expects the price to remain the same, the referring court considers that the consumer could be the victim of deception within the meaning of

Paragraph 3 of the UWG and that if the price did not increase the offer would meet the consumer's expectation but then a question would arise concerning the application of Paragraph 15 of the GWB, which prohibits manufacturers from imposing prices on retailers.

19. As regards the first possibility, it must be observed first of all that Mars has not actually profited from the promotional campaign in order to increase its sale prices and that there is no evidence that retailers have themselves increased their prices. In any case, the mere possibility that importers and retailers might increase the price of the goods and that consequently consumers may be deceived is not sufficient to justify a general prohibition which may hinder intra-Community trade. That fact does not prevent the Member States from taking action, by appropriate measures, against duly proved actions which have the effect of misleading consumers.

20. As regards the second possibility, the principle of freedom of retail trade in the matter of the fixing of prices, provided for by a system of national law, and intended in particular to guarantee the consumer genuine price competition, may not justify an obstacle to intra-Community trade such as that in question in the main proceedings. The constraint imposed on the retailer not to increase his prices is in fact favourable to the consumer. It does not arise from any contractual stipulation and has the effect of protecting the consumer from being misled in any way. It does not prevent retailers from continuing to charge different prices and applies only during the short duration of the publicity campaign in question.

The visual presentation of the '+10 per cent' marking and its alleged misleading effect

21. It is accepted by all the parties that the '+10 per cent' marking is accurate in itself.

22. However, it is contended that the measure in question is justified because a not insignificant number of consumers will be induced into believing, by the band bearing the '+10 per cent' marking, which occupies more than 10 per cent of the total surface area of the wrapping, that the increase is larger than that represented.

23. Such a justification cannot be accepted.

24. Reasonably circumspect consumers may be deemed to know that there is not necessarily a link between the size of publicity markings relating to an increase in a product's quantity and the size of that increase.

Notes

(1) It is well established case-law of the ECJ that Article 28 EC (the prohibition of quantitative import restrictions and measures having equivalent effect) prohibits national measures that affect the importation of goods from other Member States unless—in the absence of harmonisation—these measures can be justified, either on the basis of Article 30 EC (which contains a limited list of grounds of justification, including the protection of health and the protection of intellectual property) or—provided that they apply equally to domestic goods and goods imported from other Member States—on another ground of general interest recognised by Community law (the so called 'rule of reason'). The protection of the economic interests of consumers is one of the major grounds of justification under the rule of reason (see in particular *Cassis de Dijon* referred to in paragraph 15 of the annotated judgment). Measures can only be justified under Article 30 EC or the rule of reason if they are appropriate to attain the goal (of consumer protection) pursued and

proportionate to that goal. While the test of Article 28 EC was originally applied to 'all trading rules' (*Dassonville*, see paragraph 12 of the annotated judgment), in *Keck* (see ibid), the ECJ held that national rules that do not apply to goods as such, for example, to their presentation, labelling and packaging, but merely to 'selling arrangements', ie circumstances in which the goods are offered (eg sales promotion, advertising, distribution channels, shop opening hours etc) are not caught by Article 28 EC, so long as those provisions apply to all relevant traders operating within the national territory and so long as they affect in the same manner, in law and in fact, the marketing of domestic products and of those from other Member States. Provided that those conditions are fulfilled, the application of such rules to the sale of products from another Member State meeting the requirements laid down by that Member State is not by nature such as to prevent their access to the market or to impede access any more than it impedes the access of domestic products (paragraphs 16 and 17 of *Keck*).

More recently the Court has somewhat reformulated its Article 28 case-law in *Mickelsson*[16] in the following words:

> It must be borne in mind that measures taken by a Member State, the aim or effect of which is to treat goods coming from other Member States less favourably and, in the absence of harmonisation of national legislation, obstacles to the free movement of goods which are the consequence of applying, to goods coming from other Member States where they are lawfully manufactured and marketed, rules that lay down requirements to be met by such goods, even if those rules apply to all products alike, must be regarded as 'measures having equivalent effect to quantitative restrictions on imports' for the purposes of Article 28 EC (see to that effect, Case 120/78 *Rewe-Zentral (Cassis de Dijon)* [1979] ECR 649, paragraphs 6, 14 and 15; Case C-368/95 *Familiapress* [1997] ECR I-3689, paragraph 8; and Case C-322/01 *Deutscher Apothekerverband* [2003] ECR I-14887, paragraph 67). Any other measure which hinders access of products originating in other Member States to the market of a Member State is also covered by that concept (see Case C-110/05 *Commission* v *Italy* [2009] ECR I-0000, paragraph 37).

However this new formulation (in particular the addition of a third category ('any other measure', in *Mickelsson*: a prohibition of using jet-skis, on waters other than general navigable waterways) does not change the analysis made hereafter.

(2) In the case at hand the application of a national advertising rule (the prohibition of misleading advertising under German law) did affect the marketing of the good itself (its packaging). The *Keck* immunity therefore did not apply and the Court examined whether the application of the German prohibition in such a way that it restricted the importation of the products in Germany was justified in the interest of protecting consumers. In other cases the Court found that a 'selling arrangement', such as an advertising ban on television was not immune from the application of Article 28 EC, because the last condition of *Keck* was not fulfilled, ie the measure did not affect in the same manner, in law and in fact, the marketing of domestic products and of those from other Member States. In *Gourmet*,[17] for example, the Court found

[16] ECJ, 4 June 2009, Case C-142/05 *Cklagaren v Percy Mickelsson and Joakim Roos*, nyr, para 24.

[17] Case C-405/98 *Konsumentombudsmannen v Gourmet International* [2001] ECR I-1795.

that a Swedish prohibition of alcohol advertising in magazines had a greater adverse impact on the marketing of imported alcoholic beverages than on the marketing of domestic alcoholic drinks (since consumers are more acquainted with the latter and since there were other channels through which these products are brought to the attention of the public). The ECJ therefore examined whether the measure could be justified under Article 30 EC, namely for the protection of public health. The Court accepted that such a justification was possible but left it to the national court to decide whether the measure was proportionate.

(3) The annotated case is also an illustration of the benchmark consumer in the Court's case-law on free movement and consumer protection: the circumspect and well-informed consumer. That consumer will not be induced to believe that the apposition of '10 per cent' on a background that suggests a higher increase of volume means that he will get more than 10 per cent more. The ECJ has developed the notion of the average consumer who is well informed and circumspect. In Case C- 210/96 *Gut Springenheide*[18] the ECJ said:

> In those cases, in order to determine whether the description, trade mark or promotional description or statement in question was liable to mislead the purchaser, the Court took into account the presumed expectations of an average consumer who is reasonably well-informed and reasonably observant and circumspect, without ordering an expert's report or commissioning a consumer research poll. So, national courts ought, in general, to be able to assess, on the same conditions, any misleading effect of a description or statement designed to promote sales.

(4) The ECJ has consistently referred to the *Gut Springenheide* test in its case law on Article 28 EC (free movement of goods).[19] In *Estée Lauder Cosmetics*[20] the Court considered that the national court has to apply the test of the well-informed and circumspect consumer in the light of 'all relevant factors' and can take into account, in particular, social, cultural and linguistic factors.

Services Directive (2006/123/EC)[21] 1.5 (EU)

Article 16 Freedom to provide services

[18] Case C-210/96 *Gut Springenheide* [1998] ECR I-4657, para 31–32.

[19] Eg to reject a defence by a Member State in a Treaty infringement procedure: Case C-358/01 *Commission v Spain* [2003] ECR I-13145, paras 53ff: 'The Court has held that the reference consumer is an average consumer who is reasonably well informed and reasonably observant and circumspect' (see, with regard to foodstuffs, Case C-210/96 *Gut Springenheide and Tusky* [1998] ECR I-4657, para 31). That test, based on the principle of proportionality, also applies in the context of the marketing of cosmetic products where a mistake as to the product's characteristics cannot pose any risk to public health (Case C-220/98 *Estée Lauder* [2000] ECR I-117, para 28, and Case C-99/01 *Linhart and Biffl* [2002] ECR I-9375, para 31); Case C-465/98 *Darbo* [2000] ECR I-2297, para 20 and Joined Cases C-421/00, C-426/00 and C-16/01 *Sterbenz and Haug* [2003] ECR I-01065, para 43. See also (regarding foodstuff labelling) Case C-239/02 *Douwe Egberts* [2004] ECR I-7007, para 46.

[20] Case C-220/98 [2000] ECR I-117.

[21] Directive 2006/123/EC of the European Parliament and of the Council of 12 December 2006 on services in the internal market [2006] OJ L 376, 36–68.

(1) Member States shall respect the right of providers to provide services in a Member State other than that in which they are established.
The Member State in which the service is provided shall ensure free access to and free exercise of a service activity within its territory.
Member States shall not make access to or exercise of a service activity in their territory subject to compliance with any requirements which do not respect the following principles:

(a) non-discrimination: the requirement may be neither directly nor indirectly discriminatory with regard to nationality or, in the case of legal persons, with regard to the Member State in which they are established;

(b) necessity: the requirement must be justified for reasons of public policy, public security, public health or the protection of the environment;

(c) proportionality: the requirement must be suitable for attaining the objective pursued, and must not go beyond what is necessary to attain that objective. …

Article 22 Information on providers and their services

(1) Member States shall ensure that providers make the following information available to the recipient:

(a) the name of the provider, his legal status and form, the geographic address at which he is established and details enabling him to be contacted rapidly and communicated with directly and, as the case may be, by electronic means;

(b) where the provider is registered in a trade or other similar public register, the name of that register and the provider's registration number, or equivalent means of identification in that register;

(c) where the activity is subject to an authorisation scheme, the particulars of the relevant competent authority or the single point of contact;

(d) where the provider exercises an activity which is subject to VAT, the identification number referred to in Article 22(1) of Sixth Council Directive 77/388/EEC of 17 May 1977 on the harmonisation of the laws of the Member States relating to turnover taxes—Common system of value added tax: uniform basis of assessment [38];

(e) in the case of the regulated professions, any professional body or similar institution with which the provider is registered, the professional title and the Member State in which that title has been granted;

(f) the general conditions and clauses, if any, used by the provider;

(g) the existence of contractual clauses, if any, used by the provider concerning the law applicable to the contract and/or the competent courts;

(h) the existence of an after-sales guarantee, if any, not imposed by law;

(i) the price of the service, where a price is pre-determined by the provider for a given type of service;

(j) the main features of the service, if not already apparent from the context;

(k) the insurance or guarantees referred to in Article 23(1), and in particular the contact details of the insurer or guarantor and the territorial coverage.

(2) Member States shall ensure that the information referred to in paragraph 1, according to the provider's preference:

(a) is supplied by the provider on his own initiative;

(b) is easily accessible to the recipient at the place where the service is provided or the contract concluded;

(c) can be easily accessed by the recipient electronically by means of an address supplied by the provider;

(d) appears in any information documents supplied to the recipient by the provider which set out a detailed description of the service he provides.

(3) Member States shall ensure that, at the recipient's request, providers supply the following additional information:

(a) where the price is not pre-determined by the provider for a given type of service, the price of the service or, if an exact price cannot be given, the method for calculating the price so that it can be checked by the recipient, or a sufficiently detailed estimate;

(b) as regards the regulated professions, a reference to the professional rules applicable in the Member State of establishment and how to access them;

(c) information on their multidisciplinary activities and partnerships which are directly linked to the service in question and on the measures taken to avoid conflicts of interest. That information shall be included in any information document in which providers give a detailed description of their services;

(d) any codes of conduct to which the provider is subject and the address at which these codes may be consulted by electronic means, specifying the language version available;

(e) where a provider is subject to a code of conduct, or member of a trade association or professional body which provides for recourse to a non-judicial means of dispute settlement, information in this respect. The provider shall specify how to access detailed information on the characteristics of, and conditions for, the use of non-judicial means of dispute settlement.

(4) Member States shall ensure that the information which a provider must supply in accordance with this Chapter is made available or communicated in a clear and unambiguous manner, and in good time before conclusion of the contract or, where there is no written contract, before the service is provided.

(5) The information requirements laid down in this Chapter are in addition to requirements already provided for in Community law and do not prevent Member States from imposing additional information requirements applicable to providers established in their territory.

(6) The Commission may, in accordance with the procedure referred to in Article 40(2), specify the content of the information provided for in paragraphs 1 and 3 of this Article according to the specific nature of certain activities and may specify the practical means of implementing paragraph 2 of this Article.

Notes

(1) The rule of reason of *Cassis de Dijon* discussed in the preceding note has been extended by the ECJ to the free provision of services[22] and later to all the fundamental freedoms (free movement of goods, persons, services, and capital and payments).[23] Article 16 of the new Services Directive (2006/123/EC) changes that picture. The Directive, implemented by Member States at the end of 2009, applies to all service activities, except for financial services, electronic communications services and networks, services in the field of transport, services of temporary work agencies, healthcare services, audiovisual services, including cinematographic services, distribution and transmission, and radio broadcasting, gambling activities, activities which are connected with the exercise of official authority as set out in Article 45 EC, social

[22] Case C-76/90 *Säger v Dennemeyer* [1991] ECR I-4221.

[23] Case C-55/94 *Gebhard* [1995] ECR I-4165.

services relating to social housing, childcare and support of families and persons permanently or temporarily in need which are provided by the state, by providers mandated by the state or by charities recognised as such by the state, private security services and services provided by notaries and bailiffs, who are appointed by an official act of government.

(2) In the field of freedom of establishment (when a service provider operates through a permanent establishment in a Member State other than the Member State of his primary establishment) the Services Directive (2006/123/EC) maintains the (generous) rule of reason. The preamble even gives an impressive list of grounds of justification accepted so far by the ECJ:

> (40) The concept of 'overriding reasons relating to the public interest' to which reference is made in certain provisions of this Directive has been developed by the Court of Justice in its case law in relation to Articles 43 and 49 of the Treaty and may continue to evolve. The notion as recognised in the case law of the Court of Justice covers at least the following grounds: public policy, public security and public health, within the meaning of Articles 46 and 55 of the Treaty; the maintenance of order in society; social policy objectives; the protection of the recipients of services; consumer protection; the protection of workers, including the social protection of workers; animal welfare; the preservation of the financial balance of the social security system; the prevention of fraud; the prevention of unfair competition; the protection of the environment and the urban environment, including town and country planning; the protection of creditors; safeguarding the sound administration of justice; road safety; the protection of intellectual property; cultural policy objectives, including safeguarding the freedom of expression of various elements, in particular social, cultural, religious and philosophical values of society; the need to ensure a high level of education, the maintenance of press diversity and the promotion of the national language; the preservation of national historical and artistic heritage; and veterinary policy.

(3) By contrast, in the field of the free provision of services the Directive only allows Member States to impose requirements with regard to the provision of a service activity where they are justified for reasons of public policy, public security, public health or the protection of the environment and in accordance with the principles of necessity, non-discrimination and proportionality. Consumer protection is not one of the accepted grounds of justification. It has been submitted that the Directive cannot change the Treaty and that therefore the rule of reason of *Säger* would still apply.[24] This is certainly correct for Article 46 EC (not all the grounds of justification of this Article are mentioned in Article 16 of the Directive) but with regard to consumer protection it should be observed that this ground of justification is a creation of the Court 'in the absence of Community rules'. The Directive can be seen as a further step in the liberalisation of services for which the legislature is competent and which automatically excludes the rule of reason (as it existed pending further harmonisation). Davies[25] is not convinced that this exclusion (and the

[24] M Fallon and A-C Simon, 'La directive "services": quelle contribution au marché intérieur?' [2007] *Journal de Tribunaux de Droit Européen* 41.

[25] G Davies, 'The Services Directive: Extending the Country of origin Principle and reforming Public Administration' (2007) 32 *European Law Review* 235.

exclusion of other grounds of justification) matters. The only non-environmental mandatory requirement relied on to any great extent is consumer protection. Moreover the impact of removal of this exception is mitigated by several factors. First, the success rate of attempts to rely on it has not been great anyway.[26] Secondly, the Directive provides in Chapter V for detailed and comprehensive provision of information to consumers of services (Article 22 quoted here above). Thirdly, Article 16 only applies to a limited residue of services, most of which are not particularly sensitive or life threatening, and so for which information requirements may arguably be seen as an appropriate form of protection.[27] Fourthly, according to Davies, one should not forget that the myth of the approximate equivalence of standards in different Member States is not entirely without foundation. Finally Davies argues that the ECJ could well interpret the article of the Directive as it interpreted Article 49 EC by recognising additional classes of exceptions. What underlies this debate is the question of achieving a balance between the consumer interest expressed through the EC's rules on free movement and harmonised market regulation on the one hand, and on the other its expression through national rules of market regulation which are restrictive of inter-state trade. In making this balance a sensitive case- and context-specific assessment is required.

(4) The exclusion of consumer protection as a ground of justification for national restrictions affecting the free provision of services should be further put into perspective with the entry into force of the Unfair Commercial Practices Directive (2005/29/EC, discussed in chapter 2). National restrictions in the area of commercial practices (including advertising) going beyond the provisions of the Directive are not possible since the Directive is a measure of full harmonisation.

(5) Finally the Services Directive itself contains extensive information duties for suppliers vis-à-vis consumers. Chapter 3.III below contains a critical discussion of the so-called 'information paradigm', the belief that consumers' interests are best served by information duties,

I.D THE PARADIGM OF THE CONFIDENT CONSUMER

Communication from the Commission: **1.6 (EU)**
EU Consumer Policy Strategy 2007-2013. Empowering Consumers, Enhancing Their Welfare, Effectively Protecting Them[28]

The 493 million EU consumers are central to the three main challenges facing the EU: growth, jobs and the need to re-connect with our citizens. They are the lifeblood of the economy as their consumption represents 58 per cent of EU GDP. Confident, informed and empowered consumers are the motor of economic change as their choices drive

[26] See, however, *Cipolla* discussed above section I.B.

[27] See, however, for services of the professions not often life threatening except for medical services that do not come under the scope of the Directive, but sensitive and complex: again *Cipolla* for legal services.

[28] COM [2007] 99 final, summary, 1.

innovation and efficiency. But it is also in their role as consumers that the EU can most directly connect to the daily lives of our citizens and demonstrate the benefits of the EU.

The response to these challenges lies in equipping the consumer with the skills and tools to fulfil their role in the modern economy; in making markets deliver for them and in ensuring effective protection from the risks and threats they cannot tackle as individuals.

The internal market has played a central part in meeting Europe's economic challenges and delivering tangible benefits for EU citizens. But the consumer dimension of the internal market and retail markets in particular needs to be further reinforced. The new economic, social, environmental and political context calls for a change in focus of EU policy towards consumers.

T Wilhelmsson, Abuse of the Confident Consumer[29] **1.7 (EU)**

A reference to the need to create confident cross-border consumers who can contribute to the strengthening of the internal market has often been used as one of the main arguments for EC consumer policy and legislation. The argument has been presented in order to justify both the creation of a minimum safety net for consumers (the minimum confidence argument) and the current turn towards more total harmonisation of consumer protection (the harmonised confidence argument). In the paper these lines of argument are critically evaluated with reference to common sense knowledge about the behaviour of consumers as well as on the basis of Eurobarometer data concerning consumer confidence. In this light the substantive minimum harmonisation measures which have been justified with reference to the need for promoting consumer confidence seem only to a limited extent relevant with respect to the creation of such confidence. The current turn towards total harmonisation most certainly cannot be justified in this way. Other substantive measures, facilitating the access to a counterparty, would be more important in order to create consumer confidence in cross-border shopping, but the Community has almost systematically avoided adopting such measures.

T Wilhelmsson, Conclusions[30] **1.8 (EU)**

At the outset, consumer confidence reasoning appears to have at least some merits. Consumers may indeed be reluctant to acquire goods and services abroad because of a lack of confidence in the protection offered to them in foreign markets. There is some empirical evidence according to which consumers do not buy from other Member States because of difficulties relating to the exchange or repair of the goods or the settlement of disputes. Such evidence was gathered when preparing the Unfair Commercial Practices Directive. According to the survey, 76 per cent of consumers who felt less confident buying from another EU country cited as a very or fairly important factor a lack of trust in foreign sellers and a perceived greater risk of fraud or deception (COM(2003) 356 final 4). However, looking more closely at the reasons offered in studies such as

[29] T Wilhelmsson, 'Abuse of the Confident Consumer' (2004) 27 *Journal of Consumer Policy* 3, 317–37. The excerpt reproduces the abstract of the article.

[30] In G Howells, H-W Micklitz and T Wilhelmsson, *European Fair Trading Law, The Unfair Commercial Practices Directive* (Aldershot, Ashgate, 2006) 244.

these, they primarily appear to relate to problems of procedure and access—the consumer refrains from shopping abroad because of fear of practical problems related to the access to the other party and problems of access to justice resulting from the fact that the consumer and the seller are located in different countries—rather than to lack of confidence in the substantive law. [Footnote omitted]

Note

The paradigm of the confident consumer will be further discussed in the next subsection.

I.E CONSUMER PROTECTION AND HARMONISATION AT THE EC LEVEL: REVIEW OF THE CONSUMER ACQUIS

More than any other branch of the law, consumer law has been harmonised at the EC level. It is the firm belief of the EC institutions that this harmonisation (the 'consumer acquis') raises consumer confidence and thus assists cross-border purchases in the internal market. Consequently this Casebook contains a relatively high proportion of Community law texts.

The harmonisation of laws at the EC level raises questions as to the margin left to the Member States to maintain or to introduce a higher level of consumer protection than the level adopted in the harmonisation instrument. Much depends on the nature of the harmonisation.[31] The debate about 'maximum harmonisation', as a method for vertical redistribution of regulatory competence in favour of the EC in the consumer acquis, has also been connected to the bigger debate about 'Europe' (and the tension between uniformity and—cultural—diversity).

So far secondary Community law in the field of consumer protection has mostly taken the form of Directives, originally based on the old Article 100 EC Treaty (now Article 94 EC), requiring unanimity for the adoption of Directives for the approximation of laws that directly affect the common market, and later, on the basis of Article 95 (ex Article 100a) allowing the adoption of measures (including regulations) by the Council and the European Parliament (co-decision procedure) for the approximation of national provisions which have as their object the establishment and the functioning of the internal market. The alternative legal basis for consumer protective measures, Article 153(1)b, allowing specific action which supports and supplements the policy pursued by the Member States to protect health, safety and economic interests of consumers and to provide adequate information to consumers, has hardly been used. Most of the Directives, based on Article 95 EC, are minimum harmonisation Directives, leaving Member States the power to maintain or to introduce measures for a better protection of consumer and applying to all economic operators, whether established in that Member State or abroad. Today the European Commission favours full harmonisation instead of minimum harmonisation for

[31] See in particular S Weatherill, 'Maximum or Minimum Harmonisation: What Kind of "Europe" Do We Want?' in K Boele-Woelki and W Grosheide (eds), *The Future of European Contract Law; Essays in honour of Ewoud Hondius* (Alphen aan den Rijn, Kluwer, 2007) 146.

policy reasons. On the other hand it can be argued on the basis of the case law of the ECJ on Article 95 EC that this provision does not support minimum harmonisation. This will be developed hereafter.

DG Health and Consumer Protection, Preparatory Work for the Impact Assessment on the Review of the Consumer Acquis[32] **1.9 (EU)**

Although overall, the largest group of contributors favoured targeted full harmonisation [Footnote: ie harmonisation targeted to the issues raising substantial barriers to trade for business and/or deterring consumers from buying cross-border] (33 per cent), it is important to note that full harmonisation was favoured by 29 per cent of the contributors and minimum harmonisation by 24 per cent. Therefore, the majority (ie 62 per cent) favoured full or targeted full harmonisation. Minimum harmonisation, targeted full harmonisation and full harmonisation are by far the three favourite options with only 13 per cent of contributors who suggested alternative options.

Green Paper on the Review of the Consumer Acquis[33] **1.10 (EU)**

The current consumer protection directives, which are under review, are based on minimum harmonisation, ie they contain clauses under which Member States are allowed to have higher protection levels than those provided for by the directives.

Many Member States have made use of this possibility, eg by providing for longer cooling-off periods than the minimum periods laid down in the Directives on Distance Selling, Doorstep Selling and Timeshare.

Consequently consumers cannot be sure that the level of protection they are used to in their home country will apply when they shop cross-border, whereas businesses may be deterred from marketing their products or services across the EU by the fact that they have to comply with different rules in each Member State.

To remedy this problem, one option would be to revise the Consumer Acquis with a view to achieving full harmonisation. This would mean that no Member State could apply stricter rules than the ones laid down at Community level. Full harmonisation would not only entail the repeal of the minimum harmonisation clauses; it would also imply the elimination of the regulatory options available to Member States on specific aspects by some provisions in the directives, which could result in modifying the level of consumer protection in some Member States. …

Nevertheless, given that it may be difficult to achieve full harmonisation on all aspects, and in order to avoid the re-creation of barriers to the internal market, a harmonisation approach might on a case-by-case basis be complemented by a clause providing for mutual recognition for certain aspects covered by the proposed legislation but not fully harmonised.

Another option could therefore be the combination of minimum harmonisation with a mutual recognition clause. In this case, Member States would retain the possibility to introduce stricter consumer protection rules in their national laws, but they would not be

[32] Analytical Report on the Green Paper on the Review of the Consumer Acquis submitted by the Consumer Policy Evaluation Consortium. Available at the website of DG Sanco.

[33] COM [2006] 744 final, 10–11.

entitled to impose their own stricter requirements on businesses established in other Member States in a way which would create unjustified restrictions to the free movement of goods or to the freedom to provide services.

Finally, another option would be minimum harmonisation eventually combined with the country of origin approach. This combination would mean that a Member State would retain the possibility to introduce stricter consumer protection rules in its national law, but businesses established in other Member States would only have to comply with the rules applicable in their home country.

However, these options would not simplify and rationalise the regulatory environment. Regulatory fragmentation would continue to exist and its negative effects on consumers' confidence in the internal market would not be removed. In the absence of a rule designating the law of the trader as the applicable law, the judge having jurisdiction over a cross-border lawsuit (ie normally the judge of the country of destination) would have to compare systematically the law of the country of the consumer with that of the country of origin. He would then have to assess to what extent the country of destination law goes beyond the level of protection provided in the law of the country of the trader and, if the divergence constitutes an unjustified restriction, disapply the stricter requirements. This cumbersome procedure would not enhance legal certainty.

These two options would also not provide for a solution ensuring the high common level of consumer protection required by the Treaty.

Proposal for a Directive on Consumer Rights[34] **1.11 (EU)**

[Preamble] **(6)** The laws of the Member States on consumer contracts show marked differences which can generate appreciable distortions of competition and obstacles to the smooth functioning of the internal market. ...

(7) These disparities create significant internal market barriers affecting business and consumers. They increase compliance costs to business wishing to engage in cross border sale of goods or provision of services. Fragmentation also undermines consumer confidence in the internal market. The negative effect on consumer confidence is strengthened by an uneven level of consumer protection across the Community. This problem is particularly acute in the light of new market developments.

(8) Full harmonisation of some key regulatory aspects will considerably increase legal certainty for both consumers and business. Both consumers and business will be able to rely on a single regulatory framework based on clearly defined legal concepts regulating certain aspects of business-to-consumer contracts across the Community. The effect will be to eliminate the barriers stemming from the fragmentation of the rules and to complete the internal market in this area. These barriers can only be eliminated by establishing uniform rules at Community level. Furthermore consumers will enjoy a high common level of protection across the Community.

Article 4 Full harmonisation

Member States may not maintain or introduce, in their national law, provisions diverging from those laid down in this Directive, including more or less stringent provisions to ensure a different level of consumer protection.

[34] COM [2008] 614 final.

ECJ Case C- 376/98, 5 October 2000[35] **1.12 (EU)**
Commission v Germany

THE LEGAL BASIS OF THE FIRST TOBACCO ADVERTISING DIRECTIVE

Tobacco I

Article 95 EC is not the proper legal basis for an advertising ban for tobacco that does not contain a free movement provision.

Facts: In 1998 the European Parliament and the Council adopted a Directive (98/43/EC)[36] containing a (quasi) total ban on advertising for tobacco including, for example, the apposition of tobacco brands on other consumer goods. Not surprisingly the Directive was not based on Article 152 (public heath) because that provision excludes harmonisation measures. The directive was based on Article 57(2), 66 and 100a EC (which are now, after amendment Articles 47(2), 55 and 95), in other words on the provisions relating to Community legislation in the field of respectively the free provision of services and the internal market in general.

Germany had voted against the Directive and sought its annulment before the Court, under Article 230 EC, arguing that Article 95 EC was not the proper legal basis for the Directive.

Judgment: 84. Moreover, a measure adopted on the basis of Article 100a [now, after amendment, Article 95] of the Treaty must genuinely have as its object the improvement of the conditions for the establishment and functioning of the internal market. If a mere finding of disparities between national rules and of the abstract risk of obstacles to the exercise of fundamental freedoms or of distortions of competition liable to result therefrom were sufficient to justify the choice of Article 100a [now, after amendment, Article 95] as a legal basis, judicial review of compliance with the proper legal basis might be rendered nugatory. The Court would then be prevented from discharging the function entrusted to it by Article 164 [now, after amendment, Article 220] of the EC Treaty of ensuring that the law is observed in the interpretation and application of the Treaty. …

Elimination of obstacles to the free movement of goods and the freedom to provide services…

103. Under Article 5 of the Directive, Member States retain the right to lay down, in accordance with the Treaty, such stricter requirements concerning the advertising or sponsorship of tobacco products as they deem necessary to guarantee the health protection of individuals.

104. Furthermore, the Directive contains no provision ensuring the free movement of products which conform to its provisions, in contrast to other directives allowing Member States to adopt stricter measures for the protection of a general interest (see, in particular, Article 7(1) of Council Directive 90/239/EEC of 17 May 1990 on the approximation of the laws, regulations and administrative provisions of the Member States concerning the maximum tar yield of cigarettes (OJ 1990 L 137, p 36) and Article 8(1) of Council Directive 89/622/EEC of 13 November 1989 on the approximation of the laws, regulations and administrative provisions of the Member States concerning the labelling of tobacco products (OJ 1989 L 359, p 1)).

[35] ECR I-08419.

[36] Directive 98/43/EC of the European Parliament and of the Council of 6 July 1998 on the approximation of the laws, regulations and administrative provisions of the Member States relating to the advertising and sponsorship of tobacco products [1998] OJ L 213, 9–12.

105. In those circumstances, it must be held that the Community legislature cannot rely on the need to eliminate obstacles to the free movement of advertising media and the freedom to provide services in order to adopt the Directive on the basis of Articles 100a, 57(2) and 66 of Treaty. ...

Elimination of distortion of competition...

109. First, as regards advertising agencies and producers of advertising media, undertakings established in Member States which impose fewer restrictions on tobacco advertising are unquestionably at an advantage in terms of economies of scale and increase in profits. The effects of such advantages on competition are, however, remote and indirect and do not constitute distortions which could be described as appreciable. They are not comparable to the distortions of competition caused by differences in production costs, such as those which, in particular, prompted the Community legislature to adopt Council Directive 89/428/EEC of 21 June 1989 on procedures for harmonising the programmes for the reduction and eventual elimination of pollution caused by waste from the titanium dioxide industry (OJ 1989 L 201, p 56).

110. It is true that the differences between certain regulations on tobacco advertising may give rise to appreciable distortions of competition. As the Commission and the Finnish and United Kingdom Governments have submitted, the fact that sponsorship is prohibited in some Member States and authorised in others gives rise, in particular, to certain sports events being relocated, with considerable repercussions on the conditions of competition for undertakings associated with such events.

111. However, such distortions, which could be a basis for recourse to Article 100a [now, after amendment Article 95] of the Treaty in order to prohibit certain forms of sponsorship, are not such as to justify the use of that legal basis for an outright prohibition of advertising of the kind imposed by the Directive.

112. Second, as regards distortions of competition in the market for tobacco products, irrespective of the applicant's contention that such distortions are not covered by the Directive, it is clear that, in that sector, the Directive is likewise not apt to eliminate appreciable distortions of competition.

113. Admittedly, as the Commission has stated, producers and sellers of tobacco products are obliged to resort to price competition to influence their market share in Member States which have restrictive legislation. However, that does not constitute a distortion of competition but rather a restriction of forms of competition which applies to all economic operators in those Member States. By imposing a wide-ranging prohibition on the advertising of tobacco products, the Directive would in the future generalise that restriction of forms of competition by limiting, in all the Member States, the means available for economic operators to enter or remain in the market.

114. In those circumstances, it must be held that the Community legislature cannot rely on the need to eliminate distortions of competition, either in the advertising sector or in the tobacco products sector, in order to adopt the Directive on the basis of Articles 100a, 57(2) and 66 [now, after amendment Articles 95, 47(2) and 55] of the Treaty.

115. In view of all the foregoing considerations, a measure such as the directive cannot be adopted on the basis of Articles 100a, 57(2) and 66 [now, after amendment Articles 95, 47(2) and 55] of the Treaty.

S Weatherill, The Constitutional Competence of the EU to Deliver Social Justice[37] **1.13 (EU)**

Tobacco Advertising appears to insist that a harmonisation measure must ensure access to the market of conforming imported goods, and confines the application of stricter rules to domestic goods alone. The Court criticised Directive 98/43 on advertising of tobacco products because it 'contains no provision ensuring the free movement of the products which conforms to its provisions, in contrast to other Directives allowing Member States to adopt stricter measures for the protection of a general interest' (Case 376/98). This among other unfavourable findings, deprived the Directive of a valid basis. In the subsequent ruling in *ex parte BAT* a plank in the Court's reasoning approving the validity of that measure of harmonisation was the presence of a market access clause (Case 491/01). And in the wake of *Tobacco Advertising* the annulled measure was replaced by a more tightly drawn Directive which duly includes an explicit free movement/market access clause (Directive 2003/33/EC). So, it seems, it is a condition for valid resort to Article 95 that no scope is left to States to set rules stricter than the harmonised norm, other than via Article 95(4)–(9). This would harmonise the capacity of harmonisation measures to level the playing field by ruling out the possibility of national variation. It would also sharpen the distinction between the effect on national competence of legislative action undertaken pursuant to Article 95 and legislative action which belongs under the sector-specific legal bases mentioned above such as Article 153 EC which include explicit concessions to a degree of State autonomy even after the Community has acted. It would also radically transform pre-existing political bargain which has long favoured the minimum model. However, the general status of 'minimum harmonisation' was not authoritatively decided in these cases and, in particular the impact of the judgments could be confined to the particular legislation challenged. The Directive annulled in *Tobacco Advertising* was after all deeply flawed from more than one market-making perspective. And subsequently in *Doc Morris* (Case 322/01) and *Herber Karner v Troostwijk* (Case 71/02), the attack on minimum rules found in *Tobacco Advertising* was ignored. So the law is unsettled and it seems impossible to be confident about the Court's position until this case law develops further. But it would be dangerous to assume viability of the model of 'minimum harmonisation' founded on Article 95 into the future.

Notes

(1) As Weatherill explains in his note above, *Tobacco Advertising* casts doubt on the constitutionality of minimum directives (as were usual in European consumer law). This judgment is often mentioned by policymakers favouring full harmonisation. In this respect it is interesting to note that according to the Report on the Outcome of the Public Consultation on the Green Paper on the Review of the Consumer Acquis of October 2007 80 per cent of the business associations support full or targeted harmonisation (targeted to issues raising substantial barriers to trade for business and/or deterring consumers from buying cross-borders), while the majority of consumer associations support minimum harmonisation combined with the

[37] S Weatherill, 'The Constitutional Competence of the EU to Deliver Social Justice' (2006) *European Review of Contract Law* 2, 153.

application of the law of the country of destination. Some consumer associations would be ready to accept full harmonisation provided that the level of protection was high and that it was targeted at very specific issues and not extended to general principles of contract law (p 4). In the Proposal for a Directive on Consumer Rights, adopted in October 2008, the Commission nevertheless proposes to harmonise fully all aspects (including general contract law aspects) regulated in the proposal. The Proposal has, however, been received very critically.[38] Once again we can observe the thematic importance and delicacy which is involved in balancing the contributions of the EC and the Member States to the pattern of consumer protection in the internal market.

(2) The different methods of harmonisation at the EU level in consumer law will be discussed more in detail here after (IV). As to the constitutional implications, ie what kind of harmonisation in the consumer field is possible in view of the available legal bases in the EC Treaty, the following observations can be made. First it should be stressed that in *Tobacco I*[39] (the judgment discussed by Weatherill) the ECJ ruled that Article 95 EC does not vest in the Community legislature a general power to regulate the internal market.[40] A measure adopted on the basis of Article 95 EC must genuinely have as its object the improvement of the conditions for the establishment and functioning of the internal market. A mere finding of disparities between national rules, the abstract risk of obstacles to the exercise of fundamental freedoms or distortions of competition that may result therefrom will not suffice in this regard.[41] In view of the absence of an 'internal market clause', eg a provision allowing tobacco advertising conforming to the directive to freely circulate in the internal market, the Directive has no sufficient link with the internal market. On the other hand, the ECJ confirmed in *Tobacco II*[42] that recourse to Article 95 EC as a legal basis does not presuppose the existence of an actual link with free movement between the Member States in every situation covered by the measure founded on that basis. What matters is that the measure adopted on the basis of Article 95 EC must actually be intended to improve the conditions for the establishment and functioning of the internal market.[43] Be that as it may, as Weatherill rightly points out, it is uncertain (awaiting further case-law) whether Article 95 EC is a sufficient legal basis for minimum harmonisation.

[38] M Hesselink and M Loos, *Het voorstel voor een Europese richtlijn consumentenrechten* (Den Haag, Boom, 2009) 263 p; G Howells and R Schulze, *Modernising and Harmonising Consumer Contract Law* (Munchen, Sellier, 2009) 322; H-W Micklitz and N Reich, 'Crónica de una muerte anunciada: The Commission Proposal for a "Directive on Consumer Rights"' (2009) 46 *Common Market Law Review*; P Rott and E Terryn, 'The Proposal for a Directive on Consumer Rights: No Single Set of Rules' (2009) 3 *Zeitschrift fur Europaisches Privatrecht* 456–89.

[39] Case C-376/98 *Commission v Germany* [2000] ECR I-8419, see note J Usher (2000) 38 *CML Rev* 1519ff.

[40] Case C-376/98, para 83.

[41] Case C-376/98, para 84.

[42] Case C-380/03 *Germany v Parliament and Council* [2006] ECR I-11573.

[43] With reference to Joined Cases C-465/00, C-138/01 and C-139/01 *Österreichischer Rundfunk et al* [2003] ECR I-4989, paras 41 and 42, and Case C-101/01 *Lindqvist* [2003] ECR I-12971, paras 40 and 41.

If minimum harmonisation is not possible on the basis of Article 95 EC—which remains to be seen—the question arises whether Article 153(3)(b) could be the basis for minimum harmonisation directives.

EC Treaty **1.14 (EU)**

Article 153 (1) In order to promote the interests of consumers and to ensure a high level of consumer protection, the Community shall contribute to protecting the health, safety and economic interests of consumers, as well as to promoting their right to information, education and to organise themselves in order to safeguard their interests.

(2) Consumer protection requirements shall be taken into account in defining and implementing other Community policies and activities.

(3) The Community shall contribute to the attainment of the objectives referred to in paragraph 1 through:

(a) measures adopted pursuant to Article 95 in the context of the completion of the internal market;

(b) measures which support, supplement and monitor the policy pursued by the Member States.

(4) The Council, acting in accordance with the procedure referred to in Article 251 and after consulting the Economic and Social Committee, shall adopt the measures referred to in paragraph 3(b).

(5) Measures adopted pursuant to paragraph 4 shall not prevent any Member State from maintaining or introducing more stringent protective measures. Such measures must be compatible with this Treaty. The Commission shall be notified of them.

Communication from the Commission on the enforcement of the consumer acquis[44] **1.15 (EU)**

Article 153 (3)(b) EC Treaty also lays down a role for the Community in supporting, supplementing and monitoring national consumer policies. Monitoring and benchmarking enforcement is an important element in delivering an internal market that works for consumers. The Commission's tools providing supporting and supplementing measures to increase transparency have to be further evaluated. Increased transparency can be especially important where consumer detriment is neither confined to a single Member State nor related to cross-border situations, but where a given practice of a given company affects consumers in several or all Member States. In such cases with a European dimension, the Commission can usefully go first in addressing the problem and trying to identify a solution.

The same provision could also constitute a basis for future legal instruments that would enable the Commission to better support and supplement the enforcement work by Member States.

[44] COM [2009] 330 final.

Notes

(1) Although it was only in 1993, with the Treaty of Maastricht, that consumer policy made its appearance in the EC Treaty, with the introduction of a specific consumer protection chapter (now Article 153), the protection of consumers has been very present in Community law since the end of 1970s, both in the ECJ's case-law on the internal market (with ECJ Case 120/78 *Cassis de Dijon*)[45] and directives of the mid-1980s such as the Misleading Advertising Directive (84/450/EEC),[46] the Product Liability Directive (85/374/EEC),[47] the Doorstep Selling Directive (85/577/EEC)[48] and the Consumer Credit Directive (87/102/EEC).[49] In the 'rule of reason' developed by the ECJ in its case-law on free movement of goods and later the other freedoms (freedom of establishment, free provision of services and—but less important for consumer protection—free movement of capital) consumer protection has undoubtedly been the most relevant ground of justification for measures restricting free movement. Note, however, that the recent Services Directive (2006/123/EC) has excluded consumer protection as a ground of justification of national measures restricting the free provision of services (see above section I.C).

(2) Since the Treaty of Amsterdam, Community measures in the field of consumer protection shall be taken at a high level of protection (Article 153(1) EC). Article 153(3)b has hardly been used.[50] Some authors have suggested this provision as a legal basis for consumer contract law. Article 153(3)b permits consumer protection measures independent of the internal market. In addition, such measures are always 'minimum' standards (see Article 153(5)), subject to respect of general principles of Community law (including the fundamental freedoms) only. However, so far this suggestion has not been followed and the exact scope of Article 153(3)b remains uncertain. Recourse to Article 153(3)b would render the debate about 'minimum' and 'full harmonisation' to some extent superfluous.[51] The recent Commission Communication quoted above also remains extremely vague on the possible use of Article 153(3)(b).

[45] *Rewe-Zentral AG v Bundesmonopolverwaltung für Branntwein* [1979] ECR I-00649.

[46] Council Directive 84/450/EEC of 10 September 1984 relating to the approximation of the laws, regulations and administrative provisions of the Member States concerning misleading advertising [1984] OJ L 250, 17–20. In the meantime repealed by the Directive 2006/114/EC of the European Parliament and of the Council of 12 December 2006 concerning misleading and comparative advertising ('Misleading and Comparative Directive') [2006] OJ L 376, 21–27.

[47] Council Directive 85/374/EEC of 25 July 1985 on the approximation of the laws, regulations and administrative provisions of the Member States concerning liability for defective products [1985] OJ L 210, 29–33.

[48] Council Directive 85/577/EEC of 20 December 1985 to protect the consumer in respect of contracts negotiated away from business premises [1985] OJ L 372, 31–33.

[49] In the meantime replaced by the Directive 2008/48/EC of the European Parliament and of the Council of 23 April 2008 on credit agreements for consumers and repealing Council Directive 87/102/EEC ('Consumer Credit Directive') [2008] OJ L 133, 66–92.

[50] So far there is only one legislative act adopted on the basis of that article: Directive 98/6/EC on consumer protection in the indication of prices of products offered to consumers [1998] OJ L 80, 27.

[51] N Reich, 'A European Contract Law or an EU Contract Law Regulation for Consumers' [2005] *Journal of Consumer Policy* 383; H-W Micklitz, 'The Relationship between National and European Consumer Policy—Challenges and Perspectives' (2008) *Yearbook of Consumer Law* 35ff, 60–61; H-W Micklitz, N Reich and P Rott, *Understanding European Consumer Law* (Antwerpen/Oxford, Intersentia, 2009).

Questions

(1) How does competition law benefit consumers?

(2) Does Community law take proper account of vulnerable consumers?

(3) How should full harmonisation at the EC level be approached from the consumer perspective?

II. WHO IS THE CONSUMER?[52]

II.A THE NOTION OF CONSUMER

Different notions of 'consumer' exist not only between the Member States, but even within some Member States and within the EC consumer acquis.

While all definitions refer at least to natural persons acting outside a business (sometimes only if they act completely for private purposes), some other persons are sometimes included: legal persons (acting outside a business) (as in Belgium and Spain) or some legal persons, such as non-profit organisations, persons establishing a business but not yet exercising it, non-professional persons participating in a direct-selling network and earning money when they are successful in soliciting purchases, non-professionals, private investors, etc.

Where the law provides for protective rules for consumers because they lack sufficient knowledge when they enter into a transaction with a professional or because they have no bargaining power, the question arises whether the same protection should not be given to, for example, small business people who are in the same position of inferiority. On the other hand there are those who consider that small businessmen who participate in economic life should bear all risks. They therefore do not advocate the inclusion of small businessmen in the scope of the protective rules.

Some of these questions will be discussed hereafter.

ECJ Case C-541/99, 22 November 2001[53] **1.16 (EU)**
Cape v Ideal Service

A BUSINESSMAN ACTING THROUGH A COMPANY IS NOT A CONSUMER

Drink dispensers bought for staff

Professional buyers cannot benefit from the protection of the Unfair Terms Directive.

Facts: Ideal Service concluded a contract with Cape for the supply to Cape of automatic drink dispensers which were installed on the premises of Cape for use by Cape's staff. In relation to the performance of the contract, Cape instituted proceedings contesting a payment order maintaining that the clause granting

[52] See also the *Ius Commune Casebook on Contract Law*, 2nd edn, ch 4.I.A.

[53] [2001] ECR I-9049.

jurisdiction contained in the contract was unfair within the meaning of Article 1469(a) of the Italian Civil Code and could not have been enforced against the parties to the contracts by virtue of Article 1469(d) of that code. The Italian judge took the view that his jurisdiction to hear the case depended on the construction of those provisions of the Civil Code, which constitute a literal transposition of the Unfair Contract Terms Directive (93/13/EEC).[54] In particular, the term seller or supplier and consumer used in the Italian Civil Code are a literal transcription of the definitions contained in Article 2 of the Unfair Contract Terms Directive (93/13/EEC). Ideal Service contended that Cape could not be seen as a consumer within the meaning of the Directive. In addition to the fact that Cape was a company and not a natural person, Cape signed the contract at issue in the course of its business activity. The Italian judge referred the following questions to the ECJ:

(1) Is it possible to regard as a consumer an undertaking which, by a contract with another undertaking using a form produced by the latter in so far as the contract falls within the scope of its normal business activity, acquires a service or merchandise for the sole benefit of the employees, which is wholly unconnected, with and remote from its normal trade and business? Can it be said in such circumstances that that party acted for purposes which do not relate to the undertaking?

(2) If the foregoing question is answered in the affirmative, is it possible to regard any party or entity as a consumer when it is acting for purposes not relating or conducive to its normal trade or business, or does the term consumer relate only to national persons, to the exclusion of any other?

(3) Can a company be regarded as a consumer?

Judgment: 12. By its second and third questions, which it is appropriate to consider first, the national court seeks essentially to ascertain whether the term consumer as defined in Article 2(b) of the Directive must be interpreted as referring solely to natural persons.

13. Idealservice, the Italian and French Governments and the Commission contend that the term consumer refers only to natural persons.

14. The Spanish Government, on the other hand, submits that, although Community law considers that, in principle, legal persons are not consumers within the meaning of the Directive, it does not exclude an interpretation conferring that status on legal persons. Like the French Government, it contends that the definition of consumer given by the Directive does not make it impossible for Member States, when transposing it, to treat a company as a consumer in their domestic law.

15. In that connection, it must be observed that Article 2(b) of the Directive defines a consumer as any natural person who fulfils the conditions laid down by that provision, whereas article 2(c) of the Directive, in defining the term supplier or seller, refers to both natural and legal persons.

16. It is thus clear from the wording of Article 2 of the Directive that a person other than a natural person who concludes a contract with a seller or supplier cannot be regarded as a consumer within the meaning of that provision.

17. Accordingly, the answer to the second and third questions must be that the term consumer, as defined in Article 2(b) of the Directive, must be interpreted as referring solely to natural persons.

Notes

(1) Two questions were raised in this case. The first question was the following: where a businessman is buying goods or services that are totally unconnected to his professional activity or his trade, should he not be qualified as a consumer as well? The ECJ does not address this question. The second question was whether a legal person can be qualified as a consumer. The ECJ's answer is no.

[54] Council Directive 93/13/EEC of 5 April 1993 on unfair terms in consumer contracts [1993] OJ L 95, 29–34.

(2) Quite naturally the question arises whether the 'small' businessman should not be qualified as a consumer when he buys a product in the private sphere? Think of the hairdresser who is buying chairs for his private home. This question is generally answered in the affirmative. The consumer concept used in most of the European legal systems refers to natural persons that act for purposes which are outside their trade, business or profession. This is also the case with the EC consumer Directives. According to these Directives, the hairdresser in the situation described above is a consumer. Nevertheless a small businessman will often fall outside the scope of the protective rules for consumers in such a situation, because the purchase is made via a legal person (company) he has created for the exercise of his activities. Hence the purchaser is not a consumer (natural person). Small companies are very often used by small businessmen as a vehicle for private purchases (eg for tax reasons).

(3) Exceptionally the consumer concept also encompasses legal persons. Such is the case in the Belgian Trade Practices Act of 1991. Article 1(7) of this law defines a consumer as every natural or legal person buying products goods or services for exclusively non-professional purposes. In the meantime the significance of this definition—also for trade practices—has been narrowed down: a recent Act (of 2007) adapting the Trade Practices Act to the Unfair Commercial Practices Directive (2005/29/EC) (UCPD)[55] limits the notion of consumer to natural persons.

(4) In this judgment the ECJ decided that the term 'consumer', as defined in Article 2(b) of the Unfair Contract Terms Directive (93/13/EEC), must be interpreted as referring solely to natural persons. This judgment should be clearly understood: the directive on unfair contract terms is a 'minimum harmonisation' directive and leaves the Member States the freedom to provide for more protective measures. In addition this Directive only harmonises the law of the Member States concerning unfair terms in consumer contracts. Consequently the Directive does not as such prevent the Member States from providing for equivalent protection in business-to-business relationships.

UCPD (2005/29/EC) **1.17 (EU)**

Art 2 'Consumer' means any natural person who, in commercial practices covered by this Directive, is acting for purposes which are outside his trade, business, craft or profession.

Notes

(1) Most of the EC Directives contain the same definition.

(2) The question may arise whether a person acting partly, or even predominantly for a non-professional purpose is to be considered as a consumer. The so-called

[55] Directive 2005/29/EC of the European Parliament and of the Council of 11 May 2005 concerning unfair business-to-consumer commercial practices in the internal market and amending Council Directive 84/450/EEC, Directives 97/7/EC, 98/27/EC and 2002/65/EC of the European Parliament and of the Council and Regulation (EC) 2006/2004 of the European Parliament and of the Council [2005] OJ L 149, 22–39 ('UCPD').

mixed situations have been addressed by the ECJ in relation to the Brussels Convention (see section II.F and chapter 8).

(3) Another question in regard to this definition is whether a private person who is not 'consuming' but still acting outside any trade or profession can be qualified as a consumer? A typical example is the private investor (see chapter 6).

Green Paper on the Review of the Consumer Acquis[56] **1.18 (EU)**

Some businesses, such as individual entrepreneurs or small businesses may sometimes be in a similar situation as consumers when they buy certain goods or services which raises the question whether they should benefit to a certain extent from the same protection provided for consumers.

Cass civ 1e, 15 March 2005[57] **1.19 (FR)**

THE PERSONAL SCOPE OF APPLICATION OF THE RULES ON UNFAIR CONTRACT TERMS

Dairy farmers leasing computers

The small professional is not excluded from the protection against unfair contract terms.

Facts: The Syndicat départemental de contrôle laitier de la Mayenne (a professional organisation of small enterprises in the livestock business) concluded a lease contract with purchase option for IT equipment with Europe Computer Systems (ECS). According to the lease contract, the lessee had the following options at the expiry of the initial lease period: (a) purchase the leased goods, (b) return the leased goods to the lessor or (c) demand the continuation of the lease. If the lessee failed to make his choice within the time limit and according to the form specified in the contract the contract would be prolonged tacitly for an indefinite period of time with the possibility for each of the parties to terminate by giving a nine-month notice. The Syndicat failed to make a choice and was condemned by the lower court to pay ECS the contractual lease for the period of prolongation of the contract. The dispute went up to the Cour de Cassation which had to decide on the question whether the Syndicat can claim the protection of Article L 123-1 of the Code de la Consommation (unfair contract terms).

Judgment: Although in its judgment of 22 November 2001, the ECJ ruled that the notion of consumer in Article 2(b) of Directive 93/13/EEC on unfair contract terms in consumer contracts has to be interpreted in the sense that it only refers to natural persons, the distinct notion of 'professional' used by the French legislator does not exclude the protection of legal persons from the protection against unfair contracts terms. However since in this case the contract was signed by the Syndicat in its capacity of professional, the provisions of the Consumer Code do not apply.

Note

The Cour de Cassation accepted that, in spite of the ECJ decision (22 November 2001, Case C-541/99 and 542/99 *Cape* [2001] ECR I-09049) stating that the Unfair Contract Terms Directive (93/13/EEC) applied only to natural persons, the French

[56] COM [2006] 744.

[57] Pourvoi No 02-13285 (2005) D 1948, note Boujeka.

Law on Unfair Terms did not distinguish between natural persons and legal entities so that it could apply to the latter. As a result of this conflict between French and European law, the French Cour de Cassation has made a new distinction between the consumer and the non-professional ('le non-professionnel'): both a natural and a legal person can be a 'non-professional' and benefit from the protection against unfair contract terms. In the vast majority of the cases—like this case discussed above—the Cour de Cassation, however, held that the legal person acted in a professional capacity and therefore could not invoke the protection of the Code de la Consommation.[58]

Audiencia Provincial (Court of Appeal) Barcelona, 22 November 2004[59] **1.20 (ES)**

APPLICATION BY ANALOGY OF THE CRITERIA OF THE CONSUMER SALES DIRECTIVE TO SMALL PROFESSIONALS

The defective lorry

Relations between professionals are not governed by the rules on consumer sales and guarantees.

Facts: Eusebio, a professional, bought a lorry that suffered two major repairs six days after purchase. After these repairs, the lorry continued in circulation. Mr Eusebio then exercised the 'action for latent defects' (actio redhibitoria), demanding the resolution of the contract. The dispute went to the Court of Appeal of Barcelona.

Judgment: The legal relation entered into by the parties on 8 February 2000, is therefore previous to the entry into force of the Law 23/2003 of 10 July 2003 (RCL 2003, 1764), concerning Guarantees in the Sale of Consumer Goods, transposing Directive 1999/44/CE (OJ 1999, 1654) of the European Parliament and of the Council, of 25 May 1999, that has expanded the existing protection by the actio redhibitoria and the action for hidden defects of the Civil Code (LEG 1889, 27) by introducing the possibility for the buyer to request the replacement of good delivered, a possibility that was not provided for by the Code.

In the case at hand the General Consumer Protection Law (RCL 1984, 1906), Article 11 of which relates to the guarantee of durable goods does not apply because the purchaser and plaintiff does not have the quality of consumer, since he acquired the good with a view to have it integrated into his business activity.

Therefore it must be observed that there is a regulatory duality, depending on whether the buyer is a consumer or not. In the first hypothesis, where the buyer is a consumer, he will enjoy the protection organised by the Law 26/1984, already mentioned, and more recently that of the Law of 10 July 2003, also mentioned. By contrast, where the buyer is not a consumer he will have to rely on the protection granted by Art 1484ff CC on sales contracts and on the general rules on contract law of this Code. Likewise, by virtue of the second paragraph of Article 12 of the Law 7/1996 of

[58] See J Calais-Auloy and F Steinmetz, *Droit de la Consommation*, 7th edn (Paris, Dalloz, 2007) who regret that the Cour de Cassation has made this distinction and thus created legal uncertainty.

[59] (2004) AC 2161.

15 January 1996 (RCL 1996, 148 and 554) regulating retail trade, for sales that qualify under this law (Art 1–2), the buyer will benefit from a guarantee of six months as from the day of the reception of the good.

For the reasons exposed, the present dispute has to be resolved on the basis of the rules of the Civil Code.

Notes

(1) Judgments by national courts illustrate that very often the question arises as to whether a small businessman should not be treated equally to a consumer even when he buys a good that he uses in the course of his business (without processing or reselling it, but just using it as a consumer would).

(2) It has been stressed that small and medium-sized enterprises (SMEs) often lack specific expertise, experience, information and bargaining power, in a way very similar to consumers, especially when they act outside their field of usual business. This raises the question whether from the perspective of normative coherence (treating like cases alike) it is acceptable to treat SMEs in such cases so very differently from consumers as Community legislation currently does.[60] On the other hand there are many different types of SMEs. If at least some SMEs (franchisees, micro-enterprises) are as vulnerable as consumers, it remains difficult to draw the line between those SMEs that should be treated as consumers and those that should not be.[61]

II.B MIDDLEMEN

BGH, 26 January 2005[62] **1.21 (DE)**

AGENCY IN THE SALE OF SECOND-HAND CARS

The professional seller in disguise

The buyer of a second-hand car cannot invoke the legal sales guarantee against a professional car seller who merely acts as an agent for the former owner.

Facts: A consumer bought a second-hand Opel Coupé at the premises of a second-hand car salesman. The contract read: 'Sales contract for the private sale of a car' and designated a private person and his address. The contract also stipulated that the car was sold with exclusion of the legal liability for defects of the BGB (the German Civil Code). Shortly after the delivery the consumer encountered problems with the electronics of the car and demanded repair from the salesman. The salesman refused. The seller refused free repair, claiming that he is not the seller, but merely an intermediary. Thereupon the consumer claimed the rescission of the contract, arguing that the salesman is the seller because he has not drawn the consumer's attention to the fact that he merely acted as an agent and that the so-called agency is a circumvention of mandatory sales law rules. The district court rejected the claim, considering that there was no circum-

[60] M Hesselink, 'European Contract Law: A Matter of Consumer Protection, Citizenship, or Justice?' (2007) 15 *European Review of Private Law* 232–348.

[61] See M Hesselink, 'SMEs in European Contract law' in K Boele-Woelki and W Grosheide (eds), *The Future of European Contract Law. Essays in Honour of Ewoud Hondius* (Alphen aan de Rijn, Kluwer, 2007) 349ff, 360.

[62] (2005) NJW 1039.

vention but a genuine agency. The Court of Appeal confirmed the judgment. The Supreme Court confirmed that judgment.

Judgment: a) According to the content of the written sales contract, the plaintiff did not purchase the vehicle from the defendant but from M Ma, whose name and signature are entered by hand in the designated place on the form. The defendant himself is not referred to in the contractual document either by name or by the term 'C', used by him in business transactions. The colleague of the defendant, with whom the plaintiff negotiated in the matter of the vehicle, signed the contractual document on the line designated for the salesperson, with the addition 'pp'. Thus, according to the content of the contract, the defendant clearly did not appear as the seller of the vehicle. Not even an existing misconception on the part of the plaintiff would alter this. Incidentally, the plaintiff also saw the matter in this light originally, as the letter of 27/12/2002 from his lawyer to the defendant demonstrates. In reference to the sales contract, the letter states: 'Here concerned is an agency transaction, such that a sales contract was reached between MS (= plaintiff) and M Ma.'

b) Considering the terms of contract, which were subsequently also clear to the plaintiff, the attendant circumstances, from which the plaintiff now wishes to derive an individual transaction on the part of the defendant, are deemed to be of no further decisive importance. In particular it is irrelevant whether or not the defendant or his colleague indicated to the plaintiff during the course of the contract negotiations that the defendant was only acting as an agent in the sale of the vehicle. In any case it is clear that, in the given circumstances, adequate indication of this was provided, since the contract, amended in writing by the colleague of the defendant and given to the plaintiff to sign, did not describe the defendant as the seller but M Ma. The same applies to the fact cited at the appeal, that the defendant, by his own account, displayed the vehicles in the showroom in such a way that it was not clear to the customers whether the defendant was acting as the salesperson or only as the agent.

To the extent that the appeal in this context refers to the advertising conducted on behalf of the defendant's business and to the business cards previously used by him, this provides nothing which might solve the dispute, because the plaintiff did not report, after the undisputed conclusions drawn by the appeal court during the appeal, that these circumstances had created a false impression of the nature of the defendant's commercial activities.

c) The appeal cannot be accepted, in that it takes the view that commercial transactions pertaining to the sale of movable goods between a private seller and a consumer should generally be considered as circumvention transactions (§475 I 2 BGB). The appeal court rightly points out that this conception is not supported by the law.

Agency transactions, particularly in the used car business, have long been a common phenomenon. Before the introduction of differential taxation (§25a Turnover Tax Act) in 1990, they were used by the used car trade as a means of avoiding the accumulation of turnover tax when selling second-hand vehicles.

In the precedents of the adjudicating Senate they were recognized as a legitimate method of achieving this aim.

Agency transactions for the used car trade and the risk of circumventing plans to strengthen consumer protection were even referred to in the discussions concerning the revision of sales law in the course of modernizing the law of obligations. The demand made in connection with this, to avoid the possibility of circumventing the strict regulations for consumer sales by switching to agency transactions from the outset, cannot be accepted. This factor can only allow for the conclusion that agency transactions cannot generally be regarded as evasion transactions (§475 I 2 of the German Civil Code) even in the area of trade of second hand goods to private individuals.

d) According to a view predominantly represented in the literature, however, in an individual case a circumvention of the consumer protection measures aimed at the buying of consumer goods can be presumed where an agency transaction is improperly employed in order to conceal an existing transaction made, in reality, by the trader in person. ...

In connection with this, according to the opinion of the Senate, the question, as to how the prospects and risks of selling used cars from an economic perspective are divided between the previous owner of the vehicle and the vehicle dealer, is also of crucial importance. ...

If the dealer has accepted a used vehicle in part exchange, which he sells on 'in the sales order' in such a way that he has guaranteed the owner of the vehicle a certain minimum sale price for the used vehicle and has given him time to pay the appropriate share of the purchase price when buying a new vehicle, then looking at the situation from an economic perspective, it must be assumed that the dealer purchased the used vehicle, with the result that, when selling on the used car, he is to be regarded as the vendor, so that the qualification as an agency transaction chosen by the parties, cannot be accepted according to §475 I 2 of the BGB. On the other hand, if the purchaser of the new car has to bear the risk of selling on his used vehicle, then the qualification as agency must be accepted because in that case, even from an economic perspective, it cannot then be assumed to constitute circumvention.

e) On the basis of these criteria no objections can be raised to the findings of the appeal court. According to its conclusions, which are not challenged by the appeal, there are no discernible grounds for finding that the defendant ought to have borne the risk of selling the used car purchased by the plaintiff. In particular the defendant is under no obligation to assume liabilities subsequently for a minimum price when selling on the vehicle. The economic risk of the sale, therefore, lays with the vendor M Ma. A further point in its favour is that the defendant, as shown by the filed photocopy of the list of settled invoices from the 15 November 2002, only settled his account with his client M Ma after the completion of the sale to the plaintiff and that falling short of the sales price agreed with M Ma would only have been admissible after consultation with the client M Ma according to the conclusion of the appeal court, which it reached based on evidence heard at first instance and which was not objected to by the appeal. Taking all these circumstances into consideration therefore, the view of the appeal court was legally sound, namely that this is a case of genuine agency and not simply a sale carried out in person and declared as an agency transaction.

f) The appeal wrongly raises the objection to the appeal court that it cannot therefore be decisively geared to the distribution of risks between the dealer and his client, because the consumer has no insight into the privity of contract between the dealer and his client. The lawsuit in question shows that in the dispute over warranty between consumer and dealer it is entirely possible for the judge to 'illuminate' the agreement between the private vendor of the vehicle and the car dealer which underlie the agency transaction. It also does not follow from its appeal court's solution, that its warranty rights would become unenforceable because the consumer would not be able to clarify the 'actual legal position' or, therefore, who the correct opposing party is. If the consumer—as is the case here—according to the content of the sales contract did not purchase from the dealer but from a private vendor through the mediation of the dealer then from the consumer's point of view the assumption is that rights and claims as a result of faults in the purchased item can be asserted. On the other hand, if the consumer takes the view that the dealer, and not the private vendor, is in reality his contractual partner, then it is up to him to present and prove facts which argue for a case of circumvention. Even from a consumer protection perspective, a litigant is not free from the risk of not being able to prove facts that are only presumed. [references omitted]

Green Paper on the Review of the Consumer Acquis[63] **1.22 (EU)**

A consumer is not protected by the acquis when his/her contractual counterpart is another private person. The same applies to the case when an individual is represented by a commercial agent, broker or any other intermediary. A practical example of this is when a car dealer sells a second-hand car on behalf of one consumer to another consumer. It has been argued that in these cases consumers need protection similar to that of an ordinary business-to-consumer contract since the other party will benefit from the professional expertise of the intermediary and some Member States have chosen to extend consumer protection to these situations. However, it may be very difficult to establish clear criteria as to when the role of the intermediary is so strong as to warrant consumer protection. There may be a risk of unforeseen and negative knock-on effects on markets on which private persons trade with private persons.

Against applying consumer protection rules to private sellers it could also be argued that a private person might not realise that contracting a professional as her or his intermediary will put her or him in a position equivalent to a professional. On the other hand, a consumer who concludes a contract with a professional acting as intermediary for a private person may be more in need of protection than his contractual counterpart.

It should be noted that the notion of intermediary would not include trading platforms for sellers and consumers, eg on the Internet, where the platform provider is not involved in the conclusion of the contract. The role of intermediaries in electronic commerce, including search engines and auction platforms, is currently being examined in a different context and therefore not covered by this review.

Notes

(1) In the real world, where a car dealer sells a car and agrees to try to find a buyer for the consumer's old car he may prefer not to act as the seller (because in that case he will bear the legal guarantee duty provided for the Consumer Sales Directive (99/44/EC)[64] and the national laws implementing it). It may, however, also be that the consumer prefers a direct sale in order to avoid VAT. The consumer who buys a second-hand car from a new car dealer will generally know that the car dealer acts as an intermediary. Where a consumer buys a second-hand car from a second-hand car salesman he will normally assume that the dealer is the real seller of the car. The judgment of the BGH mentioned above shows that consumers may be confronted with second-hand car dealers who act as agents for private individuals who sell their cars without expecting this. The judgment of the BGH concludes that in the case at hand the agency was genuine. However, under German law the salesman may be held to be the seller when the agency is to be qualified as circumvention of sales law. This

[63] COM [2006] 744.

may be the case where the salesman, and not, as in the case at hand, the owner, bore the economic risk of the sale.

(2) In cyberspace the problems may even be much more complex. The consumer who surfs on the internet and visits a website will not always be aware of the exact identity and role of the person to whom he is giving his consent by clicking. Obviously an auction platform like eBay is a professional but not (necessarily) a professional seller; a circumstance the consumer may often not be aware of.

(3) With regard to second-hand goods, see also Article 1(3) of the Consumer Sales Directive (99/44/EC):

> Member States may provide that the expression 'consumer goods' does not cover second-hand goods sold at the public auction where the consumers have the opportunity of attending the sale in person

and Article 7(1), second subparagraph of the Directive:

> Member States may provide that, in the case of second-hand goods, the seller and consumer may agree contractual terms or agreements which have a shorter time period for the liability of the seller.

II.C THE BENCHMARK CONSUMER

The case-law of the ECJ in the field of consumer protection is particularly rich. There are basically two type of cases: judgments on direct actions brought by the Commission against Member States and preliminary rulings where the Court verifies the compatibility of national measures protecting consumers with the fundamental freedoms of the EC Treaty (in particular free movement of goods and free provision of services) on the one hand and judgments interpreting consumer protection measures at the EC level (provisions of directives).

In a recent article it is submitted that the Court has developed a two-pronged approach towards consumer protection.

H Unberath and A Johnston, The Double-Headed Approach of the ECJ Concerning Consumer Protection[65] **1.23 (EU)**

Coherence at Community level?

The starting point of our review was whether the case law revealed coherence in EC law in the field of consumer protection. Our survey confirms the finding of a double-headed approach towards consumer protection. In relation to negative harmonisation ..., we submitted that the ECJ is biased in favour of free trade and sceptical of any restrictions at national that are founded on consumer protection. In defining the need for protection, the Court has argued on the premise of a 'reference' consumer who is

[64] Directive 99/44/EC of the European Parliament and of the Council of 25 May 1999 on certain aspects of the sale of consumer goods and associated guarantees [1999] OJ L 171, 12–16.

[65] H Unberath and A Johnston, 'The Double-Headed Approach of the ECJ Concerning Consumer Protection' (2007) 44 *CML Rev* 1281–82.

reasonably circumspect and well informed. The resulting judgments can be regarded as involving a trade-oriented and liberal approach. While recognizing consumer protection as a fundamental value of EC law, the Court regularly objects to legislation at national level as being unnecessary to achieve the legislations' stated goal, and thus contrary to the principle of proportionality. Indeed, the Court has proved creative and has frequently come up with alternative measures that are less restrictive in regulating the market but just as effective in protecting consumers. Even the most serious concern justifying restrictions of human conduct, namely dangers to public health, has often failed to convince the Court, the precautionary principle notwithstanding. The Member Sates are required to establish the seriousness of the risk in relation to specific dangers and must do so on a solid scientific basis.

The case law on positive harmonisation ... rests on a fundamental different rationale. Apart from the fact that challenges to the legal validity of EC consumer protection measures are virtually absent, on the whole the Court has granted the consumer protection directives a wide scope of application and amplified their regulatory and interventionist potential .... Where the wording of the relevant provision is ambivalent, the Court has invariably opted for the most consumer-friendly and often, therefore, the most trade-restricting interpretation. Very rarely has the Court attempted to take into account possible alternatives to mandatory rules that unilaterally seek to protect the consumer. Attempts by Member States to manoeuvre within the framework of open-textured provisions to increase legal certainty or to confine interventionist legislation have regularly been rejected (often at the suit of the Commission under Art 226). One wonders what the 'reference consumer' resident in the world of negative harmonization would have thought had he been invited by the Court into the realm of positive harmonization. But he was not.

Notes

(1) Some of the cases mentioned by these authors and several issues raised by these cases, notably how to define the benchmark (average) consumer in relation to consumer law, that are liable to have an impact on free movement will be discussed throughout this chapter (see in particular the following sections) and indeed the whole Casebook.

(2) Case C-470/93 *Mars* has been discussed above section I.C. There, as in other cases, the ECJ indeed held that the average consumer is reasonably circumspect.

(3) The finding by the authors that on the whole the ECJ has granted the consumer protection Directives a wide scope of application can be nuanced by looking at the case-law regarding specific Directives (see in particular hereafter, in section IV, the case-law on the Product Liability Directive: the ECJ gives a rather restrictive interpretation of the scope of this Directive).

CFI Case T-363/04, 12 September 2007[66] *Koipe Corporacion v OHIM* 1.24 (EU)

THE RISK OF CONFUSION BETWEEN TWO TRADE MARKS

La Espanola

The Spanish consumer is not circumspect when he buys olive oil.

Facts: In 1996, Aceites del Sur SA filed an application for a Community trade mark, for several classes of foodstuffs, at the Office for Harmonisation in the Internal Market (Trade Marks and Designs) (OHIM) pursuant to Regulation 40/94.[67] The mark in respect of which registration was sought ('the mark applied for' or 'the La Española mark') is the figurative mark depicted in Figure 1. After publication of the application in Community Trade Marks Bulletin 89/98, two competitors gave notice of opposition to registration of the Community trade mark applied for. The second was by Aceites Carbonell (now Koipe Corporation SL). The ground relied on in support of the opposition was the likelihood of confusion, as provided for in Articles 8(1)b, 8(2)c and 8(5) of Regulation 40/94, between the mark applied for and the applicant's earlier figurative mark Carbonell ('the earlier mark' or 'the Carbonell mark'), depicted in Figure 2. The Board of Appeal of the OHIM considered that the overall visual impression produced by the marks at issue is different and, therefore, that their global appreciation does not reveal any similarity between them, which would exclude any likelihood of confusion. Koipe successfully appealed that decision before the CFI.

Figure 1

Figure 2

Judgment: 99. The global assessment of the likelihood of confusion must, in relation to the visual, aural or conceptual similarity of the marks in question, be based on the overall impression given by the marks, bearing in mind, in particular, their distinctive and dominant components and the fact that the average consumer normally perceives a mark as a whole and does not proceed to analyse its various details (*Sabel*, para 23, and *Lloyd Schuhfabrik Meyer*, para 25).

[66] [2007] ECR II-03355.

[67] Council Regulation (EC) 40/94 of 20 December 1993 on the Community trade mark [1994] OJ L 11, 1–36.

100. As regards the visual aspects, the Court finds that the two marks at issue have many elements in common, namely:
—they both consist of a label which is rectangular, vertical and regular, of identical size with a red border with rounded corners at the external edges;
—they both include a drawing of a woman seated in the foreground, in the vertical axis of the label, whose clothing is in similar colours and who are both dressed in a skirt, a white blouse and a red shawl with fringed edges;
—the two women depicted have their hair tied back with a flower behind their right ear and a decorative comb;
—the two women depicted have bare arms, their head turned towards the left and are seated on a wall which is ochre in colour;
—there is an olive branch in the foreground close to the heads of the two women depicted;
—there is a space for the description of the product in the upper band, which is curved toward the exterior of the label and convex towards the interior;
—the brand name appears in a white box against the red background placed on the lower part of the label;
—the shape of that box is flat on the edge nearest to the bottom of the label and convex on the edge nearest to the inside of the label;
—the brand name features in the white letters of the same height against the red background of the box;
—represented behind the woman is an olive grove in the same range of colours and the horizon of which occupies the same amount of space.

101. The Court considers that the similarity of the figurative elements at issue, both as regards the colour schemes and the drawings is more significant than small differences which become apparent only after a detailed and thorough examination.

102. As regards the conceptual aspects, the Court finds that the Board of Appeal itself held in the contested decision (paragraphs 9 and 19) that there is a conceptual link between the marks at issue, which although weak, is linked to the nature and origin of the goods protected.

103. The Court considers that the elements common to the two marks at issue, seen as a whole, produce an overall visual impression of great similarity, since the 'La Española mark' reproduces very precisely the essence of the message and the visual impression given by 'the Carbonell mark': the woman dressed in traditional clothes, seated in a certain manner, close to an olive branch with an olive grove in the background, the overall image consisting of an almost identical arrangement of spaces, colours, places for brand names and style of lettering.

104. The Court considers that that overall similar impression inescapably gives rise on the part of the consumer to a likelihood of confusion between the marks at issue.

105. That likelihood of confusion is not diminished by the existence of the different word element since, as it was held above, the word element of the mark applied for has a very weak distinctive character, since it refers to the geographical origin of the goods. ...

108. Since olive oil is a consumer product which is very common in Spain, the level of attention of the average consumer with respect to its external appearance is low (see, to that effect, Case T-283/04 *Georgia-Pacific v OHIM* (Motif gaufré) [2007] ECR I-0, paragraph 41).

109. Third, as the Board of Appeal acknowledges in the contested decision, account should be taken of the fact that olive oil is most commonly purchased in supermarkets or establishments where goods bearing different trade marks are arranged on shelves. In

this type of point-of-sale, as the applicant submits, the consumer loses little time between his successive purchases, which are made in different parts of the shop, and does not ask orally for the various goods that he is looking for, but goes to the shelves where those products are located with the consequence that phonetic differences between the marks at issue are irrelevant for the purposes of distinguishing the goods. In those circumstances, the consumer is guided more by an impression than by a direct comparison of the various marks and often does not read all the information on each olive oil container. In most cases, he merely takes a bottle whose label provides him with the visual impact of the brand he is looking for. In those circumstances, it is the figurative element of the marks at issue which acquires greater importance, contrary what was held in the contested decision, which increases the likelihood of confusion between the two marks at issue.

110. It should be noted in support of this, that where the marks at issue are examined at the distance and the speed at which the consumer in a supermarket selects the goods he is looking for, the differences between the signs at issue are more difficult to distinguish and the similarities are more apparent, since the average consumer perceives the mark as a whole and does not proceed to analyse its various details.

111. Finally, account should be taken of the fact that in light of the similarity of the signs at issue and the fact that the word element of the mark applied for has a weak distinctive character, the consumer may perceive the mark applied for as a sub-brand linked to 'the Carbonell mark' designating an olive oil of a different quality from that which is the subject of that mark (see, to that effect, *Confortflex* para 61). As it is clear from the file, 'the Carbonell mark', which has been in Spain since 1904, is identified with olive oil on the Spanish market and the image that it uses automatically identifies that mark.

Notes

(1) In this case the CFI considered that, since olive oil is a very common consumer product in Spain, the level of attention of the average consumer with respect to its external appearance is low. The CFI also observed that the product is mostly bought in supermarkets. In those circumstances, according to the CFI, the consumer is guided more by an impression than by a direct comparison of the various marks and often does not read all the information on each olive oil container. In most cases, he merely takes a bottle whose label provides him with the visual impact of the brand he is looking for.

(2) The assumption that the consumer does not pay attention to the information available on the product before buying it (when the product is one of current consumption) is in contradiction with the paradigm of the well-informed and *circumspect* consumer in the case law of the ECJ (in notably *Gut Springenheide*) (see section I.C. above) that does not differentiate according to whether the good is common or not to the relevant consumer. On the other hand, this case seems more in line with the ECJ's case-law interpreting consumer directives as explained by Unberath and Johnston in their article mentioned above.

Question

Do you think that the differentiated approach of the ECJ regarding the benchmark consumer is sustainable?

II.D VULNERABLE PARTIES

ECJ Case C-382/87, 16 May 1989[68] **1.25 (EU)**

Buet and Educational Business Services v Ministère public

THE VULNERABILITY OF CONSUMERS IN THE CASE OF CANVASSING WITH LANGUAGE COURSES

English for French unemployed

A ban on canvassing with language courses is justified since the targeted consumer is particularly vulnerable.

Facts: Mr Buet, the manager of the French company Educational Business Services (EBS), was prosecuted because representatives of that company went to the homes of potential clients for the purpose of selling them English-language teaching material. EBS earned 90 per cent of its turnover in this way and the remainder at trade fairs and exhibitions. Mr Buet was sentenced by the Tribunal de grande instance for having infringed Article 8 II of Loi No 72-1137 of 22 December 1972 on the protection of consumers with respect to canvassing and to selling at private dwellings, which prohibits canvassing for the purpose of selling educational material. Mr Buet, EBS and the Ministère public appealed against the judgment of the Tribunal de grande instance. Mr Buet claimed that application of the prohibition on canvassing to his case was contrary to the provisions of Article 28ff of the Treaty inasmuch as it forced him to abandon a particularly effective sales technique and thus restricted the marketing in France of products from another Member State. The Court of Appeal of Paris made a preliminary reference to the ECJ with regard to the interpretation of Article 28 EC (free movement of goods) in this respect.

Judgment: 12. In that respect canvassing at private dwellings exposes the potential customer to the risk of making an ill-considered purchase. To guard against that risk it is normally sufficient to ensure that purchasers have the right to cancel a contract concluded in their home.

13. It is necessary, however, to point out that there is greater risk of an ill-considered purchase when the canvassing is for enrolment for a course of instruction or the sale of educational material. The potential purchaser often belongs to a category of people who, for one reason or another, are behind with their education and are seeking to catch up. That makes them particularly vulnerable when faced with salesmen of educational material who attempt to persuade them that if they use that material they will have better employment prospects. Moreover, as is apparent from the documents, it is as a result of numerous complaints caused by such abuses, such as the sale of out-of-date courses, that the legislature enacted the ban on canvassing at issue.

14. Finally, it needs to be stressed that since teaching is not a consumer product in daily use, an ill-considered purchase could cause the purchaser harm other than mere financial loss that could be longer lasting. Thus it has to be acknowledged that the purchase of unsuitable or low-quality material could compromise the consumer's chances of obtaining further training and thus consolidating his position on the labour market.

[68] [1989] ECR 1235.

15. In those circumstances it is permissible for the national legislature of the Member State to consider that giving consumers a right of cancellation is not sufficient protection and that it is necessary to ban canvassing at private dwellings.

Notes

(1) *Buet*, together with *Oosthoek*[69] have been called exceptions[70] to a trend in the ECJ's case-law towards deregulation and a mitigation of the harsh consequences of the rule of mutual recognition inherent in *Cassis de Dijon*. It can at least been seen as the recognition by the ECJ of Member States' margin of discretion to take measures for the protection of vulnerable consumers, where such consumers can be clearly identified. *Buet* illustrates a trend in the Court's case-law that can be observed even more clearly in matters of health protection, namely that the stronger the social or societal dimension of the general interest and the national sensitivities with respect to that general interest, the greater the autonomy of the Member States to determine the measures to be taken. In these areas the ECJ will be less inclined to question the appropriateness and the proportionality of the national measure.[71] Article 5 of the Unfair Commercial Practices Directive (2005/29/EC) discussed below confirms this trend by providing that commercial practices which are likely to materially distort the economic behaviour only of a clearly identifiable group of consumers who are particularly vulnerable to the practice or the underlying product because of their mental or physical infirmity, age or credulity in a way which the trader could reasonably be expected to foresee, shall be assessed from the perspective of the average member of that group. This is without prejudice to the common and legitimate advertising practice of making exaggerated statements or statements which are not meant to be taken literally.

(2) It should be stressed that *Buet* was pronounced before *Tobacco I*,[72] a judgment that has shed some doubt on the constitutionality of minimum harmonisation directives, like the doorstep selling directive (that directive providing for a mere cooling-off period in case of doorstep selling without prohibiting this sale method as the applicable French law did with regard to educational material).

(3) It should also be mentioned that *Buet* was pronounced before Joined Cases C-267/91 and 268/91, *Keck and Mithouard*, where the Court narrowed down the scope of Article 28 EC by ruling that the application to products from other Member States of national provisions restricting or prohibiting 'certain selling arrangements' is not such as to hinder trade between Member States, within the meaning of that definition, so long as those provisions apply to all relevant traders operating within the national territory and so long as they affect in the same manner, in law and in fact, the marketing of domestic products and of those from other Member States. A

[69] Case 286/81 [1982] ECR 4575.

[70] S Weatherill, 'Recent Case Law Concerning the Free Movement of Goods: Mapping the Frontiers of Market Deregulation' (1999) 36 *CML Rev* 51–93.

[71] See J Stuyck, 'Can Consistent Legislation Be Appropriate and Proportionate to its Aim? The Case of the "loi Evin"' and the Ban on Indirect Television Advertising for Alcohol' (2005) 42 *CML Rev* 789–801ff.

[72] See s I.E. above.

sales method, such as doorstep selling, is a selling arrangement. Buet-type of national legislation that does not affect imported goods than it affects domestic goods does anymore not need to pass the proportionality test of the rule of reason of *Cassis de Dijon*.

Cass civ 1e, 21 October 2003[73] **1.26 (FR)**

THE SCOPE OF APPLICATION OF THE RULES ON CONSUMER CREDIT

The indebted physician

Applicability of the consumer credit provisions to a professional credit used for private purposes.

Facts: Mr Michel Masi, a physician, held a bank account for his professional income. In 1988 the bank allowed him an overdraft facility for FRF 80.000, which Mr Masi subsequently used to credit his personal account with the same bank. In 1996 Mr Masi was overdrawn on his professional account ti the amount of FRF 190.447,56. The bank sued Mr X. The latter invoked Articles L 311-1ff of the Code de la Consommation (Consumer Code) and claims that the action by the bank is foreclosed. The Court of First Instance and the Court of Appeal rejected Mr Masi's contention since the transfer of part of the credit from his professional account to his personal account could not change the nature of the loan (which was a professional loan). The protective measures of the Consumer Code therefore did not apply. The Cour de Cassation annuls the judgment.

Judgment: Given that Article L 311-3 of the Consumer Code excludes from the scope of application of the rules on consumer credit a credit that is destined to finance the needs of a professional activity, the professional destination of a credit, even if it is linked to a personal account, can only result from an express stipulation to that effect. …

By ruling as it did (namely that the protection of the Code did not apply) after having found that the offer which was made for an overdraft facility did not mention that the credit was destined to Mr Masi's professional activity, the Court of Appeal has made a wrong application of the above mentioned text.

The Court of Appeal has violated the consumer credit provisions of the Consumer Code by rejecting the application of these provisions without taking into account that the credit agreement did not mention that the credit was destined for the professional needs of Mr X.

Cour de Cassation, 12 October 2000[74] **1.27 (BE)**
Saint Brice v Belgian State

THE BENCHMARK CONSUMER IN CASE OF MISLEADING ADVERTISING

The mail order decoy

The consumer to be protected in the case at hand is the vulnerable consumer.

[73] (2003) Bull civ I No 208, 164; (2004) RTDcom 136, note D Legeais.
[74] Pas I, 544.

Facts: Consumers had bought goods from a mail order company attracted by the promise that they could win meaningful prizes. It turned out that in most of the cases the prizes were objects of very low value. The Minister of Economic Affairs brought an action for a cease and desist order against the mail order company for several infringement of the Trade Practices Act,[75] ie misleading advertising and acts against honest business practices that cause prejudice to consumers, ie the general clause on unfair practices. He succeeded, but the judgment was appealed. In last resort the Cour de cassation (Supreme Court) had to decide on whether the Court of Appeal had correctly applied the general clause on unfair practices. The Cour de cassation accepted that in order to judge the fairness of a commercial practice under the general clause of the Trade Practices Act, a judge could take the vulnerable consumer as a standard. Article 94 of the Trade Practices Act prohibits unfair trade practices which can harm the interests of one or more consumers.

Judgment: Given that the judgment states that the plaintiff carries out mail order trading operations under a variety of different names;

Given that the judgment rules that the surveys that were supposedly carried out (by the plaintiff) to ascertain the consumers' tastes, when in reality prizes were offered that bore no resemblance to the items originally advertised as potential prizes, as well as the publicity campaign that advertised that prizes would be awarded for early or firm orders, run contrary to honest business practices;

Given that the judgment bases its decision on article 94 Trade Practices Act which forbids any dishonest business practice on the part of a seller that harms or may harm the interests of one or more consumers;

Given that, in order to assess the extent to which a business practice can be labelled dishonest, the judge may take into consideration both the specific circumstances of some groups of consumers and the need to provide these consumers with greater protection;

Given that the judgment considers 'that the law must protect less well-educated and less well enlightened consumers, those who, without demonstrating negligence or lack of awareness, are not capable of sufficiently understanding the actual quality of the prize offered to them, of distinguishing complete and objective information from exaggerated, unlikely or frankly false information; while attracting and maintaining consumers' attention is of course an essential feature of advertising, it is important that the content of the advert does not contain 'any artifice, trickery or hidden subtleties' and that it does not seek to take advantage of the naivety of a certain type of audience; while the law does not provide a definition of those consumers in need of protection, it goes without saying that this protection must include the least well-informed consumers who, lacking the ability to critically examine an item that is skilfully presented to them, cannot detect the exaggerations, deceptive silences and traps set by the advertiser';

Based upon these considerations, the judgment legally justifies its decision that the plaintiff has breached article 94 of the Trade Practices Act.

Notes

(1) Case-law of the Cour de Cassation on the benchmark consumer for the application of the Trade Practices Act is scarce. Here the supreme court of Belgium endorses the ruling of the lower court that the Trade Practices Act aims at protecting consumers with a low education and who are not well informed, ie those who, without being negligent or inconsiderate, are unable to understand properly the real qualities of what is offered and to distinguish objective information from

[75] Loi du 14 juillet 1991 sur les pratiques du commerce et sur l'information et la protection du consommateur.

exaggerations or fraud. The Cour de Cassation accepts that when appraising a practice in the light of the Act the court can take into account the special situation of certain categories of consumers and the necessity of a stronger protection.

(2) Since the conduct under scrutiny was a mailing to the general public the judgment would seem at odds with the 'average consumer' of the ECJ's case-law (although the case at hand concerned a purely internal situation where the national judge was free to rule without taking into account the criterion developed by the Court in its case law on free movement). The judgment would seem to be in line with the Unfair Commercial Practices Directive (2005/29/EC), to the extent that the mailing was likely to 'materially distort the economic behaviour only of a clearly identifiable group of consumers who are particularly vulnerable because of … their credulity'.

UCPD (2005/29/EC) **1.28 (EU)**

Article 5 Prohibition of unfair commercial practices

(1) Unfair commercial practices shall be prohibited.

(2) A commercial practice shall be unfair if:

(a) it is contrary to the requirements of professional diligence, and

(b) it materially distorts or is likely to materially distort the economic behaviour with regard to the product of the average consumer whom it reaches or to whom it is addressed, or of the average member of the group when a commercial practice is directed to a particular group of consumers.

(3) Commercial practices which are likely to materially distort the economic behaviour only of a clearly identifiable group of consumers who are particularly vulnerable to the practice or the underlying product because of their mental or physical infirmity, age or credulity in a way which the trader could reasonably be expected to foresee, shall be assessed from the perspective of the average member of that group. This is without prejudice to the common and legitimate advertising practice of making exaggerated statements or statements which are not meant to be taken literally. …

Notes

(1) This provision should be seen against the background of the case-law of the ECJ on the relationship between national consumer and advertising law and free movement of goods. As explained above (section I.C), in its case-law concerning the compatibility of national measures to protect consumers in the field of advertising and sales promotions, the ECJ has considered that the consumer to be taken into account, in particular to determine whether consumers are misled, is the average consumer who is well informed and circumspect.

(2) Contrary to what the ECJ decided in *Buet* (see section II.D above) with regard to a particular (aggressive) sales method, the benchmark for the appraisal of advertising and sales promotion restrictions seems to be the average consumer and not the vulnerable consumer. In the line of *Buet* the Directive expressly states that where a particular group of vulnerable consumers is targeted or is the likely target of the commercial practice the average of that group is the benchmark.

II.E THE PARADIGM OF THE WEAKER PARTY

ECJ Case C-168/05, 26 October 2005[76] **1.29 (EU)**
Elisa María Mostaza Claro v Centro Móvil Milenium SL

ARBITRABILITY OF CONSUMER CLAIMS

The mobile arbitration clause

A national court must examine the validity of an arbitration agreement with a consumer even where the consumer has not pleaded the invalidity in the course of the arbitration proceedings.

Facts: On 2 May 2002, a mobile telephone contract was concluded between Móvil and Ms Mostaza Claro. The contract contained an arbitration clause under which any disputes arising from the contract were to be referred for arbitration to the Asociación Europea de Arbitraje de Derecho y Equidad (AEADE, the European Association of Arbitration in Law and in Equity). As Ms Mostaza Claro did not comply with the minimum subscription period, Móvil initiated arbitration proceedings before the AEADE. Ms Mostaza Claro presented arguments on the merits of the dispute, but did not repudiate the arbitration proceedings or claim that the arbitration agreement was void. The arbitration proceedings subsequently took place and the arbitrator found against her. Ms Mostaza Claro contested the arbitration decision delivered by the AEADE before the referring court, submitting that the unfair nature of the arbitration clause meant that the arbitration agreement was null and void. The Spanish judge made a preliminary reference to the ECJ regarding the interpretation of the Unfair Contract Terms Directive (93/13/EEC). Point 1(q) of the annex to the Directive (containing an indicative list of unfair terms) refers to terms which have the object or effect of 'excluding or hindering the consumer's right to take legal action or exercise any other legal remedy, particularly by requiring the consumer to take disputes exclusively to arbitration not covered by legal provisions'.

Judgment: 25. The system of protection introduced by the Directive is based on the idea that the consumer is in a weak position vis-à-vis the seller or supplier, as regards both his bargaining power and his level of knowledge. This leads to the consumer agreeing to terms drawn up in advance by the seller or supplier without being able to influence the content of those terms (Joined Cases C-240/98 to C-244/98 *Océano Grupo Editorial and Salvat Editores* [2000] ECR I-4941, paragraph 25).

26. Such an imbalance between the consumer and the seller or supplier may only be corrected by positive action unconnected with the actual parties to the contract (*Océano Grupo Editorial and Salvat Editores*, paragraph 27). ...

36. The importance of consumer protection has in particular led the Community legislature to lay down, in Article 6(1) of the Directive, that unfair terms used in a contract concluded with a consumer by a seller or supplier 'shall ... not be binding on the consumer'. This is a mandatory provision which, taking into account the weaker position of one of the parties to the contract, aims to replace the formal balance which the latter establishes between the rights and obligations of the parties with an effective balance which re-establishes equality between them.

37. Moreover, as the aim of the Directive is to strengthen consumer protection, it constitutes, according to Article 3(1)(t) EC, a measure which is essential to the accomplishment of the tasks entrusted to the Community and, in particular, to raising the

[76] [2006] ECR I-10421.

standard of living and the quality of life in its territory (see, by analogy, concerning Article 81 EC, *Eco Swiss*, paragraph 36).

38. The nature and importance of the public interest underlying the protection which the Directive confers on consumers justify, moreover, the national court being required to assess of its own motion whether a contractual term is unfair, compensating in this way for the imbalance which exists between the consumer and the seller or supplier.

39. Having regard to the foregoing, the answer to the question referred must be that the Directive must be interpreted as meaning that a national court seised of an action for annulment of an arbitration award must determine whether the arbitration agreement is void and annul that award where that agreement contains an unfair term, even though the consumer has not pleaded that invalidity in the course of the arbitration proceedings, but only in that of the action for annulment.

Notes

(1) The *Claro* judgment concerns arbitration clauses in consumer contracts. That subject (and the *Claro* judgment) will be discussed in chapters 4 and 8.

(2) At this point it should be stressed that the ECJ has expressly stated that the strengthening of consumer protection (Article 3(1)t) is an essential tool to achieve one of the ultimate goals of the Treaty, ie the raising of the standard of living and the quality of life. It is also noteworthy that the ECJ draws an analogy with its *Eco Swiss* judgment (Case C-126/97 [1999] ECR I-3055). In this judgment the Court held that a national court to which application is made for annulment of an arbitration award must grant that application if it considers that the award in question is in fact contrary to Article 81 EC (the prohibition of restrictive agreements), where its domestic rules of procedure require it to grant an application for annulment founded on failure to observe national rules of public policy. In other words the enforcement of the EC competition rules should be equivalent to other provisions considered under national law to relate to public policy. The ECJ refers more in particular to paragraph 36 of *Eco Swiss* where it considered that according to Article 3(1)g EC, Article 81 EC constitutes a fundamental provision which is essential for the accomplishment of the tasks entrusted to the Community and, in particular, for the functioning of the internal market. The importance and fundamental character of the prohibition of restrictive agreements in Article 81(1) also explains why the Treaty expressly provides, in Article 81(2) EC, that any agreements or decisions prohibited pursuant to that article are to be automatically void. The parallel drawn by the ECJ, in the annotated judgment, with the competition rules is remarkable. Indeed regarding consumer protection the Treaty itself does not contain any remedy, such as the automatic nullity of agreements or clauses that are unfair towards consumers. The nullity of a contract term that is unfair within the meaning of Community law, ie secondary Community law (Unfair Contract Terms Directive (93/13/EEC)) is a possible remedy according to national law, in order to give effect to Article 6(1) of the Directive that Member States shall lay down that unfair terms used in a contract concluded with a consumer by a seller or supplier shall, as provided for under their national law, not be binding on the consumer and that the contract shall continue to bind the parties upon those terms if it is capable of continuing in existence without

the unfair terms. In other words, the nullity of unfair contract terms is not a fundamental rule enshrined in the Treaty and yet the ECJ recognises that consumer protection against unfair contract terms in the field of access to justice is a 'public policy' interest obliging the national judge to examine the arbitration whether the arbitration agreement was not unfair vis-à-vis the consumer.

(3) It is also interesting to compare this case to Joined Cases C-222/05 et al, *Van der Weerd*,[77] which concerned the power of a national court to raise Community law of its own motion in legal proceedings between professionals and the state. The ECJ distinguishes the consumer law cases on the basis that the relevant consumer law Directives have the special purpose of protecting consumers as weaker parties. This justifies a more intrusive approach to the rules of national civil procedure when consumer litigation is at stake, in contrast to normal litigation such as that in the *Van der Weerd* case itself.

II.F MIXED SITUATIONS

ECJ Case C-464/01, 16 September 2004[78] **1.30 (EU)**
Gruber v Bay Wa AG

CONSUMER CONTRACTS UNDER THE BRUSSELS CONVENTION (REGULATION)

The farmer who replaced the roof tiles of his farm

No protection under the Brussels Convention for a contract that partly concerns the buyer's trade.

Facts: Mr Gruber, a farmer, owned a farm building constructed around a square ('Vierkanthof'), in Upper Austria, close to the German border. He used about a dozen rooms as a dwelling for himself and his family. In addition over 200 pigs were kept there, and there were fodder silos and a large machine room. Between 10 and 15 per cent of the total fodder necessary for the farm was also stored there. The area of the farm building used for residential purposes was slightly more than 60 per cent of the total floor area of the building. Mr Gruber wished to replace the roof tiles of his farm building, and contacted Bay Wa, a German firm publishing brochures which were also distributed in Austria. Mr Gruber made several telephone enquiries to an employee of Bay Wa concerning the different types of tiles and the prices, stating his name and address but not mentioning the fact that he was a farmer. The employee made him an offer by telephone but Mr Gruber wished to inspect the tiles on site. On his visit to Bay Wa's premises, he was given a written quotation by the employee. During that meeting Mr Gruber told Bay Wa's employee that he had a farm and wished to tile the roof of the farm building. He stated that he also owned ancillary buildings that were used principally for the farm, but did not expressly state whether the building to be tiled was used mainly for business or for private purposes. The following day a contract was concluded by correspondence. Mr Gruber considered that the tiles delivered by Bay Wa to tile the roof of his farm building showed significant variations in colour despite the warranty that the colour would be uniform. As a result the roof would have to be retiled. He therefore decided to bring proceedings on the basis of the warranty together with a claim for damages, seeking reimbursement of the cost of the tiles (ATS 258,123) and of the expense of removing them and retiling the roof (ATS 141,877) and a declaration of liability for any future expenses. Mr Gruber commenced proceedings before the Landesgericht Steyr (Austria), Bay Wa contested the court's

[77] [2007] ECR I-4233, paras 39–40.
[78] [2005] ECR I-439.

competence under Article 13 of the Brussels Convention (now the Brussels I Regulation 44/2001) on Jurisdiction and enforcement in civil matters. Article 13 of the Brussels Convention is worded as follows:

> In proceedings concerning a contract concluded by a person for a purpose which can be regarded as being outside his trade or profession, hereinafter called 'the consumer', jurisdiction shall be determined by this Section … if it is: (1) a contract for the sale of goods on instalment credit terms; or (2) a contract for a loan repayable by instalments, or for any other form of credit, made to finance the sale of goods; or (3) any other contract for the supply of goods or a contract for the supply of services, and (a) in the State of the consumer's domicile the conclusion of the contract was preceded by a specific invitation addressed to him or by advertising; and (b) the consumer took in that State the steps necessary for the conclusion of the contract.

According to the Landesgericht Steyr, the conditions for the application of Article 13(3) of the Brussels Convention were satisfied. By judgment of 1 February 2001 the Oberlandesgericht (Higher Regional Court) Linz (Austria) upheld Bay Wa's appeal, however, and dismissed Mr Gruber's claim on the ground that the Austrian courts do not have jurisdiction to hear the dispute. Mr Gruber then brought an appeal before the Oberster Gerichtshof (Supreme Court) against the judgment of 1 February 2001 of the Oberlandesgericht Linz. The Oberster Gerichtshof referred several questions to the ECJ, ia whether the rules of jurisdiction laid down by the Brussels Convention must be interpreted as meaning that a contract which relates to activities which are partly business and partly private must be regarded as having been concluded by a consumer for the purposes of the first paragraph of Article 13 of the Convention.

Judgment: 32. First of all, within the scheme of the Brussels Convention, the jurisdiction of the courts of the Contracting State in which the defendant is domiciled constitutes the general principle enshrined in the first paragraph of Article 2, and it is only by way of derogation from that principle that the Convention provides for an exhaustive list of cases in which the defendant may or must be sued before the courts of another Contracting State. As a consequence, the rules of jurisdiction which derogate from that general principle are to be strictly interpreted, so that they cannot give rise to an interpretation going beyond the cases envisaged by the Convention (see, in particular, *Bertrand*, paragraph 17; *Shearson Lehman Hutton*, paragraphs 14, 15 and 16; *Benincasa*, paragraph 13, and *Mietz*, paragraph 27).

33. That interpretation must apply a fortiori with respect to a rule of jurisdiction, such as that contained in Article 14 of the Convention, which allows a consumer, within the meaning of the first paragraph of Article 13 of the Convention, to sue the defendant in the courts of the Contracting State in which the claimant is domiciled. Apart from the cases expressly provided for, the Convention does not appear to favour the attribution of jurisdiction to the courts of the claimant's domicile (see Case C-220/88 *Dumez France and Tracoba* [1990] ECR I-49, paragraphs 16 and 19; *Shearson Lehman Hutton*, paragraph 17; *Benincasa*, paragraph 14; and Case C-168/02 *Kronhofer* [2004] ECR I-0, paragraph 20).

34. Second, the Court has repeatedly held that the special rules introduced by the provisions of Title II, Section 4, of the Brussels Convention, which derogate from the general rule laid down in the first paragraph of Article 2, and from the rules of special jurisdiction for contracts in general enshrined in Article 5(1) of the Convention, serve to ensure adequate protection for the consumer as the party deemed to be economically weaker and less experienced in legal matters than the other, commercial, party to the contract, who must not therefore be discouraged from suing by being compelled to bring his action before the courts in the Contracting State in which the other party to the contract is domiciled (see in particular *Shearson Lehman Hutton*, paragraph 18, and *Gabriel*, paragraph 39). …

36. In paragraphs 16 to 18 of the judgment in *Benincasa* the Court stated in that respect that the concept of 'consumer' for the purposes of the first paragraph of Article 13 and the first paragraph of Article 14 of the Brussels Convention must be strictly

construed, reference being made to the position of the person concerned in a particular contract, having regard to the nature and aim of that contract and not to the subjective situation of the person concerned, since the same person may be regarded as a consumer in relation to certain supplies and as an economic operator in relation to others. The Court held that only contracts concluded outside and independently of any trade or professional activity or purpose, solely for the purpose of satisfying an individual's own needs in terms of private consumption, are covered by the special rules laid down by the Convention to protect the consumer as the party deemed to be the weaker party. Such protection is unwarranted in the case of contracts for the purpose of a trade or professional activity.

37. It follows that the special rules of jurisdiction in Articles 13 to 15 of the Brussels Convention apply, in principle, only where the contract is concluded between the parties for the purpose of a use other than a trade or professional one of the relevant goods or services.

38. It is in the light of those principles that it is appropriate to examine whether and to what extent a contract such as that at issue in the main proceedings, which relates to activities of a partly professional and partly private nature, may be covered by the special rules of jurisdiction laid down in Articles 13 to 15.

39. In that regard, it is already clearly apparent from the purpose of Articles 13 to 15 of the Brussels Convention, namely to properly protect the person who is presumed to be in a weaker position than the other party to the contract, that the benefit of those provisions cannot, as a matter of principle, be relied on by a person who concludes a contract for a purpose which is partly concerned with his trade or profession and is therefore only partly outside it. It would be otherwise only if the link between the contract and the trade or profession of the person concerned was so slight as to be marginal and, therefore, had only a negligible role in the context of the supply in respect of which the contract was concluded, considered in its entirety.

40. As the Advocate General stated in paragraphs 40 and 41 of his Opinion, inasmuch as a contract is entered into for the person's trade or professional purposes, he must be deemed to be on an equal footing with the other party to the contract, so that the special protection reserved by the Brussels Convention for consumers is not justified in such a case.

41. That is in no way altered by the fact that the contract at issue also has a private purpose, and it remains relevant whatever the relationship between the private and professional use of the goods or service concerned, and even though the private use is predominant, as long as the proportion of the professional usage is not negligible.

42. Accordingly, where a contract has a dual purpose, it is not necessary that the purpose of the goods or services for professional purposes be predominant for Articles 13 to 15 of the Convention not to be applicable.

43. That interpretation is supported by the fact that the definition of the notion of consumer in the first paragraph of Article 13 of the Brussels Convention is worded in clearly restrictive terms, using a negative turn of phrase ('contract concluded ... for a purpose ...outside [the] trade or profession'). Moreover, the definition of a contract concluded by a consumer must be strictly interpreted as it constitutes a derogation from the basic rule of jurisdiction laid down in the first paragraph of Article 2, and confers exceptional jurisdiction on the courts of the claimant's domicile (see paragraphs 32 and 33 of the present judgment).

44. That interpretation is also dictated by the fact that classification of the contract can only be based on an overall assessment of it, since the Court has held on many

occasions that avoidance of multiplication of bases of jurisdiction as regards the same legal relationship is one of the main objectives of the Brussels Convention (see to that effect, in particular, Case C-256/00 *Besix* [2002] ECR I-1699, paragraph 27; *Gabriel*, paragraph 57; and Case C-18/02 *DFDS Torline* [2004] ECR I-0, paragraph 26).

45. An interpretation which denies the capacity of consumer, within the meaning of the first paragraph of Article 13 of the Brussels Convention, if the link between the purpose for which the goods or services are used and the trade or profession of the person concerned is not negligible is also that which is most consistent with the requirements of legal certainty and the requirement that a potential defendant should be able to know in advance the court before which he may be sued, which constitute the foundation of that Convention (see in particular *Besix*, paragraphs 24 to 26).

Notes

(1) For the purposes of interpreting the Brussels Convention (now Brussels I Regulation 44/2001) the ECJ has adopted a narrow interpretation of the notion of consumer (a person concluding a contract which can be regarded as being outside his trade or profession, a notion that does not differ substantially from the notion of consumer used in most EC consumer directives). Even if a consumer contracts predominantly for a purpose outside his trade or profession, the protection of the Convention is denied to him, unless the link with that trade or profession is negligible. The ECJ motivates this by considering that where a contract is entered into by a person for his trade or profession he is on equal footing with the other party to the contract but also by considering that Article 13 of the Convention is a derogation from the normal rules of jurisdiction. It remains therefore a matter of debate whether this narrow interpretation, excluding consumer protection in 'mixed situations', also applies to the consumer directives.

(2) The ECJ seems to see the consumer not as the weaker party on the basis of information asymmetry—of course a farmer does not know more about tiles than an ordinary consumer—but on the basis of the risk he is taking. A person exercising a trade or profession no longer merits the special protection of the weaker party. He is taking a professional risk and for that reason he cannot be assimilated to a person needing protection because he is not taking any business risk and is acting solely in the private sphere.

(3) In its Green Paper on the Review of the Consumer Acquis[79] the Commission reveals that the notion of consumer is not defined in an identical manner in the different consumer directives. These differences are, however, rather cosmetic. The consumer in these directives is the person acting outside a profession, trade or business. One of the questions in the Green Paper is whether the existing definitions should be maintained or, on the contrary, widened as to include natural persons acting for purposes falling primarily outside (consumer), or primarily within (professional) their trade, business and profession. It does not seem that such a widening of the definition will solve all problems. It may indeed be hard to determine in a given case whether the professional or private purpose of a given transaction is predom-

[79] COM [2006] 744 final, 16.

inant. If the widened notion of consumer were introduced in the Brussels Regulation, the *Gruber* case would be overruled where it says that where a contract has a dual purpose, it is only a consumer contract where the proportion of the professional usage is negligible. Finally the 'predominance' test does not present a solution for real mixed situations where the professional purpose and the private purpose of the transaction are equivalent.

(4) It should be noted that the recent DCRF[80] has adopted this approach and defines the consumer as 'any natural person who is acting primarily for purposes which are not related to his or her trade, business or profession'. If that definition were to apply to mixed situations as in *Gruber* the outcome may often be different, ie where the professional part of the purchase is more than marginal, but less important than the private part.

III. BASIC MODELS OF CONSUMER LAW IN THE EU

III.A INTRODUCTION

There are probably as many models of consumer protection as there are Member States in the EU. The differences are most obvious if one looks at remedies. Each Member State has its mixture of public (criminal) law and private law remedies, both in terms of sanctions and procedures. In some Member States (in particular the Nordic countries) public authorities (such as a consumer ombudsman) play a central role in the enforcement of consumer rights. In other countries (such as Germany and Belgium) this role is played by consumer organisations.

If one looks at consumer protection in private law—which is the focus of the present Casebook—there are important differences in legislative approach: ranging from many different statutes (such as in the UK), a Consumer Code (such as in France), and intermediary systems where a Consumer Protection Act containing fundamental principles or rules and remedies coexists with more specific laws.[81]

III.B CODIFICATION

In the civil law countries the codification of consumer laws cannot be seen in isolation from the debate about codification and recodification of civil law. The Netherlands adopted a new Civil Code at a moment when consumer law was emerging. Germany has recently amended the part of the BGB that deals with obligations. In France a reform of the Civil Code is in preparation. Many other countries have codified their

[80] C von Bar, E Clive and H Schulte-Nölke, *Draft Common Frame of Reference (DCRF) 'Principles, Definitions and Model Rules of European Private Law'* (Acquis Group) (München, Sellier, 2009), prepared by the Study Group on a European Civil Code and the Research Group of EC Private Law.

[81] See also F Henning-Bodewig, *Unfair Competition Law European Union and Member States* (The Hague, Kluwer, 2006).

private law, while codification is absent from common law systems.[82] Codification is also a much-debated issue in the process of building European private law.[83] The Study Group of a European Civil Code is very active in this respect. It has recently published its Principles of European Law, Sales (PEL S).[84] The Common Frame of Reference[85] can also be seen as codification in a substantive sense.[86] In 1993 France has adopted a Consumer Code. The Code de la Consommation is composed of five chapters: information of consumers and formation of contracts, conformity and security of goods and services, consumers in debt, consumers' associations and institutions. However, this Code does not contain all provisions of consumer law. The Code has been criticised for its lack of coherence, and even for being a mere compilation.[87]

J Calais Auloy and F Steinmetz, Consumer law[88] **1.31 (FR)**

As imperfect as it is, the Consumer Law Code is useful: it facilitates access to the law, in an area that is important for the day to day life of all citizens. Consumer law has also been codified in Brasil. There are codification projects in Belgium, Québec and Portugal.

III.C CONSUMER OMBUDSMAN

The Nordic countries have a long tradition of ombudsmen. An ombudsman is a kind of mediator between citizens and originally public administrations. The European Union also has an ombudsman. A Consumer Ombudsman, as this institution exists in Sweden, Denmark and Finland, acts on behalf of consumers vis-à-vis businesses. His powers are much larger than mediation. He can also bring actions in court, including group actions. In other Member States this kind of action is left to private organisations, such as consumer associations. The following abstract is taken from the website of the Swedish Consumer Ombudsman.

Swedish Consumer Agency: Swedish Consumer Policy[89] **1.32 (SW)**

Government-run activities supporting consumers are well established in Sweden. Much of the work is focused on prevention through negotiations and recommendations. However, this approach is based on the ability to use legal intervention. Solving individual disputes is another important part of national consumer policy. …

[82] See J Smits, *The Making of European Private Law* (Antwerp/Oxford, Intersentia, 2002).
[83] See eg E Hondius, 'Towards a European Civil Code' [2004] in S Vogenauer and S Weatherill (eds), *Towards a European Civil Code, The Harmonisation of European Contract Law* (Hart, Oxford, 2006).
[84] E Hondius et al (München, Sellier, 2008).
[85] See more in detail chapter 3.I.A.
[86] M Hesselink, 'The Ideal of Codification and the Dynamics of Europeanisation: The Dutch Experience' in S Vogenuaer and S Weatherill, above n 83, 52.
[87] J Calais-Auloy and F Stenmetz, *Droit de la Consommation*, 7th edn (Paris, Dalloz, 2007) 38–39.
[88] Ibid.
[89] From the website of Konsumentverket.

The Konsumentverket (Swedish Consumer Agency) provides the Swedish general public with consumer affairs assistance. The Agency acts in the collective interest of consumers but in general does not resolve individual consumer disputes. That is the task of the Allmänna Reklamationsnämnden (the National Board for Consumer Complaints).

Providing advice to individual consumers is the task of local consumer advice centres located across the country. Their staff is trained and supported by the Consumer Agency.

The Livsmedelsverket (the National Food Administration) is the supervisory agency responsible for matters relating to food.

The Consumer Agency, with a staff of around 180, works on a wide variety of consumer issues. Its fields mainly relate to advertising and contract terms, consumer information and education, domestic finances, product safety, product quality and environmental impact. The Government and the Swedish Parliament set consumer policy objectives.

The Consumer Agency is headed by a Director General, Gunnar Larsson, who is also the Konsumentombudsman (the Consumer Ombudsman). The Consumer Ombudsman represents consumer interests to the business world and pursues legal action on behalf of these interests.

The general policy goals are:

—the protection of consumers rights should be on a high level and accessible for everyone,

—consumers should make the best possible use of their own and common resources,

—producers and other traders should take their responsibility towards consumers. ...

The Consumer Ombudsman is responsible for ensuring that companies abide by the laws and rules in the consumer field and ensures that consumer rights are respected.

Consumers should neither be subjected to misleading advertisements nor to unfair sales methods, dangerous products or unfair contract terms. There are a number of laws that prohibit this. [The original excerpt continues with a list of laws: the Marketing Act, the Consumer Contract Terms Act, the Product Safety Act, the Consumer sales Act, the Consumer Services Act, the Consumer Insurance Act, the Distant Sales and Door-to-Door Sales Act].

III.D COLLECTIVE AGREEMENTS

Collective agreements defining rights and obligations of a group of persons vis-à-vis another group of persons are well known in labour law (eg collective labour agreements concluded between employers' associations and trade unions). The binding force of such agreements is often extended by decision of the competent authorities.

In France the idea of binding collective agreements between consumer organisations and professional organisations was first launched in 1990 by the Commission de refonte du droit de la Consommation (1990). This proposal was opposed by industry and has not been enacted. Québec enacted a system similar to the one proposed by the Commission de refonte in 1992 (Articles 314 and 315-1 loi sur la protection du consommateur).[90]

[90] Calais-Auloy and Steinmetz, above n 87.

In France, in a certain number of sectors (dry cleaning, car repair, after-sales service, revolving credit) collective agreements have been concluded since the 1980s. These agreements are encouraged by the state. In 1982 they were given a legal framework by the creation of 'contrats pour l'amélioration de la qualité' ('quality improvement contracts') later called 'contrats approuvés' ('approved contracts'). This technique has not been often used but a similar technique was used in 2001 for the 'engagement regularité' ('regularity undertaking') of the SNCF (the French railway company), in 2004 for the decrease of prices in large retail shops and for bank transparency, and in 2005 for the services of internet providers.

In Belgium the Act of 15 May 2007 (loi relative aux accords de la consommation)[91] inserted provisions on 'consumer agreements' into the Trade Practices Act of 14 July 1991. The binding force of agreements concluded between consumer organisations and professionals organisations can be extended by royal decree to an entire sector of the economy.

Trade Practices Act **1.33 (BE)**

Article 94 quinquies §1 A consumption agreement is an agreement concluded in the Consumer Consultative Committee between consumer organisations on the one hand and professional organisations on the other and that governs the relations between businesses and consumers in the field of goods or services or categories of goods or services.

Consumption agreements can relate to general contract terms that will be proposed to consumers, the information that will be given to them, the methods of sales promotion, the quality, conformity and safety of goods and services and the modes of dispute resolution. …

Article 94 septies General contract terms set by consumption agreements have to obtain the prior advice of the Committee on Unfair Contract Terms. The advice has to rendered within three months. If the deadline has expired the agreement can be concluded. …

Article 94 decies Subject to a unanimous advice of the Consumer Consultative Committee the King can, by decree deliberated in council of state, impose to an entire sector of economic life the application of a consumption agreement with national coverage.

Note

The Belgian law is unclear in many respects. How will agreements that have been extended by royal decree be binding? Will consumers be bound? Can it lead to a limitation of their rights? What is the precise relationship with the regulation of unfair commercial practices, etc.[92] It would also seem that such agreements are not immune from the application of antitrust law. They are liable to restrict competition between

[91] MB, 21 June 2007.

[92] See H Swennen, 'Consumentenakkoorden in België: een moeilijke weg' [2007] *Sociaal-Economische Wetgeving* 28.

undertakings, eg concerning commercial advantages given to consumers. In that case Article 81 EC (prohibition of restrictive agreements between undertakings) and its domestic equivalent may apply. Until now no such collective agreements have been concluded.

IV. LEGAL TECHNIQUES OF CONSUMER PROTECTION AT THE COMMUNITY LEVEL

It has already been mentioned that there is an ongoing debate at the EU level about the choice of method of harmonisation: minimum or full harmonisation, targeted harmonisation and other techniques (mutual recognition, country of origin principle, etc) to make the internal market work and at the same time guarantee a sufficient level of consumer protection. While most of the consumer protection Directives so far are minimum harmonisation Directives, there are a few exceptions: the Product Liability Directive (according to settled case-law of the ECJ) and the new Unfair Commercial Practices Directive (according to its express wording and rationale).

ECJ Case C-402/03, 10 January 2006[93] **1.34 (EU)**
Skov v Bilka

PERSONAL SCOPE OF APPLICATION OF THE NO-FAULT LIABILITY OF THE PRODUCT LIABILITY DIRECTIVE

Eggs contaminated with Salmonella

The no-fault liability of the Product Liability Directive cannot be extended to distributors.

Facts: After eating eggs they had bought at a shop belonging to Bilka, which had in turn obtained them from a producer, Skov, consumers fell ill with Salmonella poisoning. They brought proceedings against the supplier, Bilka, which was joined by the producer, Skov, in the proceedings. The Aalborg District Court found that the eggs had been defective, there was a causal link between the defect and the damage suffered, and no fault on the part of the injured parties had been shown. Bilka was ordered to pay compensation to the injured persons, and Skov was ordered to reimburse Bilka for that compensation. The Product Liability Directive (85/374/EEC) provides that the producer shall be liable for damage caused by a defect in his product. The importer in the EU is assimilated with the producer. Where the producer of the product cannot be identified, each supplier of the product shall be treated as its producer unless he informs the injured person, within a reasonable time, of the identity of the producer or of the person who supplied him with the product. Article 13 of the Directive provides that the Directive shall not affect any rights which an injured person may have according to the rules of the law of contractual or non-contractual liability or a special liability system existing at the moment when this Directive is notified. Pursuant to the Danish law implementing the Directive, a person who in the course of business puts a product into circulation without being regarded as a producer shall be regarded as an intermediary. An intermediary shall be directly liable for product liability to injured persons and subsequent intermediaries in the distribution chain. Before the adoption of the Directive, liability for defective products on the part of both the producer and the supplier was governed in Denmark by case-law. Under that case-law, liability for defective products was assessed by reference to the general rules of civil liability, based on the concept of fault. On appeal the Vestre Landsret

[93] [2006] ECR I-00199.

decided to stay proceedings and to refer preliminary questions to the ECJ. The Danish court asked the ECJ whether the Directive is to be interpreted as precluding a national rule under which the supplier is answerable without restriction for the no-fault liability which the Directive establishes and imposes on the producer and not on the intermediary seller.

Judgment: 33. Since the Directive, as pointed out in paragraph 23 above, seeks to achieve complete harmonisation in the matters regulated by it, its determination in Articles 1 and 3 of the class of persons liable must be regarded as exhaustive.

34. Article 3(3) of the Directive provides for the supplier to be liable only in the case where the producer cannot be identified. By laying down in Paragraph 10 of Law No 371 that the supplier is to be answerable directly to injured persons for defects in a product, the Danish legislature therefore extended the class of persons liable against whom the injured person is entitled to bring proceedings under the system of liability laid down by the Directive beyond the limits fixed by the Directive. …

37. It follows that the Directive must be interpreted as precluding a national rule under which the supplier is answerable without restriction for the liability of the producer under the Directive.

38. However, the Danish Government submits that Article 13 of the Directive, which provides that the Directive is not to affect any rights which an injured person may have according to the rules of the law of contractual or non-contractual liability, can provide a legal basis for extending to the supplier the liability which, in the system of the Directive, falls on the producer.

39. On this point, it should be recalled that in *Commission v France*, paragraph 21, *Commission v Greece*, paragraph 17, and *González Sánchez*, paragraph 30, the Court held, after analysing the wording, purpose and structure of the Directive, that Article 13 could not be interpreted as leaving it open to the Member States to maintain a general system of product liability different from that provided for in the Directive. …

40. As regards the Danish Government's argument that that interpretation of the Directive is liable to lower the level of consumer protection in Denmark, it must be stated that any extension to suppliers of the liability established by the Directive falls within the competence of the Community legislature, for whom it is to amend, if appropriate, the provisions concerned. …

45. In those circumstances, the answer to the national court's first group of questions must be that the Directive must be interpreted as precluding a national rule under which the supplier is answerable, beyond the cases listed exhaustively in Article 3(3) of the Directive, for the no-fault liability which the Directive establishes and imposes on the producer.

Notes

(1) In its Green Paper on the Review of the Consumer Acquis[94] the Commission explains that the consumer directives, which are under review, are based on minimum harmonisation, ie they contain clauses under which Member States are allowed to have higher protection levels. The Product Liability Directive (85/374/EEC), discussed in the annotated judgment, is not one of these directives. The judgment suggests that it is a full harmonisation directive, where Member States are not allowed to have a higher level of protection at least via the harmonised technique, ie strict liability. In its Article

[94] COM [2006] 774 final.

13 the Directive indeed provides that it shall not affect any rights which an injured person may have according to the rules of the law of contractual or non-contractual liability or a special liability system existing at the moment when this Directive is notified. By contrast the Directive does not allow Member States to, for example, hold an intermediary seller such as a producer strictly liable.

(2) In its Green Paper the Commission sets out two alternatives for full harmonisation: a combination of minimum harmonisation with a mutual recognition clause (Member States would be allowed to impose stricter rules in their national laws but they would not be allowed to apply them to businesses established in other Member States unless the ensuing restrictions could be justified in the general interest) and minimum harmonisation combined with the country-of-origin principle (Member States would be allowed to impose stricter rules in their national laws but they would never be allowed to apply them to businesses established in other Member States, the latter being subject to the rules of their country of origin only) (for more detail see section I.E above).

(3) In the literature there is an ongoing debate on minimum versus full harmonisation, especially in the consumer field.[95] Minimum harmonisation is said to have the advantage of allowing Member States to maintain a higher degree of consumer protection (and to prevent a 'race to the bottom') and to allow competition among lawmakers. Full harmonisation seems to be more in line with the idea of the internal market (one market with uniform conditions of competition). Legal and political preferences for harmonisation or for a particular kind of harmonisation are based on assumptions that do not always stand the test of the economics.[96]

(4) In its Green Paper the Commission shows a clear preference for full harmonisation.[97] The recent proposal for a Consumer Rights Directive has endorsed this approach (see section I.E above). A similar approach—albeit it somewhat more nuanced—can be found in the Communication from the Commission to the Council, the European Parliament and the European Economic and Social Committee—EU Consumer Policy strategy 2007-2013—Empowering consumers, enhancing their welfare, effectively protecting them.[98] The most recent initiatives in EC consumer law are based on a full harmonisation approach.[99] This can (partly) be explained by the doubts which may have been cast on the constitutionality of minimum harmonisation by the case law of the ECJ (*Tobacco Advertising*, see section I.E above).

[95] See in particular P Rott, 'Minimum Harmonisation for the Completion of the Internal Market? The Example of Consumer Sales Law 40' (2003) 40 *CML Rev* 1107 and G Howells, 'The Rise of European Consumer Law: Whither National Consumer Law?' (2006) 28 *Sydney Law Review* 63.

[96] See G Wagner, 'The Economics of Harmonization: The Case of Contract Law' (2002) 39 *CML Rev* 995.

[97] COM [2006] 744 def.

[98] COM [2007] 99 def 7.

[99] See the Consumer Credit Directive (2008/48/EC); the Unfair Commercial Practices Directive (2005/29/EC); Directive 97/55/EC of European Parliament and of the Council of 6 October 1997 amending Directive 84/450/EEC concerning misleading advertising so as to include comparative advertising ('Directive on comparative advertising') [1997] OJ L 290, 18-23; Directive 2002/65/EC of the European Parliament and of the Council of 23 September 2002 concerning the distance marketing of consumer financial services and amending Council Directive 90/619/EEC and Directives 97/7/EC and 98/27/EC ('Distance selling of financial services Directive') [2002] OJ L 271, 16–24.

(5) The difference between full and minimum harmonisation should not be exaggerated. Even full harmonisation is relative. Despite the control by the ECJ, divergent applications and interpretations in the Member States are inevitable. It is particularly unrealistic to expect full harmonisation through general clauses at the Community level such as those in the Unfair Commercial Practices Directive (2005/29/EC).[100] The experience with general clauses in several Member States can illustrate this point.[101] Moreover it is not within the province of the ECJ, when answering preliminary questions from national courts, to eliminate all obstacles in the application of general clauses. A full harmonisation measure seems more appropriate for technical and detailed measures, but in this case a rapid and flexible procedure seems necessary so that the rules can be adapted easily.[102] The present Community legislative system does not present these characteristics.

(6) Finally it should also be kept in mind that full harmonisation in the framework of the review of the consumer acquis will have effects for the Common Frame of Reference (CFR) for contract law. One of the criticisms of the Green Paper concerns its lack of clarity on its relationship with the CFR. The Commission has, however, tried to clarify its position in the following way in its Second Progress Report on the Common Frame of Reference:[103]

> The Commission considers the CFR a better regulation instrument. It is a longer-term exercise with the purpose of ensuring consistency and good quality of EC legislation in the area of contract law. It would be used to provide clear definitions of legal terms, fundamental principles and coherent modern rules of contract law when revising existing and preparing new sectoral legislation where such a need is identified. Its scope is not a large scale harmonisation of private law or a European civil code.

The Commission has also indicated that certain of the results of the CFR works will, where appropriate, be integrated in the review of the consumer acquis.[104]

UCPD (2005/29/EC) **1.35 (EU)**

Article 5(5) Annex I contains the list of those commercial practices which shall in all circumstances be regarded as unfair. The same single list shall apply in all Member States and may only be modified by revision of this Directive.

[100] On this Directive, see extensively chapter 2 below. The full harmonisation character of this Directive has been confirmed by the ECJ in its judgment of 23 April 2009, Joined Cases C-261/07 and C-299/07 *VTB-VAB v Total et al*, nyr.

[101] See eg the divergent interpretations of Art 1384 Code Napoléon (liability for damage caused by persons for whom one is responsible) by the French Cour de Cassation and the Belgian Cour de Cassation: Cass Fr, 29 March 1991 (1991) RGAR No 11.857 (general qualitative liability) and Cass Belgium, 19 June 1997 (1998–99) RW, 148 (no general qualitative liability).

[102] See J Stuyck, E Terryn and T Van Dyck, 'Confidence Through Fairness? The New Directive on Unfair Business-to-Consumer Commercial Practices' (2006) 43 *CML Rev* 143ff; See on the necessity of 'reflexible' rules in foodstuff legislation S Mahieu, *Le droit de la société de l'alimentation* (Brussel, Larcier, 2007).

[103] Report from the Commission—Second Progress Report on The Common Frame of Reference COM [2007] 447 final, see conclusions.

[104] COM [2007] 447 final, 11.

Notes

(1) Recital 17 of the Directive states that it is desirable that those commercial practices which are in all circumstances unfair be identified to provide greater legal certainty. Annex I therefore contains the full list of all such practices. These are the only commercial practices which can be deemed to be unfair without a case-by-case assessment against the provisions of Articles 5–9. The list may only be modified by revision of the Directive.

(2) Contrary to earlier Directives in the field of consumer law (in particular the Unfair Contract Terms Directive 93/13/EEC), Article 5(5) of the UCPD clearly indicates the full harmonisation character of the Directive. Member States have to provide for a general clause along the lines of Article 5(2), as well as a general prohibition of misleading respectively aggressive practices according to the criteria of Article 5(4) and Articles 6–9. The national courts will have to apply these provisions in individual cases, appraising essentially their compatibility with professional diligence. Finally the Member States have to forbid in all circumstances the 31 aggressive and misleading practices enumerated in the annex to the Directive. According to Article 5(5) this list contains the minimum and the maximum of what Member States can and shall forbid in all circumstances.

(3) The full harmonisation character of the Directive also derives from the absence of any provision, allowing Member States to take more protective measures, the Directive being based on Article 95 EC (ie Article 153(3)(a)), therefore the automatic power conferred by Article 153(4) on Member States to maintain or introduce more stringent protective measures in the field where the Community has taken action does not apply; that power only exists where the Community has taken measures which support, supplement and monitor the policy pursued by the Member States measures under Article 153(3)b.

(4) The full harmonisation character of the Directive, finally, can also be deduced from the provisions of Article 3(4) and 3(9) providing, respectively, that for a period of six years from 12 June 2007, Member States shall be able to continue to apply national provisions within the field approximated by this Directive which are more restrictive or prescriptive than this Directive and which implement directives containing minimum harmonisation clauses and that, in relation to 'financial services', as defined in the distance selling of financial services Directive (2002/65/EC), and immovable property, Member States may impose requirements which are more restrictive or prescriptive than this Directive in the field which it approximates. In other words for these two sectors the harmonisation is 'minimal'.

(5) In *VTB-VAB*[105] the ECJ confirmed the full harmonisation character of the UCPD. It ruled that the Directive must be interpreted as precluding national legislation, such as Article 54 Belgian Trade Practices Act, which, with certain exceptions, and without taking account of the specific circumstances, imposes a general prohibition of combined offers made by a business to a consumer. Indeed, combined offers are not mentioned by the Annex to the Directive, which lists exhaustively practices that are prohibited in all circumstances.

[105] ECJ, 23 April 2009, Joined Cases C-261/07 and C-299/07 *VTB-VAB v Total et al*, nyr.

Roaming Regulation (717/2007)[106] 1.36 (EU)

[Preamble] **(1)** The high level of the prices payable by users of public mobile telephone networks, such as students, business travellers and tourists, when using their mobile telephones when travelling abroad within the Community is a matter of concern for national regulatory authorities, as well as for consumers and the Community institutions. The excessive retail charges are resulting from high wholesale charges levied by the foreign host network operator and also, in many cases, from high retail mark-ups charged by the customer's own network operator. Reductions in wholesale charges are often not passed on to the retail customer. Although some operators have recently introduced tariff schemes that offer customers more favourable conditions and lower prices, there is still evidence that the relationship between costs and prices is not such as would prevail in fully competitive markets.
(2) The creation of a European social, educational and cultural area based on the mobility of individuals should facilitate communication between people in order to build a real 'Europe for Citizens'. ...
(17) The most effective and proportionate approach to regulating the level of prices for making and receiving intra-Community roaming calls is the setting at Community level of a maximum average per-minute charge at wholesale level and the limiting of charges at retail level through the introduction of a Eurotariff. The average wholesale charge should apply between any pair of operators within the Community over a specified period. ...

Article 4 Retail charges for regulated roaming calls

(1) Home providers shall make available and actively offer to all their roaming customers, clearly and transparently, a Eurotariff as provided for in paragraph 2. This Eurotariff shall not entail any associated subscription or other fixed or recurring charges and may be combined with any retail tariff.

When making this offer, home providers shall remind any of their roaming customers who, before 30 June 2007, had chosen a specific roaming tariff or package of the conditions applicable to that tariff or package.

(2) The retail charge (excluding VAT) of a Eurotariff which a home provider may levy from its roaming customer for the provision of a regulated roaming call may vary for any roaming call but shall not exceed €0,49 per minute for any call made or €0,24 per minute for any call received. The price ceiling for calls made shall decrease to €0,46 and €0,43, and for calls received to €0,22 and €0,19, on 30 August 2008 and on 30 August 2009 respectively.

Notes

(1) EC consumer law is generally a question of Directives, leaving the Member States some margin to adapt their national legislation to the Community rules with due consideration of their national legal system and tradition. Sometimes the Community legislature intervenes in consumer matters through regulations, which do not leave such flexibility.

[106] Regulation (EC) 717/2007 of the European Parliament and of the Council of 27 June 2007 on roaming on public mobile telephone networks within the Community and amending Directive 2002/21/EC [2007] OJ L 171, 32–40.

(2) In the Roaming Regulation (717/2007) the Community legislature intervenes directly to protect consumers against excessive prices for cross-border mobile calls. As far as can be seen, such a direct intervention by the EC in the fixing of retail prices is without precedent.

(3) The legal basis of this regulation is Article 95 EC on the internal market. It is interesting to note from the preamble (recital 1, see above) that: 'there is still evidence that the relationship between costs and prices is not such as would prevail in fully competitive market'. Several telecom operators have challenged the validity of the Regulation in an English court, which referred the matter to the ECJ (Case C-58/08, pending). The questions are the following:

> Is Regulation (EC) 717/2007 invalid, in whole or in part, by reason of the inadequacy of Article 95 EC as a legal basis? Is Article 4 of Regulation (EC) 717/2007 (together with Articles 2(a) and 6(3) insofar as they refer to the Eurotariff and obligations relating to the Eurotariff) invalid on the grounds that the imposition of a price ceiling in respect of retail roaming charges infringes the principle of proportionality and/or subsidiarity?

(4) It seems that the Roaming Regulation (717/2007) fixes directly retail prices for a cross-border service because the markets are not sufficiently competitive, notwithstanding the existence of competition rules that should discipline the market and of a Community framework for electronic communications from 2002 with important powers and obligations for national regulatory authorities to intervene in the fixing of prices and other conditions notably in the interest of consumers.

(5) With regard to the objectives of the Regulation, recital 2 of the preamble (see above) refers to the creation of a European social, educational and cultural area based on the mobility of individuals that should facilitate communication between people in order to build a real 'Europe for citizens'. The Regulation goes beyond the protection of consumers and the good functioning of the internal market in its economic understanding. It is an instrument for the achievement of a Europe of the citizens.

(6) This type of direct intervention by the Community to protect consumers—as the Community also did in the Denied Boarding Regulation (261/2004)[107]—can hardly serve as a model for other sections of consumer law, especially in a contractual field, where national differences rather suggest other methods of Community intervention.

(7) Yet the interventionism of the Roaming Regulation (717/2007) is limited. It only fixes prices and does not therefore (directly) affect contract law. By contrast, the Denied Boarding Regulation (261/2004) contains mandatory rules affecting contractual rights and obligations. This regulation was adopted on the basis of Article 80(2) EC (air transport policy) and establishes common rules on compensation and

[107] Regulation (EC) 261/2004 establishing common rules on the compensation and assistance to passengers in the event of denied boarding and of cancellation or long delay of flights, and repealing Regulation (EEC) 295/91 [2004] OJ L 46, 1–8; See E Varney and M Varney, 'Grounded? Air Passenger Rights in the European Union' in C Twigg-Flesner et al (eds), *The Yearbook of Consumer Law* (Aldershot, Ashgate, 2007) 171ff.

assistance to passengers in the event of denied boarding and of cancellation or long delay of flights. The regulation establishes inter alis a right to compensation in certain circumstances. It also establishes other contractual rights for consumers, such as the right to care and the right to reimbursement or rerouting. It is somewhat surprising that these direct interventions by the Community legislature (fixing prices, fixing rights to compensation, etc) do not seem to bother contract lawyers and consumer lawyers too much. The impact of these regulations on national law has hardly been examined.

V. CONSUMERS, HORIZONTAL EFFECT AND STATE LIABILITY FOR INFRINGEMENT OF EUROPEAN CONSUMER LAW

ECJ Case C-91/92, 14 July 1994[108] **1.37 (EU)**
Faccini Dori v Recreb Srl

A CONSUMER CANNOT RELY ON THE PROVISIONS OF A DIRECTIVE AGAINST A PROFESSIONAL

An English language course canvassed to an Italian consumer

No cooling-off period for Italian consumers in the absence of a national provision to that effect.

Facts: On 19 January 1989, without having been previously approached by her, Interdiffusion Srl concluded a contract with Ms Faccini Dori at Milan Central Railway Station for an English language correspondence course. Some days later, by registered letter of 23 January 1989, Miss Faccini Dori informed that company that she was cancelling her order. The company replied on 3 June 1989 that it had assigned its claim to Recreb. On 24 June 1989, Ms Faccini Dori wrote to Recreb confirming that she had cancelled her subscription to the course, indicating inter alia that she relied on the right of cancellation provided for by the Doorstep Selling Directive (85/577/EEC) to protect the consumer in respect of contracts negotiated away from business premises. Recreb asked the Giudice Conciliatore di Firenze to order Miss Faccini Dori to pay it the agreed sum with interest and costs. The judge ordered Miss Faccini Dori to pay the sums in question. She lodged an objection to that order with the same judge. She again stated that she had withdrawn from the contract under the conditions laid down by the directive. At the material time Italy had not taken any steps to transpose the directive into national law, although the period set for transposition had expired. The judge referred a preliminary question on the interpretation of the Directive: can the Directive produce effects between individuals?

Judgment: Whether the provisions of the directive concerning the right of cancellation may be invoked in proceedings between a consumer and a trader

19. The second issue raised by the national court relates more particularly to the question whether, in the absence of measures transposing the directive within the prescribed time-limit, consumers may derive from the directive itself a right of cancellation against traders with whom they have concluded contracts and enforce that right before a national court.

[108] [1994] ECR I-3325.

20. As the Court has consistently held since its judgment in Case 152/84 *Marshall v Southampton and South-West Hampshire Health Authority* [1986] ECR 723, paragraph 48, a directive cannot of itself impose obligations on an individual and cannot therefore be relied upon as such against an individual. ...

23. It would be unacceptable if a State, when required by the Community legislature to adopt certain rules intended to govern the State's relations or those of State entities with individuals and to confer certain rights on individuals, were able to rely on its own failure to discharge its obligations so as to deprive individuals of the benefits of those rights. Thus the Court has recognized that certain provisions of directives on conclusion of public works contracts and of directives on harmonization of turnover taxes may be relied on against the State (or State entities) (see the judgment in Case 103/88 *Fratelli Costanzo v Comune di Milano* [1989] ECR 1839 and the judgment in Case 8/81 *Becker v Finanzamt Muenster-Innenstadt* [1982] ECR 53).

24. The effect of extending that case-law to the sphere of relations between individuals would be to recognize a power in the Community to enact obligations for individuals with immediate effect, whereas it has competence to do so only where it is empowered to adopt regulations.

25. It follows that, in the absence of measures transposing the directive within the prescribed time-limit, consumers cannot derive from the directive itself a right of cancellation as against traders with whom they have concluded a contract or enforce such a right in a national court.

26. It must also be borne in mind that, as the Court has consistently held since its judgment in Case 14/83 *Von Colson and Kamann v Land Nordrhein-Westfalen* [1984] ECR 1891, paragraph 26, the Member States' obligation arising from a directive to achieve the result envisaged by the directive and their duty under Article 5 of the Treaty to take all appropriate measures, whether general or particular, is binding on all the authorities of Member States, including, for matters within their jurisdiction, the courts. The judgments of the Court in Case C-106/89 *Marleasing v La Comercial Internacional de Alimentación* [1990] ECR I-4135, paragraph 8, and Case C-334/92 *Wagner Miret v Fondo de Garantía Salarial* [1993] ECR I-6911, paragraph 20, make it clear that, when applying national law, whether adopted before or after the directive, the national court that has to interpret that law must do so, as far as possible, in the light of the wording and the purpose of the directive so as to achieve the result it has in view and thereby comply with the third paragraph of Article 189 of the Treaty.

27. If the result prescribed by the directive cannot be achieved by way of interpretation, it should also be borne in mind that, in terms of the judgment in Joined Cases C-6/90 and C-9/90 *Francovich and Others v Italy* [1991] ECR I-5357, paragraph 39, Community law requires the Member States to make good damage caused to individuals through failure to transpose a directive, provided that three conditions are fulfilled. First, the purpose of the directive must be to grant rights to individuals. Second, it must be possible to identify the content of those rights on the basis of the provisions of the directive. Finally, there must be a causal link between the breach of the State' s obligation and the damage suffered.

28. The directive on contracts negotiated away from business premises is undeniably intended to confer rights on individuals and it is equally certain that the minimum content of those rights can be identified by reference to the provisions of the directive alone (see paragraph 17 above).

29. Where damage has been suffered and that damage is due to a breach by the State of its obligation, it is for the national court to uphold the right of aggrieved consumers to obtain reparation in accordance with national law on liability.

30. So, as regards the second issue raised by the national court, the answer must be that in the absence of measures transposing the directive within the prescribed time-limit consumers cannot derive from the directive itself a right of cancellation as against traders with whom they have concluded a contract or enforce such a right in a national court. However, when applying provisions of national law, whether adopted before or after the directive, the national court must interpret them as far as possible in the light of the wording and purpose of the directive.

Notes

(1) Although the ECJ has consistently held that a Directive as such cannot impose obligations on an individual and cannot therefore be relied upon as such against an individual (no 'horizontal direct effect'),[109] especially in recent judgments[110] it has stressed the necessity for national courts to provide legal protection which individuals derive from the rules of Community so as to ensure that those rules are fully effective. To that effect national courts are bound to interpret national law and more in particular legal provisions that have been adopted for complying with the requirements of the Directive, so far as possible, in the light of the wording and the purpose of the Directive concerned. This obligation also requires the national courts to consider national law as a whole in order to assess to what extent it may be applied so as to avoid a result that would be contrary to the results sought by the Directive.[111] In *Berlusconi*,[112] which case concerned the First Company Directive, the Court confirmed this point of view, but it also ruled that in a situation where reliance on the Directive would lead to the applicability of manifestly more severe criminal penalty resulting from another provision of national law, this would be contrary to its standing case-law which precludes a directive from resulting in creating or increasing the liability in criminal law.[113]

(2) The duty on national courts to construe national law in conformity with a Directive can also be helpful for individuals and companies who want to object to corporate decisions (decisions taken by the board of a company) harming their interests. (eg as a shareholder). There is indeed a whole body of company law Directives on which such individuals and companies can rely to support an interpretation

[109] See M Dougan, 'When Worlds Collide! Competing Visions of the Relationship between Direct Effect and Supremacy' (2007) 44 *CML Rev* 932ff.

[110] See in particular ECJ, Case C-152/84 *Marshall* [1986] ECR 723, para 48; ECJ, Case C-91/92 *Faccini Dori* [1994] ECR I-3325.

[111] ECJ, Joined Cases C-397/01 to C-403/01 *Pfeiffer* [2004] ECR I-8835, para 111–18 (with many references to previous case-law).

[112] Eg see ECJ, joined Cases C-378/02, C-391/02 and C-403/02 *Berlusconi et al* [2005] ECR I-3565, para 73–77.

[113] With reference to ECJ, Case 80/86 *Kolpinghuis Nijmegen* [1987] ECR 3969 and ECJ, Case C-60/02 *Criminal proceedings against X* [2004] ECR I-651.

of national company law which takes sufficiently into account their rights and interest.

(3) The ECJ also ruled that mere adverse repercussions on the right of third parties, even repercussions that are certain, do not justify preventing an individual from invoking the provisions of a Directive against the Member State concerned (a so-called triangular situation).[114]

(4) In *CIA Security*, to which the ECJ refers in the judgment mentioned in the preceding note, the Court in fact recognised another type of horizontal effect of directives: an individual can use the non-conformity of a national law provision with a directive as a defence against the application of that provision. This possibility seems less relevant to consumers.[115]

(5) Finally, as the ECJ recalls in the annotated judgment, consumers who suffer prejudice from the non-transposition of a directive can, under certain circumstances claim damages from the state. That happened in, for example, *Dillenkofer*.[116] Germany had failed to implement the Package Travel Directive (90/314/EEC) correctly by not providing for a mechanism guaranteeing consumers a refund of deposits made to a tour operator in case of the latter's insolvency. The Court found that Germany had committed a serious breach of Community law and that this gave rise to a right of reparation for the individual consumers who had lost their money. Cases where consumers sue the state for compensation will remain rare, unless adequate procedures for collective redress exist (see chapter 8).

CONCISE BIBLIOGRAPHY

J Calais-Auloy and F Steinmetz, *Droit de la Consommation*, 7th edn (Paris, Dalloz, 2007).

M Hesselink, 'SMEs in European Contract Law' in K Boele-Woelki and W Grosheide (eds), *The Future of European Contract Law, Essays in honour of Ewoud Hondius* (Alphen aan den Rijn, Kluwer, 2007).

M Hesselink, 'European Contract Law: A Matter of Consumer Protection, Citizenship, or Justice?' (2007) 15 *European Review of Private Law* 232–348.

M Hesselink and M Loos, *Het voorstel voor een Europese richtlijn consumentenrechten* (Den Haag, Boom, 2009).

G Howells and S Weatherill, *Consumer Protection Law*, 2nd edn (Aldershot, Ashgate, 2005).

G Howells and R Schulze, *Modernising and Harmonising Consumer Contract Law* (Munchen, Sellier, 2009).

H-W Micklitz, 'The relationship between National and European Consumer Policy—Challenges and Perspectives' (2008) *Yearbook of Consumer Law* 35ff.

H-W Micklitz, N Reich and P Rott, *Understanding European Consumer Law* (Antwerp/Oxford, Intersentia, 2009).

N Reich and H-W Micklitz, *Europäisches Verbraucherrecht*, 4th edn (Baden-Baden, Nomos, 2003).

P Rott, 'Minimum Harmonization for the completion of the Internal Market? The Example of Consumer Sales Law' (2003) 40 *Common Market Law Review* 1107

[114] ECJ, Case C-211/02 *Delena Wells* [2004] ECR I-723, para 57, with reference to inter alia ECJ, Case 103/88 *Fratelli Costanzo* [1989] ECR I-1839, para 28 to 33; ECJ, Case C-194/94 *CIA Security* [1996] ECR I-2201, para 45- 50.

[115] See J Stuyck, case note ECJ, Case C-192/94 *El Corte InglPs* [1996] ECR I-1281; also called 'incidental direct effect', see P Craig and G De Burca, *EU Law*, 4th edn (Oxford, Oxford University Press, 2007) 296.

[116] 116ECJ, Joined Cases C-178/94ff *Dillenkofer* [1996] ECR I-4845.

I Ramsay, *Consumer Law and Policy. Texts and Materials on Regulating Consumer Markets*, 2nd edn (Oxford, Hart, 2007).

N Reich, 'A European Contract Law or an EU Contract law Regulation for Consumers' (2005) *Journal of Consumer Policy* 383.

J Stuyck, 'EC Competition Law after Modernisation: More than Ever in the Interest of Consumers' (2005) *Journal of Consumer Policy* 1ff.

S Weatherill, 'Maximum or Minimum Harmonisation What Kind of "Europe" Do We Want' in K Boele-Woelki and W Grosheide (eds), *The Future of European Contract Law, Essays in honour of Ewoud Hondius* (Alphen aan den Rijn, Kluwer, 2007) 133ff.

CHAPTER TWO
COMMERCIAL PRACTICES AND ADVERTISING

I. INTRODUCTION

Advertising and sales promotion are classical means used by manufacturers to attract the attention of consumers in a market economy. Stephen Weatherill puts it like this:[1]

> However, it has long been common for a marketing strategy to cover much more than simply the product in question. Advertising techniques are in effect part of the whole product package. Advertising is a form of consumer information. It is a method whereby the producer is able to explain to the consumer the purpose of the product. Equally, it is a method whereby a producer might seek to distinguish his or her products in the eyes of the consumer from that of a competitor. This may involve stressing quality differences or price variation, or it may involve attempts to impress the consumer in order to build consumer loyalty to a brand.
>
> As a market is integrated across borders the producer will wish to export advertising and other marketing techniques along with the products themselves. In some areas, the development of a European-wide marketing strategy is likely to parallel the development of a European-wide product strategy. The market for advertising is in this sense simply another candidate for economic integration.

[1] In H-W Micklitz and S Weatherill, *European Economic Law* (London, Dartmouth, 1997) 231.

> Is there a 'European' consumer at whom an integrated European marketing strategy may be directed? If the advertising industry believes the European consumer exists, that may begin to provide a justification for the Community institutions to respond to developing a common regulatory strategy.

However, whilst a European-wide marketing strategy might be economically efficient, it might encounter obstacles resulting from the various cultural and social backgrounds of consumers throughout the European Community. There is a fundamental tension between the constraints of economic integration via standardised marketing strategies and cultural and social resistance which might require more sophisticated marketing strategies aimed at different nations, different attitudes or different types of consumers.[2]

I.A THE DEVELOPMENT OF EC LAW ON UNFAIR COMMERCIAL PRACTICES

The development of EC law on unfair commercial practices was the idea of the European Commission right from the outset.[3] By the 1960s, the Commission had been considering problems concerned with the observance of unfair competition within the Common Market. It had asked the Max-Planck-Institut[4] to undertake a comparative analysis of the Member States' market practices law in order to ascertain the differences between the national rules liable to affect the development of the then Common Market, which led to a series of country reports and a comparative analysis under the editorship of Eugen Ulmer.[5] A more consumer-oriented approach was developed in the mid-1980s in a later study by Gerhard Schricker, the successor to Eugen Ulmerfor, the consumer directorate of the then DG Environment.[6] Inspired by the German background of the authors, the overall idea was to lay down a common framework on advertising matters for business-to-business (B2B) and business-to-consumer (B2C) relations, which includes misleading as well as unfair advertising and sales promotion strategies. It took the European Commission nearly fifty years to achieve its original idea.

The first stage was the proposal for a Council Directive relating to the approximation of the laws, regulations and administrative provisions of the Member States

[2] See T Wilhelmsson, 'Unfair Commercial Practices Law: The Cultural and Social Dimension' (2006) 44 *Osgoode Hall Law Journal* 461.

[3] A Ohly, 'Die Bemühungen um eine Rechtsvereinheitlichung auf EU-Ebene' in G Schricker and F Henning-Bodewig (eds), *Neuordnung des Wettbewerbsrechts* (Baden-Baden, Nomos, 1999) 69–81.

[4] Max-Planck-Institut für ausländisches und internationales Patent-, Urheber- und Wettbewerbsrecht in Munich, Germany.

[5] E Ulmer (ed), *Das Recht des unlauteren Wettbewerbs in den Mitgliedstaaten der Europäischen Wirtschaftsgemeinschaft* (Gutachten erstattet im Auftrag der Kommission der Europäischen Wirtschaftsgemeinschaft vom Institut für Ausländisches und Internationales Patent-, Urheber- und Markenrecht der Universität München, 1965ff, 7 vols).

[6] Unfair Advertising—Comparative Advertising, Definition of the terms and survey of the practice in Belgium, Holland, Luxembourg, Germany, France and other Member States of the EEC with a view to a harmonisation, unpublished manuscript, 1985.

concerning misleading and unfair advertising, which was submitted to the Council on 1 March 1978.[7] The objective was 'to protect consumers, persons carrying on a trade, business or profession, and the interests of the public in general against unfair and misleading advertising'. The recitals left no doubt that the harmonisation of unfair advertising was considered a prerequisite for the functioning of the Common Market and the protection of the consumer. However, the proposal did not meet with unanimous approval. The Member States cancelled the 'unfairness section'—ie also comparative advertising, which was understood as a component of unfair advertising—and finally adopted the Misleading Advertising Directive[8] relating to the approximation of the laws, regulations and administrative provisions of the Member States concerning misleading advertising, which was the sole common denominator at the time.

The second stage was the adoption of the Directive on Comparative Advertising[9] amending the Misleading Advertising Directive (84/450/EEC) so as to harmonise the rules on, and for some Member States (others had done it long before 1997) to legalise comparative advertising, which was regarded a means of improving consumer information. The third stage consisted in a piecemeal approach intended to regulate particular issues of major importance for the Internal Market. For example, the Doorstep Selling Directive,[10] which was designed to protect the consumer in respect of contracts negotiated away from business premises, was intended as a measure 'to protect consumers against unfair commercial practices in respect of doorstep selling' (recital 3). The Television Directive[11] ('Television without frontiers') as amended by Directive 97/36/EC[12] was intended to 'preserve free and fair competition' (recital 16) and to protect the consumer by various advertising provisions, such as requirements for teleshopping (Articles 10ff), a ban on tobacco advertising (Article 13) and several rules on the protection of minors (eg Article 15 lit a, Article 22). The Distance Selling Directive[13] on the protection of consumers in respect of distance contracts was aimed at providing consumers with information relating to the distance-communication means used, with due regard, in particular, to 'the principles of good faith in

[7] [1978] OJ C 70, 4.

[8] Council Directive 84/450/EEC of 10 September 1984 relating to the approximation of the laws, regulations and administrative provisions of the Member States concerning misleading advertising [1984] OJ L 250, 17–20.

[9] Directive 97/55/EC of European Parliament and of the Council of 6 October 1997 amending Directive 84/450/EEC concerning misleading advertising so as to include comparative advertising [1997] OJ L 290, 18–23.

[10] Council Directive 85/577/EEC of 20 December 1985 to protect the consumer in respect of contracts negotiated away from business premises [1985] OJ L 372, 31–33.

[11] Council Directive 89/552/EEC of 3 October 1989 on the coordination of certain provisions laid down by Law, Regulation or Administrative Action in Member States concerning the pursuit of television broadcasting activities [1989] OJ L 298, 23–30.

[12] Directive 97/36/EC of the European Parliament and of the Council of 30 June 1997 amending Council Directive 89/552/EEC on the coordination of certain provisions laid down by law, regulation or administrative action in Member States concerning the pursuit of television broadcasting activities [1997] OJ L 202, 60–70.

[13] Directive 97/7/EC of the European Parliament and of the Council of 20 May 1997 on the protection of consumers in respect of distance contracts—Statement by the Council and the Parliament re Article 6(1)—Statement by the Commission re Article 3(1), first indent [1997] OJ L 144, 19–27.

commercial transactions' (see eg Article 4). Finally, the Electronic Commerce Directive[14] recognised that commercial communications must meet a number of transparency requirements 'in the interests of consumer protection and fair trading' (recital 29). The Distance Selling of Financial Services Directive[15] contained particular rules on the distant selling of financial services.

The Green Paper on Commercial Communications in the Internal Market,[16] adopted in 1996, paved the way for a fresh consideration of the feasibility of a general legislative framework. This eventually led, after a relatively short and dense political debate, to the adoption of the Unfair Commercial Practices Directive.[17] The Directive is a broad framework Directive, based on a general clause prohibiting unfair commercial practices and including sections on misleading as well as aggressive practices. It is applicable to unfair B2C practices, before, during and after a transaction. It sets maximum standards for the admissibility of advertising and sales promotion measures in the European Community. Comparative advertising (maximum harmonisation) and sector or strategy related regulations (mostly minimum harmonisation) remain separate. There is therefore, all things considered, a dense set of EC rules.

I.B REGULATION AND SELF-REGULATION

Apart from statutory control, advertising is a prominent field of self-regulation. Codes of Conduct, as they are called in the Unfair Commercial Practices Directive (2005/29/EC) (UCPD), are also known by various other names such as Codes of Practice, Codes of Best Practice, Codes of Good Conduct, Consumer Charters, etc. When used in a general sense, the term 'code' can refer to a wide variety of documents, ranging from purely industry statements of practice to rules that have legal significance and are drawn up by governments.

Codes of Conduct in the sense that term is used in the UPCD require that the provisions are not imposed by the Member States. There are very different attitudes within the Community to codes. A comparison between the British (Advertising Standards Authority (ASA)) and German (Zentralausschuss der Werbewirtschaft (ZAW)) approaches is instructive. The British favour the use of codes, in the sense of non-binding rules, more than the Germans.[18] Indeed a study for the European

[14] Directive 2000/31/EC of the European Parliament and of the Council of 8 June 2000 on certain legal aspects of information society services, in particular electronic commerce, in the Internal Market [2000] OJ L 178, 1–16.

[15] Directive 2002/65/EC of the European Parliament and of the Council of 23 September 2002 concerning the distance marketing of consumer financial services and amending Council Directive 90/619/EEC and Directives 97/7/EC and 98/27/EC [2002] OJ L 271, 16–24.

[16] COM [1996] 192 final; see the follow-up to the Green Paper COM [1998] 121 final.

[17] Directive 2005/29/EC of the European Parliament and of the Council of 11 May 2005 concerning unfair business-to-consumer commercial practices in the internal market and amending Council Directive 84/450/EEC, Directives 97/7/EC, 98/27/EC and 2002/65/EC of the European Parliament and of the Council and Regulation (EC) No 2006/2004 of the European Parliament and of the Council [2005] OJ L 149, 22–39.

[18] G Teubner, 'Legal Irritants: Good Faith in British Law or How Unifying Law Ends Up in New Divergencies' (1998) 61 *Modern Law Review* 11.

Commission suggested that the UK had 'a virtual monopoly on the analysis of and reflection on, soft law'. The Office of Fair Trading encourages the use of Codes of Practice that are drafted in practice by trade associations. Although the codes might in appropriate circumstances be found to constitute an implied term of the consumer's contract[19] or false claims to abide by codes might breach trade descriptions legislation,[20] in principle the codes provide voluntary obligations for which there is no formal legal sanction. By contrast, Germany is characterised as having only conducted a limited experiment in self-regulation in specific areas of advertising.

Looking to the north of Europe, we see consumer ombudsmen heading the consumer authorities and playing an important role in the development of soft law rules in the Nordic countries. There are some purely voluntary self-regulatory codes here, but more distinctive is the use of guidelines negotiated by these ombudsmen with business in particular areas. The Netherlands also has an important role for self-regulation. The Self Regulation Coordination Group of the Sociaal Economische Raad develops equitable General Terms and Conditions, the key to which are the establishment of 'consumer complaints boards' under the auspices of the Foundation for Consumer Complaints Boards.[21] In Belgium, the Raad voor de Reclame/Conseil de la Publicité (Advertising Council) intends to ensure that consumers maintain confidence in commercial communications. A self-disciplinary Committee for Ethical Practices in Advertising (Jury voor Eerlijke Praktijken inzake Reclame/Jury d'Ethique Publicitaire—www.jepbelgium.be) was established by the Council.

As a rule of thumb, codes are less common the further south and east one goes in the Community,[22] although there are exceptions to this. The Schulze/Schulte-Noelke report, for instance, noted the important role self-regulation plays in Italy in relation to advertising.[23]

II. SCOPE OF EUROPEAN UNFAIR COMMERCIAL PRACTICES LAW

II.A COMMERCIAL PRACTICES AND FREE SPEECH

Not only Community legislation on unfair and misleading advertising but also ECJ case-law on Article 28 EC favours the free flow of information to the benefit of

[19] *Bowerman v ABTA*, [1996] CLC, 451.

[20] *Re VG Vehicles (Telford) Limited* (1981) 89 ITSA Monthly Review 91.

[21] See www.ser.nl.

[22] The Green Paper on European Union Consumer Protection COM [2001] 531 final at 7 refers to self-regulation in Denmark, Sweden, Finland, the United Kingdom, Ireland and Netherlands and then states it is 'less well-known in other Member States.'

[23] *An Analysis of National Fairness Laws Aimed at Protecting Consumers in Relation to Commercial Practices*, 22–23, available on the website of DG Sanco.

consumers. In an impressive series of judgments, such as *GB-INNO,*[24] *Yves Rocher,*[25] *Mars,*[26] the ECJ has struck down Member State legislation which constitutes unjustified barriers to trade. The ECJ's overall policy is to replace national bans on particular forms of advertising, such as the ban on comparing the new reduced price with the old price, as far as possible via transparent information. The role and responsibility of the consumer is strengthened, but also the trader benefits from the information paradigm. Advertising is upgraded from a marketing technique to a constitutional right or even a human right to free speech, more precisely to commercial free speech. The European Court of Human Rights (ECtHR) has paved the way for such an understanding in *Markt Intern.*[27] The point then is how far commercial free speech reaches and where the limits to commercial free speech are.

Stephen Weatherill writes:[28]

> Traders cannot invoke Community law as an indefeasible weapon for opening up markets throughout the Community. Commercial free speech is not absolute. Nevertheless the application of Community law has reduced the scope of national action which obstructs cross-border advertising campaigns. States are obliged to find justification under Community law for rules which restrict trade. Commercial free speech is a powerful weapon.

ECJ Case C-368/95, 26 June 1997[29] **2.1 (EU)**

Vereinigte Familiapress Zeitungsverlags- und vertriebs GmbH v Heinrich Bauer Verlag

RESTRICTION OF ADVERTISING MEASURES VIA HUMAN RIGHTS

Familiapress

Press diversity is more important than the chance to take part in prize games.

Facts: By order of 15 September 1995, received at the ECJ on 29 November 1995, the Handelsgericht Wien (Commercial Court, Vienna), referred a question on the interpretation of Article 28 (Article 30 prior to renumbering) of the EC Treaty to the Court for a preliminary ruling. That question was raised in proceedings brought by Vereinigte Familiapress Zeitungsverlags- und vertriebs GmbH ('Familiapress'), an Austrian newspaper publisher, against Heinrich Bauer Verlag, a newspaper publisher established in Germany, for an order that the latter should cease to sell in Austria publications offering readers the chance to take part in games for prizes, in breach of the Gesetz über unlauteren Wettbewerb 1992 (UWG, the Austrian Law on Unfair Competition). Heinrich Bauer Verlag publishes the weekly magazine *Laura* in Germany, which it also distributes in Austria. The issue of 22 February 1995 contained a crossword puzzle. Readers sending in the correct solution were entitled to be entered in a draw for two prizes of DEM 500. There were two other puzzles in the same issue, for prizes of DEM 1,000 and DEM 5,000, respectively, which were also to be awarded by drawing lots among the persons sending in the correct answers. The following issues invited readers to play similar games. Each issue indicated that there would be more puzzles the following week. According to the order for reference, such a practice is contrary to Austrian law.

[24] ECJ, 7 March 1990, Case C-362/88 [1990] ECR I-667.

[25] ECJ, 18 May 1993, Case C-126/91 [1993] ECR I-2361.

[26] ECJ, 6 July1995, Case C-470/93 [1995] ECR I-1923.

[27] ECtHR, 20 November 1989, *Markt Intern Verlag GmbH and Klaus Beermann v Germany*, [1989] Reports of Judgments and Decisions series A No 165 in particular the dissenting opinion of Judges Martens and MacDonald.

[28] In Micklitz and Weatherill, above n 1, 280.

[29] [1997] ECR I-3089.

Paragraph 9a(1)1of the UWG contains a general prohibition on offering consumers free gifts linked to the sale of goods or the supply of services. Paragraph 9a(2) 8 of the UWG authorises prize competitions and draws for which 'the value of the potential individual entries, obtained by dividing the total number of prizes at stake by the number of entry vouchers (lots) distributed, does not exceed 5 schillings and the total value of the prizes competed for does not exceed ATS 300,000'. This, however, was declared inapplicable to the press by an amending law of 1993. Consequently, there has, since then, no longer been any exception to the prohibition on publishers of periodicals inviting consumers to take part in draws. Since there is no provision to the same effect in the German Gesetz gegen den unlauteren Wettbewerb (Law against Unfair Competition), the Handelsgericht Wien took the view that the prohibition of the sale of periodicals under the UWG potentially affected intra-Community trade. It therefore stayed proceedings and referred the following question to the Court for a preliminary ruling:

> Is Article [28] of the EC Treaty to be interpreted as precluding application of legislation of Member State A prohibiting an undertaking established in Member State B from selling in Member State A, a periodical produced in Member State B, where that periodical contains prize puzzle competitions or games which are lawfully organized in Member State B?

Judgment: 24. Furthermore, it is to be noted that where a Member State relies on overriding requirements to justify rules which are likely to obstruct the exercise of free movement of goods, such justification must also be interpreted in the light of the general principles of law and in particular of fundamental rights (see Case C-260/89 *ERT* [1991] ECR I-2925, paragraph 43).

25. Those fundamental rights include freedom of expression, as enshrined in Article 10 of the European Convention for the Protection of Human Rights and Fundamental Freedoms (*ERT*, paragraph 44).

26. A prohibition on selling publications which offer the chance to take part in prize games competitions may detract from freedom of expression. Article 10 of the European Convention for the Protection of Human Rights and Fundamental Freedoms does, however, permit derogations from that freedom for the purposes of maintaining press diversity, in so far as they are prescribed by law and are necessary in a democratic society (see the judgment of the European Court of Human Rights of 24 November 1993 in Informationsverein Lentia and Others v Austria Series A No 276).

27. In the light of the considerations set out in paragraphs 19 to 26 of this judgment, it must therefore be determined whether a national prohibition such as that in issue in the main proceedings is proportionate to the aim of maintaining press diversity and whether that objective might not be attained by measures less restrictive of both intra-Community trade and freedom of expression.

28. To that end, it should be determined, first, whether newspapers which offer the chance of winning a prize in games, puzzles or competitions are in competition with those small press publishers who are deemed to be unable to offer comparable prizes and whom the contested legislation is intended to protect and, second, whether such a prospect of winning constitutes an incentive to purchase capable of bringing about a shift in demand.

29. It is for the national court to determine whether those conditions are satisfied on the basis of a study of the Austrian press market. …

34. In the light of the foregoing considerations, the answer to be given to the national court's question must be that Article 30 of the EC Treaty is to be interpreted as not precluding application of legislation of a Member State the effect of which is to prohibit the distribution on its territory by an undertaking established in another Member State of a periodical produced in that latter State containing prize puzzles or competitions which are lawfully organized in that State, provided that that prohibition is proportionate to maintenance of press diversity and that that objective cannot be achieved by less

restrictive means. This assumes, inter alia, that the newspapers offering the chance of winning a prize in games, puzzles or competitions are in competition with small newspaper publishers who are deemed to be unable to offer comparable prizes and the prospect of winning is liable to bring about a shift in demand. Furthermore, the national prohibition must not constitute an obstacle to the marketing of newspapers which, albeit containing prize games, puzzles or competitions, do not give readers residing in the Member State concerned the opportunity to win a prize. It is for the national court to determine whether those conditions are satisfied on the basis of a study of the national press market concerned.

Note

The first contentious issue concerned the question whether and to what extent the Member States might be allowed by reference to free speech as anchored in Article 10 of the European Convention of Human Rights to restrict particular advertising measures. *Familiapress* was the first opportunity to clarify the relationship. The ECJ recognised that Article 10 might indeed serve as a device to defend press diversity, thereby recognising that advertising prohibitions belong to the product and do not come under the notion of selling arrangements in the meaning of *Keck*.[30]

ECJ Case C-71/02, 25 March 2004[31] **2.2 (EU)**

Herbert Karner Industrie Auktionen GmbH v Troostwijk GmbH

RESTRICTION OF SALES PROMOTION VIA HUMAN RIGHTS

Karner

The Human Rights Convention can be invoked as a general yardstick.

Facts: Two companies, Karner and Troostwijk, were engaged in the sale by auction of industrial goods and the purchase of the stock of insolvent companies. By a sales contract of 26 March 2001, Troostwijk acquired, with the authorisation of the insolvency court, the stock of an insolvent construction company. Karner had also indicated its interest in the purchase of those goods. Troostwijk intended to sell the stock from the insolvent estate in an auction sale which was to take place on 14 May 2001. It advertised the auction in a sales catalogue, stating that it was an insolvency auction and that the goods were from the insolvent estate of the company in question. The advertising notice was also posted on the internet. In Karner's view, Troostwijk's advertising was contrary to Paragraph 30 (1) of the UWG because it gives the public concerned the impression that it was the insolvency administrator selling the insolvent company's assets. Irrespective of any risk that the public will be misled, such advertising was both contrary to the competition rules laid down in the EC Treaty and misleading within the meaning of paragraph 2 of the UWG.

Judgment: 48. ... with regard to the compatibility of the legislation in question with freedom of expression, it should be recalled that, according to settled case-law, fundamental rights form an integral part of the general principles of law the observance of which the Court ensures. For that purpose, the Court draws inspiration from the constitutional traditions common to the Member States and from the guidelines supplied by

[30] ECJ, 24 November 1993, Case C-266 and 267/91 [1993] ECR I-6097.

[31] [2004] ECR I-3025, with comment J Stuyck (2004) *CML Rev* 1683, 1695.

international treaties for the protection of human rights on which the Member States have collaborated or to which they are signatories. The ECHR has special significance in that respect (see, inter alia, Case C-260/89 *ERT* [1991] ECR I-2925, paragraph 41; Case C-274/99 *P Connolly v Commission* [2001] ECR I-1611, paragraph 37; Case C-94/00 *Roquette Frères* [2002] ECR I-9011, paragraph 25 and Case C-112/00 *Schmidberger* [2003] ECR I-5659, paragraph 71).

49. Further, according to the Court's case-law, where national legislation falls within the field of application of Community law the Court, in a reference for a preliminary ruling, must give the national court all the guidance as to interpretation necessary to enable it to assess the compatibility of that legislation with the fundamental rights whose observance the Court ensures (see, to that effect, Case C-299/95 *Kremzow* [1997] ECR I-2629, paragraph 15).

50. Whilst the principle of freedom of expression is expressly recognised by Article 10 ECHR and constitutes one of the fundamental pillars of a democratic society, it nevertheless follows from the wording of Article 10(2) that freedom of expression is also subject to certain limitations justified by objectives in the public interest, in so far as those derogations are in accordance with the law, motivated by one or more of the legitimate aims under that provision and necessary in a democratic society, that is to say justified by a pressing social need and, in particular, proportionate to the legitimate aim pursued (see, to that effect, Case C-368/95 *Familiapress* [1997] ECR I-3689, paragraph 26; Case C-60/00 *Carpenter* [2002] ECR I-6279, paragraph 42; and *Schmidberger*, cited above, paragraph 79).

51. It is common ground that the discretion enjoyed by the national authorities in determining the balance to be struck between freedom of expression and the abovementioned objectives varies for each of the goals justifying restrictions on that freedom and depends on the nature of the activities in question. When the exercise of the freedom does not contribute to a discussion of public interest and, in addition, arises in a context in which the Member States have a certain amount of discretion, review is limited to an examination of the reasonableness and proportionality of the interference. This holds true for the commercial use of freedom of expression, particularly in a field as complex and fluctuating as advertising (see, to that effect, Case C-245/01 *RTL Television* [2003] ECR I-0000, paragraph 73; judgments of the ECHR of 20 November 1989, *Markt intern Verlag GmbH and Klaus Beermann*, Reports of Judgments and Decisions series A No 165, paragraph 33; and of 28 June 2001, *VGT Verein gegen Tierfabriken v Switzerland*, Reports of Judgments and Decisions 2001-VI, paragraphs 69 to 70).

52. In this case it appears, having regard to the circumstances of fact and of law characterising the situation which gave rise to the case in the main proceedings and the discretion enjoyed by the Member States, that a restriction on advertising as provided for in Paragraph 30 of the UWG is reasonable and proportionate in the light of the legitimate goals pursued by that provision, namely consumer protection and fair trading.

53. In the light of all the foregoing considerations, the question referred to the Court must be answered as follows: Article 28 EC does not preclude national legislation, which, irrespective of the truthfulness of the information, prohibits any reference to the fact that goods come from an insolvent estate where in public announcements or notices intended for a large circle of persons, notice is given of the sale of goods which originate from, but no longer constitute part of, the insolvent estate.

Note

In *Karner*, the ECJ went beyond *Familiapress*. The ECJ took Article 10 of the Human Rights Convention as a general yardstick against which sales promotion measures may be measured—even beyond the *Keck*-doctrine. However, the Member States are granted a large margin of discretion. They may prohibit sales promotion measures which do not contribute to freedom of speech.

BGH (Federal Supreme Court), 6 December 2001[32] **2.3 (DE)**
Stern v Benetton

HIV POSITIVE

Benetton at the BGH

Moral standards limit freedom of speech.

Facts: The civil division of the German Federal Court (BGH) had to decide again whether the defendant, the distributor of the illustrated magazine *Stern*, had acted illegally by printing a Benetton advert 'HIV Positive'. The two-page advert displayed a human's posterior, stamped on its right side in bold, blue type with the abbreviation 'HIV' and, beneath that, the word 'Positive'. Just underneath this stamp, against a green background, appear the words 'United Colours of Benetton' in white type. In the left, bottom colour of the advert, the following sentence features: 'Colors, a magazine about the rest of the world, available in Benetton stores and selected newsagents.' The registered society, the Committee for the Suppression of Unfair Competition, complained that this advert was anti-competitive. Not only Benetton but also the defendant had offended the basic decencies of competition. The court of first instance upheld the complaint. The appeal of the defendant was rejected by the BGH in its judgment of 6 July 1995 (I ZR 180/94). With respect to the constitutional cross-complaint of the defendant, the German Constitutional Court suspended the decision of the lower court in a judgment of 12 December 2000 (1 BvR 1762 und 1787/95, BVerfGE 102, 347), due to a violation of Article 5(5)1 of the German Basic Law (Grundgesetz), sending the matter back to the BGH for a reconsideration of the advert's content. The defendant's appeal was unsuccessful in the new proceedings. The BGH took the view that the 'HIV Positive' advert was indecent in the sense of §1 of Unfair Competition Act (UWG); it did not enjoy the protection of the provision safeguarding freedom of expression (Article 5 German Basic Law) because it offended the human dignity of Aids sufferers (Article 1(1) German Basic Law).

Judgment: It cannot be said in refutation of the illegality of the advert that it was intended as a denunciatory, stirring, critical statement. In competition with others, where a vendor wishes to influence consumers through adverts, its advertising ought to be measured by reference to their capacity to do just that with their target audience. In an advert, only that which stems from this aim carries weight. Neither a particular statement nor a particular view can be taken from the advert—it will always be evaluated by the observer. The advert itself merely portrays a dreadful reality in a picture. Objectively speaking, it is intended only to provoke, with a strong effect.

The effect had by an advert on consumers depends definitively on how strongly it is perceived as a firm's advert. In particular, that we are concerned with an advert here which should, at least increase the profits of the trading firm is a reason for the advert's extraordinary, stirring effect in public, which the photo alone would not provoke (despite its strong provocative effect). The issue it portrays might well move people in profound ways. The connection of a photo with this intense effect with the unmistakable pursuit of profits will, for most observers, depending on their circumstances and personal views,

[32] I ZR 284/00.

evoke thoughts of a personal nature as well as strong, frequently intense reactions. Precisely therein lies the commercial effect of the advert; in the creation of a public debate, the company's name is supposed to be stamped into peoples' minds.

The advert portrays a person, who, being infected with Aids, is "stamped". This could, without more, be perceived as an expression of solidarity with Aids sufferers, as a stirring reference to the plight of a group, which not only suffers from a fatal disease, but which is also stigmatised and ostracized from society due to the danger of contagion. The advert would be unobjectionable if it could only be considered in this way or its character as a commercial advert, its meaning, and its effect, only influenced at the most insignificant parts of its target audience, because it cannot or can hardly be perceived as such.

The advert would still be overwhelmingly perceived as an advert for the relevant company, even if it were understood as a call for solidarity. It influences not only the formation of public opinion, with real or supposed good intentions, but also uses the severe suffering of people as an advertising theme (by thematising a company in the advert) in order to stir emotions. In this way, it aims to bring the company to the attention of the public, and to promote the sales of its wares, primarily clothing. Even if the solidarity point were accepted, so long as the advert's trading purpose is not missed or is only perceived in passing by its audience, functions also as a means to commercial gain, exploiting to these ends the anguish and stigmatisation of Aids sufferers.

From this perspective, the sufferers and their fate are reduced by the advert to an object for the pursuit of profits. Where it is combined with business interests, namely the increase of turnover in an unrelated market, the call for solidarity with people is cynical and denigrates their autonomous entitlement to respect and human solidarity. It could be considered injurious by those affected by the illness, to see it in an advertisement, quite possibly unprepared, in picture form, in a newspaper or in public on a billboard.

An advert like the one under consideration, risks that the method used to gain attention, through the exploitation of provocative themes and taboo topics as the object or as corollaries to adverts, has a deleterious and discriminating effect on the disabled, ethnic or political minorities, foreigners or religious groups. Only seldom will such advertising techniques be concealed, and only seldom will they send a potentially harmless message. This does not change the capacity of such adverts to have a negative effect on feelings and one deleterious to minorities. The conditions under which competition takes place would be impaired if multiple advertisers resorted to using this struggle in the nature of such an HIV Positive advert, to the cost of those traders who refrain from disrespecting others and denigrating their constitutionally enshrined rights.

Bundesverfassungsgericht (The Federal Constitutional Court), 11 March 2003[33] **2.4 (DE)**
Stern v Benetton

FREEDOM OF SPEECH UNDER THE GERMAN BASIC LAW

Benetton at the Bundesverfassungsgericht

Freedom of speech is more important than moral standards.

[33] The decision is reported in [2003] *Gewerblicher Rechtsschutz und Urheberrecht* 442.

Facts: The two-page advert displayed a human's posterior, stamped on its right side in bold, blue type with the abbreviation 'HIV' and, beneath that, the word 'Positive'. Just underneath this stamp, against a green background, appear the words 'United Colours of Benetton' in white type. In the left, bottom colour of the advert, the following sentence features: 'Colors, a magazine about the rest of the world, available in Benetton stores and selected newsagents.'

Judgment: The "HIV POSITIVE" advert falls under the protection of the press freedom of the complainant, which also encompasses the expression of the opinions of others in advertisements. The advert is expression in the sense of Art 5(1)1 of the German Basic Law as a talking picture, forming opinions and portraying a social ill with its content. This applies irrespective of the advertising context and the fact that Benetton has refrained from commenting. At first blush, the advert cannot be reduced to an attempt to make of Benetton a talking point (cf BVerfGE 102, 347, 359 f.).

The judgment of the Federal Court acknowledges the function of human dignity as a constraint on freedom of expression in competition/trading law. Human dignity is an absolute boundary on freedom of expression in this field (cf BVerfGE 102, 347, 366 f.). Art 1(1) of German Basic Law obliges the State, to protect all people from attacks upon their human dignity. Such attacks can be in the form of humiliation, stigmatisation, persecution, ostracism and so forth, which infringe a person's natural claim to dignity (cf BVerfGE 1, 97, 104). Human dignity, as the fundament of all basic rights, cannot be balanced with any single basic right. However, since the basic rights are, taken together, the crystallisation of the principle of human dignity, a careful justification is required if it is to be accepted that the exercise of a right itself injures the inalienable right to dignity (cf BVerfGE 93, 266, 293). In interpreting §1 German Unfair Competition Act, this applies *a fortiori* because if it is assumed that human dignity is violated, then the justification for derogating from freedom of expression (in this case, the impeding of free competition) necessary in other cases, is no longer required (cf BVerfG, 1. Kammer des Ersten Senats, Beschluss vom 6 Februar 2002—1 BvR 952/90, 1 BvR 2151/96 –, NJW 2002, S 1187, 1188).

The use of this standard does not entail that the advert's aim of attracting attention is inconsistent with human dignity. The advert raises the issue of the misery of Aids sufferers and leaves the interpretation to the observer. Where a message mocks, demeans or derides, or plays down or applauds or puts the suffering in a ridiculous or macabre context, the advert's profit-related purpose does not entail that it lacks the requisite respect. The mere fact of the company's intent to profit from its advertising does not justify the heavy rebuke represented by an affront to human dignity.

The Federal Court also considers the advert to be morally repugnant because it could trigger in a not insignificant part of its audience feelings of fear and endangerment as a result of Aids and confronts Aids sufferers and their relatives with their plight in an unreasonable manner. This complimentary consideration also does not exclude the conclusion that there has been a violation of the constitution.

If one wanted to prohibit the thematisation of suffering in commercial advertising, a considerable part of daily reality would be excluded from the not insignificant influence of advertising on opinions, values and preferences of people. That result cannot, given the particular interest in the thematisation of social problems, cohere with press freedom and freedom of expression (cf BVerfGE 28, 191, 202).

Notes

(1) The second set of questions has a different flavour. Here it is not so much a conflict over competences and leeway for statutory intervention to protect consumers against advertising but a matter of whether courts should limit commercial free speech or whether the consumers themselves should decide on the social acceptability of particular forms of advertising. The advertising used by Benetton serves as a prominent example. In the 1990s, the company started its shock-advertising strategy, using photographs of persons suffering from Aids or who had been killed during the Balkan conflict to attract attention to the trade mark. Shock-advertising provoked differing decisions in the Member States.

(2) Benetton has twice been before the German Federal Constitutional Court and twice before the German Federal Supreme Court (BGH).[34] In essence, the question was whether or not the advertisements were contrary to public policy. A dispute arose between the two federal courts regarding the construction of German unfair commercial practices law. Broadly speaking, it can be said that the Constitutional Court understands unfair commercial practice as market communication where the addressees are required to make their own value judgments, whereas the Supreme Court condemned the advertisements as being morally offensive.

It is interesting to look at the way Benetton was dealt with in different legal orders.

The Finnish Market Court,[35] **2.5 (FI)**
X v Benetton

MORAL OFFENSIVENESS OF ADVERTISING MEASURES

Benetton in Finland

Advertising can be prohibited where it is a clear offence against accepted principles of morality.

Facts: The consumer ombudsman requested that the company Oy UCB Finnland AB (defendant) be prohibited on the basis of Ch 2, s 1 of the Consumer Protection Act (Konsumentskyddslagen) from exploiting consumers' fear of war and violence in its marketing measures.

On 20 February 1994, the defendant launched an outdoor advertising campaign in which a blood-stained T-shirt together with a pair of camouflage trousers were depicted in front of a white background on billboards. The defendant's company logo was also displayed on the posters. According to the defendant, the clothes were worn by a Bosnian soldier, Marinko Garko, when he was shot dead in March 1993.

The Benetton company had developed its own strategy in order to attract attention. It had divided its advertising into two categories. The first category consisted of normal product advertising presenting the company's clothing, the second consisted of sensational, so-called company image advertising.

[34] The intricacies of the discussion have resulted in a number of publications. For a full account of the conflict between the German Supreme Court and the German Constitutional Court, see I Scherer, '§4-2 No 165ff' in K-H Fezer, *Gesetz gegen den unlauteren Wettbewerb* (München, Verlag CH Beck, 2005).

[35] The decision is reported in [1996] *Gewerblicher Rechtsschutz und Urheberrecht: Internationaler Teil* 251. The translation is available at the [1997] IIC 266, each of which is accompanied by comparative comments given by A Kur, 'Anmerkung' [1996] *GRUR Int* 255; 'Comment' [1997] IIC 296.

In its company image advertising, the Benetton company used depictions intended to remind the observer of newscast presentations. Generally, the depictions related to an issue that was highly likely to provoke people. For example, in the past the company employed motifs such as a moribund Aids patient surrounded by his close relatives, a lorry overloaded with refugees, and a guerrilla posing triumphantly and holding in his hands a bone (a human shinbone?). Some of these depictions were shown in Finland, others only in other countries; yet the aim of the advertising was identical in each case. The only element indicating the Benetton company was the company logo; the logo is eye-catching and it is unambiguous who is behind the advertisement: the company behind the advertisement could be readily identified. Apart from this, the use of the logo created an obvious link between the company image advertising and its product advertising. In addition, on the poster at issue in this case the technique of depiction is the same as was used in the company's product advertising.

Viewed from the perspective of the individual consumer, the aim of the defendant's company image advertising was to 'startle' consumers, to shock people with such depictions: the next time the consumer is confronted with the defendant's logo, it will already be engrained in his mind. Although the company image advertising measures were not absolutely uniform, they have nevertheless functioned in the manner intended by the defendant. Consumers remember Benetton. Hence, people's fear of war had been exploited for the commercial purposes of the company. Such advertising methods constituted a clear offence against accepted principles of morality.

At a more general level, the defendant intended to attract attention in the mass media. Hence, the company sought to achieve a secondary marketing effect. For this reason as well, the marketing methods at issue were contrary to accepted principles of morality.

Judgment: The war raging in former Yugoslavia has been communicated to Finnish consumers by the mass media. The news reports on the war may generate fear and anxiety. The reference to the war in advertising may also engender negative associations in consumers, yet as such may not be deemed an offence against accepted principles of morality or otherwise unfair to consumers. The associations made by an individual consumer when confronted with such company advertising, which operates at a more general level than does concrete product advertising, depend upon the personal experiences and values of that consumer.

[Dissenting vote of Judges Taler, Olikeinen and Mäkinen] The depiction of the blood-stained clothes of the dead Bosnian soldier who was pierced by a single bullet dominates the defendant's advertising poster. The motif on the poster has no connection with the products distributed by the company; rather, it was depicted in order to attract attention. The advertising poster reminds the consumer of the war raging in former Yugoslavia. Notwithstanding the fact that the mass media provide a constant stream of information concerning this war, in a manner that causes fear and anxiety and thus shocks people, an advertising poster depicting this war will also be understood in the same manner. The advertisement does not contain any elements that could neutralize this effect. This unusually powerful way of attracting attention and the resulting emotional effect on feelings and moral values, which are of a fundamental nature for most people, is supplemented by the defendant's logo. Consequently, the merging of such a motif with the defendant's logo constitutes a marketing measure that is contrary to accepted principles of morality; therefore the advertising poster violates Ch 2, s 1 of the Finnish Consumer Protection Act s 2b.

Raad voor Reclame (Advertising Council), 9 February 2000[36] **2.6 (BE)**
X v Benetton

ADVERTISING AND THE VIOLATION OF HUMAN DIGNITY

Benetton in Belgium

Advertising should not violate human dignity.

Facts: The poster showed a man condemned to death in the United States and displayed in large type the phrase 'Sentenced to death'. Data concerning the individual was written in small type (name, date of birth, crime, sentence). Conformity to ethical rules of advertisement must be controlled. The advert was considered a commercial exploitation of a theme linked to human dignity.

Judgment: Jury opinion: Considering that using the serious and delicate theme of death penalty with a commercial purpose is likely to upset and that the images of persons sentenced to death in the United-States may be perceived as an affront to human dignity, the Jury formulated a reserve opinion (*avis de réserves*).

Consequences: The advertiser argued that he tried to draw the public's attention to core social issues. The year 2000 being dedicated by Amnesty international and several governments to the abolition of death penalty, the advertiser intended to take part in this movement. The campaign will stop on 15 February and will not be continued.

Raad voor Reclame (Advertising Council), 10 June 1999[37] **2.7 (BE)**
X v Benetton

ADVERTISING AND THE VIOLATION OF HUMAN DIGNITY

Benetton in Belgium II

Approval of UNHCR overrules national moral reservations.

Facts: An advertisement showed the logo of the United Nations High Commissioner for Refugees (UNHCR) and the following text: 'Office of the High Commissioner of the United Nations for Refugees. Contribution for Kosovo. Citibank (Switzerland), Zurich. JNHCR bank account number: 343 140'. On a white background, a blood splash was followed by the slogan: 'United Colours of Benetton'. A complaint was received that the advert was undignified especially because it associated the UNHCR with Benetton. The advertiser submitted that the Office of the High Commissioner for Refugees confirmed that the advert, proposed and produced by Benetton to raise public awareness to the fate of Kosovo refugees and to raise funds, had been approved by it in the framework of private sector support.

Judgment: Therefore, considering that the advert did not harm the dignity of the refugees, the Jury did not formulate any remarks.

Note

In Finland, it is not so much the dimension of free speech which is at stake, but the degree to which advertising measures violate moral standards. The Finnish Market Court engaged in the moral offensiveness of the advertisement without putting

[36] Available at www.jepbelgium.be.
[37] Available at www.jepbelgium.be.

emphasis on free speech. The key of the issue was the correct interpretation of Chapter 2, section 1 of the Consumer Protection Act (KSL), under which advertising measures must be regarded as illegal if they are contrary to *bonos mores*. The majority of the judges confirmed the inadmissibility of the advertising. The Belgian Advertising Council has no regulatory power, but it also recommends the suppression of Benetton advertising. Here neither free speech nor *bones mores* lies at the forefront of the legal discourse, but the violation of human dignity. However, the Belgian Advertising Council is not willing to overrule the approval of advert sanctioned by the UNHCR.

In essence, Member States agree neither on the result nor on the legal reasoning. It seems that different cultures and traditions greatly affect the outcome of the case. The point then is to what extent these differences can be, may be or should be subject to harmonisation.

ECJ Case C-36/02, 14 October 2004[38] **2.8 (EU)**

Omega Spielhallen v Oberbürgermeisterin der Bundesstadt Bonn

INTERACTION OF FREEDOM OF EXPRESSION, PROTECTION OF FUNDAMENTAL RIGHTS AND THE FREE MOVEMENT OF SERVICES

The public policy defence

Simulated killings of human beings may violate human dignity.

Facts: Omega, a German company, had, since 1 August 1994, been operating in Bonn an installation known as a 'laserdrome', normally used for the practice of 'laser sport'. The installation continued to be used after 14 September 1994, Omega having obtained authorisation to continue its use on a provisional basis by an order of the Verwaltungsgericht Köln (Administrative Court of Cologne) of 18 November 1994. The equipment used by Omega in its establishment, which included submachine-gun-type laser targeting devices and sensory tags fixed either in the firing corridors or to jackets worn by players, was initially developed from a children's toy freely available on the market. That equipment having proved technically inadequate, Omega turned, from a date not specified but later than 2 December 1994, to equipment supplied by the British company Pulsar International Ltd (which subsequently became Pulsar Advanced Games Systems Ltd, hereinafter referred to as 'Pulsar'). However, a franchising contract with Pulsar was not concluded until 29 May 1997. Even before the public opening of the 'laserdrome', part of the population manifested its opposition to the project. At the beginning of 1994, the Bonn police authority ordered Omega to supply it with a precise description of the working of the game intended for the 'laserdrome' and, by letter of 22 February 1994, warned it of its intention to issue a prohibition order in the event of it being possible there to 'play at killing' people. Omega replied, on 18 March 1994, that the game merely involved hitting fixed sensory tags installed in the firing corridors. Having noted that the object of the game played in the 'laserdrome' also included hitting sensory tags placed on the jackets worn by players, the Bonn police authority issued an order against Omega on 14 September 1994, forbidding it from 'facilitating or allowing in its establishment' games the object of which was to fire at human targets using a laser beam or other technical devices (eg infrared), thereby, by recording shots hitting their targets, 'playing at killing people', on pain of a 10,000 DEM fine for each game played in breach of the order. That order was issued under powers conferred by §14 (1) of the Ordnungsbehördengesetz Nordrhein-Westfalen (OBG NW, the Law governing the North Rhine-Westphalia Police authorities), which provides that 'police authorities may take measures necessary to avert a risk to public order or safety in an individual case'.

[38] [2004] ECR I-9609.

Judgment: 32. In this case, the competent authorities took the view that the activity concerned by the prohibition order was a threat to public policy by reason of the fact that, in accordance with the conception prevailing in public opinion, the commercial exploitation of games involving the simulated killing of human beings infringed a fundamental value enshrined in the national constitution, namely human dignity. According to the *Bundesverwaltungsgericht*, the national courts which heard the case shared and confirmed the conception of the requirements for protecting human dignity on which the contested order is based, that conception therefore having to be regarded as in accordance with the stipulations of the German Basic Law. …

35. Since both the Community and its Member States are required to respect fundamental rights, the protection of those rights is a legitimate interest which, in principle, justifies a restriction of the obligations imposed by Community law, even under a fundamental freedom guaranteed by the Treaty such as the freedom to provide services (see, in relation to the free movement of goods, *Schmidberger*, paragraph 74).

36. However, measures which restrict the freedom to provide services may be justified on public policy grounds only if they are necessary for the protection of the interests which they are intended to guarantee and only in so far as those objectives cannot be attained by less restrictive measures (see, in relation to the free movement of capital, *Église de Scientologie*, paragraph 18). …

39. In this case, it should be noted, first, that, according to the referring court, the prohibition on the commercial exploitation of games involving the simulation of acts of violence against persons, in particular the representation of acts of homicide, corresponds to the level of protection of human dignity which the national constitution seeks to guarantee in the territory of the Federal Republic of Germany. It should also be noted that, by prohibiting only the variant of the laser game the object of which is to fire on human targets and thus 'play at killing' people, the contested order did not go beyond what is necessary in order to attain the objective pursued by the competent national authorities.

40. In those circumstances, the order of 14 September 1994 cannot be regarded as a measure unjustifiably undermining the freedom to provide services.

Note

Omega made clear that free movement of services may permissibly be restricted by national provisions on the safeguarding of human dignity—though the ECJ is careful to locate the source of the relevant fundamental rights protection at EC level, not merely at national (in this case German) level, presumably in order to avoid permitting purely national assessments of what type of interest should override trade integration. However, the Court could not have done otherwise since it refers as a general principle of Community law to the principles common to the constitutions of the Member States. To this extent, the judgment reaches beyond the overall question of the conditions under which market access is granted.

II.B PROTECTION OF INTERESTS OTHER THAN THE ECONOMIC INTERESTS OF CONSUMERS

According to Article 1, the Unfair Commercial Practices Directive (2005/29/EC) (UCPD) aims at approximating the rules on unfair commercial practices 'harming consumers' economic interests'. This means that non-economic interests are outside the scope of the Directive.

II.B.1 HEALTH AND SAFETY IN EC LAW ON UNFAIR COMMERCIAL PRACTICES

The UCPD claims not to affect certain national rules, such as rules relating to health and safety aspects. However, the scope of such aspects is contentious.

UCPD (2005/29/EC) **2.9 (EU)**

Article 3 (3) The Directive is without prejudice to Community or national rules relating to the health and safety aspects of products.

T Wilhelmsson, Scope of the Directive[39] **2.10 (EU)**

The offering of unhealthy or unsafe goods and services is not an unfair commercial practice within the scope of the Directive, but can be remedied with the help of product safety legislation, such as the General Product Safety Directive, and other similar measures. Important European legislation with an impact on health and safety issues can be found also in the areas of foodstuffs and cosmetics regulation. In addition, issues relating to public health, such as the combating of epidemics and other diseases, as well as public security issues, are outside scope of the Directive, even when the measures affect commercial practices. The Preamble to the Directive explicitly states that the Member States may, in the future and within their territory, 'retain or introduce restrictions and prohibitions ... for example in relation to alcohol, tobacco or pharmaceuticals' and that this is possible 'wherever the trader is based'. The highly topical issue of combating obesity and the over-consumption of junk food, in particular among children, might also be viewed as an issue of health policy which would fall under the health and safety exception; this would widen the scope for national measures regulating the advertising of such food.

This exception does not mean that health and safety issues are altogether outside the scope of the Directive. Misleading health claims, for example in advertising and other marketing, can be termed, under the provisions of the Directive, as misleading commercial practices. In Annex I, '[f]alsely claiming that a product is able to cure illnesses, dysfunction or malformations' is mentioned as one of the commercial practices which are under all circumstances considered unfair according to the Directive.

[39] In G Howells, H-W Micklitz and T Wilhelmsson, *European Fair Trading Law* (Aldershot, Ashgate, 2006) 74.

This means that the Unfair Commercial Practices Directive covers an area that might be covered by product safety legislation as well, because such legislation often also addresses misleading claims and misleading omission of information. As far as the product safety legislation is Community legislation, formally there is no problem as the situation may be solved with the help of the *lex specialis* provision in Article 3(4), analysed below. ... However, in relation to national legislation of the same kind, the maximum character of the Directive may cause problems that cannot be solved in an acceptable way without accepting that the 'positive' scope of the Directive is wider than its 'negative' scope, as suggested in the introduction to this chapter. 'Positively' it is clear that the Directive, and the legislation based on it, ought to be applied to misleading health claims in the marketing of products that may have an impact on health and safety. On the other hand, however, if there are stricter rules than the Directive in national product safety or health legislation concerning such marketing, they should not 'negatively' be struck down with reference to the maximum character of the Unfair Commercial Practices Directive, because they may be needed to support health policies that are intended to be outside the scope of the Directive.

And what if there are stricter general national rules on health claims than the provisions concerning misleading claims of the Directive? There may, for example, exist in national law a general rule—perhaps even based on the application of the national general clause—according to which claims that a product may cure diseases should always be considered unfair, if they cannot be very clearly substantiated. Should such a claim not be outside the scope of the Unfair Commercial Practices Directive in its negative sense, as it is 'relating to the health and safety aspects of products', and should the national rule therefore avoid assessment of its compatibility with Article 12 of the Directive that only would allow the courts to require the trader to furnish evidence concerning the health claim, if such a requirement appears appropriate?

Or should one rather—in line with the behaviour of the European Court of Justice in matters related to foodstuffs and cosmetics—apply a relatively narrow determination of what is a health policy related issue, and therefore include provisions on health claims of this nature within the maximum harmonisation scope of the Unfair Commercial Practices Directive? Partial maximum harmonisation is a difficult game.

ECJ Case C-99/01, 24 October 2002[40] **2.11 (EU)**

Criminal proceedings against Gottfried Linhart and Hans Biffl

REACH OF EUROPEAN CONSUMER LAW AND THE MARGIN LEFT TO MEMBER STATES, ECONOMISATION OF HEALTH AND SAFETY, CONSUMER CONCEPT

Dermatologically tested

The well-informed and circumspect consumer understands the limited value of references to dermatologically tested products.

Facts: By decision of 22 February 1999 of the Unabhängiger Verwaltungssenat Wien (Independent Administrative Chamber for Vienna) (Austria), Mr Linhart, the managing director of Colgate Palmolive GmbH, was found guilty of an administrative breach of §74(1) in conjunction with §§9(1) (a) and 8(f) of the

[40] [2002] ECR I-9375.

Lebensmittel- und Bedarfsgegenständegesetz (LMG, the Federal Act on trade in foodstuffs, products intended for human consumption, additives, cosmetic products and consumer goods) on the ground that the company placed on the market the cosmetic product Palmolive flüssige Seife Prima Antibakteriell (Palmolive liquid antibacterial soap) with the statement that it was dermatologically tested appearing on its packaging. By decision of 9 May 2000, the Unabhängiger Verwaltungssenat im Land Niederösterreich (Independent Administrative Chamber for Lower Austria) held Dr Biffl, as the managing director of Haarkos Parfumeriewaren und Kosmetika GmbH, to be in breach of §§74(1), 9(1)(b) and 8(f) of the LMG, on the basis that the company had distributed the product Keralogie Creme-Peeling Anti-Schuppen regulierendes Haarbad (dandruff-controlling conditioner), the packaging of which stated that it was dermatologically tested.

Opinion of AG Geelhoed: 34. As in Clinique, Unilever and Estée Lauder, the health of persons is not an actual issue in this case either. The cases concern descriptions which may, either rightly or wrongly, create the impression on the part of consumers that they possess a certain medicinal function. Measures to prevent buyers from being potentially misled or confused are not, so it would appear to me, bound up with the protection of public health, but rather with the protection of consumers and the fairness of trade.

Judgment: 29. According to the Austrian legislation and national case-law, the absence of explicit references to the contents and outcome of the medical assessment to which the cosmetic products were subject could give consumers the erroneous impression that those products had curative effects.

30. In that context, it should be determined whether the mere statement dermatologically tested appearing on the packaging of a cosmetic product is likely to attribute to that product characteristics which it does not possess, so that the national authorities can prohibit its marketing in accordance with Article 6(3) of Directive 76/768.

31. In that regard, the Court has held that the criterion of the presumed expectations of an average consumer who is reasonably well-informed and reasonably observant and circumspect also applies in the context of the marketing of cosmetic products where a mistake as to the product's characteristics cannot pose any risk to public health (*Estée Lauder*, cited above, paragraphs 27 and 28).

32. The application of such a criterion in the main proceedings makes it possible to infer that the statement 'dermatologically tested' which appears on the packaging of certain cosmetic products—in this instance, soaps and hair products—cannot suggest to the average consumer who is reasonably well-informed and reasonably observant and circumspect anything other than that the product underwent tests intended to study its effects on the skin and that, as a result, its placing on the market implies that the results of those tests were positive and that the product was well tolerated or at least harmless when applied to the skin.

33. Furthermore, the authenticity of those results is subject to monitoring by the national authorities.

34. Article 7a(1)(f) and (g) of Directive 76/768 requires the person responsible for placing the product on the market to keep information readily accessible to the competent authorities of the Member State concerning the existing data on undesirable effects on human health resulting from use of the product in question and proof of the effect claimed for it.

35. In those circumstances, the statement 'dermatologically tested' could not mislead an average consumer who is reasonably well-informed and reasonably observant and circumspect by attributing to the products in question characteristics which they do not possess and, in any event, a possible error relating to those characteristics would be unlikely to have an effect on public health.

Note

The ECJ applies in matters related to foodstuffs and cosmetics a relatively narrow determination of what is a health policy issue.[41] The ECJ is economising health and safety issues. It thereby relies on the circumspect consumer. The Advocate General even goes one step further. His interpretation highlights the importance of the judgment. There seems to exist no leeway for Member States as along as even the erroneous consumer might not endanger his or her health. The ECJ's case-law might restrict the understanding of Article 3(3) and by the same token enlarge the prospective scope of the Unfair Commercial Practices Directive (2005/29/EC). There is an obvious conflict between the broad understanding of health and safety issues suggested by Wilhelmsson and the rather narrow reading of the ECJ.

II.B.2 FOODSTUFFS, PHARMACEUTICALS, COSMETICS, TOBACCO AND ALCOHOL REGULATION

At the EC as well as at the Member State level, there are particular rules on regulating the advertising of health-related products, foodstuffs, pharmaceuticals, cosmetics, tobacco and alcohol.[42] The relevant EC rules—the numerous Directives adopted in these various fields and the UCPD—are in no way co-ordinated. That is why advertising law on foodstuffs, pharmaceuticals, cosmetics and tobacco exists side-by-side with the UCPD.

II.B.3 GENDER DISCRIMINATION IN ADVERTISING

The UCPD remains silent on the degree to which gender discrimination might come under the scope of application of the Directive. This is left to Directive 2004/113/EC.[43] The majority of Member States' courts seem quite reluctant to submit gender discrimination to market practice rules. However, the picture is rather blurred, illustrating the difficulty of relating market practice regulation to policies which are legitimate but which are not directly related to market practices. It seems as if, rather than courts, voluntary control bodies set up by the advertising industry have something to say here.

E Millan and R Elliott, Offensive Advertising, Public Policy and the Law[44] **2.12 (BG)**

In Bulgaria, in the spring of 2001, Zagorka (a brewery) launched a new television advertisement for its prime brand. The content of the advertisement can be summarised as

[41] Stated very clearly in the excerpt above (Case C-99/01 *Criminal proceedings against Gottfried Linhart and Hans Biffl* [2002] ECR I-9375 by Advocate-General Geelhoed, at 34).

[42] See for a full account of the European rules on advertising, H-W Micklitz, 'EG K Öffentliche Interessen und Verbraucherschutz' in *Münchener Kommentar zum UWG* (München, Verlag CH Beck, 2006).

[43] Council Directive 2004/113/EC of 13 December 2004 implementing the principle of equal treatment between men and women in the access to and supply of goods and services [2004] OJ L 373, 37–43.

[44] E Millan and R Elliott, 'Offensive Advertising, Public Policy and the Law: The Rulings on the Zagorka case' (2004) 27 *Journal of Consumer Policy* 477, 480.

follows: a young man is repairing an old Volkswagen Beetle. As the man lies beneath the car, two delicate female legs appear and elegantly kick the man's spanner away. The man searches for his tool, but instead of the spanner he finds a bottle of beer. The scene is followed by another one in which the man and the woman are embracing, each with a bottle of beer in their hand, and enjoying the drink. A male voiceover brings the message of the advertisement to the viewer: 'What does a human being need? A new car, a nice woman and a good beer'; the message is repeated and also displayed as a written text.

Notes

(1) The problems which arose from this advertisement can best be described in terms of the jokes which appeared in the Bulgarian media in the aftermath of this advertisement:[45] 'They sent into space first a dog, then a woman, and finally a human being', or: 'A shepherd was asked: 'Have you seen a couple passing by?' He replied: 'No. A while ago a human being and a woman passed by, but I have not seen a couple.' Only one law suit pertaining to Zagorka, which was brought by a woman, resulted in a decision against the claimant. Legal actions were brought by individual women, and one association of women, seeking damages. The then competent commission for consumer protection objected to initiating legal proceedings since there was no discrimination. The (female) vice-director stated: 'As a consumer I would not be offended by an advertisement of the kind of Zagorka.' Advertising agencies relied on the freedom of communication and the autonomy of the addressees; critics wanted to rely on unfair commercial practices law as a means of pursuing socio-political objectives.

(2) However, the Nordic countries disagree on the degree to which market practices law can be used to counteract sexist advertisements. In Finland, the Market Court has used the general clause of the Consumer Protection Act to issue injunctions against marketing that it considered unacceptable from the point of view of gender discrimination, eg when a scantily dressed female painter was used in a television advert to promote a certain house paint,[46] and when a former Miss Finland was lying on a sofa in a bikini, with the text: 'Lola is not included in the price'.[47] In contrast, the Swedish Market Court expressly refrained from issuing an injunction in a comparable case, referring to the purpose of the Marketing Act to protect consumers (and businesses), but not the integrity of women.[48] The Norwegian Marketing Act again contains an explicit provision, added to the general clause, giving the Consumer Ombudsman and the Market Council the right to interfere against marketing that is considered gender discriminating.[49]

In the UK gender advertising is subject to the UK Code of Advertising.

[45] Summary of Millan and Elliott, ibid.
[46] Finnish Market Court 1994:7.
[47] Finnish Market Court 2001:6.
[48] Swedish Market Court 1976:8.
[49] Markedsfrringsloven 1979 s 1(2).

Code of Advertising Practice (CAP)[50] **2.13 (UK)**

Rule 5. Decency (ie avoiding serious or widespread offence)

5.1 Marketing communications should contain nothing that is likely to cause serious or widespread offence. Particular care should be taken to avoid causing offence on the grounds of race, religion, sex, sexual orientation or disability. Compliance with the Code will be judged on the context, medium, audience, product and prevailing standards of decency.

5.2 Marketing communications may be distasteful without necessarily conflicting with 5.1 above. Marketers are urged to consider public sensitivities before using potentially offensive material.

5.3 The fact that a particular product is offensive to some people is not sufficient grounds for objecting to a marketing communication for it.

G Howells et al., Towards a Better Understanding of Unfair Commercial Practices[51] **2.14 (UK)**

One cinema beer advert rated 12A showed a man enjoying another beer whilst his wife tied herself to the bed and giggled mistaking the dog licking her feet for her husband. The complaint was not upheld with the adjudication stating 'children of 12 years of age and upwards were aware that adults played sexual games and believed, in a society increasingly at risk of sexually transmitted diseases, a commercial that depicted an alternative to penetrative sex was not irresponsible' [Greene King plc.] Neither was a complaint upheld regarding a food magazine advertisement showing Padma Lakshmi, the model and food writer wife of Salman Rushdie, wearing a bikini, lying on top of a metal kitchen surface, covered with lobsters surrounded by male chefs under the headline 'Dish of the day' [Guardian Newspapers Ltd]. The use of 'FCUK' has been held to refer to the brandname rather than the expletive [French Connection Ltd] ... Of course there are limits to this. A recent complaint concerned an advertisement, in Private Hire and Taxi Monthly, featuring photographs of women wearing a g-string and stockings only pulling on their g-strings accompanied by the text '... Prices Not To Pull Your Pants Down'.

Note

Self-control bodies play a major role in quite a number of the Member States in ridding the market of aggressive forms of gender discrimination. The UK example provides ample evidence. The Advertising Standards Authority (ASA) website, however, does have a separate category for complaints about the portrayal of men and women and comments that there are many complaints pertaining to this topic.[52] The ASA has 'to steer a course between companies' freedom to advertise their products and services and whether they are likely to cause serious or widespread

[50] Although the heading is simply decency in the adjudications it refers to taste and decency.

[51] G Howells, H-W Micklitz and T Wilhelmsson, 'Towards a Better Understanding of Unfair Commercial Practices' (2009) 51 *International Journal of Law and Management* 69.

[52] See www.asa.org.uk/asa/.

offence'. It commissions research to assess how offended people might be about men and women being portrayed as sex objects, as well as other factors such as the extent to which women may be portrayed as needing to look slim and attractive and holds an annual Consumer Conference, which also tests public opinion on this issue. All in all ASA's policy seems to be rather liberal.

Raad voor Reclame (Advertising Council), 2 September 2003[53] **2.15 (BE)**
X v Martini

GENDER DISCRIMINATION IN ADVERTISING

Martini

Certain sexual representations in advertising for alcoholic beverages can be contrary to the requirement of good taste.

Facts: An advertising poster for Martini shows a young woman in a bikini, sitting on a chair. Her wrists are tied to the armrests with a tie and a belt. She is leaning forward, staring with desire at the glass on the coffee table in front of her. The expression of the woman suggests that drinking alcohol enhances sexual performance. It was submitted that reducing women to being sexual symbols is humiliating. The advertiser held that he did not intend to offend or shock, which would be counter-productive insofar as women are his target group. Moreover, he maintained that this campaign is consistent with the advertising tradition of Martini, suffused with glamour, seduction, enjoyment of life and imagination, and that each individual has his/her own understanding of the advert. To him, the advertisement had nothing to do with sexism, or with submissiveness. The brand's world was one in which women know what they want and freely take part in this seduction game. It is a world in which freedom of mind prevails.

Judgment: According to the medium that has been used, which reaches a larger public than the target group, the Jury considered that the representation of the woman whose wrists are tied with a tie and a belt is not one of good taste because of the connotations that can be attached to it. Since such a communication strategy can prompt negative reactions, the Jury formulated a reserve opinion (*avis de réserve*) in accordance with article 4 of its rules.

Raad voor Reclame (Advertising Council), 8 May 2001[54] **2.16 (BE)**

GENDER DISCRIMINATION IN ADVERTISING

Taste of honey

Drastic sexual allusions are prohibited.

Facts: Advertisements with the mention 'taste of honey' showed three fashion photographs in which the hands of the models are placed next to representations of intimate parts of the body: a young woman holds the hand of a plastic bear as if it were a penis; a female hand is slipped into the vent of a tennis skirt; and a man holds a flower over his trousers as a fig leaf. It was argued that this advertisement was in bad taste because of its phallic references, and because it was likely to cause psychological damage to minors as well as to perpetuate sexist stereotypes.

[53] See www.jepbelgium.be.
[54] See www.jepbelgium.be.

Judgment: After examination of the case, the Jury considered that such images, deprived of any link to the advert's object and printed in a broadly distributed daily newspaper, are likely to hurt the public in overstepping what is allowed to be shown publicly, because of the symbolism used. On the basis of article 2 ICC (International Chamber of Commerce) Code, the Jury recommended not to distribute the advertisement anymore. The advertiser announced that the campaign had stopped and that the images would not be published again.

Jurado de Autocontrol de la Publicidad **2.17 (ES)**
(Jury for the Self-monitoring of Advertising), 8 January 2007[55]
Asociación de Usuarios de la Comunicación v Seat SA

GENDER DISCRIMINATION

Seat León

To present women or men as an object of desire is as such not illegal, provided that woman or men are not presented as mere objects of desire.

Facts: After some footage of cars on a racing circuit, a television advert showed the backside of a woman; the wind lifted her mini-skirt, and her bottom could be seen. The images of competing cars continued and some messages could be seen printed on them: 'value: guaranteed' and 'common sense: optional'. There is a final image of a professional driver making signs of satisfaction with the following text in the background: 'Congratulations to the Seat Leon team for this great season.'

Judgment: In light of this precept, and according to the practice of this Jury as exposed in prior occasions (for example, in the resolutions of the Jury Plenary of 26 January 2006 (case *AUC v Importaciones y Exportaciones Varma, SA—Ron Barceló*), and 4 July 2006 (case *Particular v Media Marka*), or in the resolution of the First Section of 26 July 2006 (case *AUC v Air Berlin*), we can affirm that there are two specific prongs in advertising contrary to women's dignity that arise from these cases. Firstly, the direct and private use of the woman's body or parts of it as a mere object disconnected to the product supposedly being promoted. And, secondly, the use of the woman's image associated with stereotyped behaviours in a way that affects the foundations of our legal order, generating gender violence. Focusing on the first of these prongs, which is the one related to the case at hand, this Body must analyze if the requirements for the occurrence of illegal publicity are present.

According to the above-cited practice of this Jury, there are three elements which in principle must concur for a publicity advert to be illicit according to article 3.a of the General Publicity Act. These are the following: i) The use of the female body, or parts of it, with erotic connotations and as an attention-capturing part of the publicity; ii) The representation of the female body as a mere object, not playing any active role in the publicity action or connected to the argument in the advertisement; and iii) The total disconnection between the female image represented and the promoted product.

[55] See www.autocontrol.es.

Note
The two Belgian cases demonstrate a degree of uncertainty as to how to decide on gender discrimination. In the first case the Commission formulated an *avis de réserve* only, although the combination of sexual symbols and alcoholic beverages is highly sensitive. The second case, on the other hand, clearly shows that the Commission is not willing to accept drastic sexual allusions. In Spain, too, there is a consolidated doctrine enforced by the 'jury of advertising self-control' on *women's dignity* and advertising. To present women or men as an object of desire is legal, even if they are nude; women or men as pure objects, however, is deemed invalid.

III. THE NOTION OF FAIRNESS

III.A THE STRUCTURE OF THE CONTROL CONCEPT

The general clause, Article 5 of the UCPD, defines the general legal framework. The Commission has decided—in conformity with the principal concept of the (continental) European Member States[56]—in favour of a general clause banning 'unfair commercial practices'. Three different levels may be distinguished: the general prohibition (the large general clause), the prohibition with regard to particular commercial practices (the small general clauses) and the list of incriminated practices.

UCPD (2005/29/EC) **2.18 (EU)**

Article 5 Prohibition of unfair commercial practices
(1) Unfair commercial practices shall be prohibited.
(2) A commercial practice shall be unfair if:
(a) it is contrary to the requirements of professional diligence, and
(b) it materially distorts or is likely to materially distort the economic behaviour with regard to the product of the average consumer whom it reaches or to whom it is addressed, or of the average member of the group when a commercial practice is directed to a particular group of consumers.
(3) Commercial practices which are likely to materially distort the economic behaviour only of a clearly identifiable group of consumers who are particularly vulnerable to the practice or the underlying product because of their mental or physical infirmity, age or credulity in a way which the trader could reasonably be expected to foresee, shall be assessed from the perspective of the average member of that group. This is without prejudice to the common and legitimate advertising practice of making exaggerated statements or statements which are not meant to be taken literally.
(4) In particular, commercial practices shall be unfair which:
(a) are misleading as set out in Articles 6 and 7, or
(b) are aggressive as set out in Articles 8 and 9.

[56] H-W Micklitz and J Keßler, *Marketing Practices Regulation and Consumer Protection in the EC Member States and the US* (Baden-Baden, Nomos-Verlag, 2002).

(5) Annex I contains the list of those commercial practices which shall in all circumstances be regarded as unfair. The same single list shall apply in all Member States and may only be modified by revision of this Directive.

Note

For the majority of Member States, the UCPD contains a number of new provisions that were not previously familiar or were not regulated so clearly. The latter is particularly true for the newly inserted element of misleading omissions. More or less unfamiliar to the legal systems of Member States is the concept of a separate general clause which prohibits aggressive trading practices, even if the advertising measures covered by the general clause are sanctioned under different terminology. Annex I illustrates that there are commercial practices that do not need to be individually assessed. Listing prohibited market practices is already known in the field of unfair contract terms but is not so familiar in the field of commercial practices.

There is not much evidence so far as to whether and to what extent the Member States' legislation will reflect the threefold structure, as to whether and to what extent Member States will take over the general cause as defined in Article 5, literally or conceptually, as to whether and to what extent they will introduce new rules on misleading omissions and aggressive practices, and last but not least on whether and to what extent they will transpose the Directive literally or conceptually into their national laws (see also section III.B.1 below).

III.B FAIRNESS, PROFESSIONAL DILIGENCE AND MATERIAL DISTORTION OF CONSUMERS

The general clause in Article 5 consists of three parts. Article 5(2)a refers to the requirements of *professional diligence* and Article 5(2)b to the *material distortion of economic behaviour of the consumer*. The terminology used in Article 5(2), professional diligence and material distortion of economic behaviour of the consumer, are further defined in Articles 2(h) and (e), respectively.

UCPD (2005/29/EC) **2.19 (EU)**

Article 2 Definitions …

(h) Professional diligence means the standard of special skill and care which a trader may reasonably be expected to exercise towards consumers, commensurate with honest market practice and/or the general principle of good faith in the trader's field of activity.

Note

The first draft proposal referred to 'normal market practice'. In its reasoning the Commission used the analogy of the widely known term as may be found in business accounting, namely good business conduct or due diligence as derived from Italian law. The finally adopted version clarifies this to the extent that the reference to customary market practice has been abandoned. Honest market practice combines both facts and norms. The normative reference system is crucial. The Directive embeds an objective review standard, which includes the interests of the consumers.

Article 5(2) refers to the material distortion of the economic behaviour of the consumer. This concept is further defined in Article 2(e).

UCPD (2005/29/EC) **2.20 (EU)**

Article 2 Definitions ...

(e) To materially distort the economic behaviour of consumers' means using a commercial practice to appreciably impair the consumer's ability to make an informed decision, thereby causing the consumer to take a transactional decision that he would not have taken otherwise.

Notes

(1) The two provisions, Article 5(2) and Article 2(e), are not entirely consistent. Article 5(2) refers to a commercial practice which materially distorts, or is likely to materially distort, economic behaviour. Article 2(e) uses 'appreciable' rather than 'material' to describe the measure of impairment. Further inconsistencies result from the economic 'behaviour' of the consumer and his ability to make an informed 'decision'. Article 2(e) refers to an 'informed decision', which is intended to be different from a 'transactional decision'. Contrariwise, the notion of informed decision seems narrower than economic behaviour. How should the interplay between economic behaviour, informed decision and transactional decision be organised? Does it suffice if the consumer's autonomy is impaired? But what does autonomy mean, and, if it is impaired, must the trader have tried to influence the consumer's autonomy intentionally? Is fault required?

(2) It is clear from the text, however, that not each and every commercial practice will impair the consumer's autonomy, but only those which *materially* distort his autonomy. Hence there is a threshold that must be met in order to label a commercial practice as unfair. It suffices if the commercial practice *potentially* effects his behaviour.

III.B.1 NATIONAL NOTIONS OF FAIRNESS

UCPD (2005/29/EC) **2.21 (EU)**

[Preamble] (5) In the absence of uniform rules at Community level, obstacles to the free movement of services and goods across borders or the freedom of establishment could be justified in the light of the case-law of the Court of Justice of the European Communities as long as they seek to protect recognised public interest objectives and are proportionate to those objectives. In view of the Community's objectives, as set out in the provisions of the Treaty and in secondary Community law relating to freedom of movement, and in accordance with the Commission's policy on commercial communications as indicated in the Communication from the Commission entitled 'The follow-up to the Green Paper on Commercial Communications in the Internal Market', such obstacles should be eliminated. These obstacles can only be eliminated by establishing uniform rules at Community level which establish a high level of consumer protection and by clarifying certain legal concepts at Community level to the extent necessary for the proper functioning of the internal market and to meet the requirement of legal certainty.

Note

The Directive strongly advocates uniformity. In practice, the wording ranges from fair commercial practices through good faith to honest practices or even illegal competition.

Cour de cassation, 2 May 1985[57] **2.22 (BE)**

ILLEGAL COMPETITION

Ostexpo Ostend

Breaches of law harming the interests of business constitute acts of unfair competition.

Facts: The operator of a sports hall organised commercial activities in excess of its permit. Its competitor claimed that the infringement of the conditions of the permit (granted under the town planning legislation) constituted an act of unfair competition.

Judgment: The decision of the Court of Appeal which considers that only the breaches of law related to trade can harm or be likely to harm the interests of a shopkeeper, infringes article 54 of the LPC (current article 94/3 Trade Practices Act). The aim of a regulation—in that case to ensure free flow—is not sufficient to establish that its breach by a shopkeeper does not harm the professional interests of other shopkeepers.

Note

Under Belgian law prior to the implementation of the UCPD, the infringement of a legal rule was held sufficient to establish a violation of honest business practices. If that violation also harms other traders in their professional interests or consumers in their interests, there is also an infringement of the general provision on unfair trade practices. The aim of the infringed provision is irrelevant. This means that, for example, an infringement of town and country planning can lead to an infringement of the general provision on unfair sales practices. If the infringement of a legal provision is established, the court will only have to determine whether that infringement causes prejudice to one or more others sellers (when applying former Article 93 of the Trade Practices Act) or one or more consumers (when applying former Article 94 of the Trade Practices Act). An important application of this

[57] 57(1985) RDC/TBH 631.

doctrine is the enforcement of the 1991 Competition Act (containing antitrust provisions very similar to Articles 81–82 EC and a regime of control of concentrations with a 'Belgian dimension' very similar to the regime of the EC Merger Regulation) and indeed Articles 81 and 82 by cease-and-desist orders for violation of former Articles 93 or 94 (consisting in an infringement of the competition rules). The Belgian consumer association Test Achats obtained a cease-and-desist order against insurance companies which had made an agreement to charge uniform minimum premiums for hospitalisation policies and to apply a common cap for interventions in execution of these policies.[58] The parallel between unfair B2B and B2C practices was abandoned with the implementation of the UCPD. For B2B practices, the former standard was maintained and former Article 93 was merely renumbered (now Article 94/3). The standard for B2C standard was replaced by the standard of the Directive (see below for the new Article 94/5). For B2B practices, the theory of 'illegal competition' is still relevant. For B2C practices, it is debated in the literature whether the new standard still allows for such reasoning.

The Member States have implemented or intend to implement the general clause as follows:

Unfair Competition Act (UWG)[59] **2.23 (AT)**

§1 Any party who in the course of business that (1) uses business practices which are *unfair* or uses other *unfair* actions that might influence competition to the disadvantage of entrepreneurs substantially, or (2) uses *unfair* business practices, that contradict professional diligence and might, with respect to the product in question, substantially influence the economic behaviour of the average consumer, whom it reaches or addresses.

Trade Practices Act[60] **2.24 (BE)**

Article 94/5 §2 A trade practice is unfair if it is contrary to the requirements of professional diligence and if it is likely to or does materially distort the economic behaviour with regard to a product of service of the consumer to whom it is addressed.

[58] Court of Appeal of Brussels, 24 May 1996, (1996) RDC/TBH 637, annulled, but only in so far as the judgment qualified the Belgian association of insurance companies as a 'seller' within the meaning of the Trader Practices Act, by Cass 13 March 1998 (1999) Revue des Assurances/Tijdschrift voor Verzekeringen 21, with annotation J Stuyck.

[59] Bundesgesetz gegen den Unlauteren Wettbewerb, Bundesgesetzblatt für die Republik Österreich 13 November 2007, Teil 1, No 79, 1.

[60] MB 21 June 2007, 34.272.

Consumer Code (Code de la Consommation)[61] **2.25 (FR)**

Article L 120-1 Unfair trade practices are prohibited. A trade practice is unfair when it is contrary to the requirements of professional diligence and when it is likely to or does materially distort the economic behaviour with regard to a product of service of the normally informed, reasonably circumspect and considerate consumer.

Consumer Protection Act[62] **2.26 (FI)**

Chapter 2 Regulation of marketing

Section 1 (1) No conduct that is inappropriate or otherwise unfair from the point of view of consumers shall be allowed in marketing.

Unfair Competition Act (Gesetz gegen den unlauteren Wettbewerb, UWG)[63] **2.27 (DE)**

§3 Any *unfair* competition action that might substantially influence competition to the disadvantage of the members of the market, the consumer or other members of the market, is prohibited.

Law 29/2009 on Unfair Competition[64] **2.28 (ES)**

Article 4 Any behaviour that objectively infringes the requirements of *good faith*. Similarly, article 6, paragraph b) of the General Law on advertising (1988 as amended in 2002), which before 2002 only referred to the advertising which infringe the norms on correction and good commercial uses.

The Consumer Protection from Unfair Trading Regulations 2008[65] **2.29 (UK)**

Regulation 3 Prohibition of unfair commercial practices

(1) Unfair commercial practices are prohibited.

(2) Paragraphs (3) and (4) set out the circumstances when a commercial practice is unfair.

(3) A commercial practice is unfair if—

(a) it contravenes the requirements of professional diligence; and

(b) it materially distorts or is likely to materially distort the economic behaviour of the average consumer with regard to the product.

[61] Loi No 2008-776 du 4 août 2008 pour le développement de la concurrence au service des consommateurs, JORF No 0003 du 4 janvier 2008.

[62] 38/1978, as amended in 2008, see www.finlex.fi.

[63] Bundesgesetzblatt 19 April 2006 (BGBl I 866) (BGBl I 1414).

[64] Boletín Oficial del Estado, 31 December 2009, No 315.

[65] Statutory instruments 2008 No 1277.

Note

The situation did not change much after the implementation period expired. So far, 20 Member States have taken implementing measures.[66] There is an overall tendency to maintain national wording that go back to particular traditions and legal cultures.[67]

III.B.2 IS THERE AN OBLIGATION TO INTRODUCE THE CONCEPT OF FAIRNESS *TEL QUEL*?

The following excerpts demonstrate the degree of controversy in the Austrian/German academic environment.

T Lettl, Community Law and the New UWG[68] **2.30 (DE)**

Also those unfair competition events in the draft proposal of the Unfair Commercial Practice Directive do not set any requirements for changes in the UWG in case the Directive is implemented.

F Henning-Bodewig, Reform of the UWG and the Proposal for a Directive[69] **2.31 (DE)**

It is of crucial importance whether the content of general clauses [the national and the European] match, and whether the wording of §3 UWG may be interpreted in the sense of Art 5 of the draft proposal. In my opinion, despite some differences, this is the case [a detailed analysis of the two general clauses follows subsequently].

D Seichter, The Implementation of the UCPD[70] **2.32 (DE)**

[With regard to professional diligence] Since the definition does not increase clarity it might be permissible from the perspective of European law that the German legislator sticks to his approach not to provide any definition of fairness.

[66] See the overview on the website of DG Sanco, available via www.europa.eu.

[67] for a critical account of the implementation of the UCPD in the United Kingdom, Germany, the Netherlands, Belgium and France, see B Keirsbilck, 'Towards a Single Regulatory Framework on Unfair Commercial Practices?' [2009] *European Business Law Review, 507–64.*

[68] 'Gemeinschaftsrecht und neues UWG' (2004) 9 *Wettbewerb in Recht und Praxis* 1132.

[69] 'UWG-Reform und Richtlinienvorschlag' [2004] *GRUR Int* 183, 190.

[70] 'Der Umsetzungsbedarf der Richtlinie über unlautere Geschäftspraktiken' (2005) 9 *WRP* 1087, 1090.

J Glöckner, The Proposal for an Unfair Commercial Practices Directive, The German UWG or The Difficult Implementation of European Open Norms[71] **2.33 (DE)**

However, the terminological 'mimikri' [with reference to Article 5 (2)], should be criticised: Unfairness is defined as the offence against the professional duties to exercise diligence, that means with the offence against decent market customs respectively good faith. That only means that a general term replaces another one. ... A literal assumption of a Directive is demanded only if their meaning cannot be seized with the use of other terminology.

H Gamerith, The Proposal for an Unfair Commercial Practices Directive—Possibilities for a Harmonious Implementation[72] **2.34 (AT)**

With regard to possible differences between fairness and bonos mores: The term of fairness is better than the one of bonos mores to avoid a possible equating with offences against a commercial custom, a professional or public policy.

Note

Given the diversity of concepts, it might be for the European Commission to check once all Member States have implemented the Directive, how far diversity reaches. Ultimately the question can only be decided by the ECJ.

III.B.3 THE ROLE AND FUNCTION OF THE GENERAL CLAUSE—SAFETY NET?

As Schünemann puts it with regard to the German law, but in view of the then ongoing work on the EC Directive:[73]

WB Schünemann, Unfairness **2.35 (DE)**

§3 UWG [the prominent general clause] is without doubt suitable to judge whether a competition action that is not prohibited by other regulations concerning unfair competition is deemed unfair. Therefore, one may conclude that in case the less prominent general clauses and other regulations do not prohibit a respective action it might be prohibited by §3 UWG instead of §1 UWG (old system) ... Having this in mind it seems senseless or even useless to discuss ... the legal sample prohibitions at all.

[71] 'Richtlinienvorschlag über unlautere Geschäftspraktiken, deutsches UWG oder die schwierige Umsetzung von europarechtlichen Generalklauseln' (2004) 8 *WRP* 936, 939.

[72] 'Der Richtlinienvorschlag über unlautere Geschäftspraktiken—Möglichkeiten einer harmonischen Umsetzung' (2005) 4 *WRP* 395, 419, 431.

[73] WB Schünemann, '"Unlauterkeit" in den Generalklauseln und Interessenabwägung nach neuem UWG' (2004) 8 *WRP* 925, 927.

Note

Schünemann interprets the general clause in Article 5 as a means of last resort, eg the Directive must be read from the end: the first step is to look at the list of incriminated practices; if the commercial practice to be assessed cannot be found there, the next step is to look into the small general clauses (eg prohibition of misleading actions/omissions and aggressive practices). Only in extreme cases would the general clause be applicable. Generally, practices which are neither forbidden under the list of incriminated practices nor under the small clauses must be regarded as being legal. Their illegality cannot be based on the general clause. Such a reading would considerably reduce the scope of the general clause.

Glöckner[74] discusses the relationship between the new German law rules on misleading advertising and the possible need to adapt them to the requirements of the Directive.

J Glöckner, Introduction[75] **2.36 (DE)**

In the area of special clauses, particularly misleading clauses, one may find a large number of deviating details in the UWG to the provisions of the Directive. However, for a proper implementation of the Directive it should suffice if, on the one hand, the misleading criterion in the UWG complies with the criterion of the average consumer in Art 6 in connection with 2 lit b of the draft Directive, and, on the other hand, all other misleading criteria are in fact fulfilled. This may be affirmed in principle: potential gaps in German law may be closed through the application of the general clause. Furthermore, it has no effect if German regulations go beyond Art 6, 7 of the draft Directive as the draft Directive does not regulate all cases of misleading advertisement. The general clause remains the catchall element. In this case indeed one may identify a difference in the Member State's duties to implement Directives because of the use of the general clause.

Note

The second variant results in exactly what Schünemann fears: the broad general clause of Article 5 would allow national courts to fill the gaps left by the small general clauses and the list of incriminated practices.

Stuyck, Terryn and Van Dyck provide a third interpretation.

J Stuyck, E Terryn and T van Dyck, Confidence through Fairness?[76] **2.37 (EU)**

In practice, it can be expected that both traders and consumers will first resort to the black list, for a simple reason: if a certain practice is caught by the blacklist, it will be

[74] J Glöckner, 'Einl B Rn 192' in H Harte-Bavendamm and F Henning, *Gesetz gegen den unlauteren Wettbewerb* (München, Verlag CH Beck, 1994).

[75] B para 192.

[76] J Stuyck, E Terryn and T van Dyck, 'Confidence through Fairness? The New Directive on Unfair Business to Consumer Commercial Practices in the internal Market' (2006) 43 *CML Rev* 107, 134.

deemed unfair, without discussion. Whether it will be possible to use various legal grounds in a cascade reasoning (ie, arguing that y applies but if y does not apply x will apply) or in a cumulate reading (ie, arguing that both x and y apply) will depend on the concrete implementation of the UCPD in the Member States. Nevertheless, we believe that the framework and the wording of the UCPD suggests that both a cascade reasoning and a cumulate reasoning should be possible, especially because the grand general clause is designed to function as a safety net and catch-all for unfair commercial practices; it will catch practices which are not aggressive or misleading within the meaning of Articles 6-9, but which are more generally contrary to the requirements of professional diligence and materially distort the economic behaviour of consumers.

Note

The first case decided by the ECJ offered the opportunity to clarify the relationship between the grand and the small general clauses as well as between the general clauses and the list of incriminated practices. At stake was the question whether promotional sales are fully harmonised via the list of incriminated practices thereby setting aside the leeway for Member States to maintain more stringent national rules.

Case C-261/07 and C-299/07, 23 April 2009[77] **2.38 (EU)**
Galatea BVBA v Sanoma Magazines Belgium NV and VTB-VAB v Total Belgium

STRUCTURE OF THE DIRECTIVE

VTB-VAB

The structure of Directive 2005/29/EC implies a cascade approach to assess the fairness of a commercial practice.

Facts: Does Directive 2005/29 of the European Parliament and of the Council concerning unfair commercial practices preclude a national provision such as Article 54 of the Belgian Law of 14 July 1991 on commercial practices, consumer information and consumer protection, which, subject to the exhaustive list of exceptions contained within that Law, prohibits any collateral offer by a seller to a consumer, including an offer in which goods which the consumer has to buy are tied to a free service, the acquisition of which is linked to the purchase of the goods, notwithstanding the circumstances of individual cases, in particular notwithstanding the possible influence of the actual offer on the average consumer, or whether, in the actual circumstances, that offer may be regarded as contravening the professional duty of care and genuine commercial custom?

Opinion of Advocate General Trstenjak: (79) For purposes of the application of law by the national courts and administrative authorities, it therefore follows that the first point of reference must be the list of 31 cases of unfair commercial practices contained in Annex I. If a commercial practice can be subsumed under one of those constituent elements, it must be prohibited; prohibition does not depend on a further examination of, for example, the effects. If the actual situation is not covered by that list of prohibited practices, it is necessary to consider whether one of the regulated illustrative cases in the generalprovision—misleading and aggressive commercial practices—is present. Only

[77] ECJ, 23 April 2009, Joined Cases C-261/07 and C-299/07, nyr.

when that is not the case does the general provision in Article 5(1) of Directive 2005/29 apply directly.

Note

In her opinion Advocate General Trstenjak strongly advocated a cascade understanding. The ECJ, whilst following the Advocate General in substance, was much less outspoken (see below section VIII.E for the judgment of the ECJ). It remains to be seen whether and to what extent the interrelationship between the different general clauses and the black list needs further clarification.

III.C FAIRNESS, TASTE, DECENCY AND CULTURE: HOW ARE THEY INTERRELATED?

'Fairness' under the UCPD needs to be established autonomously. Whilst this might ideally provide a European understanding free from national concepts, in practice there is a link between that European concept and national concepts. The UCPD cannot and should not 'reinvent the wheel'; that is why national concepts of fairness still matter. It is at this point that things become complicated. The UCPD seems to leave Member States the choice between honest business practices and good faith.

National legal orders have used different methods for controlling 'unfair' commercial practices: some are market-based, others are value-based. This is made explicit in the difference between banning *unfair* marketing practices on the one hand, and striking down marketing practices that are not in compliance with *bonos mores* on the other. Through *bonos mores* a moral dimension is inserted into the control of commercial practices. The Directive does not provide much guidance in finding out whether or not its notion of fairness is morally bound. However, there are two references in the recitals which might help to clarify the notion of fairness: one to '*taste and decency*', the other to '*social, cultural and linguistic factors*'.

Recital 7 refers to matters of 'taste and decency' and Recital 18 points to 'social, cultural and linguistic factors':

UCPD (2005/29/EC) **2.39 (EU)**

[Preamble] (7) This Directive addresses commercial practices directly related to influencing consumers' transactional decisions in relation to products. It does not address commercial practices carried out primarily for other purposes, including for example commercial communication aimed at investors, such as annual reports and corporate promotional literature. It does not address legal requirements related to *taste and decency* which vary widely among the Member States. Commercial practices such as, for example, commercial solicitation in the streets, may be undesirable in Member States for *cultural* reasons. …

(18) It is appropriate to protect all consumers from unfair commercial practices; however the Court of Justice has found it necessary in adjudicating on advertising cases since the enactment of Directive 84/450/EEC to examine the effect on a national, typical

consumer. In line with the principle of proportionality, and to permit the effective application of the protections contained in it, this Directive takes as a benchmark the average consumer, who is reasonably well-informed and reasonably observant and circumspect, taking into account *social, cultural and linguistic factors*, as interpreted by the Court of Justice, but also contains provisions aimed at preventing the exploitation of consumers whose characteristics make them particularly vulnerable to unfair commercial practices. [emphasis added]

ECJ Case C-220/98, 13 January 2000[78] **2.40 (EU)**
Estée Lauder Cosmetics GmbH & Co OHG v Lancaster Group GmbH

ON THE ROLE OF SOCIAL CULTURAL AND LINGUISTIC FACTORS IN ADVERTISING

Lifting Cream

Differing cultures can justify obstacles to the free movement of goods resulting from advertising rules.

Facts: Lancaster marketed a firming cream for the skin, Monteil Firming Action Lifting Extreme Creme, the name of which incorporates the term 'lifting'. In the main proceedings, Estée Lauder argued that the term 'lifting' was misleading because it gave purchasers the impression that use of the product would yield results which, above all in terms of their lasting effects, were identical or comparable to surgical lifting, whereas this was not the case as far as the cream in question was concerned. It sought an order restraining the defendant from engaging in the commercial marketing, distribution and promotion of cosmetic products the name of which incorporates the term 'lifting' (in particular, the cream in question) on the ground that this is incompatible with §3 of the UWG, §27(1) of the Lebensmittel- und Bedarfsgegen-ständeGesetz (Act on Trade in Foodstuffs) and Directive 76/768/EEC.[79]

Whilst admitting that the cream in question did not have the same long-term effect as surgical lifting, Lancaster maintained that it nevertheless had a significant firming effect. It denied that the expectations entertained by the public with regard to this cream were those alleged by Estée Lauder. It submitted that, in any event, the order sought would, if granted, be contrary to Articles 30 and 36 (now, after amendment, Articles 28 EC and 30 EC) of the EC Treaty. Nor was there any justification for the expenditure that would be entailed by the adoption of a new name for the product if Lancaster had to repackage it solely for distribution in Germany, when no objection to the current name had been raised in the other Member States. The prohibition sought would amount to a disproportionate restriction, given the minor importance of the public interest to be protected, which consists in preventing consumers from being mistaken solely as to the duration of the product's effects.

Judgment: 27. It should be borne in mind that when it has fallen to the Court, in the context of the interpretation of Directive 84/450, to weigh the risk of misleading consumers against the requirements of the free movement of goods, it has held that, in order to determine whether a particular description, trade mark or promotional description or statement is misleading, it is necessary to take into account the presumed expectations of an average consumer who is reasonably well-informed and reasonably observant and circumspect (see, in particular, Case C-210/96 *Gut Springenheide and Tusky* [1998] ECR I-4657, paragraph 31).

28. That test, based on the principle of proportionality, also applies in the context of the marketing of cosmetic products where, as in the case in the main proceedings, a mistake as to the product's characteristics cannot pose any risk to public health.

[78] 78[2000] ECR I-117.

29. In order to apply that test to the present case, several considerations must be borne in mind. In particular, it must be determined whether social, cultural or linguistic factors may justify the term 'lifting', used in connection with a firming cream, meaning something different to the German consumer as opposed to consumers in other Member States, or whether the instructions for the use of the product are in themselves sufficient to make it quite clear that its effects are short-lived, thus neutralising any conclusion to the contrary that might be derived from the word 'lifting'.

30. Although, at first sight, the average consumer—reasonably well-informed and reasonably observant and circumspect—ought not to expect a cream whose name incorporates the term 'lifting' to produce enduring effects, it nevertheless remains for the national court to determine, in the light of all the relevant factors, whether that is the position in this case.

31. In the absence of any provisions of Community law on this matter, it is for the national court—which may consider it necessary to commission an expert opinion or a survey of public opinion in order to clarify whether or not a promotional description or statement is misleading—to determine, in the light of its own national law, the percentage of consumers misled by that description or statement which would appear to it sufficiently significant to justify prohibiting its use (see *Gut Springenheide and Tusky*, cited above, paragraphs 35 and 36).

32. The reply to the question put to the Court must therefore be:

—Articles 30 and 36 of the Treaty [now, after amendment, Articles 28 EC and 30 EC] and Article 6(3) of Directive 76/768 do not preclude the application of national legislation which prohibits the importation and marketing of a cosmetic product whose name incorporates the term 'lifting' in cases where the average consumer, reasonably well-informed and reasonably observant and circumspect, is misled by that name, believing it to imply that the product possesses characteristics which it does not have.

—It is for the national court to decide, having regard to the presumed expectations of the average consumer, whether the name is misleading.

—Community law does not preclude the national court, should it experience particular difficulty in deciding whether or not the name at issue is misleading, from commissioning, in accordance with its national law, a survey of public opinion or an expert opinion for the purposes of clarification.

Wilhelmsson argues that taste, decency and culture remain outside the scope of the Directive.[80]

T Wilhelmsson, Scope of the Directive **2.41 (EU)**

The main consequence for the sphere of application of the Directive of the reference to consumers' economic interests in Article 1 is that, as a main rule, 'matters of taste, decency and social responsibility will be outside [its] scope'. According to the Preamble the Directive 'does not address legal requirements related to taste and decency which vary widely among the Member States' and the Member States are therefore able to continue to ban commercial practices on these grounds, regardless of the Directive. The

[79] Council Directive 76/768/EEC of 27 July 1976 on the approximation of the laws of the Member States relating to cosmetic products [1976] OJ L 262, 169–200.

[80] In Howells, Micklitz and Wilhelmsson, above n 39, 59, 62.

Directive's basic purpose, to address issues of market transparency and oppressive practices, naturally leaves issues of taste and decency, as well as social responsibility, outside its scope. As long as there does not exist a common European understanding of moral questions concerning taste, decency and social responsibility there is also no basis for harmonisation of this area. The basic idea of a Europe 'united in its diversity' speaks for the continuance of a decentralised approach to this area, even though this approach may be at odds with the demands of the Internal Market ...

Even though mostly only issues of taste and decency (often understood very broadly) have been commented upon in relation to the delimitation of scope at hand, some other kinds of issues appear to fall outside the scope of 'consumers' economic interests' as well. The reference in the Preamble to 'cultural reasons' appears to be a far wider concept than 'taste and decency'. Regulations concerning advertising and other commercial practices that aim to protect features of the national culture beyond the requirements of taste and decency are also left outside the scope of the Directive. Already, at an early stage of the preparation of the Directive, the Commission signalled that issues related to 'pluralism' and to 'the protection of culture' should be excluded from its scope.

Notes

(1) If matters of taste, decency and culture remain outside the scope of application, then the point is to keep them distinct from the notion of fairness. It is not difficult to predict that it will become one of the major battlefields of EC law to decide what is within the scope of the Directive and what is outside it, what is fair or unfair and therefore within the Directive and what is the advertising that concerns matters of taste, decency and culture.

(2) Two examples might illustrate the difficulty, the first comes from both Finland and Sweden, the second is a more general one that concerns each and every national legal order. The Finnish Market Court has in several cases forbidden the use of violent scenes in marketing. It has considered it unacceptable to use such scenes to attract the consumers' attention. Violence should therefore not be shown, if it has no connection with the product.[81] Somewhat similarly, the Swedish Market Court has forbidden marketing that can be considered to encourage violence against persons.[82]

(3) The second example deals with the overall problem of the extent to which producers shall provide guidance on the conditions under which the product has been produced, ie information on the quality of the product process (environmental conditions, 'fair trade' ie fair recompensation of the producers of, for example, coffee beans, etc). The question is whether this sort of conflict falls under the scope of the Directive—is the value judgment one of fairness or is it taste and decency? There is no clear-cut answer to such a conflict. In one way or another the European Court of Justice will have to face the challenge of defining whether and to what extent Member States might prohibit commercial practices interfering with national cultures.

[81] See eg Finnish Market Court Decisions 1984:5 and 1998:18, as well as 1988:11 which concerned violence in marketing to children.

[82] Swedish Market Court 1996:7.

III.D THE AVERAGE CONSUMER AND PARTICULARLY VULNERABLE GROUPS

Almost no other topic of European unfair marketing practices law has been dealt with in legal literature to such an extent as the consumer image, the *Verbraucherleitbild*. During the *travaux préparatoires* on the Directive it became apparent that the Commission's efforts to codify in a Directive the image of the average consumer as created by the ECJ met strong opposition. The finally adopted version of the UCPD provides for a general yardstick where the practice is targeted at all consumers—this is dealt with in chapter 1—and for a particular one where so-called 'vulnerable groups' of consumers are approached, Article 5(3). The *Verbraucherleitbild*, the average consumer, and the vulnerable consumer are discussed in chapter 1.I.2. As the concept of the vulnerable consumer might in particular be discussed in the field of unfair commercial practices, some further discussion of the case-law might illustrate the inherent dynamics of this concept.

BGH, 22 September 2005[83] **2.42 (DE)**

THE LINE BETWEEN THE AUTONOMY AND RESPONSIBILITY OF THE YOUNGER GENERATION

Sunglasses

Teenagers are not misled if they buy a youth magazine with free sunglasses.

Facts: The plaintiff published the monthly magazine *BM*, the paid circulation of which was 225,000 by mid-2001. The magazine was offered at a fixed price of DEM 4.30; the magazine's target group was girls and young women. The defendant published the magazine *1.* which targeted female teenagers. The magazine was offered at a fixed price of DEM 4.50. The paid circulation was 181.000 in the second half of 2001. In the August 2001 issue the defendant published his magazine with sunglasses—available in the colours 'black' and 'purple'—fixed to the title page. The defendant maintained the magazine's usual cover price of DEM 4.50. In connection with the sunglasses, one could read on the title page, among other things: 'Extra! Designer-Glasses!'. On page 3 was an article, which provided hints for the female reader on how to use these glasses.

The plaintiff considered the selling of the magazine in conjunction with the sunglasses anti-competitive because it represented an exaggerated attraction. The regular price of comparable sunglasses would be approximately DEM 30. For this reason, a large part of the target group bought the magazine only because of the sunglasses. The risk of recurrent infringement may not be excluded through signing a cease-and-desist order on the 11 December 2001, because the scope of the order was limited to the use of the term 'designer glasses'. The defendant claimed the glasses were highly valuable. Additionally, the defendant infringed the Unfair Competition Act (UWG), because it is illegal to give away a product not subject to price-fixing together with a price-fixed magazine.

Judgment: In business, an exploitation of inexperienced children and teenagers in the sense of §4 No 2 [UWG] may not be assumed, if a magazine is sold in connection with sunglasses. The norm (§30 (1) GWB) aims at protecting the freedom of press, which also embraces the distribution of press products. Subject to protection is the historically grown distribution system that is typical for newspapers and magazines, whereby press products are available everywhere to standardized prices, so that all citizens in all parts of

[83] BGH I ZR 28/03 (2006) WRP 69.

the country may form their opinion under the same circumstances ... Here this may be affirmed as the magazine was distributed through the usual way of distribution and the sunglasses were evidently only used as a gratis addition to increase the attractiveness of the press product.

BGH, 6 April 2006[84] **2.43 (DE)**

THE LINE BETWEEN THE AUTONOMY AND RESPONSIBILITY OF THE YOUNGER GENERATION

Ring-tone advertising

Teenagers are misled if they are unable to identify the price when downloading ring-tones.

Facts: The plaintiff was an umbrella organisation of 16 consumer associations and 18 other consumer- and socially oriented associations. The defendant distributed, among other things, ring-tones, logos and SMS pictures to the end-consumer, which a purchaser could download onto a mobile phone by calling a 0190 number at a cost of €1.86 (DEM 3.63) a minute. The defendant argued that the download of such a ring-tone lasted on average 110 seconds at a cost of €3.40 (DEM 6.66), and could be increased as a result of typing errors. The defendant advertised its offer in September 2001 in, among other places, the magazine *BRAVO Girl*.

According to the plaintiff's pleadings, *BRAVO Girl* was a magazine for teenagers. It considered the advertisement in question of the defendant to be an infringement of *bones mores*, because it targeted teenagers who were especially susceptible to such advertising. In business, the knowing exploitation of an inexperienced target group is unfair. An average, rational, informed consumer would never buy a ring-tone via a telephone call for €1.86 a minute, especially because it was not clear through the mere indication of a minute's price how much the ring-tone would in fact cost. In contrast, the defendant argued that the advertisement was aimed neither exclusively nor predominantly at minors, but at all adults, as there were comparable advertisements published in a large number in magazines accessible to all. Furthermore, teenagers did not need any special legal protection regarding competition law as they were in a perfect position to correctly evaluate advertisements.

Judgment: According to §4 No 2 UWG especially such competition actions are unfair that are suitable to exploit the inexperience of children and teenagers in business matters ... The prerequisite of such unfairness in the sense of §4 No 2 UWG is that advertisement—at least also—aims at children and teenagers directly, as the regulation's goal is to anticipate an exploitation of the inexperience of the respective target group.

According to the statement of the Court of Appeal, the over 50% of the readership of the magazine 'BRAVO Girl', which published the complained advertisement, are teenagers. ... However, according to §4 No 2 UWG not each purposeful influence of minors is unfair. The concrete action must be rather suitable to exploit the inexperience. ...

From this viewpoint, higher demands according to transparency must be made if an advertisement addresses minors. Their possible financial obligations must be made sufficiently clear to the children and teenagers. (see BGH GRUR 2006, 161 Tz 22—sunglasses); ... The objected advertisement does not meet these standards. It is not traceable for the users of the defendant's offer how much the costs amount in the end, since the relevant duration of the loading procedure is unknown to them and it depends, in addition, on the skills of the user. In contrast to normal telephone calls, the costs are also not controllable. It seems to make little sense to cancel the download after a certain amount of time, because in such a case one would have to pay the respective rate without obtaining

[84] BGH I ZR 15/03 (2006) WRP 885.

any service in return. The fact that a consumer is only able to obtain information about his full financial burden through a bill he receives much later increases the importance of the consideration of the uncertainty about the emerging costs. As the Court of Appeal pointed out with good reason this will lead to the fact that many minors will not think about the evolving costs at first instance. Additionally, a special risk exists because the offer of the defendant may be obtained regardless limits of time and space. For this reason, advertisements for ring tones of mobile phones that only state the unimportant costs for a minute call and do not specify the expected higher costs might in principle exploit the inexperience of minors. (see for the same result also OLG Hamm MMR 2005, 112; KG MD 2005, 1045; ... Harte/Henning/Stuckel, UWG, §4 No 2 Rdn 14; Benz, WRP 2003, 1160, 1165; Klees/Lange, CR 2005, 684, 686).

The situation in Finland is described in Keßler/Wilhelmsson as follows:[85]

J Keßler and T Wilhelmsson, Country Report **2.44 (FI)**

Despite there being no special provisions aimed at protecting children in the CPA, the Act has to be interpreted in the light of public policy and the ICC rules of conduct. For this reason, advertising targeted at children or minors is subject to strict criteria. Considering the objectives of the CPA the advertiser by marketing its product has to take into consideration the inexperience and the lack of knowledge typical for this particular group of consumers. Advertising must not result in any physical, mental or moral harm to the recipients. Advertising to children may not be suggestive or make use of emotional elements like the fear of loneliness. Advertising contravening this stipulation violates the General Clause of the CPA.

Note

The concept of the vulnerable consumer needs to be clarified. The UCPD provides little guidance. Annex I of the UCPD blacklists certain aggressive commercial practices (see also section VIII below) including direct pressure on children to buy products or to persuade their parents or other adults to buy advertised products for them (Annex I, 28). Further clarification of the meaning is, however, needed. Children are certainly primary targets of advertising measures.[86] The legal difficulty is to decide when and under what circumstances an advertising measure is directed at children. The two conflicting decisions of the German Supreme Court show how difficult it is to decide. In a way, it is hard to understand that a measure in a particular journal designed to reach young consumers is regarded as fair, whereas the advertising of selling particular ring-tones for mobile phones is supposed to mislead young consumers. One might, however, argue that the selling of particular ring-tones is not limited to the young consumer. Young adults and even others may equally be affected by this sort of advertising. In that case, however, the concept of the vulnerable consumer might

[85] J Keßler and T Wilhelmsson, 'Country report' in Micklitz and Keßler, above n 56, 71.

[86] See K Viitanen, 'The Unfair Commercial Practices Directive and Marketing Targeted at Minors' in Th Wilhelmsson, E Paunio and A Phjolainen (eds), *Private Law and the Many Cultures of Europe* (Kluwer Law International, 2008) 283.

become a device to strengthen advertising control, by using the vulnerable consumer as a device to circumvent the concept of the average consumer.

IV. MISLEADING PRACTICES

IV.A DEFINITION

UCPD (2005/29/EC) **2.45 (EU)**

Article 6 (1) A commercial practice shall be regarded as misleading if it contains false information and is therefore untruthful or in any way, including overall presentation, deceives or is likely to deceive the average consumer, even if the information is factually correct, in relation to one or more of the following elements, and in either case causes or is likely to cause him to take a transactional decision that he would not have taken otherwise.

Consumer Code[87] *(Code de la Consommation)* **2.46 (FR)**

Article L 121-1 A commercial practice is misleading if it is executed under one of the following conditions: (1) if it creates confusion with another good or services, trade mark, commercial name or another distinctive sign of a competitor, (2) if it is based on allegations, indications, or false representations or of a nature to produce an error resulting from one or several following elements: a) the existence, the availability or the nature of the good or service, b) the main characteristics of the product or service, its substantial qualifications, its composition, its accessories, its origin, its quantity, its method and date of manufacture, conditions of usage and fitness for purpose, its properties and the results to be expected from its usage, as well as the results and principal characteristics of tests or checks carried out on the product or service; c) the price or the mode of price calculation, the promotional character of the price and the selling, payment and delivery conditions of the good or service, d) the after sales services, the need for a service, part, replacement or repair, e) the extent of the advertiser's commitment, the nature, the procedure or the motives for the selling or the presentation of the service, f) the identity, qualifications, attributes and the rights of the professional, g) the complaint handling and the rights of the consumer, (3) if the person on whose account the action is taken is not clearly identifiable.

Cass crim, 14 October 1998[88] **2.47 (FR)**

ADVERTISING AND LABELLING ACCORDING TO ARTICLE L121-1

Fictitious rebates

The nature of advertising does not depend on truthful and verifiable information.

Facts: A furniture outlet advertised high rebates which in practice no consumer ever received. The Court of Appeal held that the mere indication of a price is not advertising absent accompanying circumstances setting an incentive to purchase a product or service. The Court of Cassation disagreed.

[87] As amended by Loi 2008-776, 4 August 2008.
[88] Bull crim, No 262; (1999) JCP E 462, note Conte.

Judgment: Advertising can be any means of information in the meaning of Article L 121-1 Code de la Consommation intended to enable the potential client to form himself an opinion on the characteristics of the goods or services which are offered to him.

Note

The definition of misleading actions in Article 6 is obviously intended to be understood rather broadly. It not only covers cases where false or misleading information is actually given concerning a product or service, or concerning some other elements of a consumer transaction, but also extends to 'practices' that are likely to deceive the consumer. For example, in the Annex, marketing methods such as bait advertising, bait and switch advertising, advertorials and pyramid promotional schemes are mentioned as misleading commercial practices. French law is very much in line with the Directive's concept and might be understood as being indicative for the situation in the other Member States. A new Article L 121-1 has been inserted into the Code de la Consommation which implements the blacklisted misleading practices of the UCPD.[89]

IV.B UNTRUTHFULNESS/DECEPTIVENESS CONDITION

The Directive uses in Article 6(1) both the notions of 'untruthfulness' and of 'deceptiveness' and relates them to 'false information'. Obviously, deceptiveness does not require untruthfulness. That is why the consumer might even be misled 'if the information is factually correct'.

Hanseatisches OLG (Court of appeal), 15 January 2007[90] **2.48 (DE)**

ADVERTISING WITH TEST RESULTS

FACTS-good

The reference to the test results must be given in the advertising.

Facts: The defendant ran an internet direct-selling company and advertised a computer printer in several trade journals as having a rating 'good', such as the advertisement 'FACTS-good'. However, there was no reference as to in which issue of the trade journal *FACTS* this printer had been rated. The plaintiff objected that this was unfair. The claim (inter alia to cease and desist) was successful in its main parts before the Court of First Instance. The appeal was withdrawn upon the declaratory judgement of the Senate to dismiss the appeal according to §522(2) ZPO (*Zivilprozessordnung*, Code of Civil Procedure).

Judgment: The contested advertisement of the defendant is an advertisement with a trade journal's test results without proper reference and therefore unfair regarding to §3 UWG. Regarding the old version of §1 UWG, the BGH already showed—without special reference to aspects of comparative advertising—that advertising with test results of the *Stiftung Warentest* (foundation for product testing) without a proper reference are

[89] Art 121-1 Loi 2008-776 of 4 August 2008, available at www.legifrance.gouv.fr.

[90] Az 3 U 240/06, [2003] *Medien, Internet und Recht* 3.

contrary to good business practice. Through the missing reference it is not only significantly more difficult for interested people to obtain the test. Additionally, *Stiftung Warentest* advises in its guidelines on the 'advertisement with test results' that all data obtained from test results must be easily and clearly verifiable, which embraced the publishing of month and year of the test's first publication. Additionally, the people greet research of the *Stiftung Warentest* with great interest and acceptance, therefore there is a special need to simplify the finding of all test results for the consumer.

These principles that were developed according to the test results of *Stiftung Warentest* are transferable to the so-called *Testhinweiswerbung* (test result advertisement) with test results in trade journals. Also in the case of the so-called *Testhinweiswerbung* the advertiser refers to an independent third person, which adds *quasi*-objective authority to the information in the advertisement. Also in so far as there is a special need of the addressed people to obtain the respective test in full.

The difference with respect to the test results of *Stiftung Warentest* is the lack of a special guideline of the journal FACTS on how to use the respective reference for advertising purposes. However, the same reasons as to the recommendations of the *Stiftung Warentest* apply to the so-called *Testhinweiswerbung*.

Providing the source of the information, which is clearly demanded by *Stiftung Warentest*, also guarantees the verifiability of the test's structure, its procedure and the test results to establish transparency. Especially because, from a view of the respective costumers, a third person adds special authority to the information in the test results these results have to be verifiable, at least as far as this is possible through the indication of the source of information.

Therefore, the lack of reference, as far as it was subject to this dispute, is unfair in the sense of §3 UWG. [references omitted]

Cass crim, 21 May 1984[91] **2.49 (FR)**
X v Samsonite

ADVERTISING WITH FALSE INFORMATION

Football match between bulldozers

Consumers do not necessarily believe what they see.

Facts: A Samsonite suitcase was featured in a television commercial as escaping unharmed from a football match between bulldozers, where it had been used as a ball.

Judgment: The advertiser was not guilty of misleading advertising, since the commercial's unreal and imaginary character could not escape an average viewer, who therefore could not have been misled.

Note

The German and the French cases indicate that the information in advertising may have a twofold character. 'Information' means first of all statements concerning facts that can be empirically proven or at least can be understood as such. However, not

[91] Bull crim, No 185, (1985) D 105, note Marguery; (1985) RTDcom 379, note Bouzat.

only general commercial exaggeration of the more imprecise type—'our product is the best!'—but also more concrete false statements may be acceptable, if they are not intended to be taken literally, so long as this intention was discernible for the average consumer. This is the message to be learned from the Court of Cassation. The extent to which such aesthetic and emotional assessments are regarded as implied and statements of facts as deceptive always depends on the consumer and the context.

ECJ Case C-470/93, 6 July 1995[92] **2.50 (EU)**
Mars v Verein gegen Umwesen in Handel und Gewerbe Köln eV

MISLEADING ADVERTISING BY WAY OF OVERSIZED MARKING ON PACKAGING

+10% Mars

The consumer will not be mislead by oversized markings on packaging.

Facts: By order of 11 November 1993, received at the ECJ on 17 December 1993, the Landgericht Köln (Regional Court, Cologne) referred to the Court for a preliminary ruling under Article 177 (now, after amendment, Article 234) of the EC Treaty a question relating to the interpretation of Article 30 (now, after amendment, Article 28) of that Treaty. The question was raised in proceedings between an association for combating unfair competition, the Verein gegen Unwesen in Handel und Gewerbe Koeln eV, and Mars GmbH (hereafter 'Mars') concerning the use of a certain presentation for the marketing of ice-cream bars of the Mars, Snickers, Bounty and Milky Way brands. Mars imported those goods from France where they were lawfully produced and packaged by an undertaking belonging to the US group, Mars Inc, Mc Lean, in uniform packaging for distribution throughout Europe. At the material time, the ice-cream bars were packaged in wrappers marked '+10 per cent'. That format had been chosen as part of a short publicity campaign covering the whole of Europe during which the quantity of each product was increased by 10 per cent.

Under §1 UWG (Unfair Competition Act) proceedings may be brought in order to restrain improper competitive practices while under §3 of that Act proceedings may be brought in order to restrain the use of misleading information. Furthermore, under §15 of the Gesetz gegen Wettbewerbsbeschränkungen (GWB, Law on Restraints on Competition), agreements between undertakings restricting the freedom of one of the parties to fix prices in contracts concluded with third parties for the supply of goods are void. The plaintiff association brought proceedings under those provisions before the Landgericht Köln in order to prevent the '+10 per cent' marking from being used in Germany. It contended first of all that the consumer was bound to assume that the advantage indicated by the '+10 per cent' marking is granted without any price increase, since a product whose composition is only slightly changed and which is sold at a higher price offers no advantage. So, in order not to mislead the consumer, the retailer should maintain the final price previously charged. Since the marking in question was binding on the retail trade as regards the fixing of the price for sale to the ultimate consumer, it constituted a breach of §15 of the GWB which had to be brought to an end in accordance with §1 UWG. Secondly, the plaintiff in the main proceedings contended that the way in which the '+10 per cent' marking was incorporated in the presentation gave the consumer the impression that the product had been increased by a quantity corresponding to the coloured part of the new wrapping. The coloured part occupied considerably more than 10 per cent of the total surface area of the wrapping and this, in the plaintiff' s view, was misleading and therefore contrary to §3 UWG.

Judgment: 21. It is accepted by all the parties that the '+10 per cent' marking is accurate in itself.

22. However, it is contended that the measure in question is justified because a not insignificant number of consumers will be induced into believing, by the band bearing

[92] [1995] ECR I-1923.

the '+10 per cent' marking, which occupies more than 10 per cent of the total surface area of the wrapping, that the increase is larger than that represented.

23. Such a justification cannot be accepted.

24. Reasonably circumspect consumers may be deemed to know that there is not necessarily a link between the size of publicity markings relating to an increase in a product's quantity and the size of that increase.

Audiencia Provincial (Court of Appeal) Alicante, 19 September 2002[93] **2.51 (ES)**

MISLEADING ADVERTISING THROUGH USE OF LEGAL CONCEPTS

Multi-property timeshare

Timeshare advertising featuring the term property is misleading.

Facts: Two consumers signed a contract for a time-sharing property with a company on 30 May 1999. The company brought a lawsuit against them demanding the performance of the contract, since it was signed before the Law of 1998 transposing Directive 94/47/EC. The consumers responded claiming the nullity of the contract since it contains the word 'ownership', which is legally prohibited because it is misleading. The appellant company lost in the first instance and in its appeal.

Judgment: In the only argument of the appeal, the legal regime applied in the judgment of First Instance to the contract concluded by the parties on 30 May 1999 is challenged. The appellant argues that the right transmitted by virtue of this contract is not that regulated in the Act 42/1998, of 15 December (RCL 1998, 2916), but that this right was constituted by virtue of a pre-existing regime and is of a different nature from that regulated by this Act.

In the legal regime established in the Act 42/1998 one can distinguish, on the one hand, the rules (Articles 4–7), referring to the constitution of the regime for the enjoyment in turns; and on the other, the rules (Articles 8–15) regulating the promotion and transmission of these rights. Related to this double regulation, the Second and Third Transitional Provisions of the cited Act require that the pre-existing regimes adapt to the new legal requirements; and the First Transitional Provision 3 of the afore-mentioned Act establishes that for the promotion and transmission of these rights articles 2 and 8–12 of the Act will be applicable in all cases.

This means that any contract on the promotion or transmission of rights celebrated after the entry into force (as in the contract object of this case), independently of that the pre-existing regime has not yet adapted to the new Act, Articles 8–12 apply in all their force. Proof of this is that, in the contract, Articles 10–12 of the Act 42/1998 are quoted *in verbis*.

Paragraph 1 of Article 8 relative to the general duty of information declares expressly that 'the transmission of rights of enjoyment by turns is forbidden under the denomination of multi-property or any other denomination containing the word property'. In the contract, as indicated in the judgment of First Instance, it is mentioned repeatedly that the contractors will become the proprietors or co-proprietors and that the object transmitted is that of multi-property.

[93] Judgment of the Province Court number 545/2002 (5th Division) of 19 September 2002.

Notes

(1) Consumers might be deceived not only by statements and other linguistic information. A common practice is the use of boxes for products that are much larger than the amount of the product they contain. In light of *Mars*, one might wonder, however, to what extent national rules comply with ECJ case-law if they regard packaging as deceptive, even if the correct quantity of the product is printed on the box. The Swedish Marketing Act of 27 April 1995, for example, contains an explicit prohibition on the marketing of misleading packaging sizes (section 7).

(2) Easier are cases in which advertisers refer to legal concepts to make the consumer believe that he is in a better legal position than is actually the case. Article 8 of the Spanish Law 42/1998 on timeshare rights forbids the use of the word 'property', 'shared-property', 'ownership' or derivative terms that could induce the consumer to misinterpret nature of his rights. If the timeshare right is advertised as a kind of 'property', the consumer is deemed to have been mislead.

IV.C THE MATERIALITY CONDITION

Not all false or deceptive information is prohibited by Article 6 of the Directive.

ECJ Case C-373/90, 16 January 1992[94] **2.52 (EU)**
Criminal proceedings against Nissan

RELEVANCE OF INFORMATION

Nissan

Vehicles registered for the purpose of importation are legally new vehicles.

Facts: By a letter of 12 December 1990, which was received at the ECJ on 17 December 1990, the Juge d'Instruction (Examining Magistrate) at the Tribunal de Grande Instance (Regional Court), Bergerac, referred to the Court for a preliminary ruling under Article 177 (now, after amendment, Article 234) of the EEC Treaty a question on the interpretation of the Misleading Advertising Directive

The question arose in the context of a complaint lodged against X, together with a claim for civil indemnity, by Jean-Pierre Richard, the Chairman of the Board of Directors of the Société Richard-Nissan, which enjoyed an exclusive importation contract for Nissan vehicles on French territory. The complaint, brought under Article 44 of French Act No 73-1193 of 27 December 1973 on the Orientation of Business and Crafts, known as the 'Loi Royer', alleged untruthful and unlawful advertising.

The French legal provision in question was communicated by the French Government to the Commission as the legislative measure implementing the Directive. The complaint concerned a garage in Bergerac which placed display advertisements in the press with the words 'buy your new vehicle cheaper', followed by the words 'one year manufacturer's guarantee'. It transpired from the letter containing the reference that the advertising referred to vehicles imported from Belgium, registered for import purposes but never having been driven, being sold in France below local dealers' prices because Belgian basic models have fewer accessories than the basic models sold in France.

Judgment: 11. In interpreting this provision [Article 2 (2) of Directive 84/450/EEC] in relation to the features of advertising such as that at issue in the main proceedings, one must consider in turn the three claims made in the advertising, namely that the cars in

[94] [1992] ECR 131.

question are new, that they are cheaper, and that they are guaranteed by the manufacturer.

12. Before embarking on such an examination, it should be emphasized that these aspects of the advertising are of great practical importance for the business of parallel car importers, and that, as the Advocate General has pointed out in paragraphs 5 and 6 of his Opinion, parallel imports enjoy a certain amount of protection in Community law because they encourage trade and help reinforce competition.

13. On the first point, concerning the claim that the cars in question are new, it should be noted that such advertising cannot be considered misleading within the meaning of Article 2 just because the cars were registered before importation.

14. It is when a car is first driven on the public highway, and not when it is registered, that it loses its character as a new car. Moreover, as the Commission has pointed out, registration before importation makes parallel import operations considerably easier.

15. It is for the national court, however, to ascertain in the circumstances of the particular case and bearing in mind the consumers to which the advertising is addressed, whether the latter could be misleading in so far as, on the one hand, it seeks to conceal the fact that the cars advertised as new were registered before importation and, on the other hand, that fact would have deterred a significant number of consumers from making a purchase, had they known it.

16. On the second point, concerning the claim that the cars are cheaper, such a claim can only be held misleading if it is established that the decision to buy on the part of a significant number of consumers to whom the advertising in question is addressed was made in ignorance of the fact that the lower price of the vehicles was matched by a smaller number of accessories on the cars sold by the parallel importer.

17. Thirdly and finally, regarding the claim about the manufacturer's guarantee, it should be pointed out that such information cannot be regarded as misleading advertising if it is true.

18. It should be remembered in this respect that in Case 31/85 *ETA v DK Investment* [1985] ECR 3933 the Court held that a guarantee scheme under which a supplier of goods restricts the guarantee to customers of his exclusive distributor places the latter and the retailers to whom he sells in a privileged position as against parallel importers and distributors and must therefore be regarded as having the object or effect of restricting competition within the meaning of Article 85(1) [now, after amendment Article 81(1)] of the Treaty (paragraph 14).

19. In answer to the question referred to the Court for a preliminary ruling it must therefore be held that Council Directive 84/450 of 10 September 1984 must be interpreted as meaning that it does not preclude vehicles from being advertised as new, less expensive and guaranteed by the manufacturer when the vehicles concerned are registered solely for the purpose of importation, have never been on the road, and are sold in a Member State at a price lower than that charged by dealers established in that Member State because they are equipped with fewer accessories.

Note

In *Nissan* the ECJ went quite far. However, the decision must be read in its particular context. *Nissan* deals in parallel imports—an area where the ECJ usually takes a rather critical position against all attempts to defend national markets. Thus, the decision might not be paradigmatic for the future shaping of the materiality criterion.

The threshold for intervention indeed seems to be put rather high in this case,[95] and it should not necessarily determine the approach to the Unfair Commercial Practices Directive (2005/29/EC)

IV.D WHAT INFORMATION?

The provision on misleading actions enumerates the types of issues to which misleading actions can relate.

UCPD (2005/29/EC) **2.53 (EU)**

Article 6 (1) A commercial practice shall be regarded as misleading if it contains false information and is therefore untruthful or in any way, including overall presentation, deceives or is likely to deceive the average consumer, even if the information is factually correct, in relation to one or more of the following elements, and in either case causes or is likely to cause him to take a transactional decision that he would not have taken otherwise:

(a) the existence or nature of the product;

(b) the main characteristics of the product, such as its availability, benefits, risks, execution, composition, accessories, after sale customer assistance and complaint handling, method and date of manufacture or provision, delivery, fitness for purpose, usage, quantity, specification, geographical or commercial origin or the results to be expected from its use, or the results and material features of tests or checks carried out on the product;

(c) the extent of the trader's commitments, the motives for the commercial practice and the nature of the sales process, any statement or symbol in relation to direct or indirect sponsorship or approval of the trader or the product;

(d) the price or the manner in which the price is calculated, or the existence of a specific price advantage;

(e) the need for a service, part, replacement or repair;

(f) the nature, attributes and rights of the trader or his agent, such as his identity and assets, his qualifications, status, approval, affiliation or connection and ownership of industrial, commercial or intellectual property rights or his awards and distinctions;

(g) the consumer's rights, including the right to replacement or reimbursement under Directive 1999/44/EC of the European Parliament and of the Council of 25 May 1999 on certain aspects of the sale of consumer goods and associated guarantees, or the risks he may face.

Note

The provision does not make clear whether and to what extent the list is exhaustive. One might argue that it is due to the lack of any restrictive wording, such as 'in particular' or the like. The question might remain a purely theoretical one, as the list

[95] A Bakardjieva Engelbrekt, *EU and Marketing Practices Law in the Nordic Countries—Consequences of a Directive on Unfair Business-to-Consumer Commercial Practices* (Report for the Nordic Council of Ministers Committee on Consumer Affairs, 2005) 35.

is long and seems to be exhaustive. However, one important item that seems to be lacking from the enumeration is information concerning competitors.[96] In the area of comparative advertising this should not be a problem, as the Unfair Commercial Practices Directive (2005/29/EC) and the Directive on Comparative Advertising (97/55/EC) are mutually interlinked.[97]

V. MISLEADING OMISSION

V.A A EUROPEAN DUTY TO DISCLOSE INFORMATION?

UCPD (2005/29/EC) **2.54 (EU)**

Article 7 (1) A commercial practice shall be regarded as misleading if, in its factual context, taking account of all its features and circumstances and the limitations of the communication medium, it omits material information that the average consumer needs, according to the context, to take an informed transactional decision and thereby causes or is likely to cause the average consumer to take a transactional decision that he would not have taken otherwise.

(2) It shall also be regarded as a misleading omission when, taking account of the matters described in paragraph 1, a trader hides or provides in an unclear, unintelligible, ambiguous or untimely manner such material information as referred to in that paragraph or fails to identify the commercial intent of the commercial practice if not already apparent from the context, and where, in either case, this causes or is likely to cause the average consumer to take a transactional decision that he would not have taken otherwise.

T Wilhelmsson, European Fair Trading Law[98] **2.55 (EU)**

The cited provision indicates that 'hidden' information can render an omission as misleading as well as information that is omitted altogether. Information may be hidden in various ways. Providing information in small print in some less eye-catching part of the marketing materials is just one example. The information should also be understandable. Unclear, unintelligible and ambiguous information may be treated as omitted information ... One might assume that the issue of how information given is understood is an issue where there is a strong need for diverging national assessments related to variations in national consumer cultures ...

The required information should also be given in a timely manner, in order not to be irrelevant. This provision shows that separate pieces of the trader's activity should be judged independently when applying Article 7. Article 2(d) of the Directive [2005/29/EC] provides that a practice means 'any act, omission, course of conduct or representation,

[96] H Köhler and T Lettl, 'Das geltende europäische Lauterkeitsrecht, der Vorschlag für eine EG-Richtlinie über unlautere Geschäftspraktiken und die UWG-Reform' (2003) 9 *WRP* 1039.

[97] Misleading Advertising Directive, Art 3a(1)(a).

[98] In Howells, Micklitz and Wilhelmsson, above n 39, ch 5, s (c)(ii).

commercial communication' … For example, it is a well-recognised fact that information given at very late stages of the process, when the consumer has effectively made up his mind, often does not have any impact. Such information may therefore not be sufficient to cure an omission and make the practice as a whole acceptable. Finally, the provision mentions as a particular example of a misleading omission that the trader 'fails to identify the commercial intent of the commercial practice if not already apparent from the context'. This sentence repeats in a more general form the principle that marketing should always be identifiable as marketing, which was mentioned already above.

However, there is also the question of where to draw the line between misleading action and misleading omission.

J Stuyck, E Terryn and T van Dyck, Confidence through Fairness?[99] **2.56 (EU)**

Briefly summarised, the test to assess whether the commercial practice is a misleading action is so see whether it contains false information and is therefore untruthful or in any way, including overall presentation, deceives or is likely to deceive the average consumer even if the information is factually correct, in relation to one or more of a set of elements detailed in Art 6(1); and in either case causes or is likely to cause him to take a transactional decision that he would not have taken otherwise. To the extent that a commercial practice causes or is likely to cause the average consumer to take a transactional decision that he would not have taken otherwise, Article 6(2) furthermore prohibits practices that create confusion with any products, trade marks, trade names or other distinguishing marks of a competitor and in certain circumstances by non-compliance with commitments contained in codes of conduct by which the trader has undertaken to be bound. An omission on the other hand, is misleading if its factual context, taking account of all its features and circumstances and the limitations of the communication medium, omits material information that the average consumer needs to take an informed transactional decision, (Art 7(1)) or if material definition is given in an unclear, unintelligible, ambiguous or untimely manner (Art 7(2)). In both cases, one needs to establish that the omission has caused or is likely to cause the average consumer to take a transaction decision that he would not have taken otherwise.

Notes

(1) There has been much debate as to what extent advertising law should oblige advertisers to disclose information relevant to consumers. Scholars made a strong plea for introducing not only a duty to disclose information but also to grant consumers a positive and enforceable right to information. The European Commission chose a rather cautious approach, introducing what has been termed 'an indirect duty to inform'.[100] However, this does not prevent the academia from discussing whether

[99] Stuyck, Terryn and van Dyck, above n 76, 128.
[100] The wording stems from T Wilhelmsson in Howells, Micklitz and Wilhelmsson, above n 39, ch 5, s (i).

and to what extent the established prohibition of misleading omissions contains a positive right to information.[101]

(2) The UCPD is not very clear on the distinction between misleading action and misleading omission. The key question is when exactly an advertising measure is lacking information which is material. Whenever advertising measures are linked to information, the debate is open as to whether these suffice to meet the information needs of the consumer. But what is material? The yardstick is the average consumer but in interpretations of Article 5(3) it might also be the vulnerable consumer. When and under what conditions shall the supplier be obliged to disclose information, ie, hidden information? The standard to be applied will decide on the role and the importance of Article 7(1) to level up consumer protection in the field of advertising law. Article 7(2) clarifies that there can be a misleading omission even though the material information is given, but not in a sufficiently clear manner.

V.B MEMBER STATES' APPROACHES TO THE DISCLOSURE OF INFORMATION

The implementation of Article 7 will be the cornerstone in the ongoing debate in the Member States on whether and to what extent national laws need to be amended. Some Member States have already gone a long way in linking the prohibition of misleading advertising to the disclosure of information; others are lagging behind.

Marketing Act (2008:486)[102] **2.57 (SW)**

Section 10, subsection 3 A trader must not omit material information in the marketing of his or her own or someone else's trade. A misleading omission includes situations where material information is provided in an unclear, unintelligible, ambiguous or otherwise untimely manner.

Note

In *Nordic law*, it has been relatively self-evident, since the beginning of consumer protection in the 1970s, that withholding important information from consumers can be regarded as an unfair commercial practice. The UCPD did not make any radical change in Scandinavian law even though wordings were made clearer in the Directive. Even the old Swedish version of this information duty, which dates back to 1975, seems to go further than what is now prescribed in the UCPD. Since 1995, the Swedish Marketing Act contains a provision, in connection with the general clause on unfair marketing, according to which the business shall give such information that is of particular importance from the point of view of consumers.[103]

[101] See K-H Fezer, 'Das Informationsgebot der Lauterkeitsrichtlinie als subjektives Verbraucherrecht—Zur Umsetzung des Art 7 der Richtlinie über unlautere Geschäftspraktiken in §5 UWG' (2007) *WRP* 1021.

[102] Marknadsföringslag.

[103] Marknadsföringslag (1995:450) s 4(2). The same provision was included already in the 1975 Marketing Act; on the history, see U Bernitz, *Marknadsföringslagen* (Stockholm, Norstedts, 1997) 80.

Consumer Protection Act[104] **2.58 (FI)**

Chapter 2, Section 7 Omission of material information
Omission of material information that the consumer needs to take a decision to buy or any other decision concerning consumer goods and services is prohibited in marketing and in relations to clients, if the omission might cause the consumer to take a decision that he would not have taken had proper information been given.

As to whether sufficient information is provided, matters to be considered include whether the information provided is clear, intelligible and timely as well as the limitations of the medium used to communicate and other measures taken by the trader in order to provide the consumer with material information.

Relevant Information in respect of the health and economic security of consumers shall never be omitted.

Note
Since its adoption in 1978, the Finnish Consumer Protection Act has in a similar vein to Sweden introduced an information obligation. The requirement of 'economic security' has been interpreted fairly widely, referring not only to information needed in connection with economically important consumer decisions, but also to information required for rational decision-making of consumers when acquiring goods and services of lesser value.[105] The Consumer Protection Act also makes possible the issuing of more concrete decrees concerning provision of information.[106]

Similar provisions exist in other jurisdictions.

Trade Practices Act **2.59 (BE)**

Article 30 At the latest, at the time of the conclusion of a sale, the seller shall, in good faith, supply to the consumer all useful information concerning the characteristics of the product or the service and concerning the contract terms, taking into account both the need for information as expressed by the consumer and the specific use of the product or the service as stated by the consumer or as reasonably foreseeable by the seller.

In Spain, the general information duty is located in Art 13 LGDCU (General Consumer Protection Act).

General Consumer Protection Act[107] **2.60 (ES)**

Article 60 Information prior to the contract.

[104] 38/1978, as amended in 2008, available at: www.finlex.fi.
[105] For example, Finnish Market Court decision 1981:12, requiring information that a cheap decorative telephone could not be connected to the telephone net.
[106] Ch 2, s 6.
[107] Enacted by Royal Legislative Decree 1/2007 of 16 November.

1. Prior to the contract, the provider must make available to the consumer and user the relevant, truthful and sufficient information on the essential features of the contract, particularly on its legal and economic conditions, and those of the goods and services that are the object of the contract, in a manner clear, understandable and appropriate to the circumstances.

2. For these purposes the duties of information about the goods and services established by this provision and rules resulting from practice will be relevant, and, furthermore:

a) The name, company name and full domicile of the responsible for the contractual offer and, according to the specific case, the name, company name and full address of the businessman on whose account the one responsible for the offer operates.

b) The full price, including taxes, or budget, according to the case. In all information to the consumer on the price of goods and services, including advertising, it is mandatory to inform the final full price, expressly showing, according to the case, the amount of the increases or discounts that will be applied, of the expenses to be afforded by the consumer and user and the additional expenses for accessory services, financing or other similar payment conditions.

c) The date of delivery, performance of the contract and duration.

d) The procedure available to the consumer to terminate the contract.

e) The warranties offered.

f) The language or languages in which the contract can be formalized, when this is not the language in which the information prior to contracting has been offered.

g) The existence of the right to recede from the contract that can be available to the consumer and user, the deadlines and form of exercising the right.

3. The pre-contractual information must be given to the consumer free of charge.

Germany has introduced a new rule in the 2004 Act.

Gesetz gegen den Unlauteren Wettbewerb **2.61 (DE)**
(Unfair Competition Act)

§5 (2) To judge whether the concealing of a fact is misleading, special account must be taken of its relevance for the decision to enter into a contract judged upon common opinion and the appropriateness of concealing the fact.

Note

The finally adopted Act to implement the UCPD in Germany provides for a more or less literal translation of Article 7 of the UCPD.[108]

It is interesting to contrast the Belgian and Spanish solutions with the German formula. The former countries have relatively broad rules on consumer information which would then have to be adapted to unfair commercial marketing practices. In Germany, the starting point was different. The German Supreme Court in very well-established case-law held that the advertiser cannot be legally obliged per se to disclose information which sheds a negative light on his products or services.[109] The

[108] See §5 a BGBl I 28 December 2008, 2949.

[109] See BGH (1989) GRUR 683; BGHZ 15 July 1999, 104, 185, 188.

courts are balancing the consumers' interest in receiving as much information as possible, also on negative aspects of the products, against the advertisers' interests legitimately to hide pejorative information and their desire to use easy placard-style messages. The courts insist that not merely particular aspects of the advertising should be highlighted to justify claims of misleading omissions, but rather that it is the general impression of the advertising as a whole which counts. In sum, the advertiser is said to mislead the consumer only if the non-disclosure of material facts might provoke the wrong general impression that the advertising is misleading. It remains to be seen to what extent the intended revision will have an impact on the role and function of information in advertising measures.

Twigg-Flesner says this of the situation in the UK:

C Twigg-Flesner, Consumer Product Guarantees[110] **2.62 (UK)**

In *Breed v Cluett* (1970), a vendor of a house had falsely stated that the house was covered by the National House-Builders' Registration Council ten-year guarantee. In a very brief judgment, Lord Parker CJ suggested that this statement fell within s 14(1) of the Trade Descriptions Act 1968. If so, the provision of a guarantee would, indeed, be a 'service', and false statements about a guarantee could be dealt with under this section. This question was revisited in *Ashley v London Borough of Sutton* (1994). In this case, a book containing a betting strategy was advertised in a mailshot. The mailshot contained a satisfaction guarantee:

Our guarantee is straightforward and unmatched by any other publication known today. [We] invite you to try out the complete Formula 2 strategy for a whole 90 days. Then if you for any reason feel it is not the most powerful and profitable strategy you have ever seen, just return it. We'll be happy to buy it back from you right away, for the full price you paid.

When consumers who bought the book tried to invoke the guarantee, this was refused by the defendant. He was convicted by magistrates of a breach of s 14(2)(b). The Divisional Court was asked whether it was correct to decide that the guarantee constituted a service within the meaning of s 14 TDA. Unfortunately, Scott Baker J. did not consider whether the guarantee itself constituted the service, but rather focused on whether a consumer who bought the book had bought 'goods' or a service, ie, the betting strategy contained in the book. Surprisingly, he concluded that the book was a service and that s 14 applied. This decision has been much criticised. Oughton and Lowry (2000, p 524) take the view that it was incorrect to find that the book was a service, and instead, there was merely the supply of goods, that is, the book itself. This view is shared by Cartwright (1996, p 60). This appears to be the correct view. The Divisional Court clearly misunderstood the question it had been asked. However, the case is still of some value for the present discussion. *Ashley* concerned a money-back (or 'satisfaction') guarantee, and it is difficult to describe the service provided in this context. Indeed, in *Dixons Ltd v Roberts* (1984), the Court of Appeal held that an offer by Dixons to pay the difference in price should a customer be able to find a product purchased at Dixons at a lower price elsewhere did not constitute a provision of a service. In *Newell and Taylor v*

[110] C Twigg-Flesner, *Consumer Product Guarantees* (Aldershot, Ashgate, 2003), 202ff.

Hicks (1984), it was noted that a service should be regarded as 'doing something for somebody' (Goff LJ at p 313). The promise to provide a refund did not constitute a service within that definition. Cartwright comments that had this been cited to the court in *Ashley*, it would have come to the conclusion that the money-back guarantee would not be a service within the meaning of s 14 after all (Cartwright, 1996, p 61).

In contrast, manufacturers' guarantees do not normally promise a refund, but instead offer repair or replacement of products which are not working in the way promised by the guarantor. Surely, there can be no doubt that this *would* constitute the provision of a service, or a facility, within the meaning of s 14, and therefore any failure to honour a guarantee could be a breach of this section.

Harvey and Parry (2000, p 404, No 6) query whether the failure by Ashley to honour the money-back guarantee, rather than being a criminal offence under the TDA, should be treated simply as a breach of contract. There can be little doubt that such a refusal to honour a guarantee will be a breach of contract, and that it may be possible to rely on regulatory enforcement instead.

Notes

(1) The UK case-law shows no clear trend. Liability for half-truths is not the same thing as a duty to disclose, though it is sometimes an approximation. For instance, in *Farrand* v *Lazarus*[111] it was held that the only way to counter the impression of a materially understated odometer reading on a car was to state the true mileage where this was known.

(2) The Trade Descriptions Act 1968 still provides the model for regulation of marketing practices, combining strict criminal liability, subject to a due diligence defence, with a test of whether the statement is false or misleading.[112] The extension to misleading as well as false descriptions allows some scope for control of omissions that amount to half-truths.[113] A true impression of marketing law in the United Kingdom requires knowledge of the important role played by the self-regulatory Advertising Standards Authority (ASA).[114] Article 7(1) of its Code of Advertising Practice states: 'No marketing communication should mislead, or be likely to mislead, by inaccuracy, ambiguity, exaggeration, omission or otherwise.' The self-regulatory system is backed by injunction powers under the Control of Misleading Advertisements Regulations 1988 and the Government has stated 'it is widely recognised that advertisements which mislead by omission would already be unlawful' under those Regulations.[115] The UK implemented the UCPD literally. Again, it is an open question to what extent the new regulation affects control in practice.

[111] [1976] 1 WLR 1243.

[112] The 1968 Act governs goods and services; prices are covered by Part III of the Consumer Protection Act 1987 and estate agency by the Property Misdescriptions Act 1991. All but the 1991 Act are planned to be repealed as part of the implementation of the Unfair Commercial Practices Directive (2005/29/EC): see *Government Response to the Consultation Paper on Implementing the Unfair Commercial Practices Directive* available at: www.dti.gov.uk.

[113] D Roberts, 'Trade Descriptions: False by Reason of What it Omits' (1988) 6 *Trading Law* 145.

[114] G Howells and S Weatherill, *Consumer Protection Law* (Aldershot, Ashgate, 2005).

[115] *Consultation on Implementing EU Directive on Unfair Commercial Practices Directive and Amending Existing Consumer Legislation* (DTI, 2005) para 99.

V.C THE INVITATION TO PURCHASE

The informational needs of consumers depend on *what phase* of the relationship the commercial practice relates to ('according to the context'). Article 7(4) contains a list enumerating the information that shall be regarded as material in the specific situation of *an invitation to purchase.*

UCPD (2005/29/EC) **2.63 (EU)**

Article 7 (4) In the case of an invitation to purchase, the following information shall be regarded as material, if not already apparent from the context:

(a) the main characteristics of the product, to an extent appropriate to the medium and the product;

(b) the geographical address and the identity of the trader, such as his trading name and, where applicable, the geographical address and the identity of the trader on whose behalf he is acting;

(c) the price including taxes, or where the nature of the product means that the price cannot reasonably be calculated in advance, the manner in which the price is calculated, as well as, where appropriate, all additional freight, delivery or postal charges or, where these charges cannot reasonably be calculated in advance, the fact that such additional charges may be payable;

(d) the arrangements for payment, delivery, performance and the complaint handling policy, if they depart from the requirements of professional diligence;

(e) for products and transactions involving a right of withdrawal or cancellation, the existence of such a right.

Notes

(1) The term 'invitation to purchase', which delimits the scope of Article 7(4), is defined in Article 2(i) of the Directive. According to that provision it

> means a commercial communication which indicates characteristics of the product and the price in a way appropriate to the means of the commercial communication used and thereby enables the consumer to make a purchase.

(2) Article 7(3) puts emphasis on the *medium* used to communicate the commercial practice:

> Where the medium used to communicate the commercial practice imposes limitations of space or time, these limitations and any measures taken by the trader to make the information available to consumers by other means shall be taken into account in deciding whether information has been omitted.

(3) Article 7(4) introduces a new concept into unfair commercial practices. The invitation to purchase is a concept which is very much related to contract law. It refers to the pre-contractual stage. The overall logic of Article 7(4) is clearly that the advertiser has to provide more information the closer the conclusion of a contract. What exactly is an invitation to purchase and how is it linked to the information duties enshrined in Article 7(5)?

V.D ESTABLISHED INFORMATION REQUIREMENTS, ARTICLE 7(5)

UCPD (2005/29/EC) **2.64 (EU)**

Article 7 (5) Information requirements established by Community law in relation to commercial communication including advertising or marketing, a non-exhaustive list of which is contained in Annex II, shall be regarded as material.

Note

The list in Annex II includes: Provisions of the Distance Selling Directive, Package Tour Directive, Timeshare Directive, Price Indication Directive, Medicinal Products Directive, Electronic Commerce Directive, Consumer Credit Directive, Distance Selling of Financial Services Directive, Transferable Securities Directive, Insurance Mediation Directive, Life Assurance Directive, Financial Instruments Directive, Third Non-life Insurance Directive and Prospectus Directive.

Stuyck, Terryn and Van Dyck provide the following understanding of the interplay between Articles 7(4) and (5).[116]

J Stuyck, E Terryn and T Van Dyck, Confidence through Fairness? **2.65 (EU)**

The rules relating to invitation to purchase go far in imposing positive disclosure duties on traders ... Article 7(5) further provides information requirements established by Community law in relation to commercial communication which shall be regarded as material: a non-exhaustive list of such Community law information requirements is contained in Annex II of the UCPD. Recital 15 implies that only omission of the information in this wide-ranging list will automatically constitute a misleading omission. Recital 15 further explains that 'Member States will be able, when allowed by the minimum clauses in Community law' to maintain or introduce more stringent provisions in conformity with Community law so as to ensure a higher level of protection of consumers' individual contractual rights'.

Recital 15 is quite problematic. Presently various Member States attach contract law consequences to failure to comply with these disclosure duties. Recital 15 could be read as implying that Member States would no longer be allowed to attach contract law consequences to disclosure requirements in B2C relationships unless when allowed by the minimum clauses in Community law. Consequently, absent of minimum clauses stemming from a sector-specific Directive, Member States would only be allowed to attach contractual consequences to omission of information, if these are either misleading omissions within the meaning of Art 7(1) UCPD or if the omission is an unfair commercial practice under the general clause.

We nevertheless doubt that Recital 15 should be read in this sense. The impact of such interpretation would be immense and involve far-reaching consequences in shaping

[116] Stuyck, Terryn and Van Dyck, above n 76, 129, 130.

disclosure duties stemming from general contract law. In that sense, such interpretation would be disproportionate to the objectives and rationale of UCPD which clearly states that '(t)his Directive is without prejudice to contract law.' In any event, we expect and enduring discussion on this subject—a discussion that makes it clear the apparent straightforward line between regulation of marketing practices and general contract law does not exist. The UCPD may have an impact, even a major and shaping impact, on general private law.'

Notes

(1) The Annex is quite comprehensive. However, it does not mention provisions of the Distance Selling Directive (97/7/EC), nor of the Consumer Sales' Directive (99/44/EC) nor of the Data Protection Directive (95/46/EC). These gaps might easily be filled as the Annex is explicitly not meant to be exhaustive. However, it seems much more difficult to decide what sort of EC and national rules could equally be regarded as information requirements under Article 7(5). Under EC law, prime candidates are the different product-related labelling Directives which contain various consumer relevant information. National law varies considerably with regard to the minimum character of most of the consumer law Directives.

(2) The relationship between 'misleading omissions' and 'invitation to purchase' and 'the list of information duties in the Annex' may serve as a striking example where the official statement in the Directive—that the Directive does not affect general contract law—is nothing more than paying lip-service to the Member States reservations. The UCPD clearly oversteps the boundaries between marketing practices and general contract law and will affect our understanding of both fields of law, at least in the long-run.

VI. LANGUAGE IN COMMERCIAL PRACTICES

The Directive remains silent on the significance of language in advertising. However, it should therefore not be concluded that language is irrelevant in evaluating fairness. The Community legislator has rather put aside the question—in compliance with the established policy on language—of whether the use of a particular language, or of linguistically alienated messages, is likely to distort commercial transactions. As a matter of fact, the problem arises with advertising measures which provide information.

An Act of 4 August 1994[117] makes the use of the French language compulsory when advertising a product or a service and makes violation a criminal offence. Article 2 provides:

[117] Loi Tourbon, Act No 94-665 of 4 August 1994 concerning the use of the French language (Loi relative B l'emploi de la langue française—Loi Toubon), Circulaire 19 March 1996 (1996) JCP(G) II, 67801.

It is obligatory to use the French language for the specification, offer, presentation, instructions, description of the scope and conditions of the guarantee of goods, a product or service, as well as for bills and receipts.

The same provisions apply to all written, oral or audiovisual advertising.

ECJ Case-366/98, 12 September 2000[118] **2.66 (EU)**
Criminal proceedings against Yannick Geoffrey

COMPATIBILITY OF NATIONAL LANGUAGE REQUIREMENTS WITH EC LAW

Geoffrey

The law should not impose a specific language for labelling if another language is used which is easily understood by consumers.

Facts: At an inspection carried out on 5 June 1996 at the Géant Hypermarket (Casino chain) in Clermont-Ferrand, officials of the Direction de la Concurrence, de la Consommation et de la Répression des Fraudes (Department of Competition and Consumer Protection and Suppression of Fraud; hereinafter 'the Department') of Puy-de-Dôme found: that the labelling on certain drinks, namely 432 bottles of Coca-Cola, 47 bottles of Merry Down cider and 22 bottles of Red Raw ginger ale, was not in French, save for the indications of volume and, in the case of the ginger ales, the alcohol content; that advertisements showed bottles of cider of the brands OD Pirat and Shock, which, according to the officials of the Department, did not correspond to the 'cider description', which is reserved for alcoholic drinks made of apples; that the shelf labels for the products OD Pirat, Snake Bite and Blackadder also misleadingly represented them as cider. The national court sought to determine whether certain provisions of Community law preclude the application of national legislation such as Decree No 84-1147. It stated that that decree, which has been codified as part of the French Consumer Code, requires, in particular, that all particulars which are made compulsory by French legislation must be written in French.

Judgment: 24. As to the language requirements concerning the labelling of foodstuffs which a Member State is entitled to impose, the Court has already ruled on this matter a number of times.

25. First, in Case C-369/89 *Piageme* v *Peeters* [1991] ECR I-2971, the Court ruled that Article 30 [now, after amendment Article 28] of the Treaty and Article 14 of Directive 79/112 preclude a national law from requiring the exclusive use of a specific language for the labelling of foodstuffs, without allowing for the possibility of using another language easily understood by purchasers or of ensuring that the purchaser is informed by other means.

26. The Court then further ruled in Case C-85/94 *Piageme* v *Peeters* [1995] ECR I-2955 that Article 14 of Directive 79/112 precludes a Member State, as regards the requirement of a language easily understood by purchasers, from requiring the use of the language most widely spoken in the area where the product is offered for sale, even if the use at the same time of another language is not excluded.

27. Finally, in Case C-385/96 *Goerres* [1998] ECR I-4431, the Court ruled that Article 14 of Directive 79/112 does not preclude national legislation which, as regards language requirements, prescribes the use of a specific language for the labelling of foodstuffs but which also permits, as an alternative, the use of another language easily understood by purchasers.

[118] [2000] ECR I-6579.

28. It follows from that case-law that Article 30 [now, after amendment Article 28] of the Treaty and Article 14 of Directive 79/112 must be interpreted as precluding a national rule, such as that at issue in the main proceedings, from requiring the use of a specific language for the labelling of foodstuffs, without allowing for the possibility of using another language easily understood by purchasers or of ensuring that the purchaser is informed by other means.

Notes

(1) Following the ECJ decision, a new sentence was added to Article R 112-8 of the Code de la Consommation,[119] which now reads:

> All the labelling statements provided for by this chapter must be easily understandable, written in French and be free of abbreviations other than those provided for by regulations or international conventions. They shall be written in an obvious place and are clearly visible, legible and indelible. They must not, in any way, be concealed, masked or separated by other indications or images.
>
> The labelling statements provided for by this chapter may furthermore appear in one or several other languages.

(2) The lack of EC requirements means that Member States' rules on language in commercial communications that primarily aim at safeguarding the position of the national language or of a recognised minority language cannot be set aside using the Directive.[120] On the other hand, if language requirements are issued as a means to improve transparency in relation to consumers, they obviously fall within the ambit of the Directive. As the purpose of language rules is not always clearly expressed, and as such rules sometimes may even be adopted for both of the reasons mentioned, this might result in difficult legal problems in drawing the borderline between the acceptable and the forbidden.[121] Again, these difficulties are connected with the decision to make the Directive a maximum harmonisation Directive.

(3) French law may serve as an example of how difficult it is to draw a line, although the ECJ has already had several occasions to decide on language issues.[122] On 14 November 2000, the Cour de Cassation[123] ruled that the requirement to use French is compatible with the principle of free circulation of goods, as it is justified by the necessity to protect consumers.[124] This decision was taken six weeks after the

[119] Available at www.legifrance.gouv.fr.

[120] But may of course be in conflict with the basic freedoms of the Treaty; see the *Piageme* doctrine elaborated first in Case C-369/89 *Piageme et al v BVBA Peeters* [1991] ECR I-2971, according to which '[t]he obligation exclusively to use the language of the linguistic region constitutes a measure having equivalent effect to a quantitative restriction on imports, prohibited by Article [28] of the Treaty' (at 16). See also the concretisation in Piageme II, Case C-85/94 *Groupement des Producteurs, Importateurs et Agents Généraux d'Eaux Minérales EtrangPres, VZW (Piageme) et al v Peeters NV*[1995] ECR I-2955.

[121] Illuminating is the analysis of the relationship between the French language law (Loi Toubon) and European law in H-W Micklitz, 'Zum Recht des Verbrauchers auf die eigene Sprache' (2003) 11 *ZEuP* 635.

[122] ECJ, 18 June 1991, *Piageme v Peeters*, Case C-369/89 [1991] ECR I-2971; ECJ, 12 October 1995, *Piageme v Peeters* II, Case C-85/94 [1995] ECR I-2955; and ECJ, 3 June 1999, *Colim v Bigg's*, Case C-33/97 [1999] ECR I-3175.

[123] Cass crim, 14 November 2000, (2001) JCP 940.

[124] Micklitz, above n 120.

ECJ decided in *Yannick Geoffrey* on a relatively similar issue. Both cases deal with mandatory language requirements on labelling. They seem to comply with Directive 79/112/EEC[125] (which has become now Directive 2000/13/EC[126]) as it requires the possibility for using another language easily understood by purchasers outside and beyond the specific language of the country. However, the Cour de Cassation does not mention the ECJ decision at all. The strong link of the UCPD to information requirements in Articles 7(4) and (5) provides ample ground for possible conflicts over the use of language.

(4) The use of languages: in Spain, the languages of the Autonomous Communities are all official within the Spanish territory, according to Article 3(1) of the Spanish Constitution. Article 13 LGDCU does not say anything about the language in which the information should be presented to consumers. There are a number of scattered administrative rules on this in the normative codes on labelling of different products, namely the rule that the duty of information would be fulfilled in the language of any EU member, or in any of the languages of the Autonomous Communities (Basque, Catalonian, Galician, etc) if that information is also provided in the Spanish language.

VII. COMPARATIVE ADVERTISING

The European Commission regards comparative advertising as a means of consumer information. The respective standards are laid down in the Directive on Comparative Advertising (97/55/EC),[127] linked via the UCPD (2005/29/EC) to B2C transactions.

Directive on Comparative Advertising (97/55/EC) **2.67 (EU)**

Article 3a (1) Comparative advertising shall, as far as the comparison is concerned, be permitted when the following conditions are met:

(a) it is not misleading according to Articles 2(2), 3 …

(b) it compares goods or services meeting the same needs or intended for the same purpose;

(c) it objectively compares one or more material, relevant, verifiable and representative features of those goods and services, which may include price.

[125] Council Directive 79/112/EEC of 18 December 1978 on the approximation of the laws of the Member States relating to the labelling presentation and advertising of foodstuffs for sale to the ultimate consumer [1979] OJ L 33, 1–14.

[126] Directive 2000/13/EC on the approximation of the laws of the Member States relating to the labelling, presentation and advertising of foodstuffs [2000] OJ L 109, 29 as well as Directive 76/768/EEC on the approximation of the laws of the Member States relating to cosmetic products [1976] OJ L 262, 169.

[127] Directive 97/55/EC of European Parliament and of the Council of 6 October 1997 amending Directive 84/450/EEC concerning misleading advertising so as to include comparative advertising [1997] OJ L 290, 18–23.

ECJ Case C-356/04, 19 September 2006[128] **2.68 (EU)**
Etablissementen Franz Colruyt NV v Lidl Belgium GmbH & Co KG

PRICE COMPARISONS IN SUPERMARKETS

Lidl

The products which are compared must be clearly identified.

Facts: Lidl Belgium GmbH & Co KG ('Lidl') and Etablissementen Franz Colruyt NV ('Colruyt') each operated in Belgium a chain of stores which essentially retail basic consumables, under the names Lidl and Colruyt, respectively. On 19 January 2004, Colruyt sent its customers a mailshot ('the letter at issue') worded as follows:

> ... Last year, 2003, you were able once again to make significant savings with Colruyt. On the basis of our average price index for the past year we have calculated that a family spending €100 each week in Colruyt stores: saved between €366 and €1,129 by shopping at Colruyt's rather than at any other supermarket (such as Carrefour, Cora, Delhaize, etc); and saved between €155 and €293 by shopping at Colruyt's instead of a hard discounter or wholesaler (Aldi, Lidl, Makro). On the reverse side you will see the evolution of the price differential vis-à-vis other stores in the course of 2003. The figures indicate that the price differential between Colruyt and the other stores has increased even further over the last few months. In order to be able to continue to guarantee the lowest prices, we compare daily 18,000 prices in other stores. In addition, we also collect all promotions. Our data are thus very much up-to-date. We store all the prices in our central computer. Each month we use those prices to calculate the price differential between Colruyt and the other stores. We refer to this as our price index which is certified by Quality Control (Instituut voor Kwaliteitscontrole), an independent body. The result: at Colruyt's you enjoy, every day and at any time of the year, the lowest prices. In 2004 also we remain true to this guarantee.'

The reverse side of the letter at issue featured two charts. The first set out the price differential between Colruyt and its competitors as at 22 December 2003, a differential which was stated to have been calculated by it on the basis of a daily comparison of the prices, including promotional prices, of comparable products sold in each Colruyt store and in the competing stores located in the region. The second illustrated the development of that differential over the whole of 2003. In addition, the following text appears on the checkout receipts issued at stores operated by Colruyt:

> 'How much did you save in 2003? If you spent €100 at Colruyt's each week, then, according to our price index, you will have saved: between €366 and €1,129 in comparison with another supermarket (such as Carrefour, Cora, Delhaize, etc); between €155 and €293 in comparison with a hard discounter or wholesaler (Aldi, Lidl, Makro).'

Judgment: 19. It should be noted at the outset, first, that two separate methods of comparative advertising are at issue in the main proceedings.

20. The first method involves comparing the general level of the prices charged by competing chains of stores in respect of their ranges of comparable products and inferring therefrom the amount that consumers can save on an annual basis depending on whether they purchase their basic consumables each day from one rather than another of those chains ('the first method of comparison at issue'). Those general price levels are determined monthly, then annually, on the basis of a daily record of the individual prices of a very wide sample of basic consumables, whether identical (branded products) or similar (unbranded products or the chain's own brand), sold by both the advertiser and each of its competitors. In order to determine the general price levels, the individual prices thus recorded are weighted according to the quantities of each product that are purchased from the advertiser.

[128] [2006] ECR I-8501.

21. The second method of advertising is based on the assertion that all of the advertiser's products that have a red label bearing the word 'BASIC' are sold by it at the lowest price in Belgium ('the second method of comparison at issue'). This selection of products consists of, first, branded products and, second, products sold unbranded or under the advertiser's own brand name. The price comparison relates, in the case of the first category, exclusively to identical branded products sold by both the advertiser and its competitor and, in the case of the second category, to products of comparable quality sold by the advertiser and its competitor.

22. The second preliminary point to note is that, given the objectives of the Directive and in particular the fact that, as the second recital in the preamble to Directive 97/55 points out, comparative advertising helps to demonstrate objectively the merits of the various comparable products and thus stimulate competition between suppliers of goods and services to the consumer's advantage, it is settled case-law that the conditions required of comparative advertising must be interpreted in the sense most favourable to it (Case C-112/99 *Toshiba Europe* [2001] ECR I-7945, paragraphs 36 and 37, and Case C-44/01 *Pippig Augenoptik* [2003] ECR I-3095, paragraph 42; see also Case C-59/05 *Siemens* [2006] ECR I-2147, paragraphs 22 to 24). …

82. The Court has thus already been led to state that advertising relating to the lower prices of cars that are parallel imports can be considered to be misleading only if it is established that the decision to buy on the part of a significant number of consumers to whom the advertising in question is addressed was made in ignorance of the fact that the lower price of the vehicles was matched by a smaller number of accessories on the cars sold by the parallel importer (*X*, paragraph 16).

83. Analogously, comparative advertising relating to the general level of the prices charged by competing chains of stores in respect of their comparable ranges of products and to the amount that can be saved by consumers purchasing their basic consumables from one of those chains rather than the other should, for example, be considered to be misleading if it is established, in the light of all the relevant circumstances of the particular case, that the decision to buy on the part of a significant number of consumers to whom that advertising is addressed is made in the mistaken belief that all the advertiser's products have been taken into account in calculating the general price level, and the amount of savings, that are claimed by the advertising. The same must be true if it is established that such a decision is made in the mistaken belief that that amount will be saved by consumers irrespective of the nature and quantity of the products which they acquire from the advertiser or, for example, in the mistaken belief that all the advertiser's products without exception are cheaper than those of his competitors.

84. Such advertising will also be misleading if it is established that the collective reference which it contains to a range of amounts that may be saved by consumers who purchase their basic consumables from the advertiser rather than from competing chains of stores and the failure to specify individually the general level of the prices charged by each of those chains in competition with the advertiser and the amount that can be saved in relation to each of them are such as to deceive a significant number of persons to whom the advertising is addressed as to the amount that they are actually liable to save by purchasing their basic consumables from the advertiser rather than from some particular competitor or other, and to affect their economic behaviour to that extent.

85. Accordingly, the answer to the first question should be that Article 3a(1)(a) of the Directive must be interpreted as meaning that comparative advertising claiming that the advertiser's general price level is lower than his main competitors', where the comparison has related to a sample of products, may be misleading when the advertisement: does

not reveal that the comparison related only to such a sample and not to all the advertiser's products, does not identify the details of the comparison made or inform the persons to whom it is addressed of the information source where such identification is possible, or contains a collective reference to a range of amounts that may be saved by consumers who make their purchases from the advertiser rather than from his competitors without specifying individually the general level of the prices charged, respectively, by each of those competitors and the amount that consumers are liable to save by making their purchases from the advertiser rather than from each of the competitors.

86. It is for the referring court to determine whether the advertisements at issue in the main proceedings display such characteristics.

Note

From a consumer point of view it is plain that price comparisons are only helpful if the consumer gets to know which products are compared. Quite often price comparisons are limited to particular items out of a large scale of products which appear to shed a favourable light on the advertiser's product. In *Pippig*,[129] the ECJ seemed to have recognised such a highly selective comparison to the detriment of consumers. However, in *Lidl*,[130] the ECJ took a different stance with regard to comparisons suggesting that all products of a particular supplier are as favourable as particularly selected items. In essence, the consumer may request full disclosure of the information.

The degree to which comparative advertising is used as a means of consumer information differs considerably in the Member States.

Tribunal Supremo (Supreme Court), 24 February 1997[131] **2.69 (ES)**

ILLICIT ADVERTISING, NON-EXISTENCE, NON-COMPARATIVE, DENIGRATING OR MISLEADING PUBLICITY

Coca Cola

No denigration without a clear-cut comparison.

Facts: In an advertisement for Pepsi Cola a famous rap singer is drinking Pepsi during a concert. Suddenly, he changes the rhythm of the performance and starts singing a melodic song ('Feeling') while sipping some other beverage in a white glass. A background voice announces that he is drinking 'another cola drink'. After seeing bored faces in the public, one of the fans throws him a 'Pepsi Cola' can and he recovers his normal way of singing to the excitement of the public. The background voice underlines the slogan: 'Pepsi is today's'. The Coca-Cola company claimed that there was an implicit denigrating comparative advertisement, due to the exaggeration of the stimulating effects of the other product, associated with a music style preferred by young people, thus suggesting that Coca-Cola is an old-fashioned drink.

[129] ECJ, 8 April 2003, Case C-44/01 [2003] ECR I-3095.

[130] ECJ, 19 September 2006, Case C-356/04 *Etablissementen Franz Colruyt NV v Lidl Belgium GmbH & Co KG* [2006] ECR I-8501.

[131] RJ 1997\1195.

Judgment: There is no discrepancy between the parties about the emission, content of the advert and its identification. The discrepancy arises about the reach of the content and the possible weakening of the legality, by the concurrence or not of the comparative, denigrating and misleading character, with respect to the refreshing beverage elaborated by the applicant.

The advert consists of the performance of a singer of a modern type of music, known as 'rap', called MCH., who, during a concert or festival before a large crowd drinks the refreshing beverage 'Pepsi Cola'; in a given moment a background voice announces the change of the drink 'for another cola drink' at the moment in which the lead singer in the advert drinks from a white-colored glass, without any brand or reference, abruptly changing the rhythm of the performance, and singing a melodic song before an astonished audience, until one of the people in the audience throws a 'Pepsi' bottle on stage. Upon tasting the contents of the bottle, MCH turns back to the rap performance, ending with the sentence 'Pepsi is today's'. ...

The character of the advert is considered to be exaggerated, naive and improbable, and the criterion suggested by the claimant does not support the manipulation of young people, which the applicant considers easily manipulated. The claimant considers that young people consume those products mainly due to their stimulating effects, and not by their self-definition as soft drinks. This is the reason why the stimulating feature is a must to be advertised in order to increase sales.

[The effectiveness of the advert] will depend on the maturity of the addressees, as some will follow the supposed habits of the artist making the advert by his popularity, others will believe what he says and others, lastly, will know that the advert is selling popularity and not the manifestation of his own tastes.

Further, the publicity does not make any comparisons, because it does not identify the competing brands, either explicitly or impliedly, because it does not mention its name or allude to the applicant's product the consumers of which are perfectly aware of the effects produced by its consumption.

There is no denigration, no actual harm, no deception (except if the deception is the generic one of all advertisers that lead people to think about the beneficial effects of their product for their consumers).

Nor is the music undesirable, or denigrating, or must be rejected by youth ...

Nor is there conduct forbidden by the Consumer and User Act, legitimating '*Coca Cola de España, SA*' to invoke its provisions against another multinational company, because its relation is not that of user and provider.

For all these reasons the appeal is rejected.

Tribunal Supremo (Supreme Court, Private Law Chamber), 4 June 2002[132] **2.70 (ES)**

ILLICIT ADVERTISING AND DISLOYAL PUBLICITY

Good Price SA but bad publicity

Price comparisons based on partially false or manipulated facts are misleading.

[132] No 575/2002, RJ 2002\4978.

Facts: A supermarket ('Bon Preu SA'—literally 'Good Price SA') in Catalonia (Spain) published an advertisement in a local journal in July 1994 with the main heading: 'Playing with health is not fair'. In the content of this advertisement, Bon Preu compared its own hygiene protocols with those of its competitor (DIA supermarkets) and referred to the closing of DIA's supermarkets for hygiene reasons. However, the fact that the only supermarket of its competitor that had been closed (in May 1994) had been already reopened at the time of the publication and that it was not located in the same region but in Madrid was not mentioned in the advertisement. The Supreme Court held that despite the existence of some true information in the comparative publicity, the way in which it was presented and the omitted facts constituted denigrating comparative publicity.'

Judgment: In the advert, *Bon Preu, SA*, compares its own performance with that of the applicant, in terms that constitute 'the paradigm of denigrating, comparative publicity'. The judge comes to this conclusion after analyzing the characteristics of the advert, its format, with reference to the font size and, also the relevant guidelines of the message and its contrasts and contents, which highlight the differences between the respondent's services as patterns of identity control and the plaintiff's services, which are depicted as rendered in unhygienic facilities, with a deficient state of conservation and cleaning. Moreover, the appealed judgment echoes the issue of the exception of truth (*exceptio veritatis*), which is expressly admitted as an argument to reject claims based on denigrating and disloyal competence, despite the silence of the legal article applied to this case. That judgment denies this issue as a problem, since a) the partial or biased reproduction of true data or facts is against the truth; b) the ambiguity of the advert easily induces the consumer to believe in the permanence of the closing on the day of the advert's publication ...; c) the publication of the news became outdated—since the advert is included in the edition of 8th July 1994, whereas the closing took place on May, 24th –; and d) for the accurateness in the treatment of the story the geographical abstraction or de-contextualization is not immaterial. ...

The manipulation deriving from the lack of truth originated from the use without nuances of the present tense and not indicating the date of closing, the extemporaneity of the story and the omission of additional complementary data—not secondary to the story—more specifically the reopening of the facilities—... to which the appellant wants to attribute similar effects to the correctional publicity—since: a) if on the one hand it is indifferent to the extemporaneity; b) on the other it becomes insufficient to destroy the harmful effects of the denigrating publicity message, one can only conclude, logically, that the diffusion was manipulated precisely to mislead the consumer. For all these reasons, the appeal cannot be granted.

Note

The Spanish Supreme Court declared in *Coca-Cola* that there is no negative comparison when no express comparison exists. The 2002 reform (Law 39/2002 of 28 October) of the General Law on advertising now refers to comparative publicity as that which alludes 'in a express or implied way' to a competitor (Art 6bis), following the Directive. Aggressive advertising against competitors is allowed when the statements are 'true and correct' with regard to defects in the competitors' products or services, not as to personal qualities. *Bon Preu* is in line with the ECJ in *Lidl* in its holding that price comparisons which reveal the competitor and are based on partially false or manipulated facts, are misleading. However, price comparisons are permissible if they provide useful information to consumers.

VIII. AGGRESSIVE PRACTICES AND SALES PROMOTION

One of the problems with including 'aggressive practices' is that the term is not a developed concept within most Member States or in European law. It potentially covers a wide array of practices and legal instruments, some of which are only tangentially related to trade law. Many practices that might potentially be labelled 'aggressive' would have fallen within the scope of the originally envisaged Sales Promotions Regulation.[133] But beyond this, the Green Paper pointed to rules on lotteries and gambling, mock auctions, pyramid-selling and multi-level marketing and 'bait and switch' tactics.[134] Indeed the Green Paper provided case studies on multi-level distance selling and power shopping (or co-shopping).[135] It talked about a general clause in a framework Directive potentially covering undue influence and said it would draw upon national examples covering, inter alia, undue influence and pressure, vulnerable consumers, equitable bargains and good faith.

The Explanatory Memorandum to the first proposal for a Directive[136] actually gave surprisingly few hints as to what amounted to aggressive practices. It did offer some examples of undue influence. These turned on whether the practice could have significantly limited the consumer's ability to make an informed decision. Perhaps the best overall rationalisation of what constitutes an aggressive practice is found in Recital 16 to the Directive, which states that provisions on aggressive practices should cover practices which significantly impair the consumer's freedom of choice.

VIII.A AGGRESSION

UCPD (2005/29/EC) **2.71 (EU)**

Article 8 A commercial practice shall be regarded as aggressive if it, in its factual context, taking account of all its features and circumstances, by harassment, coercion, including the use of physical force, or undue influence, significantly impairs or is likely significantly to impair the average consumer's freedom of choice or conduct with regard to the product and thereby causes him or is likely to cause him to take a transactional decision that he would not have taken otherwise.

Article 9 In determining whether a commercial practice uses harassment, coercion, including the use of physical force, or undue influence, account shall be taken of:

(a) its timing, location, nature and persistence;

(b) the use of threatening or abusive language or behaviour;

(c) the exploitation by the trader of any specific misfortune or circumstance of such gravity, of which the trader is aware, as to impair the consumer's judgement to influence the consumer's decision with regard to the product;

[133] Proposal for a European Parliament and Council Regulation concerning sales promotions in the Internal Market COM [2001] 546, [2002] OJ C 75E, 11–16.

[134] COM [2001] 546 at 7.

[135] COM [2001] 546 at 8.

[136] COM [2003] 356.

(d) any onerous or disproportionate non-contractual barriers imposed by the trader where the consumer wishes to exercise rights under the contract, including rights to terminate a contract or switch to another product or another trader;

(e) any threat to take action that cannot be legally taken.

Note

Article 8 sets out three conditions that have to be fulfilled before a commercial practice is regarded as aggressive. There must have been (i) harassment, coercion or undue influence; (ii) that significantly impairs or is likely to impair the average consumer's freedom of choice or conduct; and (iii) which causes or is likely to cause him to take a transactional decision that he would not otherwise have taken. The practice has also to be assessed in its factual context. Article 9 lists factors that have to be taken into account in assessing whether there has been harassment, coercion and undue influence.

VIII.B HARASSMENT

Harassment concerns the invasion of an individual's private space. There are extreme cases of the trader coming up to someone in the street and forcing themselves on consumers or refusing to leave a consumer's home until a contract has been signed. However, the term harassment is broader and covers many annoying trade practices, such as spam. There is a potential problem of aligning the well-meaning broad scope of this provision with the wording of Article 8 as many of these objectionable practices will not affect the consumer's transactional decision. The average consumer is simply irritated by these practices and ignores them. Some examples will be given of harassment that might be considered aggressive because of the means of communication used or the place where the practice takes place. There may be interesting debates as to whether a practice can be unfair because of the way it is carried out even if formally permitted under specific Directives.

VIII.B.1 MEANS OF COMMUNICATION

The Directive on Privacy and Electronic Communications (2002/58/EC)[137] prohibits automatic calling machines, or the sending of faxes or e-mail without prior consent. Article 13(3) of the Directive gives Member States the option with respect to other unsolicited forms of direct marketing either to introduce an opt-in system requiring prior consent or an opt-out system allowing subscribers to indicate they do not want to receive such communications. Member States disagree on whether unsolicited phone calls should be per se admissible. Under EC law, they are free to decide.

[137] Directive 2002/58/EC of the European Parliament and of the Council of 12 July 2002 concerning the processing of personal data and the protection of privacy in the electronic communications sector [2002] OJ L 201, 37–47.

Act on Data Processing and Fundamental Rights of 6 January 1978[138] **2.72 (FR)**

Article 38 Any individual is entitled, without paying charges, to refuse that his or her data be used for canvassing by the person responsible of the current or future instruction of this data.

BGH, 27 January 2000[139] **2.73 (DE)**

UNSOLICITED PHONE CALLS

Cold calling prohibited

A pre-formulated term in standard contract conditions may not be considered as a consent to be called.

Facts: The plaintiff was a registered association. Its statutory business was, inter alia, to represent consumer interests. The defendant was a credit union. It also sold insurance treaties for the R life insurance company as an agent. A female customer of the defendant signed two applications to open a savings account in autumn 1994. The pre-printed text read: 'The account/depot owner agrees/disagrees with the bank providing help in person and via telephone.' In both applications the box 'agrees' was checked. A member of staff of the defendant called the customer in November 1995 and scheduled a meeting because of a 'tax saving issue'. He offered to sign a permanent insurance with the R life insurance company during the visit. The plaintiff considered that the call violated §1 UWG because its purpose was to enter into a new business. The consent that was given in the standardised application to receive consulting in money matters would cover only telephone calls connected to banking business, not insurance issues.

Judgment: The Court of Appeal correctly assumed that a telephone call for advertising purposes in the private sector in principle infringes *bones mores* of competition and is exceptionally permissible only if the person called consented to such a call before its being made. This corresponds to the consistent jurisprudence of the Bundesgerichtshof on the limits of business telephone advertisement. This also applies to phone calls that—such as here—are the prelude to a salesman's visit. Presumed consent to the call may justify a telephone advertisement in business matters, however, not within the private sector.

The Court of Appeal's interpretation of the standardised declaration of consent of the customer has to be tested by the supreme Court of Appeals without reservation, as the general business terms are, as the Court of Appeal decided, used by all V banks nationwide.

According to §8 AGBG the clause is to be tested by reference to the measure in §9 AGBG, because it deviates from §1 UWG in the way the regulation was shaped through the courts in that telephone advertisement in the private sector is generally prohibited. Therefore, a generalising balancing that takes into account the interests of both parties has to be applied, as it is regularly conducted in representative collective redress procedures according to §13 (2) No 3 UWG and §13 (2) No 1 AGBG. According to §9 (1) AGBG regulations in general business terms are void if they discriminate against the contracting party of the user of standard business terms contrary to *bones mores*; according to §9 (2)

[138] Loi informatique et libertés.
[139] I ZR 241/97 (2000) WRP 722.

No 1 AGBG in case of doubt, this is to be applied if it does not comply with the fundamental ideas of the changed provision. This is the case here.

The disapproval of anti-competitive unrequested telephone advertisement within the private sector is based on the idea that the protection of the individual sphere enjoys priority over competitor's profit motives and that the entitled interests of the commercial economy to advertise their products does not require, it in view of the variety of the advertising methods, to enter the private sphere of the targeted consumer. After a generalising balancing under consideration of the mutual interests it is therefore inadequate especially in view of the advertising addressee's protection of privacy if applications to open a bank account contain pre-formulated declarations of customer's consent that shall enable the bank to undertake telephone advertising for conclusions of contracts in other financial matters that go beyond the contractual relation with the bank, with which the declaration of consent stands in connection. The clause remains inadequate although some authors argue on the contrary that pre-formulated declarations of consent may be always be revoked. If one affirmed this argument, the initiative to recover undisturbed privacy would be illegitimately displaced in the sphere of the affected. [references omitted]

The United Kingdom makes use of voluntary controls such as the Mailing, E-mail and Telephone Preference Services. The following is an explanation of the Telephone Preference Service.

Telephone Preference Service (TPS)[140] **2.74 (UK)**

The Telephone Preference Service (TPS) is the central opt out register on which you can record your preference not to receive unsolicited sales and marketing telephone calls to your home or mobile telephone numbers. It is a legal requirement that all organisations (including charities, voluntary organisations and political parties) do not make such calls to numbers registered on the TPS unless they have your consent to do so.

Organisations with which you have an ongoing relationship, for example those who regard you as a customer, (or in the case of charities—a donor) may well gather your consent during the early stages of your relationship with them and will therefore be entitled to call you even if your number is registered on TPS, unless you have previously told them specifically that you object to them calling you for marketing purposes.

The TPS can accept the registration of mobile telephone numbers, however it is important to note that this will prevent the receipt of marketing voice calls but not SMS (text) messages. If you wish to stop receiving SMS marketing messages, please send an 'opt-out' request to the company involved.

As TPS registration only prevents marketing calls, organisations will still be able to call you for the purposes of genuine market research.

Before you register with TPS …

It is worth reflecting on the fact that registering may well prevent you from receiving relevant and worthwhile information. For instance charities find telemarketing to be an economical way to raise awareness and much needed support.

140 Available at: www.mpsonline.org.uk.

If you are happy to receive telemarketing calls from some companies but not others, contact the companies who you do *not* wish to hear from and ask them to remove your details from their call lists. All companies—including charities and voluntary organisations—are required to respect your wishes.

The Information Commissioner's Office (ICO) is responsible for the enforcement of these regulations. Please click on the useful links page on this site for their details and for more information on this area of the law.

Note

The three regimes described represent different approaches and traditions. Article 38 of the French law on data processing establishes an opt-out system. An opt-in system (see Article L 121-20-5 Code de la Consommation) applies to the use of automated calling systems without human intervention (automatic calling machines), fax or e-mail, in accordance with Article 13 of the Directive on Privacy and Electronic Communications (2002/58/EC). Germany and Austria stick to the prohibition of cold calling. The consumers have to give their consent, otherwise the advertising is regarded as unfair. The UK relies on voluntary rules, but in essence allows cold calling. The differences between the Member States stem from different traditions and behaviour of consumers in the different countries.

VIII.B.2 PLACE: DIRECT SELLING

UCPD (2005/29/EC) **2.75 (EU)**

[Preamble] **(7)** Commercial practices such as, for example, commercial solicitation in the streets, may be undesirable in Member States for cultural reasons. Member States should accordingly be able to continue to ban commercial practices in their territory, in conformity with Community law, for reasons of taste and decency even where such practices do not limit consumers' freedom of choice.

Annex 1 Commercial practices which are in all circumstances considered unfair ...

Aggressive commercial practices

(25) Conducting personal visits to the consumer's home, ignoring the consumer's request to leave or not to return except in circumstances and to the extent justified, under national law, to enforce a contractual obligation.

Note

Is selling away from trade premises (in the home, workplace or street) to be treated as an aggressive practice, and if so under what conditions? There are no EC rules on direct selling methods, apart from contract law rules on cancellation found in the Doorstep Selling Directive (85/577/EEC) and Member States therefore have leeway on how to deal with these practices. Annex 1 No 25 explicitly confirms these reservations. Most solicitations away from trade premises will not be aggressive per se. Rather the timing, manner and nature of the practice will determine in particular instances whether the practice will be deemed to be aggressive in the circumstances.

Nevertheless for policy reasons some forms of selling away from trade premises are banned. For instance, Denmark and Luxembourg ban doorstep selling, whilst most states ban some forms of soliciting on the street.[141] Whether these rules are in compliance with the UCPD remains to be seen (see section VIII.E above).

ECJ Case 382/87, 16 May 1989[142] **2.76 (EU)**

Buet and Educational Business Services (EBS) v MinistPre Public

COMPATIBILTY OF NATIONAL CONTROLS ON DOORSTEP SELLING WITH EC LAW

Educational materials

Rules prohibiting certain selling methods can be justified.

Facts: A French law prohibiting the doorstep selling of education material was upheld as compatible with EC rules on the free movement of goods.

Judgment: 11. It is common ground that the French legislature adopted the prohibition of canvassing in question out of concern to protect consumers against the risk of ill-considered purchases. However, as the Court has repeatedly held (see in particular the judgment of 14 July 1988 in Case 407/85 3 *Glocken GmbH* [1988] ECR 4233) such rules must be proportionate to the goals pursued, and if a Member State has at its disposal less restrictive means of obtaining the same goals, it is under an obligation to make use of them.

12. In that respect canvassing at private dwellings exposes the potential customer to the risk of making an ill-considered purchase. To guard against that risk it is normally sufficient to ensure that purchasers have the right to cancel a contract concluded in their home.

13. It is necessary, however, to point out that there is greater risk of an ill-considered purchase when the canvassing is for enrolment for a course of instruction or the sale of educational material. The potential purchaser often belongs to a category of people who, for one reason or another, are behind with their education and are seeking to catch up. That makes them particularly vulnerable when faced with salesmen of educational material who attempt to persuade them that if they use that material they will have better employment prospects. Moreover, as is apparent from the documents, it is as a result of numerous complaints caused by such abuses, such as the sale of out-of-date courses, that the legislature enacted the ban on canvassing at issue.

14. Finally, it needs to be stressed that since teaching is not a consumer product in daily use, an ill-considered purchase could cause the purchaser harm other than mere financial loss that could be longer lasting. Thus it has to be acknowledged that the purchase of unsuitable or low-quality material could compromise the consumer's chances of obtaining further training and thus consolidating his position on the labour market.

[141] For instance, in relation to money loans in the United Kingdom.

[142] [1989] ECR 1235.

Note

The decisions in *Keck* and *Mithouard*[143] have added another opportunity to resist attacks on national controls on selling methods because if they affect the freedom of trade in the same manner, in law and in fact, the marketing of domestic products and products from other Member States, they will not even fall within the scope of Article 28 and therefore do not need to be justified. This was an issue in recent ECJ decisions upholding national restrictive legislation on doorstep selling in *Burmanjer*[144] and *A-Punkt Schmuckhandel*.[145] However, as the latter case, indicates it might still be necessary to consider justifications: sometimes the national rules might be found to impact differently on domestic and community rules. In doing so the level of protection afforded by EC legislation will be a relevant consideration in determining whether additional national rules are really necessary, but the ECJ seems willing to accept there are some types of selling practices that justify such national measures.

VIII.C COERCION

In combination with Article 8, Annex 1 might provide some hints as to what might be understood by coercion.

UCPD (2005/29/EC) **2.77 (EU)**

Annex 1 Commercial practices which are in all circumstances considered unfair ...

Aggressive commercial practices

(28) Including in an advertisement a direct exhortation to children to buy advertised products or persuade their parents or other adults to buy advertised products for them. This provision is without prejudice to Article 16 of Directive 89/552/EEC on television broadcasting.

(29) Demanding immediate or deferred payment for or the return or safekeeping of products supplied by the trader, but not solicited by the consumer except where the product is a substitute supplied in conformity with Article 7(3) of Directive 97/7/EC (inertia selling).

(30) Explicitly informing a consumer that if he does not buy the product or service, the trader's job or livelihood will be in jeopardy.

Notes

(1) It is clear from the wording of Article 8 that coercion can include the use of physical force, but is not limited to physical coercion. The use of violence, or the threat of violence to force someone to enter into a contract, or the more likely scenario of threatening them to extract a payment, are obvious examples of coercion. Coercion can, however, be of a psychological nature. Where this exploits a position of power it may be possible to characterise it as undue influence, but in many cases it will

[143] ECJ, 24 November 1993, Joined Cases C-267/91 and C-268/91 [1993] ECR I-6097.

[144] ECJ, 26 May 2005, Case C-20/03 [2005] ECR I-4133.

[145] ECJ, 23 February 2006, Case C-441/04 [2006] ECR I-2093.

be easier to treat these as examples of coercion in order to avoid possible arguments as to the meaning of 'position of power'. It may be possible to give 'position of power' a very broad reading which would include most consumer transactions given the natural imbalance of power between consumers and traders, but the concept must be intended to cover a narrower range of situations.

(2) Coercion must significantly impair or be likely significantly to impair the average consumer's freedom of choice or conduct. This does not mean that coercion must overwhelm the consumer. Often the consumer will have the choice of ignoring the pressure, but a practice will still be aggressive if there is significant impairment either as a direct reaction to the coercion or because the consumer calculates that it is in his interests to accept the outcome being aggressively forced upon him by the trader.

(3) Coercion is not defined, but can impliedly be understood to refer to means other than harassment used to impair the consumer's freedom of choice or conduct that do not rely on abuse of a position of power. The difficulty is that in most cases there will in theory be freedom on the consumer's part not to give in to the practice; the problem is that the consumer will in practice feel pressured or 'coerced' to act in the way the trader wants. The task for the Directive is to establish what pressure is legitimate and what is coercion. Marketing is after all about making people feel that they should buy your products.

(4) Annex 1 provides some useful examples of when the line between legitimate and illegitimate marketing may be overstepped. Thus, whilst advertising must be accepted as part of the marketplace, direct exhortations to children to buy products or persuade their parents to buy products are not allowed.[146] Of course, parents might be able to resist such pressure, but they can feel coerced. Equally, inertia selling can make consumers feel they have to buy the goods or at least be responsible for their safekeeping or return.[147] Similarly, informing the consumer that the trader's job or livelihood will be at jeopardy is viewed as coercive.[148]

(5) Categories of commercial practices that play on *emotions*, *fears* and the *exploitation of trust of third parties* will have to be reviewed according to this standard. Most cases will not be clear cut and there will have to be a concrete assessment of whether the trader has overstepped the mark of what is illegitimate. The Explanatory Memorandum to the First Proposal suggested that offering incentives such as a free bus to an out-of-town store or refreshments whilst shopping might influence consumers, but not unduly so because their ability to make an informed transactional decision would not be impaired.[149] More generally, it is argued that sales promotions could not be considered aggressive practices per se. This issue was referred to the ECJ (see section VIII.E below).

[146] Item 28, Annex I.
[147] Item 29, Annex I.
[148] Item 30, Annex I.
[149] COM [2003] 356 at 15.

VIII.D UNDUE INFLUENCE

VIII.D.1 THE DEFINITION

'Undue influence' is the only one of the three concepts within the 'aggressive practices' definition to be specifically defined in the Directive (Article 2(j)). Annex 1 blacklists some similar practices.

UCPD (2005/29/EC) **2.78 (EU)**

Article 2 (j) Exploiting a position of power in relation to the consumer so as to apply pressure, even without using or threatening to use physical force, in a way which significantly limits the consumer's ability to make an informed decision.
Annex 1 Commercial practices which are in all circumstances considered unfair ...

Aggressive commercial practices

(27) Requiring a consumer who wishes to claim on an insurance policy to produce documents which could not reasonably be considered relevant as to whether the claim was valid, or failing systematically to respond to pertinent correspondence, in order to dissuade a consumer from exercising his contractual rights ...

(30) Explicitly informing a consumer that if he does not buy the product or service, the trader's job or livelihood will be in jeopardy.

Notes

(1) It is apparent that undue influence can involve force or the threat of force. The wording in Article 2(j) 'even without ... physical' suggests that if physical force was also involved, there would certainly be undue influence. This of course makes the drafting of Article 8 perplexing, for whilst it specifically states that coercion should include the use of physical force, and above it was argued that harassment must also potentially include such violence or potential violence, it seems to suggest undue influence does not include physical force. Yet here the definition of undue influence leads to the opposite conclusion and physical force seems to be included.

(2) The fundamental questions about the undue influence concept are: what is meant by a position of power and when does conduct amount to exploitation of that position?

(3) It would be unrealistic to argue that because of the structural inequalities of the market all traders are always in a position to unduly influence consumers. The Directive's definition of undue influence undoubtedly includes situations where traders have some particular suasion over the consumer. For example, item 27 of Annex 1 refers to insurance companies requiring documents that could not reasonably be considered relevant before fulfilling their obligations. This is an example of an insurance company aggressively exploiting the vulnerable position of the consumer. In a similar vein, factors to be taken into account by virtue of Article 9 are any onerous or disproportionate non-contractual barriers imposed by the trader where a customer wishes to exercise rights under the contract.[150]

(4) Sometimes traders use psychological tools, based around the notion of 'fictive friendships' to exhort the consumer to buy in order to maintain the relationship or even assist the trader who is described as being in need of the consumer's purchase. Item 30 of Annex 1 covers situations where traders explicitly inform the consumer that their job or livelihood will be in jeopardy if they do not buy the product. This can amount to coercion. It would in common parlance be said to be a means of unduly influencing the consumer, but it may be difficult to say it is exploiting a position of power unless the relationship can be viewed as one where the consumer has become psychologically dependent on the trader.

VIII.D.2 FREE GIFTS IN THE CASE-LAW OF THE ECJ

ECJ Case 286/81, 15 December 1982[151] **2.79 (EU)**
Criminal proceedings against Oosthoek

COMPATIBILITY OF NATIONAL PROHIBITION ON SALES PROMOTION MEASURES WITH EC LAW

Oosthoek

Consumers may need protection against seemingly attractive free gifts.

Facts: The Gerechtshof (Regional Court of Appeal), Amsterdam, asked the Court of Justice whether Dutch legislation intended to restrict the freedom to offer or give free gifts within the framework of a commercial activity was compatible with Community law. Article 2(1) of that law prohibits the offering or giving of products as free gifts within the framework of a commercial activity. There are, however, several exceptions to that prohibition, in particular that provided for in Article 4(3) of the law which permits a free gift to be offered or given provided that it is usually used or consumed at the same time as all the products in respect of the purchase of which it is offered or given (a criterion usually described as related consumption or use—in Dutch *Consumptieverwantchap*), if it bears a mark which is indelible and clearly visible when it is used in the normal way and which clearly shows that it is intended for advertising purposes, and if its value does not exceed 4 per cent of the sale price of all the products with which it is offered or given.

Oosthoek marketed in the Netherlands, in Belgium and in a small part of northern France, various encyclopedias in the Dutch language, which were produced partly by Oosthoek in the Netherlands and partly by a company affiliated to Oosthoek in Belgium. In its newspaper and magazine advertisements and advertising brochures, Oosthoek had since 1974 offered a dictionary, a universal atlas or a small encyclopedia as a free gift to all subscribers to an encyclopedia. Following the entry into force of the Wet Beperking Cadeaustelsel 1977 (Act Limiting Free Gifts) and in the light of that practice, proceedings were instituted against Oosthoek in the Netherlands for infringement of that law.

Judgment: 14. As regards the restrictions on imports referred to in Article 30 [now, after amendment Article 28] of the EEC Treaty, it must be remembered that the Court has repeatedly held, since its Judgment of 20 February 1979 in Case 120/78 *Rewe* [1979] ECR 649, that in the absence of Common rules relating to Marketing, obstacles to movement within the Community resulting from disparities between national rules must be accepted in so far as those rules, being applicable to domestic products and imported products without distinction, are justifiable as being necessary in order to satisfy mandatory requirements relating, *inter alia*, to Consumer Protection and Fair Trading.

[150] Art 9(d).
[151] [1982] ECR 4575.

15. Legislation which restricts or prohibits certain forms of advertising and certain means of sales promotion may, although it does not directly affect imports, be such as to restrict their Volume because it affects marketing opportunities for the imported products. The possibility cannot be ruled out that to compel a producer either to adopt advertising or sales promotion schemes which differ from one Member State to another or to discontinue a scheme which he considers to be particularly effective may constitute an obstacle to imports even if the legislation in question applies to domestic products and imported products without distinction.

16. It is therefore necessary to consider whether a prohibition of a free gift scheme, such as that contained in the Netherlands legislation, may be justified by requirements relating to Consumer Protection and Fair Trading.

17. In that regard, it is clear from the evidence before the Court that the *wet Beperking Cadeaustelsel* 1977 pursues a twofold objective which is, in the first place, to prevent the disruption of normal competition by undertakings which offer products as free gifts or at very low prices with a view to promoting the sale of their own range of goods and, secondly, to protect consumers by the attainment of greater market transparency.

18. It is undeniable that the offering of free gifts as a means of sales promotion may mislead consumers as to the real prices of certain products and distort the conditions on which genuine competition is based. Legislation which restricts or even prohibits such commercial practices for that reason is therefore capable of contributing to Consumer Protection and Fair Trading.

19. The question raised by the National Court with regard to legislation of that kind concerns, in particular, the criterion of related consumption or use the purpose of which, in the present case, is to define the scope of one of the exceptions relaxing the rule which in principle prohibits the offering of free gifts.

20. Even though no such criterion has been incorporated in the Laws of other Member States, and in particular that of Belgium, it does not appear to be unrelated to the above-mentioned objectives of the Netherlands legislation or, in particular, to the desire to achieve market transparency to the extent considered necessary for the Protection of consumers and to ensure fair trading. Accordingly, the incorporation of such a criterion in national legislation in order to define the scope of an exception to a rule which prohibits the offering of free gifts does not exceed what is necessary for the attainment of the objectives in question.

Note

Traditional and new techniques of sales promotion, such as free gifts (bundling with sale of goods) and premiums, rebates, promotional contests and promotion games, premiums could equally come under the notion of undue influence. They play an increasing role in contemporary business practice. In *Oosthoek* the ECJ adopted a relatively generous position which left Member States leeway to restrict commercial practices. In *Familiapress*[152] it granted Austria the power to maintain its strict rules on banning particular forms of promotional games. Member States are therefore still in a position to maintain particular rules on sales promotion measures—at least with regard to premiums which are not blacklisted in the UCPD. It remains to be seen to

[152] ECJ, 26 June 1997, Case C-368/95 [1997] ECR I-3089.

what extent the UCPD sets limits to the Member States' powers in regulating sales promotion (see section VIII.E below).

VIII.D.3 NATIONAL LAWS ON SALES PROMOTIONS

The majority of Member States have adopted extensive legislation on all forms of sales promotion measures. Belgium and France seem to be particularly strict.

Trade Practices Act **2.80 (BE)**

Article 54 A joint offer exists, in the meaning of the present article, when the acquisition—free or not—of goods, services or any other advantages, or of documents which entitle to goods, services or other advantages, is linked to the acquisition of other goods or services, even of identical goods or services.

Apart from the exceptions listed below, any joint offer to the consumer is prohibited. Any joint offer to the consumer made by several sellers acting with a common intention is also prohibited.

Article 55 It is allowed to jointly offer, for a global price:

1. Goods or services constituting a whole; The King may, on proposition of the competent Ministers and of the Finance Minister, indicate the financial services that constitute a whole;

2. Identical goods or services, if:

a) each product or service may be acquired separately at its usual price in the same establishment;

b) the buyer is clearly informed of this possibility, as well as of the unit price of each product and service;

c) the potential discount offered when buying the whole of the products or services does not exceed one third of the added up prices.

Article 56 It is allowed to offer for free, with a principal product or service:

1. the accessories of a principal product, especially adapted to this product by its manufacturer and delivered with the principal product to extend or facilitate its use;

2. the packaging or the containers used to protect the goods, taking the nature and the price of these goods into account;

3. small goods and services accepted by trade custom as well as the delivery, the installation, the control and the maintenance of the goods sold;

4. samples from the stock of the manufacturer or the distributor of the principal goods, if they are provided in the quantity or size strictly needed to test the qualities of the good;

5. chromolithographs, stickers and other images of minor trade value;

6. legally authorised lottery tickets;

7. goods with permanent and clearly apparent advertisement inscriptions, which cannot be purchased, if they do not cost the offeror more than five per cent of the price of the principal product or service which they come with.

Article 57 It is also allowed to offer for free, with a principal product or service:

1. Documents entitling to acquire an identical product or service, if the discount does not exceed the percentage in article 55(2);

2. Documents entitling to advantages mentioned in article 56(5) and (6);
3. Documents only entitling to a discount in cash, if:
a) they mention the cash amount they represent;
b) in the establishments where the goods and services provided are sold, the rate or the amount of the discount is clearly indicated, as well as the goods or services which acquisition allows to receive these cash discount documents.
4. Documents entitling to, after the acquisition of a certain number of goods or services, a free offer or a discount on the acquisition of a similar or identical product or service, if this advantage is conceded by the same distributor and does not exceed one third of the price of the goods or services previously acquired.
The documents must mention their maximum period of validity, if any, as well as the conditions of the offer.
When the seller interrupts the offer, the consumer must get the promised advantage in proportion to his or her actual purchases.

Note

There is a general prohibition on premiums in Belgium. Article 54 Trade Practices Act sets out the general prohibition, Articles 55–57 Trade Practices Act formulate a number of exceptions to the prohibition. Tying is only allowed if the trader can invoke one of the exceptions mentioned in these articles. In view of the limited scope of the exceptions of Article 55ff, the prohibition of Article 54 renders many fidelity schemes impossible. That is why the two articles have been subject to constant litigation. The two rules form the background to the reference before the ECJ (see under section VIII.E below).

Consumer Code (Code de la consommation) **2.81 (FR)**

Article L 121-35 All sales or offers for sale of goods or any provision or offer to provide services made to consumers and giving entitlement, free of charge, immediately or at the end of a fixed period, to a bonus consisting of products, goods or services, unless these are identical to those forming the subject of the sale or the service provision, are prohibited. This provision does not apply to small objects or low value services or samples.

Article L 121-36 Written sales promotions which are likely to engender hope of gain for each of the participants, whatever the procedures of random selection, may only be used if they do not require any financial consideration or outlay whatsoever from participants. The entry form must be separate from any purchase order for goods or services.

Article L 121-41 Organisers of the promotions defined in the first paragraph of article L 121-36 who have failed to adhere to the conditions required by this section shall be punished with a fine of €37,500. The court may order its decision to be published, at the expense of the convicted party, by any appropriate means. In the event of a particularly serious breach, it may order the decision to be sent to all persons solicited by said promotions. Where the court orders the decision to be displayed on a poster, this is carried out in accordance with the conditions and subject to the penalties provided for by article 131-35 of the Penal code.

[Specific rules apply to authorised *lotteries*, ie, to those which do not require any financial consideration or outlay from participants:]

Article L 121-37 The documents presenting the sales promotion must not be likely to engender confusion with an administrative or banking document made out in the name of the addressee or with an informative press article.

They must include a legible inventory of the lots which may be won specifying, for each one, their nature, their exact number and their commercial value.

They must also reproduce the following wording: 'Rules governing the promotion will be sent, free of charge, to anyone who asks for them'. They must, in addition, specify the address to which this request may be sent as well as the name of the public officer with whom said regulations have been lodged in application of article L 121-38.

Article L 121-38 The sales promotions rules as well as a copy of the documents sent out to the public must be lodged with a public officer who checks that they are in order. The above rules must be sent, free of charge, to anyone who requests them.

Note

Despite its extensive rules French law has been confronted with a kind of sweepstake which is not specifically regulated by the Code de la Consommation: an organiser sends to many people a document indicating that they have won a prize or that they have a great chance winning a prize in a forthcoming sweepstake. But, of course, this is not true, and the document always comes along with a proposal to buy some products or services. The Cour de Cassation ruled that such a practice constitutes misleading advertising in the sense of Article L 121-1 Code de la Consommation. But this does not offer any remedy to the persons abused, who have been led to believe that they had won a prize. Courts, including the Cour de Cassation, have explored several paths in order to enable the victims to obtain compensation from the organisers. Civil liability was a possibility (Article 1382 Civil Code), but if the courts apply this provision, the victim cannot claim the full prize which had been promised to him. Another possibility would be to recognise the existence of a contract between the organiser and the victim, or the existence of a unilateral undertaking, according to which the organiser is bound to deliver the prize, but this solution has finally been discarded as being a fiction, since the organiser's intention is precisely *not* to give the prize to the victim. After some hesitation, the Cour de Cassation finally resorted to the notion of '*quasi-contrat*'. It discovered a new *quasi-contrat*, unheard of in the Code civil, according to which

> the organiser of a sweepstake who informs a denominated person of a gain without making clear the existence of a chance, obliges himself, because of this purely voluntary fact, to deliver this gain.[153]

[153] Cass ch mixte, 6 September 2002, Bull ch mixte No 4, (2002) D 2963, note D Mazeaud ; JCP (E) No 1687, note G Viney.

VIII.E NATIONAL SALES PROMOTION LAW AND THE SCOPE OF UCPD

The original idea of the European Commission was to supplement the envisaged EC rules on unfair commercial practices by a separate regulation on sales promotion. That is why on the very same day, 2 October 2001, the Commission published two documents: the Green Paper on Consumer Protection[154]—which paved the way for the Directive 2005/29/EC—and the Proposal for a Regulation on Sales Promotion in the Internal Market.[155]

The draft regulation was originally based on a problem-related approach, thereby heavily relying on the Green Paper on Commercial Communication.[156] Eight forms of sales promotion are subject to regulation:[157] (i) simple price reductions; (ii) quantity discounts; (iii) coupons and vouchers; (iv) free gifts, ie gifts offered unconditionally on sale; (v) premiums considered to be offers other than discounts which are provided to the consumer once the latter has ordered or bought the promoted product or service; (vi) promotional contests involving questions to consumers, the answer to which require certain skills; (vii) promotional games, where the winner is designated by chance and where no payment is required to participate; and (viii) promotional games, where the winner is designated by chance and where no payment nor obligation to buy is required to participate. In the meantime, the European Commission has withdrawn the proposal.[158] However, the question remains to what extent the UCPD (2005/29/EC) which is meant fully to harmonise commercial practices regulation within its scope covers sales promotion measures as well.

Stuyck, Terryn and Van Dyck are underpinning the far-reaching problems which result from the failure of the draft regulation on sales promotion.

J Stuyck, E Terryn and T Van Dyck, Confidence through Fairness?[159] **2.82 (EU)**

7. The UCPD in the broader legal context: its relationship with other Community Acts, contract law and international private law.

Although the *Green Paper on European Union Consumer Protection*—which eventually led to the UCPD—and the Proposed Regulation on Sales Promotions were published on the same day, the relationship of the UCPD with the Proposed Regulation is a very uneasy one. In the Green Paper, the framework directive was presented as a safety net to cover practices where cross-border restrictions are identified and which fall outside the coordinated fields of the sector-specific directives. The Proposed Regulation then seems to be regarded as a sector specific initiative and a complement to such a

[154] COM [2001] 531 final.

[155] COM [2001] 546 final.

[156] COM [1996] 192 final.

[157] Communication on Sales Promotions, COM [2001] 546 final, 4.

[158] Outcome of the screening of legislative proposals pending before the Legislator COM [2005] 462 final (27 September 2005).

[159] Stuyck, Terryn and van Dyck, above n 76, 141.

framework directive. Although the Commission stressed the need to ensure overall coherence in a consumer protection system based on a mixed approach (a framework directive and sector specific directives), this consistency is lacking. Not only is the scope of application different—the Proposed Regulation does not exclude B2B practices—there is also a lack of consistency in the definitions and terminology used. It will be difficult to apply both instruments at the same time (for instance, the unconditional prohibition in the Proposed Regulation to limit the value of a sales promotion can be in conflict with the notion of appreciable impairment of the consumer's ability to make an informed decision of the UCPD). Even more importantly, the total harmonisation nature of the UCPD seems to suggest that Member Sates have lost the competence to regulate methods of sales promotion beyond the application of rules implementing the Directive ... In this respect, the Proposed Regulation's aim to force Member States to abolish certain restrictions on sales promotions may have become redundant.

As mentioned above, many other directives exist in the field of fair trading law which have dealt with i.a. distance selling, doorstep selling, misleading advertising, timesharing etc. In case of conflict, those directives take precedence for the specific aspects regulated therein. Article 3(4) merely spells out the more general '*lex specialis derogat legi generali*' principle, which is well-known at EC level. An important proviso to this principle was, however, made in the original Proposal. Although the specific directives would take precedence over the current Directive, according to the Commission, Member States would no longer be able to use the minimum clauses to impose additional requirements in the harmonized field. This would have meant that the adoption of a total harmonisation framework directive would lead to the transformation of the more specific directives from minimum harmonisation into total harmonisation directives, without much debate or in-depth discussion. This approach was no longer followed in the UCPD as finally adopted. Article 3(5) now provides for a temporary derogation and allows Member States to continue to apply national provisions within the harmonised field which are more restrictive or prescriptive than this Directive and which implement directives containing minimum harmonisation clauses for a period of six years from 12 June 2007. This derogation can possibly be prolonged. The derogation is in our opinion to be welcomed. Although the transformation of the minimum harmonisation consumer protection directives into total harmonisation directives is—and should be—on the agenda, this discussion should take place in the process of a substantive revision of these existing Directives. This transformation should definitely not be achieved through the backdoor.

By the time the question of whether and to what extent the Directive fully harmonised sales promotion measures seems to be most debated within the new regime. The first case ever brought to the ECJ deals with Belgian law that puts heavy restrictions on sales promotion measures:

ECJ Case 261/07 and C-299/07, 23 April 2009[160] **2.83 (EU)**
Galatea BVBA v Sanoma Magazines Belgium NV and VTB-VAB v Total Belgium

FULL HARMONISATION OF SALES PROMOTION MEASURES

VTB-VAB

The UCPD does not allow a Member State to maintain a per se prohibition of combined offers.

Facts: See above 2.38 (EU).

Judgment: 51. … it must first be recalled that the Directive is intended to establish, in accordance with recitals 5 and 6 in the preamble thereto and Article 1 thereof, uniform rules on unfair business-to-consumer commercial practices in order to contribute to the proper functioning of the internal market and to achieve a high level of consumer protection.

52. Thus, the Directive fully harmonises those rules at the Community level. Accordingly, as Article 4 thereof expressly provides and contrary to the assertions of VTB and the French Government, Member States may not adopt stricter rules than those provided for in the Directive, even in order to achieve a higher level of consumer protection.

53. Next, Article 5 of the Directive provides that unfair commercial practices are to be prohibited and sets out the criteria on the basis of which practices are to be classified as being unfair. …

56. Annex I to the Directive also establishes an exhaustive list of 31 commercial practices which, in accordance with Article 5(5) of the Directive, are regarded as unfair 'in all circumstances'. Consequently, as recital 17 in the preamble to the Directive expressly states, these are the only commercial practices which can be deemed to be unfair without a case-by-case assessment under the provisions of Articles 5 to 9 of the Directive.

57. Finally, it should be noted that combined offers are not included in the practices listed in Annex I to the Directive.

58. It is therefore in the light of the content and the general scheme of the provisions of the Directive noted in the preceding paragraphs that the questions referred by the national court must be examined.

59. In that regard, clearly, by establishing a presumption of unlawfulness of combined offers, national legislation such as that at issue in the main proceedings does not meet the requirements of the Directive.

60. In the first place, Article 54 of the 1991 Law lays down the principle that combined offers are prohibited, notwithstanding the fact that such practices are not referred to in Annex I to the Directive.

61. As has been pointed out in paragraph 56 of the present judgment, that annex exhaustively lists the only commercial practices which are prohibited in all circumstances and accordingly do not have to be assessed on a case-by-case basis.

62. Thus, the Directive precludes the system implemented by Article 54 of the 1991 Law in so far as that article prohibits, generally and pre-emptively, combined offers without any verification of their unfairness in the light of the criteria laid down in Articles 5 to 9 of the Directive.

[160] ECJ, 23 April 2009, Joined Cases C-261/07 and C-299/07, nyr.

63. Next, by operating in that manner, a rule of the type at issue in the main proceedings runs counter to the content of Article 4 of the Directive, which expressly prohibits Member States from maintaining or adopting more restrictive national measures, even where such measures are designed to ensure a higher level of consumer protection.

64. Finally, it should be added that such an interpretation cannot be called into question by the fact that the 1991 Law provides, in Articles 55 to 57 thereof, for a number of exceptions to that prohibition of combined offers.

Note

The ECJ fully accepted the argumentation of the Attorney General. The hidden message behind the judgment is that Member States have to raise their voice in the Council if they do not agree to the proposal of the European Commission. They are barred from referring to the history of the Directive which might shed light on particular rules of the Directive; here the original idea of two competing projects, one devoted entirely to sales promotion measures. The ECJ takes the full harmonisation principle seriously. To this extent, it is not at all surprising that the Directive will become the battlefield for all sorts of national sales promotion measures which reach beyond the few rules set out in the Annex to the Directive.

CONCISE BIBLIOGRAPHY

A Bakardjieva Engelbrekt, *EU and Marketing Practices Law in the Nordic Countries—Consequences of a Directive on Unfair Business-to-Consumer Commercial Practices* (Report for the Nordic Council of Ministers Committee on Consumer Affairs, 2005), www.norden.org/konsum/sk/rappdownload.asp.

G Howells and S Weatherill, *Consumer Protection Law*, 2nd edn (Aldershot, Ashgate, 2005).

G Howells, H-W Micklitz and T Wilhelmsson, *European Fair Trading Law* (Aldershot, Ashgate, 2006).

H-W Micklitz and J Keßler, *Marketing Practices Regulation and Consumer Protection in the EC Member States and the US* (Baden-Baden, Nomos-Verlag, 2002).

J Stuyck, E Terryn and T van Dyck, 'Confidence through fairness? The new Directive on unfair Business to Consumer Commercial Practices in the internal Market' (2006) *Common Market Law Review* 141.

T Wilhelmsson, 'Unfair Commercial Practices Law: The Cultural and Social Dimension' (2006) 44 *Osgoode Hall Law Journal* 461.

CHAPTER THREE
CONSUMER CONTRACT LAW

This chapter starts with a general introduction that explains the role of consumer law in the ongoing process of harmonisation of contract law at EU level (section I) and then deals with formation of contract (section II) and information duties (section III). The chapter discusses general contract law issues but naturally focuses on their relevance to consumer contracts. Chapter 4 deals with issues that are more consumer-specific (rights of withdrawal and standard terms). Chapters 5 and 6 will focus on specific contracts.

I. CONSUMER PROTECTION AND THE EVOLUTION OF EUROPEAN CONTRACT LAW

I.A THE EMERGING EU CONTRACT LAW: TOWARDS A 'COMMON FRAME OF REFERENCE'

I.A.1 EUROPEAN COMMISSION COMMUNICATIONS 2001–03

After several years during which European Parliament proposals 'on an effort to harmonise the Private Law of the Member States' were not directly included on the political agenda of the Community institutions, the European Commission set about analysing and debating its Communication on 'European Contract Law' of 11 July 2001[1]. While the Resolutions of the European Parliament of 26 May 1989 and 6 May 1994[2] called for the elaboration of a 'Common European Code of Private Law', the European Commission, in its 2001 Communication, focused exclusively on contract law; in particular, the Commission sought to broaden the debate and proposed four

[1] COM [2001] 398 final, 13 September 2001, OJ C 255.

[2] EP Resolution A2-157/89, 26 June 1989, OJ C 158 and EP Resolution A3-0329/94, 25 June 1994, OJ C 205.

possible alternatives: (1) no action on the part of the European Community (convergence through market competition); (2) promotion of common non-binding principles; (3) the improvement of existing legislation; or (4) the approval of a detailed legislative instrument (opt-in or opt-out).

In view of the resulting debate, during which options (2) and (3) received most support, the Commission published another Communication on 'A More Coherent European Contract Law. An Action Plan' on 12 February 2003, in which it announced various measures (financial promotion of research, creation of a standard database of contract terms—later apparently discarded or postponed, etc), including the original decision to create a type of 'Code' or 'Restatement' on general contract law, enigmatically entitled a 'Common Frame of Reference' (CFR). Although the Commission has always maintained a policy of calculated ambiguity on the structure, form, validity and purposes of this text, its content aims to

> provide clear definitions of legal terms, fundamental principles and coherent model rules of contract law, drawing on the EC acquis and on best solutions found in Member States' legal orders.[3]

Moreover, in addition to sales, services and other contracts, it aims to incorporate

> general rules on the conclusion, validity and interpretation of contracts, as well as performance, non-performance and remedies should be covered as well as rules on credit securities on movable goods and the law of unjust enrichment.[4]

The subject matter thus extends far beyond the scope of the existing consumer protection directives, although these are, in turn, related to types of contracts and phases of contracts already regulated sectorially in these directives. In designing the CFR, the Commission has taken advantage of the academic experience offered by different research groups in this area.

I.A.2 ACADEMIC PROJECTS AS INPUT FOR FUTURE HARMONISATION

CFI (5th Chamber) Case T-333/03, 16 November 2006[5] **3.1 (EU)**
Masdar (UK) Ltd v European Commission

STUDY GROUP RULES AS A SOURCE OF LAW?

Benevolent intervention in another's affairs

The negotiorum gestio civil action can only be used very exceptionally to claim liability according to the principles common to the laws of the Member States and the principles of European law.

[3] EU Commission's Communication of 11 October 2004 (The Way Forward) COM [2004] 651, 3.

[4] COM [2003] 68 final. A more detailed list of issues (which largely coincide with the structure and content of the PECL) can be found in Appendix I of the 2003 Communication (The Way Forward) COM [2004] 651.

[5] [2006] ECR II-04377, but appeal brought on 2 February 2007 by Masdar, OJ C-82/20.

Facts: The case concerned a claim for payment by the Commission of services supplied by a sub-contractor.

Judgment: 89. According to the Commission, the civil action based on *negotiorum gestio* is not intended to deal with a situation in which a sub-contractor does work pursuant to a contract for the benefit of a third party. The Commission refers to the articles prepared in October 2003 by the Study Group on a European Civil Code concerning the Principles of European Law on Benevolent Intervention in Another's Affairs. Those articles exclude liability at the outset 'where the intervener is under a duty to a third party to act'. In this case, since the applicant was simply performing its obligations under its contract with Helmico, the *negotiorum gestio* type of liability is excluded without more. ...

100. Similar reasoning may also be used to rule out the application of the principles of the *negotiorum gestio* civil action which, according to the general principles common to the laws of the Member States, lends itself only very exceptionally as a means to establish liability on the part of the public authorities in general, and more particularly in the factual and legal context of this action. The conditions governing the civil action based on *negotiorum gestio* are manifestly not satisfied.

Tribunal Supremo (Supreme Court), 31 October 2006[6] **3.2 (ES)**
Tomás and Almudena v Casimiro and María Milagros

SALE OF AN ALREADY SOLD FLAT IS NON-PERFORMANCE THAT ALLOWS TERMINATION?

Principles of European Contract Law (PECL) to the rescue of the deceived buyer

The claim to terminate a contract requires that non-performance must be essential and this is a standard established in international provisions (such as the PECL) which are used to integrate the Civil Code.

Facts: Tomás and Almudena concluded a private sale-purchase contract and, shortly before the envisaged date for execution of the corresponding public deed, they discovered that the property to which the contract pertained was affected by a lawsuit instigated by third parties seeking to establish another public deed on the same property by virtue of another supposed verbal sale agreement concluded with the same sellers. In these circumstances, unknown to the buyers Tomás and Almudena, the other buyers considered that the sellers had breached the agreement and called for termination of the contract and double the amount paid as compensation, as established in the penalty clause contained in the contract. The proceedings focused on the possibility of terminating the contract (Article 1124 of the Civil Code) instead of other less drastic measures, such as payment deferral (Article 1502), until the question of the double sale was resolved, as occurred five months later.

Judgment: This trend, as declared by the Spanish Supreme Court on 5 April 2006, complies with the criteria on non-performance contained in the United Nations Convention on Contracts for the International Sale of Goods [CISG], of 11 April 1980 (ratified by Spain via the corresponding Instrument on 17 July 1990); Article 25 of the aforementioned Convention classifies contractual non-performance as essential (by virtue of which the buyer may declare a contract terminated: Article 49), stating that Article 8:103 of the Principles of European Contract Law has the same purpose, according to which non-performance of the obligation is essential. ...

[6] (2006) RJ 8405.

The criterion established in a conventional international provision contained in our legal code and also reflected in a document formulating the legal principles integrating the so-called *lex mercatoria* common to the different legal systems, insofar as they reflect and attempt to order, in order to develop uniform rules, the practice to be adopted in supra-state commercial relations, must be used to integrate Article 1124 CC pursuant to the obligation to interpret that article in accordance with the social reality in which it is applied.

Notes

(1) Efforts to promote the elaboration of the CFR are based fundamentally on the results of two research groups financed by, among other institutions,[7] the European Commission: (a) the Study Group on a European Civil Code,[8] created in 1998 and co-ordinated by Professor von Bar. This group succeeded the Lando-Commission, created in 1980, and, in addition to reviewing and updating PECL rules, proposes new 'model rules' in other areas of contract law and property law; (b) the 'Acquis Group' ('European Research Group on Existing EC Private Law'),[9] founded in 2001 and co-ordinated by Professor Schulte-Nölke, aims to develop coherent principles drawn exclusively from EU legislation and case-law. The group applies these principles, rules and common terminology (published at the end of 2007) to co-operate in the simplification, improvement and coherence of the *acquis communautaire* (the total body of EU law) in contract matters, mainly in EC consumer law. In addition to these two groups, which reflect the dichotomy of issues involved in the elaboration of genuine European contract law (contract law in general, on the one hand; and consumer contract law, on the other), other European research networks have been established with different methodologies and objectives, such as the Academy of European Privatists in Pavia, the Trento Group on the 'Common Core of European Private Law' (comparative law studies without proposing uniform rules), SECOLA (Society of European Contract Law), etc. These academic studies are not just useful for constructing an official European contract law, they also aspire (especially the studies that propose rules or principles) to achieve a certain degree of spontaneous convergence, inspiring national and international courts and national legislators, providing guidance to contracting parties and contributing to the teaching of European private law. Incipient influence has been achieved in recent years in this area, as shown in the two judgments cited.

(2) The Spanish judgment, one among more than 20 along the same lines, illustrates a nascent and pioneering tendency of certain national tribunals to use the PECL or the work of the Study Group on a European Civil Code (as exemplified by the judgement handed down by the European Court of the First Instance) with one of the following two objectives: either to support or strengthen principles or rules contained in national legislation or in jurisprudential criteria on legal institutions not

[7] All the groups belonging to the so-called Joint Network on European Private Law, financed with the Sixth Framework Programme of the European Union, are listed at http://www.copecl.org/.

[8] See information and drafts in http://www.sgecc.net/.

[9] See http://www.acquis-group.org.

regulated by law; or to integrate or fill gaps in the Civil Code or national laws.[10] See also in *Hamilton v Volksbank Filder eG*,[11] where A-G Poires Maduro (paragraph 24) cites a future Draft Common Frame of Reference (DCFR) to support time limits for the exercise of a right (in a doorstep contract with a consumer) as being a 'principle common to the law of the Member States'. This type of reference to the PECL, the DCFR or similar initiatives, as an argument to support judgments, is evident in the case-law of other countries, such as the judgment handed down by the Lithuanian Supreme Court on 6 November 2006 or the judgment issued by the Tribunal of Padova (Italy) on 10 January 2006[12] (which mentions Article 7:101(1)(B) PECL). A third reason for tribunals to use the PECL could even be considered. This would be riskier and would favour spontaneous harmonisation, consisting in the use of these types of soft law principles to contradict or correct a national legal rule or consolidated case-law. This has recently been exemplified in numerous English judgments, based on the UNIDROIT Principles of International Commercial Contracts (and on the CISG), questioning the previously solid doctrine that prior negotiations (pre-contractual dealings) cannot be used to interpret a contract under English Law.[13]

(3) It is worth bearing in mind that these English judgments and the Spanish judgment transcribed above both mention the CISG and the PECL or UNIDROIT Principles. Two aspects must be considered in this context: (i) respect for the use of soft law as a means for integrating or completing (and not just interpreting) national jurisdiction—as a harmonisation or spontaneous convergence factor—and tribunals take special care to justify, for this delicate task, the use of the CISG, which is also national law (ratified international convention), unlike the other Principles, Restatements or Model Laws, which do not form part of national legislation; and (ii) while the CISG or UNIDROIT Principles deal with business-to-business (B2B) contracts, in contrast, the PECL (or the rules of the Study Group or the future CFR of the European Commission) encompass not just business-to-business relations but also business-to-consumer (B2C) contracts. This gives the latter texts additional value for use in case-law in order to create an effective consumer contract law in the European Union, beyond the approved Directives, based on the exemplary value of certain academic texts or, where appropriate, texts approved by the European Commission with no direct legal validity.

I.A.3 THE COMMON FRAME OF REFERENCE ('CFR'), 2007–09

Ever since the announcement by the European Commission of the creation of the CFR in 2003, the *legal nature* of this instrument has been extremely ambiguous: originally, it was assumed that the CFR 'is an intermediate step towards improving

[10] See MP Perales Viscasillas, 'La aplicación jurisprudencial en España de la Convención de Viena de 1980 sobre compraventa internacional, los principios de Unidroit y los Principios de Derecho Contractual Europeo: de la mera referencia a la integración de lagunas' (31 May 2007) *La Ley* 6725, 1ff.

[11] ECJ, Case C-412/06 *Hamilton v Volksbank Filder eG* [2008] ECR I-02383.

[12] Judgments referred to in the text of MP Perales Viscasillas, above n 10.

[13] See Court of Appeal (Civil Division) of 17 February 2006, *Proforce Recruit Ltd v The Rugby Group Ltd* [2006] EWCA Civ 69 (No 57) [per Arden LJ] and Court of Appeal (Civil Division), *The Square Mile Partnership Ltd v Fitzmaurice McCall Ltd* of 18 December 2006 [2006] EWCA Civ 1689.

the quality of the EC *acquis* in the area of contract law'.[14] Moreover 'the Commission considers at this stage that the CFR would be a non-binding instrument. However … this question might be raised again.'[15] Additionally, it has repeatedly affirmed that the

> CFR is intended to be a 'toolbox' or a handbook for the Commission and the EU legislator to be used when revising existing and preparing new legislation in the area of contract law … to provide clear definitions of legal terms, fundamental principles and coherent modern rules of contract law.[16]

However, together with this primary objective, which falls within the scope of the competences of the Community legislator, certain official declarations suggest that the European Commission may have other, more ambitious objectives for the CFR, including 'other possible roles' (similar to those to which the above-mentioned soft law texts previously aspired): 'national legislators could use the CFR when transposing EU directives' or 'when enacting legislation on areas of contract law which are not regulated at Community level'; the CFR could be used in arbitration; or 'would be likely to serve as the basis for the development of a possible optional instrument'; the CFR 'based on EC *acquis* and on best solutions identified as common to Member States contract laws, could inspire the European Court of Justice when interpreting the *acquis* on contract law'.[17] As can be seen, the Commission dreams of making the CFR a factor for achieving latent or indirect harmonisation.

However, in terms of the *issues contained* in the CFR (see section I.A above), the Commission continues to be more restrictive than the Parliament would like; the latter

> strongly supports an approach for a wider CFR on general contract law issues going beyond the consumer protection field [and] underlines that, besides the work on revision of the consumer *acquis*, the work on a wider CFR should go on … taking into account the fact that the final long-term outcome could be a binding instrument.[18]

In terms of the proposed *form* of the CFR, the design was based on the texts with rules and comments provided by the 'Joint Network on European Private Law' (which integrates the above-mentioned research groups). These rules are critically examined by the CFR-net, which is comprised of stakeholders and practitioners (no academics) who contribute their practical experience. Expert representatives from the Member States are also consulted regularly. The research groups submitted a first 'Draft' of the CFR (the DCFR)[19] at the end of 2007 and a final draft at the end of

[14] COM [2003] 68 final, para 53.

[15] COM [2004] 651 final, 5.

[16] COM [2007] 447 final, 10–11; EU Commission, *Second Progress Report on The Common Frame of Reference*, 25 July 2007.

[17] COM [2004] 651 final, 5.

[18] EU Parliament Resolution on European Contract Law, September 2006, P6_TA(2006)0352, paras 3–5. See also Resolution of 23 March 2006, P6_TA(2006)0109.

[19] Study Group on a European Civil Code and Acquis Group, *Draft Common Frame of Reference (DCFR). Principles, Definitions and Model Rules of European Private Law* (München, Sellier, 2008 and final outline edition 2009).

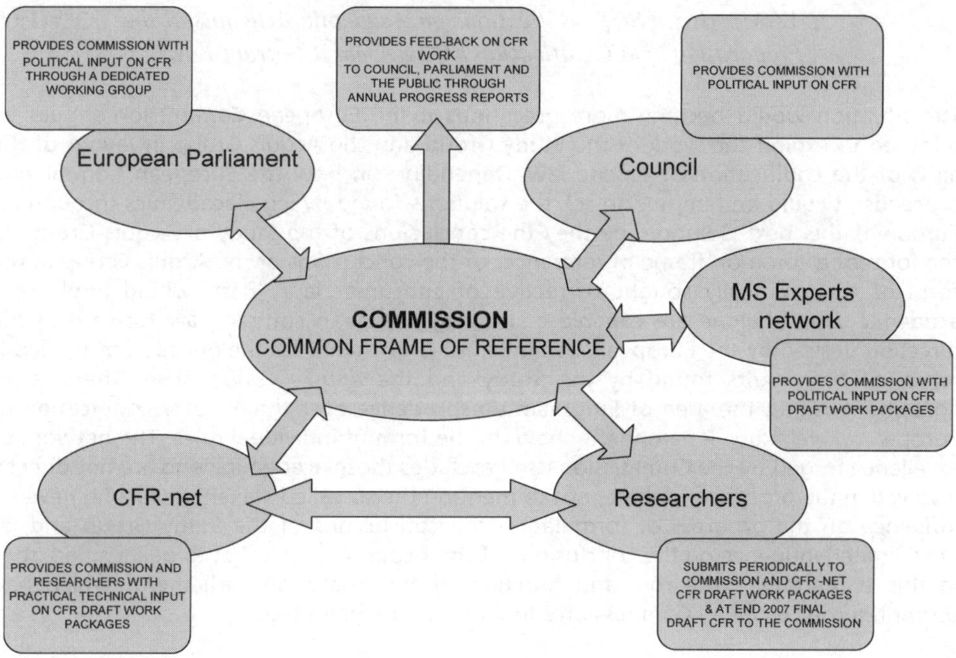

Figure 3.1

2008. The Commission will take this draft, without being bound by it, and will modify it by selecting 'very carefully the parts of this draft that correspond to the common legislative objectives'. After this selection and consultation process, 'the Commission could submit its approach in the form of a White Paper'.[20]

Figure 3.1 shows the complex network created to provide the CFR with scientific authority, practical guarantees, representativeness and legitimacy.[21]

The CFR's relationship with the 'optional instrument' that was also announced has yet to be defined; this was another measure contained in the 2003 Action Plan and the Commission was unsure whether to approve it as a Regulation or a Recommendation.[22] Interest in this instrument, resulting from an idea to encode private law that was on the agenda in 2001 and 2003, has gradually diminished in recent years and is no longer a priority.

[20] COM [2007] 447 final, 10. See also COM [2004] 651 final, 12.

[21] Figure included in COM [2007] 447 final, 12.

[22] See COM [2003] 68 final, paras 89–97 on the various hesitations of the Commission on the shape, content, scope of application (consumers, transnational contracts, mandatory rules?) of this 'optional instrument'.

H-W Micklitz, (Self-) Reflections on Academic Attempts at the Preparation of a Codification of European Contract Law[23] **3.3 (EU)**

The situation would become more precarious if the European Commission should be tempted to exploit the work of the Study Group and the Acquis Group in favour of the aims of the codification of private law. Depending on how the European Commission proceeds, it could be tempted to sell the solutions found by legal academics throughout Europe as the 'best' solution, be they the conclusions of the Study or Acquis Group, in the form of a common frame of reference, or the conclusions of the Acquis Group in the form of the politically sought corrective of consumer law. 'Best' would imply that academic experts alone are capable of moving European contract law forward in the direction desired by the European Commission. Only then does the question of the legitimacy of the results found by the Study and the Acquis Group arise. There is no agreement within the area of European jurisprudence over the 'if' of a codification of European private law, let alone the 'how' in the form of individual rules. The network of excellence forged by the Commission itself excludes those academics who are not directly involved in the process of debate, not to mention the so-called stakeholders who have no influence on the progress of formulating the conclusions of the Study Group and, at best, limited influence on the conclusions of the Acquis Group ... Yet to be included at all in this scenario are the role and function of the European Parliament, which had prompted the European Commission's initiative in the first place.

R Zimmermann, European Contract Law: General Report[24] **3.4 (EU)**

It is widely felt that there is too little real transparency. And there is widespread uncertainty about what the Commission really wants. *If* it ultimately envisages an optional code that can be chosen by businesses in cross-border transactions I would say: There is no real need for it. After all, we have CISG and the UNIDROIT Principles of International Commercial Contracts. *If* the Commission thinks that it has to unify contract law in order to remove trade barriers within the internal market, it will have to change gear and adopt the strategy of full harmonization. The consequences would, ultimately, be a European Contract Code enacted by way of regulation. The Commission has, however, repeatedly and emphatically denied that it intends to codify European contract law. *If* the Commission wants to increase consumer confidence, and ensure a decent level of consumer protection across the Union, it should do so in so many words and not hide that intention behind Art 95 EC Treaty. The Commission should continue to use the vehicle of the Directive and it should continue to pursue the path of minimum harmonization. *If* the law in the field of consumer contract law has become messy and incoherent, the Commission should engage in a tidying-up exercise. No voice has been raised against that specific project and against the plan to prepare a consolidated consumer law Directive, as envisaged in the Green Paper [see below, I.B.3]. The opportunity should then, however, be taken to do what the Green Paper says it wants to do: to revise and not merely to rearrange the consumer *acquis*.

[23] '(Selbst-)Reflektionen über die wissenschaftlichen Ansätze zur Vorbereitung einer europäischen Vertragsrechtskodifikation' (2007) GPR 1, 2ff, 14-15.

[24] 'European Contract Law: General Report' [2007] EuZW 15, 462.

I.A.4 THE EUROPEAN CIVIL CODE IN THE BACKGROUND

Numerous aspects reveal the initial interest of Community institutions in the approval of a type of 'European Civil Code' or European Contract Law Code to strengthen the internal market rather than simply to provide protection to consumers. This is shown by the Parliament's Resolutions, the name of the Study Group, whose work would serve as a basis for the CFR, its consideration as a type of 'pre-code',[25] or the plan to develop an 'optional instrument'; the British House of Lords has even described the CFR as 'a Trojan horse for a future European Civil Code'.[26] However, opposition from different sectors to the idea of a Private Law Code has prompted the European Commission recently to insist on denying its 'intention to propose a "European Civil Code" which would harmonise contract laws of Member States'[27] and to also insist that the purpose of the CFR 'is not a large scale harmonisation of private law or a European Civil Code'.[28]

I.B CONSUMER PROTECTION DIRECTIVES

I.B.1 A FRAGMENTED APPROACH

After a long period of specific consumer directives (1984–2001), a new phase was inaugurated in 2001, which has been defined by the redrafting and systematisation of consumer regulations in the quest for an internal market with a more organic and coherent common law. This phase is characterised by interaction between consumer regulations and the creation of a new European Contract Law; the 'diagnostic' stage (defects, incoherencies, needs) of this phase is reaching its conclusion[29] and will imminently make way for new legal measures.

However, the Member States are currently governed by the transposition of existing directives included in the previous phase. The core of the *acquis communautaire* of consumer contract law comprises the following rules:

(a) eight consumer directives currently under review—six on pure contact law: Doorstep Selling Directive,[30] Package Travel Directive,[31] Unfair Contracts Terms

[25] E Hondius, 'Towards a European Civil Code' in A Hartkamp et al (eds), *Towards a European Civil Code*, 3rd edn (Nijmegen/Den Haag, Kluwer Law International, 2004) 13.

[26] House of Lords, *European Union Twelfth Report Session 2004–5 European Contract Law—The Way Forward?* para 62ff, as quoted by G Howells, 'The Scope of European Consumer Law' (2005) 1 *ERCL* 368. As for a critical examination of the content of the DCFR (also with opposition even to an optional instrument based on it), see House of Lords, *European Union Twelfth Report Session 2008–2009 European Contract Law; The Draft Common Frame of Reference* [HL Paper 95] 10 June 2009.

[27] COM [2004] 651, 8.

[28] COM [2007] 447 final, 11.

[29] COM [2004] 651 final, 4 (The Way Forward) and COM [2006] 744 final, 8 February 2007.

[30] Council Directive 85/577/EEC of 20 December 1985 to protect the consumer in respect of contracts negotiated away from business premises [1985] OJ L 372, 31–33.

[31] Council Directive 90/314/EEC of 13 June 1990 on package travel, package holidays and package tours [1990] OJ L 158, 59–64.

Directive,[32] Timeshare Directive,[33] Distance Selling Directive,[34] Consumer Sales Directive;[35] plus Price Indication Directive[36] and Injunctions Directive.[37]

(b) Three more Directives on pure consumer law with certain special characteristics compared to previous directives,[38] and which reveal certain potential features of the current phase: Distance Selling of Financial Services Directive,[39] Unfair Commercial Practices Directive[40] and Consumer Credit Directive.[41]

(c) Various Directives applicable to both consumer and business relations, and which also provide protection for the weak party; hence proposals have been presented for its inclusion, instead of consumer law, in a general 'Customer Law', 'Business Law' or 'Market Law', such as, for example, the Directives on advertising, e-commerce or insurance.

With all these regulations in view, the aim is to cover the harmonisation 'deficit' with initiatives to achieve a coherent European Contract Law. Moreover, the harmonisation 'surplus' is to be improved through refinement and simplification. On the shortcomings of the current Community patrimony, with respect to consumer law, namely the insufficiencies of the directive as a harmonising instrument and the weaknesses of the system created by these directives, see chapter 1.IV above.

[32] Council Directive 93/13/EEC of 5 April 1993 on unfair terms in consumer contracts [1993] OJ L 95, 29–34.

[33] Directive 94/47/EC of the European Parliament and the Council of 26 October 1994 on the protection of purchasers in respect of certain aspects of contracts relating to the purchase of the right to use immovable properties on a timeshare basis [1994] OJ L 280, 83–87, repealed by Directive 2008/122/EC of the European Parliament and of the Council of 14 January 2009 on the protection of consumers in respect of certain aspects of timeshare, long-term holiday product, resale and exchange contracts [2009] OJ L 33, 10-30.

[34] Directive 97/7/EC of the European Parliament and of the Council of 20 May 1997 on the protection of consumers in respect of distance contracts [1997] OJ L 144, 19–27.

[35] Directive 99/44/EC of the European Parliament and of the Council of 25 May 1999 on certain aspects of the sale of consumer goods and associated guarantees [1999] OJ L 171, 12.

[36] Directive 98/6/EC of the European Parliament and of the Council of 16 February 1998 on consumer protection in the indication of the prices of products offered to consumers [1998] OJ L 80, 27–31.

[37] Directive 98/27/EC of the European Parliament and of the Council of 19 May 1998 on injunctions for the protection of consumers' interests [1998] OJ L 166, 51–55.

[38] Ie *maximum harmonisation* in distance selling of financial services, unfair commercial practices and consumer credit; *horizontal approach* or 'Framework Directive' in the case of unfair commercial practices.

[39] Directive 2002/65/EC of the European Parliament and of the Council of 23 September 2002 concerning the distance marketing of consumer financial services and amending Council Directive 90/619/EEC and Directives 97/7/EC and 98/27/EC [2002] OJ L 271, 16–24.

[40] Directive 2005/29/EC of the European Parliament and of the Council of 11 May 2005 concerning unfair business-to-consumer commercial practices in the internal market and amending Council Directive 84/450/EEC, Directives 97/7/EC, 98/27/EC and 2002/65/EC of the European Parliament and of the Council and Regulation (EC) 2006/2004 of the European Parliament and of the Council (Text with EEA relevance) [2005] OJ L 149, 22–39.

[41] Directive 2008/48/EC of the European Parliament and of the Council of 23 April 2008 on credit agreements for consumers and repealing Council Directive 87/102/EEC [2008] OJ L 133, 66–92.

I.B.2 TOWARDS A NEW COMPREHENSIVE APPROACH: GREEN PAPER OF 2001 AND COMMUNICATION OF 2004 (REVISION OF THE ACQUIS)

The transition from the former phase to the current one could be defined by three characteristics that are today at the core of the debate:

(i) The creation of framework directives or horizontal directives, whose scope of application is uniformly superimposed on existing consumer-related directives (see the Green Paper on EU Consumer Protection of October 2001[42] and its result, the Unfair Commercial Practices Directive (2005/29/EC), Articles 3.5 and 18).

(ii) The change from minimum harmonisation to maximum harmonisation in which the Member States cannot increase the level of protection of the directive (see chapter 1, sections I.E and IV above).

(iii) Review of the existing *acquis* to achieve greater coherence and to update and simplify consumer directives. This review was identified as an absolute priority in the Commission's document entitled 'European Contract Law and the Revision of the Acquis: The Way Forward'.[43] Proposals and reports were presented for the review of eight consumer directives. One of the first results is the so-called 'EC Consumer Law Compendium', which is a public database on the *acquis*, including national legislation and case-law, a bibliography and a comparative analysis of the implementation of the directives in practice; it has been available online since December 2006[44] and may also be a useful tool to further the teaching method propounded by these Casebooks, since it contains references to many judgments handed down by national tribunals, translated into various languages, on the application of the consumer directives.

I.B.3 THE GREEN PAPER ON THE REVIEW OF THE CONSUMER ACQUIS AND THE PROPOSAL FOR A DIRECTIVE ON CONSUMER RIGHTS[45]

This document represents a definitive commitment to the modernisation, simplification, improvement and extension of consumer protection provided by existing directives. Therefore, these 'are being reviewed as a whole and individually to identify regulatory gaps and shortcomings'. Different modern factors that were not taken into account when the Consumer Directives were approved will be given special consideration for review, namely the following: e-commerce, the impact of copyright, technological advances in the market (digital services, such as music download; new channels of transaction, such as online auctions—see the case-law, below in this chapter; software excluded from the scope of the Consumer Sales Directive (99/44/EC), etc).

The Green Paper of 8 February 2007 considers the possibility of adopting a 'vertical approach', consisting in a separate directive-by-directive approach or of adopting a 'mixed approach' ('horizontal instrument combined, where necessary,

[42] COM [2001] 531.

[43] 11 October 2004, COM [2004] 651. Absolute priority, relegating any other progress in general Contract Law that is not relevant for the review of the Consumer *acquis*, was declared more categorically in subsequent documents, such as in the Second Report Progress on the CFR, COM [2007] 447 final, 2.

[44] www.eu-consumer-law.org.

with vertical action'), thus revealing its preference for the latter. The Commission argues that the directives share various common aspects (notion of consumer/professional, length of cooling-off periods, the modalities for the exercise of the right of withdrawal, etc), which could be regulated jointly in a single instrument. Its structure could be divided into a general part, which would include the Unfair Commercial Practices Directive (2005/29/EC) and these horizontal concepts, and a specific part dealing with contracts of sale. Finally, the Green Paper considers different questions (similar to those that could be considered parallel to the CFR), such as its territorial scope of application (only to transnational or also to national transactions or operations or only to distance purchases?) or the desirable degree of harmonisation (minimum or maximum?), as well as different questions regarding specific modifications to the existing directives. For the time being, a Proposal for a Directive on Consumer Rights has been published (8 October 2008)[46] which purports to replace several Directives—on consumer sales, unfair terms, doorstep and distance contracts—and includes a general part with definitions, information duties and rules on the right of withdrawal. The Proposal adopts a maximum harmonisation approach.

I.B.4 A 'EUROPEAN CONSUMER CODE' IN THE BACKGROUND?

Although the latest European Commission declarations only suggest, as immediate measures, the review of eight Consumer Directives (taking into account the rules on general contract law envisaged in the CFR) and an eventual horizontal 'Framework Directive', on general matters of consumer law (a Proposal for a Directive on Consumer Rights is currently on the table), other aspects could point to the existence of a hypothetical European Consumer Code based on the existing revised *acquis*. The shift since 2004 towards the prioritisation of redrafting consumer law or declarations on its content in the Proposed Directive on services of 2004[47] (which is declared to be 'coherent with the revision of the *acquis* in respect of consumer protection, including the move towards full harmonisation, notably in the area of contract law') or the ambitious reference to the fact that the '*consolidation, codification and recasting* of existing instruments, focused on transparency and clarity, will have to be considered where appropriate',[48] suggest the possibility of such a 'codification', with the features of a truly coherent system. *Quid iuris* if there is a European Consumer Code and a (real or watered-down) European Civil Code? Should they be kept separate or is recasting or harmonising existing instruments preferable?

[45] COM [2006] 744 final.
[46] COM [2008] 614, 3.
[47] 5 March 2004, COM [2004] 2 final/3, 16.
[48] COM [2003] 68 final (Action Plan) para 77, where these three concepts are defined.

I.C CO-ORDINATION BETWEEN EUROPEAN CONTRACT LAW AND EUROPEAN CONSUMER LAW? QUESTIONS AND TRENDS

This evolution, presented as a dichotomy of scopes that have alternately been drawn closer and pulled further apart in the *desiderata* of the Community institutions, reveals the difficulties involved in harmonising private law on a larger scale. The core of the debate is whether or not the rules protecting consumers should be kept separate from the general rules in the law of obligations and contract law. Increasingly, doctrine maintains that the construction of a future European private law necessarily requires a review of the underlying values and ideologies of the legal rules on contract law[49] (currently different from the liberal nineteenth-century ideas on which many national contract laws are based). In this connection, various authors argue that the purposes of 'solidarity', the 'redistribution of wealth', the creation of a real 'social contract law' or the 'protection of contractual fairness' ('party protection'), so present in consumer law, should pervade any future European contract law (even in B2B relations):[50] the principle of 'freedom of contract' should not enjoy a pre-eminent position above the principle of protection of the weak party. However, other authors argue that it is preferable to keep the scopes of consumer contract law and general contract law completely separate.[51] As can be seen, the choice of one legislative technique or the other (Consumer Protection Code, Civil Code or Restatement-CFR incorporating consumer regulations) is not purely formal but rather may have deep axiomatic fundamentals and consequences.

Study Group on Social Justice in European Private Law, Social Justice in European Contract Law: A Manifesto[52] **3.5 (EU)**

Why should the principle of freedom of contract have such a privileged position, so that proposals for constraint must satisfy the heavy burden of proof that they can be justified with good reasons? Why not reverse the burden, so that those who wish to deregulate market transactions should have the burden of explaining the potential advantages to be gained by the parties to these transactions from the absence of mandatory rules? These

[49] As a summary, see M Hesselink (ed), *The Politics of a European Civil Code* (Den Haag, Kluwer Law International, 2006).

[50] Eg B Lurger, *Vertragliche Solidarität* (Nomos, Baden-Baden, 1998); B Lurger, *Grundfragen der Vereinheitlichung des Vertragsrechts in der Europäischen Union* (Wien, Springer Verlag, 2002); B Lurger, 'The "Social" Side of Contract Law and the New Principle of Regard and Fairness' in Hartkamp et al (eds), *Towards a European Civil Code*, 3rd edn (Antwerpen, Kluwer Law International, 2004) 273ff; T Wilhelmsson, *Social Contract Law and European Integration* (Ashgate, Aldershot, 1995); T Wilhelmsson, 'Consumer Law and Social Justice' in Ramsay (ed), *Rethinking Consumer Law in the Global Economy* (1997), also in T Wilhelmsson, *Twelve Essays on Consumer Law and Policy* (Helsinki, 1996) 191ff. There are also voices against this: F Gómez Pomar, 'European Contract Law and Economic Welfare: A View from Law and Economics' (2007) 1 *Indret* 1ff, available at www.indret.com.

[51] In this sense, Howells, above n 26, 369 and 372: 'Consumer Law has developed to meet the particular social concerns of consumer protection. The danger must be that if these are universalised there will be a tendency to water them down so that they are acceptable also in business-to-business transactions.'

[52] Study Group on Social Justice in European Private Law, 'Social Justice in European Contract Law: A Manifesto' (2004) 10(6) *ELJ*, 653ff, 663–664 and 667.

are indeed the deeper questions raised by the agenda for constructing a European contract law, but they are not questions ever raised in the Commission's agenda set by the *Action Plan*. By its fleeting reference to such questions, the Commission implicitly acknowledges that they are present, but clearly it has no desire to initiate any debate about them. …

The values of negative integration and competition were never intended to provide an exhaustive scheme of social justice for a market order. They should not be used now as the exclusive determinative foundations for a consensus of values underpinning European contract law.

Questions

(1) What are your views on the fundamental question posed by this excerpt?

(2) How will existing consumer protection rules be incorporated in the CFR?

(3) Are the Study Group and Acquis Group truly co-ordinated in this sense?

(4) Is coherence (codification) an intrinsic value in this process or should the pure opportunity and effectiveness of diverse rules be prioritised (sectorial fragmented approach)? Maximum/minimum harmonisation?

(5) Is it preferable to separate or recast consumer rules and general contract rules?

(6) Should a future horizontal directive on consumer law (the so-called 'mixed approach') go further and integrate all consumer contract law rules into an organised instrument? Does the Proposal for a Directive on Consumer Rights play this role? Which are the main innovations contained in this text as compared with the former directives?

II. FORMATION OF CONTRACT

II.A INTRODUCTION: NON-NEGOTIATED CONTRACTS WITH CONSUMERS

L Cavalaglio, Formation of contract[53] **3.6 (IT)**

With subtle rhetoric refinement, not absent of the intellectual mood of *èpater les bourgeois*, there have been attempts to frame the modern methods of acquiring goods and services (in supermarkets, in TV-shopping, in telecommunication exchanges) into the category of 'exchange/trade without agreement' (*scambi senza accordo*): it has been contended that it is not possible to do without the presence of a *dialogue* between the parties in the definition of the contractual agreement … which is substituted with other tools, easier to foresee, faster and more functional to fulfil the exchange. …

It is said that the phenomena described in Articles 1341 and 1342 of the [Italian] Civil Code [which govern standard contract terms] are the first step towards sacrificing the

[53] L Cavalaglio, *La formazione del contratto. Normative di protezione ed efficienza economica* (Milano, Giuffrè, 2006) 120–21.

freedom represented by the dialogue on the altar of market efficiency and they mark 'the fall of the *homo loquens*', who would find himself overwhelmed by the physical aspect of things (and definitively substituted by the *homo videns*) when acquisitions in supermarkets or, even worse, in television or electronic networks are brought to mind.

Notes

(1) All European jurisdictions share the view that the consensus or *agreement* on which contracts are based is reached by an offer made by one party (the offeror) followed by its acceptance by the other party (the offeree). This traditional approach to the formation of agreement is confirmed in the context of consumer contracts by a handful of rules scattered across some EC consumer Directives and by some statements of the ECJ.[54] Given that the rules governing offer and acceptance purport to apply generally to all contracts and not just to some,[55] the following pages will emphasise only how the particular needs of consumer protection affect the operation of the rules of offer and acceptance.

(2) At first sight, B2B and B2C contracts are not very different in this respect, but there is at least one major difference: in most (but not all) consumer contracts there is *no negotiation phase at all*. This means that some problems specific to contracts concluded between similar categories of contractor *inter pares* (trader to trader or individual to individual), such as letters of intent, a purported acceptance which differs from the offer (the so-called 'battle of forms') or the restrictive interpretation of public statements, are simply not encountered in the consumer context. Moreover, means by which to conclude contracts that are widely used by consumers, notably when concluded electronically via the internet, must comply with the 'mirror image' rule (according to which there must be an exact correspondence between offer and acceptance); this avoids the problems otherwise encountered in terms of counter-offers. This being the case, the *Casebook on Contract Law* should be consulted for materials dealing with these aspects of contract formation.

(3) As Malaurie and Aynès put it, nowadays a great number of massive non-negotiated contracts are concluded without prior contractual dealings. In some extreme cases, such as sales by automatic distributors, a new label has been created: the so-called *réification* of the contract, which gives the impression that the contract is not concluded with a person but with a machine, as is apparently the case for the sale of goods in a shop at a fixed price, or with a train ticket for a fixed price.[56]

[54] See s 2(1) and 9(2) of the Distance Selling Directive (97/7/EC), Art 9(2) of the Distance Selling of Financial Services Directive (2002/65/EC) and Art 7(1) of the Consumer Sales Directive (99/44/EC). In ECJ case-law, see *Rudolf Gabriel* judgment (C-96/00, paras 48ff: the parties' agreement gives rise to 'reciprocal and interdependent obligations') and *Francesco Benincasa* judgment (C-269/95, para 29 referring to 'consensus formed between the parties'). Those sources are quoted, for instance, in the '*Acquis Principles*' (München, Sellier, 2007) I, 129 to ground similar rules to Art II—4:201 DCFR quoted in the text.

[55] E McKendrick, *Contract Law* (Oxford, Oxford University Press, 2003) 52, although 'the supposed universality of these rules is, in itself, a source of difficulty.'

[56] P Malaurie, L Aynès and P Stoffel-Munck, *Les obligations*, 2nd edn (Paris, Defrénois, 2005) 227.

II.B OFFER

II.B.1 THE CONCEPT OF AND REQUIREMENTS FOR AN OFFER ('OBJECTIVE' ELEMENTS)

DCFR **3.7 (EU)**

Article II.—4:201: Offer

(1) A proposal amounts to an offer if:

(a) it is intended to result in a contract if the other party accepts it; and

(b) it contains sufficiently definite terms to form a contract.

(2) An offer may be made to one or more specific persons or to the public.

(3) A proposal to supply goods from stock or a service at a stated price made by a business in a public advertisement or a catalogue, or by a display of goods, is treated, unless the circumstances indicate otherwise, as an offer to supply at that price until the stock of goods, or the business's capacity to supply the service, is exhausted.

Notes

(1) The *concept* of an 'offer'—defined as an expression of willingness to contract on specified terms made with the intention that it is to become binding as soon as it is accepted by the person to whom it is addressed—is widely used in many national case-laws.[57] However, while there is also a well-established distinction between 'offer' on the one hand and 'invitation to treat' or 'preliminary dealings' (*offre*, *pourparlers*, *promesse*, etc) on the other, this distinction is applied differently in certain types of situation depending on the jurisdiction in question (see below on the treatment of advertisements, the display of items in a shop with a price indication, etc). An agreement in the sense of the meeting of offer and acceptance can be reached with or without preliminary dealings (unilateral imposition of the contract/offer).

(2) The concept of an 'invitation to treat', which is mainly used in the context of proposals to the public at large, resorts to the idea of public statements so as to justify the assertion that the real offer is sent by a consumer to the trader who made the previous statement: the consumer's reply is not treated as an acceptance of an offer, but rather as an offer which the professional may choose to accept or reject. This is supported by the traditional approach in most Member States that an offer must be addressed to one or more specific persons, whereas a declaration addressed to the public is treated as an invitation to make an offer (*invitatio ad offerendum*). Nevertheless, even under this traditional approach there are exceptions (such as an announcement of a reward which is considered to be an offer despite being addressed to the public) and over the last few years there has been a tendency in the courts of

[57] [England] *Storer v Manchester CC* [1974] 1 WLR 1403 (*ex* Treitel, below n 98, 8); [Belgium] Hof van Cassatie (Court of Cassation), 23 September 1969 (1971) RCJB 216 (with emphasis added in the fact of containing all essential elements in the offer); [Spain] Tribunal Supremo (Supreme Court), 2 February 1990, RJ 199052; [Germany] see EA Kramer, in K Rebmann and F Säcker (eds), *Münchener Kommentar zum BGB*, 4th edn (München, Beck, 2000) §146, 6–9.

some Member States to treat proposals to the public in general as offers.[58] EU consumer law also tends to make these exceptions to the traditional approach the new rule and paradigm so as to protect consumers (see Article 3 of the Package Travel Directive (90/314/EC) and Articles 2(2)d, 2(4) and 6 of the Consumer Sales Directive (99/44/EC); see also its special treatment in the Unfair Commercial Practices Directive (2005/29/EC) and further references in chapter 2.V.C above)

(3) As can be seen from comparative law studies[59] and from Article II 4:201 DCFR and Article 4:103 of the 'Acquis Principles' (both using similar wording to the PECL), there are at least two elements necessary for a proposal to amount to an offer: an intention to be bound and the supply of information on its essential elements (it must be 'sufficiently definite').[60]

II.B.2 INTENTION TO BE BOUND AND CONSUMER DIRECTIVES WHICH REQUIRE CLARIFICATION OF A PARTY'S INTENTION

DCFR **3.8 (EU)**

Article II—4:102: How intention is determined

The intention of a party to enter into a binding legal relationship or bring about some other legal effect is to be determined from the party's statements or conduct as they were reasonably understood by the other party.

Distance Selling Directive (97/7/EC) **3.9 (EU)**

Article 4 (2) The information referred to in paragraph 1, the commercial purpose of which must be made clear, shall be provided in a clear and comprehensible manner in any way appropriate to the means of distance communication used, with due regard, in particular, to the principles of good faith in commercial transactions, and the principles governing the protection of those who are unable, pursuant to the legislation of the Member States, to give their consent, such as minors.

Electronic Commerce Directive (2000/31/EC)[61] **3.10 (EU)**

Article 6 Information to be provided ...

58 O Lando and H Beale, *Principles of European Contract Law. Parts I and II* (The Hague, 1999) 161–63; P Møgelvang-Hansen, 'The Binding Effects of Advertising' in R Schulze, *New Features in Contract Law* (München, Sellier, 2007) 175.

59 Eg AT Von Mehren, 'The Formation of Contracts' in AT Von Mehren (ed) *International Encyclopedia of Comparative Law* (Tübingen/Dordrecht, Nijhoff, 1992) 25ff; RB Schlessinger (ed), *Formation of contracts* (New York, Oceana, 1968); A Farnsworth, 'Comparative Contract Law' in M Reimann and R Zimmermann, *The Oxford Handbook of Comparative Law* (Oxford, Oxford University Press, 2006) 915.

60 Both requisites also in Art 14 CISG, which describes 'sufficiently definite' as 'if indicates the goods and expressly or implicitly fixes or makes provision for determining the quantity and the price'.

61 Directive 2000/31/EC of the European Parliament and of the Council of 8 June 2000 on certain legal aspects of information society services, in particular electronic commerce, in the Internal Market [2000] OJ L 178, 1-16.

(a) the commercial communication shall be clearly identifiable ...

(c) promotional offers, such as discounts, premiums and gifts, where permitted in the Member State where the service provider is established, shall be clearly identifiable as such, and the conditions which are to be met to qualify for them shall be easily accessible and be presented clearly and unambiguously.

Note

Some EU consumer directives impose an obligation to indicate the existence of an 'offer' when it is addressed to a consumer (or to indicate its 'commercial purpose' while excluding the classification of 'offer').[62] Here, the established aim is one of transparency.

Cass civ 2e, 11 February 1998[63] **3.11 (FR)**
Fonvieille v France Direct Service (FSD)

OFFER AND UNILATERAL PROMISE

False reward becomes true

The appearance of an unambiguous winning of a prize must be deemed a contractual agreement that binds the offeror.

Facts: After sending an order to FSD (a distance seller), Mme Fonvieille received official notice that she had won FRF 250,000 in a ballot organised by that company. The winner tried unsuccessfully to obtain this prize. She claimed against FSD.

Judgment: Considering the argument that a mail order company that organises competitions can only be required to uphold a contractual agreement to pay a fixed sum if the firm and clear offer of payment of this amount does not contain any ambiguity or terms and conditions; that the Court of Appeal had announced in its judgment of 18 October 1995 and after having conducted a full analysis of the letter sent by FSD on 25 March 1992, that Mme Fonvieille was only presented as a potential winner of the prize of FRF 250.000, which she would have to share with other winners, and that the letter was only a 'notification of the possibility of participating in a competition to win FRF 250.000', and that she could only receive the prize money 'if your personal number is recognised as the winning one,' which constitutes a violation of Articles 1134 and 1147 of the Civil Code;

Whereas, since the judgment states that it can be necessarily deduced from the positive and unambiguous terms employed by the company FDS that this company sought to lead its customer to believe that she had won the promised sum, and that the company could not have been mistaken about the extent of the implications of the letter, which were clear;

Considering that, from the above findings and considerations, and without contravening the arguments raised, the Court of Appeal was able to conclude that because of the meeting of both wills, the company FSD was bound to its contractual agreement, accepted by Mme Fonvieille, to pay the latter the promised sum of FRF 250.000.

[62] On the value of a term excluding the qualification of 'offer' to a commercial communication, when the content requisite suffices, see below.

[63] Bull civ II 55.

Cass Ch mixte, 6 September 2002[64] **3.12 (FR)**
Union fédérale des consommateurs Que Choisir (UFC) v Maison Française de Distribution

OFFERS/PROMISES AS QUASI-CONTRACTS

Prize won or pure sweepstake participation?

The organiser of a sweepstake, who announced a gain to a consumer without specifying the gain is only an eventuality, is committed by his own voluntary act to deliver what he promised.

Facts: Mr X received from a professional distance seller (Maison Française de Distribution) two documents in which he was nominated in big letters and with his own name as the winner of FRF 105,750, with the promise of immediate payment if he sent an attached document within a certain period. Mr X did so, but the seller never replied nor paid. Mr X sued the trader on the ground of misleading advertising (confusion between a consolidated winning and participation in a sweepstake). The consumer association Que Choisir (UFC) claimed the payment of FRF 100,000 as compensation in the collective interest of consumers.

Judgment: In light of Article 1371 of the Civil Code;

Considering that quasi-contracts are purely voluntary acts of man which lead to an obligation to a third party;

Considering that, in order to obligate the company to pay Mr X a fixed sum of money in damages, the judgment maintains that by announcing in positive terms what was only a possible eventuality, the company committed a non contractual fault since it created the illusion that Mr X had won a large amount of money, and the judgment also maintains that the damages could not correspond to the amount that Mr X had envisaged winning.

That by thus deciding, whereas the organiser of a sweepstake that informs a particular person that he or she has won a prize without indicating that this announcement carries no guarantee is obliged by his own voluntary action to deliver on his promise, the Court of Appeal violated the aforementioned text.

Court of Appeal, 1982[65] **3.13 (UK)**
Lambert v Lewis

LACK OF INTENTION TO BE BOUND BY ADVERTISEMENTS

Foolproof towing hitches

Full safety of a product in any context stated in written advertising cannot be understood as a binding promise, an offer or a warranty.

Facts: Manufacturers of towing hitches had claimed in advertising leaflets that their towing hitches were foolproof and required no maintenance. The claimants argued that these statements had been made

[64] (2002) D 2963 note D Mazeaud; JCP(E) No 1687 note G Viney.
[65] [1980] 2 WLR 289, reversed on different grounds [1982] AC 225.

seriously and with the intention that they would be relied on. The Court of Appeal agreed with the defendants' argument that there was insufficient evidence of an intention to create a contract.

Judgment: [Stephenson LJ] But the difficulty is to show that what the manufacturers stated in the literature advertising and accompanying their products as to their safety and suitability was intended to be a contractual warranty or binding promise. It is one thing to express or imply it in a contract of sale, another to treat it as expressed or implied as a contract, or a term of a contract, collateral to a contract of sale. ... In *Carlill v Carbolic Smoke Ball Co* [1893] 1 QB 256, this court had no difficulty in holding that the suppliers of the ball made a binding promise to pay GBP 100 to any users of the ball on the stated conditions if it failed to prevent them from getting influenza. Their statement that they had deposited GBP 1.000 with a bank showed that their statements were not a mere 'puff' but a sincere promise ... . That case is no authority for holding that the manufacturers were saying to the retailers: 'If you acquire our product we promise it is safe and merchantable and if it is not we will pay you such damages as the law requires.'

A statement relating to the marketed product may be more than a puff and less than a warranty: it may be so important that it may induce a contract, may now amount to a negligent misrepresentation, and may nearly amount to a warranty: *Howard Marine and Dredging Co Ltd v A Ogden & Sons (Excavations) Ltd* [1978] QB 574 ... But whether the statement is oral or written, made contemporaneously with the contract or earlier, the question is whether it is intended to be binding. When it is written, as here, we doubt if parol evidence of the intention of the person who made it is admissible, though here admitted without objection, but the intention must, we think, be inferred from the construction of the writings against the background of all the circumstances. The construction of these documents in the circumstances of this case leads us to the same conclusion as the judge, that the claims in them 'were not intended to be, nor were they acted upon as being express warranties, and' (though this further finding, if it adds anything, is not strictly necessary) 'the retailers did not purchase the coupling in reliance on such warranties'.

Court of Appeal, 25 November 1995[66] **3.14 (UK)**
Bowerman v Association of British Travel Agents Ltd (ABTA)

INTENTION TO BE BOUND BY A NOTICE

Who pays for my failed travel?

A notice displayed before contracting must be construed as the average reader would and therefore an intention to be bound (offer) could be found in the form of an enforceable promise.

Facts: ABTA travel agents displayed a notice in their offices with this wording: 'Where holidays or other travel arrangements have not yet commenced at the time of failure [of the tour operator], ABTA arranges for you to be reimbursed the money you have paid in respect of your holiday arrangements.' Ms Bowerman, who had booked a holiday with an ABTA tour operator which became insolvent, claimed that this notice constituted a contractual offer by ABTA to those who booked their holidays through an ABTA agent to protect them financially should the agent go out of business. ABTA denied this and relied on *Carlill* (see below).

[66] [1996] CLC 451.

Judgment: [Waite LJ] The central issue in this appeal is whether the ordinary member of the public, reading the notice as a whole, would regard it as intended to create legal relations between ABTA and those who buy tours or holidays through its members … . In the end this case depends, as with so many questions involving construction of a document, upon impression—in this instance an impression gained by the court at one remove through the eyes of the hypothetical member of the public … My own view is that the notice—notwithstanding the bewildering miscellany it contains of information, promise, disclaimer and reassurance would be understood by the ordinary member of the public as importing an intention to create legal relations with customers of ABTA members. The words that are crucial to the present case [see facts] would in my judgment be understood by the ordinary reader as words of clear promise which do not lose their significance or their promissory character through being associated in the same context with words connoting a lesser degree of commitment. I would allow the appeal and substitute for the order made by the judge a declaration in the terms prayed that ABTA is obliged to reimburse to the plaintiffs the cost of providing insurance cover for the lost holiday with Adventure Express.

[Hobhouse LJ] … Whether it contains an offer, whether it is sufficiently clear to be legally enforceable, and whether it discloses an intention to enter into legal relations, all depend upon the evaluation of what is said in this written document. … In my judgment this document is intended to be read and would be reasonably be read by a member of the public as containing an offer of a promise which the customer is entitled to accept by choosing to do business with an ABTA member. A member of the public would not analyse his situation in legal terms but he would clearly understand that this notice would only apply to him if he should choose to do business with an ABTA member and he would also understand that if he did do so he would be entitled to hold ABTA to what he understood ABTA to be promising in this document. In my judgment it satisfies the criteria for a unilateral contract and contains promises which are sufficiently clear to be capable of legal enforcement. The principles established in the Carbolic Smoke Ball case apply. The plaintiffs are entitled to enforce the right of reimbursement given to them in para 5.

This conclusion also covers ABTA's further argument that it had no intention to create legal relations. The document as reasonably read by a member of the public would be taken to be an offer of a legally enforceable promise. Given that this is the effect of the document which ABTA has chosen to publish, it does not advance ABTA's case to say that ABTA privately did not intend to expose itself to any legal liability to the public. It suffices that ABTA intentionally published a document which had that effect. A contracting party cannot escape liability by saying that he had his fingers crossed behind his back.

Notes

(1) In this set of judgments different approaches to the same problems can be seen, even within the same jurisdiction. The first problem deals with the significance of *unilateral promises* and their possible classification as 'offers' with binding effect from the standpoint of the intention of the promisor to be bound by his public statement. A usual context in which this theory is developed is found in rewards and promised winnings in sweepstakes or lotteries. Some countries recognise the binding nature of these kinds of promises, as is the case in Germany (for rewards or *Auslobungen*; see §661a BGB), in Nordic law (where the so-called *Løfte-teori* or promise

theory applies) and in England (only in a restrictive way for those kinds of reward which need no acceptance to be binding on the offeror, as in *Carlill* below). Article 4:109(1) ACQP tries to follow this view: 'A valid unilateral promise or undertaking is binding on the person giving it, if it is intended to be legally binding without acceptance.'

(2) The example of French law shows the difficulties of classifying such public rewards from the point of view of the requisite of the intention to be bound. The technique of ambiguous sweepstakes (some of which are regulated in the French Consumer Code, Article L 121-36/41) is analysed in chapter 2, section VIII.D.3, where further references are given.

(3) The second problem refers to the wider field of advertisements and public statements made before the contract is concluded relating to the quality or characteristics of goods or services. The test of an intention to be bound by those statements becomes crucial, as shown in the two English cases mentioned. General approaches to the value of advertisements differ depending on national legal systems: according to English law and German law they are invitations to treat (with a few exceptions which will be seen later in this chapter), whereas for French law they are normally regarded as offers as long as they contain information on all essential elements of the contract (a certain thing at a fixed price) and there is an intention to be bound.

Questions

(1) In cases of rewards and apparently won sweepstakes, how many legal techniques to guarantee the consumer's position can you identify?[67] Do all of them achieve the same results, ie full recognition of the price for the consumer?

(2) According to the ECJ case-law (on jurisdiction over consumer contracts according to the Brussels I Regulation 44/2001), what is the legal nature of the communication of prizes apparently won? Do the different facts in the cases justify a qualification of those communications as giving rise to contractual or non-contractual liability? Contrast the reasoning of the ECJ in the following judgments: *Ilsinger* (Case C-180/06 of 14 May 2008), *Engler* (Case C-27/02 of 20 January 2005) and *Gabriel* (Case C-96/00 of 11 July 2002) (see chapter 8 below).

(3) To determine the existence of a genuine intention to be bound by an offeror, should we use an 'objective test' (ie using only the external manifestation to check whether the *declared* intention was as anyone would understand it) or should we use a 'subjective test' (proving the genuine internal intention of the offeror and how the addressee actually understood it)? What are the pros and cons of either test? You must take into account the fact that there is no uniform approach to a subjective/objective test on intention in the different jurisdictions.[68] Do you share the reasons underlying the test used by the DCFR?

[67] See eg unfair commercial practice no 31 of the Annex I in Unfair Commercial Practices Directive (2005/29/EC).

[68] See for explanation, J Cartwright, *Contract Law. An Introduction to the English Law of Contract for the Civil Lawyer* (Oxford/Portland, Hart Publishing, 2007) 86ff.

Some directives have an effect on the legal qualification of advertisements or public statements.

Package Travel Directive 90/314 **3.15 (EU)**

Article 3(2) When a brochure is made available to the consumer, it shall indicate in a legible, comprehensible and accurate manner both the price and adequate information concerning:

(a) the destination and the means, characteristics and categories of transport used;

(b) the type of accommodation, its location, category or degree of comfort and its main features, its approval and tourist classification under the rules of the host Member State concerned;

(c) the meal plan;

(d) the itinerary;

(e) general information on passport and visa requirements for nationals of the Member State or States concerned and health formalities required for the journey and the stay;

(f) either the monetary amount or the percentage of the price which is to be paid on account, and the timetable for payment of the balance;

(g) whether a minimum number of persons is required for the package to take place and, if so, the deadline for informing the consumer in the event of cancellation.

The particulars contained in the brochure are binding on the organizer or retailer, unless:

—changes in such particulars have been clearly communicated to the consumer before conclusion of the contract, in which case the brochure shall expressly state so,

—changes are made later following an agreement between the parties to the contract.

Notes

(1) See also, similarly, Article 3(3) of the Distance Selling of Financial Services Directive (2002/65/EC); Article 5(2) of the Timeshare Directive (2008/122/EC): 'The information referred to in Article 4(1) shall form an integral part of the contract.' For another long list of information items which must be provided, see also Article 4(1) of the Distance Selling Directive (97/7/EC) (see below 3.51 (EU)).

(2) The outcome at EU level differs from some of the national approaches, this outcome being based on the specific need to protect consumers. Accordingly, some directives treat the supply of legally required pre-contractual information for the benefit of consumers as amounting to an offer. This will normally happen when there is a comprehensive commercial proposal which does not exclude expressly the qualification of an offer. There are even some directives which directly provide for the binding character of any information supplied in this way, as the quoted ones reveal.

(3) The proposed rules on European contract law include this requirement (DCFR, ACQP, PECL). From a national standpoint, it is interesting to contrast the examples of French and English law. According to Article 1583 of the French Civil Code, a sale contract 'is complete between the parties, and ownership is acquired as

of right by the buyer as against the seller, as soon as the thing and the price have been agreed upon'. To illustrate the consequences of this rule, the judgment of the Cour d'appel (Court of Appeal) Paris, 29 January 1996[69] can be mentioned: 'Where an owner of immovable property fails to make any indication of its price in writing, any proposal by him can constitute only an invitation to negotiate.' By contrast, section 8(2) of the UK Sale of Goods Act 1979 provides that if no price is fixed by the contract, a reasonable price must be paid; an agreement for the sale of goods may be binding as soon as the parties have agreed to buy and sell, the remaining details being determined by the standard of reasonableness or by law.

Question
In the light of the European provisions, is it possible to see different effects as regards the classification of 'offers' when directives merely require the supply of comprehensive information or when they expressly declare that this information is binding?

II.B.3 'SUBJECTIVE' ELEMENTS OF AN OFFER

II.B.3.a The addressee: offers to the public, to undetermined consumers and to determined consumers

Cass civ 3e, 28 November 1968[70] **3.16 (FR)**
Maltzkorn v Braquet

OFFER TO THE PUBLIC BINDS AS AN OFFER TO A PARTICULAR PERSON

Trapped by a press announcement

An announcement in a newspaper proposing the sale of a piece of land to anyone who accepts the deal has to be considered an offer made to the public that binds the offeror and not a pure invitation to treat.

Facts: Mr Braquet published an announcement in a newspaper proposing the sale of a particular piece of land at a price of FRF 25,000. Mr Maltzkorn communicated his acceptance of this offer to the seller. Mr Braquet rejected this acceptance, alleging that he did not intend to be bound by his earlier proposal. The Cour de Cassation quashed the judgment of the Court of Appeal which had rejected the claim of Mr Malzkorn by asserting that an offer made in a newspaper could not be treated in the same way as an offer made to a particular person

Judgment: An offer that is made to the public binds the offeror to the first person that accepts the offer under the same conditions as an offer made to a particular person.… Considering that, in order to disregard Mr Malzkorn's request to regularise the sale, the judgment states that when a sale offer is made in a newspaper, of a good that can only be acquired by one person, such offer cannot be treated in the same way as an offer made to a particular person. …

[69] Defrénois 1996, Art 36434, No 144.
[70] Bull civ III No 507, 389; (1969) JCP II, 15797.

Since the Court of Appeal did not show how it reached the conclusion that the advertisement only amounted to an invitation to open negotiations and that the original advertisement contained reservations and qualifications, it is decided that the Court of Appeal did not provide a legal basis for its decision.

Cour d'appel (Court of Appeal) Paris, 2 March 1992[71] **3.17 (FR)**
Euromarché v Inter Discount France

OFFER TO A RESTRICTED PUBLIC

Video recorder for consumers, not for resellers

An offer to the public may be implicitly restricted as not addressed to other businesses or competitors.

Facts: Euromarché (a commercial centre) published a catalogue with items on special offer at reduced prices from 13 to 22 December 1991. One of the items so offered was a video recorder at a price of FRF 1,490, instead of the normal FRF 1,790. On 13 December Inter Discount France (a retailer) placed an order for 500 video recorders and on 18 December sent a cheque for FRF 745,000. Euromarché refused to sell the items to Inter Discount France, who claimed enforcement of their alleged contract.

Judgment: The order of 500 VCRs, placed on 13 December 1991 by Inter Discount France, who, as a specialist retailer, does not belong to the company's usual clientele, meant that, in order for Inter Discount France to benefit from the discount, Euromarché would be forced to part with almost all of its stock on the very first day of the promotional offer and would consequently risk not being able to satisfy its usual customers, thereby endangering its promotional offer; even if it were possible for other Euromarché stores to restock the store in question, the volume of FSDs order was still unprecedented in relation to the expected number of VCR orders that are usually placed during a promotional sale.

Considering that it would seem that a promotional sale organised by a supermarket for New Year celebrations seeks to attract customers and persuade them to shop at their supermarket because of the low prices it offers on certain items; Considering that it would be out of the question to reproach Euromarché for not having specified in its catalogue that its products were only offered to certain customers and in limited amounts since this company was able to satisfy the demands of the particular group of customers to whom the offer was naturally addressed, which, in addition to television and radio products also applied to food and clothes; Considering that, the order of 500 VCRs placed by Inter Discount clearly surpassed the context of retailing and did not fall within Euromarché's expected range; Inter Discount's intention appears increasingly to be that of a competitor who sought to block and damage Euromarché's promotional sale by putting the company in the impossible position of either running out of all of its sales products or not being able to satisfy its regular customers.

The refusal to sell the ordered products in bulk under the conditions specified in the offer (which reveals the bad faith of Inter Discount), does not amount to any obvious illegal conduct that must be stopped.

[71] (1992) D 152; JurisData No 1992-020478.

Notes

(1) While the requirements as to intention and sufficiently definite terms are not controversial almost irrespective of the national law examined, there are conflicting solutions to the problem whether a declaration which is addressed to the public (and so to undetermined persons) should be treated as an 'offer'. In line with the tendency of many national courts to recognise such declarations as offers even though this departs from the traditional requirement that an offer must have an actual and determined addressee, Article II 4:201(3) DCFR, Article 4:103(2-3) ACQP and Article 2:202(3) PECL accept that those declarations are 'offers' where they fix a price, even where the statement is made in public advertisements, catalogues or displays of goods. This more consumer-friendly solution is not the one adopted by Article 14(2) CISG, which affirms that 'a proposal other than one addressed to one or more specific persons is to be considered merely as an invitation to make offers, unless the contrary is clearly indicated by the person making the proposal'—a solution that also seems to be the position of English law and German law which treat this as a simple invitation to make an offer.[72] By contrast, French law seems more in line with DCFR and Acquis Principles on this point as the cited cases illustrate.

(2) A case from the Danish Supreme Court decided in 1991[73] concerns chocolate bars that were advertised at prices below the wholesale price in door-to-door leaflets and by signs in the potential seller's discount store. The owner of a chocolate shop wanted to buy the discount store's entire stock of 4,000 bars of chocolate, but the discount store refused to sell. The Danish Supreme Court held that the display in the shop was an offer, but six of the Court's judges considered that the owner of the chocolate shop should have understood that the advertising was aimed at its ordinary clientele which consisted of private consumers and also that the seller had not intended the sale of large quantities to competitors and therefore that the offer was incapable of being accepted by a business buyer. By contrast, three of the judges did not want to interpret the offer in this restrictive way and would have decided in favour of the chocolate shop owner, the potential buyer.

Questions

(1) What do you think of these ways of reasoning from the point of view of the intention to be bound by the offeror?

(2) If an offer may be interpreted by reference to the implicit intention of the offeror so as to restrict its number of addressees, can you imagine or give an example of a reported case where an offer is restricted only to others in business and is not open to consumers?

(3) Can you think of an example of an offer which should be restricted by implication to a certain group or category of consumers even though the external

[72] F Terré, P Simler and Y Lequette, *Droit civil. Les obligations*, 8th edn (Paris, Dalloz, 2002) 120.

[73] Reported in *Ugeskrift for Retsvaesen* (1991) 43, as cited by P Møgelvang-Hansen, 'The Binding Effects of Advertising' in R Schulze, *New Features in Contract Law* (München, Sellier, 2007) 176.

manifestation of the offeror's intention is apparently addressed to consumers in general?

(4) Which one of the contrasting solutions (DCFR/PECL versus CISG) accords better with modern ways in which commercial transactions are made and/or with a fair balance of the interests of the parties?

II.B.3.b The role of the prior activity of the consumer (passive/active)

OGH (Supreme Court), 8 July 2003[74] **3.18 (AT)**
Verein für Konsumenteninformation v I AG

A CONSUMER'S REPLY TO AN OFFER MAY NOT ITSELF CONSTITUTE AN OFFER

Talking to an automated message: who makes the offer?

When a trader offers the consumer—via telephone calls by means of automated systems—the opportunity to claim a prize on a premium rate telephone number, the subsequent telephone call made by the consumer accepting this offer must be considered the moment of conclusion of the contract.

Facts: The defendant was a mail order firm and telephoned consumers to inform them that they had won a prize. At the same time, the consumers were informed that they would be sent a letter. The telephone call used a tape-recorded message and was made without the permission of the consumer. The person called was not informed of the defendant's name, address or headquarters. The people who were called were requested to claim their prize by dialling a premium-rate number and the call charges were specified. While no goods or services were offered during the telephone calls, subsequent written correspondence did contain the relevant offers. The Austrian Consumers' Association brought an action for an injunction to order the defendant to desist from concluding contracts with consumers by distance selling without first informing them of the firm's name and operating address. The Association also applied for the defendant to refrain from using automated messages as a means of communicating with consumers. The main issue was to determine whether a request to call a number and claim a prize constitutes a contract in accordance with §5a(1) KSchG whenever the consumer states his intention to accept the offer.

Judgment: Directive 97/7/EC from 20 May 1997 on the protection of consumers when concluding contracts in distance selling was implemented through §§5a to 5j and §31a of the KSchG (Austrian Consumer Protection Act). §5c KSchG regulates the duties of a trader to provide information. The consumer must be informed in good time prior to making a contractual statement of the name (firm) and an address to which summons can be sent (§5c(1) l.1 KSchG). Use of an automated interlocutor with a consumer requires the latter's prior consent which may be withdrawn at any time (§5c(3) KSchG). The defendant asserts that the prerequisites for application of §5c(3) KSchG were not fulfilled and that the disputed automated telephone calls had no connection with the conclusion of any contract; the consumer did not even have the opportunity at this stage to make any statement constituting a legal transaction. The information required before a contractual statement can be made did not have to be given at that time, even if a contract were to be reached later. Only claiming the prize by telephone is considered a

[74] 4 Ob 149/03w. Full text in the original language and facts/abstract in English (by P Bydlinski and M Stefula) in *EC Consumer Law Compendium* (http://www.eu-consumer-law.org).

subsequent contract. There were no assertions or declarations, however, on what information was forthcoming in subsequent conversations before making the contractual statement. This means that the grounds for finding an offence against the duty of disclosure under §5c(1) KSchG are lacking. According to the defendant, the wording of the law clearly states that information in the course of such a subsequent conversation would be sufficient. In any case, merely claiming the possibility of requesting a prize by telephone does not constitute a distance contract because the law on distance selling is only aimed at contracts in which the mutual contractual statements are made by way of distance communication, but not at contracts which would restrict themselves to the use of distance communication as such. Hence the German legislature under §312c(3) of the BGB (German Civil Code) excluded services from the duty to inform which are rendered directly through the use of means of distance communication. If only because of the European legal background, the Austrian regulations also need to be teleologically and restrictively construed. …

The defendant first offers the consumer by telephone the opportunity to claim his prize on a premium rate telephone number; the consumer accepts this offer by calling the premium rate telephone number (Lütke, Distance Selling Law §312b BGB para 43, according to whom the acceptance of a contractual offer can also be an implied acceptance for distance contracts); before the conclusion of a contract, personal contact between consumer and trader, which would exclude the use of §§5c to 5i KschG, does not occur. The contract is therefore concluded "under exclusive use" of a means of distance communication. The contract for services offered by the defendant—the claiming of a prize by telephone—is concluded by the call to a premium rate telephone number. The consumer would receive information during the following conversation only once the contract has been concluded. The content of the subsequent conversation has, therefore, no relevance for the judgement on whether the offer of the possibility of claiming a prize by telephone must comply with the duty to provide information under §5c KschG. The only decisive factor is the conversation in which the defendant, by means of an automated system, offers the consumer the possibility of claiming a prize by telephone. This conversation is not "merely the prelude to a possible contractual relationship", but represents the offer of a service which is conclusively accepted by calling a telephone number disclosed as premium rate, with the subsequent conclusion of the contract in direct conjunction with this.

Note

The moment at which an offer has taken place and the question on who is the offeror when the consumer has a certain active role poses many problems, as the Austrian case reproduced shows in the context of distance selling. Also the right of withdrawal of the consumer depends on who made the offer, as another Austrian OGH 29 November 2000[75] demonstrates; on these specific problems, see below, chapter 4.

[75] 5 U 17/04; 3 Ob 94/00w (which concludes that the placing by a consumer of an advertisement in a newspaper for the sale of immovable property is not tantamount to initiating an estate agency contract). Full text in the original language and facts/abstract in English (by P Bydlinski and M Stefula) in *EC Consumer Law Compendium* (www.eu-consumer-law.org).

II.B.4 FORMAL REQUIREMENTS/RESTRICTIONS OF OFFERS

Distance Selling Directive (97/7/EC) **3.19 (EU)**

Article 5 (1) The consumer must receive written confirmation or confirmation in another durable medium available and accessible to him of the information referred to in Article 4(1)(a) to (f), in good time during the performance of the contract, and at the latest at the time of delivery where goods not for delivery to third parties are concerned, unless the information has already been given to the consumer prior to conclusion of the contract in writing or on another durable medium available and accessible to him.

OLG (Court of Appeal) Hamburg, 23 December 2004[76] **3.20 (DE)**

MOMENT OF THE DELIVERY OF INFORMATION

The cost of a woman's pullover and wristwatch

The delivery of information must be prior to the conclusion of the contract: 'in good time' before being bound, not necessarily in advertising.

Facts: The parties were competitors, who distributed fashion garments and accessories by distance means. In May 2003, the respondent advertised a special offer for a woman's cashmere pullover and a woman's quartz wristwatch in various Hamburg media. The first matter at issue concerned an advertisement in the press. This contained a depiction and accompanying brief description of the products as well as their respective prices without reference to the fact that these prices contained Value Added Tax. Next to the price details, an asterisk referred to a footnote which stated that postage cost €5 per delivery. The website and the telephone number of the respondent for placing orders were highlighted. Furthermore, the respondent also commissioned radio and television advertising for the same products. These gave the prices and made a reference to the postage cost. The applicant claimed that this advertising was contrary to fair competition and sought an injunction against the respondent. It contended that the aforementioned forms of advertising by the respondent failed to satisfy the information duties towards consumers required by §§312b, 312c(1) BGB, §1 BGB-InfoV ('Regulation on Information Duties and Obligations to Produce Supporting Documents According to Civil Law'). In addition, it submitted that the respondent had failed to comply with the duties found in §§1(2), 6 PAngV (Preisangabeverordnung—'Price Details Regulation') in respect of the pricing information. As §§312b and c deal with distance contracts, the interpretation of these articles in conformity with Directive 97/7/EC on distance selling was also discussed.

Judgment: The regional court has accurately started from the assumption that, in not providing in the disputed forms of advertising the items of information, notes or details listed in these claims, the conduct of the respondent is not unfair with regard to competition law, now §3 UWG (Unfair Competition Act). In particular, the respondent is not violating statutory regulations in the terms of §4 no 11 of the UWG. To elaborate on the district court's grounds in detail, the following applies (to which is referred incidentally): a) For the respondent §§312b, 312c(1) no 1 BGB do not constitute a legal obligation to provide the information specified under §1(1) BGB-InfoV, in the means of advertising in dispute. According to §312c(1) no 1 BGB, the trader must, 'in good time before the conclusion of a contract', provide the information in accordance with §1(1) BGB-InfoV. ... It follows from this that the consumer must have all the necessary information at the

[76] (2005) MMR 318ff. Full text in the original language and facts/abstract in English (by C Rodorff and J Mertens) in *EC Consumer Law Compendium* (www.eu-consumer-law.org).

moment the contract is concluded. To what extent, however, the requirement for information to be provided 'in good time' requires this information to be given at an earlier moment can be inferred neither from the wording of the national law nor from that of the EC Directive. Thus the expression 'in good time' in the terms of §312c(1) BGB is to be interpreted in line with the aims of the European directive. ... b) An interpretation of the expression 'in good time' which preserves the aims of the EC Directive does not demand that the information owed must already be provided without exception within an advertising measure. Although such an approach taken by the trader would satisfy the demands of §312c(1) no 1 BGB, no obligation to that effect exists according to the EC Directive or national legislation. ...

What is crucial is that the consumer receives the necessary information in any case, before he himself offers the trader the conclusion of a distance contract (§145 BGB) or accepts a corresponding offer from the trader (§§147ff BGB). The consumer must be advised of the necessary information at a point in time when he still in no way feels obligated to enter into a contract or even in any way already contractually obliged. ... Such a disclosure of the information can also still be effected in good time directly after contact has been established by the consumer in response to a means of advertising. ...

Product advertising, which—as in this case—is transmitted through advertisements in the print media, television or radio and contains an invitation to order the product and enter into a distance contract, is in cases of doubt not to be understood as an offer in accordance with §145 BGB but as an invitation to treat. Routinely the trader does not want to be irrevocably bound at this stage because he may not have sufficient stock or because there may exist concerns about particular customers. When the trader, does not make an offer to conclude a distance contract with an advertisement he can still fulfil the pre-contractual duties to provide information by giving that information at a later time.

This shall not apply when the advertisement is designed in such a way that it does not simply invite the consumer to enter into contact with the trader with the aim of ordering, but stipulates that the consumer alone can make a binding proposal to conclude a distance contract in accordance with §145 BGB on the basis of the information provided in the advertisement and without further contact with the trader. This is the case for example, when an advertisement contains an order form with which the consumer bindingly offers the trader the conclusion of a distance contract by returning it completed. In these circumstances there is no longer any possibility for the trader still to inform the consumer in good time in accordance with §312c(1) BGB, if he does not do this in the advertisement itself. In particular it would be too late if the necessary information were only given to the consumer with the declaration of acceptance in accordance with §§147ff. BGB or even when the goods were sent. ...

The fact that giving the owed pre-contractual information purely by telephone may be less helpful for the consumer when compared to written notification does not lead to other conclusions. According to §312c(1) sentence 1 BGB the consumer should be informed in a way appropriate to the means of distance communication used, hence also by way of telephone contact. Furthermore, the standardized requirement to provide information in text form at the time of delivery at the latest, set out under §312c(1) BGB, shows that the law regards information given pre-contractually by telephone as sufficient. A written pre-contractual notification, even if it were technically possible, is not required. Further, the claimant is also incorrect in asserting that the consumer, having dialled the ordering hotline and thereafter been informed in accordance with §1(1) BGB-InfoV, is subsequently no longer able to make an informed, well considered decision for or against the contract during the course of the telephone call. ...

The respondent is only required to inform the consumer 'in good time', as has been demonstrated in detail above. Whether he does this in the advertisement or at a later point (while still in good time) is left to him. ...

The applicant is entitled to an injunction according to §§3, 4 no 11, 8(1), (3) no 1 and §1(2) no 1 of the PAngV. The forms of advertising which were the subject of complaint contravene §1(2) no 1 PAngV because when a price is quoted in an advertisement in distance selling the respondent must specify that this price includes value-added tax. ...

No objections can be raised against the respondent's practice ... of referring to a footnote on the same page, in which the shipping expenses which arise are indicated by means of an asterisk following the respective price. Through the presence of the asterisk the consumer unmistakably recognises that he must take note of further price quotations, namely the costs of shipping as per the footnote, in order to be able to assess the value for money offered in the advertised product. The respondent is at least satisfying the demands of §1(6) of the PAngV with the concrete graphic presentation of the advertisement. The observer's attention is directed to the statements on shipping expenses by virtue of the layout of the advertisement, conforming to the clarity demanded. The same is true of the graphic insertion of the reference to the shipping expenses in the challenged television advertisement.

Electronic Commerce Directive (2000/31/EC)[77] **3.21 (EU)**

Article 7 (2) ... Member States shall take measures to ensure that service providers undertaking unsolicited commercial communications by electronic mail consult regularly and respect the opt-out registers in which natural persons not wishing to receive such commercial communications can register themselves.

Distance Selling Directive (97/7/EC) **3.22 (EU)**

Article 10 (1) Use by a supplier of the following means requires the prior consent of the consumer:

—automated calling system without human intervention (automatic calling machine),

—facsimile machine (fax).

(2) Member States shall ensure that means of distance communication, other than those referred to in paragraph 1, which allow individual communications may be used only where there is no clear objection from the consumer.

Notes

(1) On the *substantial requirements* of the offer in the sense of pre-contractual information duties, see below section III.C and see, for example, Article 3 of the Consumer Credit Directive (2008/48/EC). The language of the offer addressed to consumers has been analysed in chapter 2, see, for example, Article 4 of the Timeshare Directive (2008/122/EC). Some rules establish *measures to ensure that some professionals provide information/offer in a document when requested by a*

[77] See also Art 3(3) of the Distance Selling of Financial Services Directive (2002/65/EC) on distance marketing of financial services.

consumer. At an EU level, a good example would be Article 3(3) of the Timeshare Directive (2008/122/EC):

> Member States shall ensure that any advertising specifies the possibility of obtaining the information referred to in Article 4(1) and indicates where it can be obtained.

(2) The main special features governing formal requirements of offers addressed to consumers lie in the field of distance communications and electronic commerce. Three issues deserve special attention according to the EU directives. First, the set of *formal requirements governing the display of information on the steps* to reach agreement ('crumb trail' system in e-commerce: Article 10 of the Electronic Commerce Directive (2000/31/EC), Article II—3:105 DCFR); on the kind of offer ('clearly identifiable as such', Articles 6–7 of the Directive on Electronic Commerce (2000/31/EC)); on transparency requirements, etc. An example may be found in Article 4(3) of the Distance Selling Directive (97/7/EC):

> Moreover, in the case of telephone communications, the identity of the supplier and the commercial purpose of the call shall be made explicitly clear at the beginning of any conversation with the consumer.

Second, it is required that information should at least be confirmed in a 'durable medium' in distance contracts (see definition in Article 2(f) of the Distance Selling of Financial Services Directive (2002/65/EC)); on this see the cited Article 5(1) of the Distance Selling Directive (97/7/EC) and the OLG Hamburg, 23 December 2004 (above 3.20 (DE)) as for the moment of delivery of information. Third, the restriction of some offers and proposals in the context of some means of distance communication, which is illustrated by the quoted Article 7(2) of the Electronic Commerce Directive (2000/31/EC) and Article 10 of the Distance Selling Directive (97/7/EC) and by 'the insistent e-mail' case (see the analysis of those aggressive practices in chapter 2). For further reading on transparency requirements, see OLG München 11 September 2003[78] (information on provider identification, accessed on the internet through a double link via 'contact' and 'impressum') dealt with later in this chapter, 3.53 (DE).

II.B.5 THE BINDING CHARACTER OF AN OFFER (AND OF AN ADVERTISEMENT?): CASES INVOLVING UNWILLING SELLERS

Distinguishing between a genuine offer and other types of public pre-contractual statements made by a professional or a business (such as advertisements, labelling, brochures and catalogues) is not always easy in practice. Some EU rules, and some national rules—not implementing these European rules—have established the binding effect of some types of declarations, such as advertisements and information supplied to the public in certain circumstances, even where there is evidence of an implied intention not to be bound on the part of the person who makes the statement as long as the content of the information which it provides was sufficiently definite.

[78] 29 U 2681/03.

Where this is the case, these national or European rules classify public declarations which lack one of the two traditional elements of offers under general contract law as offers in order to ensure a higher level of consumer protection.

II.B.5.a Limits on the binding character of public statements (legal and contractual limits)

Consumer Sales Directive (99/44/EC) **3.23 (EU)**

Article 2 (4) The seller shall not be bound by public statements, as referred to in paragraph 2(d) if he:

—shows that he was not, and could not reasonably have been, aware of the statement in question,

—shows that by the time of conclusion of the contract the statement had been corrected, or

—shows that the decision to buy the consumer goods could not have been influenced by the statement.

Cour d'appel (Court of Appeal) Toulouse, 6 December 1995[79] **3.24 (FR)**
Comptoir général d'ameublement Teisseire v Union Fédérale des Consommateurs (UFC)

RESERVATIONS TO ACCEPT ACCEPTANCE

***Sine die* cooker installation**

A term subjecting a consumer's acceptance to confirmation is unfair.

Facts: A trader sold cookers and promised to install these. His standard form of contracts and order forms included a term by which the professional reserved his consent to contract at his own discretion with this wording: 'every order becomes final only after confirmation by the board of directors'. The UFC claimed this contract term was unfair and ought to be omitted from the contracts and offers to contract used by the trader.

Judgment: The Commission on unfair terms has found such a clause unfair. The appellant maintains that this is not sufficient to lead to a conviction and emphasises that it was justified to include such a clause because of the need to check the feasibility of an order.

This last consideration cannot prevail, since the order is necessarily formalised after an examination of the location where the installation is envisaged, and the professional is unable to hide behind a supposedly bad description of the technical constraints by the client.

The abusive nature of the litigious clause arises from the fact that the conclusion of a contract depends solely on the will of the seller who is in a situation where an offer is being made to him on a continuous basis.

[79] JurisData No 1995-052910.

Notes

(1) The point about a term such as 'No contract without our confirmation' is that it attempts to make the real offeree into an offeror. In some jurisdictions the possibility of excluding the binding character of an offer is clearly established (eg §145 BGB),[80] but in a consumer law context (unlike contracts made B2B) in some countries such a term is considered vulnerable as an unfair term, reference being made to term (c) of the Annex to the Unfair Contract Terms Directive (93/13/EEC) ('making an agreement binding on the consumer whereas provision of services by the seller or supplier is subject to a condition whose realization depends on his own will alone'). The judgment of the Toulouse Court of Appeal, 6 December 1995, is a good example of the application of this negative approach, as is Article 32(1) of the Belgian Trade Practices Act, which blacklists such a clause as unfair in all circumstances.

(2) Contractual limits on an offer may be set by the offeror to safeguard his position. Depending on the terms on which an offer is made by a trader, the latter may be bound either by the first person who purports to accept (as in the case of auction sales where it is understood that each item put forward constitutes a single offer capable of acceptance by the highest bidder) or by any person who purports to accept. Therefore, apart from the *'reservation to accept' (by the offeror)* clauses dealt with in the cited French case, other common contractual limitations are introduced by the *'limited stock'* clauses: European contract law texts have provisions concerning public proposals to supply goods or services at stated prices which are described as 'offers' but then restricted as being open only 'until the stocks of goods, or the business's capacity to supply the service is exhausted' (Article 4:103(3) ACQP and Article II—4:201(3) DCFR, similar to Article 2:201(3) PECL). Except where they are used as a covert means of refusing to conclude the contract at the whim of the trader[81] or where they involve a misleading commercial practice (see 'bait advertising', fifth forbidden practice of Annex I of the Unfair Commercial Practises Directive (2005/29/EC), though not affecting contract law according to Article 3(2) of this directive), these clauses validly limit the offer and may be expressly established in the proposal itself or—according to DCFR, ACQP and PECL—be implicitly construed from it. It is usually accepted that the courts may assess what constitutes reasonable availability for this purpose in objective terms (the usual number of items for a standard competitor under similar circumstances).[82] And 'limited stock' clauses raise the question of the effect of offers addressed to consumers in general or only to a restricted number or category of consumers.

[80] But see BGH 8 March 1984 (1984) NJW 1885, where despite the use of the word 'without engagement', the court stated that this does not necessarily remove the character of offer (subject to revocation). It was a B2B case, available in H Beale, A Hartkamp, H Kötz and D Tallon (eds), *Cases, Materials and Text on Contract Law* (Oxford, Hart Publishing, 2002) 183ff; See also H Kötz, A Flessner, *European Contract Law*, translated by T Weir (Oxford, Clarendon Press, 1997) I, 19.

[81] Terré, Simler and Lequette, above n 72, 118.

[82] In this sense, for instance, Italian or Spanish doctrine: G Cian, 'L'offerta al pubblico e l'art 3 del D Legisl 31 maggio 1998, n 114, in materia di vendite al dettaglio' (2001) *Rivista di Diritto Civile* 322–23; A González Gozalo, *La formación del contrato tras la Ley de servicios de la sociedad de la información y de comercio electrónico* (Granada, Comares, 2004) 21.

(3) As regards legal limits, the cited Article 2(4) of the Consumer Sales Directive (99/44/EC) provides concrete rules of its general requirement that the goods supplied should be in conformity with the contract. See also Article 3(2) of the Package Travel Directive (90/314/EEC) (see above section II.B.2).

II.B.5.b Is the trader/offeror bound by mistakes in the declaration and by typing errors?

BGH, 26 January 2005[83] **3.25 (DE)**

TYPING ERRORS DO NOT AMOUNT TO OFFERS

The €2,650 computer offered at €245

The erroneous advertising of the price of a notebook computer should be regarded as a mistake in the act of declaration, not a mistake in motivation or in intention; therefore, the purchaser cannot claim the wrong price stated.

Facts: Due to a transmission error, a notebook computer normally offered at €2.650 was advertised on the internet for €245 and was sold at this price. The seller then purported to annul the contract on the ground of mistake (§119 BGB).

Judgment: 15. The corruption of the declaration, which had originally been correct, on the way to the recipient via software that no one had realised was faulty should be regarded as a mistake in the act of declaration. It makes no difference whether the maker of the declaration writes incorrectly or mistypes or whether the divergence from the desired facts of the declaration occurs later on the way to the recipient. This also results from §120 BGB, according to which a declaration of intent which has been incorrectly conveyed by the person or device used to send it can be challenged under the same condition, as in the case of a mistakenly made declaration of intent in accordance with §119 BGB. …

16. … This declaration—accepting the order at a price of €245—did not correspond to what the claimant wanted to declare. He wanted to sell the notebook, as is explained, at a price of €2.650. He had planned the programme sequence of his ordering system in such way that the value entered into the merchandise information system should be transferred to the product database and be binding as the sales price of subsequent orders. In line with his intended programme sequence, the claimant wrongly assumed that the sales price which had automatically been transferred to the product database was consistent with the value entered into the data processing system, as is usually the case, and that the respondent's order was therefore carried out at the price of €2.650 which he had determined. His intention was to declare his acceptance at the price he had determined. Nonetheless, by accepting the respondent's order in execution of the programme sequence—at a price of €245—the claimant's mistake was carried forward.

17. … What is at issue is not a mistake in the decision-making process or in the preparation of a declaration. The claimant formed his intention for a declaration faultlessly as the colleague responsible determined the sales price for the notebook at €2.650 and this sum was to be transferred to the product database on the website after running the

[83] (2005) MMR 233.

computer programme. For this reason the present case is not comparable with a (hidden) pricing error ..., where the mistake already made at the decision-making stage does not categorically give the right to annul as an error of motivation even if the incorrect calculation is based on errors in software used by the declarant (cf BGHZ 139, 177, 180ff). Stating the wrong value of €245 was not based on an incorrect calculation of the price at the decision-making stage of the claimant, but on the subsequent mistake during the transferral of data.

Cour d'appel (Court of Appeal) Angers, 8 January 2001[84] **3.26 (FR)**
SA Castorama v Mr X

PRICE-TAGGING ERRORS LEAD TO A DEFECT OF CONSENT WHICH INVALIDATES THE OFFER

Swimming pool at bargain price

Labelling mistakes reveal a lack of intention of the seller to sell at a fixed and absurd price. The sale is void due to a mistake vitiating consent or due to a sale 'without cause'. The awareness of the buyer, who hired a bailiff to witness the refusal to sell, introduced undue pressure that showed the existence of a defect in the consent of the seller.

Facts: Mr X, with the company of a bailiff, went to a shop to buy some flagstones to build his swimming pool. The fixed price tagged for the flagstones was FRF 22 per square metre (FRF 3.52 per flagstone). Mr X ordered 1,250 flagstones at 3.52 each. The shop refused to deliver the items on the ground of a mistake in the labelling process, but nevertheless did so under pressure from the buyer. The shop had itself bought each flagstone from its own supplier at the price of FRF 92 each. The first instance court ordered the shop to deliver the items at the price on the label. The Court of Appeal reversed this decision and ordered the customer to pay the shop FRF 5,000 under Article 700 of the New Civil Procedure Code, declaring the nullity of the sale.

Judgment: The price being fixed at FRF 22 per square metre (FRF 3,52 per flagstone) arose from a purely material error which, as opposed to the error relating to the value of the sold good, affects consent (which is not disputed). The buyer was clearly aware of this error since he went to the trouble of hiring a bailiff before he had any contact with the seller (as the findings of the verbal hearings show), fearing that his offer may be refused (which rules out any notion of good faith on the part of the interested party);

The price was absurd since it represented a mere 16% of the actual price (that is to say, FRF 4.400 as opposed to FRF 27.500—the first judge having made a calculation error).

The conditions in which the manager of the shop, who had been called by a shop assistant, finally authorised the sale price of the goods at the erroneous price—which the respondent took advantage of as further proof of consent of sale in the full knowledge that the price was wrong—do not allow him to be considered as having freely given his consent to the sale. The client was accompanied to the place of sale (which, by definition, is a place open to the public that may witness the difficulties the seller is faced with) by a bailiff whose status and qualifications imply a certain degree of authority and competence and who was hired to record an eventual refusal of sale, which—without

[84] (2001) JCP IV.2857.

any attestation being necessary—led to threats, without there being any support for the allegation that the co-contractor would have had time to reflect upon the matter.

Reversing the prior judgment, the sale must be considered void, whether this be because of a mistake that vitiated the seller's consent to the sale or because of the absurd compensation, which could be assimilated with a sale 'without cause' or may be bound up with the extremely low price of the goods.

Note

(1) The following English cases were reported in newspapers:

(a) Argos, a leading retailer, mistakenly offered and sold through its website television sets priced at GBP 3 instead of GBP 299.99.

(b) Compaq offered and sold a computer at GBP 1 instead of GBP 530. Both companies refused to carry out these orders.[85]

(c) Due to a website blunder, for a short period Kodak offered a digital camera for GBP 100 when it should have been GBP 329; several hundred consumers who rushed to buy the camera for GBP 100 threatened to sue the company unless it delivered, which it then did, though under pressure.[86]

(2) None of these cases with different endings reached the courts.

ACQP **3.27 (EU)**

Article 4:107 Pre-contractual statements by a contract party

(1) Any public statement which a business, prior to the conclusion of the contract, makes about the specific characteristics of the goods or services, which it supplies is binding under the contract unless:

(a) when the contract was concluded, the other party was aware, or should have reasonably been aware that the statement was incorrect, or

(b) the other party's decision to conclude the contract could not have been influenced by the statement, or

(c) the statement had been corrected by the time of conclusion of the contract.

Notes

(1) Different solutions can be found. German law contains a specific rule governing 'declaration mistakes' (mistakes made in the process of making a declaration) where annulment is permitted, as opposed to mistakes related to the motives for entering into a transaction: see §§119 and 122 BGB. The German courts consider cases of mistyping and price-tagging errors as 'declaration mistakes'. A similar solution was followed by the French courts. English law provides no similar rule and would, for example, treat a web proposal not as an offer, but as mere advertising or as an invitation to treat, with the result that a consumer could not normally claim in reliance on it (although it should be noted that a trader could fall foul of the criminal

[85] Both in BBC News 1999 and 2000, at http://news.bbc.co.uk/2/hi/business/441740.stm and http://news.bbc.co.uk/2/hi/business/736295.stm.

[86] More information at http://news.bbc.co.uk/2/hi/science/nature/1795624.stm.

offence of section 20 of the Consumer Protection Act 1987 which makes it a criminal offence to give consumers a misleading price indication). In some Nordic countries, such as Denmark, the doctrine of mistake is also seen as way of escape for an offeror in these circumstances on similar lines as are found in German and French law, though in the Danish context this is buttressed in some cases where the offeror's mistake was obvious due to the fact that the offerees were aware or ought to have been aware of this mistake. So, for instance, in a Danish Supreme Court decision of 1985,[87] the offerees had taken a snapshot photograph of the offeror's window display of television sets which bore a price tag of DKK 1,695 instead of the real price of 5,421; the Court held that this behaviour showed that they realised that there might be later dispute as to the validity of the offer.

(2) PECL echoes this kind of nuanced approach, placing the key issue of the knowledge or possible knowledge of a mistake in the offer by the addressee under the guidance of the principle of good faith and fair dealing (Article 4:103); the DCFR provides for similar treatment (Article II—7:201).[88] In line with this rule, but specifically dealing with public statements, see the quoted Article 4:107 ACQP.

(3) Other judgments can be cited with similar approaches to the quoted judgments. The BGH 26 January 2005[89] dealt with a contract of sale concluded through the internet, where it was held that the seller has a right to nullify the contract under §120 BGB where the price which was accepted by the buyer was shown as lower than it really should have been owing to a change in the provider's software. In the tribunal d'instance (First Instance Court) of Strasbourg, 24 July 2002,[90] a video projector was offered on a website at a ludicrous price when compared with the price fixed by competitors. Again, a mistake in the electronic price-tagging was considered as a lack of consent and the sale was nullified, despite the electronic confirmation automatically sent by the website.

Questions

(1) In this tension between the protection of consumers by keeping offers binding on their makers and the protection of the quality of consent of both parties following the general contract law, is it significant that a party's mistake occurs at the very moment of making the offer or at an earlier stage?

(2) Should the fact that it is one of the employees of the trader who is responsible for the error in an offer change the position? Or the fact that it is a third party

[87] Reported in *Ugeskrift for Retsvaesen* (1985) 877.

[88] Art II—7:201 DCFR: '(1) A party may avoid a contract for mistake of fact or law existing when the contract was concluded if: (a) the party, but for the mistake, would not have concluded the contract or would have done so only on fundamentally different terms and the other party knew or could reasonably be expected to have known this; and (b) the other party: (i) caused the mistake; (ii) caused the contract to be concluded in mistake by leaving the mistaken party in error, contrary to good faith and fair dealing, when the other party knew or could reasonably be expected to have known the mistake; (iii) caused the contract to be concluded in mistake by failing to comply with a pre-contractual information duty or a duty to make available a means of correcting input errors; or (iv) made the same mistake ...'

[89] (2005) NJW 976, confirming OLG Frankfurt, 20 November 2002 (2003) CR 450.

[90] (2003) D 2434.

for whom the trader is not responsible, for instance, possible hackers changing data on a website, as was alleged in the Strasbourg First Instance Court of 24 July 2002 (mentioned above)?

(3) What is (and should be) the role of the good faith of the consumer in relation to the question whether or not he had the chance to know that the mistake was an obvious one?

II.B.5.c Controversial types of 'offers'

Privy Council, 25 February 1974[91] **3.28 (UK)**
New Zealand Shipping Co Ltd v AM Satterthwaite & Co Ltd

OFFER, ACCEPTANCE AND CONSIDERATION

Practical English law

Not all situations fit easily into the marked slots of offer, acceptance and consideration.

Judgment: [Lord Wilberforce] It is only the precise analysis of this complex of relations into the classical offer and acceptance, with identifiable consideration, that seems to present difficulty, but this same difficulty exists in many situations of daily life, e.g., sales at auction; supermarket purchases, boarding an omnibus; purchasing a train ticket; tenders for the supply of goods; offers of rewards; acceptance by post; warranties of authority by agents; manufacturers' guarantees; gratuitous bailments; bankers' commercial credits. These are all examples which show that English law, having committed itself to a rather technical and schematic doctrine of contract, in application takes a practical approach, often at the cost of forcing the facts to fit uneasily into the marked slots of offer, acceptance and consideration.

(i) Advertisements

Consumer Sales Directive (99/44/EC) **3.29 (EU)**

Article 2 (2) Consumer goods are presumed to be in conformity with the contract if they:

(a) comply with the description given by the seller and possess the qualities of the goods which the seller has held out to the consumer as a sample or model;

(b) are fit for any particular purpose for which the consumer requires them and which he made known to the seller at the time of conclusion of the contract and which the seller has accepted;

(c) are fit for the purposes for which goods of the same type are normally used;

(d) show the quality and performance which are normal in goods of the same type and which the consumer can reasonably expect, given the nature of the goods and taking into account any public statements on the specific characteristics of the goods made about them by the seller, the producer or his representative, particularly in advertising or on labelling.

[91] [1975] AC 154 (PC) 167.

Cour d'appel (Court of Appeal) Mons, 6 February 1996[92] **3.30 (BE)**
Etat belge v SA Movitex

DISTANCE MAILING AS OFFER

The binding brochure

The consumer's obligation to call or to go to a store to find out the payment conditions does not prevent the offer from being binding when it is sent out to consumers.

Facts: Movitex was a mail-order firm. In a mailing, sent to all of the customers in its database, Movitex advertised several of its products. In this mailing, Movitex offered its customers three different ways of payment: payment at the time of placing the order; payment at the time of delivery, for which the consumer had to pay an additional sum of BEF 55 (€1,5); and payment after delivery. In the event of payment after delivery, the brochure referred to the firm's general conditions which obliged the consumer to telephone DAXON or visit a shop of that firm to find out the additional costs of this method of payment.

Judgment: Given that Article 79 §1 [of the 14 July 1991 Trade Practices Act now article 78 of that Act], states that 'in the event of a mail order sale, the consumer must receive clear and unambiguous information, in particular about the following elements ... the price ... the methods of payment ...'

Given that, on this occasion, the order form mentioned a number of different methods of payment, as has already been stated; given that, for payments made after delivery, the consumer must consult 'the general sales conditions' which themselves state that the consumer must call Daxon or go to one of its stores to get the necessary information;

Given that Article 79 §1 states that clear and specific information must be provided at the time of a mail order sale transaction, not after;

Given that the respondent claims that the offer cannot be considered as having been fully and effectively completed since the necessary information must be obtained over the telephone or in one of the Daxon stores;

Given that, for there to be an offer, three conditions must be fulfilled: all of the essential elements of the contract must be specified in the offer, one of the parties must show an definite intention of committing itself by accepting the other party's offer, the offer must be brought to the attention of the beneficiary by the offeror himself;

Given that, as soon as the consumer receives the brochure sent to him by Movitex, all of these factors are brought together; given that the consumer's obligation to call or to go to a Daxon store to find out the payment conditions for a payment after delivery does not prevent the offer from being effective when it is sent out to consumers since the only condition the buyer must agree to is to enter into a contract; given that the methods of payment are not part of the essential elements of the contract and do not therefore delay the creation of the offer until the moment the consumer receives the complimentary information;

Since there is no doubt that it follows from Article 79 §1 that it is important that the consumer be clearly and fully informed about the price and the methods of payment when the offer is made (and therefore when the brochure is received); since it is of no use to investigate whether Article 79 §1 contains any formal requirements; since in any

[92] (1996) DCCR 124. Full text in the original language and facts/abstract in English (by G Straetmans) in *EC Consumer Law Compendium* (www.eu-consumer-law.org).

case, it is certain that the obligation to include information must occur concurrently with the offer, and therefore with the receipt of the brochure in this case;

The litigious practice that involves obliging consumers to call or to go to one of the Daxon stores (whose address is not indicated) in order to obtain the information specified in Article 79 §1 violates this provision, since there is no reason why this obligation should exist and it reveals the director of Movitex's bad faith.

Note

(1) Some legal systems establish by law that the trader or professional will be bound by any statement made in the advertising of his products. Thus, Article 94/14 of the Belgian Trade Practices Act sets that the information relating to the contract and provided in advertising and other trade practices may be taken into account when interpreting the contract. Similarly, the Spanish General Consumer Protection Act (Recasted Text of 2007) declares in Article 61:

> The content of the offer, promotion or advertising, the features of each good or service, the legal or economic terms and the offered guarantees are suitable to be claimed by the consumers and users, even when those aspects are not expressly included in the concluded contract or in the document or receipt received and they have to be taken into account when applying the principle of conformity with the contract.

(2) Danish courts reach the same result. The rule in many systems, however, is that advertisements do not constitute 'offers' with the result that their content can not be claimed as forming part of the contract.

(3) Recent French case-law has increasingly accepted that promotional documents are a source of solid agreements.[93]

(4) According to the prevailing opinion, German law remains firmly attached to the rule which denies the classification of 'offer' to newspapers advertisements, catalogues and prospectuses.[94] Although the same approach is taken by the common law so that the general rule holds that advertisements are mere invitations to treat (eg *Partridge v Crittenden* of 5 April 1968:[95] a newspaper advertisement of birds for sale), some *exceptions* have been consistently recognised by the English case-law for cases where the intention of the potential offeror to be bound is sufficiently proved (as in the case of advertisements of rewards to the finder of lost property, unilateral promises, etc, see above), the classic judgment on this point being *Carlill*:[96] an advertisement promised anyone who used the 'smoke ball' according to its instructions a sum of GBP 100 if they contracted influenza. Mrs Carlill satisfied these conditions and successfully claimed this sum on the basis that the advertisement constituted a unilateral offer which had been accepted by performing the required act (using the

[93] Eg where the price is contained in the advertisement: Cass com, 17 June 1994, Bull civ IV No 195, 170, (1998) JCP I.144 No 8; Cass civ 3e, 17 July 1997 (1998) RTDciv 363.

[94] See K Muscheler and M Schewe, 'Die invitatio ad offerendum auf dem Prüfstand' (2000) 11 *Jura* 566 although the qualification of other devices such as automatic machines, web pages and self-service shops are under discussion.

[95] [1968] 2 All ER 421; 1 WLR 1204; 132 JP 367.

[96] *Carlill v The Carbolic Smoke Ball Company* of 7 December 1892 [1893] 1 QB 256.

smoke ball). It was intended by the Smoke Ball Company to be understood by the public as an offer which was to be 'acted upon' (*per* Bowen LJ); the 'sincerity' of which had been manifested by the statement that a sum of money had been deposited with a specific bank to satisfy any demands. In *Wood v Letrik* [1932],[97] an advertisement stated that an electric comb would cure grey hair after 10 days' use and guaranteed payment of GBP 500 if it failed to do so. This was held enforceable. See also *Bowerman v Association of British Travel Agents Ltd (ABTA)* (Court of Appeal, 1996), cited above.

(5) Some directives deal with the binding character of public statements or advertising made by a trader and addressed to consumers. Apart from the quoted Article 2(2) of the Consumer Sales Directive (99/44/EC), see also Article 3(2) of the Package Travel Directive (90/314/EEC). The Acquis Principles, drawing on these scattered pro-consumer rules, propose as a general rule that public advertisements and catalogues should be considered as offers to sell or supply and as binding (with a few exceptions): Article 4:103 and 4:107 (see above).

Questions

(1) Under the solutions adopted by the Directives and the rules of some national laws, according to which advertisements are considered binding offers, which remedy would be or should be available when performance of the announced features is impossible? Do the rules on misleading advertising offer any specific remedy for this situation? (See chapter 2 above.)

(2) Are pre-contractual statements by third parties (eg the producer of goods, other persons in the supply chain, or marketing communicators) which differ from what is said by the final seller or supplier also binding on them and enforceable by the consumer? Should they be? See Articles 2 and 6 of the Consumer Sales Directive (99/44/EC), and Article 4:108 ACQP.

(ii) Display of goods for sale in a shop (supermarket, shop-window, shelves in a self-service shop, etc)

G Treitel, The Law of Contract[98] **3.31 (UK)**

The general rule is that a display of price-marked goods in a shop window is not an offer to sell goods but is an invitation to a customer to make an offer to buy. Similarly, the display of goods on the shelves of a self-service shop is merely an invitation to treat; the customer makes an offer to buy when he presents the goods for payment; at this stage, the retailer may accept or reject it. Similar principles would seem to apply where a supplier of goods or services indicates their availability on a website. …

The general rule relating to shop and similar displays is well established, but the reasons given for it are not entirely convincing. One reason is that 'a shop is a place for bargaining, nor for compulsory sales.' But the modern English shop, in which goods are

[97] *The Times* 13 January 1932.

[98] G Treitel, *The Law of Contract*, 11th edn (London, Thomson/Sweet & Maxwell, 2003) 12.

generally bought on the retailer's terms, is scarcely a place for bargaining; and even if the display of goods were an offer, any resulting sale would not be compulsory: the shopkeeper need not display goods which he does not want to sell. Another argument is that if the display were regarded as an offer, the retailer might be exposed to many actions for damages if more customers purported to accept than his stock could satisfy. But such an offer could be construed as one which automatically expired when the retailer's stock was exhausted: this would probably be in keeping with the common expectation of both retailer and customer. It has also been said that, if a display in a self-service shop were an offer, the undesirable result would follow that the customer would be bound to buy as soon as he picked up the goods to examine them. But if the display were an offer, it could be argued that there was no acceptance until the customer did some less equivocal act, such as presenting the goods for payment. Finally, it may be asked whether the general rule does not sometimes cause injustice. Customers may be induced by a window display to believe that they will be able to buy goods at exceptionally low prices and to wait outside the shop for many hours in reliance on that belief. Is it right to allow the retailer to go back on such statement at the very moment when the customer demands the goods? ... The customer might indeed, still lose his bargain since the offer could be withdrawn at any time before it was accepted; but if it is so withdrawn the person displaying the notice may incur criminal liability under legislation passed for the protection of consumers [Consumer Protection Act 1987, s 20(1): see *R v Warwickshire Cc, ex p Johnson* [1993] AC 583 at 588; contrast *Link Stores Ltd v Harrow BC* [2001] 1 WLR 1479].

Notes

(1) Again, different approaches can be traced depending on the jurisdiction in question: in English law the display constitutes an invitation to treat and not an offer (leading case: *Pharmaceutical Society of Great Britain v Boots Cash Chemists (Southern) Ltd of 5 February 1953*[99] on medicines displayed on open shelves in a self-service shop; see also *Fisher* v *Bell of 10 November 1960*,[100] on a flick-knife displayed in a shop window). The position is the same in German law.[101] These laws are in line with the approach of the CISG, which concerns international trade between professionals (B2B) and is oriented accordingly. According to Article 14(2) CISG, 'a proposal other that one addressed to one or more specific persons is to be considered merely as an invitation to make offers, unless the contrary is clearly indicated by the person making the proposal.' The reproduced excerpt by Treitel shows the criticism and arguments against this rule in the English context.

(2) On the other hand, under the legislative rules of some other countries such a display is held clearly to be an offer with the result that the potential seller cannot refuse to perform the contract. This is a more consumer-law-oriented approach and is found in the Swiss Code of Obligations (Article 7(3): 'The display of goods with price

[99] [1953] 1 QB 401; 1 All ER 482, Court of Appeal.

[100] [1961] 1 QB 394; 3 All ER 731.

[101] One argument *ex* §2.1 of the regulation on price details (*PreisangabeVerordnung)* which imposes the obligation not to change prices tagged to products currently exhibited. More doubtful is the qualification of pure invitation to treat for self-service shops (*Selbstbedienungsladen*): see K Muscheler and M Schewe, 'Die *invitatio ad offerendum* auf dem Prüfstand' [2000] *Jura* 567.

indication shall be considered as an offer'), in Article 1336 of the Italian Civil Code (which is more general) and in Article 9 of the Spanish Law on Retail Trade (which is very specific and consumer friendly).[102] Also under French case-law a display of goods in a shop amounts to an offer[103] (Cass civ 1e, 20 October 1964).[104] As already seen, the Acquis Principles also adopt this solution.

(3) The moment when the consumer is said to accept such an offer is also disputed. For instance, in the view of the French case which has just been noted, it was held to have been the moment the buyer placed the goods in the supermarket basket (for the purposes of imposing contractual liability when the goods—a lemonade bottle—exploded). Sometimes Italian courts have held for the purposes of the criminal law that a customer does not acquire property in the goods when he gets possession of them, but only on payment to the cashier. According to the English case *Pharmaceutical Society of Great Britain v Boots Cash Chemists (Southern) Ltd* which has already been noted, the *consumer* is not held to make an offer for goods in supermarket until he puts them forward to the cashier, who then may reject or accept this offer.

(iii) Auctions

BGH, 7 November 2001[105] **3.32 (DE)**

PLACING GOODS IN AN INTERNET AUCTION IS AN OFFER

Ricardo.de, internet auction of a new car

The seller's declaration of his anticipated acceptance of the highest bid in an online auction, without reserve price, represents a real offer that binds him, and not an 'invitatio ad offerendum' even when the price reached is really low.

Facts: The defendant was an economics student and part-time car dealer who used an online auction website run by a third party, Ricardo, to sell a new car. He refused to deliver the car for the price (DEM 26,350) bid by the highest bidder, the claimant. The latter's claim failed at first instance but succeeded on appeal and before the Supreme Court. The cost of the new Volkswagen Passat Variant TDI was listed locally as being DEM 57,000. The opening price for the auction was DEM 10 and the defendant did not specify any reserve (minimum) price, despite the fact that Ricardo's standard terms allowed sellers to do so. These terms also provided that any seller on submitting an item for sale declares his anticipated acceptance of the highest valid bid made during the auction (5 days and 963 valid bids in this case). The defendant denied the existence of a valid contract and tried to rescind any agreement on the basis of mistake.

[102] Art 9 of the Spanish Retail Trade: 'Obligation to sell: 1. The public offer to sell or the exhibition of items in commercial premises means the duty of the titleholder to sell to the persons who fulfil the conditions to acquire, attending in the second case to the temporal order of the applications. Objects in which it is expressly warned that they are not for sale or that clearly form part of the decoration are exceptions to this rule. 2. Traders will not be allowed to limit the quantity of items that may be acquired by every buyer nor to establish higher price nor suppress reductions or promotions to sales that overpass a certain volume. In case of lack of stock to cover the orders, temporal priority in the orders will apply.'

[103] P Malaurie, L Aynès and P Stoffel-Munck, *Les obligations*, 2nd edn (Paris, Defrénois, 2005) 231; Terré, Simler and Lequette, above n 72, 119.

[104] (1964) Bull civ No 461.

[105] NJW 2002, 263.

Judgment: As far as the declaration, which was made by the defendant at activation, is identified as an acceptance in §5 IV of the terms and conditions, this is a legally harmless false description; in fact this declaration already fulfils all requirements for a legally binding offer and is not purely an invitation to treat. Even if the defendant's declaration connected to the activation of the auction site is not regarded as an offer in the sense of §145 BGB, it constitutes in any event an anticipated statement of acceptance with regard to the offer effectively made by the last bidder, ie the claimant.

Court of Appeal, 2000[106] **3.33 (UK)**
Barry v Davies (Trading as Heathcote Balls & Co)

A CONTRACT IS CONCLUDED WHEN A BID IS MADE TO THE AUCTIONEER/OFFEROR

Auction of machines without reserve price

The auctioneer makes a real offer to sell to the highest bidder; if he does not transfer property to this bidder but sells to a third person there is a breach of contract.

Facts: HM Customs and Excise put up two engine analysers for sale by auction, without a reserve price. The price of the machines new was GBP 14,521 each. The claimant bid GBP 200 for each machine after the auctioneer tried and failed to get bids of GBP 5,000 and GBP 3,000 for each machine. The auctioneer refused to sell the machines to the claimant for such a low price and they were subsequently sold to a third party for GBP 1,500 each. The claimant brought an action against the *auctioneer* for breach of contract. The claim succeeded. The claimant was held to be entitled to recover GBP 27,600 by way of damages, being the difference between the amount he would have had to pay to obtain the machines in the ordinary way.

Judgment: [Sir Murray Stuart-Smith] The judge held that it would be the general and reasonable expectation of persons attending at an auction sale without reserve that the highest bidder would and should be entitled to the lot for which he bids. Such an outcome was in his view fair and logical. As a matter of law he held that there was a collateral contract between the auctioneer and the highest bidder constituted by an offer by the auctioneer to sell to the highest bidder which was accepted when the bid was made. In so doing he followed the views of the majority in the Court of Exchequer Chamber in *Warlow v Harrison* (1859) 1 E& E 309. …

The authorities, such as they were, do not speak with one voice. The starting point is section 57 of the Sale of Goods Act 1893 (56 &57 Vic c 71), itself in this section a codification of the common law. I have already referred to the effect of subsection (2). Subsections (3) and (4) are also important. They provide:

(3) A sale by auction may be notified to be subject to a reserve or upset price, and a right to bid may also be reserved expressly by or on behalf of the seller.

(4) Where a sale by auction is not notified to be subject to the right to bid by or on behalf of the seller, it is not lawful for the seller to bid himself or to employ any person to bid at the sale, or for the auctioneer knowingly to take any bid from the seller or any such person. …

As to consideration, in my judgment there is consideration both in the form of detriment to the bidder, since his bid can be accepted unless und until it is withdrawn,

[106] [2000] 1 WLR 1962.

and benefit to the auctioneer as the bidding is driven up. Moreover, attendance at a sale is likely to be increased if it is known that there is no reserve.

As to the agency point, there is no doubt that, when the sale is concluded, the contract is between the purchaser and the vendor and not the auctioneer. Even if the identity of the vendor is not disclosed, it is clear that the auctioneer is selling as an agent. It is true that there was no such contract between vendor and purchaser. But that does not prevent a collateral agreement existing between the auctioneer and bidder. A common example of this is an action for breach of warranty which arises on a collateral contract.

For these reasons I would uphold the judge's decision on liability.

Notes

(1) Both German and English law take the view that auction bids are offers, which lapse the moment a higher valid bid is made, and that no contract is formed unless and until the auctioneer decides to conclude the auction by bringing down the hammer, which marks the final acceptance (§156 BGB and section 57(2) of the Sale of Goods Act 1979). *Barry v Davies* established, after a century of doubt, that the majority's reasoning (though *obiter*) in *Warlow* v *Harrison*[107] was correct and that in an auction sale without reserve there is an offer by the auctioneer to sell to the highest bidder.[108]

(2) EU consumer law has not dealt with these problems as yet. Article 3(1) of the Distance Selling Directive (97/7/EC) declares: 'This Directive shall not apply to contracts: … concluded at an auction.'[109] Therefore, this is a realm still fully in the hands of national legislation and/or case-law. The Green Paper on the Review of the Consumer Acquis of 8 February 2007[110] draws attention to the new problems created by new means by which transactions between business and consumers are concluded arising from technological developments which were not considered by existing Directives (notably, the Distance Selling and Electronic Commerce Directives): 'as confirmed by the evaluation of the national laws, the different usage of this regulatory option by the Member States creates fragmentation and has led to a rise in consumer complaints in respect of these on-line auctions'.[111] Further definition of the notion of 'public auctions' and a separate regulation of online auctions are currently under scrutiny by the European Commission.

[107] [1858] 1 EE 309; 120 ER 92.

[108] A Burrows, *A Casebook on Contract* (Oxford/Portland, Hart Publishing, 2007) 19.

[109] Furthermore, Art 1.3 of this Directive allows Member States to provide that the definition of consumer goods does not cover 'second-hand goods sold at public auctions where the consumer has the opportunity to attend the sale in person'. This exemption is a source of uncertainty both for businesses and consumers and, in consequence, the Green Paper on the Review of the Consumer Acquis (25) raises the question on the necessity of defining the notion of 'public auctions' in order to remove this uncertainty. The Green Paper also considers that it may be necessary to follow a specific and different approach for online auctions.

[110] COM [2006] 744 final.

[111] See the Communication from the Commission on the implementation of the Distance Selling Directive (1997/7/EC).

(3) In fact, both old and new questions are raised by online auctions, which are increasingly being used by consumers as a way of acquiring goods: at what time is the contract concluded? Where a seller receives bids at a much lower level than he expects, and therefore appears to be bound to sell, can he revoke the offer or rescind the contract? At what moment does the offer take place? When the bidder contacts the intermediary auctioneer or when the call of the bid on a lot is made public?[112] The two judgments noted above illustrate eloquently these problems and their differing reasoning is worth comparing.

Questions

(1) Check the standard terms of an online auctioneer (eg eBay) on its website and compare the sets of terms displayed for four different countries as regards the questions as to what are considered as offer and acceptance and when. Are there differences in the wording and the legal timing, even within the same auctioneer's site? If so, how do you account for these differences?

(2) What is the role of the intermediary 'auctioneer' in an online auction?[113] Can such an auctioneer be considered an offeror, and, if so, of what?

(iv) Webpages

There is considerable discussion in the literature in most countries on this point. For instance, taking Belgium as an illustration, the debate concerns the possibility of assimilating the legal nature of a webpage to the legal nature of a catalogue. With regard to catalogues, some authors say these are mere 'proposals' or invitations to offer;[114] other authors say these are offers;[115] and a third group says one has to check on a case-by-case basis whether the elements constitutive of an offer are present[116] (which seems to be the most sensible solution). Some legal systems consider that webpages deserve the same treatment as shop-window displays with price tags (eg in Denmark: binding offers).[117]

(v) Automatic distributors/machines

Like the case of online auctions, sales of goods by automatic vending machines are not dealt with separately by EC Directives, although the Green Paper on the Review of the Consumer Acquis is considering their regulation. Article 3(1) of the Distance Selling Directive 97/7/EC states:

[112] See G Spindler and A Wiebe, *Internet-Auktionen* (Köln, Otto Schmidt, 2001) 69ff.

[113] This is now under revision by the European Commission: conclusions will be announced in the Second Report on the application of the Directive 2000/31/EC.

[114] Kh Brussel 9 april 1964 (1965) JCB 193.

[115] R Kruithof, 'Overzicht van rechtspraak (1965/1973) Verbintenissen' (1975) TPR 453; F Kint in X Dieux, M Fontaine and PA Foriers (eds), *Les obligations contractuelles* (Editions du Jeune Barreau, Brussel, 1984) No 46, 33–34.

[116] Y Schoentjes-Merchiers (1971) RCJB 229–30.

[117] P Møgelvang-Hansen, 'The Binding Effects of Advertising' in R Schulze, *New Features in Contract Law* (München, Sellier, 2007) 177–78.

> This Directive shall not apply to contracts: … concluded by means of automatic vending machines or automated commercial premises.

An illustration of the problems to which these devices give rise in terms of the formation of the contract is demonstrated by the cases of car parks with coin machines. In *Thornton* v *Shoe Lane Parking*,[118] Lord Denning MR said that the offer is made when the proprietor of the machine holds it out as being ready to receive the money, and acceptance takes place when the customer puts his money into the slot:

> assuming, however, that an automatic machine is a booking clerk in disguise—so that the old fashioned ticket cases still apply to it.

This scheme of offer (by the proprietor) and acceptance (by the customer) is also the general view in German law, although some conditions are required to avoid the inappropriate imposition of liability, such as the validity of the offer when three conditions are met: adequate use by the customer, capacity of working (not a vandalised machine) and the availability of goods (not empty);[119] however, a few German scholars have challenged this scheme and hold the opinion that putting money in the slot is the offer and the acceptance is produced by the functioning of the machine.[120] Anyway, under either interpretation, in Germany if the customer inserts money and receives no goods due to a failure in the machine, no contract is concluded. Discussion in other jurisdictions on who offers and who accepts runs normally parallel to the general position of each system on what is to be considered as an offer or as an invitation to treat.

(vi) Tacit offers (offers by conduct)

Cass civ 1e, 2 December 1969[121]
Ms Jean Jacques X v Société des Autoplaces **3.34 (FR)**

A PURE FACT MAY BE DEEMED AS AN OFFER

Dangerous taxi for old ladies

The simple fact of parking a taxi in a designated parking space constitutes an offer and the opening of the door by the customer means her acceptance.

Facts: An old lady was injured when she was getting into a taxi which began moving due to the road inclination, since the driver had taken off the handbrake. When the lady sued the taxi company, the main legal question was whether a contract of transport had been concluded between the parties so as to give rise to a contractual duty of safety on the part of the company (a duty whose non-performance gave rise to strict contractual liability). The Court of Appeal accepted the conclusion of the contract and the contractual liability of the taxi company, without any fault of the victim. The Cour de Cassation confirmed this decision.

118 [1971] All ER 686; 2 QB 163; 2 WLR 585 (CA).

119 Eg OLG Düsseldorf, 16 October 1986 (1987) ZMR 328.

120 D Medicus, *Allgemeiner Teil des BGB*, 7th edn (Heidelberg, Müller, 1997) para 362; Erman-Hefermehl, *BGB*, 10th edn (Münster, Aschendorff, 2000) §145, para 5.

121 Bull civ I No 281; (1970) D 104.

Judgment: Since the conclusion of a transport contract arises from the offer of the carrier and the acceptance of the traveller;

Since the appeal judges, who autonomously appreciate the intention of both parties to conclude an agreement, state that, first, the simple fact of parking a car in a designated parking space, with the driver at the wheel and the meter not yet engaged, constitutes an offer, and that, secondly, Mrs Jean Jacques had displayed her intention of sitting down in the taxi by opening the door, an 'unequivocal gesture';

For that reason, the first argument must be disregarded. …

Given that the Court of Appeal, which, contrary to what is stated in the order, has decided that both parties intended to conclude an agreement, has rightly decided that the moment Mrs Jean Jacques began to get into the taxi the carrier had an obligation to ensure her security. The Court of Appeal has also rightly concluded that in this case, the victim cannot be reproached for any fault in her behaviour that would exempt the debtor from his obligation to her.

II.B.6 LAPSE OF AN OFFER

An offer may come to an end on a number of grounds, such as a refusal to accept an offer, the death or incapacity of the parties (though this varies from legal system to legal system), the expiry of the time for acceptance or the revocation of the offer. We will focus here on the last two issues.

An offer may be set with or without a fixed period of validity, at the expiry of which it lapses. Legal systems seem to be quite uniform on the default rules (without particular reference to consumer rules in EU Directives). According to comparative case-law, every offer has an express or implicit maximum time-limit, after which acceptance is ineffective: in this sense, French case-law states that in the case of absence of an express period set for acceptance, there must be a 'délai raisonnable'.[122] §§146 and 148 of the German BGB are very similar. English case-law emphasises that the default period of a reasonable time should be assessed by the court according to all the circumstances of the transaction;[123] and some English decisions even hold that both the circumstances existing at the time of the offer and the circumstances arising thereafter should be considered.[124] This sort of common core on the reasonable default period of time for acceptance of an offer can also be seen, with different nuances of wording, in international texts such as in Articles 2:206 ('time limit for acceptance') and 2:207 ('late acceptance') PECL, in Article II—4:206 and II—4:207 DCFR and also in definitely B2B-oriented texts, such as Articles 17, 18 and 21 CISG. Due to the lack of specific rules in the consumer *acquis communautaire*, no particular rule can be found in the Acquis Principles.

The examples in certain countries show that *sometimes legal time-limits for acceptance are imposed for the benefit of consumers*. Two instances coming from French law may illustrate this. On one hand, there are *periods for acceptance directly imposed by law:* some offers must be maintained for a period of days from the

[122] Cass civ, 8 February 1968, Bul civ III, No 52, 44 and 21 October 1975, Bull civ III, No 302, 229; Cass civ 3e, 10 May 1972, Bull civ III, 207; Cass civ 3e, 20 May 1992, Bull civ II, 164.

[123] *Ramsgate Victoria Hotel Co Ltd* v *Montefiore* [1866] 1 LR 1 Exch 109.

[124] *Manchester Diocesan Council* v *Commercial Investment* [1969] 3 All ER 1593 (Chancery Division).

moment of sending the offer so as to allow the consumer to examine it calmly. Thus, 15 days in consumer credit contracts (Article L 311-8 of the French Consumer Code); 30 days from receipt if the offer deals with a loan for the purpose of acquiring immovable property (Article L 312-10(1)c of the French Consumer Code). In Spanish Law, an offer of consumer credit is irrevocable for 10 days after it is made (Article 16 of the Law 7/1995 of 22 March 1995 on consumer credit). On the other hand, in certain situations, the law imposes on the offeror a duty to fix the time-limit of his offer: for instance, Article L 121-18 of the French Consumer Code, which provides that a trader in a distance contract must fix the period of validity of the offer. If he does not fix it, the courts may assess what is a reasonable period.[125]

II.B.7 REVOCABILITY OF AN OFFER

Once again, no particular EU consumer law rules apply here, but on the topic of revocability there exists 'a major difference among legal systems'.[126] Whereas in German law, the *Angebot* binds the offeror and is irrevocable in the absence of an express reservation: §§145-148 BGB (also Article 3 of the Swiss Civil Code), in English law an offer can be withdrawn at any time before it has been accepted, even if the offer states otherwise,[127] although much of the gap between English and German law is bridged or mitigated by the English posting or 'mailbox' rule (according to which acceptance is effective when is posted).[128] French law on public offers is more similar to English law than to German law: offers are revocable as long as they have not been accepted,[129] though French law is unclear as to whether an acceptance is effective on posting or on receipt. Similarly, Article 1328(1) of the Italian Civil Code. Article 2:203(3) PECL and Article II—4:202 DCFR take a more English/French approach to this point.

DCFR **3.35 (EU)**

Article II—4:202: Revocation of an offer

(1) An offer may be revoked if the revocation reaches the offeree before the offeree has dispatched an acceptance or, in cases of acceptance by conduct, before the contract has been concluded.

(2) An offer made to the public can be revoked by the same means as were used to make the offer.

(3) However, a revocation of an offer is ineffective if:

[125] Terré, Simler and Lequette, above n 72, 121.

[126] A Farnsworth, 'Comparative Contract Law' in M Reimann and R Zimmermann, *The Oxford Handbook of Comparative Law* (Oxford, Oxford University Press, 2006) 915.

[127] *Routledge v Grant* [1828] 4 Bing 653, 3 C&P 267, 6 LJOS 166, 1 Moo&P 717; *Dikinson v Doods* [1876] 2 Ch D 463. This surprising effect is due to the doctrine of consideration (although some limits can be found, for instance, under the doctrine of promissory estoppel).

[128] G Dannemann, *An Introduction to German Civil and Commercial Law* (London, BIICL, 1993) 12.

[129] Cass civ, 3 February 1919 (1923) DP I.126. However, under some circumstances, revocation may be regarded as a *faute* and illegitimate if abusive (for instance, if the offer fixed a period of irrevocability).

(a) the offer indicates that it is irrevocable;
(b) the offer states a fixed time for its acceptance; or
(c) it was reasonable for the offeree to rely on the offer as being irrevocable and the offeree has acted in reliance on the offer.

(4) Paragraph (3) does not apply to an offer if the offeror would have a right under any rule in Books II to IV to withdraw from a contract resulting from its acceptance. The parties may not, to the detriment of the offeror, exclude the application of this rule or derogate from or vary its effects.

II.C ACCEPTANCE

II.C.1 REQUIREMENTS FOR EXPRESS ACCEPTANCE

The *substantive requirement* is again that the acceptor has an intention to be bound. As national and international rules usually put it, '(1) Any form of statement or conduct by the offeree is an acceptance if it indicates assent to the offer. (2) Silence or inactivity does not in itself amount to acceptance' (Article II—4:204(1) DCFR = Article 2:204(1) PECL). It is not enough if he simply acknowledges receipt of the offer, since a genuine intention or 'will' to be contractually bound is needed. This intention or will can be expressed in words or by conduct alone (see, for instance, the case already noted of Cass civ 1e, 2 December 1969: acceptance produced simply by the opening of a taxi's door). However, in the field of consumer law, purely passive behaviour (such as silence) is much more restricted in its capability of binding than is the case as a matter of general contract law (see chapter 2). Together with the intention issue, consumer law is particularly demanding as regards the offeree's knowledge of the whole offer and makes special requirements in relation to the incorporation or transparency of standard terms (see chapter 4).

As to the *formal requirements* for acceptance, although the rule is that this declaration may be expressed in any way, frequently the law imposes a written form or special means so as to guarantee the existence of the consumer's intention or will. For instance, in French law, *postal* acceptance of an offer of credit to purchase immovable property must be no earlier than 10 days after the offer was made (Article L 312-10(2) French Consumer Code). For instance, the French judgement in Cass civ 29 October 2002[130] states:

> in view of articles L 312-10(2) and L 312-33 Consumer code; according to the first text, the acceptance of a loan for immovable property, to be given within 10 days of receipt, must be given by letter that must be postmarked; in application of the second text, the only private law remedy of infringement of that formal condition is the loss, total or partial, of the right to interest payments in such proportion as determined by the judge.

Another source of formal requirements can arise from contractual practice. For instance, in French practice, in many consumer contracts it is required that a

[130] Bull Civ I No 255; (2002) D 2076.

consumer who accepts an offer must write before his or her signature that he or she has 'read and approved' it ('lu et approuvé').[131]

II.C.2 REQUIREMENTS FOR IMPLIED ACCEPTANCE: SILENCE, INERTIA SELLING AND UNWILLING BUYERS

G Dannemann, Formation of Contracts on the Internet[132] **3.36 (EU)**

Unwilling buyers will usually have paid on-line by credit or debit card. If they seek some form of restitution, they will quickly learn that much of the regulatory function of the law is replaced by the practice of credit card companies. These act as unappointed arbiters who decide whether customers have presented reasonable grounds as to why they did not agree to this transaction, or why the goods or services did not conform. Their practice may be sufficiently generous for the buyers to prevent them from litigating in court.

Note

The well-settled principle in all jurisdictions, in EU consumer law Directives and in uniform and international texts is that 'silence or inactivity does not in itself amount to acceptance'.[133] See also Article 9 of the Distance Selling Directive (97/7/EC), Article 9(2) of the Distance Selling of Financial Services Directive (2002/65/EC) and the classification of some unsolicited sales as unfair commercial practices or aggressive practices under numbers 20, 21, 26 and 29 of Annex I to Directive 2005/29/EC. Consumer law rules try to be particularly firm in this respect and so avoid exceptions as much as possible. For more information on this principle and aggressive practices against it, see chapter 2.

Questions

(1) Do you think that claims by a business for the deterioration, diminished value for use or loss in the hands of a consumer would also fail as a result of these European rules on unsolicited goods? What about the costs of sending back the unsolicited item?

(2) Does obvious evidence of a mistake made by a business in sending property play any role for this purpose (eg where a parcel appears in the mailbox of the consumer which is clearly addressed to a neighbour)? Can you cite any judgment on this question?

(3) Would it be regarded as an unsolicited supply if a business supplies goods which are different from those which were ordered, but of a similar price and character (see §241(a)(3) of the German BGB)?

[131] S Jacquin, 'Les mentions contractuelles "coutumières', un droit imaginaire' (2001) I *JCP* 288.

[132] In P Birks and A Pretto (eds), *Themes in Comparative Law in Honour of Bernard Rudden* (Oxford, Oxford University Press, 2002) 180. See also R Brownsword and G Howells, 'When Surfers Start to Shop: Internet Commerce and Contract Law' (1999) 19 *Legal Studies* 287–315.

[133] Art II—4:204(2) DCFR = Art 2:204(2) PECL, similar in Art 18.1(2) CISG and see also Art 4:106 ACQP.

II.C.3 CORRECTION OF INPUT ERRORS

Electronic Commerce Directive (2000/31/EC) **3.37 (EU)**

Article 11 Placing of the order

(2) Member States shall ensure that, except when otherwise agreed by parties who are not consumers, the service provider makes available to the recipient of the service appropriate, effective and accessible technical means allowing him to identify and correct input errors, prior to the placing of the order.

(3) Paragraph … 2 shall not apply to contracts concluded exclusively by exchange of electronic or by equivalent individual communications.

DCFR[134] **3.38 (EU)**

Article II—3:201: Correction of input errors

(1) A business which intends to conclude a contract by making available electronic means without individual communication for concluding it has a duty to make available to the other party appropriate, effective and accessible technical means for identifying and correcting input errors before the other party makes or accepts an offer.

(2) Where a person concludes a contract in error because of a failure by a business to comply with the duty under paragraph (1) the business is liable for any loss caused to that person by such failure. This is without prejudice to any remedy which may be available under II—7:201 (Mistake).

(3) In relations between a business and a consumer the parties may not, to the detriment of the consumer, exclude the application of this Article or derogate from or vary its effects.

Note

Consider the possible remedies and sanctions of non-performance of this duty and compare those remedies in the DCFR, in the ACQP and in Article 20 of the Directive on Electronic Commerce (2000/31/EC).

II.C.4 PERIOD OF TIME FOR PRIOR REFLECTION ('DÉLAI DE RÉFLEXION PRÉALABLE')

Another device to safeguard the consumer's consent is, for instance, what in French law is called a '*délai de réflexion préalable*' which differs from the right of withdrawal ('*droit de rétractation*') on the basis that consumer's consent is 'postponed' in the former and 'precarious' in the latter. During this period, a consumer is forbidden to accept for a fixed period of time after receipt of the offer. This technique is used only in the case of some types of contract and is set at different lengths of time:

[134] See also similarly Art 2:301 of the 'Acquis Principles' (the provision is currently under review).

(a) Seven days in contracts for distance learning.[135]

(b) Ten days when contracting a credit to buy immovable property.[136]

(c) Seven days when contracting for purchase or the construction of a residential house by notarial deed.[137]

II.C.5 CONFIRMATION OF THE ACCEPTANCE (ACKNOWLEDGEMENT OF RECEIPT)

Directive on Electronic Commerce (2000/31/EC) **3.39 (EU)**

Article 11 Placing of the order

(1) Member States shall ensure, except when otherwise agreed by parties who are not consumers, that in cases where the recipient of the service places his order through technological means, the following principles apply:

—the service provider has to acknowledge the receipt of the recipient's order without undue delay and by electronic means,

—the order and the acknowledgement of receipt are deemed to be received when the parties to whom they are addressed are able to access them. ...

(3) Paragraph (1) ... shall not apply to contracts concluded exclusively by exchange of electronic or by equivalent individual communications.

ACQP **3.40 (EU)**

Article 4: 110 Acknowledgment of receipt

(1) A business which offers the facility to conclude a contract by electronic means and without individual communication must acknowledge by electronic means the receipt of an offer or an acceptance by the other party. Article 1:303 (Electronic notice) applies.

(2) If the other party does not receive such an acknowledgment or an acceptance without undue delay, that other party may withdraw its offer or acceptance and may also claim damages.

(3) Paragraphs (1) and (2) are mandatory in the sense of Article 1:203 (Mandatory nature of consumer rules) in relations between businesses and consumers.

[135] Art 9 of the Act of 12 July 1971, which became Art L 444-8 of the Education Code.

[136] Art 7 of the Act of 13 July 1979, which became Art L 312-10(2) of the French Consumer Code: see Cass civ 1e, 30 March 1994 (1994) Bull civ I No 130, 96.

[137] Art L 271-1(5) of the Code on building, according to the modification by Law 2006-872 of 13 July 2006.

AG (Court of First Instance) Butzbach, 14 June 2002[138] **3.41 (DE)**

CONFIRMATION OF AN ORDER IN E-COMMERCE IS NOT NECESSARILY AN ACCEPTANCE BY THE TRADER

Thank you for your e-mail

Automatic e-mails to confirm receipt of an order do not amount to an acceptance of that order when there was a mistake in the price shown on the webpage.

Facts: On 20 October 2001 at 7:53 am the claimant ordered online ten television sets at €270,47 each as set out on the website of the defendant (the offeror) (this being 1/10th of the normal market price). On the same day at 8:43 am he received by e-mail the following communication: 'Thank you very much for your e-mail. We will process your order immediately.' The next day at 15:31 pm the defendant sent another e-mail with the following content: 'Thank you very much for your order. Regretfully we cannot confirm your order at that price. That price was placed on our web-site by a temporary mistake. The correct price for this model amounts to DEM 5,295. We respectfully ask for your understanding and we will be glad to hear from you again.' The court rejected the claim of the claimant-buyer.

Judgment: 20. According to the concrete wording of the message in the defendant's e-mail of 20 October 2001, however, the defendant stated that the claimant's order had been received and that his order would now be promptly processed further. Theoretically this choice of wording allows—albeit only with a little imagination—for an interpretation which could go in two directions, the first being that the defendant is now beginning the concrete handling of the order (preparation of the goods, shipping, accounting etc)—which implies that the offer has been accepted—and the other being that the defendant is checking whether it will agree to the terms of the contract inherent in the offer. In principle an acceptance of an offer aimed at the conclusion of a contract can only be perceived in a declaration of the unreserved acceptance of the offer. Bearing in mind the particular customary practices of electronic commerce already set out above, one cannot infer from the statement contained in the defendant's e-mail of 20 October 2001 a declaration to the effect that the claimant's offer was accepted unreservedly.

Notes

(1) The aim of the Electronic Commerce Directive's rule is not to modify the normal procedure by which a contract is formed (which rests on the national rules of each country governing who offers/accepts and when agreement is formed), but to impose clearly a new formal information requirement, on the ground that it may be doubtful whether an order or an acceptance sent by electronic means has actually reached its addressee. The 'double-click' requirement underwent an important modification in the course of the negotiations on the Electronic Commerce Directive. In the amended Proposal of 1999,[139] Article 11 stated that '*the contract is concluded* when the recipient of the service has received from the service provider, electronically, an acknowledgement of receipt of the recipient's acceptance' and the 'acknowledgement of receipt is deemed to be received when the recipient of the service is able

[138] (2003) VuR 34.

[139] Amended proposal for a European Parliament and Council Directive on certain legal aspects of electronic commerce in the Internal Market, OJ C [2000] 69–96, COM [1999] 427 final.

to access it'. Therefore, the amended proposal opted for a rule of receipt, rather than a rule of acceptance, but in such a way that the conclusion of the contract was left entirely at the option of the offeror. This was changed on the adoption of the Common Position on the Directive by the Council on 28 February 2000.[140] The Council relied to a considerable extent on the diversity of national positions governing the time at which a contract is concluded and 'considered that it was not appropriate to harmonise national law regarding the moment at which a contract is concluded. For this reason Article 11 has been renamed and now limits itself to certain requirements regarding the placing and receipt of orders on-line'. As a result, Article 11 as enacted imposes a simple obligation of information in that the offeror must send an acknowledgement of receipt.[141]

(2) The *Butzbach* case illustrates the ineffectiveness of an acknowledgement of receipt in forming a part of the agreement process in a system, such as the German one, where a consumer's electronic order may be deemed to be an offer (rather than an acceptance as in other systems). The question of determining the significance of the receipt itself depends on whether it is an automated message or a personal communication. Other judgments in different jurisdictions have noted the minor importance of automated acknowledgements of receipt as evidence of an intention to be bound on the part of the offeror: see in this sense the Strasbourg First Instance Court judgment of 24 July 2002 (cited above).[142] Note the contrast between Article 11 of the Electronic Commerce Directive (2000/31/EC) and Article 5 of the Distance Selling Directive (97/7/EC) (written confirmation of information during the performance of contract).

(3) As regards the comparison between Article 11 of the Directive on Electronic Commerce (2000/31/EC) and the proposed Article 4:110 ACQP, two features deserve attention, both of which underline possible weaknesses in the European norm: on the one hand, the Principles explicitly establish remedies and sanctions for the case of infringement of the trader's duty to acknowledge receipt of the customer's communication, whereas the Electronic Commerce Directive does not specify any sanctions (see Article 11 of the Distance Selling of Financial Services Directive (2002/65/EC)); this has been the subject of criticism and suggestions for reform of the European text. On the other hand, the Principles deviate slightly from the model adopted by the Directive (receipt of the recipient's 'order'), when they require receipt of an 'offer or an acceptance by the other party.' This difference allows the application of the rule without taking a position as to how the conclusion of the contract takes place, ie which party makes or accepts the offer.[143]

[140] OJ C 128 of 8 May 2000.

[141] See J Huet, 'Encore une modification du Code Civil pour adapter le Droit des contrats à l'électronique. Loi LCEN n° 2004-575 du 21 juin 2004' (2004) 47 *JCP* 2086, who criticises the wording of Art 1369-2 of the French Civil Code with some expressions inherited from the amended proposal ('confirmation de l'acceptation'). On invitation to purchase and the Unfair Commercial Practices Directive (2005/29/EC) see chapter 2, section V.C.

[142] (2003) D 2434.

[143] S Leible, J Pisulinski and F Zoll, 'Comments on Art 4:108' in Acquis Group (ed), *Principles of Existing EC Contract Law* (München, Sellier, 2007) 150.

Question
Compare the articles cited from the directive and the Acquis Principle with Article II—4:210 DCFR ('Formal confirmation of contract between businesses'). Are the grounds for different solutions between B2B and B2C sufficiently justified? Would the *Butzbach* case be solved differently applying Article II—4:210 DCFR?

II.C.6 MOMENT AND PLACE OF CONCLUSION OF THE CONTRACT

This issue is determined by the national legal systems. The typical approach is that the national rules rely on their general principles of contract law to set the moment and place of conclusion of the contract, without any special rules for the consumer context, but there are some special features provided for consumers in some systems. Therefore, the differences between the 'reception rule' (§§130 and 147(2) German BGB, Article 1335 Italian Civil Code, Article 18.2 CISG, Article 2:205 PECL) and the 'dispatch or postal acceptance rule' (English law; Article 1263(3) Spanish Civil Code;[144] in French law the case-law is divided) in distance contracts and electronic commerce should be taken into account: on those rules, see the Contract Law Casebook.

III. INFORMATION DUTIES

III.A INTRODUCTION

The classical way of thinking about contract law used to stress the importance of contractual freedom, that used to be seen as a sufficient guarantor of contractual justice: 'Qui dit contractuel dit juste.'[145] This classical belief started from the presumption that parties were free to enter into a contract, and equal, so that they could influence the content of the contract to the same degree. This classical model soon proved not to match reality and adjustments were deemed necessary, inter alia in the form of information duties.

[144] After the transposition of the Electronic Commerce Directive in Spain by the Law 34/2002 of 11 July, the diverging criteria of the Civil Code and the Commercial Code were unified, but differences remain between electronic or contracts (posting or expedition rule, for 'contracts concluded via automatic devices') and other distance contracts (reception rule). A summary with criticism in Arroyo i E Amayuelas, 'Le contrat électronique en droit espagnol' (2007) *Revue Lamy Droit de l'immatériel*, suppl no 29, 30ff.

[145] See A De Bersaques, 'L'oeuvre prétorienne de la jurisprudence en matière de lésion' in *Mélanges Jean Dabin* II (Brussel, Larcier, 1963) 491.

R Sefton-Green, Duties to Inform versus Part Autonomy. Reversing the Paradigm: From Free Consent to Informed Consent? A Comparative Account of French and English Law[146] **3.42 (EU)**

In order to explain why party autonomy and duties to inform are in opposition with one another the motto of *'Liberté, Egalité, Fraternité'* will be used as a metaphor. Party autonomy can be assimilated to freedom of contract: here is *liberté*. In the classical version of contract, freedom of contract and the autonomy of the parties are paramount. The classical belief presumes that the parties are equal: here is *égalité*. However, these two presumptions have long since been decreid; an awareness of the parties' inequality highlights the deficiency of classical contract values. It is widely admitted that in an increasing number of contractual situations the parties are neither free nor equal. Next, it is contended that the classical paradigm needs to be reversed, inter alia, since the prevailing value of party autonomy is anachronistic. Indeed very few contracts actually fit the classical model today: it represents myth rather than reality. Moreover, greater recognition of the need for contractual fairness means that the paradigm must be changed because party autonomy and freedom of contract often lead tot contractual unfairness.

It is submitted that contractual fairness may be achieved by putting a greater emphasis on contractual solidarity: here is *fraternité*. Freedom, equality and solidarity must all be present in order to achieve this ideal. This needs explaining. Schematically, there are two conceptions of contract: the first where the binding force of contract is based on party autonomy and free consent. This model represents the contract of conflicting adversarial interests from which it is inferred that each party behaves individualistically. The rule of *caveat emptor,* long prevailing in the English contract of sale, sums up this viewpoint: the parties do not have a duty to inform one another of facts unknown to the other and each person looks after his own interests. The second conception posits that solidarity lies at the heart of the contract on the basis that each party has a positive duty to help an cooperate with the other contracting party; that the parties must behave transparently towards one another. Duties to inform must be imposed to produce informed consent and to enable the parties to work together. It follows that the model focusing on duties to inform as means of achieving contractual solidarity, is opposed to that of party autonomy.

Linked with the evolution towards more solidarity in contracts is the evolution from free consent towards informed consent—an evolution that is not only present in general contract law, but also and very prominently in consumer contracts. An evolution that is moreover not only present in national law, but also and very prominently in European law. At the European level, there is a very strong emphasis on informed consent and on information provision as a means of protecting consumers in the internal market as the following excerpt illustrates:

[146] R Sefton-Green, 'Duties to Inform versus Part Autonomy. Reversing the Paradigm: From Free Consent to Informed Consent? A Comparative Account of French and English Law' in G Howells, A Janssen and R Schulze, *Information Rights and Obligations* (Aldershot, Ashgate, 2005) 171–72.

G Howells and T Wilhelmsson, EC Consumer Law: Has it Come of Age?[147] **3.43 (EU)**

The information paradigm underlines transparency as the main method of consumer protection. It is closely connected with the emphasis on party autonomy as an important value of the internal market. As is well known, this approach is typical of the consumer protection legislation in the European Union. The European Court of Justice has even in a well-known case expressly stated that: 'under Community law concerning consumer protection the provision of information to the consumer is considered one of the principal requirements' (Case C-362/88 *GB Inno BM* [1990] ECR 667). The strong emphasis on transparency and of information can be seen both in the practice of the Court of Justice when outlawing trade barriers on the basis of the Treaty as well as in much of the secondary legislation in the consumer law area.

The proliferation of information duties both at national and at European level as an instrument of consumer protection has not received complete support. The use of information obligations as a means of consumer protection has important advantages as it is considered to be the least intrusive instrument to achieve consumer self-determination and it potentially leads to maximisation of consumer choice. Information remedies moreover allow consumers to protect themselves according to personal preferences rather than place on regulators the difficult task of compromising diverse preferences with a common standard.[148] The disadvantages are unfortunately also present. There is firstly a problem of unnecessary overlap and a lack of consistency in the existing national and Community instruments imposing information requirements. These are technical problems that should in theory be relatively easy to overcome. But there is also the more fundamental problem of the effectiveness and efficiency of information requirements as a means of consumer protection:

G Howells and T Wilhelmsson, EC Consumer Law: Has it Come of Age?[149] **3.44 (EU)**

The criticisms of the information paradigm are also well-known. As many have noted, necessary information may not reach consumers, they may have difficulties in understanding and using the given information, and they may not even find it worthwhile to make use of the information considering the relatively small advantages it may bring. These kinds of problems also seem to accumulate in the most disadvantaged groups of consumers. … The regulation of information also lacks relevance if the consumer does not have any alternatives in practice. …

Indeed, there is evidence from the developing literature on behavioural economics to suggest that information provision may not be the total panacea even for the confident

147 G Howells and T Wilhelmsson, 'EC Consumer Law: Has it Come of Age' (2003) 4 *ELRev* 380.

148 H Beales, R Craswell and S Salop, 'The Efficient Regulation of Consumer Information' (1981) *Journal of Law and Economics* 513.

149 G Howells and T Wilhelmsson, above n 147, 380–81.

and well-educated consumers, who might be expected to gain most from it. This is because consumers often interpret information in ways that suit their prejudices. Thus information that might cause them to change approach will sometimes be ignored or downplayed. In other words, consumers interpret information to justify their consumption behaviour and do not always use it in the rational manner, as neutral advice, that traditional economists suggest they ought to. Businesses of course know this and are keen to ensure their legal obligations to inform are carried out in a manner which as far as possible supports the favourable images consumers have of their products.

Similar reservations as to what an information-based approach towards consumer protection can achieve stem from the behavioural law and economics literature.

GK Hadfield, R Howse, M Trebilcock, Information-Based Principles for Rethinking Consumer Protection Policy [150] **3.45 (EU)**

Although there was early recognition that information problems in consumer markets were compounded by the ability of consumers to process and make use of information, the early analyses tended to see these problems as ones of education or sophistication or class. We now have a greater appreciation of the routine obstacles that any consumer faces in processing complex information, such as information about product risks or market uncertainty. Information processing is costly and so consumers economize on the care with which information is processed. There is evidence that people rely on various heuristics and other devices to govern their interpretation of the great quantities of information they confront daily, and that these devices systematically lead to bad choices as sellers exploit their weaknesses. In some cases, consumers may need substantive protection, not because they are members of a vulnerable group such as the poorly educated, but because as a class consumers are systematically unable to adequately process the information they need to make good decisions. ...

As a first principle, consumer protection instruments that actually generate information that is costly for consumer to interpret or access may be counterproductive. This principle may imply a reevaluation of quite a wide range of consumer protection laws and regulations, especially those that mandate detailed disclosure of contents or ingredients, complex details of price, terms and conditions of a transaction or very specific caveats about the use of a product. ... The corollary proposition is that cruder instruments which often actually restrict consumer choice (such as bans of hazardous products) may in fact be more successful in lowering information costs. There may thus be a trade-off of some importance between reducing information costs effectively and maximizing consumer choice.

[150] GK Hadfield, R Howse and M Trebilcock, 'Information-based Principles for Rethinking Consumer Protection Policy' (1998) *Journal of Consumer Policy* 145 and 159.

III.B GENERAL INFORMATION DUTIES

III.B.1 INTRODUCTION

Although important differences can be seen between the different legal systems, all legal systems now recognise a duty to disclose information in pre-contractual relationships, but the legal basis for such duty varies as well as the scope and the limits to such duty.

England and Wales Court of Appeal, 27 February 2004[151] **3.46 (UK)**
Sykes v Taylor-Rose

CAVEAT EMPTOR?

Dead body parts

There is no legal obligation on vendors to disclose the history of the property.

Facts: Mr and Mrs Sykes bought a house from Mr and Mrs Taylor Rose. They lived there for a couple of months and then saw a documentary programme that revealed that a particularly gruesome murder of a young girl had taken place at the house. The victim had been dissected and some parts had been hidden around the house, but not all parts had been discovered. They were horrified and took the view that they could not longer live in the house and put in on the market. They felt that they could not in conscience dispose of the property without disclosing what they had found out. After trying to sell the property for six months, they sold it to an investor for GBP 75,000 although they claimed that the market value without its history was GBP 100,000. They now asked damages from Mr and Mrs Taylor Rose who had sold them the house without disclosing the murder. Mr and Mrs Taylor Rose had also bought the house without knowing its history and were informed of the murder by an anonymous note with press cuttings. They moved out for some days but then returned and continued to live in the house for 18 months. When they sold the house, they had been informed by their family solicitor that there would be no duty to disclose the history of the house when they sold it. The 'Seller's Property Information Form' included a question: 'Is there any other information to which you think the buyer may have a right to know?' They answered: 'no'. The judge in first instance concluded that the Taylor-Roses were not under a duty to disclose that the murder had taken place at the property nor what had happened. The judge also concluded that the question was a subjective question and had to be answered honestly. The appeal against the judgment was dismissed.

Judgment: [Sir William Aldous] 13. The judge concluded that the respondents were not under a duty to disclose that the murder had taken place at the property, nor what had happened. He said this in paragraph 14:

14. Mr Toone, on behalf of the claimants, accepts that there is no general duty on a vendor to disclose defects in the quality or expected enjoyment of land which he is selling, or matters which may affect the value of the land. He says, however, that: '[the] particulars facts [of this case] are so heinous that they cannot be withheld because there is no other way [by] which the reasonably prudent purchaser would be able to discover them' (written submissions, para 5.14).

15. Mr Toone frankly accepts that he is asking the court to take a great leap forward in the development of the law. He says that the principle of caveat emptor, hallowed though it may have been in the past, is nearing the end of its useful life. The terminal state of the principle is demonstrated, it is submitted, by the recent decision of the majority of the Court of Appeal in *Taylor v Hamer* [2002] EWCA Civ 1130. I have

[151] [2004] EWCA Civ 299.

considered that case. It does not, in my judgment, mark the sea-change for which Mr Toone contends. It seems to me that the decision in Taylor v Hamer depended on the interplay of three relevant considerations. These were the definition of the property to be sold in the contract; a clause in that contract which stated that the purchaser was deemed to have inspected the property; and the giving of an answer regarding fixtures, surreptitiously removed by her husband, which the vendor was found to have given fraudulently. The case does not, in my judgment, have any wider significance.
16. Accordingly, I reject the first basis of the claim made in this case.
There is no appeal against the judge's conclusion upon that matter. …

48. [Lord Justice Peter Gibson] I feel a good deal of sympathy for the appellants. I can well understand their horrified reaction to learning that their recently purchased house had been the scene of so gruesome a murder, made all the more vivid by the details given in the documentary shown on television and with the possibility that parts of the victim's body might still lie undiscovered in their house. I can well understand their indignation that although the value of the house has fallen so sharply in the light of its history once revealed, the respondents might not be liable to them to make good that loss.

49. However, the question for this court is a dry question of law as to whether the respondents incurred a liability to the appellants in answering question 13 of the Seller's Property Information Form in the negative. The answer to that question cannot be affected by my sympathy for the appellants.

50. Because the caveat emptor rule can work harshly on purchasers, whose knowledge of material facts affecting the property they are purchasing is almost certain to be considerably less than that of the vendors, the practice of sending pre-contract enquiries has become standard and the scope of the enquiries has been extended over a period of time. It is for the buyer to decide what enquiries to raise and in what form. It cannot be doubted that a more specific and less subjective question going to the value of the property or to the ability of the purchaser to enjoy the property could have been asked. Unhappily, question 13 in the Law Society's form at that time (we are told that it is no longer in use) did allow the answer to be given in a way which only required, in my view, the vendor to answer the question honestly.

51. For the reasons given by Sir William Aldous, I too would hold that this court cannot interfere with the conclusion of the judge on the main issue in the light of his finding that the vendors were honest in answering that question.

Notes

(1) This case, where all judges consented, illustrates the traditional 'caveat emptor' rule in English sales law and the rather hostile English approach toward information duties. Courts in several other jurisdictions have been more inclined to accept information duties, as will be illustrated below. This does not imply that information duties are non-existent in English law. The cases below will illustrate that—although the 'caveat emptor' rule has not totally disappeared—it is under attack from several sides and several exceptions to the principle exist.

(2) Whereas in general it can be said that English law is rather hostile toward pre-contractual information duties, French, Belgian and German law take a much more positive attitude towards pre-contractual information requirements. In Nordic

countries, information duties are underlined as part of a general emphasis on honesty in transactions.[152]

III.B.2 BASED ON GENERAL CONTRACT LAW

III.B.2.a Existence and legal basis

Duties to disclose can and have been linked to different doctrines or principles in the different legal systems. They are often linked to the notion of good faith in pre-contractual relationships or to the theory of the *culpa in contrahendo* (fault in concluding a contract). This has clearly been the case in the Nordic countries, where the good faith provision has been used as a vehicle to introduce pre-contractual duties of disclosure.[153] This has also been the case in Germany, where the jurisprudential rules on *culpa in contrahendo* have been codified in §311(2), §241 (2) and §280 BGB.[154] The French and Belgian courts have deduced information obligations from Article 1134(3) Civil Code that requires 'contracts to be *executed* in good faith'. The Article is considered also to be applicable in the pre-contractual phase.[155]

In the UK, courts have also been willing to demand active disclosure of certain (particularly onerous) terms and conditions in order to be enforceable. Failure to bring such terms adequately to the attention of the consumer will result in their exclusion from the binding terms of the agreement.[156] *Thornton v Shoe Lane Parking*,[157] which is dealt with in chapter 4 below, illustrates the increasing willingness of the (English) courts to accept that more activism may be required on behalf of the trader to bring certain information to the attention of the consumer and to depart from the fiction that all contracts result from free bargaining with full information on all conditions. Indirect duties to disclose have furthermore been constructed with the help of concepts as 'mistake' or 'misrepresentation'. It will be a misrepresentation to make statements which are true but misleading because they do not reveal all relevant facts.[158] Misrepresentation is also possible by conduct. This was, for example, accepted in the *Spice Girls* case.[159] A company had been induced to enter into a contract with the Spice Girls band on the assumption that all five girls would continue working together. All the girls had participated in the commercial photocall that induced the company to conclude the contract. Ginger Spice left the band some

[152] T Wilhelmsson and C Twigg-Flesner, 'Pre-contractual Information Duties in the Acquis Communautaire' (2006) 2(4) ERCL 455 and S van Erp, 'The Pre-contractual Stage' in A Hartkamp et al (eds), *Towards a European Civil Code* (Den Haag, Kluwer law international, 2004) 376–77.

[153] See Wilhelmsson and Twigg-Flesner, above n 152, 450. The Swedish and Finnish version of s 33 of the Contracts Act provides that: 'An act that would otherwise be binding shall not be enforceable if it was done under circumstances that would make it incompatible with honour and good faith for anyone knowing of those circumstances to invoke the act and the person to whom the act was addressed must be presumed to have known of the circumstances.'

[154] V Rieble, 'Die Kodifikation der culpa in contrahendo' in B Dauner-Lieb, H Konzen and K Schmidt, *Das neue Schuldrecht in der Praxi* (Köln, Heymans, 2003) 137.

[155] Terré, Simler and Lequette, above n 72, No 258.

[156] G Howells and S Weatherill, *Consumer Protection Law* (Aldershot, Ashgate, 2005) 23.

[157] [1971] 2 QB 163.

[158] See eg *Dimmock v Hallet* [1866] LR 2 Ch App 21.

[159] EWCA *Spice Girls v Aprilia World Service* [2002] EMLR 27.

weeks later. It was held that there was misrepresentation by conduct, which creates indirect duties to disclose: once it had been confirmed that one of the girls was to leave, this should have been disclosed to the company before the contract had been concluded.

Similarly, the French and Belgian courts have deduced information obligations from Articles 1108 and 1109 Civil Code ('vices de consentement'), that require consent that has been formed without mistake, violence or fraud ('erreur', 'violence', 'dol'). The impact of these notions has been extended in the late twentieth century. 'Dol' for example, was at first interpreted as requiring positive action (eg a false statement), similar to the English concept of fraud. It has, however, been extended so as to also allow the invalidation of contracts on the ground of failure to speak in circumstances where courts found that a party should have spoken ('dol par réticence').[160]

Cass civ, 18 February 1997[161] **3.47 (FR)**

Caisse régionale de Crédit agricole mutuelle la Gironde v Mme Dorian

NULLITY FOR FAILURE TO DISCLOSE

Badly informed guarantor

For a bank not to inform a guarantor of the bad financial position that the debtor is in, is contrary to the obligation to contract in good faith and constitutes fraud by concealment.

Facts: Mme Dorian entered into a suretyship contract with the Caisse regionale. The bank did not inform her that the person she was standing surety for was in a bad financial position. She was guaranteeing a loan to finance the acquisition of a business, but had not been informed that there was a provisional financial report on the commercial establishment of the debtor, nor had she been informed of the existence of another loan, so that the reimbursement of all loans taken out implied monthly payments of FRF 6,713 for a monthly income of FRF 8,750. The Court of Appeal annulled the suretyship contract on the basis of 'dol par réticence' (fraud by concealment). The Cour de Cassation upheld the decision.

Judgment: Considering the claimant's sole argument in its four parts.

According to the pronouncements of the contested judgement (Bordeaux, 29 November 1994), the bank Caisse régionale de Crédit agricole mutuel de la Gironde (Crédit Agricole) concluded a suretyship contract with Mrs Dorian for a loan of FRF 160.000. On 20 July 1989, the loan agreement was concluded with Mrs Sanz for the acquisition of a business. Since some of the repayments were outstanding, Crédit Agricole sent two formal notices to Mrs Sanz on 13 and 14 December 1989. The bank then took legal action against both Mrs Sanz, who was declared bankrupt by the court on 27 April 1990, and Mrs Dorian for recovery of the money owed. Mrs Dorian invoked the nullity of the suretyship contract on the basis of fraud by concealment.

[160] S Whitakker, 'The Relationship of the Unfair Commercial Practices Directive to European and National Contract Law' in S Weatherill and U Bernitz, *The Regulation of Unfair Commercial Practices under EC Directive 2005/29* (Oxford, Hart Publishing, 2007) 152. Similarly, it is accepted under German law, that *Täuschung* leading to the avoidability (*Anfechtung*) of the contract, is also possible by failure to act (§123 BGB—see Staudinger, *Kommentar zum BGB* (Berlin, Sellier/De Gruyter, 2005) §123 No 10).

[161] Bull civ I No 61, 39; (1997) JCP(E) No 68-70, 114; (1997) JCP(G) IV No 806, 125.

Whereas Crédit Agricole opposed the judgement on the grounds that it permitted the request for annulment since, first, by stating that, according to expert opinion, the turnover should be multiplied by three after the first financial year, the Court of Appeal would have undermined its decision by altering the study of the aforementioned turnover; secondly, in asserting that the valuer's report stated that the turnover should be multiplied by three after the first financial year, but in failing to specify the basis the expert used to reach its decision, as had been asked by the lender in his appeal statement, the Court of Appeal would have undermined the legal basis of its decision in view of Article 1116 of the Civil Code. Thirdly, by stating that 'the scale of concealed information' characterised the fraud, without investigating whether the guarantor made the conclusion of the contract dependant on the debtor's creditworthiness, the Court of Appeal would have further undermined the legal basis of its decision in view of the aforementioned text. Finally, in failing to specify in what way the bank's concealing of the debtor's financial position was responsible for the establishment of the suretyship contract, the Court of Appeal would further have undermined the legal basis of its decision.

However, a bank that, in the full knowledge that its debtor was financially compromised beyond repair, or at least, had fallen into considerable debt, omits to communicate this information to the guarantor, thus inciting the guarantor to conclude the contract, fails to contract in good faith and commits 'dol par réticence' (fraud by concealment). As the judgement, states that, first, the bank Crédit Agricole, who did not disclose the information obtained from the study of the accounts of Mrs Sanz's business at the time the suretyship was established, did not inform Mrs Dorian that Mrs Sanz had taken out an additional loan of FRF 25.000 that was repayable up until 10 February 1990 and states second, that the repayment of the two loans, as well as a monthly rental payment of FRF 2.800, obliged Mrs Sanz to monthly instalments of FRF 6.713 to be paid from an expected monthly turnover of FRF 8.750, making it clear that Mrs Sanz was unable to repay the loan of guaranteed by Mrs Dorian, the Court of Appeal has, on the above considerations, legally justified its decision. Consequently, given that the argument's first part is inoperative, the argument is unfounded with regard to the other three parts.

Notes

(1) The annotated case illustrates the link between information duties implied in the notion of good faith and the 'vices de consentement'. 'Dol par réticence' includes cases where a potential party to a contract is under a legal duty to inform the other party. The Cour de Cassation here refers to the general notion of good faith.

(2) Consumer protection instruments that are at first sight without prejudice to contract law can nevertheless indirectly affect contract law. The Unfair Commercial Practices Directive (2005/29/EC) is such an instrument. Article 3(2) states expressly that it is without prejudice to contract law. However, it creates positive information requirements, especially through its provisions on misleading omissions. This makes it easier for a consumer who concluded a contract although certain information the national implementing legislation requires to be provided has not been given, to plead the nullity of the contract because of 'dol par réticence', both under French and Belgian law.[162]

[162] See Whitakker, above n 160.

III.B.2.b Scope

Whether an obligation to provide information to the other contract party actually exists in general contract law is in many jurisdictions linked with the knowledge that parties to the contract have or ought to have.

In a number of jurisdictions, the existence of a duty to disclose is therefore more easily accepted if the (potential) information provider is a professional and the absence of a duty to seek for information oneself or the possibility to rely legitimately on the information provided by the other party is more easily accepted when the recipient of the information is *not* acting in a professional capacity.[163] Even in the UK, with its traditional hostile attitude towards duties to disclose, it is accepted that in a relationship of special confidence (eg between a solicitor and a client), there is a duty of disclosure of all material facts.[164]

The obligations on the professional may in certain jurisdictions go beyond a mere duty to inform. Thus, the French courts not only accept that the professional has a duty to inform his non-professional counterpart on all elements that will allow him to conclude the contract *and* to execute the contract, they also accept that the professional is under an obligation to consult and advise the layman. This obligation is considered to be an accessory to the obligations to deliver and warranty (obligation de délivrance et de garantie) in a sales contract of a certain technicality (eg hardware);[165] it is also considered to be part of certain services contracts, as illustrated by the following case.

Cass civ, 2 May 2001[166] **3.48 (FR)**

DUTY TO ADVISE

Broken clutch

Article 1135 of the Civil Code implies a duty to advise for a garage owner. This involves obtaining the approval of the client before executing an important repair.

Facts: A car broke down because of problems with the clutch. The clutch was replaced and this was billed by the garage owner. The car owner challenged the opportunity of the replacement. The lower court had condemned the car owner as the garage owner had not infringed any duty to advise as on the one hand, the car had been consigned to him without any reservations on the costs of the intervention and on the other

[163] See for Belgium, eg D Freriks, 'Onderzoeks- en mededelingsverplichting in het contractenrecht' (1992) TPR 1187-1260; for France, eg G Raymond, V *Jurisclasseur, Concurrence, Consommation,* fasc 845, information du consommateur, No 18; J Ghestin, *Conformité et garantie dans la vente* (Paris, LGDJ, 1983) No 142; for Germany, BGH (1971) NJW 1795, 1799, BGH (1977) NJW 1055, BGH (1974) NJW 849, 851 and BGH (1992) NJW 300, 302.

[164] J Poole, *Textbook on Contract Law* (Oxford, Oxford University Press, 2006) 525.

[165] Cass civ 1e, 25 June 1996 (1996) Bull Civ I No 274. See also Cass civ 1e, 13 October 1993 (1993) Bull civ I, No 287; Cass civ 1e, 13 April 1999 (1999) CCC comm 127, note L Leveneur (the legal basis for the obligation to inform and advise the seller was found in Article 1602 Code Civil that holds an obligation for the seller to explain clearly to the buyer the scope of his obligations).

[166] (2001) CCC comm 132.

hand, given the age and value of the car, there could be no discussion on the opportunity of the replacement. The Cour de Cassation annulled the judgment

Judgment: Considering that in July 1997, Mr Diverres's car broke down because of a problem with the clutch; the garage (Jamain) charged Mr Diverres FRF 3.163,91 for the repair of the clutch. Mr Diverres, who had had the clutch repaired at another garage in the previous June of the same year, contested that such a replacement was appropriate. He based his claim upon the conclusions reached by the expert of his insurer, Mr Le Ven. Mr Le Ven attributed the break down to a problem with the cable and therefore did not consider the repair works justified. However, the expert provided by the garage's insurance company reached the opposite conclusion and deemed the repair work necessary...

However, given the argument's fourth part:

In light of Article 1135 of the Civil Code;

Whereas, in ruling as it did, the contested judgement holds that the garage owner cannot be held to have failed to meet his obligation to advise, as on the one hand, the car was entrusted to him by the owner without any reservations about the price of the intervention and as, on the other hand, given the age and the value of the vehicle, the appropriateness of repairing was not under discussion;

In ruling in this way the Court of Appeal violated the above stated text since the garage owner, who is bound by an obligation to advise, must seek his client's consent before carrying out an important repair job.

Notes

(1) Article 1135 Civil Code, which was relied on in this case to impose a duty to advise the client of a garage owner, says that 'contracts not only bind parties to perform what is stated in the contract, but also of all the consequences that equity, customs or the law link to such obligation by its nature'. Other grounds that have been used by the French and Belgian courts to imply information obligations have been mentioned above.

(2) The duty to advise thus goes beyond the mere duty to inform. The layman not only needs to receive all elements that enable him to conclude and execute a contract; he must also receive additional information: the consequences of the contract for his personal situation or needs must be pointed out, so that he is in a position to make adequate choices.

(3) This case illustrates that the obligation to advise customers has not only been read into contracts with professionals whose primary job is to advise their clients (eg lawyers, public notaries), but also into contracts that would not at first sight be considered to imply such an obligation.[167] Similar decisions can be found in Germany, where courts have also been rather generous in assuming pre-contractual (and also contractual) information duties and have accepted that, for example, banks and insurance companies were under a duty not only to inform but also to advise clients (*Beratungspflichten*)—see also chapter 6 in this regard.[168] Nevertheless a duty

[167] Raymond, above n 163, nos 21–22.

[168] See Staudinger, *Kommentar zum BGB, §241* (Berlin, Sellier/De Gruyter, 2005) No 477–78.

to advise, going beyond a duty to inform, remains the exception and not the general rule.

III.B.3 BASED ON EXPLICIT STATUTORY PROVISIONS

III.B.3.a National law

In a number of jurisdictions, a general obligation to provide pre-contractual information to a consumer has been codified.

Code de la Consommation **3.49 (FR)**

Article L 111-1 Every professional seller of goods or services must, before the conclusion of the contract, enable the consumer to know all essential characteristics of the good or service.

Note

This article of the French Code de la Consommation is considered to be a codification of the obligations to inform that have been developed by the courts. A similar provision exists in Belgium.[169] Although the wording of Article L 111-1 seems narrower than the general contract law obligations to inform, the Article was meant to reinforce consumer protection. Consumers continue to benefit both from the general contract law obligations and from this provision, which is specified in the following articles of the Code de la Consommation.

The scope of this obligation is illustrated by the following excerpt.

Cass civ, 1 March 2005[170] **3.50 (FR)**

PROFESSIONAL CAPACITY SUFFICES

Concrete

A professional who sells goods must enable the non-professional buyer to know all the essential characteristics of the goods before the conclusion of the contract.

Facts: In this case, the seller, a constructor, had bought some concrete for his professional use, ie construction; he had then sold some of it to a consumer who had been hurt when using the concrete. The seller had not informed the consumer of the essential characteristics of the goods. The seller argued in his defence that he was not a professional seller of concrete but a construction company. The Court of Appeal

[169] See Article 30 of the Belgian Trade Practices Act which is seen by some as the codification of a jurisprudential duty. This Article provides that: 'At the latest, at the time of the conclusion of a sale, the seller shall, in good faith, supply to the consumer all useful information concerning the characteristics of the product or the service and concerning the contract terms, taking into account both the need for information as expressed by the consumer and the specific use of the product or the service as stated by the consumer or as reasonably foreseeable by the seller.'

[170] Bull Civ I, No 109; (2005) RDC 1051, note D Fenouillet.

found that Article L 111-1 Code de la Consommation had not been infringed as the company was a general construction company and not a professional concrete seller. The Cour de Cassation quashed the decision.

Judgment: In light of the Article L 111-1 of the Consumer Code;

Considering that, as the above stated text indicates, a professional seller or a professional service provider must ensure that the consumer has access to all essential features of the goods or services, before the contract is concluded;

Considering that since, in order to deny Mr X the right to hold the company Scarna and son responsible for not complying with the provisions of the above stated text, the judgement states only that this company was a construction company and not a professional concrete seller, so that the company cannot be held to have failed to fulfil the provisions of the above stated text;

However, whereas the Court of Appeal, who qualified Mr X as a non-professional, and held that Mr X's injuries were caused by handling the concrete that had been sold to him by the company Scarna and son, who had ordered it from the supplier in its capacity of a construction company;

In ruling in this way, while it follows from its own observations that the use of the concrete can in fact be considered to be part of the professional activities of the company Scarna and son, so that the latter company, in its capacity as a professional seller of the material to a non-professional, is obliged to ensure that Mr X had access to the essential features of the aforementioned material before the sales contract was concluded, the Court of Appeal violated the above stated text.

Note

The Cour the Cassation accepted that an information duty exists whenever the product sold to a consumer is 'within the field of the seller's professional activity', even if the seller has no special knowledge about the product or service. This case illustrates that the codification of such general contract law principles may not be an entirely neutral operation. The case-law obligations to disclose apply to every person, provided he or she is aware or should have been aware, in particular because of his professional capacity, of certain facts. The obligation in Article L 1111-1 of the Code de la Consommation, on the other hand, *only* applies to professionals, but it does apply to *all* professionals. By imposing an obligation on *all* professionals to provide information on the essential characteristics of the product or service, without actually enquiring whether this professional was actually aware of these characteristics, the legal obligation extends the presumption of awareness to *all* professionals in their relationship with consumers.[171]

III.B.3.b EC law

There is no general obligation in the current EC directives to provide pre-contractual information to a consumer.[172] One does, however, have to keep in mind that the

[171] N Rzepecki, *Droit de la consommation et théorie générale du contrat* (Aix-Marseilles, Presses Universitaires d'Aix-Marseilles, 2002) 72.

[172] T Wilhelmsson, 'Private Law Remedies Against the Breach of Information Requirements of EC Law' in R Schulze, M Ebers and C Grigoleit, *Informationspflichten und Vertragsschluss in Acquis Communautaire* (Tübingen, Mohr, 2003) 247; Wilhelmsson and Twigg-Flesner, above n 152, 456.

UCPD goes quite far in prohibiting misleading omissions (see Article 7 UCPD), which comes quite close to imposing positive information duties on a seller.[173] See chapter 2 on this issue.

III.C SPECIFIC INFORMATION DUTIES

Whereas there is a tendency in most jurisdictions towards accepting the existence of more elaborate information obligations, especially in the relationship between a professional and a person acting outside his professional activities, only a limited number of jurisdictions have gone so far as to enact a general obligation for the business to provide information to the consumer. Statutory requirements to disclose information, relating to specific contracts or relating to specific situations in which the contracts are concluded, are, however, present in all jurisdictions. Specific information requirements are mainly imposed where this is deemed necessary (1) because the consumer is at a disadvantage because of the nature of the contract (eg timeshare contracts and more generally complex contracts) and (2) where the consumer is considered to be at a disadvantage because of the specific situation in which the contract is concluded (eg doorstep contracts, distance contracts).[174]

Such information requirements can, for example, be found in most countries with regard to contracts for the provision of services (eg consumer credit, travel contracts and of course financials services (see below chapter 6)). Moreover in most jurisdictions, there are statutory provisions regulating indication of prices and quantity. Specific information requirements are also very prominent in the EC Directives that protect the consumer. As mentioned, the idea of the informed consumer again plays a very prominent role at EC level, and information requirements are heavily relied on as a means of consumer protection. This is apparent from the extensive information requirements in most consumer directives.[175]

Distance Selling Directive (97/7/EC) **3.51 (EU)**

Article 4 Prior information

(1) In good time prior to the conclusion of any distance contract, the consumer shall be provided with the following information:

(a) the identity of the supplier and, in the case of contracts requiring payment in advance, his address;

(b) the main characteristics of the goods or services;

(c) the price of the goods or services including all taxes;

(d) delivery costs, where appropriate;

[173] On this, J Stuyck, E Terryn and T Van Dyck, 'Confidence through Fairness? The European Directive On Unfair Commercial Practices' (2006) CML Rev 105.

[174] See Wilhelmsson and Twigg-Flesner, above n 152, 441–70.

[175] Such as the Package Travel Directive (90/314/EEC); the Consumer Credit Directive (2008/48/EC); the Timeshare Directive (94/47/EC); the Price Indication Directive (98/6/EC); the Distance Selling Directive (97/7/EC); the Distance Selling of Financial Services Directive (2002/65/EC); the Electronic Commerce Directive (2000/31/EC) (though not exclusively applicable in B2C relationships), etc.

(e) the arrangements for payment, delivery or performance;

(f) the existence of a right of withdrawal, except in the cases referred to in Article 6(3);

(g) the cost of using the means of distance communication, where it is calculated other than at the basic rate;

(h) the period for which the offer or the price remains valid;

(i) where appropriate, the minimum duration of the contract in the case of contracts for the supply of products or services to be performed permanently or recurrently.

(2) The information referred to in paragraph 1, the commercial purpose of which must be made clear, shall be provided in a clear and comprehensible manner in any way appropriate to the means of distance communication used, with due regard, in particular, to the principles of good faith in commercial transactions, and the principles governing the protection of those who are unable, pursuant to the legislation of the Member States, to give their consent, such as minors.

Article 5 Written confirmation of information

(1) The consumer must receive written confirmation or confirmation in another durable medium available and accessible to him of the information referred to in Article 4(1)(a) to (f), in good time during the performance of the contract, and at the latest at the time of delivery where goods not for delivery to third parties are concerned, unless the information has already been given to the consumer prior to conclusion of the contract in writing or on another durable medium available and accessible to him.
In any event the following must be provided:

—written information on the conditions and procedures for exercising the right of withdrawal, within the meaning of Article 6, including the cases referred to in the first indent of Article 6(3),

—the geographical address of the place of business of the supplier to which the consumer may address any complaints,

—information on after-sales services and guarantees which exist,

—the conclusion for cancelling the contract, where it is of unspecified duration or a duration exceeding one year.

Electronic Commerce Directive (2000/31/EC) **3.52 (EU)**

Article 5 General information to be provided

(1) In addition to other information requirements established by Community law, Member States shall ensure that the service provider shall render easily, directly and permanently accessible to the recipients of the service and competent authorities, at least the following information:

(a) the name of the service provider;

(b) the geographic address at which the service provider is established;

(c) the details of the service provider, including his electronic mail address, which allow him to be contacted rapidly and communicated with in a direct and effective manner;

(d) where the service provider is registered in a trade or similar public register, the trade register in which the service provider is entered and his registration number, or equivalent means of identification in that register;

(e) where the activity is subject to an authorisation scheme, the particulars of the relevant supervisory authority;

(f) as concerns the regulated professions:

—any professional body or similar institution with which the service provider is registered,

—the professional title and the Member State where it has been granted,

—a reference to the applicable professional rules in the Member State of establishment and the means to access them;

(g) where the service provider undertakes an activity that is subject to VAT, the identification number referred to in Article 22(1) of the sixth Council Directive 77/388/EEC of 17 May 1977 on the harmonisation of the laws of the Member States relating to turnover taxes—Common system of value added tax: uniform basis of assessment.

(2) In addition to other information requirements established by Community law, Member States shall at least ensure that, where information society services refer to prices, these are to be indicated clearly and unambiguously and, in particular, must indicate whether they are inclusive of tax and delivery costs.

Notes

(1) These Articles illustrate that the information requirements in the current Directives often overlap. In many situations, more than one piece of legislation will apply, which leads to an accumulation of information obligations. Traders selling their products or services to consumers through the internet will, for example, have to comply with both the Distance Selling Directive (97/7/EC) and the Electronic Commerce Directive (2000/31/EC). The recent Proposal for a Directive on Consumer Rights now has the aim of harmonising information requirements and even to provide for maximum harmonisation.[176]

(2) Even detailed provisions such as Article 5 of the Electronic Commerce Directive (2000/31/EC) give rise to interpretation problems. The ECJ recently decided that Article 5(1)(c) of Directive 2000/31/EC does not necessarily require a service provider to give a telephone number as a means to be contacted rapidly. It may also be an electronic enquiry template through which the recipients of the service can contact the service provider via the internet, to whom the service provider replies by electronic mail. A German consumer organisation had argued that a service provider operating exclusively on the internet is under an obligation to communicate its telephone number to clients prior to the conclusion of a contract.[177] Specific statutory requirements often impose the use of particular forms, as is illustrated in the Articles above. Such formal requirements may have several functions: they can warn the consumer to be on his guard, and they can try ensure that the consumer effectively gets the information in a way that he can absorb it and/or later retrieve it.

(3) Both national and EC law provisions often require the information to be provided in a clear and precise form and in plain and intelligible language; see, for example, the above provisions but also Article 5 of the Unfair Contract Terms

[176] COM [2008] 614 final. For criticism see inter alia P Rott and E Terryn, 'The Proposal for a Directive on Consumer Rights: No Single Set of Rules' (2009) ZEup 3; C Twigg-Flesner and D Metcalfe, 'The Proposed Consumer Rights Directive—Less Haste, More Thought?' (2009) *ERCL*.

[177] ECJ, 16 October 2008, Case C-298/07 *Bundesverband der Verbraucherzentralen v Deutsche internet versicherung AG*, nyr.

Directive (93/13/EEC). The requirement that information must be clear and intelligible has also been deduced by the courts from more general provisions, such as the above-mentioned Article L 111-1 Code de la Consommation. This requirement was held also to imply that when photographs are used to reinforce a textual message, such images should be clear and not misleading. This will be particularly relevant in the case of distance selling or e-commerce.[178] The following cases illustrate the possible divergences in interpretation of a 'clarity' requirement.

OLG (Court of Appeal) München, 11 September 2003[179] **3.53 (DE)**

TRANSPARENCY OF ONLINE INFORMATION

Transparent weblink

The transparency requirement can be met when the identification details of a provider can be accessed through a double link.

Facts: A centre against unfair competition brought an action for an injunction and argued that the information a supplier provided on its website with regard to its identity was insufficient. The Landgericht granted the injunction and ordered the supplier to cease offering online ordering facilities for periodicals and books when identification details are only available indirectly via the link 'contact' and then via a further link 'impressum'. The respondent appealed the decision. The Oberlandesgericht (OLG) partially annulled the decision.

Judgment: The supplier identification on the respondent's internet domain, which was objected to in the application for an injunction, is accessible through a double link via 'contact' and 'impressum' according to the findings of the court of first instance (Judgment of 5 March 2003, UA p 3) and is sufficient according to §6(1) of the Teleservices Act (Teledienstegesetz) (TDG), §10(2)(1) of the Interstate Media Services Agreement (Mediendienste-Staatsvertrag) (MDStV).

For commercial teleservices, according to §6(1) TDG, service providers must keep at least the information as described in this provision in an easily discernible and directly accessible manner constantly available; according to §10(2)(1) of the MDStV the same is true for commercial media services. The information according to §6 of the TDG, §10(2) MDStV must be in an easily noticeable place and retrievable at all times without lengthy searching (cf Official Records of Parliament 14/6098, 21; cf also Art 5 of the Electronic Commerce Directive, according to which the service provider must render the information mentioned 'easily, directly and permanently accessible' to the recipients of the service). These requirements were complied with, according to the facts established by the regional court. The information pertaining to supplier identification in this case is easily discernible because of the headings 'contact' and 'impressum'. There is no legal requirement as to under which heading the supplier identification should be provided. … When offering teleservices or media services the descriptions 'contact' and 'impressum' have become accepted in trade for referring the user to the personal details of the supplier …; this is proven by the hard copies of prominent internet service providers

[178] For an illustration, Orléans 15 November 1995 (1995) *Contrats concurrence consommation* 118, note G Raymond.

[179] (2004) NJW-RR 913-915; (2004) MMR 36-38.

presented by the respondent in his written submissions of 3 September 2003. The headings 'contact' and 'impressum' are understood by the average, reasonably observant, and informed user of the internet (World Wide Web) as a reference to the information on supplier identification in accordance with §6(1) of the TDG, §10(2)(1) of the MDStV (...). This does not conflict with the fact that 'contact' sometimes signifies an e-mail link.

The supplier identification objected to on the respondent's internet domain, which is accessible through a double link via 'contact' and 'impressum', also satisfies the prerequisites of the transparency requirement in accordance with §312c(1)(1) of the German Civil Code. The entrepreneur must in this respect inform the consumer clearly and comprehensibly (§312c(1)(1) of the German Civil Code, with which Art 4(2) of Directive 97/7/EC of the European Parliament and Council on the protection of consumers in respect of distance contracts (OJ L 144, 19) was implemented; according to this provision the information in question must be given in a clear and comprehensible manner in any way appropriate to the means of distance communication used). The prerequisites of this transparency requirement do not go beyond the transparency requirement contained in §6(1) of the TDG, §10(2)(1) of the MDStV. Reference is made to the above remarks on the criteria 'easily discernible', 'directly accessible' and 'permanently accessible'.[180]

OLG (Court of Appeal) Karlsruhe, 27 March 2002[181] **3.54 (DE)**

TRANSPARENCY OF ONLINE INFORMATION

Opaque weblink

The transparency requirement is not met when the identification details of a provider can be accessed through a link.

Facts: The claimant organised lottery pools; the respondent ran an internet portal, where he offered lottery tips to lottery pools for payment. To use these services, registration with the respondent was required. Upon registration, a lottery ticket could be completed online. All pages contained the link 'search—themes—services—freemail—help—contact' at the top of the page and in a bar at the bottom. Clicking on 'contact' led to a page where the user could send a request to the respondent. In a frame on the right of that page under the title 'Impressum' the name of the respondent's company, their address and the names of the members of the board of directors could also be retrieved. One of the issues under dispute was whether the respondent satisfied the requirements of §§2 and 3 FernAbsG (Distance Selling Act) as it then applied.

Judgment: Details of the firm and the address are not given clearly and unambiguously. Providing this data under the heading 'Impressum' on a particular webpage, which can be accessed via the link 'Contact' at the top of a page and in the bar at the bottom, is not sufficient. The Act does not define in detail when the trader has informed the consumer in a satisfactory manner. Even Art 4(1) and (2) of directive 97/7/EC of the European Parliament and Council on the protection of consumers in respect of distance contracts (Distance Selling Directive), whose implementation served §2(2) of the Distance Selling Act (today §312c(1)(1) no 1 German Civil Code in connection with Art 240 of the Introductory Act to the German Civil Code and §1(1) no 1 to 3 of the BGB-InfoV (Regulation

[180] The TDG was replaced by the Telemediengesetz (TMG) in 2007 without changes in substance relevant for this case.

[181] (2002) CR 682.

on Information Duties and Obligations to Produce Supporting Documents According to Civil Law)), does not offer a more exact indication. The grounds for the government's drafting of a law only expounds the problem as to whether the use of the German language will always be necessary and merely explains that as a rule it will have to be regarded timely if the information, on the basis of which the consumer decides to place an order, is contained in prospectuses, catalogues or on websites on the internet. The aim of the legal obligation to provide information on identity and address is that the trader voluntarily indicates to the consumer, in a clear and unambiguous manner, with whom he has come into commercial contact. Thus it is not sufficient if the trader merely enables the consumer to find this information for himself. Therefore it is necessary for the information—if it is not expressly pointed out, as in this case—to be displayed, at the very least, in a place which stands out clearly enough on the online form that the consumer is bound, so to speak, to find it. It is unnecessary to decide here whether or not it is even required that the user be forced to request the data. In any case, the provision of information under 'Impressum' on a webpage accessible via the link 'Contact' is not clear and unambiguous. According to what is now firmly established usage on the World Wide Web when using the German language, 'Contact' indicates a website which is supposed to enable the user to come into contact with the person appearing on the internet. The fact that in this case it refers not only to an e-mail link, but also to information on the company and its address, remains concealed from large sections of the targeted consumers, of which the members of the Senate form also part. Moreover, the heading 'Impressum' also gives rise to misunderstandings because in the 'Impressum' of a publication it is customary to name the persons who are responsible according to press law. At any rate, it is unclear for a large number of consumers that in this case it is in fact the same person with whom one can conclude a service contract for the 'online release of a lottery ticket'. [references omitted]

Notes

(1) The annotated cases illustrate that the opinions of the national courts as to what is to be considered as a 'clear and comprehensible manner' may differ, even when national courts are applying provisions that implement the same rule of an EC Directive (Article 4 Distance Selling Directive (97/7/EC)) and that there are even differences in application between courts in one and the same Member State. The BGH has in the meantime decided the question and followed the interpretation of the München OLG. The BGH, moreover, decided that there was no need to refer the question to the ECJ as it found that it is not the task of the ECJ to decide in individual cases what conditions have to be met to comply with the transparency requirements of the Distance Selling Directive (97/7/EC) and the Electronic Commerce Directive (2000/31/EC).[182]

(2) In addition to the requirement that the information has to be clear and comprehensible, certain jurisdictions have strict requirements with regard to the language that is to be used. This was dealt with in chapter 2.

[182] BGH 20 July 2006 (2006) NJW 3633.

III.D REMEDIES

III.D.1 INTRODUCTION

There are several ways in which information duties are not be complied with. In essence, three situations can be distinguished: either

(1) the required information is not provided or is not provided in a timely fashion or in the form required; or

(2) the information provided is misleading; or

(3) the information is provided before the contract is concluded, but the professional refuses to perform the contract in conformity with that information.

In the EC Directives, remedies for failure to provide information are either not provided for or are dealt with inconsistently. A remedy that we do find in the Directives is the prolongation of the right of withdrawal (see below, chapter 4). It should be mentioned that—although the European Commission proposed in its Green Paper on the Review of the Consumer Acquis to deal also with general contractual remedies at EU level—no comprehensive system of remedies was included in the Proposal for a Directive on Consumer Rights. The national law remedies vary widely within the different jurisdictions. In some instances, specific remedies are provided. Thus, for example, under Belgian law, omission to include the withdrawal clause in the written confirmation of the information in case of distance selling (see Article 4(2) Distance Selling Directive (97/7/EC)) entails a specific sanction: the product or service is deemed to be delivered without the prior request of the consumer, and the consumer can keep the product or service without paying its price, or send it back to the seller (Article 79(1) Trade Practices Act). Similarly, German consumer credit legislation provides for very specific sanctions: thus, giving the wrong average percentage rate results in a reduction of the interest rate provided by the law in §246 BGB; forgetting to name specific costs of the contract would mean that the consumer does not owe them, etc. In other instances, general private law remedies are relied on. These vary widely and are discussed below.

III.D.2 GENERAL PRIVATE LAW REMEDIES

The remedies that are available to a consumer in the case of infringement of information duties depend to a large extent on the general private law system. Actions in contract and/or in tort may be open to the consumer and grant him a claim for damages. He may also have a right of avoidance or even a right to specific performance. This will all depend to a large extent on the concrete nature of the information obligation that was infringed, on the availability of remedies under the general law of obligations, on the question of whether a breach of information obligations amounts to a breach of contract under the legal system concerned, and whether such a breach leads to a concrete damage or disadvantage to the consumer.[183]

[183] Consumer law compendium.

III.D.2.a Avoidance

If the information that had not been provided, or had wrongly been provided, would influence the will of the negotiating party, violation of the duty to provide this information may lead to a *vice de consentement* and possibly to the invalidity or avoidance of the contract. The following case illustrates such a mechanism.

Audiencia Provincial (Court of Appeal) Castellón, 1 July 1999[184] **3.55 (ES)**

Juan Bautista RR and Teresa GM v Mundivac, SA and Acualandia, SA

VITIATED CONSENT

Voidable timeshare contract

Fraud by concealment renders the contract voidable.

Facts: Two consumers concluded a timeshare contract at a time when the Timeshare Directive 94/47/EC had not yet been transposed into Spanish law and the period for transposition had also not expired. A withdrawal clause stipulating a penalty of 25 per cent in case of withdrawal was included in the contract but in much smaller print than the rest of the contract, in a deliberate attempt to conceal this from the consumer. The consumers wanted to cancel the contract. Although the provisions of the Timeshare Directive could not be applied, the consumers were held no longer to be bound by the contract, which was considered to be void.

Judgment: The plaintiffs did not claim the recognition of a right to withdraw [from the Timeshare directive that was not implemented], but solely the nullity of the contract as they contest the validity of the consent given.

The fact that the contract was concluded during a free stay of the buyers in a hotel in Peñíscola, on condition that they would attend an event to promote the product—the timeshare apartement—should be taken into account. At this event, in the wording of the Appeal Court of Zaragoza in its judgment of 4 November 1997, took place 'a clearly aggressive marketing technique, that aims—if not at vitiating consent, then at least at altering the capacity to decide, that normally recommends the use of a correction mechanism consisting of a certain period for reflection that allows to quietly consider the advantages and the disadvantages of one's acts'. That is the 'ratio legis' of the right to freely withdraw from the contract during a certain period of time, that is set out in the Directive and in the current Act. …

The miniscule characters of an essential clause have been deliberately used in order to go unnoticed by the buyer. For that reason, when the plaintiffs confirm in their demand that they were only informed of the possibility to withdraw at any moment, but not of the penalty provided if they would do so, this is a credible statement given the atmosphere created by the seller during the promotional event, and given the way the clauses are incorporated in the written contract, where the clauses that are particularly onerous for the buyer are included in a format that is reduced or unappropriate in view of their importance for the contract. In no other paragraph in both contracts, the sales contract and the maintenance contract, are such small characters used as for these clauses and that—and the indications in former Art 1253 Civil Code—leads to the

[184] AC 1999553.

conclusion that in reality the plaintiffs were not informed of the penalty their withdrawal from the contract implied.

To proceed in such a fraudulent way is a serious offence and causes the buyers to make a mistake with regard to a specific condition so that they conclude the contract whereas the impression is wrongfully created that it is possible to withdraw from the contract some days laters, so that the contract is void because it infringes the articles 1265, 1266 and 1200 of the Civil Code. Also, the content of the withdrawal clause that provides that a penalty is due in case of withdrawal of 25 % of the contract price leads to a contractual imbalance and is an unfair term. … In this case must be declared void, not only the withdrawal clause … but the nullity also affects the entirety of both contracts as in the best case Art 10(4) of the Act on Consumer and User Protection (Ley de Defensa de los Consumidores y Usuarios Protection) would apply.

Note

In the annotated case, the court considered that the seller had acted in bad faith by deliberately concealing information on a penalty clause and that this vitiated the consent of the consumer, thus leading to the nullity of the contract on the basis of the general provisions of the Spanish Civil Code. Although the specific requirements may differ, similar remedies exist in other jurisdictions. Under French and Belgian law, 'dol' or 'fraud' vitiates consent and leads to the nullity of the contract, 'when the stratagems practised by one of the parties are such, that it is evident that without such stratagems the other party would not have contracted' (Article 1116 Civil Code). It has been mentioned above that the omission of information can also constitute 'dol' or 'fraud' and lead to the nullity of the contract. The situation is similar in the UK where a misrepresentation, also by conduct, renders the contract voidable (eg see the *Spice Girls* case above). Similarly, under German law, a consumer that has been induced to conclude a contract by deceit, may avoid the contract (§123 BGB).

Failure to provide the required information may also lead to avoidance of the contract even if it has not been demonstrated that this failure has affected the consent. Such consequence may be expressly provided for in the statutory provisions,[185] but it can also be implied, a 'nullité tacite' or 'implied nullity'. The following case is an illustration of a 'nullité tacite'.

Cass civ 1e, 7 December 2004[186] **3.56 (FR)**

TACIT NULLITY

Trade in furniture

When the information required is not provided, the contract may be void even though the applicable legislation only sanctions such infringement by a penalty.

[185] Art 88, in fine of the Belgian Trade Practices Act, for example, states that a doorstep selling contract in which the required information on the right of withdrawal has not been provided is void.

[186] Bull civ I No 303, 253; (2005) RDC 323, note D Fenouillet.

Facts: According to French law, and more specifically the Decree of 14 March 1986 concerning the trade in furniture, certain specific information needs to be included in a purchase order ('bon de commande'). A consumer had ordered several pieces of furniture but all the required information was not included in the purchase order, nor were certain technical indexes attached, as required by the decree. The consumer now invoked the nullity of the contract although the relevant provisions did not explicitly state that a failure to provide the information was sanctioned by the nullity of the contract.

Judgment: Considering the sole argument:

In light of Article L 214-1 of the Consumer Code, Articles 2 and 5 of decree number 86-583 of 14 March 1986, L 214-2, paragraph 1 of the aforementioned code and paragraph 6 of the Civil code; ...

Given that on 11 January 1997, Mr X signed a purchase order for the purchase of several items of furniture which were on sale in a shop run by the company Elmo meubles; the purchase order, which stated 'cash sale, firm and definite sale', also included the following information: the furniture that was sold, the price of the sale (FRF 30.000), the total amount of the deposit paid (FRF 10.000), and the delivery time; since Mr X subsequently displayed his intention of obtaining an annulment of the sale, the company took legal action against him for recovery of the balance of the price of sale and payment of damages;

Whereas, in order to amend the judgment which, following Mr X's counterclaim, declared the aforementioned sale void on the grounds that the purchase order signed by the latter did not contain the full range of 'quotes' outlined in the decree of 14 March 1986 and on the grounds it had not been established that the datasheets for the furniture had been delivered to Mr X and in order to accept the company's claim, the contested judgment maintains that neither the decree of 14 March 1986, nor its application explicitly ordered the annulment as a sanction for non-observance of the provisions of Article 2 of the aforementioned decree, and that the latter provisions refer to Article L 213-1 of the consumer code, which only contains penal sanctions, and that Article L 311-1 of the aforementioned code, does not specify annulment either.

In basing its judgement on the above considerations, the Court of Appeal violated the aforementioned texts by failing to apply their provisions.

Based on the above considerations:

The judgment is declared null and void.

III.D.2.b Specific performance

The information given in a pre-contractual phase as well as in advertising may be binding on the professional. This may follow from general contract law. Thus in the UK, statements in the pre-contractual phase or in advertising may become terms of the contract if the statement-maker intended to guarantee the truth of the statement. The binding character may also result from specific provisions. The Timeshare Directive (2008/122/EC), for example, states that the information given in the information documents forms an integral part of the contract (Article 5(2)). More general provisions can be found in national law (see Article 8 of the Spanish General Consumer Protection Act (1984); Article 94/14 of the Belgian Trade Practices Act, discussed above at section II.B.5.c)

III.D.2.c Damages

Damages will be available for breach of information duties in certain circumstances in the various jurisdictions. The sort of harm that will be compensated for (material/ immaterial harm), the level of the damages and the way in which the damages are calculated may differ in from jurisdiction to jurisdiction. In some jurisdictions, the seriousness of the wrong will also influence the level of damages. Moreover, it will not always be easy to classify information duties as contractual/pre-contractual. Either an action in contract or in tort, and in some cases both in contract and in tort, may be available. This may also influence the level of the damages as contract law rather protects an expectation interest and tort law a reliance interest.[187] Thus, under English law, a person who is induced to enter a contract as a result of a false pre-contractual statement may be able to claim damages in tort,[188] or on the basis of a contractual warranty.[189] In French and Belgian law, pre-contractual liability is in general considered as extra-contractual,[190] while in principle any liability arising after the contract has been concluded will only be contractual. This results from the rule that excludes (in most cases) the combination of contractual and non-contractual liability (*non-cumul des responsabilités contractuelle et délictuelle*).[191] Under German law, a contractual claim for damages would be available (*culpa in contrahendo*, as mentioned above), and possibly, in cases of fraud, tort as well. The principle of *non-cumul* is not applied so that courts can apply both contract and tort law.

Hof van Beroep (Court of Appeal) Brussel, **3.57 (BE)**
1 December 2006[192]
Axa Belgium v Langendonck

DAMAGES FOR BREACH OF OBLIGATION TO INFORM

Underinsured car

Breach of a pre-contractual information duty gives rise to an obligation to compensate for all losses that the prejudiced party would not have sustained without the breach.

Facts: Ms Langendonck bought a secondhand car for BEF 525,000 (VAT included) and took out insurance for this car. When asked to declare the value of the object to be insured in the insurance documents, she mentioned BEF 500,000, VAT excluded. A couple of months later, the car was stolen and an expert estimated the loss at BEF 346,600, VAT excluded. Ms Langendonck was then informed by the insurer that

[187] On this and for more details on the different national regimes, see W van Gerven, P Larouche and J Lever, *Tort Law* (Oxford, Hart Publishing, 2000) 33ff.

[188] Three main bases for such a tort claim exist: the tort of deceit (*Derry v Peek* [1889] LR 14 App Cas 337), the tort of negligence (*Hedley Byrne & Co v Heller & Partners Ltd* [1964] AC 465) and the Misrepresentation Act 1967, s 2.

[189] *Esso Petroleum v Mardon* [1976] QB 801.

[190] For Belgium, see Hof van Cassatie (Court of Cassation), 10 December 1981 (1981–82) Arr Cass 502; (1982) Pas I, 494; (1982-83) RW 1065.

[191] S Whitakker in S Weatherill and U Bernitz (eds), *The Regulation of Unfair Commercial Practices under EC Directive 2005/29. New Rules and New Techniques* (Oxford, Hart Publishing, 2007) 147.

[192] (2007) DCCR 77, note C Verdure.

her car had been underinsured. It appeared that according to the general terms and conditions, the 'value of the object to be insured' was the listed value or catalogue value of the year that the car was first brought into circulation. This value amounted to BEF 1,088,799. Furthermore, the general conditions set out that there was underinsurance when the declared value was smaller than the 'value of the object to be insured' as defined in the general terms and conditions. The insurance company therefore applied a proportionality rule and claimed it only had to reimburse part of the BEF 346,600: BEF 159,166. Ms Langendock nevertheless claimed the whole sum. A first issue to be decided was whether the concept of underinsurance actually had to be interpreted in the way set out in the contract. This issue went up to the Cour de Cassation, which decided that the contract was binding in this regard and quashed the decision of the Ghent Court of Appeal. The discussion before the Brussels Court of Appeal to which the case was returned now turned upon the question whether there had been a breach of a pre-contractual information duty.

Judgment: In the intermediate decision of 18 January 2006 it was already decided that:

—it is the appellant's duty as an insurer to point out explicitly to the candidate insurance taker—prior to the conclusion of the insurance policy—the very specific meaning of the 'value to be insured' in the policy, also taking into account the far reaching consequences with regard to underinsurance that the declaration of a lower value than the catalogue value when first brought into circulation could entail;

—it was not argued nor proven that the appellant complied with this pre-contractual information duty;

—in these circumstances, it must be accepted that the defendant meant the actual value of the insured object at the time of conclusion of the contract with the 'declared value'; that it is excluded in the given situation that the defendant would consciously have chosen only to insure a part of the vehicle and to take the risk of underinsurance;

—by omitting to point out explicitly and prior to the conclusion of the policy to the defendant as a candidate insurance taker the very specific definitions of the 'value to be insured' and 'underinsurance' in the general terms and conditions and as a consequence the far reaching consequences of declaring the 'value to be insured', appellant committed a pre-contractual fault;

—committing a pre-contractual fault gives rise to an obligation to indemnify the aggrieved party for the damages he would not have sustained without the pre-contractual fault.

It is considered proven that, if the appellant had pointed out explicitly and prior to the conclusion of the insurance policy to the defendant, candidate insurance taker, the very specific definitions of the 'value to be insured' and 'underinsurance' in the general terms and conditions and as a consequence the far reaching consequences of declaring the 'value to be insured', the latter:

—would either have declared as 'value to be insured' the catalogue value of the vehicle when first brought into circulation in accordance with Art 5 of the general terms and conditions, that is the amount of BEF 1.088.799;

—or would not have taken out a fire and theft insurance policy with the appellant but with another insurer on the usual conditions applicable in case of compensation of the actual value, whereby the value to be insured is defined as the actual value of the object to be insured at the time of conclusion of the contract and whereby there underinsurance only occurs when the insured sum, as declared by the insurance taker, is lower than the value of the good insured when the damage occurs.

In both cases the insurer would not have been able to invoke the proportionality rule that applies in case of underinsurance.

Notes

(1) The Brussels Court of Appeal decided that a breach of a pre-contractual information duty gives rise to an obligation to compensate the party that was prejudiced for all losses that it would not have sustained without the breach of the pre-contractual information duty. In this case these losses were rather easy to quantify and the insurer had to reimburse to actual value of the car. It other cases, this may be far more difficult and losses may be determined *ex aequo et bono*.

(2) A similar outcome could have been reached by declaring the clause void as it was not transparent. This would probably have been the approach under German law. If the clause had nevertheless been upheld, under German law, damages could also have been obtained as wrong advice by insurers (or their intermediaries) is a case of §311(2) BGB (*culpa in contrahendo*).

(3) In these cases, the question of causation frequently arises. What would the consumer/customer have done if he had been properly advised. German courts have developed the *Prinzip aufklärungsrichtigen Verhaltens* to help in this respect, ie the assumption that the consumer would have done the right thing, in particular in insurance law.[193]

CONCISE BIBLIOGRAPHY

G Dannemann, 'Formation of Contracts in the Internet' in P Birks and A Pretto (eds), *Themes in Comparative Law in Honour of Bernard Rudden* (Oxford, Oxford University Press, 2002) 179ff.

G Howells, A Janssen and R Schulze, *Information Rights and Obligations* (Ashgate, Aldershot, 2005).

A Farnsworth, 'Comparative Contract Law' in M Reimann and R Zimmermann (eds), *The Oxford Handbook of Comparative Law* (Oxford, Oxford University Press, 2006) 899ff.

H-W Micklitz, 'The Visible Hand of European Regulatory Private Law' (2008) *European University Institute (EUI) Working Papers*, Law 14, 1ff (available at http://www.eui.eu).

P Møgelvang-Hansen, 'The Binding Effects of Advertising' in R Schulze, *New Features in Contract Law* (München, Sellier, 2007) 169ff.

RB Schlessinger (ed), *Formation of Contracts* (New York, Oceana Publications, 1968).

Study Group on a European Civil Code and Acquis Group, *Draft Common Frame of Reference (DCFR). Principles, Definitions and Model Rules of European Private Law* (München, Sellier, 2009).

R Zimmermann, 'European Contract Law: General Report' (2007) *Zeitschrift für Gemeinschaftsprivatrecht* 2ff.

[193] See eg BGHZ 61, 118; BGHZ, 94, 356.

CHAPTER FOUR
RIGHT OF WITHDRAWAL AND STANDARD TERMS

Chapter 3 provided for an introduction into some general contract law aspects; this chapter is concerned with two issues in contract law that are particularly relevant for consumers: rights of withdrawal and standard terms. Rights of withdrawal are a relatively recent phenomenon and in most countries are enjoyed only by consumers, and then only in specific situations. A discussion of their rationale (I.A), an overview of the situations in which the consumer enjoys a right of withdrawal (I.B) and of the regulation of such rights (I.C) could therefore not be omitted from this Casebook on consumer law. This chapter also deals with standard terms. These terms are of course not solely used in consumer contracts, but are nevertheless very frequently so used. Businesses often impose identical contractual conditions on a large number of consumers that often lack the bargaining power to enforce their own terms. The second part of this chapter focuses on control of standard terms.

I. RIGHT OF WITHDRAWAL

I.A RATIONALE

A right of withdrawal gives the consumer the possibility, without giving any reasons and without incurring any penalty, of no longer being bound by a contract into which he has entered. This right aims to put the consumer in a position which makes it more likely that his consent will be free, well considered and informed. The right of withdrawal can hence be seen as a means to ensure the right to self-determination, a function information requirements can also fulfil. This right at first sight seems to imply that in (certain) consumer contracts, the basic principle that contracts are binding (*pacta sunt servanda*) is no longer applicable.

B Stauder, Pacta sunt Servanda and the Right of Withdrawal[1] **4.1 (CH)**

The principle of autonomy of the will is not a purely formal principle. The recognition of this principle is based on the presupposition that its responsible exercise is the best guarantor of contractual justice. However, in certain cases, only the right of withdrawal permits the consumer to exercise this responsibility. This is about his 'economic and legal self-determination'. But if, once the period for withdrawal has lapsed, he did not revoke the decision that was formally taken, 'pacta sunt servanda'. Instead of contradicting this principle, the right of withdrawal instead, in a new context, gives the principle an additional justification and confirms its role as a pillar of our private law in a free economy.

Note

As explained by Stauder, the right of withdrawal is thus not a real exception to the principle of *pacta sunt servanda*. It can instead be seen as a nuance to this principle. Only those contracts where the consent that has been given was real and informed are considered to be binding.

The situations in which the consumer enjoys a right of withdrawal do vary in the various jurisdictions. Broadly speaking, however, two categories of situations in which the consumer enjoys such a right can be distinguished:

(i) Situations in which there is a *psychological deficit*. Due to certain factors, the consumer is deemed not to be in a position to take a rational decision, most often because sales practices considered to be aggressive have been used (eg doorstep selling, timesharing). The period for withdrawal is then a real 'cooling-off' period. The factors that barred the consumer from taking a rational decision are no longer present during the period for withdrawal so that he can reconsider in peace whether the decision he took was in accordance with his preferences.

(ii) Situations in which there is an *information asymmetry*. A second category of situations are those in which the consumer is deemed to have insufficient information to take a well-considered decision. This could be due to the sales method used (eg distance selling), but also because of the complexity of the contract at stake (eg consumer credit, life assurance). The period for withdrawal should then allow the consumer to obtain the information required or to assess the information already received.[2]

[1] B Stauder, 'Pacta sunt servanda et le droit de repentir' (1982) 32 *La semaine judiciaire* 481–500.

[2] See J Drexl, *Die wirtschaftliche Selbstbestimmung des Verbrauchers* (Tübingen, Mohr Siebeck, 1998); G Reiner, 'Der verbraucherschützende Widerruf im Recht der Willenserklärungen' [2003] *Archiv fur die civilistische Praxis* 1–45; P Rekaiti and R Van den Bergh, 'Cooling-off Periods in the Consumer Laws of the EC-Member States. A Comparative Law and Economics Approach' [2000] *Journal of Consumer Policy* 371–407.

I.B SITUATIONS IN WHICH THE CONSUMER ENJOYS A RIGHT OF WITHDRAWAL

I.B.1 OVERVIEW

The right of withdrawal is not an invention of the European Union. Most countries first introduced a cooling-off period for doorstep selling in the 1960s and 1970s—some time before the right of withdrawal first emerged at European level with the Doorstep Selling Directive (85/577/EEC). More specific legislation that introduced new rights of withdrawal soon followed, sometimes in order to implement EC consumer law directives (inter alia the Timeshare Directive (94/47/EC),[3] the Distance Selling Directive (97/7/EC), the Life Assurance Directive (2002/83/EC)[4] and recently also the Distance Selling of Financial Services Directive (2002/65/EC) and the Consumer Credit Directive (2008/48/EC)).

Many countries also introduced the right of withdrawal in contracts where there is no EU law requirement to do so. In Germany, for example, the right of withdrawal was also introduced for distance learning contracts,[5] for insurance contracts[6] and for consumer credit contracts.[7] Consumers in the Netherlands also have a right of withdrawal when buying immovable property.[8] In France, the consumer also has a right of withdrawal for, for example, consumer credit, language courses,[9] for contracts with dating agencies, and also for private contracts for the purchase or construction of a house.[10] In Spain, the consumer also enjoys a right of withdrawal for package holidays—this is a special right of withdrawal (not linked to alteration of terms or any other non-performance) without limitations in time, though the consumer does have to pay a small amount of compensation to exercise this right (Article 9.4 of the Law 21/1995).

I.B.2 OBJECTIVE SITUATIONS

The right of withdrawal is meant to ensure that the consent of the consumer is free and well considered. The question then arises whether it is necessary for the consumer to prove that his consent was somehow vitiated in order to be able to exercise a right

[3] In the meantime repealed by Directive 2008/122/EC of the European Parliament and of the Council of 14 January 2009 on the protection of consumers in respect of certain aspects of timeshare, long-term holiday product, resale and exchange contracts [2009] OJ L 33, 10–30.

[4] Directive 2002/83/EC of the European Parliament and of the Council of 5 November 2002 concerning life assurance [2002] OJ L 345, 1–51.

[5] §4 of the Distance Learning Act (Fernunterrichtsgesetz, FernUSG).

[6] §8 of the Insurance Contract Act (Versicherungsvertragsgesetz, VVG).

[7] §7 of the Consumer Credit Act (Verbraucherkreditgesetz, VerbrKrG).

[8] Art7:2 NBW (Dutch Civil Code). See M Loos, 'Consumentenbescherming bij de koop van onroerende zaken en aanneming van werk: een nog altijd onevenwichtig en onvoldoende doordacht voorstel' (2002) 8 *Nederlands Tijdschrift voor Burgerlijk Recht* 356–67.

[9] See Art L 311-15 Code de la consommation (crédit mobilier à la consommation); Art L 121-33 Code de la consommation (démarchage de méthodes de libre apprentissage des langues étrangères ou régionales).

[10] Contrats de courtage matrimonial (Act of 23 June 1989 on marriage brokers, Art 6-II); actes sous seing privé d'achat ou de construction d'un immeuble à usage d'habitation (Art L 271-1 Code de la construction et de l'habitation).

of withdrawal. Similarly, the question arises whether the state of mind of the trader is at all relevant.

ECJ Case C-423/97, 22 April 1999[11]
Travel-Vac SL v Sanchis

4.2 (EU)

IRRELEVANCE OF THE STATE OF MIND OF THE CONSUMER

Timeshare at the doorstep

The consumer can withdraw from a contract concluded in the circumstances described in Article 1 of the Doorstep Selling Directive without having to prove that he was influenced or manipulated by the trader.

Facts: Mr Antelm Sanchis concluded a contract with Travel Vac under the terms of which he acquired a right to use immovable property on a timeshare basis and rights to certain services. Mr Sanchis wanted to withdraw from the contract. The contract had been concluded in 1996, before the Timeshare Directive had been and had to be transposed in Spanish law. It was agreed between the parties that Mr Sanchís was to appear at the bank to sign the document confirming the contract within three days of signing it, therefore by 17 September 1996 at the latest. However, Mr Sanchís did not appear at the bank within the period prescribed, but, instead, went to the vendor's offices on 17 September 1996 and stated orally that the whole contract was of no effect and that the documents he had signed should be returned to him. Travel Vac then applied for an order for enforcement against Mr Sanchís. The national court raised the question whether the Doorstep Selling Directive (85/577/EEC) applied to the case and, if so, whether it could grant the counterclaim for cancellation of the contract made by Mr Sanchís. It therefore decided to stay proceedings and referred a number of questions to the ECJ for a preliminary ruling on, inter alia, whether timeshare contracts could fall within the scope of the Doorstep Selling Directive; and also on the link between the right of renunciation of the Directive and some general provisions of the Spanish Civil Code on deliberate deceit and the need for a freely given consent that forms part of any contract (Article 1269 and Articles 1254, 1258, 1261ff of the Spanish Civil Code). Only the latter issue is dealt with in the excerpt below.

Judgment: 39. By its fourth question, the national court is asking essentially whether it is sufficient, in order for a consumer to be able to exercise his right of renunciation under Article 5(1) of Directive 85/577, for the contract to have been concluded in circumstances such as those described in Article 1 of that directive, or whether it must also be shown that the consumer was influenced or manipulated by the trader.

40. The Spanish Government states that account should be taken of the fact that the right of renunciation granted to the consumer is intended to meet the risk of abusive commercial practices, so that the right arises simply if he is a consumer and the contract falls within the directive, without his needing to prove that such abusive practices took place and even if there were no such practices.

41. The Commission claims that the right of renunciation is unconditional inasmuch as its exercise in no way depends on the existence of any false pretences on the part of the trader or on the trader's intention to manipulate the consumer in order to force him to make a decision in the trader's interest. The right of renunciation is implicit in any contract covered by Directive 85/577.

42. The fourth recital of Directive 85/577 explains that, when a contract is concluded away from a trader's business premises, the consumer is unprepared for the contract negotiations, and that he is often unable to compare the quality and price of the offer

[11] [1999] ECR I -2195.

with other offers. For that reason, according to the fifth recital of the directive, the consumer should be allowed a right of cancellation over a period of at least seven days in order to enable him to assess the obligations arising under the contract.

43. It follows that, in order for the consumer to have the right of renunciation provided for by Directive 85/577, it is sufficient for him to be in one of the situations described in Article 1 of that directive. Specific conduct or an intention to manipulate on the part of the trader are not, however, required and do not therefore have to be proved.

Note

Although there are clear links between a right of withdrawal and general contract law requirements that consent needs to be freely given, the right of withdrawal is an autonomous remedy. In most jurisdictions, when a contract has been entered into but the consent of one of the parties has been vitiated by mistake or undue influence, remedies will be available to that party under certain conditions. Consent was then not freely given. When granting the consumer a right of withdrawal, the legislator goes one step further: it presumes that in certain objective situations, the consent of the consumer cannot be freely given. This can be because the sales method used is presumed to influence the consumer or because the consumer is presumed not to have sufficient information to give informed consent. There is, however, no need actually to prove that the consent of the consumer was indeed influenced or not free. It suffices that the consumer was in one of the objective situations set out in the statutory instrument granting the consumer a right of withdrawal. Even if he would in the given situation not be able to rely on general contract law remedies, a right of withdrawal will be available. On the other hand, failure to withdraw in a timely fashion from a contract should not deprive the consumer of general contract law remedies. The Court of Appeal in Versailles thus decided that the fact that a consumer had not exercised its right of withdrawal in a doorstep selling contract did not mean that the contract could no longer be annulled because the consent of the consumer had been vitiated. The contract was indeed annulled both on the basis of mistake, deceit and undue influence.[12] This case thus illustrates that the existence of a right of withdrawal does not deprive consumers of general contract law remedies.

ECJ Case C-229/04, 25 October 2005[13] **4.3 (EU)**
Crailsheimer Volksbank eG v Klaus Conrads et al

IRRELEVANCE OF THE STATE OF MIND OF THE TRADER

Junk immovables

When a third party intervenes in the name of or on behalf of a trader in the negotiation or conclusion of a contract, the application of the Doorstep Selling Directive cannot be

[12] Court of Appeal Versailles, 15 September 1995, unpublished, cited by J Mestre, 'Jurisprudence en matière de droit civil. Obligations et contrat spéciaux' [1996] *Revue Trimestrielle de Droit Civil* 147–48.

[13] [2005] ECR I-09273.

made subject to the condition that the trader was or should have been aware that the contract was concluded in a doorstep selling situation.

Facts: In the early 1990s a property development company built an apartment complex. The apartments were sold on a joint ownership basis to individuals as an investment entailing tax advantages. The property development company used a sales company under its supervision which set up a 'timetable' for the various steps necessary to arrange the purchase and its financing. The sales company, in turn, used independent intermediaries, including a broker, who negotiated the purchases at issue in the main proceedings. In most cases the purchase of the apartments was financed by the DSL-Bank which undertook part of the expenditure with preferential security, while the Crailsheimer Bank, which had already provided the finance for the property development company to construct the complex, financed the remainder of the expenditure with a lower-ranking charge as security. In the cases in the main proceedings, the broker's method was to make appointments with the borrowers at their home in order to show them calculation models and compile information concerning their solvency in order to draw up an application for financing. The broker would return several weeks later to have the loan agreements, which had been drawn up in the meantime by the Crailsheimer Bank, signed. Some months after the building was completed, the operating company discontinued the rental payments and became insolvent; the property development company paid the agreed rent for some months and then also became insolvent. The anticipated rate of occupation was never achieved. Subsequently, the revenue derived from the investment proved insufficient. The borrowers also discontinued their payments to the Crailsheimer Bank. Following the termination of the loan agreements by the borrowers, the Crailsheimer Bank brought proceedings against each of the borrowers for payment of what was owed to it with interest. In first instance, the Bank's applications were upheld. Appeals against the judgments followed and in the further proceedings the Hanseatische Oberlandesgericht referred several questions to the ECJ. One of the questions concerned the conditions under which a lender must be considered responsible for a doorstep selling situation.

Judgment: 41. By this question the referring court essentially seeks to know whether Articles 1 and 2 of the Directive must be interpreted as meaning that, when a third party intervenes in the name of or on behalf of a trader in the negotiation or conclusion of a contract, the application of the Directive can be made subject not only to the condition that the contract has been concluded in a doorstep-selling situation defined in Article 1 of the Directive but also to the condition that the trader was or should have been aware that the contract was concluded in that situation.

42. In that regard, suffice it to observe that there is no basis in the wording of the Directive for inferring the existence of such an additional condition. Article 1 of the Directive provides that it applies to contracts concluded between a trader and a consumer in a doorstep-selling situation and, under Article 2 of the Directive, for the purposes thereof, 'trader' means any person who acts in the name or on behalf of a trader.

43. Moreover, to accept such an additional condition would be contrary to the objective of the Directive which is to protect the consumer from the element of surprise inherent in doorstep selling.

44. That interpretation is borne out by paragraph 43 of the judgment of 22 April 1999 in Case C-423/97 *Travel Vac* [1999] ECR I-2195, according to which, in order for the consumer to have the right of renunciation, it is sufficient for him to be in one of the situations described in Article 1 of the Directive and there is no need to require in addition that he was influenced or manipulated by the trader.

Note

The German courts started from the well-established premise that the third party action (door-to-door selling via independent representatives) can only lead to the liability of the contracting party if the latter knew or could have reasonably known that the independent representative is using direct selling methods. In reaction to the ECJ judgment, the German Supreme Court has revised its case-law.[14]

I.B.3 SOLICITED VISITS

Whether the situations in which the consumer ought to enjoy a right of withdrawal are correctly defined can be subject to discussion. This is, inter alia, the case for doorstep selling contracts. The right of withdrawal that is granted to the consumer in doorstep situations is deemed to be necessary as the consumer is 'taken by surprise' in a doorstep selling situation and is therefore unable to take a rational, well-considered decision. The logical consequence is then that the consumer is not in need of protection if he has asked himself for a visit by the seller. The consumer has then taken the initiative and therefore no longer needs to be protected. Article 1(1) 2nd indent of the Doorstep Selling Directive (85/577/EEC) provides that the consumer does not enjoy the protection of the Directive where the visit by the business takes place at the express request of the consumer. The burden of proof that the consumer has expressly requested a business visit with regard to the contract lies with the business. If the consumer asked for a visit only in order to obtain more information and not with the intention to negotiate a contract, then the business visit does not fall within the exception. The application of the exception for solicited visits leads to interpretation problems. Under the Belgian provisions implementing the Doorstep Selling Directive, the seller does not only need to prove the express request of the consumer for a visit by the seller but also the intent of the consumer to negotiate the conclusion of a contract (Article 87 Trade Practices Act). The onus of proof is, however, interpreted very differently by the courts: certain lower courts have held that if the consumer sent a written request for a visit to the seller, the intent to negotiate the conclusion of the contract must follow from the wording of such writing;[15] the Court of Appeal has held that not only the wording of the written request can be looked at, but also the circumstances of the case[16] and even that a standard clause stating 'the consumer has expressly requested the visit of the seller in order to conclude the contract' may be sufficient as proof.[17] Similar difficulties to distinguish requests for information from requests to be visited have arisen in other jurisdictions.

[14] See BGH, 15 December 2005 (2006) NJW 497.

[15] Kh (Commercial Court) Leuven, 1 June 1993 (1993) DCCR 527, note P De Vroede (1993) *Jaarboek Handelspraktijken* 291.

[16] Eg the fact that a contract was immediately signed; the fact that a prepayment was made can indicate that the request was not merely a request for information: Hof van Beroep (Court of Appeal) Gent, 3 February 2004, (2005) DCCR 46, note J Stuyck.

[17] Hof van Beroep (Court of Appeal) Gent, 23 March 2005 (2006) DCCR 70, note E Terryn.

Audiencia Provincial (Court of Appeal) Burgos, 26 October 2001[18] **4.4 (ES)**
Entidad técnica de distribución X SL v María Cruz SR y Raúl AS

UNSOLICITED VISIT

Doorstep course

A 'request for free personal information' is not the same as a request for a visit from a business or the person acting on the latter's behalf.

Facts: Mr Raúl AS signed a contract for a course with a company (Distribución X). Mr Raúl did not pay for the course. The material delivered by the contracting company did not correspond to the material requested and was not accepted (or at least this was not accredited by signature) by the defendant. Distribución X presented a complaint against Mr Raúl requesting payment of the amount due. During the proceedings the parties debated the possibility of applying the exception envisaged in Article 1(b) of Law 26/1991 on contracts negotiated away from commercial premises, which establishes, as an exception to the scope of application that law, 'that the visit by the business or the person acting on his/her behalf has been requested expressly by the consumer'.

Judgment: As the aforementioned article indicates [Art 1(b) of Law 26/1991 of 26 November: 'the consumer must explicitly request a visit from a businessman or from the person acting on the latter's behalf'] the request for the visit must be explicit, that is to say unequivocal, with no doubts as to the purpose of the request; moreover, the fact is that, in this case, the form, which requests personal and free information has no other aim than that which is obvious: to obtain information, not to conclude a contract. This act has no other meaning than the one objectively revealed.

This legal result, which seeks to reconcile what was intended with what was said, neither bars nor makes invalid the introduction of evidence of facts to the contrary, which is a positive fact such as the evidence of the explicit request of the visit. The burden of proof lies with the plaintiff not only due to the essential and positive features of the fact to be proved, but also due to the legal requirements in Article 2(2) of the Law 26/1991, which includes within the scope of this law all contracts and offers concluded outside of the commercial premises and determines that evidence to the contrary must be given by the business. Therefore, if evidence to the contrary is not provided, the business must endure the effects of the burden of proof, as occurs in this case.

If the legal requisites stated in Article 3 of the Law of 26/1991 are not fulfilled, for contracts that fall within its ambit, the result is their nullity. This is stated in Article 4 of the aforementioned law.

Notes

(1) Similar cases exist in the UK: in *Havair Ltd v Vile*, for example, it was held that a visit whereby only a flyer is given which the recipient is requested to return does not exclude application of the exception.[19] For Germany, see, for example, a decision of the OLG Dresden where it was held that no '*vorhergehende Bestellung*' exists when the consumer merely replies to a voucher in which a present was promised.[20]

[18] (2001) JUR 332674.
[19] [2000] 5 CL 114 (Basildon County Court).
[20] OLG Dresden, 8 November 1995 (1996) NJW-RR 758.

(2) Not all Member States have, however, adopted the exception for solicited visits of the Doorstep Selling Directive (85/577/EEC).[21] The minimum harmonisation character of the Directive allows Member States to go further in protecting the consumer. There do indeed seem to be good reasons to extend the protection to solicited visits. In the UK, a large study on doorstep selling demonstrated that consumers are also subject to high-pressure selling when they request the visit themselves.[22] The OFT has therefore proposed to abandon the exception. In its response to the public consultation on doorstep selling and cold calling in September 2006, the DTI has accepted extending to solicited visits the cooling-off period and cancellation rights which currently apply to unsolicited visits by traders. The new regulations (Cancellation of Contracts Made in a Consumer's Home or Place of Work etc Regulations 2008)—with extended scope of application—entered into force on 1 October 2008. In the ACQP it was proposed to abolish this exception in order to improve EC law. The same choice is reflected in the DCFR (see Article II—5:201 DCFR). The recent Proposal for a Directive on Consumer Rights also abolished the general exception for solicited visits.

Questions

Should consumers also enjoy a right of withdrawal for solicited visits? Will this not make urgent repairs of the consumer's property difficult?

I.C REGULATION AND HARMONISATION OF THE RIGHT OF WITHDRAWAL

I.C.1 INTRODUCTION

There are blatant inconsistencies in the way the 'right of withdrawal' is regulated in different Directives:[23] different terminology is used to denominate the right, cooling-off periods are calculated in different ways, the notice of the right of withdrawal differs (both as to content and timing of formal requirements), a failure to inform the consumer of his right of withdrawal is sanctioned in different ways, etc. At national level, the situation is often even worse. These inconsistencies have made it very difficult to fit such a right into general contract law.

Germany was the first jurisdiction that perceived this as a problem and attempted to deal with the right of withdrawal in a harmonised way in §355ff BGB (§361 old

[21] Denmark, France, Italy, Latvia and Poland have, for example, decided not to include such an exception when implementing the Doorstep Selling Directive (87/577/EEC) and have thus extended the protection to solicited visits (H Schulte-Nölke, C Twigg-Flesner, M Ebers (eds), *Consumer Law Compendium* (Munich, Sellier, 2008) 180).

[22] 'Studies on Doorstep Selling' (OFT, 2004).

[23] See, amongst others, K Riesenhuber, 'System and Principles of EC Contract Law' [2005] *ERCL* 297; M Loos, 'The Case for a Uniform and Efficient Right of Withdrawal from Consumer Contracts' [2007] *ZEuP* 3–35; E Terryn, *Bedenktijden in het consumentenrecht. Het herroepingsrecht als instrument van consumentenbescherming,* (Antwerp/Oxford, Intersentia, 2008) 686.

BGB). This harmonisation also ended the discussion whether the contract had to be considered as 'schwebend unwirksam' or 'schwebend wirksam'.

P Rott, The Right of Withdrawal in Germany[24] **4.5 (DE)**

In the year 2000, a 'critical mass' of such specific legislation was reached, and the legislator decided that central notions and concepts of the various rights of withdrawal should be harmonised, and that this should occur through provisions to be included into the BGB. Thus, with the implementation of the Distance Selling Directive 97/7/EC, a first step was made. In particular, the new §§361a and 361b BGB largely harmonised the legal nature of the right of withdrawal, the normal period of withdrawal, some rules on the information to be supplied by the trader, and the consequences of the withdrawal.

This process was intensified when Germany prepared for the implementation of the Consumer Sales Law Directive 1999/44/EC. In the context of implementing this Directive, the German law of obligations was modernised. The opportunity was also taken to integrate fields of private law that had developed outside the BGB, in order to make the BGB a comprehensive codification of private law again. Amongst others, specific consumer legislation was transferred into the BGB, and the Unfair Contract Terms Act, the Doorstep Selling Act, the Distance Selling Act, the Time-sharing Act and the Consumer Credit Act were repealed. In the course of this process, the partly harmonised rules dealing with the right of withdrawal—§§361a and 361b BGB of 2000—were replaced by the new provisions of §§355 to 357 BGB.

Further amendments were made following the *Heininger* judgment of the ECJ, in June 2002, and in the course of the implementation of Directive 2002/65/EC on the distance marketing of financial services. …

When the right to withdrawal was first introduced in doorstep selling law, the German Supreme Court (Bundesgerichtshof, BGH) held that contracts concluded at the doorstep were not fully valid until the right of withdrawal was expired. Until that moment, the validity of contracts would be pending ('schwebend unwirksam'), a concept that is used in German law for contracts concluded by minors, or by agents that are not entitled to act. This concept of postponed validity had some legal consequences. In principle, a consumer who bought goods at the doorstep was only entitled to performance once the contract was fully valid, and so was the trader with a view to payment. This was perceived to be a problem, at least by some authors, who accordingly argued that the consumer should be allowed to refrain from his right to withdrawal in order to be able to claim immediate performance of the contract; an opinion that was clearly ignoring EC law requirements.

Certainly, the concept of pending validity could not be reconciled with the Distance Selling Directive 97/7/EC. It was therefore given up for all the different rights of withdrawal when this Directive was implemented and a first round of harmonisation took place. Nowadays, contracts that are subject to a right to withdrawal are fully valid from the beginning but they can be invalidated by the consumer by exercising his right to withdrawal. Therefore, both parties can now claim performance immediately after the conclusion of the contract, unless they agree otherwise.

[24] P Rott, 'Le droit de rétractation en Allemagne' in E Terryn (ed), *Le droit de rétractation* (Brussel, Larcier, 2008).

Note

(1) In other jurisdictions, eg France and Belgium, discussion on the contractual qualification of the right of withdrawal is ongoing. Different terminology is used to denote the right of withdrawal. Moreover, the terms of the relevant articles sometimes imply that a contract has not been concluded until the period for withdrawal has lapsed, whereas other provisions oblige the trader to perform before the period for withdrawal can commence.[25] Opinions differ: according to some authors, the contract only comes into existence or is only effective when the period for withdrawal has lapsed (see the German concept of 'schwebende Unwirksamkeit'); according to other authors the contract is fully effective but withdrawing from the contract unwinds the contract retroactively. Many aspects (eg the consequences of exercising the right of withdrawal) are not regulated explicitly in the relevant statutory provisions.

(2) In the UK, the situation is somewhat different. The different Acts giving the consumer a right of withdrawal (eg the Consumer Protection (Distance Selling) Regulations 2000, the Cancellation of Contracts made in a Consumer's Home or Place of Work etc Regulations 2008, the Consumer Credit Act 1974) do provide detailed rules on the exercise and consequences of this right. However, there are also differences in the provisions of these acts that are not policy based and moreover the Acts do not deal with all possible situations.[26] In the Netherlands, the right of withdrawal is (quasi-)uniformly qualified as a right to terminate the contract,[27] but the exact consequences of such a termination are, however, disputed—as termination normally requires a breach of contract, the rules on restitution after termination are therefore not adequate. Some authors therefore argue for the application of the rules of restitution in case of avoidance.[28]

(3) The need to provide for common rules is now also strongly felt at EC level. The European legislator has been aware for some time of the discrepancies in the way the right of withdrawal is regulated,[29] and recently steps have been taken for a more comprehensive reform of the right of withdrawal.[30] The recent Green Paper on the review of the Consumer Acquis proposes to deal with the right of withdrawal in a

[25] For France, see R Baillod, 'Le droit de repentir' [1984] *RTDCiv* 227ff; V Christianos, 'Délai de réflexion: théorie juridique et efficacité de la protection des consommateurs' (1993) VIII *D Chron* 28–32; P Malinvaud, 'Droit de repentir et théorie générale des obligations' in *Scritti in onore di Rodolfo Sacco* (Milano, Giuffre, 1994) 744–62; S Detraz, 'Plaidoyer pour une analyse fonctionnelle du droit de rétractation en droit de la consommation' [2004] *Contrats Concurrence Consommation* 7–13; for Belgium: for an overview, see Terryn, above n 23.

[26] See the criticism of P Hellwege, 'Consumer Protection in Britain in Need of Reform' [2004] *Cambridge Law Journal* 712–42.

[27] See J Hijma and W Valk, *Wettelijke bedenktijd* (Deventer, Kluwer, 2004) 30. This appeared to be a rather arbitrary decision.

[28] Ibid.

[29] See the statement by the Council and the Parliament that 'the Commission will examine the possibility and desirability of harmonizing the method of calculating the cooling-off period under existing consumer-protection legislation, notably Directive 85/577/EEC on 'door-to-door sales' that was already added to the Distance Selling Directive (97/7/EC).

[30] Communication from the Commission to the European Parliament and the Council—A more coherent European contract law—An action plan, COM [2003] 68 final, OJ 15 March 2003, para 16.

horizontal instrument. Common rules are envisaged for the timeframes for exercise of the right of withdrawal, for the modalities of exercising the right of withdrawal and for the contractual effects of withdrawal.[31] The approach there proposed is similar to the current German legislation. In the Proposal for a Directive on Consumer Rights that followed the Green Paper, the 'harmonised' rules on withdrawal were, however, limited to distance and off-premises contracts.[32]

(4) In the ACQP, the researchers of the Acquis Group have tried to develop a general set of rules based on the current Directives.[33] The relevant provisions of the DCFR are based on these principles.[34]

I.C.2 NOTIFICATION OF WITHDRAWAL

I.C.2.a Introduction

The consumer will only be able to exercise his right of withdrawal if he is aware of such a right. Most Directives and national provisions therefore provide for more or less extensive obligations for the seller to inform the consumer. However, there is considerable variety as to the content of such notice, the time at which the consumer needs to be informed, the formal requirements of such notice as well as with regard to the sanction when the information has not been given. Some of these elements are illustrated below.

I.C.2.b Content

The content of the notice of withdrawal varies in the different Directives as well as in the different national regulations.

Doorstep Selling Directive (85/577/EEC) **4.6 (EU)**

Article 4 In the case of transactions within the scope of Article 1, traders shall be required to give consumers written notice of their right of cancellation within the period laid down in Article 5, together with the name and address of a person against whom that right may be exercised. Such notice shall be dated and shall state particulars enabling the contract to be identified. It shall be given to the consumer: (a) in the case of Article 1(1), at the time of conclusion of the contract; (b) in the case of Article 1(2), not later than the time of conclusion of the contract; (c) in the case of Article 1(3) and 1(4), when the offer is made by the consumer. Member States shall ensure that their national legislation lays down appropriate consumer protection measures in cases where the information referred to in this Article is not supplied.

31 COM [2006] 744 final, 20–21.

32 COM [2008] 614 final.

33 See Acquis Group (ed), *Principles of the Existing EC Contract Law—Contract I (Acquis Principles—ACQP)* (München, Sellier, 2007).

34 For comments, see E Terryn, 'The Right of Withdrawal, the Acquis Principles and the Draft Common Frame of Reference' in R Schulze (ed), *Common Frame of Reference and Existing EC Contract Law* (München, Sellier, 2008).

Distance Selling of Financial Services Directive (2002/65/EC) **4.7 (EU)**

Article 3 Information to the consumer prior to the conclusion of the distance contract

1. In good time before the consumer is bound by any distance contract or offer, he shall be provided with the following information concerning: …

(3) the distance contract

(a) the existence or absence of a right of withdrawal in accordance with Article 6 and, where the right of withdrawal exists, its duration and the conditions for exercising it, including information on the amount which the consumer may be required to pay on the basis of Article 7(1), as well as the consequences of non-exercise of that right; …

(d) practical instructions for exercising the right of withdrawal indicating, inter alia, the address to which the notification of a withdrawal should be sent; …

2. The information referred to in paragraph 1, the commercial purpose of which must be made clear, shall be provided in a clear and comprehensible manner in any way appropriate to the means of distance communication used, with due regard, in particular, to the principles of good faith in commercial transactions, and the principles governing the protection of those who are unable, pursuant to the legislation of the Member States, to give their consent, such as minors.

Note

As an overload of information makes it less likely that the consumer will actually read the information, a delicate balance must be struck. It seems crucial in any event that the consumer is aware that he has a right of withdrawal, that he knows the length of the period for withdrawal and the way in which he needs to exercise his right of withdrawal. There also seems to be consensus that such information should be given in a clear way. There is considerably more discussion as to the need to point out to the consumer what the consequences are (in terms of restitutionary obligations—see the Distance Selling of Financial Services Directive (2002/65/EC)) if he exercises his right of withdrawal.

The German legislator has harmonised the different provisions dealing with the notice on the right of withdrawal, but the case-law illustrates that this notice is not so evident for traders seeking to comply with these requirements.

BGB **4.8 (DE)**

§355 Right of withdrawal in consumer contracts

(2) The period begins when the consumer has been informed in textual form by a clearly formulated notice of his right of withdrawal which makes clear to him the nature of his rights in accordance with the requirements of the means of communication used, which also states the name and address of the person to whom withdrawal is to be declared and refers to the beginning of the period and the rules in subsection (1), sentence 2 above. Except in the case of contracts authenticated by a notary, it is to be signed separately by the consumer or provided by him with a qualified electronic signature. If the contract is to be made in writing, the period does not begin until the consumer has also been provided with a contract document, his written application or a

copy of the contract document or of the application. If the beginning of the period is disputed, the businessperson bears the burden of proof.

BGH, 18 April 2005[35] **4.9 (DE)**

CLARITY REQUIRED

Blurry notification

Notification of the right of withdrawal is not in accordance with the requirements of the Doorstep Selling Act when it is unclear whether the period for withdrawal starts when the consumer signs, when the seller signs or when the contract is handed over to the consumer.

Facts: A consumer invested money in a company that was active in, inter alia, the acquisition of real estate. The contract was concluded in a doorstep situation. The consumer wanted to withdraw from the contract years after it had been concluded. The BGH accepted that the consumer could validly withdraw from the contract.

Judgment: The week-long withdrawal period of §1(1) of the Doorstep Selling Act (Haustürwiderrufsgesetz) had not yet expired when the claimant announced his withdrawal. According to §2(1) of the Doorstep Selling Act, the period for withdrawal only begins when the customer is handed a notification on the right of withdrawal, which is typographically clearly set out and which is able thoroughly, accurately and unambiguously to advise an offeree with no legal training on the conditions of his right of withdrawal … The notification on the right of withdrawal reads: 'I can withdraw my declaration of accession in writing within a period of one week after signing. The period begins once a copy of this notification on the right of withdrawal is handed over.' Before this text one finds on the subscription forms not only the signature line for the investor but also—directly before the text—the signature line for the acceptance of the defendant or the defendant's predecessor in title. It is therefore unclear for an impartial reader with no legal training as to whether the period for withdrawal begins with his signature, with the signature of the contracting partner's representative or with the handing over of the notification on the right of withdrawal that precedes the countersignature. …

In this respect what is missing is a typographically clear form in the terms of §2(1) s 2 of the Doorstep Selling Act. Moreover, these notifications on the right of withdrawal do not meet the conditions of §2(1) s 3 of the Doorstep Selling Act, according to which the notification must not contain any other declarations and should be signed by the customer.

[35] (2005) DB 1516.

BGH, 4 July 2002[36] **4.10 (DE)**

ADDITIONS CAN MISLEAD

Blurry notification 2

Notification of the right of withdrawal is inadequate if it contains additions that do not clarify its content, but can mislead the average consumer.

Facts: An employee of a roofing company contacted a consumer at his house and offered to improve his roof for a fixed price. On the order form, which was signed by the consumer during their discussions, there was information on the right of withdrawal in a black box in the following terms: 'You can withdraw from the order within one week by addressing a written notice to the Company… It suffices to dispatch your withdrawal within this period to do so timely. The period for withdrawal starts when the contract is handed over, but not before the customer has consented to conclude the contract.' The roofing company was challenged by several consumer organisations who claimed that the information on the right of withdrawal was not in accordance with the relevant legislation. The last part of the last sentence ('but not before …') was claimed to be an illegitimate addition to the legal requirements and to mislead the consumer. The consumer organisations won their case at first instance but then lost on appeal (OLG Naumburg 27 January 2000). The Federal Supreme Court quashed the latter decision.

Judgment: 3. What is decisive, therefore, is whether the aim of the law, in allowing a right of withdrawal in favour of the consumer, is reached with the notification on the right of withdrawal used by the defendant. This is not the case.

a) The right of withdrawal, now set out in §355 of the German Civil Code and in provisions—as in this case §312(1) s 1 of the German Civil Code—which refer to this regulation, aims to achieve protection for the consumer, just like the earlier right of withdrawal, set out, inter alia, in §2 of the Doorstep Selling Act old version, §7 of the Consumer Credit Act old version and also in §1b of the Instalment Act old version. This protection requires a notification which must be as comprehensive, unambiguous and clear from the point of view of consumers as possible. The formal requirements which must be legally observed when explaining the right of withdrawal, and the demands as regards content allow for this (cf BGHZ 121, 52, 54ff—Notification on the Right of Withdrawal 1). Not only is the consumer supposed to acquire an understanding of this right of withdrawal through the notification, but he should also be enabled to exercise it. In addition, even before the standardization of the right of withdrawal in consumer contracts, through §361a of the German Civil Code old version, it corresponded to the aim of the Doorstep Selling Act and of the Consumer Credit Act, as well as to that of the former Instalment Act, to inform the consumer, who is typically untrained in legal matters, clearly about the beginning of the period for withdrawal and to ensure that he is not left in the dark about how it is calculated (cf BGHZ 121, 52, 54ff—Notification on the Right of Withdrawal 1; BGHZ 126, 56, 62). This is now made explicit by §355(2) s 1 of the German Civil Code. In order that the clarification of the right of withdrawal aimed for by the law should not be impaired, the notification on the right of withdrawal categorically must not contain any other declarations. The revision of the law has done nothing to change this requirement, expressly standardized in §2 (1) s 3 of the Doorstep Selling Act (cf Bülow, Verbraucherkreditgesetz, 4th ed, §7 para 117). In it, it now clarifies that §355 (2) s 1 of the German Civil Code demands that the notification be in a form which makes the consumer's rights clear to him. This regulation does not exclude absolutely

[36] I ZR 55/00.

any type of addition to the notification, however. In accordance with its aim, addenda which clarify its content should be seen as permissible. Statements which have their own content, however, and which have no relevance for either the understanding or the effectiveness of the notification of the right of withdrawal and which, therefore, distract from it, are not counted among these permitted additions.

b) The notification of the right of withdrawal used by the defendant does not meet these requirements, because it suggests the incorrect interpretation that cases are even conceivable, where the period of withdrawal does not begin when the contractual document, containing the notification, is handed over, but only once the consumer's declaration of intention to conclude the contract has subsequently been submitted in good time. This is incorrect, however, in such a way that the addition objected to by the claimant does not clarify the notification of the right of withdrawal in its required content, but, to the contrary, is misleading for the consumer who, as a rule, has no legal training.'

Notes

(1) The requirements as to clarity of information are very strict and the sanction severe. The German legislator therefore introduced a mechanism that had to reduce the risk for traders. An optional standard form or 'Musterbelehrung' was created (Annex to the 'Verordnung über Informations- und Nachweispflichten nach bürgerlichem Recht, BGB-InfoV'). If this form was used, then the requirements of §355(2) BGB would be met, according to §14 BGB-InfoV. Although, as such, a good initiative, the model form attracted both praise and heavy criticism. It was very complicated because it catered, with various options in the text and with ten, sometimes lengthy, footnotes, for all the various rights of withdrawal with their remaining differences. It also contained a few flaws.[37] Moreover, it appeared too technical and did not really explain to the consumer in sufficient detail the costs he may incur or how these can be avoided. Some authors even considered the model form void, arguing that it violated the BGB (a superior law).[38] In 2006, a lower instance court followed this argument[39] and in the meantime, several other courts have followed suit.[40] Even the BGH has expressed doubts as to the conformity of the model form with the BGB but could not decide the matter because the trader withdrew his appeal.[41] Therefore, the German Ministry of Justice opened a consultation concerning the revision of the model form in October 2007. In the meantime, a new model form was designed; this came into effect on 1 April 2008.

(2) Standard forms for notification of withdrawal (and also allowing the consumer to exercise his right of withdrawal) have recently also been introduced at European level (see the Timeshare Directive 2008/122/EC, Annex V and the Proposal for a Directive on Consumer Rights).

[37] Rott, above n 24.

[38] See A Masuch, 'Musterhafte Widerrufsbelehrung des Bundesjustizministeriums' [2002] *Neue Juristische Wochenschrift* 2931–32.

[39] See LG Halle, 13 May 2006 (2006) VuR 411.

[40] See LG Halle, 13 May 2006 (2006) VuR 411; LG Koblenz, 20 December 2006 (2007) BB 239.

[41] See BGH, Az VIII ZR 25/07.

In the DCFR, the following Article tries to harmonise the diverging provisions relating to the content of the notification of the right of withdrawal.

DCFR **4.11 (EU)**

Article II—5:104: Adequate notification of the right to withdraw

An adequate notification of the right to withdraw requires that the right is appropriately brought to the entitled party's attention, and that the notification provides, in textual form on a durable medium and in clear and comprehensible language, information about how the right may be exercised, the withdrawal period, and the name and address of the person to whom the withdrawal is to be communicated.

Questions

(1) Do you think this provision rightly balances the interests of the consumer and the business?

(2) Do you think the consumer will have all relevant information if the business complies with this provision?

I.C.3 PROLONGATION OF THE RIGHT OF WITHDRAWAL

Failure to inform the consumer of his right of withdrawal makes such a right ineffective. A remedy that is specific for consumer contracts is the extension of the right of withdrawal if the required information has not been provided: the period for withdrawal in such case never starts. This implies an indefinite period for withdrawal and a clash with the principle of legal certainty. Some authors have therefore argued for the introduction of a maximum time limit for the exercise of the right of withdrawal to balance the interests of consumers with the need for legal certainty. Some EC directives provide for an explicit time limit themselves. Such is, for example, the case for the Distance Selling Directive (97/7/EC) and the Timeshare Directive (2008/122/EC).

Distance Selling Directive (97/7/EC) **4.12 (EU)**

Article 6 Right of withdrawal

(1) For any distance contract the consumer shall have a period of at least seven working days in which to withdraw from the contract without penalty and without giving any reason. …

If the supplier has failed to fulfil the obligations laid down in Article 5 [information requirements], the period shall be three months. The period shall begin:

—in the case of goods, from the day of receipt by the consumer,

—in the case of services, from the day of conclusion of the contract.

If the information referred to in Article 5 is supplied within this three-month period, the seven working day period referred to in the first subparagraph shall begin as from that moment.

In other Directives, no explicit extension of the period for withdrawal has been foreseen, but these Directives do determine that the period for withdrawal only starts running once certain information has been provided. This is the case for the Doorstep Selling Directive (85/577/EEC) and the Distance Selling of Financial Services Directive (2002/65/EC).

ECJ Case C-481/99, 13 December 2001[42] *Heininger v Bayerische Hypo- und Vereinsbank AG* — 4.13 (EU)

NO MAXIMUM PERIOD FOR WITHDRAWAL FOR DOORSTEP SELLING

National time limits

The Doorstep Selling Directive precludes the national legislature from imposing a one-year time limit for the right of cancellation where the consumer has not received the information required.

Facts: By a contract dated 28 April 1993 and 7 May 1993 (the 'loan agreement'), Mr and Mrs Heininger took out a loan from the bank in order to finance the purchase of a flat. The loan was secured by means of a *Grundschuld* (charge on the property) in the same amount. By an action brought in January 1998, Mr and Mrs Heininger revoked their declaration of intent to enter into the loan agreement, pursuant to §1 of the HWiG (Doorstep Selling Act). They claimed that, on several occasions, an estate agent known to them and acting on a self-employed basis as agent for the bank, called uninvited at their home, and there induced them to purchase the flat in question and to enter into the loan agreement. They maintained that he did not inform them of their right of cancellation. Mr and Mrs Heininger sought an order that the bank reimburse to them the sums paid by way of capital and interest and refund to them the costs they incurred in connection with the execution of the loan agreement, the total sum claimed being DEM 118,443.81. They further sought a declaration that no rights accrued to the bank under the loan agreement. Their application was dismissed both at first instance and upon appeal. Mr and Mrs Heininger then brought an appeal on points of law (Revision) before the Bundesgerichtshof (BGH). The BGH decided to stay proceedings and to refer the several questions to the ECJ for a preliminary ruling. By its first question, the BGH essentially asked whether the Doorstep Selling Directive (85/577/EEC) also covered agreements for the grant of credit secured on immovable property and, as far as the right of cancellation provided for in Article 5 is concerned, whether it takes precedence over the Consumer Credit Directive (87/102/EEC). If that question was answered in the affirmative, the BGH also wanted to know whether national legislature was precluded by the Doorstep Selling Directive from applying the time limit for exercising the right of cancellation provided for in the third sentence of §7(2) of the VerbrKrG (Consumer Credit Act) also in cases where the subject of the doorstep transaction is credit secured by immovable property within the meaning of §3(2) of the VerbrKrG, and the information required under Article 4 of that directive was not given.

Judgment: 44. In that regard, it should first be observed that the first paragraph of Article 4 of the doorstep-selling directive provides that traders shall be required to give consumers written notice of their right of cancellation within the period laid down in Article 5 and that the third paragraph of Article 4 of the same directive provides that Member States shall ensure that their national legislation lays down appropriate consumer protection measures in cases where the information referred to in this Article is not supplied. Article 5(1) of the directive provides that [t]he consumer shall have the right to renounce the effects of his undertaking by sending notice within a period of not less than seven days from receipt by the consumer of the notice referred to in Article 4, in accordance with the procedure laid down by national law.

[42] [2001] ECR I-9945.

45. It should next be pointed out that the doorstep-selling directive thus expressly provides that the minimum period of seven days prescribed for cancellation must be calculated from receipt by the consumer of the notice concerning his right of cancellation, and that it is on the trader that the obligation falls to provide that information. Those provisions are explained by the fact that if the consumer is not aware of the existence of the right of cancellation, he will not be able to exercise that right.

46. Having regard to the wording and purpose of Article 5 of the doorstep-selling directive, it is not possible to construe the third paragraph of Article 4 as enabling the national legislature to provide that the consumer's right of cancellation must in any event be exercised within a period of one year, even if the trader has not notified the consumer of the existence of that right.

47. Finally, as regards the argument that it is essential, for reasons of legal certainty, to restrict the period within which the right of cancellation may be exercised, such reasons cannot prevail since they imply a limitation of the rights expressly conferred on consumers by the doorstep-selling directive in order to protect them against the risks arising from the fact that the credit institutions have chosen to enter into agreements away from their business premises. If those institutions choose such methods in order to market their services, they can easily safeguard both the interests of consumers and their own requirements as to legal certainty by complying with their duty to supply consumers with information.

48. In the light of those considerations the answer to the second question must be that the doorstep-selling directive precludes the national legislature from imposing a time-limit of one year from the conclusion of the contract within which the right of cancellation provided for in Article 5 of that directive may be exercised, where the consumer has not received the information specified in Article 4.

Notes

(1) The ECJ thus decided that it was impossible for national legislators to impose a maximum time limit as the period for withdrawal did in any event did not start until the information had been provided, thus leading to a possibly eternal right of withdrawal. The problems that may arise when unravelling contracts that are withdrawn from, possibly after a longer period of time, are dealt with in the following part of this chapter.

(2) The issue of the prolongation of the right of withdrawal is one that could be harmonised relatively easily. Legal certainty argues in favour of a maximum time limit. One then still has to decide how long this limit should be and different proposals have been made, ranging from three months to one year.[43] Others have argued against a maximum time limit: traders can easily avoid the indefinite extension of the period for withdrawal by providing the information required. In the DCFR, the following Article tries to harmonise the currently diverging provisions in the directives.

[43] See eg M Loos, above n 23, 5ff.

DCFR **4.14 (EU)**

Article II—5:103: Withdrawal Period

(1) A right to withdraw may be exercised at any time after the conclusion of the contract and before the end of the withdrawal period.

(2) The withdrawal period ends fourteen days after the latest of the following times;

(a) the time of conclusion of the contract;

(b) the time when the entitled party receives from the other party adequate information on the right to withdraw; or

(c) if the subject matter of the contract is the delivery of goods, the time when the goods are received.

(3) The withdrawal period ends no later than one year after the time of conclusion of the contract.

(4) A notice of withdrawal is timely if dispatched before the end of the withdrawal period.

Questions

(1) Do you think this provision correctly reflects the current provisions in the directives?

(2) Do you think this provision fairly balances the need for legal certainty and the need for consumer protection?

The ECJ has in the meantime decided that not all maximum time limits in national law are contrary to the Doorstep Selling Directive (85/577/EEC).

ECJ Case C-412/06, 10 April 2008[44] **4.15 (EU)**
Hamilton v Volksbank Filder

MAXIMUM PERIOD FOR WITHDRAWAL FOR DOORSTEP SELLING FROM TOTAL PERFORMANCE OF THE CONTRACT

Fully performed contract

The national legislature is entitled to provide that the right of cancellation may be exercised no later than one month from the time at which the contracting parties have performed in full their obligations under a contract for long-term credit where the consumer has been given defective notice concerning the exercise of that right.

Facts: In 1992 Ms Hamilton signed, at her home, a contract for a loan with a bank to finance the acquisition of shares in a property fund. In accordance with then applicable law on consumer credit the contract contained the following notice concerning the right of withdrawal: 'If the borrower has received the loan, cancellation shall be deemed not to have taken place unless he repays the loan either within two weeks of giving notice of cancellation or within two weeks of the paying out of the loan.' At the end of April 1998, Ms Hamilton had entirely repaid the loan and the security for the loan was returned. In 2002, Ms Hamilton cancelled the loan contract on the basis of the judgment in Case C-481/99 *Heininger*. In 2004, Ms Hamilton brought an action against Volksbank, on the one hand, for reimbursement of the interest paid under the

[44] [2008] ECR I-2383.

loan contract at issue and the amount of the loan that she had paid back, and, on the other, for compensation for the interest she had paid to the building society with which she had concluded the savings contract. In these proceedings, the Oberlandesgericht Stuttgart had doubts as to whether the provisions laid down in the fourth sentence of §2(1) HWiG could be regarded as 'appropriate consumer protection measures' because they provided that, in a case such as that before it, the right of cancellation was to lapse. The Oberlandesgericht stayed the proceedings and referred, inter alia, the following question to the ECJ for a preliminary ruling:

May the first paragraph of Article 4 and Article 5(1) of [the Doorstep Selling Directive] be interpreted as meaning that the national legislature is not precluded from placing a time-limit on the right of cancellation given by Article 5 of the directive, despite the consumer having been given defective notice, so that it expires one month after both parties have performed their obligations under the agreement in full?

Judgment: 35. As the Advocate General points out in points 18 and 19 of his Opinion, incorrect information concerning exercise of the right of cancellation is equivalent to no information, since both situations are equally misleading for the consumer as regards his right of cancellation.

36. For such situations, the third paragraph of Article 4 of the doorstep selling directive provides that 'Member States shall ensure that their national legislation lays down appropriate consumer protection measures'.

37. The question therefore arises in the main proceedings whether a measure which provides that the right of cancellation given by Article 5(1) of that directive is to expire one month after both parties have performed in full their obligations under a long-term loan contract, when the consumer has been given defective notice concerning the exercise of that right, may none the less be regarded as an appropriate consumer protection measure within the meaning of the third indent of Article 4 of that directive.

38. It should be pointed out in that regard that the concept of 'appropriate consumer protection measures', to which the third paragraph of Article 4 of the doorstep selling directive refers, indicates that the Community legislature wished to give those measures a uniform scope at Community level.

39. Moreover, the term 'appropriate' in the abovementioned provision indicates that such measures do not seek to provide absolute protection for consumers. The Member States must exercise their discretion in accordance both with the principal aim of the doorstep selling directive and with the other provisions thereof.

40. Although it is true, as has been pointed out in paragraph 32 of the present judgment, that the principal aim of the doorstep selling directive is to protect consumers, it should be pointed out that both the general structure of the directive and the wording of several of its provisions indicate that such protection is subject to certain limits.

41. Thus, with regard, specifically, to the purpose of the time-limit for cancellation, the fifth recital in the preamble to the directive states—as has been pointed out in paragraph 33 of the present judgment—that that time-limit enables the consumer 'to assess the obligations arising under the contract' concluded at the doorstep. The reference in that recital to the concept of 'obligations arising under the contract' indicates that the consumer may cancel such a contract during the time that it is in effect.

42. Similarly, the provision which governs the exercise of the right of cancellation—namely, Article 5(1) of the doorstep selling directive—provides, inter alia, that '[t]he consumer shall have the right to renounce the effects of his undertaking'. The use in that provision of the term 'undertaking' indicates, as Volksbank argued at the hearing before the Court, that the right of cancellation may be exercised as long as the consumer is not bound, at the time that the right is exercised, by any undertaking under the cancelled contract. That logic flows from one of the general principles of civil law, namely

that full performance of a contract results, as a general rule, from discharge of the mutual obligations under the contract or from termination of that contract.

43. Moreover, according to Article 5(2) of the directive, which governs the consequences of the exercise of the right of cancellation, the giving of cancellation notice has the effect of releasing the consumer from 'any obligations under the cancelled contract'. The reference to the concept of 'obligation' in that provision indicates that the existence of the abovementioned consequences presupposes that the consumer has exercised his right of cancellation in regard to a contract which was in the process of being performed, whereas after the full performance of the contract, there is no further obligation.

44. Furthermore, with regard to the legal effects of cancellation, particularly in regard to the reimbursement of payment for goods or services provided and the return of goods received, Article 7 of the doorstep selling directive refers to the national laws.

45. It follows that an 'appropriate measure' within the meaning of the third paragraph of Article 4 of the doorstep selling directive is one which provides that the performance in full by the parties of their obligations under a long-term loan contract causes the right of cancellation to lapse.

46. That interpretation is not weakened by the judgments in *Heininger* and *Schulte* or in Case C-229/04 *Crailsheimer Volksbank* [2005] ECR I-9273. It can be seen from paragraphs 16 and 18 of *Heininger*, paragraph 26 of *Schulte* and paragraph 24 of *Crailsheimer Volksbank* that the interpretation of the doorstep selling directive provided by the Court in those judgments concerns loan contracts which had not been fully performed. However, that is not the position in the case before the referring court.

47. With regard, specifically, to *Heininger*, the Court held in that judgment that the doorstep selling directive precludes the national legislature from imposing a time-limit, of one year from the conclusion of the contract, within which the right of cancellation provided for in Article 5 of that directive must be exercised, where the consumer has not received the information specified in Article 4 of that directive. As Volksbank, the German Government and the Commission were fully entitled to argue, that is not the position in the case before the referring court. In that case, the national legislature applies a time-limit of one month from the time at which the contracting parties have performed in full their obligations under a contract.

48. It should be borne in mind—with regard to the one-month time-limit provided for by the national legislation at issue in the main proceedings, which runs from the performance in full by the parties of their obligations under the contract—that, under Article 8 of the doorstep selling directive, that directive does not prevent Member States from adopting or maintaining more favourable provisions to protect consumers in the field which it covers.

49. In the light of all the foregoing, the answer to the first question referred to the Court must be that the doorstep selling directive must be interpreted as meaning that the national legislature is entitled to provide that the right of cancellation laid down in Article 5(1) of the directive may be exercised no later than one month from the time at which the contracting parties have performed in full their obligations under a contract for long-term credit, where the consumer has been given defective notice concerning the exercise of that right.

Questions

(1) Do you agree with the ECJ that when a consumer has not been informed of his right of withdrawal, different rules should apply depending on whether the

contract has been fully performed? The Court uses this argument to distinguish this case from the *Heininger* and *Schulte* and *Crailsheimer* cases.

(2) Should full performance have an effect on the possibility of exercising a right of withdrawal (cf what the Court seems to imply in paragraph 43 above)? In the case at issue, a long-term credit contract was at stake. Suppose goods are sold on the doorstep at an excessive price (which is not unusual for doorstep selling), delivered and immediately paid for. The contract is thus fully performed. Should this influence the possibility for the consumer to exercise his right of withdrawal? If the right of withdrawal lapses when the contract is fully performed, even if the consumer was not informed of his right of withdrawal, could this not be an incentive for rogue traders to quickly deliver the goods and demand (often excessive) payment?

(3) The issue of performance during the period for withdrawal is further dealt with below, section I.C.4.

The following case of the French Cour de Cassation, in which a similar French rule of prolongation of the period for withdrawal was applied, illustrates that there is a potential risk for abuse when the period for withdrawal is prolonged.

Cass civ, 7 March 2006[45] **4.16 (FR)**

EXTENSION OF RIGHT OF WITHDRAWAL

Downward life insurance

The right of withdrawal can be exercised at the discretion of the insured person, who is not required to act in good faith. This is also the case when the period for withdrawal is prolonged.

Facts: M Senacq concluded a contract for a 'multisupport life insurance' on 5 November 1999. On the application form, he acknowledged he had 'received and read the standard terms and annexes'. He chose a system where he could manage approximately half of the funds himself. He paid an amount of FRF 2,020,202 at the time of subscription and some months later another FRF 2,500,000. Dissatisfied with the evolution of the capital invested, he wanted to exercise his right of withdrawal on 6 November 2001, arguing that the company had not respected its pre-contractual information requirements. He relied on Article L 132-5-1 and Article L 132-5-2 Code des assurances. These Articles state that if the required information has not been provided, the period for withdrawal of 30 calendar days only runs as from the date the information has effectively been provided (Article L 132-5-2). Article L 132-5-1 further provides that the sums paid by the consumer must be entirely reimbursed when the consumer exercises his right of withdrawal. The Court of Appeal accepted that the required information had not been provided and that the consumer could exercise his right of withdrawal and was entitled to the entire reimbursement of the sums paid. The judgment was challenged on several grounds, inter alia on the ground that the consumer had waived its right of withdrawal as the contract had been in operation for two years and as the consumer himself had carried out several transactions in which he himself had changed the underlying stock basis and had chosen new stocks. The judgment was also challenged in that it had not accepted that the exercise of the right of withdrawal in the circumstances was an abuse of right. The Cour de Cassation dismissed the appeal.

[45] (2006) JCP(G) 737 II 10056. See also the very similar case of the same date Cass civ 2e, 7 March 2006, pourvoi No 05-10366 (2006) RGAR 2.

Judgment: Considering the fifth argument: The judgement is contested for having accepted Mr X's demands, on the following grounds:

1. that according to paragraph 3 of Article 1134 of the Civil Code, all obligations must be performed in good faith; that an insured party fails to meet the obligation to act in good faith if—in a situation where he is perfectly capable of obtaining the required documents and information the insurer allegedly did not communicate to him within the time limit of 30 days, as is stated in the first paragraph of Article L 132-5-1 of the Insurance Law Code—he instigates, within the context of the contract, speculative and repeated arbitrage transactions and shows, by acting in such a way, that first, he was not in fact lacking information that would not have been given to him and that second, he had a perfect understanding and a good grasp of the insurance contract, and then decides, two years after the conclusion of the contract, under the pretext of lacking information, to withdraw from the contract in order to avoid the consequences of the financial risks he incurred following a decline in the value of the financial instruments, which he freely chose. That the Court of Appeal violated Article 1134 of the Civil Code in maintaining—in order to reject La Mondiale's claim that Mr X's acted in bad faith—that the legislator intended to oblige the insurance company to provide the subscriber with enough information and has chosen to couple this obligation with an automatic sanction, a sanction that cannot be made dependant on the circumstances of the case in question.

2. that, as emphasised by La Mondiale in its conclusions, as the purpose of the right of withdrawal is to ensure the protection of the subscriber against an ill-considered engagement, without well informed consent. This represents a departure from the provisions of Article L 132-5-1 of the Insurance Law Code and an improper use of the right of withdrawal, it institutes the subscriber's use of this right for the sole aim of forcing the insured party to accept the financial consequences of his choices on the stock market. In refraining from investigating, as the Court was invited to do by the company La Mondiale, whether Mr X had not abused his rights by invoking his right of withdrawal not because he could not understand the operation of the insurance contract to which he was bound at the time it was concluded, but because the execution of the aforementioned contract on the basis of his own financial choices, later turned out to be damaging to his own interests, the Court of Appeal undermined the legal basis of its decision with respect to Article L 132-5-1 of the Insurance Law Code;

However, it follows from Article L 132-5-1 of the Insurance Law Code, a public policy provision, and it is in line with Directive 2002/83/EEC of 5 November 2002, that the exercise of the prolonged right of withdrawal, automatically granted to the insured as a sanction for the failure to submit the documents and the information stated in this text, is at the insured party's discretion and that good faith is not required.

Moreover, given that the judgement states explicitly that, under the provisions laid out in the above stated article, the legislator wanted to oblige the insurer to provide the subscriber with enough information and has linked this obligation to an automatic sanction, the application of which cannot be made subordinate to the specific circumstances of the case;

It thus follows that the argument is unfounded;

Based on the above considerations:

The appeal is declared null and void.

Note

This case illustrates the risk of abuse by the consumer when the period for withdrawal is prolonged. The case also provides some indications on the nature of the right of withdrawal. The Cour de Cassation held that the right of withdrawal is a 'discretionary right' that does not require good faith. Although no reasons need to be given for the exercise of this right, the Cour de Cassation goes one step further and seems to imply that the right cannot be abused. In France, as well as in several other countries, legal doctrine has argued for the opposite result: there may be situations in which the exercise of a right of withdrawal can be an abuse of right.[46]

I.C.4 PERFORMANCE DURING THE PERIOD FOR WITHDRAWAL

There is a clear tension between, on the one hand, ensuring that the consumer can effectively exercise his right of withdrawal, and, on the other hand, the desire not to hinder trade and economic activities or the normal performance of contracts. If performance is allowed during the period for withdrawal, this will make it harder for the consumer to withdraw without any costs. Services that have been provided will have to be reimbursed, thus complicating the exercise of the right of withdrawal. On the other hand, if performance is prohibited during the period for withdrawal, this may actually harm consumers, who may, for example, need urgent repairs to their houses, or may need a loan quickly. This issue will be illustrated, focusing on doorstep contracts.

Consumer Code (Code de la consommation) **4.17 (FR)**

Article L 121-26 Prior to the expiration of the cooling-off period as specified in Article L 121-25, no person or entity shall demand or obtain from the client, whether directly or indirectly, on any grounds, any remuneration or any undertaking nor provide any service of any kind.

However, a subscription taken out at home to a daily publication, in the sense of Article 39 of the General Tax Code, is not subject to the provisions of the preceding paragraph if the consumer has a permanent right to cancel the subscription, without any charges, with repayment within two weeks, of the total sums paid for the portion of the subscription period, which has not elapsed.

Moreover, the undertakings or orders of payment must not be carried out before the time limit specified in Article L 121-25 has expired and must be returned to the consumer within two weeks of his or her withdrawal.

[46] For the Netherlands: Hijma and Valk, above n 27, 76. For Belgium: Terryn, above n 23, No 160. For Germany: M Schmidt-Kessel, 'Die gesetzliche Ausweitung der Widerrufsrechte nach Heininger' [2002] *Zeitschrift fur die gesamte Staatswissenschaft* 313; P Mankowski, *Beseitigungsrechte* (Tübingen, Mohr Siebeck, 2003) 840. In France legal doctrine is divided. Compare F Descorps Declère, 'La Cour de Cassation sanctionne le défaut d'information de souscripteurs de contrats d'assurance sur la vie' (2006) II *La Semaine Juridique: Juris Classeur Periodique* 10056, 737 with S Mirabail, *La rétractation en droit privé français* (Paris, LGDJ, 1997) 188.

The provisions laid out in the second paragraph apply to subscriptions taken out at home offered by the associations and businesses pre-approved by the State, whose objective is to provide the services mentioned in Article L 129-1 of the Labour Code.

Note

In France, a prohibition on providing services during the period for withdrawal exists. No such prohibition on the trader performing a doorstep contract, or claiming payment, exists in Germany, although consumer lawyers have occasionally called for such a provision.[47] In the UK, the OFT conducted extensive market research on doorstep selling and has proposed amending the doorstep selling regulations and including a prohibition on performance (with some exceptions) during the period for withdrawal.[48] Such a proposal was, however, rejected by the government. It was considered that the UCPD's prohibition on aggressive trade practices would help to tackle the considerable consumer detriment suffered in this area, that an outright prohibition on performance would reduce consumer choice, and that exceptions to such a prohibition would in any event be necessary. Such exceptions (including a possible waiver of the right of withdrawal) would only create new loopholes to be exploited by rogue traders.[49] The 2008 Cancellation of Contracts Made in a Consumer's Home or Place of Work etc Regulations does, however, require the consumer's written agreement to performance of certain specified contracts beginning before the end of the cooling-off period.

In other countries, however, the period for withdrawal only starts running when the goods have been delivered.

Door-to-Door Sales Act 1981 **4.18 (SW)**

Article 7 [F]or movables, the cooling off period runs from the day on which the consumer took delivery of the goods or a material part thereof, or prior thereto, examined the goods or similar goods.

Questions

(1) In the case of distance selling of goods, the rationale for the period for withdrawal only starting when goods have been delivered is clear: it is only then that the consumer will be able to verify the quality of the goods. Do you think similar arguments exist in the case of doorstep selling contracts?

(2) In the DCFR, the rule of Article 6(1) the Distance Selling Directive (97/7/EC) was generalised: if the subject-matter of the contract is the delivery of

[47] See eg P Rott, 'Widerruf und Rückabwicklung nach der Umsetzung der Fernabsatzrichtlinie und dem Entwurf eines Schuldrechtsmodernisierungsgesetzes' [2001] *Verbraucher und Recht* 87.

[48] Above n 22.

[49] Available at www.dti.gov.uk/files/file33819.pdf.

goods, the period for withdrawal can only start at the time when the goods are received (see above Article II—5:103 DCFR). Do you think this is a good rule?

(3) A more limited prohibition on performance by the consumer and, more specifically, a prohibition to ask for payment during the period for withdrawal is more common in national law (see above, Article L 121-26 for France; Article 89 Trade Practices Act for Belgium). At EC level, the Timeshare Directive (2008/122/EC) is the only Directive having such a prohibition. Some countries, eg Belgium, also have such a prohibition for distance selling.[50] In the DCFR, the rule of the Timeshare Directive prohibiting payment during the period for withdrawal was not generalised but only kept in relation to timeshare contracts. Do you think this choice rightly balances the interests of businesses and consumers?

I.C.5 EXERCISE OF THE RIGHT OF WITHDRAWAL

The Directives mainly leave this issue to the Member States. There is a wide variety with regard to formal requirements between countries and often even within one and the same country. Thus, under Spanish law, although no formal requirements are imposed with regard to doorstep selling, such requirements do exist with regard to timeshare sales. Similar variations exist in Belgian law. In the ACQP and DCFR, the following solution has been proposed:

DCFR **4.19 (EU)**

Article II—5:102: Exercise of right to withdraw

(1) A right to withdraw is exercised by notice to the other party. No reasons need to be given.

(2) Returning the subject matter of the contract is considered a notice of withdrawal unless the circumstances indicate otherwise.

Note

No formal requirements have thus been imposed on the consumer. Although this is also one of the issues that could easily be harmonised, it is also an issue over which opinions differ. Introducing formal requirements could help the consumer to prove that he has exercised his right of withdrawal. However, it would also make it more difficult for the entitled party actually to exercise its right of withdrawal and would complicate matters for the seller as he would also need to inform the consumer of such formal requirements. The absence of formal requirements ensures that the

[50] See, however ECJ, 16 December 2008, Case C-205/07 *Lodewijk Gysbrechts and Santurel Inter BVBA,* nyr where it was held that Art 29 EC does not preclude national rules which prohibit a supplier, in cross-border distance selling, from requiring an advance or any payment from a consumer before expiry of the withdrawal period, but that Art 29 EC does preclude a prohibition, under those rules, on requesting, before expiry of that period, the number of the consumer's payment card. The case concerned a preliminary reference on the compatibility of the (strict interpretation) of the Belgian prohibition on requiring advance payment during the period for withdrawal.

exercise of the right of withdrawal is not barred merely because the right form has not been respected.

I.C.6 EFFECTS OF WITHDRAWAL

I.C.6.a General

Having a *theoretical* right of withdrawal is one thing. Having an *actual* right of withdrawal is another. Whether the exercise of a right of withdrawal will actually benefit a consumer depends to a large extent on the effects of exercising such a right and the liability in restitution. These aspects are hardly dealt with in the Directives granting consumers a cooling-off period where national rules on liability in restitution seem to be presupposed, but similar lacunae also exist in certain national jurisdictions. Germany is one of the countries that does provide detailed rules regulating the consequences of exercising a right of withdrawal (§357 BGB juncto §346 BGB).

BGB **4.20 (DE)**

§357 Legal consequences of withdrawal and return

(1) Save where otherwise provided, the provisions on statutory termination apply mutatis mutandis to the right of withdrawal and return. The period laid down in §286(3) begins upon the consumer's declaration of withdrawal or return.

(2) In the event that he exercises the right of withdrawal the consumer is bound to return the goods if they can be sent as a parcel. The cost and risk of return is borne by the businessperson in the event of withdrawal and return. If a right of withdrawal exists, the normal costs of return may be imposed by contract on the consumer where the value of his order does not exceed €40, unless the goods delivered do not correspond to the goods ordered.

(3) In derogation from §346(2), sentence 1, No 3, the consumer must pay compensation for value in respect of a deterioration in the goods as a result of their proper use, if his attention has previously been drawn in textual form to this legal consequence and to a means of avoiding it. This does not apply if the deterioration is due exclusively to inspection of the goods. §346(3), sentence 1, No 3 does not apply if the consumer has been properly informed of his right of revocation or he has become aware of it in another way.

(4) More extensive claims do not exist.

The compatibility with EC law of the German provisions on restitution was the subject of the preliminary references in the cases below.

ECJ Case C-350/03, 25 October 2005[51] 4.21 (EU)
Schulte v Deutsche Bausparkasse Badenia AG

RESTORATION OF THE STATUS QUO ANTE

Junk immovables continued

The exercise of the right of cancellation has the effect of releasing the consumer from any obligations under the cancelled agreement, which implies the restoration of the status quo ante.

Facts: Deutsche Bausparkasse Badenia (the 'Bank') had financed the purchase of old apartments since the end of the 1980s. These properties were generally blocks of flats constructed as social housing which were purchased by Allgemeine Wohnungsvermögens AG, partly renovated and then offered for sale. Heinen & Biege GmbH handled the marketing of the properties and arranged finance. In the context of this marketing scheme, Mr and Mrs Schulte were contacted in February 1992 by a representative of Heinen & Biege. On 28 April 1992 Mr and Mrs Schulte purchased an apartment and took out a loan, solely in order to finance the purchase, from the Bank, secured by a charge on the property. The loan agreement contained no information regarding the right of cancellation within the meaning of the Hausturwiderrufgesetz (HWiG).

Once all the agreements had been concluded and the securities provided, the Bank made a direct payment to the company selling the immovable property, in accordance with written instructions from Mr and Mrs Schulte. As Mr and Mrs Schulte failed to meet their monthly repayment obligations under the loan agreement, the Bank terminated the agreement, demanded immediate repayment of the loan and, in the absence of any payment, sought to enforce payment. In November 2002 Mr and Mrs Schulte cancelled the loan agreement on the basis of §1 of the HWiG and instituted proceedings against the enforcement before the Landgericht Bochum. They submitted before that court that they were contacted at home by a representative of Heinen & Biege who presented a tax-saving scheme to them and that they were offered, also at their home, complete financing, which was in the event solely that provided by the Bank. They were informed that, under the chosen financing scheme, the property would be financed by the associated tax advantages and the rental income. Both the loan agreement and the real estate savings agreement were signed at their home. They considered that the Bank must take responsibility for the doorstep selling situation, since it had worked closely with the company acting as an intermediary for many years, and the entire negotiation phase of the contracts was conducted on behalf of the Bank. Mr and Mrs Schulte also submitted that the purchase contract and the loan agreement must be regarded as a single economic entity and that they were therefore merely required to retransfer ownership of the property pursuant to the fourth sentence of §9(2) of the VerbrKrG (Consumer Credit Act) which applies in any event by analogy.

The Landgericht Bochum referred several questions to the ECJ. It asked for clarification on the scope of application of the Doorstep Selling Directive (85/577/EEC). The other questions mainly concerned the effects of cancellation. Under German law, the cancellation of a secured credit agreement results in the voiding of the contract, so that, under §3 of the HWiG, each party must return to the other whatever it has received and must pay for the use of what was supplied up to the date of cancellation. It follows that, in the event of the cancellation of a secured credit agreement, the lending Bank has a right to repayment of the net amount of credit paid with interest at the market rate. According to the settled case-law of the Bundesgerichtshof, the secured credit agreement and the purchase of immovable property financed by the loan are moreover not deemed to be linked agreements constituting a single economic entity. Consequently, the cancellation of the secured credit agreement does not affect the validity of the purchase contract for immovable property financed by that credit agreement.

The Landgericht Bochum therefore wanted to know whether such rules were compatible with the requirements of a high level of protection in the field of consumer protection and the effectiveness of consumer protection safeguarded by the Directive.

Judgment: 88. In that regard, it must be borne in mind that, as the Bank, the German Government and the Commission pointed out, under Article 5(2) of the Directive, the giving of notice of cancellation has the effect of releasing the consumer from any

[51] [2005] ECR I-09215.

obligations under the cancelled contract. Such cancellation of the obligations of the consumer entails, for the consumer and for the lender, the restoration of the status quo ante.

89. Accordingly, the Directive does not preclude an obligation on the consumer to repay to the lender immediately the amount he borrowed, in the event of cancellation of a secured credit agreement.

90. Third, the referring court seeks to know whether, in a situation such as that in the main proceedings, the Directive precludes national legislation which provides for an obligation on the consumer, in the event of cancellation of the contract, not only to repay the amounts received under the contract but also to pay to the lender interest at the market rate.

91. In the view of Mr and Mrs Schulte, such legislation is contrary to the principle of effective consumer protection laid down by the Directive. In the view of the Bank and the German Government, even when account is taken of the effectiveness of the consumer protection which it guarantees, the Directive contains no requirement which would preclude such national legislation.

92. In that regard, it must be observed that the exercise of the right of cancellation provided for by Article 5(1) of the Directive, in the case of a loan agreement, has the effect under Article 5(2) of releasing the consumer from any obligations under the cancelled agreement, which implies the restoration of the status quo ante.

93. Accordingly, the Directive does not preclude national legislation which provides for an obligation on the consumer, in the event of cancellation of a secured credit agreement, not only to repay the amounts received under the contract but also to pay to the lender interest at the market rate.

The requirements under the Directive in the event of failure to comply with the obligation to inform the consumer of his right of cancellation

94. Although the Directive does not generally preclude the application of national rules under which a consumer who cancels a credit agreement must immediately repay the loan in full with interest at the market rate in circumstances in which the trader has complied with the obligation to inform the consumer incumbent on him under Article 4 of the Directive, the same is not necessarily true where the trader has not complied with that obligation.

95. In that connection, it must be observed that under the third paragraph of Article 4 of the Directive, Member States are to ensure that their national legislation lays down appropriate consumer protection measures in cases where the information referred to in this article is not supplied

96. It must be observed that, if the referring court takes the view that the cancellation was valid, the fact that the Bank did not inform Mr and Mrs Schulte of their right of cancellation and that they cancelled the credit agreement after several years is relevant for the assessment of the dispute in the main proceedings.

97. If the Bank had informed Mr and Mrs Schulte of their right of cancellation under the HWiG at the correct time, they would have had seven days to change their minds about concluding the loan agreement. If they had chosen then to cancel it, it is common ground that, given the link between the loan agreement and the purchase contract, the latter would not have been concluded.

98. In a situation where the Bank has not complied with the obligation to inform the consumer incumbent on it under Article 4 of the Directive, if the consumer must repay the loan under German law as construed in the case-law of the Bundesgerichtshof, he

bears the risks entailed by financial investments such as those at issue in the main proceedings, as described in paragraph 52 of this judgment.

99. However, in a situation such as that in the main proceedings, the consumer could have avoided exposure to those risks if he had been informed in time of his right of cancellation.

100. In those circumstances, the Directive requires Member States to adopt appropriate measures so that the consumer does not have to bear the consequences of the materialisation of those risks. The Member States must therefore ensure that, in those circumstances, a bank which has not complied with its obligation to inform the consumer bears the consequences of the materialisation of those risks so that the obligation to protect consumers is safeguarded.

101. Accordingly, in a situation where, if the Bank had informed the consumer of his right of cancellation, the consumer would have been able to avoid exposure to the risks inherent in investments such as those at issue in the main proceedings, Article 4 requires Member States to ensure that their legislation protects consumers who have been unable to avoid exposure to such risks, by adopting suitable measures to allow them to avoid bearing the consequences of the materialisation of those risks.

Notes

(1) A similar conclusion was reached in the *Crailsheimer* case of the same date and these cases are a follow-up to the *Heininger* case (see above 4.13 (EU)).[52] The ECJ did clarify some aspects with regard to the effects of withdrawal but left many questions open. It thus follows from *Crailsheimer* and *Schulte* that, in principle, the exercise of a right of withdrawal can give rise to restitutionary obligations that must ensure a return to the status quo ante. This could be considered to be the point of departure in all situations where the consumer has a right of withdrawal. However, other Directives use different wording and the answer to the question as to whether (national) restitutionary obligations are compatible with (other) Directives is therefore not necessarily the same. In Germany, for example, it is often argued that Article 6(2) of the Distance Selling Directive (97/7/EC)—which says that 'the only charge that may be made to the consumer because of the exercise of his right of withdrawal is the direct cost of returning the goods'—stands in the way of an obligation for the consumer to compensate for damages to the goods through the use of those goods.[53] This issue is dealt with in the following section.

(2) The general principle of the return to the status quo ante was somehow mitigated when the consumer has not been informed of his right of withdrawal. The ECJ based the need for limitations to such restitutionary obligations if the consumer has not been informed of his right of withdrawal specifically on Article 4(3) of the Doorstep Selling Directive (85/577/EEC) and not on the more general principle of the *effet utile* of EC law and more concretely the need to ensure the effectiveness of the right of withdrawal. This again makes it difficult to use the *Schulte* and *Crailsheimer* case-law to interpret the effects of the right of withdrawal in other Directives, which lack similar wording.

[52] Case C-481/99, *Heininger v Bayerische Hypo- und Vereinsbank AG* [2001] ECR I-9945.
[53] An obligation provided in §357(3) BGB. This provision is dealt with below (s I.c.6.B).

(3) The ECJ also does not seem to have provided a conclusive answer to the question whether withdrawal operates prospectively or whether it also has retrospective effect. Whereas the Advocate General in *Crailsheimer* did state that withdrawal 'has the effect of making the agreement void from the outset', and thus operated retrospectively, the wording of the ECJ in that case was not conclusive. The ECJ did not refer to the voidness of the contract, but merely referred to the restoration of the *status quo ante*. This *status quo ante* can be achieved both by considering that the contract has never existed and is to be regarded as void (claims for restitution are then often based on principles of unjustified enrichment), or through the establishment of specific legal obligations to return what one has received under the contract. Different systems can indeed be found in the Member States. Thus in Germany, the right of withdrawal has been construed as a slightly modified *Rücktrittsrecht* (right of termination)[54] and the rules on termination (§§346ff BGB) apply to the right of withdrawal, except where otherwise provided for (see §357(1) s 1 BGB).[55] Exercise of the right of withdrawal operates *ex nunc* and brings the parties in an *Abwicklungsverhältnis*, which replaces the original contractual duties to perform by duties to return and to reimburse.[56] Exercise of the right of withdrawal does not have retroactive proprietary effect. In other jurisdictions, there can be more uncertainty as to the effects of withdrawal. Thus in the Netherlands, although the right of withdrawal is systematically referred to as an *ontbindingsrecht* (right of termination),[57] this terminology seems to have been adopted without giving thorough thought to the exact consequences to be attached to it.[58] The terminology seems to imply that the rules governing restitution upon termination (Article 6:269ff Dutch Civil Code) would also apply upon withdrawal and withdrawal would terminate the contract *ex nunc*.[59] Some authors, however, do not accept that the rules that govern the effects of termination for non-performance should also govern the effects of withdrawal, claiming rather that the rules on termination are meant to deal with a situation where performance was problematic. The absence (or irrelevance) of non-performance is exactly what distinguishes the right to terminate the contract from the right of withdrawal.[60] Other Dutch authors have argued to qualify the right of withdrawal as a right to avoid the contract retrospectively. The rules on unjustified enrichment (Article 6:201 Dutch Civil Code) would then govern the effects of withdrawal.[61] Many authors have indeed pointed out the similarities between the situations in which a party can avoid a contract because his consent was vitiated (*vices de consentement*) and situations in which the consumer has a right of withdrawal.[62]

[54] G Ring in Dauner-Lieb, *Schuldrecht* (Bonn, DeutscherAnwaltVertrag, 2002) 546.

[55] §357 BGB indeed derogates to some extent from the rules of §§346ff BGB.

[56] J Staudinger, *Kommentar zum BGB*, 14th edn (Berlin, Sellier/De Gruyter, 2001) §355 No 21.

[57] With the exception of the recent Act on Financial Supervision (Wet Financieel Toezicht (WfT)) that implemented the Distance Selling of Financial Services Directive (2002/65/EC). See Art 4(63) WfT.

[58] Hijma and Valk, above n 27, 30.

[59] Although the Doorstep Selling Act deviates in this regard and provides that withdrawal operates retrospectively (Art 25(5) Doorstep Selling Act (Colportagewet)).

[60] C Sander, *Consumentenbescherming bij transacties op afstand* (Den Haag, Sdu, 2001) 58–59.

[61] Hijma and Valk, above n 27, 33.

[62] See eg ibid, 33; G Reiner, above n 2; Terryn, above n 23, 54ff.

The latter situations can be considered as situations in which the legislator *presumes* that the consent of the consumer was vitiated. Avoidance operates retrospectively and this is indeed the position that has been taken in several other jurisdictions with regard to the effect of withdrawal. In the UK, as a general rule, exercise of the right of withdrawal has as an effect that the contract is treated as if had never been entered into, except as otherwise provided.[63] In Belgium and France, there is considerable discussion as to the effects of withdrawal, but some authors have argued that withdrawal should be considered to work retrospectively and that the contract should be regarded as if it had never been entered into.[64]

In the DCFR detailed rules have been adopted to deal with the effects of the right of withdrawal, although the *acquis* does not provide for a clear answer to many questions that may arise:

DCFR **4.22 (EU)**

Article II—5:105: Effects of withdrawal

(1) Withdrawal terminates the contractual relationship and the obligations of both parties under the contract.

(2) The restitutionary effects of such termination are governed by the rules in Book III, Chapter 3, Section 5, Sub-section 4 (Restitution) as modified by this Article, unless the contract provides otherwise in favour of the withdrawing party.

(3) Where the withdrawing party has made a payment under the contract, the business has an obligation to return the payment without undue delay, and in any case not later than thirty days after the withdrawal becomes effective.

(4) The withdrawing party is not liable to pay:

(a) for any diminution in the value of anything received under the contract caused by inspection and testing;

(b) for any destruction or loss of, or damage to, anything received under the contract, provided the withdrawing party used reasonable care to prevent such destruction, loss or damage.

(5) The withdrawing party is liable for any diminution in value caused by normal use, unless that party had not received adequate notice of the right of withdrawal.

(6) Except as provided in this Article, the withdrawing party does not incur any liability through the exercise of the right of withdrawal.

(7) If a consumer exercises a right to withdraw from a contract after a business has made use of a contractual right to supply something of equivalent quality and price in case what was ordered is unavailable, the business must bear the cost of returning what the consumer has received under the contract.

[63] See eg Reg 8(2) of Cancellation of Contracts made in a Consumer's Home or Place of Work etc Regulations 2008.

[64] See for Belgium: Terryn, above n 23. For France: S Detraz, 'Plaidoyer pour une analyse fonctionnelle du droit de rétractation en droit de la consommation' [2004] *Contrats Concurrence Consommation* 7–13 (who argues for a qualification of the right of withdrawal as an avoidance of a contract).

Question
The DCFR provisions refer to the rules on restitution upon termination and in the system of the DCFR this implies that the right of withdrawal is considered only to have prospective effect. Should such questions on contractual qualification be dealt with at EU level?

I.C.6.b Compensation for normal use

The gaps in the current Directives continue to give rise to debate on the compatibility with EC law of certain national provisions on liability in restitution. One issue already mentioned is whether the consumer should and can be charged for (normal) use of the goods, or more importantly for the loss of value that is due to the use of the goods (which can be fairly high). The Directives do not deal with this matter explicitly. According to some authors, Article 6(2) of the Distance Selling Directive (97/7/EC) would exclude such a possibility.[65]

Distance Selling Directive 97/7/EC **4.23 (EU)**

Article 6 Right of withdrawal

(2) Where the right of withdrawal has been exercised by the consumer pursuant to this Article, the supplier shall be obliged to reimburse the sums paid by the consumer free of charge. The only charge that may be made to the consumer because of the exercise of his right of withdrawal is the direct cost of returning the goods. Such reimbursement must be carried out as soon as possible and in any case within 30 days.

Other authors, and the German and Austrian legislators, are in any event not of that opinion as the following excerpts will illustrate. The German harmonised provisions of the right of withdrawal have a special paragraph dealing with this issue.[66]

BGB **4.24 (DE)**

§357 Legal consequences of withdrawal and return

(3) In derogation from §346(2), sentence 1, No 3, the consumer must pay compensation for value in respect of a deterioration in the goods as a result of their proper use, if his attention has previously been drawn in textual form to this legal consequence and to a means of avoiding it. This does not apply if the deterioration is due exclusively to

[65] See on this discussion H-W Micklitz, 'La directive 97/7/CE sur les contrats à distance' in H and B Stauder (eds), *La protection des consommateurs acheteurs à distance. Analyse du droit suisse à la lumière du droit communautaire et du droit comparé* (Brussel, Bruylant, 1999) 37; C Gössmann, 'Electronic commerce. Die EU Fernabsatzrichtlinie und ihre Auswirkungen auf den Handel über die neue Medien' [1998] *MMR* 90–91.

[66] On this provision see inter alia G Ring, 'Wertminderung infolge bestimmungsgemässe Ingebrauchname nach §357 Abs 3 BGB—Unternehmerschutz statt Verbraucherschutz?' in B Dauner-Lieb and K Schmidt, *Das neue Schuldrecht in der Praxis* (Köln, C Heymans Verlag, 2003) 356; H-W Micklitz and N Reich, 'Umsetzung der EG-Fernabsatzrichtlinie' [1999] *Der Betriebs-Berater* 2095; P Mankowski, *Beseitigungsrechte* (Tübingen, Mohr Siebeck, 2003) 893.

inspection of the goods. §346(3), sentence 1, No 3 does not apply if the consumer has been properly informed of his right of revocation or he has become aware of it in another way.

The following case illustrates the concrete consequences of such a rule.

OGH (Supreme Court), 27 September 2005[67] **4.25 (AT)**
VKI v W

COMPENSATION FOR NORMAL USE

43½ hours of flat screen viewing

If a consumer uses and not merely tests a good bought through distance selling during the period for withdrawal, so that the seller can only resell it as 'used', compensation for use and loss of value is due according to §5g KSchG, a norm which does not conflict with Article 6 of the Distance Selling Directive.

Facts: A consumer bought a flat screen television through the internet for €2,179.46. He used it for 43½ hours and then withdrew from the contract. The seller only reimbursed €1,499.96. The consumer claimed full reimbursement of the price. The claim was rejected in first instance. On appeal, the consumer's claim was upheld but so was the counterclaim of the trader for compensation for the use of the screen by the consumer, rendering the item 'used'. The Court of Appeal estimated compensation for use at 15 per cent of the original price (€330) as appropriate. Both parties asked the Supreme Court to revise the decision.

Judgment: The government proposal for the provisions of the Austrian Consumer Protection Act [Konsumentenschutzgesetz, KSchG] on the conclusion of distance selling contracts … states with regard to the right of withdrawal that the period for withdrawal, which begins when the good is handed over, does not prevent the consumer from using the good. Although the use of the good does not lead to the forfeiture of the right of withdrawal, the consumer should, however—in accordance with §4 of the Austrian Consumer Protection Act—be obligated to pay possible compensation for use and loss of value to the extent to which he used the good. Furthermore it is explained that the directive allows such a provision, especially as it (only) excludes further demands on the part of the trader for expenses (a handling fee or transfer fee for example), but not claims for damages and enrichment. The 'appropriate compensation for use' in the sense of §5g of the Austrian Consumer Protection Act, should be qualified as a payment on the part of the consumer in return for the use of the contractual service, which is why one cannot speak of 'costs' in this connection. With an interpretation in the light of the directive, imposing compensation for use or loss of value in §5g of the Austrian Consumer Protection Act would only be incompatible with the aim of the right of withdrawal according to Art 6 of the directive, if the obligation to pay compensation for use as well as to offset any loss of value were imposed on the consumer if all he did was to examine the good or take it for the purpose of testing it for a short time, in accordance with the terms of the contract. Such financial burdens, which the consumer would routinely be exposed to when exercising his right of withdrawal, would constitute a sanction that is not in conformity with the directive and that circumvents the right of withdrawal or impedes the ability to exercise this right. Since goods can regularly be examined, without

[67] 1 Ob 110/05s.

having to pay compensation, when concluding contracts of sale in the physical presence of both parties (if it can be tried on for example), this must also be possible in the case of contracts of sale concluded via distance selling, otherwise this would place the consumer at a disadvantage.

The facts of the case to be decided upon here are entirely different, however: The buyer operated the flat screen which he had bought through a distance transaction during, eight working days for approximately 43½ hours, which corresponds to full-time operation during an (entire) working week. Therefore, this clearly no longer constitutes a test, but usage of the monitor. It is possible to establish whether the features of the monitor (speed of image formation, resolution) matched the features specified in the product description and whether it corresponds to the subjective requirements and perceptions of the consumer as well, after a much shorter period of use. With regard to this extensive usage, questions which prove to be at best problematic in other cases, arise as to the boundary between testing and using. In cases where such intensive usage of the item of purchase takes place before the declaration of withdrawal is made, the directive provides no provision, so that the national legislator had scope to add to the directive. It is not discernible in the case at hand that §5g of the Austrian Consumer Protection Act exceeds this scope for regulation. The aim of the directive to protect the consumer from pressure for a decision when exercising his right of withdrawal is not called into question if appropriate compensation for the use of a good which is liable to wear, in accordance with the law of unjustified enrichment, is imposed on him, including indemnity for loss of base value linked to usage. A penalty, frowned upon by the directive, would only be imposed if the regulation allowed the consumer to be forced to pay such a high level of compensation for use that this would take on the appearance of a penalty payment, whereby the consumer would, in effect, be deprived of the possibility of withdrawing from the contract for financial reasons. This is countered, however, by the limitation to an 'appropriate' level of compensation for use. §5g of the Austrian Consumer Protection Act consequently prevents a one-sided shifting of the risk to the disadvantage of the trader in cases of extensive usage and thereby brings about a balance of interests between consumer and trader. …

So if, as is the case here, the consumer has used an item of purchase—which is liable to wear and lose value—for many hours during the period of withdrawal such that the trader can no longer sell it as new, but can only sell it on as 'used' at a considerably lower purchase price, the imposition of an appropriate level of compensation for use, including indemnity for loss of base value linked to usage in accordance with §5g of the Austrian Consumer Protection Act is in conformity with Art 6(2) of the directive. …

In summary, neither party's appeal is valid.

Notes

(1) The OGH did not consider it necessary to refer the matter to the ECJ for a preliminary ruling on the compatibility of the relevant Austrian provision (§5g KSchG) with Article 6 of the Distance Selling Directive. In *Mesner*,[68] the ECJ was asked to rule on the compatibility of the German rule allowing the seller to claim compensation for the value of the use of consumer goods during the period for

[68] Case C-489/07, *Pia Messner*, nyr, casenote P Rott [2010] ERPL 185-194.

withdrawal. Such a *general* requirement to pay compensation was held incompatible with Article 6(1) 2nd sentence and 6(2) of the Distance Selling Directive. However, the ECJ emphasized that the Directive is not intended to grant the consumer rights going beyond what is necessary to allow him effectively to exercise his right of withdrawal. Therefore, the Directive was held not to preclude, in principle, a national rule which requires a consumer to pay fair compensation in case he has made use of the goods in a manner incompatible with the principles of civil law, such as those of good faith or unjust enrichment on condition that the functionality and efficacy of the right of withdrawal are not adversely affected, this being a matter for the national court to determine. National rules on compensation may therefore in any event not make it impossible or excessively difficult to exercise a right of withdrawal.

(2) In a similar decision, a court of first instance in Germany had to apply §357(3) BGB.[69] A lorry was sold for €25,897 and then registered. The purchaser withdrew from the contract. The seller claimed compensation of €3,000 for the reduced value of the lorry. The court accepted the claim and held that it was sufficient to inform the purchaser in a standard clause (small print) of this consequence. In another, more recent German case, a question on the compatibility of a national provision allowing a claim for reduced value with the Distance Selling Directive has now also been referred to the ECJ.[70]

(3) In other jurisdictions, eg the Netherlands, Belgium and France, legislation often does not explicitly deal with the problem of loss of value due to normal use during the period for withdrawal and the opinions in the literature differ as to whether the consumer can even still exercise his right of withdrawal once he has used the goods.[71] This issue, which can to a major extent determine whether a consumer's right of withdrawal is a right he can really exercise or just a theoretical one, is one that the legislator might want to deal with.

(4) For a similar question, namely whether a seller may require the consumer to pay compensation for the use of goods that are not in conformity until their replacement with new goods, see chapter 5.VII.A.3 (*Quelle*).

I.C.7 LINKED CONTRACTS

The contract the consumer withdraws from often does not stand alone. An insurance contract may be linked to a purchase contract for a car; a credit agreement may have been concluded to finance a timeshare contract. Specific provisions are then needed to determine the effect of withdrawal from one contract on linked transactions. The effect on linked contracts determines to a large extent the effectiveness of a right of withdrawal.

69 LG Trier, 20 July 2004, (2004) NJOZ 3887.

70 See AG Lahr, 26 October 2007, [2008] *MMR* 271.

71 Loos, for example, is of the opinion that when the consumer has done more than merely testing the goods, he should lose his right of withdrawal even is he has not been informed of his right of withdrawal: Loos, above n 23, 15.

In some jurisdictions, national law deals with linked contracts in detail. This is the case in Germany, where §358 BGB deals with linked contracts. This Article codified the concept that contracts that form a commercial unit should follow the same fate, an idea that had been worked out in the case-law and that could already be found in §9 VerbrKrG. In other countries, general contract law has to be relied on in the absence of explicit provisions dealing with the fate of linked contracts in case of withdrawal.[72]

BGB **4.26 (DE)**

§358 Linked contracts

(1) If the consumer has effectively revoked his declaration of intention to enter into a contract for the supply of goods or for the provision of a service by a business, he is also no longer obliged by his declaration of intention to enter into a consumer credit contract linked to this contract.

(2) If the consumer has effectively revoked his declaration of intention to enter into a consumer credit contract, he also ceases to be obliged by his declaration of intention to enter into a contract linked to that consumer credit contract for the supply of goods or for the provision of a service. If the consumer may revoke the declaration of intention to enter into the linked contract under this subtitle, only subsection (1) applies, and his right of withdrawal under §495(1) is excluded. If the consumer in the case of sentence 2 nevertheless withdraws from the consumer credit contract, this is treated as withdrawal from the linked contract in relation to the business under subsection (1).

(3) A contract for the supply of goods or for the provision of some other performance and a consumer credit loan contract are linked, if the loan fully or partially serves to finance the other contract and both contracts constitute an economic unit. An economic unit is to be assumed in particular if the business himself finances the consideration of the consumer or, in the case of financing by a third party, if the lender in preparation for or for entering into the consumer credit contract uses the services of the business. In the case of a financed acquisition of a plot of land or of an equivalent right, an economic unit is only to be assumed if the lender himself provides the plot of land or the equivalent right, or if he, beyond the provision of the loan, promotes acquisition of the plot of land or the equivalent right in cooperation with the business, by making the interest of the business in its disposal his own, in full or in part, by assuming functions of the disposing party in planning, advertising or carrying out the project, or by unilaterally favouring the disposing party.

(4) §357 applies to the linked contract with the necessary modifications. In the case of subsection (1), however, claims for payment of interest and costs arising from the reversal of the consumer credit contract are excluded against the consumer. With regard to the legal consequences of withdrawal or return, the lender assumes the rights and duties of the business under the linked contract if the loan has already flowed to the business when the withdrawal or return becomes effective.

(5) The necessary instruction on the right of withdrawal or the right of return must draw attention to the legal consequences under subsections (1) and (2) sentences 1 and 2 above.

[72] For the Netherlands, see Hijma and Valk, above n 27, 85; for Belgium: Terryn, above n 23, ch V.

Note
The regulation of linked contracts in the existing EC Directives is currently incoherent and insufficient. Whereas some Directives do not provide for specific provisions dealing with linked agreements (eg the Doorstep Selling Directive (85/577/EEC)), the provisions in other Directives vary widely in scope and with regard to the consequences of the exercise of a right of withdrawal on linked contracts. The Distance Selling Directive (97/7/EC), for example, only mentions credit agreements as linked contracts. In the Distance Selling of Financial Services Directive (2002/65/EC), a wider concept of linked contracts has been adopted. Article 6(7) mentions 'another distance contract [that] has been attached concerning services provided by the supplier or by a third party on the basis of an agreement between the third party and the supplier' without further defining what the exact link between the main contract for financial services and the attached contract ought to be. Contracts other than credit agreement can indeed be linked contracts (eg insurance contracts, maintenance contracts); the Distance Selling of Financial Services Directive (2002/65/EC) does not define the exact relationship between the contracts.

In the *Schulte* and *Crailsheimer* cases, one of the problems the ECJ had to deal with was the effect of cancellation of a secured credit agreement concluded in a doorstep selling situation on the contract for the purchase of immovable property.

ECJ Case C-350/03, 25 October 2005[73] **4.27 (EU)**
Schulte v Deutsche Bausparkasse Badenia AG

EFFECT OF WITHDRAWAL ON LINKED CONTRACTS

Junk immovables continued

The Doorstep Selling Directive does not preclude national rules which limit the effect of cancellation of the loan contract to the avoidance of that agreement.

Facts: See above 4.21(EU).

Judgment: The first and second questions, concerning the effect of cancellation of the loan agreement on the purchase contract

72. By its first question, the referring court seeks an interpretation of Article 3(2) of the Directive, which excludes from the scope of the Directive, inter alia, contracts for the sale of immovable property. It asks whether that exclusion also covers contracts for the purchase of immovable property which must be regarded as merely a component of an investment scheme financed by a loan for which the negotiations prior to the conclusion of the contract were held in a doorstep-selling situation, both as regards the contract for the purchase of the immovable property and the loan agreement serving solely to finance that purchase.

73. By its second question, the referring court asks essentially whether the Directive precludes national rules which limit the effect of cancellation of the loan agreement to

[73] [2005] ECR I-09215.

the avoidance of that agreement, even in the case of investment schemes in which the loan would not have been granted at all without the acquisition of the immovable property.

74. According to the order for reference, that court referred those two questions on the basis of its view that in circumstances such as those of the main proceedings, the two contracts could constitute contracts forming a single economic unit, so that the cancellation of the loan agreement could affect the validity of the purchase contract and, as a result of his cancellation of the first contract, the borrower could no longer be bound by the second.

75. In that connection, it must first be found that the Directive expressly and unequivocally excludes contracts for the sale of immovable property from its scope.

76. While other Community directives intended to protect the interests of consumers, inter alia Directive 87/102, contain rules concerning connected contracts, the Directive contains no rule of that type and provides no basis for an assumption that such rules are implied.

77. In some of the observations submitted to the Court, inter alia those of the French Government, it is stated that it follows from the judgment in Case C-423/97 *Travel Vac* [1999] ECR I-2195 that the Directive applies to a doorstep-selling situation which results in the conclusion of a contract for sale of immovable property, which is an integral part of a larger group of contracts also including a loan agreement secured by a charge, a real estate savings agreement and a contract for the administration of the property, where those contracts must be construed as a contract for the provision of services whose value is higher than that of the immovable property.

78. That view cannot be upheld. The timeshare contract at issue in *Travel Vac*, which was held not to fall within the exclusion provided for by Article 3(2) of the Directive, is not comparable to the contracts at issue in the main proceedings, if only because that judgment concerned a single contract for property rights and services in which the latter were predominant, whereas, in the case in the main proceedings, there were two legally separate transactions with different purposes.

79. Moreover, the Court has already pointed out, in paragraph 35 of its judgment in Heininger, that the effects of a cancellation of a secured credit agreement in accordance with the directive on the contract for the purchase of the immovable property and on the provision of security in the form of a charge on it fall to be governed by national law.

80. Accordingly, while the Directive does not preclude national law from providing, where the two contracts form a single economic unit, that the cancellation of the secured credit agreement has an effect on the validity of the contract for sale of the immovable property, it does not require such an effect in a case such as that described by the referring court.

81. The answer to the first two questions should therefore be that:

—Article 3(2)(a) of the Directive must be interpreted as excluding from the scope of the Directive contracts for the sale of immovable property even where they are merely a component of an investment scheme financed by a loan for which the negotiations prior to the conclusion of the contract were held in a doorstep-selling situation, both as regards the contract for the purchase of the immovable property and the loan agreement serving solely to finance that purchase;

—the Directive does not preclude national rules which limit the effect of cancellation of the loan contract to the avoidance of that agreement, even in the case of investment schemes in which the loan would not have been granted at all without the acquisition of the immovable property.

Notes

(1) The case illustrates that, in the absence of explicit provisions in a Directive, the general concept of effectiveness of Community law can in principle not be relied on to determine the fate of linked contracts as this remains a question of national law.[74]

(2) The ECJ nevertheless did impose some limits on the discretion of the national legislator to determine the effects of the exercise of a right of withdrawal in the case where the necessary information with regard to the right of withdrawal had not been provided. As mentioned before, it decided that

> in a situation where, if the Bank had complied with its obligation to inform the consumer of his right of cancellation, the consumer would have been able to avoid exposure to the risks inherent in investments such as those at issue in the main proceedings, Article 4 of the [Doorstep Selling] Directive requires Member States to ensure that their legislation protects consumers who have been unable to avoid exposure to such risks, by adopting suitable measures to allow them to avoid bearing the consequences of the materialisation of those risks.

(3) Such 'suitable measures' could be, for example, to accept an effect on linked contracts, but other measures (eg an action for damages) can also be envisaged. The German courts have chosen to make it easier for consumers in such cases to ask for damages for infringement of information obligations.[75]

II. STANDARD TERMS

Standard terms—understood as pre-formulated terms imposed by one contracting party—are of course not solely used in consumer contracts. Such terms are nevertheless very frequently used in consumer contracts: businesses impose identical contractual conditions on a large number of consumers who often lack the bargaining power and the economic incentives to enforce their own terms.[76] Both the national legislators and the EU have been particularly active in regulating standard terms in the last decades, thereby using several models, depending on the underlying policy.

M Ebers, Unfair Contract Terms Directive (93/13/EEC)[77] **4.28 (EU)**

If one enquires into the policy reasons for monitoring pre-formulated contract terms, two primary lines of argument come to the fore.

[74] A similar decision was reached in ECJ, 25 October 2005, Case C-299/04 *Crailsheimer Volksbank eG v Klaus Conrads ea* [2005] ECR I-9273.

[75] See eg BGH, 16 May 2006 (2006) NJW 2099.

[76] H-W Micklitz, N Reich and P Rott, *Understanding EU Consumer Law* (Antwerp/Oxford, Intersentia, 2009) 122.

[77] M Ebers, *Consumer Law Compendium* (München, Sellier, 2008) 203.

The first theory is based on a consideration of transaction costs: A party using pre-formulated terms is usually better informed about the content of the terms than the other party (whether a consumer or business). By drafting terms just once for several transactions, the user can spread costs an infinite number of times, whereas for the other party it is often too expensive to obtain the information required for negotiating on the conditions of the transaction. Informational asymmetries—disparities in the level to which each party is familiar with the terms of the contract—and the uneven distribution of transaction costs therefore have to be balanced by reviewing pre-formulated terms.

A series of legal systems, especially German, Dutch and Portuguese law, were based on this model even before transposition of the Directive 93/13. Characteristic of these countries is that in principle only standard terms are subject to review, ie terms pre-formulated for a multitude of contracts, but not individual agreements. This is due to the fact that an uneven distribution of transaction costs regularly results only where standard terms are used, and not with individually negotiated clauses. At the same time however standard terms are capable of endangering not only the consumer, but any contractual partner against whom they are used. Therefore, the protection afforded by monitoring of terms in the aforementioned countries extends not only to B2C transactions, but also to B2B and P2P transactions. According to the second model ('abuse theory') the control of pre-formulated contract terms is based in contrast upon the notion that unfair terms are often used against weaker parties. The main catalyst for control of terms is not the dangerousness of standard terms, but rather the protection of a specified class of persons. In view of the economic, social, psychological and intellectual superiority of the business the customer has no choice other than to submit to the clauses in question. A review of validity shall accordingly counter an imbalance in bargaining power and knowledge. This fundamental notion underpinned the laws of some countries, namely France, Belgium, Luxembourg, even prior to transposition of the Directive 93/13. Characteristic of these countries is that in principle they only protect the consumer, as the inferior party ... Consequently this protection does not only cover standard terms, but rather all clauses, whether pre-formulated or individually negotiated.

Alongside both these models many other mixed systems exist as well as the model of the Nordic States, where according to the general clause (Contract Acts, Art 36) it is possible even in B2B contracts to review individually negotiated standard terms.

At EU level, standard terms have been regulated by the Unfair Contract Terms Directive (93/13/EEC).[78] Thus, certain issues have been taken out of the competence of the Member States. However, the Directive does not touch on all issues related to standard terms. The Directive also does not set absolute standards but allows Member States to adopt or maintain more stringent rules related to the protection of consumers. Quite a few Member States indeed provide for increased consumer protection in this field.[79] This mixed competence in the field of standard terms is reflected under the various sub-points below. It should be noted that the recent Proposal for a Directive on Consumer Rights now, however, wants to fully harmonise control of unfair contract terms in consumer contracts.[80]

[78] [1993] OJ L 95, 29.
[79] See Ebers, above n 77, for an overview.
[80] COM [2008] 614 final.

In the *Casebook on Contract Law* (1st edn, chapter 3.4), the historical development of the control of unfair clauses is dealt with in detail, and the reader will find a detailed discussion of the indirect control of unfair clauses through general contract law doctrines there. In addition to general contract law doctrines, many Member States already had some system in place for the control of unfair terms even before the adoption of the Directive.

In Germany, where the courts had initially used the rules on immorality (§138 BGB) and on good faith (§242 BGB) to deal with standard terms (cf *Casebook on Contract Law*, 509ff), the Standard Terms Act (Gesetz über Allgemeine Geschäftsbedingungen, AGBG) was enacted in 1976. It included rules on incorporation, surprising clauses and the *contra proferentem* rule, but also provided substantive rules, namely a blacklist of totally prohibited terms, a greylist of terms that were presumed to be unfair, and a general clause. The general clause also applied in B2B relationships. Moreover, collective procedures with which consumer organisations could seek injunctions against traders were introduced by the AGBG. In many ways, the AGBG served as a model for subsequent EC legislation.

In the UK, the Unfair Contract Terms Act was adopted in 1977 and it established a rather complex system of control of certain contract terms and of certain terms in non-contractual notices. The Act does not allow the control of unfair terms in general and mainly focuses on limitation and exclusion clauses. Outside the scope of the Act, no general contract law doctrine of unfairness or unreasonableness exists to which a party that seeks to set aside a term can appeal (see below, section II.B for the implementation of the Unfair Contract Terms Directive 93/13/EEC).

In France, the Loi Scrivener (Act No 78-23 of 10 January 1978) introduced a system of administrative control of standard terms. Its Article 35 allowed the government to issue decrees prohibiting specific terms in B2C contracts. Clauses prohibited by such decree were then to be treated as of no effect. The Loi Scrivener also created a Commission des clauses abusives, a body whose main task is to advise the government and other organisations; it can also issue non-binding recommendations on the unfairness of certain terms. The lower courts had not interpreted this Act as granting the civil courts a statutory mandate to control the fairness of contract terms, but the Cour de Cassation decided differently in a judgment of 14 May 1991.[81] Article 35 of the Loi Scrivener was from then on used not only as an administrative instrument to control standard terms but also as an instrument for control by the civil courts. The text of the Article 35 became Article L 132-1 Code de la Consommation, which was amended when the Directive was implemented (see below section II.B).

In this section, we will focus on the incorporation of standard terms as an illustration of general private law doctrines controlling contract terms (II.A) and on some key features of the control of standard terms in consumer contracts now that the Unfair Contract Terms Directive (93/13/EEC) has been implemented in the Member States (II.B). Control of standard terms in collective litigation is dealt with in chapter 8.IV, and arbitration and jurisdiction clauses also get special attention in that chapter (sections III.E and VII.B).

81 (1991) D 449.

II.A INCORPORATION OF STANDARD TERMS

Incorporation of standard terms into the contract as such is not dealt with by the Unfair Contract Terms Directive (93/13/EEC).[82] The reason is that Member States were afraid that the EC could interfere with national rules on the conclusion of contracts. The only provision of EC law that might be mentioned in this context is Article 10(3) of the Electronic Commerce Directive (2000/31/EC). According to this provision, contract terms and general conditions provided to the recipient must be made available in a way that allows him to store and reproduce them. In contrast, the provision does not deal with the incorporation of standard terms as such.

II.A.1 GENERAL REQUIREMENTS

Generally speaking, all Member States seem to recognise that standard terms must be brought to the attention of consumers, although the rules—partly legislative provisions, partly rules developed by case-law—differ in detail.

BGB **4.29 (DE)**

§305 (2) Standard terms only become part of a contract, if the user when entering into the contract

1. refers the other contracting party to them explicitly or, where explicit reference due to the nature of the conclusion of the contract is only possible with considerable difficulties, by posting a clearly visible notice at the place of the conclusion of the contract, and

2. provides the other contracting party with the opportunity, in an acceptable manner, that also appropriately takes into account a physical handicap of the other contracting party discernible by the user, of taking notice of their contents

and if the other contracting party is in agreement with their application.

Only in the cases of approved terms and conditions in the transportation, postal services, telecommunications, electricity and gas sectors do exceptions apply under §305a BGB.

French law adopts a similar position. If a document was signed, the terms in that document are still generally accepted to be incorporated.[83] However, courts do take into account the legibility, accessibility and the onerous character of the terms (see also section II.A.3 below). It will be easier to invoke the nullity of clauses in unsigned documents that were submitted after the conclusion of the contract: if the business does not succeed in proving that the term was known to the consumer at the time of conclusion of the contract, the term will not bind the consumer.[84] Similarly, terms on

[82] The question is nevertheles unanswered as to what extent the way of incorporating standard terms forms an element of the notion of good faith; see H-W Micklitz, 'Anmerkung' [2003] *ZEuP* 881ff.

[83] J Calais-Auloy and F Steinmetz, *Droit de la consommation* (Paris, Dalloz, 2006) 197.

[84] Ibid; A Karimi, *Les clauses abusives et la théorie de l'abus de droit* (Paris, LGDJ, 2006) 167.

a noticeboard or poster are only incorporated if the business can prove that they were known to the consumer and accepted before the conclusion of the contract.[85]

Cour d'appel (Court of Appeal) Bourges, 4 February 1963[86] **4.30 (FR)**

INCORPORATION OF STANDARD TERMS—LEGIBILITY

Illegible clauses

Illegible clauses will not bind a party to a contract as consent cannot be established.

Judgment: In order to be effective, a jurisdiction clause that deviates from the general rules must have been accepted;

If such acceptance may be tacit if must nevertheless be certain;

In this case, the term was printed in characters that were not very noticeable; it is therefore uncertain that the attention of X was drawn …

Cass civ 1e, 3 May 1979[87] **4.31 (FR)**

INCORPORATION OF STANDARD TERMS—PLACE

Reverse side clauses

Illegible clauses will not bind a party to a contract as consent cannot be established.

Facts: The court dealing with the substance of the case had declared an exoneration clause to be ineffective as it was a standard term that was on the reverse side of an order form signed by the client. The case was brought before the Cour de Cassation.

Judgment: The judges of the court dealing with the substance of the case found that the clause in Article 8 of the standard terms of the sales contract was among numerous other provisions on the reverse side of the order form that was only signed on the front by the buyer, who when signing the order form, lacking a precise reference, certainly did not find out that there were provisions on the reverse side;

The judges could therefore conclude that the buyer did not consent to these provisions and these provisions can therefore not be invoked against him.

The general rule in English law is that terms in unsigned documents will be incorporated if reasonable steps are taken to bring the attention of the other party to the existence of the term. The term will then be incorporated even if the other party has not read it.[88] Nevertheless, English law appears to be slightly less formal than German law, as the following case illustrates.

[85] Calais Auloy and Steinmetz, above n 83; Karimi, above n 84, 167.
[86] Cour d'Appel (Court of Appeal) Bourges, 4 February 1963 (1963) D 239.
[87] Bull Civ I No 128; (1980) RTDcom 140, note J Hérmard.
[88] *Thompson v LMS Ry* [1930] 1 KB 41.

High Court, 18 November 1971[89] **4.32 (UK)**
Hollier v Rambler Motors

INCORPORATION OF STANDARD TERMS—COURSE OF DEALING

Car on fire

A consistent course of dealing between the parties can make it imperative for the court to read into the contract the condition over which the sellers are contending.

Facts: The plaintiff had had his car repaired at the defendants' garage on three or four occasions over a period of five years. On at least two of the occasions he had signed a form, but had not read the printed words: 'The company is not responsible for damage caused by fire to customers' cars on the premises.' By an oral agreement made between the plaintiff and the defendants, the defendants agreed to repair his car and, while at their premises, the car was damaged by a fire caused by the defendants' negligence. The plaintiff claimed damages for breach of the implied term that the defendants would take reasonable care of his car. The defendants relied on the condition excluding responsibility for damage to cars caused by fire which they contended was incorporated into the oral agreement because of the previous course of dealing between the parties.

Judgment: We have been referred to *Hardwick Game Farm v Suffolk Agricultural Poultry Producers Association.* ... That was a case in which some feeding-stuff was sold by some merchants to a farmer. The feeding-stuff was found to be defective. The farmer sued the merchants. ... It is to be observed that in that case there had been three or four dealings each month between the parties during the previous three years. The course of dealing had been that the feeding-stuff was ordered orally by the buyer and the order was accepted orally by the suppliers. Then on the day of the oral contract, or perhaps the next day, the suppliers sent on to the buyer a sold note. One of the terms appearing on the sold note was that the buyer under the contract took the responsibility for any latent defects. Three or four times each month, year in and year out for three years, sold notes had been sent on to the buyer, and the buyer had never raised any protest or said anything which would have led the sellers to assume that the buyers were doing anything other than accepting the terms of the contract which appeared on the sold note. ... The House of Lords decided that the fact that the buyer had not read the condition on the sold notes, having had every opportunity of doing so, did not avail him, because any reasonable seller in circumstances such as those, having had no intimation from the buyer that he took any objection to the condition, would have had good cause to assume that the buyer was agreeing to the condition.

That case is obviously very different from the present case. The *Hardwick Game Farm* case seems to be a typical case where a consistent course of dealing between the parties makes it imperative for the court to read into the contract the condition for which the sellers were contending. Everything that the buyer had done, or failed to do, would have convinced any ordinary seller that the buyer was agreeing to the terms in question. The fact that the buyer had not read the term is beside the point. The seller could not be expected to know that the buyer had not troubled to acquaint himself with what was written in the form that had been sent to him so often, year in and year out during the previous three years, in transactions exactly the same as the transaction then in question.

The sellers in that case sought to rely on *McCutcheon v David MacBrayne Ltd* [1964] 1 WLR 125, which was also a decision of the House of Lords. ... *McCutcheon v David*

[89] [1972] 2 QB 71.

MacBrayne Ltd is an example of a case in which dealings between the parties prior to the contract in question cannot be relied upon to import a term into the relevant contract. In that case the appellant had asked his brother-in-law to have a car shipped from Islay to the mainland. The appellant had personally consigned goods on four previous occasions. On three of them he was acting on behalf of his employer; on the other occasion he sent his own car; and each time he signed what was called a 'risk note.' The risk note made it plain that the respondents were accepting the goods on their ship on the condition that they would not be responsible for any damage by negligence that the goods might suffer during the course of the voyage. In that case, through negligence, the ship sank and the car was lost. … He said that on the occasion in question no risk note was put before him. Apparently, unknown to him, the purser, by mistake, had taken the car on board without asking him to sign the risk note. The House of Lords held, as I have already indicated, that there was no previous course of dealing from which the term of exclusion could be implied into the contract which had been made on behalf of the appellant by his brother-in-law. …

It seems to me that if it was impossible to rely on a course of dealing in *McCutcheon v David MacBrayne Ltd*, still less would it be possible to do so in this case, when the so-called course of dealing consisted only of three or four transactions in the course of five years.

II.A.2 STANDARD TERMS IN A FOREIGN LANGUAGE

Language requirements are an issue that the EC hesitates to touch upon. Except for some specific Community instruments—such as the Timeshare Directive 2008/122/EC and the Payment Services Directive 2007/64/EC—the issue is mainly left to the Member States. In the case of standard terms, the question is in which language the terms must be made available. The Unfair Contract Terms Directive 93/13/EEC does not deal with this issue explicitly. To some extent, a requirement to draft terms in a comprehensible language from the consumer's point of view could be inferred from Article 5, sentence 1, requiring that terms must always be drafted in plain, intelligible language.[90] German courts have dealt with this issue in a number of cases. As a general rule, they have established that German is the appropriate language when contracts are concluded in Germany even if the contracting partner obviously has only little knowledge of German.[91] Cross-border cases are treated differently. Here, courts have not assumed comprehension of any language other than a mother tongue, not even in commercial contracts.[92]

II.A.3 SURPRISING OR PARTICULARLY ONEROUS CLAUSES

Even if standard terms are incorporated in general, they may still include terms that are so surprising that they do not form part of the contract. The following English case illustrates this.

[90] Ebers, above n 77, 413.

[91] See eg OLG Bremen, 22 June 1973 (1973) WM 1228, 1229.

High Court, 17 December 1970[93] **4.33 (UK)**
Thornton v Shoe Lane Parking

INCORPORATION OF PARTICULARLY ONEROUS TERMS

Car park accident

A particularly onerous term will only be incorporated into a contract if this term has been pointed out to the contracting partner in the most explicit way (red ink rule).

Facts: The plaintiff drove his car into a new automatic car park. He had not been there before. A notice on the outside gave the charges and stated that all cars were 'parked at owner's risk.' A traffic light on the entrance lane showed red and a machine produced a ticket when the car drew up alongside it. The plaintiff took the ticket and, the light having turned green, he drove on into the garage and parked his car. On the plaintiff's return to collect the car there was an accident and he was severely injured. The plaintiff claimed damages from the defendant garage. The defendants contended, inter alia, that the ticket incorporated a condition exempting them from liability. The ticket stated the car's time of arrival and that it was to be presented when the car was claimed. In the bottom left-hand corner of the ticket in small print it was said to be 'issued subject to conditions ... displayed on the premises'. On a pillar opposite the ticket machine a set of eight printed 'conditions' was displayed in a panel. In the second condition it was stated that the garage would not be liable for any injury to the customer occurring when his car was on the premises.

Judgment: [per Lord Denning MR] All I say is that [the term] is so wide and so destructive of rights that the court should not hold any man bound by it unless it is drawn to his attention in the most explicit way. ... In order to give sufficient notice, it would need to be printed in red ink with a red hand pointing to it—or something equally startling.

Notes

(1) Germany has included a similar rule in §305c(1) BGB, which reads: Provisions in standard terms which in the circumstances, in particular with regard to the outward appearance of the contract, are so unusual that the other party to the contract need not expect to encounter them, are not part of the contract.

(2) In France, judges also take the surprising or unreasonable character of the clause into account when deciding whether a consumer can be considered to have accepted a clause.[94]

II.B CONTROL OF STANDARD TERMS IN INDIVIDUAL LITIGATION

With a view to creating substantive law, the Unfair Contract Terms Directive (93/13/EEC) has introduced minimum requirements for the control of standard terms. Article 3 of the Directive generally defines the factors that make a term unfair (see below section II.B.2). Article 4 specifies that this unfairness is to be assessed, taking into account the circumstances attending the conclusion of the contract. Article 5 lays down a requirement for clarity in the drafting of the terms offered to

[92] For an overview, see P Rott, 'Informationspflichten in Fernabsatzverträgen als Paradigma für die Sprachenproblematik im Vertragsrecht' [1999] *Zeitschrift fur Vergleichende Rechtswissenschaft* 382, 388 ff.

[93] [1971] 2 QB 163.

[94] Karimi, above n 84, 164.

the consumer and determines that where there is doubt about the meaning of a term, the interpretation most favourable to the consumer shall prevail. This so-called *contra proferentem* rule already formed part of many national legal orders.[95] The Directive follows to some extent the German model, although it does not copy it.

All Member States have in the meantime implemented the Directive. In Germany, the directive required minor amendments of the Standard Terms Act (AGBG). The main changes include a presumption that standard terms were to be regarded as having been presented by the trader unless they were introduced into the contract by the consumer (§24a Standard Terms Act). For B2C contracts the Standard Terms Act also applied even if the terms have been used only once, whereas the Standard Terms Act in general only applied to terms that are used several times. The transparency principle was only expressly included in 2000, with the reform of the law of obligations. In France, Article L 132-1 Code de la Consommation was amended so that judicial control of unfair terms now got a firm statutory basis (cf above). In the UK, a new statutory instrument was adopted: the Unfair Terms in Consumer Contracts Regulations 1994, later replaced by the 1999 Regulations. The text of the Regulations is quite close to the text of the Directive. The Unfair Contract Terms Act 1977 was not repealed, hence in the UK both instruments operate alongside each other.[96]

II.B.1 STANDARD TERMS VS INDIVIDUALLY NEGOTIATED TERMS

Contrary to the original intentions of the Commission,[97] the Unfair Contract Terms Directive (93/13/EEC) does not apply to clauses that have been negotiated individually. Where the distinction between standard terms and individually negotiated terms is relevant, that distinction can be tricky, as the following case from Germany illustrates.

BGH, 3 December 1991[98] **4.34 (DE)**

STANDARD TERM OR INDIVIDUALLY NEGOTIATED TERM

Ticking boxes

A term is not individually negotiated if the customer only has the choice between specific alternatives offered by the user of the term.

Facts: The defendant, an agricultural credit bank, used credit agreement forms from 1977 to 1980 which had blank columns in the section at the top for entering the conditions agreed upon when concluding an individual contract, including, among others, type and amount of credit, rate of interest and payment and

[95] See eg §5 of the German Standard Terms Act (AGBG) of 1976 (now §305c(2) BGB); the English case of *Alisa Craig Fishing Co Ltd v Malvern Fishing Co* [1983] 1 All ER 92 and Art 1162 French and Belgian Civil Code: 'in the event of an uncertainty, an agreement is to be construed against the party stipulating an obligation and in favour of the party entering into that obligation'.

[96] For details, see the *Casebook on Contract Law*.

[97] See H-W Micklitz in Reich, Micklitz and P Rott, above n 76, 123ff.

[98] (1992) NJW 503.

final repayment. The column 'Repayment' was subdivided into 'Amount/Start/Deadline'; the following footnote referred to the details given on the repayment deadline: 'm = monthly, q = quarterly, b = biannually, y = yearly'. Towards the centre of the form was the following clause, with blank spaces to be filled out: 'The interest accrued on the loan is calculated from the day the loan is received, and subsequently … yearly, calculated each time on the balance of debt to the … of the month/quarter/half-year/year.

Judgment: The defendant unsuccessfully claims that on the basis of the typewritten additions this is an individual agreement which is not subject to review according to the Standard Terms Act [Gesetz zur Regelung des Rechts der Allgemeinen Geschäftsbedingungen, AGBG]. In the case of such additions the following must be distinguished: if the text on the form already contains the clause which is to be objected to, the character of a clause as a general condition is not brought into question by dependant additions which only substantiate the subject of the contract in individual cases. If the inadequacy of a clause, on the other hand, results from the additions themselves, particular scrutiny is needed to establish whether the requirements of §1(1) or (2) of the Standard Terms Act are fulfilled. In particular cases there can be an individual agreement …. A term is however a standard term if the customer only has a choice between particular alternatives offered by the user. At the same time it cannot be decisive whether the user makes use of a separate form for each of the alternatives or whether he prints all the alternatives onto one form and has the customer mark the ones he wants, or whether the choice between several given alternatives—as in the design of the defendant's form—is filled out by hand or typed in the blank spaces left for this purpose on the form.

Notes

(1) There has been a similar debate in England involving construction contracts where the consumer took professional advice from a surveyor or architect in finding an appropriate contractor, and in selecting particular terms from a choice of standard terms. In *Bryen & Langley Ltd v Martin Boyston*,[99] Judge Seymour QC commented obiter that it was 'at least arguable' that the consumer had been able to influence the substance of a term and that this term could therefore be regarded as having been 'individually negotiated'.

(2) Some Member States have extended the scope of application of their national laws on unfair contract terms to individually negotiated clauses as the directive did not pre-empt the field of individually negotiated clauses.[100] One example is Belgium where Articles 31 and 32 of the Trade Practices Act (the general prohibition on unfair contract terms and the blacklist) are also applicable to individually negotiated contract terms, but this is also the case in France, Luxembourg, the Czech Republic, Latvia, Malta and Slovenia.[101] The Nordic countries allow for the adjustment of unfair contracts (even if they are individually negotiated and in all types of

[99] [2004] EWHC 2450 (TCC).

[100] See recital 16 of Directive 93/13/EEC: '[W]hereas, however, as they now stand, national laws allow only partial harmonization to be envisaged; whereas, in particular, only contractual terms which have not been individually negotiated are covered by this Directive; whereas Member States should have the option, with due regard for the Treaty, to afford consumers a higher level of protection through national provisions that are more stringent than those of this Directive.'

[101] See Acquis Group (ed), above n 33, 215.

contractual relationships) on the basis of §36 of the Contracts Act (which is similarly worded in the Nordic countries).

(3) Individually negotiated terms are excluded from review under German law, but what is 'individually negotiated' is narrowly interpreted. The BGH has held that the customer needs to fully understand the content of the contract and to be aware of the legal consequences if a term is individually negotiated.[102]

II.B.2 THE UNFAIRNESS TEST

The general clause defining the standard of the unfairness test is a central provision in the Unfair Contract Terms Directive.

Unfair Contract Terms Directive 93/13/EEC **4.35 (EU)**

Article 3 (1) A contractual term which has not been individually negotiated shall be regarded as unfair if, contrary to the requirement of good faith, it causes a significant imbalance in the parties' rights and obligations arising under the contract, to the detriment of the consumer.

The provision was transposed in a number of very different forms in the Member States. The ECJ has been asked a few times about the unfairness of specific terms but has not yet had an opportunity to clarify the general terms used in Article 3(1) of Unfair Contract Terms Directive (93/13/EEC). In fact, the question is whether or to what extent such broad concepts as 'good faith' can be clarified at all without reference to the circumstances of a particular case, an issue that is discussed below (at section II.B.5.).

The House of Lords gave its opinion on this issue in the case of *Director General of Fair Trading v First National Bank plc*.[103]

House of Lords, 25 October 2001 **4.36 (UK)**
Director General of Fair Trading v First National Bank plc

FAIRNESS TEST IN UNFAIR CONTRACT TERMS LAW

Interests and no end

The case reflects an open debate on the fairness test.

Facts: First National Bank plc (FNB, the 'Bank') was licensed to carry on consumer credit business. It was a major lender in the market and had lent large sums to borrowers under credit agreements regulated under the UK Consumer Credit Act 1974. Such agreements were made on its printed form which contained a number of standard terms. Condition 4 of the Bank's standard form provided that: 'The rate of interest will be charged on a day to day basis on the outstanding balance and will be debited to the Customer's account monthly in arrears …' Condition 8 of the agreement was in these terms:

[102] BGH, 19 May 2005 (2005) NJW 2543.
[103] [2002] 1 AC 481.

> Time is of the essence for making all repayments to FNB as they fall due. If any repayment instalment is unpaid for more than 7 days after it became due, FNB may serve a notice on the Customer requiring payment before a specified date not less than 7 days later. If the repayment instalment is not paid in full by that date, FNB will be entitled to demand payment of the balance on the Customer's account and interest then outstanding together with all reasonable legal and other costs charges and expenses claimed or incurred by FNB in trying to obtain the repayment of the unpaid instalment of such balance and interest. Interest on the amount which becomes payable shall be charged in accordance with Condition 4, at the rate stated in paragraph D overleaf (subject to variation) until payment after as well as before any judgement (such obligation to be independent of and not to merge with the judgement).

The last sentence of the clause deviated from the otherwise applicable rules under the law of England. In the absence of such a clause, once a judgment is obtained under a loan agreement for a principal sum and judgment is entered, the contract merges in the judgment and the principal becomes owed under the judgment and not under the contract. This means that after the judgment the contractually agreed interest rates are replaced by (lower) statutory interest rates on judgment debts. To ensure that they were able to recover not only the full sum of principal outstanding but also any interest accruing on that sum after judgment as well as before, it became the practice for lenders to include in their credit agreements a term to the effect of the term here at issue.

Judgment: [Lord Bingham of Cornhill] The requirement of significant imbalance is met if a term is so weighted in favour of the supplier as to tilt the parties' rights and obligations under the contract significantly in his favour. This may be by the granting to the supplier of a beneficial option or discretion or power, or by the imposing on the consumer of a disadvantageous burden or risk or duty. The illustrative terms set out in Schedule 3 to the Regulations provide very good examples of terms which may be regarded as unfair; whether a given term is or is not to be so regarded depends on whether it causes a significant imbalance in the parties' rights and obligations under the contract. This involves looking at the contract as a whole. But the imbalance must be to the detriment of the consumer; a significant imbalance to the detriment of the supplier, assumed to be the stronger party, is not a mischief which the Regulations seek to address. The requirement of good faith in this context is one of fair and open dealing. Openness requires that the terms should be expressed fully, clearly and legibly, containing no concealed pitfalls or traps. Appropriate prominence should be given to terms which might operate disadvantageously to the customer. Fair dealing requires that a supplier should not, whether deliberately or unconsciously, take advantage of the consumer's necessity, indigence, lack of experience, unfamiliarity with the subject matter of the contract, weak bargaining position or any other factor listed in or analogous to those listed in Schedule 2 to the Regulations. Good faith in this context is not an artificial or technical concept; nor, since Lord Mansfield was its champion, is it a concept wholly unfamiliar to British lawyers. It looks to good standards of commercial morality and practice. Regulation 4(1) lays down a composite test, covering both the making and the substance of the contract, and must be applied bearing clearly in mind the objective which the Regulations are designed to promote.

[Lord Steyn] The twin requirements of good faith and significant imbalance will in practice be determinative. Schedule 2 to the Regulations, which explains the concept of good faith, provides that regard must be had, amongst other things, to the extent to which the seller or supplier has dealt fairly and equitably with the consumer. It is an objective criterion. Good faith imports, as Lord Bingham of Cornhill has observed in his opinion, the notion of open and fair dealing: see also Interfoto Picture Library Ltd v Stiletto Visual Programmes Ltd [1989] QB 433. And helpfully the commentary to *Lando & Beale, Principles of European Contract Law, Parts I and II* (combined and revised 2000), p 113 prepared by the Commission of European Contract Law, explains that the purpose of the provision of good faith and fair dealing is 'to enforce community standards of decency, fairness and reasonableness in commercial transactions'; a fortiori that is true of consumer transactions. Schedule 3 to the Regulations (which corresponds to the annex to the Directive) is best regarded as a check list of terms which must be regarded as potentially vulnerable. The examples given in Schedule 3 convincingly demonstrate that the argument of the bank that good faith is predominantly concerned with procedural defects in negotiating procedures cannot be sustained. Any purely procedural or even predominantly procedural interpretation of the requirement of good faith must be rejected.

Notes

(1) The House of Lords concluded unanimously that the above-mentioned term was not unfair.

(2) Read Micklitz's analysis of this case[104] in which he not only discusses the different approaches taken by Lord Bingham of Cornhill and Lord Steyn but also the question as to whether the House of Lords should have referred the case to the ECJ and to what extent the ECJ could have clarified the underlying Europeanised concept of good faith.

Question

Contrast the speeches of Lord Bingham of Cornhill on the one hand and of Lord Steyn on the other.

II.B.3 BLACKLISTS, GREYLISTS, INDICATIVE LISTS

Lists of (potentially) unfair clauses make it easier for traders, consumers, and courts or authorities to determine the meaning of the general clause. It is possible to distinguish so-called 'blacklists' of absolutely unlawful clauses, 'greylists' of clauses that are presumed to be unfair, and 'indicative lists' of clauses that may be unfair. The Annex to the Unfair Contract Terms Directive (93/13/EEC) provides an 'indicative and non-exhaustive list of the terms which may be regarded as unfair' (Article 3(3) of this Directive).

ECJ Case C-478/99, 7 May 2002[105] **4.37 (EU)**
Commission v Sweden

CHARACTER OF THE ANNEX

Black, grey or neither?

The list in the Annex to the Directive is an indicative list.

Facts: Sweden had not reproduced the Annex to the Unfair Contract Terms Directive (93/13/EEC) in its Unfair Contract Terms Act. It appears, with a commentary, in the statement of reasons for the draft.

[104] H-W Micklitz, 'Case Note' [2006] *ERCL* 471ff.
[105] [2002] ECR I-4147.

Judgment: 20. ...a term appearing in the list need not necessarily be considered unfair and, conversely, a term that does not appear in the list may none the less be regarded as unfair. ...

22. Inasmuch as the list contained in the annex to the Directive is of indicative and illustrative value, it constitutes a source of information both for the national authorities responsible for applying the implementing measures and for individuals affected by those measures.

Notes and Questions

(1) Thus, the Annex neither contains a blacklist nor a greylist, which is in line with the emphasis that Article 4(1) puts on the particular circumstances of each individual case.

(2) In *Océano Grupo*,[106] the ECJ used the annex to establish the unfairness of a jurisdiction clause that deprived the consumer of the competence of his local court and forced him to travel. The ECJ held that such a clause fell into the category of terms 'excluding or hindering the consumer's right to take legal action or exercise any other legal remedy' of lit (q) of the Annex.

(3) Member States can go beyond this minimum requirement and establish blacklists (eg Spain and Belgium)[107] or greylists (France), or a combination of both blacklists and greylists (eg Germany). In the mentioned 'blacklist' countries, the list of unfair terms exceeds the list of terms provided by the Annex to the Unfair Contract Terms Directive (93/13/EEC).

(4) English law provides for a shorter blacklist, focusing on exemption clauses, in the Unfair Contract Terms Act 1977 but has otherwise implemented the flexible test of Article 4(1) in the Unfair Terms in Consumer Contract Regulations 1999.

(5) The recent Proposal for a Directive on Consumer Rights wants to introduce a short blacklist and a greylist at European level. Member States could no longer provide for different or additional national lists. Do you think it is feasible and desirable only to have a European blacklist or greylist (excluding national lists) in the absence of a totally harmonised contract law, especially in view of the case of *Freiburger Kommunalbauten* (see section II.B.5 below)?

II.B.4 CORE TERMS

Following the German model,[108] Article 4(2) of the Unfair Contract Terms Directive (93/13/EEC) provides that assessment of the unfair nature of the terms shall relate neither to the definition of the main subject matter of the contract nor to the adequacy of the price and remuneration, on the one hand, as against the services or goods supplied in exchange, on the other, in so far as these terms are in plain intelligible language. This provision has been implemented in most Member States, including the UK (see the next excerpt) and France (cf Article 132-1 (al 7) of the

[106] ECJ, 27 June 2000, Joined Cases C-240/98 to C-244/98 *Océano Grupo Editorial SA v Rocío Murciano Quintero* and *Salvat Editores SA v José M. Sánchez Alcón Prades ea* [2000] ECR I-4941.

[107] Art 32 of the Belgian Trade Practices Act.

[108] §8 AGBG (old version). Germany had insisted on including this restriction into the directive.

Code de la consommation). For France, this merely ensures that consumer contract law stays in line with general contract law: as the fact that a contract is burdensome is not a ground for nullity of the contract in general contract law either. The underlying policy being that free competition should sufficiently ensure an adequate price/quality relationship.[109]

II.B.4.a Control of price-related terms

Traders frequently rely on this provision or its national implementation when it comes to price-related standard terms such as variation terms, terms concerning default interests, etc, as shall be illustrated with the following case.

House of Lords, 25 October 2001[110] **4.38 (UK)**
Director General of Fair Trading v First National Bank plc (per Lord Steyn)

CONTROL OF PRICE-RELATED TERMS

Expensive banking

Price escalation clauses are subject to the fairness provision.

Facts: See above 4.36 (UK). The controversial clause was: 'Interest on the amount which becomes payable shall be charged in accordance with Condition 4, at the rate stated in paragraph D overleaf (subject to variation) until payment after as well as before any judgement (such obligation to be independent of and not to merge with the judgement).'

Judgment: In any event, regulation 3(2) must be given a restrictive interpretation. Unless that is done regulation 3(2)(a) will enable the main purpose of the scheme to be frustrated by endless formalistic arguments as to whether a provision is a definitional or an exclusionary provision. Similarly, regulation 3(2)(b) dealing with 'the adequacy of the price or remuneration' must be given a restrictive interpretation. After all, in a broad sense all terms of the contract are in some way related to the price or remuneration. That is not what is intended. Even price escalation clauses have been treated by the Director as subject to the fairness provision … It would be a gaping hole in the system if such clauses were not subject to the fairness requirement. For these further reasons I would reject the argument of the bank that regulation 3(2), and in particular 3(2)(b), take clause 8 outside the scope of the Regulations.

Notes

(1) The Finnish Market Court had to deal with contract terms regarding a deposit relationship between a bank and a consumer. The problem centred on the calculation of interest on the deposit. Incoming deposits were only valued on the following date, whereas withdrawal deposits were valued immediately. Thus, in a case where deposits came in on one day and deposits were withdrawn on the same day, the consumer was fictitiously in debt, and the bank could claim compensation in the form

[109] Calais-Auloy and Steinmetz, above n 83, 212.
[110] [2002] 1 AC 481.

of interest. The relevant term was obviously not a 'core term', and the Market Court held that it was unfair.[111]

(2) Equivalent terms were struck out by German courts.[112]

The issue frequently arises in banking law but there are also other examples, as the following English case demonstrates.

High Court, 20 February 2004[113] **4.39 (UK)**

Bairstow Eves London Central Limited v Smith, Stacy Hill and Darlingtons

PRICE OPTIONS OR DEFAULT RULE

The impatient estate agent

Regulation 6(2) of the Unfair Terms in Consumer Contract Regulations 1999, under which no price control takes place, may be unlikely to shield terms as to price escalation or default provisions from scrutiny under the fairness requirement contained in Regulation 5(1).

Facts: The vendors wished to sell their property, a flat in Leytonstone. To this end, they entered into an agreement. Commission was payable at a rate of 1.5 per cent if paid in full within 10 working days of completion or any agreed alternative payment date. If it was not so paid, then the vendors became liable to pay commission at 3 per cent on the entirety of the final sale price of the property. But matters did not stop there; if the full 1.5 per cent commission was not paid within the 10-day period, then interest was to be paid on any outstanding sums at 3 per cent above the base rate as defined. In such circumstances, therefore, Bairstow would be entitled to receive not only the full 1.5 per cent commission but an additional 1.5 per cent commission plus interest on all outstanding sums.

Judgment: The object of the Regulations is not price control nor are the Regulations intended to interfere with the parties' freedom of contract as to the essential features of their bargain. But, that said, regulation 6(2) must be given a restrictive interpretation; otherwise a coach and horses could be driven through the Regulations. So, while it is not for the Court to re-write the parties' bargain as to the fairness or adequacy of the price itself, regulation 6(2) may be unlikely to shield terms as to price escalation or default provisions from scrutiny under the fairness requirement contained in regulation 5(1). I say 'may be unlikely' because, of course, much depends on the individual contract under consideration. When, however, regulation 6(2) is inapplicable so that regulation 5(1) is engaged, it does not follow that a term will be adjudged unfair; whether or not a term is unfair involves a separate inquiry but one which cannot be undertaken at all insofar as regulation 6(2) is applicable and bars the way.

To my mind, in the present case the applicability of regulation 6(2) turns on the following question: (1) did the agreement provide for a 3 per cent commission rate (or price) with the vendors having an option but no obligation to pay 1.5 per cent? Or: (2) did the agreement place the vendors under an obligation to pay a price of 1.5 per cent, with a 'default' provision exercisable at Bairstow's option to insist on payment of 3 per cent? If the former, then regulation 6(2) would be applicable and the appeal must be

[111] Market Court (1984) MT 12.

[112] See eg BGH, 17 January 1989, BGHZ 106, 259, 263ff.

[113] [2004] ECHC 263 (QB).

allowed. If the latter, then regulation 6(2) would be inapplicable and the appeal must be dismissed.

On the available material, it seems plain to me that both parties contemplated an agreed operative price of 1.5 per cent with a default provision of 3 per cent. First, the market. On a fair reading of the transcript of his evidence, Mr Farquharson, the branch manager of Bairstow, recognised that it would have been unlikely to obtain such business at a commission rate of 3 per cent in the then prevailing market. Secondly, it was not or not seriously in dispute that the negotiation focused exclusively on the 1.5 per cent. ... Thirdly, both parties proceeded on the assumption that the 1.5 per cent commission would be paid within 10 days of completion; they had indeed no reason to assume otherwise; the completion moneys would necessarily be available from day one of the period. Unless something went wrong, the 3 per cent rate would never become relevant.

In any event, I am not persuaded that the language of the agreement—even considered in isolation—compels the conclusion that the price was a 3 per cent commission with a vendors' option to pay 1.5 per cent within the defined period. ...

Notes

(1) The Appeal Court of Asturias in Spain[114] declared unfair a term included in a credit contract, according to which the bank was entitled to charge 29 per cent penalty interest in the case of non-performance or delayed performance, regarding this term as price-related and not a core term. The German Bundesgerichtshof has taken the same view.[115]

(2) Spanish law has also applied the distinction between core terms and price-related terms to mobile phone contracts, parking fees, etc. After a recent amendment of unfair contract terms law,[116] terms that allow the trader to charge round-off fees for a service that is potentially not supplied in full are subject to unfair contract term control. Examples would be fees per minute in mobile phone contracts where the consumer has only made a phone call of a few seconds, or fees per hour for parking where the consumer has only stopped for a couple of minutes.

II.B.4.b Insurance contracts

Another field where 'core terms' are an issue is insurance contracts. Insurance contracts frequently exclude insurance coverage in specific situations. Do such exclusions specify the content of the contract (and are therefore 'core terms'), or do they exclude the insurer's liability and are therefore subject to unfair terms control? Contrast the two following cases.

[114] SAP Asturias, 20 September 2004 (2004) JUR 277965. See also SAP Murcia, 1 February 2000 (2004) AC 1163.

[115] BGH, 9 November 1978 (1979) NJW 805; BGH, 17 May 1979 (1979) NJW 2092.

[116] Law 44/2006 of 29 December 2006.

High Court, 7 March 2003[117] **4.40 (UK)**
Bankers Insurance Company Ltd v South and Gardner

CORE TERMS

Jet-ski accident

The exclusion of liability in insurance contracts can be seen as specification of the risks covered by the policy.

Facts: Kenny Brennan booked a holiday for himself and six other young men. He also purchased insurance. The group departed for Ayia Napa, Cyprus. On 15 July one member of the group, Mr South, was involved in a serious accident. A jet-ski which he had hired and was riding was in collision with another jet-ski being ridden by Mr Gardner who was seriously injured. When the insured sought to invoke the insurance policy, the insurer, Bankers Insurance Company Ltd, refused to pay and pointed to their standard terms, section 9 of which provided: '[W]e will not pay for: … Compensation or other costs arising from accidents involving your ownership or possession of any … mechanically propelled vehicles and any trailers attached thereto, aircraft, motorised waterborne craft or sailing vessels or windsurfing.

Judgment: It was agreed that the insurance policy in this case was subject to the Unfair Terms in Consumer Contract Regulations 1994. The Court also held that section 9 of the policy contained terms which 'defined the main subject matter of the contract'.

BGH, 21 April 1993[118] **4.41 (DE)**

CORE TERMS

Stolen treasures

A clause in an insurance contract is a core term if the contractual promise cannot be determined without this clause. Otherwise it merely modifies the contractual promise and is subject to the fairness test.

Facts: R, M and E broke into the claimant's house. They cut open a safe and stole valuables. The insurer refused to pay and pointed to its standard terms. The regulations of §9 of the Insurance Liability Conditions 84 read in extracts: '3. The insurance coverage against theft by housebreaking or robbery, regardless of contributive causes, does not apply to a) losses resulting from theft by housebreaking or robbery through the deliberate actions of domestic employees or persons living in the home of the policy holder; …'

Judgment: These clauses are not excluded from the control of unfairness by §8 of the Standard Terms Act [Gesetz zur Regelung des Rechts der Allgemeinen Geschäftsbedingungen, AGBG]. Certainly, mere descriptions of service are not subject to the review. Such descriptions establish type, scope and quality of the services owed, but do not affect the legal provisions which apply to the service. Clauses, which limit, change, develop or modify the principal promise of service are, in contrast, subject to control. Because of this, only the descriptions of service without whose existence an effective contract cannot be concluded in the absence of certainty or determinability of the essential content of the contract, are excluded from review.

[117] [2003] EWHC 380 (QB).
[118] (1993) NJW-RR 1049.

The provisions of §§9 no 1a and 9 no 3a of the Insurance Liability Conditions 84 do not belong to this narrow area of the description of services. They limit the insurance coverage by denying payment if domestic employees or people living with the policy holder caused the insurance claim. Through this provision, the principal promise of service is merely modified. Even without this clause an effective contract, whose essential content is determinable, can be concluded.

Note

In earlier German case-law, the debate had turned on the question as to whether one should distinguish between terms that positively determine the coverage and terms that exclude coverage in certain situations, a distinction that appears somewhat arbitrary.[119] The BGH has in the past assessed the unfairness of exclusion clauses.[120] Only terms without which the content of the contract can no longer be determined fall outside the control of standard terms.[121] In contrast, the High Court of England and Wales has excluded the unfairness test for an exclusion clause, ie a term that excludes liability in certain situations that would otherwise be covered by the insurance policy. The control was therefore limited to the question as to whether the term was in plain and intelligible language, see Article 4(2) of Directive 93/13/EEC.

II.B.5 ROLE OF THE ECJ

Although the ECJ has once ruled out, in *Océano Grupo*,[122] a jurisdiction clause that deprived the consumer of the competence of his local court and forced him to travel, the ECJ seems to be of little help in finding a Community-wide standard of unfairness of standard terms.

ECJ Case C-237/02, 27 June 2000[123] **4.42 (EU)**

Freiburger Kommunalbauten GmbH Baugesellschaft & Co KG v Ludger Hofstetter and Ulrike Hofstetter

INTERPRETATION OR APPLICATION OF EC CONSUMER LAW

Payment or nothing?

The ECJ does not apply the unfairness test to particular standard terms.

Facts: By notarial contract of 5 May 1998, Freiburger Kommunalbauten, a municipal construction company acting in the course of its business, sold to Mr and Mrs Hofstetter, who were dealing as

[119] In fact, the same term included in a travel insurance contract was held to be a positive description by LG Paderborn, 21 December 1984 (1986) VersR 481, but seen as an exclusion clause by LG München I, 18 May 1983 (1983) NJW 1685.

[120] Landmark cases are BGH, 21 April 1993 (1993) NJW-RR 1049 and BGH, 23 June 1993 (1993) NJW 2369.

[121] See BGH, 23 November 1994, BGHZ 128, 54, 59.

[122] ECJ, 27 June 2000, Joined Cases C-240/98 to C-244/98 *Océano Grupo Editorial SA v Rocío Murciano Quintero* and *Salvat Editores SA v José M. Sánchez Alcón Prades ea* [2000] ECR I-4941.

[123] [2004] ECR I-3403.

consumers, a parking space located in a multistorey car park that Freiburger Kommunalbauten was to build. Under clause 5 of the contract, the whole of the price was due upon delivery of a security by the contractor. In the event of late payment, the purchaser was liable to pay default interest. The security took the form of a bank guarantee and was delivered to Mr and Mrs Hofstetter on 20 May 1999. The guarantor undertook, as a primary liability, to guarantee any claims Mr and Mrs Hofstetter might assert against Freiburger Kommunalbauten for repayment of the purchase price paid to it or of which it was entitled to dispose. Mr and Mrs Hofstetter refused to make the payment. They claimed that the provision requiring payment of the whole of the price was contrary to paragraph 9 of the Gesetz zur Regelung des Rechts der Allgemeinen Geschäftsbedingungen (AGBG, the Standard Terms Act).

Judgment: 21. As to the question whether a particular term in a contract is, or is not, unfair, Article 4 of the Directive provides that the answer should be reached taking into account the nature of the goods or services for which the contract was concluded and by referring, at the time of conclusion of the contract, to all the circumstances attending the conclusion of the contract. It should be pointed out in that respect that the consequences of the term under the law applicable to the contract must also be taken into account. This requires that consideration be given to the national law.

22. It follows ... that in the context of its jurisdiction under Article 234 EC to interpret Community law, the Court may interpret general criteria used by the Community legislature in order to define the concept of unfair terms. However, it should not rule on the application of these general criteria to a particular term, which must be considered in the light of the particular circumstances of the case in question.

Notes

(1) Advocate General Geelhoed had stressed that national courts must be able to fulfil their role in applying the Directive without constantly having to refer questions on the unfairness of particular clauses to the ECJ, and that the multiplicity of terms which currently appears in consumer agreements could give rise to continual references for preliminary rulings under Article 234 EC.

(2) This reasoning of the ECJ in *Freiburger Kommunalbauten* was recently confirmed, although obiter, in the case of *Mostaza Claro*.[124] Again, the Advocate General made it clear that only obvious cases, such as the case of *Océano Grupo*, could be decided by the ECJ itself.

(3) In the recent case of *Pannon*, the ECJ has even applied its *Freiburger Kommunalbauten* line of reasoning to a jurisdiction clause, such as the one in *Océano Grupo*. Referring to *Freiburger Kommunalbauten*, the ECJ held that it was for the national (Hungarian) court to determine whether the jurisdiction clause in question satisfied the criteria of unfairness within the meaning of Article 3(1) of the Directive. In so doing, the national court had to take account of the fact that a term, contained in a contract concluded between a consumer and a seller or supplier, which has been included without being individually negotiated and which confers exclusive jurisdiction on the court in the territorial jurisdiction of which the seller or supplier has his principal place of business, might be considered to be unfair.[125]

[124] ECJ, 26 October 2006, Case C-168/05 *Elisa María Mostaza Claro v Centro Móvil Milenium SL* [2006] ECR I-10421, para 22.

[125] ECJ, 4 June 2009, Case C-243/08 *Pannon GSM Zrt v Erzsébet Sustikné Gyorfi*, nyr, paras 42 to 44.

II.B.6 LEGAL CONSEQUENCES OF UNFAIRNESS

The legal consequences of a breach of law are frequently not spelt out very clearly in EC consumer law, as we have seen earlier in this chapter. This also applies to some extent to the consequences of the unfairness of a standard term.

Under Article 6 of the Unfair Contract Terms Directive (93/13/EEC), unfair terms shall not be binding on the consumer, and the contract shall continue to bind the parties upon those terms if it is capable of continuing in existence without the unfair terms.[126] In contrast, the Directive leaves it to the Member States to determine the exact legal consequences. Varying systems can be found in the Member States. 'Absolute nullity' is a concept found in many Member States. This implies that a unfair term is automatically considered null and void. This is the system in, inter alia, Germany,[127] and the French system whereby the unfair terms are considered non-existent (*non écrites*) has similar consequences. 'Relative nullity' is the system other Member States have chosen (with variations). This implies that the term is initially valid and that the consumer needs to invoke its non-binding or invalid character. This is the system that seems to apply in the Netherlands, where such terms are voidable (*vernietigbaar*).[128] In other countries, there is considerable discussion on the exact legal consequences of unfairness, especially in view of the ECJ case-law, discussed below, which is not always easy to align with nation legal concepts. Before turning to that case-law, it should be mentioned that the Nordic countries (Denmark, Finland and Sweden) adopt a more flexible approach whereby the courts are entitled not only to declare an unfair term null and void, but also to alter, amend and adjust the particular term, other terms or the entire contract, thereby taking into account circumstances that have arisen after the contract was entered into.[129]

II.B.6.a *Ex officio* control

Furthermore, the ECJ has already spelt out limitations to the regulatory freedom of the Member States with a view to determining the national courts' competence to control the fairness of standard terms *ex officio*. In *Océano Grupo*, the ECJ argued that a court's power to determine of its own motion whether a term is unfair had to be regarded as constituting a proper means both of achieving the result sought by Article 6 of the Unfair Contract Terms Directive (93/13/EEC), namely preventing an individual consumer from being bound by an unfair term, and of contributing to achieving the aim of Article 7, since if the court undertakes such an examination, that may act as a deterrent and contribute to preventing unfair terms in contracts concluded between consumers and sellers or suppliers.[130] This was then clarified and

[126] This is an objective approach, see AG Tizzano, Opinion of 22 September 2005, ECJ, 10 January 2006, Case C-302/04 *Ynos Kft v János Varga* [2006] ECR I-371. The ECJ declined jurisdiction to decide the case.

[127] §307(1) s 1 BGB.

[128] See Art 6:233 NBW (Dutch Civil Code). See also, on Hungarian law, ECJ, 10 January 2006, Case C-302/04 *Ynos Kft v János Varga* [2006] ECR I-371.

[129] Ebers, above n 77, 409.

[130] ECJ, 27 June 2000, Joined Cases C-240/98 to C-244/98 *Océano Grupo Editorial SA v Rocío Murciano Quintero* and *Salvat Editores SA v José M. Sánchez Alcón Prades ea* [2000] ECR I-4941, para 28.

confirmed in *Cofidis* and *Mostaza Claro*. In *Cofidis*,[131] the ECJ added that a procedural rule which prohibits the national court, on expiry of a limitation period, from finding of its own motion or following a plea raised by a consumer that a term sought to be enforced by a seller or supplier is unfair is against the principle of effectiveness and cannot therefore be applied.

ECJ Case C-168/05, 26 October 2006[132] **4.43 (EU)**
Elisa María Mostaza Claro v Centro Móvil Milenium SL

EX OFFICIO CONTROL OF UNFAIRNESS

Disconnected phone

The courts have the right and the duty to assess the unfairness of pre-formulated terms ex officio.

Facts: See 1.29(EU). In the order for reference, the Audiencia Provincial (Court of Apeal) de Madrid (Spain) stated that there was no doubt that the arbitration agreement included an unfair contractual term and was therefore null and void. However, as Ms Mostaza Claro did not plead that the agreement was invalid in the context of the arbitration proceedings, and in order to interpret the national law in accordance with the Directive, the Audiencia Provincial de Madrid decided to stay the proceedings and to refer the following question to the ECJ for a preliminary ruling.

Judgment: 25. The system of protection introduced by the Directive is based on the idea that the consumer is in a weak position vis-à-vis the seller or supplier, as regards both his bargaining power and his level of knowledge. This leads to the consumer agreeing to terms drawn up in advance by the seller or supplier without being able to influence the content of those terms (Joined Cases C-240/98 to C-244/98 *Océano Grupo Editorial and Salvat Editores* [2000] ECR I-4941, paragraph 25).

26. Such an imbalance between the consumer and the seller or supplier may only be corrected by positive action unconnected with the actual parties to the contract (*Océano Grupo Editorial and Salvat Editores*, paragraph 27).

27. It is on the basis of those principles that the Court has ruled that the national court's power to determine of its own motion whether a term is unfair constitutes a means both of achieving the result sought by Article 6 of the Directive, namely preventing an individual consumer from being bound by an unfair term, and of contributing to achieving the aim of Article 7, since if the court undertakes such an examination, that may act as a deterrent and contribute to preventing unfair terms in contracts concluded between consumers and sellers or suppliers (*Océano Grupo Editorial and Salvat Editores*, paragraph 28, and Case C-473/00 *Cofidis* [2002] ECR I-10875, paragraph 32).

28. That power of the national court has been regarded as necessary for ensuring that the consumer enjoys effective protection, in view in particular of the real risk that he is unaware of his rights or encounters difficulties in enforcing them (*Océano Grupo Editorial and Salvat Editores*, paragraph 26, and *Cofidis,* paragraph 33).

29. The protection which the Directive confers on consumers thus extends to cases in which a consumer who has concluded with a seller or supplier a contract containing an

[131] ECJ, 21 November 2002, Case C-473/00 *Cofidis SA v Jean-Louis Fredout* [2002] ECR I-10875, para 36.

[132] [2006] ECR I-10421.

unfair term fails to raise the unfair nature of the term, whether because he is unaware of his rights or because he is deterred from enforcing them on account of the costs which judicial proceedings would involve (*Cofidis*, paragraph 34).

30. Under those circumstances, the result sought by Article 6 of the Directive which, as was recalled at paragraph 27 of this judgment, requires the Member States to ensure that consumers are not bound by unfair terms, could not be achieved if the court seised of an action for annulment of an arbitration award was unable to determine whether that award was void solely because the consumer did not plead the invalidity of the arbitration agreement in the course of the arbitration proceedings.

31. Such an omission by the consumer could not then, under any circumstances, be compensated for by action on the part of persons not party to the contract. The regime of special protection established by the Directive would be definitively undermined. ...

36. The importance of consumer protection has in particular led the Community legislature to lay down, in Article 6(1) of the Directive, that unfair terms used in a contract concluded with a consumer by a seller or supplier 'shall ... not be binding on the consumer'. This is a mandatory provision which, taking into account the weaker position of one of the parties to the contract, aims to replace the formal balance which the latter establishes between the rights and obligations of the parties with an effective balance which re-establishes equality between them.

37. Moreover, as the aim of the Directive is to strengthen consumer protection, it constitutes, according to Article 3(1)(t) EC, a measure which is essential to the accomplishment of the tasks entrusted to the Community and, in particular, to raising the standard of living and the quality of life in its territory (see, by analogy, concerning Article 81 EC, *Eco Swiss*, paragraph 36).

38. The nature and importance of the public interest underlying the protection which the Directive confers on consumers justify, moreover, the national court being required to assess of its own motion whether a contractual term is unfair, compensating in this way for the imbalance which exists between the consumer and the seller or supplier.

Note

In *Pannon*, the ECJ clarified that where a court considers a standard term to be unfair, it must not apply it, except if the consumer opposes that non-application.[133] In *Rampion and Godard*,[134] the ECJ has transferred the requirement on courts to apply EC consumer law of their own motion to consumer credit law, arguing that a consumer may not be aware of the provisions of linked contracts, and most recently, in *Martín Martín*, the ECJ has also applied this in the context of doorstep selling law.[135]

II.B.6.b Partly unfair terms

The question remains how to deal with terms that are partly unfair or terms that, for example, unfairly exclude liability for all negligence whereas it would have been acceptable to exclude liability for gross negligence only. German courts have long

[133] ECJ, 4 June 2009, Case C-243/08 *Pannon GSM Zrt v Erzsébet Sustikné Gyorfi*, nyr, para 35.

[134] ECJ, 4 October 2007, Case C-429/05 *Max Rampion, Marie-Jeanne Rampion, née Godard v Franfinance SA, K par K SAS* [2007] ECR I-8017.

[135] AG Trstenjak, opinion of 7 May 2009, Case C-227/08 *Eva Martín Martín v EDP Editores, SL*, nyr, para 90.

excluded the possibility of reducing the meaning of a clause to the acceptable degree of contractual freedom ('Verbot geltungserhaltender Reduktion').[136] This used to be the line of thinking of English courts as well.[137] In contrast, the judge in the English case of *Bankers Insurance Company*[138] thought that it was possible to declare a term unfair only to the extent that it denied recovery 'whatever the consequences of the breach'. He was influenced by the fact that holding the term inapplicable in its entirety would be 'unfair' on the seller/supplier.

Other Member States explicitly accept the possibility of reducing an unfair term to a legally permitted version; thus Article 3:42 of the Dutch Civil Code allows the replacement of an invalid contractual term by a contractual term that would have been agreed on by the parties to the contract.

Question

Do you think that allowing a reduction of an invalid term to an acceptable and legally permitted variation provides an incentive to use unfair terms?

CONCISE BIBLIOGRAPHY

R Baillod, 'Le droit de repentir' [1984] *Revue trimestrielle de droit civil* 227.

J Calais-Auloy and F Steinmetz, *Droit de la consommation*, 7th edn (Paris, Dalloz, 2006).

P Hellwege, 'Consumer Protection in Britain in Need of Reform' [2004] *Cambridge Law Journal* 712–42.

A Karimi, *Les clauses abusive et la théorie de l'abus de droit* (Paris, LGDJ, 2006).

M Loos, 'The Case for a Uniform and Efficient Right of Withdrawal from Consumer Contracts' [2007] *Zeitschrift für Europäisches Privatrecht* 5–36.

P Malinvaud, 'Droit de repentir et théorie générale des obligations' in *Scritti in onore di Rodolfo Sacco* (Milano, Giuffre, 1994) 744–62.

H-W Micklitz, N Reich and P Rott, *Understanding EU Consumer Law* (Antwerp/Oxford, Intersentia, 2009).

N Reich, 'The Implementation of Directive 93/13/EEC on Unfair Terms in Consumer Contracts in Germany' [1997] *European Review of Private Law* 165–72.

G Reiner, 'Der verbraucherschützende Widerruf im Recht der Willenserklärungen' [2003] *Archiv der civilistischen Praxis* 1–45.

H Schulte-Nölke, C Twigg Flesner and M Ebers (eds), *EC Consumer Law Compendium* (München, Sellier, 2008).

E Terryn (ed), *Le droit de rétractation. Une analyse de droit compare. Droits européen, allemand, français, néerlandais et belge* (Brussel, Larcier, 2008).

[136] Established case-law since BGH, 20 January 1983, BGHZ 86, 297.

[137] See eg *Stewart Gill Ltd v Horatio Myer & Co Ltd* [1992] 2 All ER (CA) 257 at 263 (per Stuart-Smith LJ): 'Nor does it appear to me to be consistent with the policy and purpose of the Act to permit a contractor to impose a contractual term, which taken as a whole is completely unreasonable, to put a blue pencil through the most offensive parts and say that what is left is reasonable and sufficient to exclude or restrict his liability in a manner relied upon.'

[138] 7 March 2003 [2003] EWHC 380 (QB).

CHAPTER FIVE
SALE OF GOODS

This chapter is concerned with consumer-specific issues regarding contracts of sale. In particular, it will consider some of the difficulties associated with the different legal transactions which can be used to supply goods to consumers (II). It will consider the requirement that goods must be in conformity with the contract (IV) and the remedies available to a consumer for non-conformities (VI). There will also be a brief discussion of consumer guarantees (IX).

I. EU LEGISLATION ON CONSUMER SALES

As with many other areas of consumer law discussed in this book, the European Community has created legislation to deal with aspects of consumer sales—in other words, there has been a significant 'top-down' effect in the Europeanisation of this area of law. The Consumer Sales Directive (99/44/EC)[1] entered into force in 2002 and applies in all the Member States of the European Union.[2] This measure deals with three central aspects of any contract of sale: the standard of quality a consumer can

[1] Directive 99/44/EC of the European Parliament and of the Council of 25 May 1999 on certain aspects of the sale of consumer goods and associated guarantees [1999] OJ L 171, 12–16.

[2] See eg S Grundman and M Bianca (eds), *EU Sales Directive—Commentary* (Antwerp/Oxford, Intersentia, 2002); H-W Micklitz, 'Ein einheitliches Kaufrecht für Verbraucher in der EG?' (1997) 8 *EuZW* 229; C Twigg-Flesner, 'The EC Directive on Certain Aspects of the Sale of Consumer Goods and Associated Guarantees' (1991) 7 *Consumer Law Journal* 177–92; D Staudenmeyer, 'The Directive on the Sale of Consumer Goods and Associated Guarantees—A Milestone in the European Consumer and Private Law' (2000) 4 *ERPL* 547–64.

reasonably expect of the goods; remedies where goods fall below that standard; and voluntary guarantees. This chapter will consider these core areas in depth, drawing on case-law from both before and after the adoption of the Directive.

The Directive marked the most significant intervention yet by the European Community in the substantive contract laws of the Member States. Although heavily influenced by the UN Convention on the International Sale of Goods 1980 (CISG)—arguably because of its familiarity to most legal systems within the European Union—the Directive's provisions have been modified in order to fit the particular needs of consumers, which are, of course, not always the same as those of non-consumers. The impact of the Directive has been significant—in Germany, for example, it became the trigger for a major reform of parts of its law of obligations, whereas its impact on English law has been more muted. On the whole, however, the Directive has had a noticeable impact across all the Member States, but it is beyond the scope of this chapter to examine this in depth.[3]

The European Commission has started the process of revising the existing acquis communautaire in the consumer law field, undertaking first a study on the implementation of eight consumer law Directives,[4] including the Consumer Sales Directive, and then a Green Paper on the Review of the Consumer Acquis.[5] These will be referred to, where appropriate.

In October 2008, the European Commission presented its proposal for a Consumer Rights Directive.[6] This includes a new chapter IV on sales. Whilst this largely restates the provisions from Directive 99/44/EC, there is one significant development with regard to the remedies for a lack of conformity: it would be for the trader, rather than the consumer, to choose whether to provide repair or replacement in the first instance. In addition, there would be specific rules on delivery as well as the passing of risk. The proposals are likely to be controversial,[7] and one can expect considerable debate and modification to the individual provisions before a final directive is agreed.

II. CONTRACTS OF SALE

II.A DEFINING 'SALE'

It is first necessary to consider what makes a contract for the supply of goods a contract of sale, as opposed to some other transaction (hire, lease, hire-purchase, etc).

[3] For a detailed overview, see H Schulte-Nölke, C Twigg-Flesner and M Ebers (eds), *EC Consumer Compendium* (München, Sellier, 2008).

[4] Ibid. See also ch 1.I.E.

[5] COM [2006] 744 final. See C Twigg-Flesner, 'No Sense of Purpose or Direction? The Modernisation of European Consumer Law' (2007) 3 ERCL 198–213.

[6] COM [2008] 614 final.

[7] See C Twigg-Flesner, 'Fit for Purpose? The Proposals on Sales' in G Howells and R Schulze (eds), *Modernising and Harmonising Consumer Contract Law* (München, Sellier, 2009).

There is no coherent definition in the Consumer Sales Directive itself, although it is clear that it only applies to contracts involving the sale of 'consumer goods'.[8]

With regard to German law, one can identify the hallmarks of a contract of sale from this provision:

BGB **5.1 (DE)**

§433 Typical Contractual Duties in a Contract of Sale

(1) Under a contract of sale, the seller of a good is obliged to deliver the thing to the buyer and to procure ownership of the thing for the buyer. The seller must procure the thing for the buyer free from material and legal defects.

(2) The buyer is obliged to pay the seller the agreed purchase price and to accept delivery of the thing purchased.

In English law, the central definition of a contract of sale is as follows.

Sale of Goods Act 1979 **5.2 (UK)**

Section 2 Contract of sale

(1) A contract of sale of goods is a contract by which the seller transfers or agrees to transfer the property in goods to the buyer for a money consideration, called the price.

And in French law, the following two articles from the Civil Code provide a definition:

Code civil **5.3 (FR)**

Article 1582 A sale is an agreement by which one person binds himself to deliver a thing, and another to pay for it. It may be made by an authentic instrument or by an instrument under private signature.

Article 1583 It is complete between the parties, and ownership is acquired as of right by the buyer with respect to the seller, as soon as the thing and the price have been agreed upon, although the thing has not yet been delivered or the price paid.

Note

We can see from these provisions that a contract of sale involves two things: the handing over of a physical item (the good), and also the transfer of the legal interest ('property') in that item, from seller to buyer.

Consequently, not all contracts involving the supply of goods are treated as 'sales'—if, for example, there is no agreement to transfer the property in the goods to the buyer, the contract is not one of sale, but may, instead, be one of hire, or

[8] Art 1(1) and (2)(b) of the Consumer Sales Directive (99/44/EC).

hire-purchase. This is a contract under which the consumer would acquire goods for a limited period of time, permitting the consumer to use those goods, but he would not acquire outright ownership of these goods and cannot treat them as his own. This is significant for many consumer transactions for high-value goods, such as cars. Often, a consumer will not have the financial resources available to pay for such goods outright at the time of acquiring them. A contract of hire would enable the consumer to obtain the benefit of the goods in return for a regular instalment payment, but the consumer would be obliged to return the goods at the end of the hire-period. A hire-purchase agreement is similar to a contract of hire, except that the consumer will have the option of acquiring the property in the goods at the end of the contract period in return for the payment of an additional sum.

As such, contracts are not regarded as contracts of sale; the degree of consumer protection may be less than would be the case with sales. The Consumer Sales Directive (99/44/EC) does not extend to such contracts. This means that the remedies for a consumer may differ where the goods are supplied by way of hire or hire-purchase, because the remedies provided for in the Consumer Sales Directive (99/44/EC) do not have to be made available for such contracts.[9]

II.B BROADENING THE DEFINITION: GOODS TO BE MANUFACTURED OR PRODUCED

Although the Consumer Sales Directive does not contain a definition of 'sale' itself, Article 1, paragraph 4 specifies that:

Consumer Sales Directive (99/44/EC) **5.4 (EU)**

Article 1 (4) Contracts for the supply of consumer goods to be manufactured or produced shall also be deemed contracts of sale for the purpose of this Directive.

Notes

(1) This can cover a wide range of circumstances, from items made-to-order (but otherwise standardised), to custom-designed goods made specifically for one particular consumer. It reflects the overall result of the transaction, ie the transfer of property in a finished item to the consumer.

(2) This marks a change from the position in many jurisdicitons. For example, English law has historically adopted a 'substance of the contract' test in establishing whether a contract is one of sale or for work and materials, but there has been a lack of consistency, and the case-law is difficult to reconcile. For example, it was held that a contract for a painter to paint a portrait was a contract for work and materials, because central to the contract was the painter's skill.[10] Other cases have focused on

[9] For a comparative study, see A Sandrock, *Vertragswidrigkeit der Sachleistung* (Tübingen, Mohr-Siebeck, 2003).

[10] *Robinson v Graves* [1935] 1 KB 579.

the fact that the contract ultimately results in the transfer of property in finished goods, and have concluded that such contracts are sales, even though the supplier's skill was relevant to producing the finished item.[11] This now seems to be the accepted approach.

In French law, the distinction between contracts of sale and contracts of services has also not always been an easy one. The main criterion used to distinguish between them is based on a comparison of the value of materials and the value of work. If the value of the material is higher, the contract can be defined as a contract of sale of goods. If not, then it will be classified as a services contract. The case below is an example; here, the Cour d'appel (Court of Appeal) held that the material supplied was of higher value than the work. The Cour de cassation (Supreme Court) approved the classification as a sale of goods.

Cass civ 1e, 27 April 1976[12] **5.5 (FR)**

DIFFERENCE BETWEEN A CONTRACT OF SALE OF GOODS AND A CONTRACT OF SUPPLY OF SERVICES

The unfit curtain

Where the material supplied is of higher value than the work the contract is a contract for the sale of goods.

Facts: Mr da Silva had ordered some curtains from Mrs Vinay. Mrs Vinay had made them but had also supplied the fabric. Mr da Silva refused to accept the curtains on delivery and asked, inter alia, for rescission of the contract as provided by a regulation concerning hire purchase and applying only to sale of goods.

Judgment: Considering the claimant's first argument in each of its two subdivisions: according to the contested judgement, Mr da Silva ordered a set of curtains, double-sided curtains, valances and lace trimmings from Mrs Vinay, the director of the Sovitex group. Mrs Vinay supplied the fabric herself and had it cut and fashioned according to the specified measurements;

The price was fixed at FRF 149, with a down payment of FRF 100. It was also agreed that the total sum would be paid over a series of 21 equal monthly instalments;

When he received these items, Mr da Silva refused to accept them and, once Mrs Vinay had issued summons, he requested that the contract be terminated.

The Court of Appeal was incorrect for having granted this request by applying the provisions of the decree of 4 August 1956 concerning hire-purchases on the grounds that the interest rate of the credit agreement in this case exceeded the statutory interest rate.

On the one hand, a contract in which a person agrees to perform a service by providing both his or her services and the material at a higher service price constitutes a contract for services and not a sales contract (as indicated by the terms stated in article

[11] *Lee v Griffin* [1861] 1 B & S 272 (contract for a dentist to make and supply a set of dentures was a contract of sale); *J Marcel Furriers Ltd v Tapper* [1953] 1 WLR 49 (contract to make and supply a coat).

[12] Bull civ I No 143, 114.

1787 of the Civil Code). On the other hand, the hire-purchase rules must be applied in a restrictive manner because of their exorbitant nature with regard to the principle of the freedom of contract;

This case concerns a mixed agreement involving items for the home, the 'judges' in lower instance could not have refused to acknowledge that the hire purchase rules did not apply to the items on the basis that the list of exempt objects was exhaustive;

However, first, the Court of Appeal correctly decided that a contract in which a person provides both services and delivers movable property must be regarded in law as a sale when the service is not of primary importance in the transaction. Following an evaluation that is outside the Court of Cassation's competence, the Court of Appeal decided that on this occasion, this was the case, because the material required for the transaction took precedence over the actual service.

Second, if the decree of 4 August 1956 intended to exempt certain items 'of family or educative value' from the hire purchase rules, there is no mention of decorative pieces, such as those under dispute, in the list provided in the regulation of 11 January 1957.

The Court of Appeal rightly decided that this list, which constituted an exception to the principle outlined in the decree of 4 August 1956, which regulates all hire purchases, was restrictive.

The claimant's first argument cannot therefore be accepted; ...

Given the above considerations, the appeal against the judgement delivered on 30 April 1974 by the Court of Appeal of Grenoble is rejected.

The Cour de Cassation has sometimes held that a contract involving a sale and a supply of services is to be submitted to the rules governing the sale for its 'sale part' and the ones applying to the services contract for the 'services part'. The following case (not a consumer case) illustrates this.

Cass civ 3e, 16 March 1977[13] **5.6 (FR)**

DIFFERENCE BETWEEN A CONTRACT FOR THE SALE OF GOODS AND A CONTRACT FOR THE SUPPLY OF SERVICES

Thermal power station

Where one part of the contract has the nature of a contract for the sale of goods and the other part the nature of a contract for the supply of services, the rules concerning the sale of goods will apply for one part and the rules concerning the supply of services will apply for the other part.

Facts: Papeterie de France had ordered Tunzini enterprises to build and install a thermal power station. Once installed, the station did not operate properly. Papeterie de France sued for compensation. The Court of Appeal of Grenoble held that this could be awarded on the basis of the rules governing the contract of sale of goods and the contract of supply of services on the ground that the contract was an hybrid one (sale and services). Tunzini took the view that the rules of the sale of goods could not apply, relying on the fact that the work supplied was of higher value than the material sold.

Judgment: Considering the claimant's first argument: given what emerges from the contested judgement, ... the company Papeterie de France ordered the company

[13] Bull civ III No 131, 101.

Tunzini-enterprises to construct a thermal power station. Tunzini-enterprises subcontracted the firm Aeg Kanis Turbimen Fabrik to supply the turbo-alternator;

The 'preliminary' delivery document containing a number of reservations was signed on 26 June 1970. The 'definite' delivery, foreseen by the parties for 30 June 1971, after repeated postponements, never occurred since the results of the tests carried out were inconclusive. Various operational hitches occurred repeatedly up until the end of the year 1972.

The judgement is challenged on the grounds that it required the company Tunzini-enterprises to repair the damage suffered by Papeterie de France between 1 June 1971 and the end of the year 1972, which were the result of faulty installation. According to the claimant's argument, on the one hand, 'faced with a complex but unique agreement, the Court cannot accept the dual quality of a services and a sale contract. The Court cannot hold the company Tunzini-enterprises responsible as both the supplier of services and as a professional seller. In this case, the contract should have been classified as a services contract on the basis of both the requirements of the tender that provided that an installation was to be constructed on the client's land, and on the basis of the economic criterion regarding the value of the service and the material respectively, and because there was no action for annulment of the sale brought by the plaintiff, which thus excluded the seller's guarantee for hidden defects. On the other hand, in requiring the company Tunzini-enterprises to pay an amount determined on the basis of the main causes of harm or loss—without specifying in what capacity the latter company was responsible—the contested judgement, does not allow the Court of Cassation to check the legitimacy of the ruling. Moreover, the contested judgement contradicts itself in that it acknowledges the principal causes of harm or loss as a judgement that would only have accepted the classification as a contract for services'.

However, the Court of Appeal—that could classify the complex agreement between the company Papeterie de France and the company Tunzini-enterprises as a services contract and a contract for the sale of goods—has declared that its capacity of project manager, which arose from the services contract, made the company Tunzini-enterprises responsible for the management of the installation and supervision of the operations, an obligation that was not satisfactorily fulfilled.

The Court of Appeal deemed the company Tunzini-enterprises responsible for four different sets of defaults that, according to expert report, the company itself created through managerial and installation faults. Moreover, the Court of Appeal based its decision to condemn the company on the sole ground that it failed to fulfil the obligations stemming from the contract for the provision of services;

Based on the above considerations, it follows that the claimant's argument cannot be accepted in any of its parts. ...

Given the above considerations, the appeal against the judgement of 28 May 1975, issued by the Court of Appeal of Grenoble, is rejected.

Another criterion used in French law is that one of 'spécifications', ie instructions given by the client. If the client has given special instructions to the contractor, then the contract will be considered as a services contract since there is no possibility of mass production.[14] But if there is a possibility of mass production, the Cour de

[14] Eg Cass civ 1e, 14 December 1999, Bull civ I No 340.

Cassation will define the contract as a 'sale of goods'.[15] The following case is an illustration.

Cass comm, 3 January 1995[16] **5.7 (FR)**

DIFFERENCE BETWEEN A CONTRACT FOR THE SALE OF GOODS AND A CONTRACT FOR THE SUPPLY OF SERVICES

Cereal bars

Where the client gives special instructions to his contractor who will supply goods and work on them in accordance with the contract, the contract will be a contract for the supply of services and not a contract for the sale of goods.

Facts: The Société Diététique had ordered cereal bars from the Société nouvelle Dupont d'Isigny. The cereal bars were to be produced by the Société nouvelle Dupont d'Isigny according to special instructions given by the Société Diététique. When delivered, the cereal bars were found to be contaminated. The Société Diététique sued the Société nouvelle Dupont d'Isigny on the ground of provisions of the Civil Code concerning the sale of goods. The Société nouvelle Dupont d'Isigny contested the application of these provisions but the Cour d'appel held that the contract was a sale of goods contract. The Société nouvelle Dupont d'Isigny asked the Cour de cassation to reconsider the nature of the contract.

Judgment: Considering the claimant's argument in its first part:

In light of articles 1582, 1779 and 1787 of the Civil code;

According to the contested judgement, the company Société nouvelle Dupont d'Isigny (SNDI) delivered contaminated cereal bars to the company Société Diététique et santé. The produce in question was made by SNDI using cereal that had been prepared by Société Diététique et santé using wheat flakes produced by the company Etablissements Favrichon (Favrichon company) on the basis of deliveries to the latter company by Mr Lerat, acting under the company name of L'Etablissements Minoterie Lerat (M Lerat).

Seeking recovery for the damages it suffered, Société Diététique et santé called upon the following companies: SNDI and its insurer, Compagnie Abeille Paix (now Compagnie Abeille assurances), Société Favrichon and its insurer, Les Mutuelles du Mans, and Etablissements Minoterie Lerat. During the appeal, Société Diététique et santé claimed that, bound to SNDI by a sales contract, the latter failed to perform its delivery obligation. SNDI maintained that it only agreed to a contract for the provision of services.

In order to decide whether or not SNDI and Société Diététique et santé had concluded a sales contract, as opposed to a contract for the provision of services, the judgement holds that 'making the cereal bars according to the special instructions laid out by Société Diététique et santé and using the latter's equipment and produce, does not constitute a contract for the provision of services as described in article 1787 of the Civil Code'.

By ruling this way and by holding that the cereal bars were made using bars supplied by Société Diététique et santé, according to a process outlined and halted by the latter company and using the latter company's equipment, from which it follows that these products cannot be deemed to have been made according to a process chosen by their producer, but rather that they were intended to meet the specific requirements of the

[15] Cass comm, 6 March 2001, pourvoi No 98-17015, on telecommunication wires.

[16] Bull civ IV No 2, 1.

company Société Diététique et santé, the Court of Appeal failed to consider the legal consequences of its observations. ...

Based on these grounds, and without it being necessary to examine the other elements of the appeal:

The appeal is rejected and annulled

Note

Under the Consumer Sales Directive (99/44/EC), the seller is liable for the conformity with the contract of the finished item, and this may entail liability for design faults, as well as faults in the component parts or materials used to manufacture the finished item. However, if the consumer has furnished the seller with the materials that are to be made into a finished item (eg fabric to be used for making a suit), then there is no liability on the seller for a lack of conformity of the end-product if this is caused by the materials supplied by the consumer.[17]

II.C CONTRACTS INVOLVING THE INSTALLATION OF GOODS

Although there is no clear statement in the Directive that contracts involving an element of 'installation' of the goods sold are also to be treated as contracts of sale, it seems from Article 2(5) that this is the intention. The relevant parts of this Article provide that:

Consumer Sales Directive (99/44/EC) **5.8 (EU)**

Article 2 (5) Any lack of conformity resulting from incorrect installation of consumer goods shall be deemed to be equivalent to lack of conformity of the goods if installation forms part of the contract of sale of the goods and the goods we installed by the seller or under his responsibility.

Contracts for the supply and installation of goods may contain a significant service element, and in national law it may be difficult to distinguish between circumstances where the installation is only a minor part of the contract (eg a television set that is delivered and connected to the aerial or satellite receiver) and where it forms a significant aspect of the transaction (eg the supplying and fitting a kitchen, which usually involves the assembly of the various units, connecting of appliances, and fixing of cupboards to the kitchen walls). It seems that, under the Directive, it is irrelevant whether the service aspect of the transaction (ie the installation) constitutes a substantial part of the seller's obligations under the contract, although the position is not entirely clear. It is arguable that, once the installation element is significant, the contract is really one for work and materials, but it may then be the case that the contract would be one for 'goods to be manufactured', which, under the Directive, should also be treated as sales.

[17] Art 2(3) final part, Consumer Sales Directive.

Queen's Bench Division, 20 November 1969[18] **5.9 (UK)**
Philip Head & Sons Ltd v Showfronts Ltd

THE SUPPLY AND FITTING OF A CARPET WAS A SALE

The unfitted carpet

Where the service element of a contract involving the supply of goods and their installation is a small one, the contract is one of sale.

Facts: The (non-consumer) buyer had contracted with the supplier to provide and lay carpets in an office building it was refurbishing, but the materials were stolen between delivery and laying. The key issue was whether ownership had passed and whether the relevant rules on contracts of sale applied. About 10 per cent of the contract value was for planning and laying the carpeting, with the remainder relating to the materials provided. It was held that this was a contract of sale.

Judgment: [Mocatta J] I was referred to a number of authorities dealing with the question whether this contract was one to which the Sale of Goods Act 1893, applied or not. It is often difficult to determine this matter; there are some fascinating cases in the books dealing with dentures, paintings, pictures and so forth in which that matter had to be decided. It usually became material in the old days when a defendant relied upon the now repealed sec 4 of the statute. The cases are thus summarized in Chalmers on the Sale of Goods Act, 15th ed (1967) at p 7:

'Opinions have differed much about the test for distinguishing between these two contracts [that is to say the contract for sale of goods and the contract for the supply of work and materials] but the general rule deducible from the cases seems to be that if the main object of the contract is the transfer from A to B, for a price, of the property in a thing in which B had no previous property, then the contract is a contract of sale; but if the real substance of the contract is the performance of work by A for B, it is a contract for work and materials notwithstanding that the performance of the work necessitates the use of certain materials and that the property in those materials passes from A to B under the contract.'

It is unnecessary to mention specifically the cases on this point cited to me, mainly by Mr Braithwaite, but the conclusion I have come to is that notwithstanding that the planning in connection with this carpeting and the laying of the carpeting (which, of course, included cutting, stitching and so forth) were of very great importance, and that similar remarks may be made in relation to the tiling part of the contract, nevertheless this was a contract of sale and one to which the Sale of Goods Act 1893, applied.

Notes

(1) In *Jones v Gallagher (t/a Gallery Kitches and Bathrooms)*,[19] a contract involving the supply and installation of a handmade pine fitted kitchen, appears to have been treated by the Court of Appeal as a contract for work and materials, rather than sale, although the reasoning is confused as there is also discussion of a specific restriction on a consumer's right to terminate a contract for breach which only applies in relation to contracts for sale.

[18] [1970] 1 Lloyd's Rep 140.
[19] [2004] EWCA Civ 10.

(2) Although the Consumer Sales Directive takes a broad view of what might constitute a contract of sale, there are difficulties with this when compared to established positions in national law. Often, distinctions drawn in national sales law may have been based on factors which may no longer have any relevance today—but is a top-down change required by a Directive the best way to modernise the law?

III. WHAT ARE 'CONSUMER GOODS'?

The next matter to consider is whether the type of goods a consumer seeks to buy may affect the classification of the contract of sale as a consumer or non-consumer contract. In the Consumer Sales Directive, the definition of 'consumer goods' is very broad, covering any tangible movable item, with the exception of goods sold by way of execution or otherwise by authority of law; water and gas not sold in a limited volume or set quantity; and electricity.[20] Whilst French law follows the definition of the Directive,[21] neither German nor English law have adopted a specific definition of 'consumer goods'.

In Germany, the definition of goods is rather broader.

BGB **5.10 (DE)**

§90 Concept of the Good

Only corporeal objects are goods as defined by law.

The same is true of English law.

Sale of Goods Act 1979 **5.11 (UK)**

Section 61 Interpretation

(1) 'goods' includes all personal chattels other than things in action and money, and in Scotland all corporeal moveables except money; and in particular 'goods' includes emblements, industrial growing crops, and things attached to or forming part of the land which are agreed to be severed before sale or under the contract of sale and includes an undivided share in goods.

However, despite this broad approach to the notion of goods, there are limitations which are of considerable relevance to the Directive: the first is the distinction between new and second-hand goods; and the second relates to the classification of computer software.

[20] Art 2(2)(b).

[21] Art L 211-1 and 2 Code de Consommation.

III.A SECOND-HAND GOODS

The Consumer Sales Directive contains two provisions affecting second-hand goods, although there is no definition of this term in the Directive. First, Article 1(3) grants Member States the option of excluding from the definition of 'consumer goods'—and therefore the rules on consumer sales—'second-hand goods sold at public auction where consumers have the opportunity of attending the sale in person'. Only one-third of Member States have made use of this option, including France (but only with regard to the specific rules which implement the Directive), Germany and the United Kingdom, but the vast majority have chosen not to implement this restriction.[22] Indeed, in France, the crucial distinction is between *contrats de droit commun* (contracts governed by Civil Code provisions) and consumer contracts (theoretically contracts governed by Consumer Code provisions). This distinction is particularly important in the field of conformity (see below).

Secondly, whilst the Directive generally imposes liability on the seller for any lack of conformity that arises within two years of delivery, Article 7(1) includes a further option for the Member States to provide in their domestic law that this liability period may be reduced in the case of second-hand goods. However, the period may not be less than one year. This option has been implemented by just over half of all the Member States, including Germany, but not France or the United Kingdom.[23]

With no definition of second-hand goods, the question arises whether there should be an objective test for considering whether goods are second-hand, or whether this should be a matter for the parties, ie a subjective approach. In favour of the former, one may argue that classifying goods as 'second-hand' can benefit the seller because the period of liability is reduced. A subjective approach would create the risk that a seller could take advantage of the possibility to designate even new goods as 'second-hand', thereby reducing consumer protection. On the other hand, if goods are sold as second-hand goods, their price will usually be lower, and this may be sufficient to deter a seller from seeking to take advantage of this. The following two cases offer contrasting opinions.

OLG (Court of Appeal) Schleswig-Holstein, 13 December 2005[24] **5.12 (DE)**

ARE ANIMALS NEW OR SECOND-HAND GOODS?

Horse with faulty heart-valve

Animals are not to be treated as second-hand goods immediately after birth, although the parties may agree that in the circumstances of a particular case an animal is no longer new.

[22] Schulte-Nölke, Twigg-Flesner and Ebers, above n 5, 667.
[23] Ibid.
[24] 3U 42/05 (2006) OLG-report Schleswig 193.

Facts: A six-month old horse, which had not been used for riding or breeding, was sold at an auction. Some time later, it was discovered that the horse suffered from a faulty heart-valve. The seller refused to accept the buyer's claim on the basis that the horse was second-hand goods, and the limitation period had already expired.

Judgment: The six month old colt is not objectively a used good. According to §90a of the German Civil Code, animals should be governed by the provisions that apply to goods. The boundary between new and used goods when dealing with animals is, however, disputed. … The reason for the different handling is not, therefore, dependent on the nature of the thing for sale, but on the particular dangers or risks resulting from use. … According to the then view of the German Civil Code, working or saddle horses can still be regarded as new goods up until the first time they are put to their respective uses. Accordingly, the court of first instance of Aschaffenburg … also considered 9-week-old puppies as newly produced goods. The literature has also argued in part that animals, with the exception of previously used working animals, should be classified as newly produced goods …

As far as is apparent, two voices in the literature represent, without further explanation, the view that whether a good is used or not is only determined objectively and not according to an agreement on quality. 'Used', as a characteristic, cannot be determined by an agreement on quality between the parties … The senate takes the opposing view …, which is based convincingly on the idea that it is always in the hands of the parties to determine the quality owed. In the area of application of §474(1) s 2 of the German Civil Code, one need hardly be concerned that the vendor would auction new things off as used, in order to avoid the application of the law on the purchase of consumer goods, since he would normally obtain a lesser price. Furthermore, in the same area of application of §474(1) s 2 of the German Civil Code, i.e. at a public auction, the typical advantage in knowledge the vendor has over the purchaser is not assured. Conversely, the purchaser who buys an item for sale through public auction knows that a certain speculative element is inherent in the auction and regularly shows less confidence in the item than he would in a normal sale. The Senate is convinced of this because of the lesser need for protection of the buyer, and also to the general freedom of the parties to make agreements on quality. It is the very auctioning of animals, and the difficulty of defining boundaries which arises in this area, that lead clearly to relevant solutions if it is left to the parties to determine whether they want to start out on the basis of new or used animals. Wording and the legislative history of §474(1) s 2 do not conflict with this interpretation.

Notes

(1) This case was primarily concerned with the exclusion from the consumer sales rules of contracts for second-hand goods concluded at a public auction. The goods in this case were a horse, but for the purposes of sales-law, animals are treated as goods. Indeed, historically, sales law has evolved out of cases dealing with the sale of animals, including horses.[25]

(2) The court rejected the suggestion that the determination of goods as 'second-hand' should be approached objectively. Although it acknowledged the difficulty of adopting a satisfactory approach with regard to animals, it did consider

[25] For an English perspective, see P Mitchell, 'The Development of Quality Obligations in Sale of Goods' (2001) 117 *LQR* 645–63.

generally that the question of whether goods are properly regarded as 'second-hand' is for the parties to resolve. It may have been a factor that the sale took place at an auction.

(3) The German Federal Supreme Court (BGH), on appeal in this case,[26] took the view that animals should not as a general rule be regarded as 'used' or 'second-hand' goods. In particular, a young animal, or one that had, at the time of sale, not yet been used, for example, for breeding or—in the case of a horse—riding purposes, cannot be regarded as second-hand. Consequently, an animal which is objectively regarded as 'new' cannot be deemed by the parties as 'second-hand' by the terms of their contract.

LG (Court of first instance) Oldenburg, 30 March 2006[27] **5.13 (DE)**

SALE OF ANIMAL AT PUBLIC AUCTION

Horse with poor legs

The sale by auction of a horse which had been used for riding purposes was a sale of second-hand goods at a public auction and therefore not a consumer sales contract.

Facts: A horse was sold at public auction for €18,500. The terms and conditions of the auction stated that this was a public auction and that all horses were second-hand. The rules on consumer sales were excluded. The horse had various problems with its legs, but not all of these were known to the purchaser at the time of the auction. She therefore sued for the return of the purchase price.

Judgment: The horse in question is a used good as defined by §474(1) s 2 of the German Civil Code. The use of this classification for animals and the boundary with newly produced goods may well pose problems when dealing with foals. The definition under letter B of the defendant's conditions of auction, according to which horses, foals included, are considered as 'used goods as defined by law', does not help. Here an objective model must be applied irrespective of the terms and conditions of the defendant. The horse in question was already trained as a saddle horse before the auction. In this respect it is a used good. Ultimately the claimant does not manage to cast any serious doubt on this.

Note

In contrast to the previous case, the court here took the view that an objective standard has to be applied in determining whether the goods (another horse!) should be regarded as second-hand or not.

III.B SOFTWARE AND OTHER DIGITAL CONTENT

A difficult issue is the treatment of computer software and what has become known as 'digital content': should software and digital content be regarded as 'goods', or

[26] (2007) NJW 674–78.
[27] 9 O 2979/05 (2006) RdL 152; (2006) AUR 294.

would this be inappropriate? Answering this question is not straightforward. An initial distinction may be drawn between contracts for the sale of goods which incorporate software (such as a washing machine or a car, as well as a personal computer with pre-loaded software), and contracts for the separate supply of software (such as a wordprocessing package for a personal computer). In respect of the latter, a further distinction can be made between software supplied on a tangible medium (such as a CD-ROM) and software downloaded from the internet. Generally speaking, there is some uncertainty as to whether a contract involving the supply of software can properly be classified as a sale of goods. Where physical items are supplied (eg the washing machine, or the PC, or a CD-ROM), there can be little doubt that these physical items are, indeed, 'goods', but whether the software supplied in the same transaction is also 'goods' is unclear. Usually, software is not 'sold' in the sense that no property in the software is transferred—the user merely acquires a licence. Treating the supply of software and digital content as a 'sale of goods' could therefore cause conceptual difficulties. Arguably, the main concern, however, is not so much whether software is 'goods', but rather whether a supplier of software should be held to the same standard of liability as the seller of physical goods, and, if so, how this could best be achieved. If the concern is predominantly with subjecting a supplier to the obligation to supply software that is in conformity with the contract and make available remedies also available in contracts of sale, then it may be possible to apply the existing conformity requirement and remedies to contracts for the supply of software mutatis mutandis, but without confusing the essential definition of a contract for the sale of goods.

Court of Appeal, 26 July 1996[28] **5.14 (UK)**

St Albans City and District Council v International Computers Ltd

THE CLASSIFICATION OF SOFTWARE DEPENDS ON THE METHOD OF SUPPLY

No taxation with faulty software?

A contract for the supply of a program is subject to an implied term that it will be reasonably fit for achieving the intended purpose.

Facts: The supplier had provided the council (a public authority) with faulty computer software which resulted in a shortfall in the collection of local taxation.

Judgment: 'Is software goods?' To seek to answer this question, it is necessary first to be clear about the meaning of some of the words used in argument. In his judgment, Scott Baker J adopted a description of a computer system which contains the following passage which I have found helpful:

'By itself hardware can do nothing. The really important part of the system is the software. Programs are the instructions or commands that tell the hardware what to do. The program itself is an algorithm or formula. It is of necessity contained in a physical

[28] [1997] FSR 251.

medium. A program in machine readable form must be contained on a machine readable medium, such as paper cards, magnetic tapes, discs, drums or magnetic bubbles.' ...

Under the contract, [the claimants] were licensed to use the program. ... In both the Sale of Goods Act 1979 section 61 and the Supply of Goods and Services Act 1982 section 18 the definition of 'goods' 'includes all personal chattels other than things in action and money ...'. Clearly a disc is within this definition. Equally clearly, a program, of itself, is not. If a disc carrying a program is transferred, by way of sale or hire, and the program is in some way defective, so that it will not instruct or enable the computer to achieve the intended purpose, is this a defect in the disc? Put more precisely, would the seller or hirer of the disc be in breach of the terms as to quality and fitness for purpose implied by section 14 of the Sale of Goods Act and section 9 of the Act of 1982? ... There is no English authority on this question, and indeed we have been referred to none from any Common Law jurisdiction. ... Suppose I buy an instruction manual on the maintenance and repair of a particular make of car. The instructions are wrong in an important respect. Anybody who follows them is likely to cause serious damage to the engine of his car. In my view the instructions are an integral part of the manual. The manual including the instructions, whether in a book or a video cassette, would in my opinion be 'goods' within the meaning of the Sale of Goods Act, and the defective instructions would result in a breach of the [contract]. If this is correct, I can see no logical reason why it should not also be correct in relation to a computer disc onto which a program designed and intended to instruct or enable a computer to achieve particular functions has been encoded. If the disc is sold or hired by the computer manufacturer, but the program is defective, in my opinion there would prima facie be a breach of the terms as to quality and fitness for purpose implied by the Sale of Goods Act or the Act of 1982.

As I have already said, the program itself is not 'goods' within the statutory definition. Thus a transfer of the program [by the supplier installing the software directly on the claimant's computer] does not, in my view, constitute a transfer of goods. ... The answer must be sought in the Common Law ...In the absence of any express term as to quality or fitness for purpose, or of any term to the contrary, such a contract is subject to an implied term that the program will be reasonably fit for, i.e. reasonably capable of achieving the intended purpose.

Notes

(1) As will be seen below, English law utilises the 'implied terms' technique to provide for the conformity of the goods with the contract. Although mainly based on legislation, these terms evolved from common law, and the common law can be used to fill gaps in the legislation where necessary.

(2) Contrast this view with a Scottish case, *Beta Computers (Europe) Ltd v Adobe Systems Ltd*,[29] where Lord Penrose, the Lord Ordinary, suggested that the answer would not be in the law of sale, and that instead a contract for the supply of software should be regarded as a contract sui generis, with some of the characteristics of a sale and some of a licence. Do you think that this provides a better analysis?

In France, there is an example where the Cour de cassation applied *garantie des vices cachés* (Article 1641 of the Civil Code, see below), which is a remedy specific to sales

[29] [1996] SLT Rep 604.

contracts, in a case concerning the sale of a floppy disk containing a virus. There is an extract of the case below, but the application of *garantie des vices cachés* is very questionable.[30]

Cass comm, 25 November 1997[31] **5.15 (FR)**

LATENT DEFECTS

Floppy disk containing a virus

The garantie des vices cachés (as provided by Article 1641 of the Civil Code and following) applies to the sale of a floppy disk containing a virus even though the floppy disk had not been manufactured by the seller.

Facts: A floppy disk was sold with a computing magazine. The Agi 32 Company bought the magazine and as a consequence its computing system was infected by the virus. It brought an action against the publisher of the magazine who claimed that the floppy disk had not been manufactured by him. The Cour d'appel d'Agen (Court of Appeal) found the publisher liable on the ground of Article of the 1641 Civil Code. According to the Court of Appeal, the supply of the floppy disk could not be dissociated from the sale of the magazine and its supply was moreover advertised in the magazine itself in order to increase the sales. The seller asked the Cour de Cassation (Supreme Court) to review the decision of the Court of Appeal.

Judgment: According to the contested judgement (Agen 20 February 1995), the company Agi 32 bought an edition of a monthly computing magazine published by the company Exa publications, whose 'rights' were acquired by the company Excelsior. This magazine contained a floppy disk which was infected with a virus. Agi 32 instituted legal proceedings … Considering the claimant's second argument in its two subdivisions: The companies Exa publications and Excelsior informatique both objected to the judgement on the grounds that it ruled that the disputed floppy disk was part of the sales contract and that the company Excelsior informatique is liable for the damage caused to the company Agi 32 by the virus.

According to the appellant, on the one hand, since the disputed floppy disk, which was offered as a free gift (the price of the magazine remained unchanged), was not made by the company Excelsior informatique and since the default that arose from the virus was not linked to the sale of the product, the Court could not, without violating articles 1134 and 1641 of the Civil Code, find that the floppy disk was part of a sales contract and that the company was bound by the legal obligations of a seller. On the other hand, since the presence of the virus in the floppy disk arose from a fraudulent interference (which is why its producers have been prosecuted) which was beyond the control of the company that distributed the magazine, the Court of Appeal could not, without violating articles 1134 and 1641 of the Civil code a second time, find that an unavoidable and unforeseeable act of a third party was not proven.

However, on the one hand, the judgement states that given that the floppy disk was fixed in the middle of the magazine, it could not be physically disassociated from the magazine before it could be used independently. In addition, the judgment states that the magazine contained an advertisement on the front of the cover which drew attention

[30] See further P Jourdain, 'Le virus informatique, la force majeure et le risque de développement' [1998] *RTDciv* 386–88.

[31] [1998] CCC commentaire 43.

to the free floppy disk. This advertisement was clearly designed to increase sales. The logo 'Soft et micro' was displayed on the floppy disk, which indicated the participation of the company Exa publications in its distribution. Given all of these considerations, the Court of Appeal rightly decided that the floppy disk constituted a component of the sales contract, and that from that moment onwards the company Exa publications was bound by the legal obligations of a seller.

On the other hand, the judgment maintains that the risk of contamination by a virus is a known risk in the IT industry (in recent years much literature on the subject has been produced, antivirus software has been brought up to date, and a real defence strategy against the risk of contamination has been put in place). It also states that the company Excelsior had created an antivirus software, which confirms its competence in this area and underlines its professional qualities. The judgment also discloses that the company had tested a 'trial' disk in order, illustrating that such a check was common and feasible.In light of all of these considerations. The Court of Appeal has therefore been able to conclude that an unavoidable and unforeseeable act of a third party was not proven.

It follows that none of the arguments' subdivisions are founded …

Given these considerations:

The appeal is rejected.

Note

The question of how digitial content/software should be treated was raised in the Green Paper on the reform of the consumer acquis (2007).[32] In considering whether to adopt legislation on this matter, the Commission said the following (at 25):

> The lack of coverage of contracts for the supply of software and data (so called 'contracts providing digital content') is a particularly important problem. With the increase in digital content consumption, questions of liability (eg when software damages hardware) and guarantee from defects will grow in importance. Several consumer complaints point, for instance, to problems with music downloaded from the internet or used in MP3 players, software and digital content to be used in mobile phones (eg ring tones). An extension of the coverage of consumer protection rules to such situations would allow consumers to make use of remedies for nonconformity and obtain damages. Such an extension of the scope of the Directive may, however, require specific rules since digital content is usually licensed rather than sold to the consumers.

For a similar discussion in the context of product liability, see chapter 7.III.B.

IV. GOODS MUST BE IN CONFORMITY WITH THE CONTRACT

The main obligation of the seller is to deliver goods which are in conformity with the contract. This test encapsulates the statutory quality standard required of the goods. The relevant parts of Article 2 of the Consumer Sales Directive provide as follows.

[32] COM [2006] 744.

Consumer Sales Directive (99/44/EC) **5.16 (EU)**

Article 2 (1) The seller must deliver goods to the consumer which is in conformity with the contract of sale.

(2) Consumer goods are presumed to be in conformity with the contract if they:

(a) comply with the description given by the seller and possess the qualities of the goods which the seller has held out to the consumer as a sample or model;

(b) are fit for any particular purpose for which the consumer requires them and which he made known to the seller at the time of conclusion of the contract and which the seller has accepted;

(c) are fit for the purposes for which goods of the same type are normally used;

(d) show the quality and performance which are normal in goods of the same type and which the consumer can reasonably expect, given the nature of the goods and taking into account any public statements on the specific characteristics of the goods made about themby the seller, the producer or his representative, particularly in advertising or on labelling. …

(4) The seller shall not be bound by public statements, as referred to in paragraph 2(d) if he:

—shows that he was not, and could not reasonably have been, aware of the statement inquestion,

—shows that by the time of conclusion of the contract the statement had been corrected, or

—shows that the decision to buy the consumer goods could not have been influenced by the statement.

(5) Any lack of conformity resulting from incorrect installation of the consumer goods shall be deemed to be equivalent to lack of conformity of the goods if installation forms part of the contract of sale of the goods and the goods were installed by the seller or under his responsibility. This shall apply equally if the product, intended to be installed by the consumer, is installed by the consumer and the incorrect installation is due to a shortcoming in the installation instructions.

Notes

(1) Perhaps the most significant aspect of this test is the express inclusion of 'public statements' (Article 2(2)(d)), whether made by the seller or the producer, about the goods. Thus, general advertising can affect a consumer's expectation regarding the quality of the goods, and this is reflected in the criteria to be applied in establishing the goods' conformity with the contract. However, this is mitigated somewhat by Article 2(4), according to which such public statements will not be relevant where the seller (!) could not have been aware of the statement or where the statement had been corrected (which raises the question of the steps that would have to be taken to satisfy this exclusion), as well as where the consumer's decision to buy could not have been influenced by the statement. With regard to the consumer's position, it remains to be seen when a consumer could not have been influenced: this might simply be the case where the evidence shows that the consumer did not know of the statement at all, but perhaps also where the statement is obviously exaggerated (an advertising puff). Note that the burden of proof in all cases is on the seller.

(2) It was seen earlier that the Directive extends to circumstances where goods have to be installed, and incorrect installation resulting in a lack of conformity effectively means that the goods are not in conformity with the contract according to Article 2(5). Note that this does not mean that a consumer can claim that the goods were not in conformity simply because the installation instructions had a shortcoming (eg by being unclear or missing out information), but rather because the shortcomings caused the consumer to undertake the installation in a manner to resulted in a lack of conformity.[33]

(3) Interestingly, the transposition of this requirement into both German and English law departs from this provision significantly. German law starts with the qualities of the goods as agreed between the parties—party autonomy remains paramount. Insofar as there is no agreement, criteria equivalent to those in Article 2(2) lits (c) and (d) apply, although there is no equivalent to lits (a) and (b)—these matters are part of the 'agreed qualities'.

IV.A NO 'CONFORMITY' REQUIREMENT IN ENGLISH LAW

English law does not adopt a 'conformity with the contract' requirement at all, relying instead on the statutorily implied terms that have developed over several centuries and were first codified in 1893 and modernised in 1994. The relevant provisions of English law are as follows.

IV.A.1 CORRESPONDENCE WITH DESCRIPTION

Sale of Goods Act 1979 **5.17 (UK)**

Section 13 Sale by description

(1) Where there is a contract for the sale of goods by description, there is an implied term that the goods will correspond with the description.

Notes

(1) The case-law on section 13 has refined the scope of that section. It is clear that not every description applied to particular goods is regarded as a description for the purposes of the section. Thus, it has been held that it requires a broad commercial definition of the goods, but should not be approached in an excessively technical manner[34]—the description should identify the essential commercial characteristics of the goods.[35]

[33] Generally, C Willett and D Oughton, 'Liability for Incorrect Installation and Other Services Associated with Consumer Goods' in G Howells, A Nordhausen, D Parry and C Twigg-Flesner (eds), *The Yearbook of Consumer Law 2007* (Aldershot, Ashgate, 2007).

[34] *Ashington Piggeries Ltd v Christopher Hill Ltd* [1972] AC 441.

[35] *Reardon Smith Lines v Hansen Tangen* [1976] 1 WLR 989.

(2) In *Harlingdon Leinster Ents v Christopher Hull Fine Arts*,[36] the (non-consumer) buyer was an expert in German expressionist paintings interested in a painting labelled 'painted by Gabriele Münter'. The seller emphasised that he had no expertise in German expressionist painting, and that the attribution of the painting to Münter was based on the auction catalogue. It was discovered subsequently that that painting was not by Münter after all and not worth very much. The Court of Appeal reaffirmed the fact that section 13 was concerned with the essential commercial characteristics of the goods, and added to this that the description must be one on which the parties would reasonably expect the buyer to rely. As the buyer was himself an expert in the the style of painting, there was no reliance, and consequently no breach of the term implied by section 13.

IV.A.2 QUALITY AND FITNESS FOR PARTICULAR PURPOSE

Sale of Goods Act 1979 **5.18 (UK)**

Section 14 Implied terms about quality or fitness

(2) Where the seller sells goods in the course of a business, there is an implied term that the goods supplied under the contract are of satisfactory quality.

(2A) For the purposes of this Act, goods are of satisfactory quality if they meet the standard that a reasonable person would regard as satisfactory, taking account of any description of the goods, the price (if relevant) and all the other relevant circumstances.

(2B) For the purposes of this Act, the quality of goods includes their state and condition and the following (among others) are in appropriate cases aspects of the quality of goods—

(a) fitness for all the purposes for which goods of the kind in question are commonly supplied,

(b) appearance and finish,

(c) freedom from minor defects,

(d) safety, and

(e) durability. …

(2D) If the buyer deals as consumer or, in Scotland, if a contract of sale is a consumer contract, the relevant circumstances mentioned in subsection (2A) above include any public statements on the specific characteristics of the goods made about them by the seller, the producer or his representative, particularly in advertising or on labelling.

(2E) A public statement is not by virtue of subsection (2D) above a relevant circumstance for the purposes of subsection (2A) above in the case of a contract of sale, if the seller shows that—

(a) at the time the contract was made, he was not, and could not reasonably have been, aware of the statement,

(b) before the contract was made, the statement had been withdrawn in public or, to the extent that it contained anything which was incorrect or misleading, it had been corrected in public, or

(c) the decision to buy the goods could not have been influenced by the statement.

[36] [1990] 1 All ER 737.

(2F) Subsections (2D) and (2E) above do not prevent any public statement from being a relevant circumstance for the purposes of subsection (2A) above (whether or not the buyer deals as consumer or, in Scotland, whether or not the contract of sale is a consumer contract) if the statement would have been such a circumstance apart from those subsections.

(3) Where the seller sells goods in the course of a business and the buyer, expressly or by implication, makes known—

(a) to the seller, or

(b) where the purchase price or part of it is payable by instalments and the goods were previously sold by a credit-broker to the seller, to that credit-broker,

any particular purpose for which the goods are being bought, there is an implied term that the goods supplied under the contract are reasonably fit for that purpose, whether or not that is a purpose for which such goods are commonly supplied, except where the circumstances show that the buyer does not rely, or that it is unreasonable for him to rely, on the skill or judgment of the seller or credit-broker.

Notes

(1) In *Jewson Ltd v Boyhan*,[37] the (non-consumer) buyer had acquired a building that he converted into flats. Each flat was to have individual heating boilers, and he asked the defendant builders' merchant for advice. The seller identified an electric boiler which, according to the promotional literature, would be a cost-effective alternative to gas boilers. However, after their installation, it was discovered that the boilers did not provide acceptable energy-efficiency ratings, making the flats less attractive to potential buyers. It was argued that the boilers were neither of satisfactory quality, nor fit for purpose, but this was rejected by the Court of Appeal. The Court commented on where it thought the dividing line between the terms implied by sections 14(2) and 14(3) should lie: the former section laid down a general quality standard, whereas the latter section was relevant to the particular circumstances affecting the specific case. In short, section 14(2) focused on the intrinsic aspects of the goods, whereas section 14(3) was concerned with their extrinsic features. The impact on the flats' energy efficiency ratings was an extrinsic factor and did not affect the boilers' functionality as such. Quite where the line between 'intrinsic' and 'extrinsic' aspects is to be drawn may be difficult to determine in individual cases.

(2) Although there is no 'conformity with the contract' requirement, there is a definition of this notion in section 48(F) of the Sale of Goods Act 1979, which states that

> [f]or the purposes of this Part [dealing with the consumer-specific remedies], goods do not conform to a contract of sale if there is, in relation to the goods, a breach of an express term of the contract or a term implied by s 13, 14 or 15 above.

This is only relevant for the specific remedies applicable in consumer sales contracts.

(3) The technique used here is that of the 'implied term'. Every contract of sale will therefore automatically contain these terms.

[37] [2004] 1 Lloyd's Rep 505.

The position in France is also rather complex. Since the implementation of the Consumer Sales Directive in 2005, there are now three types of requirements to be considered when dealing with the conformity with the contract under French law. As a consequence of the implementation of the directive in the Consumer Code rather than in the Civil Code, the remedies first introduced in 1804 still exist. They are to be found in Articles 1604, 1641 and 1642. Some provisions exclusively relating to consumer sales are to be found in Articles L 211-1ff of the Consumer Code. According to Article L 211-13 of the Consumer Code, the plaintiff has the possibility to choose between the remedies provided by the Civil Code or the Consumer Code.

Code civil **5.19 (FR)**

Article 1604 Delivery is the transfer of the good sold into the power and possession of the buyer.

Article 1641 A seller is bound to a warranty on account of the latent defects of the good sold which render it unfit for the use for which it was intended, or which so impair that use that the buyer would not have acquired it, or would only have given a lesser price for it, had he known of them.

Article 1642 A seller is not liable for defects which are patent and which the buyer could ascertain for himself.

Notes

(1) The Consumer Sales Directive (99/44/EC) was implemented in France in 2005 by Decree No 2005-136 of 17 February 2005 concerning the warranty for non-conformity of goods sold to a consumer.[38] The provisions of the Decree were inserted in the Consumer Code. It is still too early for leading case-law on these provisions to have emerged. In particular, consumers can still rely the Civil Code provisions, and these, to some extent, better protect their interests than the provisions of the Consumer Code.

(2) The main problem concerning the warranties provided by the French Civil Code is to understand which rules apply when there is a non-conformity problem.

(3) Conformity under Article 1604: theoretically speaking, Article 1604 only deals with delivery. However, case-law relating to non-conformity issues developed on this ground. The reason is that the concept of delivery has been interpreted as delivery in conformity with the parties' expectations. The Cour de cassation held that if there is non-conformity with the contract of the good delivered, there is no delivery in the sense of Article 1604. In order to comply with the provisions of Article 1604, the good delivered has to be in conformity with 'the exact aim intended by the buyer'.[39] As a consequence, the distinction between the conformity requirement of

[38] Ordonnance relative à la garantie de la conformité du bien au contrat due par le vendeur au consommateur, JORF 18 February 2005.

[39] 'chose qui correspond en tous points au but recherché par lui', Cass civ 1e, 20 March 1989, Bull civ I No 140.

Article 1604 as interpreted by the Cour de cassation and the conformity requirement of Article 1641 became difficult to understand, especially because the remedies related to Article 1604 were more convenient to the buyer because of the time limits (see below). The third chambre civile dissented, considering that the requirement of delivery in conformity was met if the nature and quality of the good were in conformity with the contract.[40] The Cour de cassation later draws a clear distinction between the two concepts (see below). Article 1615 of the Civil Code states that the obligation to deliver also includes the accessories and all that was designed for the perpetual use of the good.

(4) Conformity under Article 1641: the provisions of Article 1641 are quite clear. The good is said not to be in conformity where the latent defects of the good render it unfit for the use for which it was intended, or impair that use. The main issue was, however, to distinguish this type of conformity (*garantie des vices cachés*) with the one provided by Article 1604, especially with regard to the decision of the first chambre civile mentioned above of 20 March 1989. A consensus was eventually reached when the first chambre civile agreed with the third one by holding that a defect of the good could not be considered as a non-conformity at delivery in the sense of Article 1604.

Cass civ 1e, 5 May 1993[41] **5.20 (FR)**

APPLICATION OF ARTICLE 1641 OF THR CIVIL CODE WHERE THE GOOD IS 'UNFIT FOR NORMAL USE'

The frozen tiles

Hidden defect claims are not a non-conformity at delivery issue.

Facts: Mr and Mrs Gosse bought tiles and installed them on the roof of their house. The tiles appeared to be defective: they had been broken by the frost, and BMB, the company which sold them, agreed to give the Gosses 1,000 free tiles. The free tiles were also defective, and the Gosses eventually brought a suit against the BMB company to obtain compensation. The Cour d'Appel (Court of Appeal) of Amiens held that the Gosses were not entitled to compensation since they did not meet the requirements set by Article 1648 of the Civil Code. According to this Article at that time, any action under Article 1648 had to be brought within a short period after the discovery of the defect. Mr and Mrs Gosse appealed to the Cour de cassation (Supreme Court), invoking Article 1604, which does not provide for a time limit.

Judgment: Considering the claimant's sole argument in its three parts:

According to the judgment of the lower instance judges, in April 1974, the Gosses bought tiles from the company Blocs et matériaux du Beauvaisis (BMB). The Gosses installed the tiles themselves on the roof of their house. Defects appeared on the tiles in 1976 and BMB gave them 1000 free tiles. This cracking of tiles spread in 1982 when almost the entire roof was affected. On 9 September 1983, the Gosses filed a claim against BMB to compensate for the damages they suffered. The contested judgement (Amiens, 29 May 1990) dismissed their action, on the grounds that it had not been brought during the short time limit provided for in article 1648 of the Civil Code;

[40] Cass civ 3e, 23 October 1991, Bull civ III No 249.

[41] Bull civ I No 158.

The Gosses raised objection to the judgement for having ruled in such a way. First, according to their argument, a seller cannot be said to have fulfilled his delivery obligations if he delivers a faulty item which does not correspond in any way to the item originally ordered by the customer. In restricting the delivery obligation to the matters anticipated and accounted for in the contracts of the two parties, the contested judgement violated Article 1603 of the Civil Code.

Secondly, the purchaser to whom a faulty good has been delivered can bring an action against the seller for a warranty against hidden defects, as set out in Article 1641 of the Civil Code, and an action for contractual liability, as set out in Article 1147 of that code. In acknowledging only the first of these claims, the Court of Appeal violated the aforementioned articles. Finally, the Gosses did not bring an action for annulment of the sale, but only asked that the damage they suffered be repaired. In subordinating the admissibility of this action to Article 1648 of the Civil Code, when in fact it was a contractual liability claim under general contract law rules, the contested judgement violated Articles 1147, 1641 and 1648 of the Civil Code;

However, hidden defects (defined as defects which rendered the goods unfit for the use for which they were intended) do not allow for a claim to be brought in contract. Rather, they allow for a warranty under the conditions set out in Article 1641ff of the Civil Code. Having disclosed that BMB had provided the tiles, the inadequate quality of which had been recognized by an expert, and having acknowledged that more than a year had elapsed between the discovery of the defect and the issuing of the summons, the Court of Appeal could decide that the claim was not brought during the time period specified in Article 1648 of the Civil Code. The Court thus legally justifies its decision. It follows that none of the argument's elements can be upheld.

Given these considerations: the appeal is rejected.

Note

This case was then identified as a leading one since the chambre commerciale followed it[42] as well as further decisions of the first chambre civile.[43] The criterion of conformity with the contract under Article 1604 is now the agreed specifications (*spécifications convenues*),[44] ie the specifications agreed by the parties. However in case of existing business relationships the court used the criterion of 'usual contractual specifications'.[45]

The following extract is from an English case involving a consumer and is of considerable relevance even today.

[42] Cass comm, 26 April 1994, Bull civ IV No 159; Cass comm, 31 May 1994, Bull civ IV No 199.

[43] Cass civ 1e, 27 October 1993, Bull civ I No 305; Cass civ 1e, 8 December 1993, Bull civ I No 362.

[44] Cass civ 1e, 16 June 1993, Bull civ I No 287.

[45] Cass civ 1e, 30 March 1999, Bull civ I No 118.

Court of Appeal, 5 November 1986[46] **5.21 (UK)**
Rogers v Parish (Scarborough) Ltd

CRITERIA RELEVANT TO ESTABLISHING CONFORMITY

Range Rover with faults

Goods may not be in conformity with the contract despite the fact that several minor defects could be repaired easily.

Facts: The claimants bought a new Range Rover, but the car had several defects. The dealer replaced the car, but the replacement vehicle also had many faults. Eventually, the consumer rejected the car, arguing that it was not of merchantable (now: satisfactory) quality.

Judgment: There are two respects in which the judge in my opinion applied a test which was not that of section 14(6) ... He gave much weight to the fact that the defects were capable of repair and that the first defendant had in some measure been able to repair them. Yet the fact that a defect is reparable does not prevent it from making the res vendita unmerchantable if it is of a sufficient degree: see *Lee v. York Coach and Marine* [1977] RTR 35.

The fact, if it was a fact, that the defect had been repaired at the instance of the purchaser, which in the present case does not appear to be so, ... cannot in my view be material to the question of merchantability which falls to be judged at the moment of delivery. Furthermore, the judge applied the test of whether the defects had destroyed the workable character of the car. No doubt this echoed an argument similar to the one developed before us that if a vehicle is capable of starting and being driven in safety from one point to the next on public roads and on whatever other surfaces the car is supposed to be able to negotiate, it must necessarily be merchantable. I can only say that this proposition appears to have no relation to the broad test propounded by section 14(6) even if, in certain particular circumstances, the correct inference would be that no more could be expected of the goods sold.

This being so, I think it legitimate to look at the whole issue afresh with direct reference to the words of section 14(6). Starting with the purpose for which 'goods of that kind' are commonly bought, one would include in respect of any passenger vehicle not merely the buyer's purpose of driving the car from one place to another but of doing so with the appropriate degree of comfort, ease of handling and reliability and, one might add, of pride in the vehicle's outward and interior appearance. What is the appropriate degree and what relative weight is to be attached to one characteristic of the car rather than another will depend on the market at which the car is aimed.

To identify the relevant expectation one must look at the factors listed in the subsection. The first is the description applied to the goods. In the present case the vehicle was sold as new. Deficiencies which might be acceptable in a secondhand vehicle were not to be expected in one purchased as new. Next, the description 'Range Rover' would conjure up a particular set of expectations, not the same as those relating to an ordinary saloon car, as to the balance between performance, handling, comfort and resilience. The factor of price was also significant. At more than GBP 14,000 this vehicle was, if not at the top end of the scale, well above the level of the ordinary family saloon. The buyer was entitled to value for his money.

[46] [1987] QB 933.

With these factors in mind, can it be said that the Range Rover as delivered was as fit for the purpose as the buyer could reasonably expect? The point does not admit of elaborate discussion. I can only say that to my mind the defects in engine, gearbox and bodywork, the existence of which is no longer in dispute, clearly demand a negative answer.

Notes

(1) This case was decided before the current version of section 14(2) had been adopted. Prior to 1995, the test applied by the English courts was whether goods were of 'merchantable' quality. This was defined in section 14(6) thus:

> Goods of any kind are of merchantable quality … if they are as fit for the purpose or purposes for which goods of that kind are commonly bought as it is reasonable to expect having regard to any description applied to them, the price (if relevant) and all the other relevant circumstances.

Although the current test is worded differently, the decision in *Rogers v Parish* remains a good illustration of how various factors need to be taken into account and balanced to come to a conclusion on whether goods are satisfactory or not. However, as emphasised in *Thain v Anniesland Trade Centre* (below), all the cases on satisfactory quality turn on their facts, and earlier decisions are of limited value as precedents.

(2) In *Lee v York Coach and Marine*[47] (referred to in the judgment above), the consumer had bought a second-hand car which was seven years old. It was supplied with a new MOT certificate. The car had to be returned twice during the following fortnight for repairs, and was only used for a few short journeys. When the defendant refused to carry out further repairs, it was discovered that the car was not in a condition in which an MOT certificate should have been issued. The Court of Appeal held that the car, whilst it could be driven, was not in a roadworthy condition and therefore not of merchantable quality.

(3) In this case, the Court emphasised that the fact that a defect can be repaired does not mean that the goods are in conformity with the contract. The reason for this view is that the quality of the goods has to be assessed at the time of delivery. If goods are faulty at that point in time, they are not in conformity with the contract, even though the non-conformity could easily be cured by repair.

(4) The Court also considered the relevance of a manufacturer's guarantee in establishing whether the goods had reached the statutory quality standard. This aspect of the case is discussed below at 5.49 (UK).

UK law does not have a reduced liability period for second-hand goods; instead, it relies on a flexible application of the 'satisfactory quality' test, as illustrated by the following case.

[47] [1977] RTR 35.

Sheriff Court of Glasgow and Strathkelvin, 7 August 1997[48] **5.22 (UK)**
Thain v Anniesland Trade Centre

QUALITY TO BE EXPECTED FROM SECOND-HAND GOODS

Second-hand car with faulty gearbox

It is reasonable to expect that a second-hand car may break down soon after purchase.

Facts: The consumer had bought a second-hand car which was five years old and had travelled around 80,000 miles (120,000 kilometres). Soon after, it developed a fault in the gearbox which was uneconomic to repair, rendering the car useless. The consumer claimed that the car was not of satisfactory quality.

Judgment: [The Sheriff Principal (N D MacLeod, QC)] ... two aspects of quality, fitness and durability, were explored at the proof ... the [consumer]'s solicitor's argument in respect of fitness and his argument in respect of durability were based upon the simple fact that a car costing GBP 2,995 gave acceptable service for only a few weeks. That fact, he submitted, indicated that the Renault had not been reasonably fit for its purpose and that it had not been of reasonable durability when supplied. Within a very few weeks a component wore out with the result that the Renault could no longer be used. ... The solicitor for the defenders drew attention to the facts on which the sheriff had reached his conclusion. The sheriff had found that the price, GBP 2,995, was reasonable for a secondhand Renault 19 automatic between five and six years old which had done approximately 80,000 miles. ... What [the sheriff] required to consider was whether, when supplied, the Renault failed the standard that a reasonable person would regard as satisfactory in respect of its fitness for its purpose and its durability. ... The Renault was tested before purchase by witnesses experienced in judging secondhand cars. ... None of them detected then any of the symptoms of the defect which manifested themselves later. After acquiring the Renault the pursuer drove it for a period. During that period of use the Renault proved reasonably fit for its purpose. The pursuer apparently found it capable of being driven safely and effectively, and drove it from A to B with the degree of comfort, ease of handling and reliability that one might reasonably demand. The symptoms that, according to the expert evidence before the sheriff, indicated wear developing in a differential bearing were not apparent when the car was tested before purchase. They appeared only after the pursuer began to use the car. That does seem to me to provide a justifiable basis for the sheriff's conclusion that the defect was not present when the Renault was supplied to the pursuer but developed after a period of use by the pursuer, albeit a very short period of use. The fact that it gave such a very short period of use before developing the defect complained of is a fact which, it seems to me, in the circumstances of this case, relates to durability as an aspect of reasonable quality rather than to fitness. ... If one buys a new car one can reasonably expect to use it for at least the guarantee period without experiencing the failure of an important component or system. But if one continues to run that car for five or six years until it has something like 80,000 miles on the clock, one has run it well into the area of risk that a component or system may fail. That failure may prove expensive, even uneconomic to rectify. Cars vary in the length of trouble free use they provide, even within the same marque and model, but the 'reasonable person' accepts that the risk of failure and the need for expensive repair increases with the increasing age and use of a car. People who

48 [1997] SLT (Sh Ct) 102.

are sufficiently well off financially to do so usually replace their cars before they reach the age and mileage that involves them in that risk. People who buy secondhand cars get them at less than the original price in large part because secondhand cars have attached to them increased risk of expensive repairs. The price of the Renault, GBP 2,995, was considered reasonable because there was the risk of expensive repair attached to the Renault. In choosing to buy the Renault the pursuer accepted the risk of expensive repair inevitably attaching to a car that was between five and six years old which had over 80,000 miles on the clock.

Notes

(1) This case was decided by a Scottish court, rather than an English court, but it involves the application of provisions of the Sale of Goods Act 1979 which are applicable in both jurisdictions.

(2) This was also the first reported case in the United Kingdom on the new requirement that goods must be of satisfactory (as opposed to merchantable) quality. In *Thain*, the judge took the view that earlier case-law was of limited assistance, although it remains the position that earlier cases are considered by the courts when applying the current test. Also, the judge emphasised that each case will turn on its own facts, which means that even similar cases may produce contrasting outcomes on the question of whether goods are of satisfactory quality.[49]

IV.B LOWERING EXPECTATIONS

The 'conformity with the contract' standard is inherently flexible to suit the circumstances of each particular case. Consequently, establishing whether goods are in conformity requires that the factors listed in Article 2(2) of the Consumer Sales Directive (or in the corresponding national legislation) are taken into account. Of particular significance is the description of the goods. We have already seen that in English law, the descriptive words that are relevant are those identifying the essential characteristics of the goods and are intended to be relied upon by the buyer. In addition, the way the goods are described can affect the assessment of whether they are of 'satisfactory quality'. Similarly, in German law, the 'agreed qualities' of the goods will be based on the way they have been described. This raises the interesting issue of just how significant a description will be, and—perhaps more significantly—how accurate it should be. Invariably, if the description promises more than the goods can offer, the consumer will have a remedy, but what would be the case if the description of the goods indicated that they are of very low quality (even when their actual quality is higher)? The following case offers a good example.

[49] See JN Adams and R Brownsword, 'Law Reform, Law Jobs, and Law Commission No 160' (1988) 51 *Mod LR* 481–92.

OLG (Court of Appeal) Oldenburg, 22 September 2003[50] **5.23 (DE)**

IMPACT OF DESCRIPTION ON CONFORMITY

Kit-car for the road

A general description intended to lower or exclude the conformity requirement is ineffective if that description is incompatible with all the relevant circumstances of the sale.

Facts: A second-hand car described as a *Bastlerfahrzeug* (kit-car) was sold for €4,900. The seller was a car-dealer rather than a scrap-metal dealer, and the consumer had acquired the car for use on the road, rather than to harvest parts for use on another vehicle.

Judgment: In accordance with §475 I 1 of the German Civil Code, the defendant cannot claim to have sold the vehicle without warranty as a kit-car. As the claimant is a consumer and the defendant a seller, the sales contract concluded between the parties should be qualified as a sale of consumer goods as defined by §§474ff of the German Civil Code. This means that the defendant cannot categorically exclude the warranty for possible defects, and that circumventing this prohibition is ineffective (§475 I 2 German Civil Code). The description of the car as a kit-car represents one such circumvention of §475 I 1 of the German Civil Code. The defendant itself admits in its written submissions that the formulation 'kit-car' was selected by her because it felt unable to warrant that the car was free from defects, and not, therefore, because it was thought that the car was no longer fit for use on the road due to its condition. The claimant, who is not a car mechanic but a sailor, was only interested in purchasing a car for driving and not for parts. This should moreover live up to business expectations when a potential customer, as in this case, approaches a professional car dealer and not a scrap dealer. This consideration is confirmed in the price demanded for the vehicle by the defendant, namely 4.900. As a brief internet search on relevant sites will prove, this is consistent with the current price for used cars of the model sold, with corresponding mileage. In other words, the defendant asked the current market price for a used car of equivalent quality. The defendant, who carries the burden of proof in this respect, did not give any other reasons to believe that in fact the parties could only have intended a car for parts and not for driving on the road.

The aforementioned considerations, which result in the liability of the defendant, cannot be successfully challenged by arguing that the claimant entered the agreement voluntarily, because it follows from §475 of the German Civil Code that in case of a sale of consumer goods, the waiver of the legal warranty claims is withdrawn from a private, autonomous agreement, so that the question, disputed in this context, as to whether the claimant grasped the meaning of the description at all, no longer needs to be investigated.

Note

In this case, the court had an opportunity to address a debate as to whether the required level of quality can be lowered below what would be regarded as a usual standard through an agreement between the parties, eg by describing a car as 'wreck',

[50] (2004) DAR 92.

or, as in the present situation, a 'kit car'. Such a description has the effect of considerably reducing the level of quality that might be expected. If the goods are, indeed, 'wrecks', then such a description would be accurate, but if, as in this case, the description does not bear any relation to the actual state of the goods, then using such a description could be equivalent to an attempt to exclude the legal rights of consumers altogether.

IV.C DISCLOSURE OF FAULTS

The rationale for the general conformity standard is that the description of goods, advertising and other public statements, and other factors, create certain expectations regarding the quality of the goods. If the goods meet such expectations, then they are in conformity with the contract. This does not mean that the goods have to be perfect, but they should not have any significant shortcomings.

The conformity requirement is often regarded as a form of disclosure rule. In that sense, the seller has information about the quality of the goods to which the consumer is not privy. The consumer—with more limited information—has certain expectations regarding the goods. This creates an incentive for the seller to disclose relevant information about the goods, particularly if the availability of this information would affect the consumer's expectations. In the literature, this has variously described as a duty of disclosure,[51] an 'indirect information requirement'[52] or an 'encouragement to provide information'.[53] This is further reinforced by provisions such as Article 2(3) of the Consumer Sales Directive, according to which a consumer is unable to raise a lack of conformity of which he had knowledge at the time the transaction was entered into.

Consumer Sales Directive (99/44/EC) **5.24 (EU)**

Article 2 (3) There shall be deemed not to be a lack of conformity for the purposes of this Article if, at the time the contract was concluded, the consumer was aware, or could not reasonably be unaware of, the lack of conformity, or if the lack of conformity has its origin in materials supplied by the consumer.

A similar provision, which is perhaps more favourable to a consumer than the Consumer Sales Directive, can be found in English law.

[51] For relevant further analysis, see eg K Riesenhuber, 'Party Autonomy and Information in the Sales Directive' in S Grundmann, W Kerber and S Weatherill (eds), *Party Autonomy and the Role of Information in the Internal Market* (Berlin, De Gruyter, 2001) or S Hedley, 'Quality of Goods, Information, and the Death of Contract' [2001] *J Bus Law* 114–25.

[52] T Wilhelmsson, 'Private Law Remedies against Breach of Information Requirements of EC Law' in R Schulze, M Ebers and HC Grigoleit (eds), *Informationspflichten und Vertragsschluss in Acquis communautaire* (Tübingen, Mohr Siebeck, 2003).

[53] C Twigg-Flesner, 'Information Disclosure about the Quality of Goods—Duty or Encouragement?' in G Howells, A Janssen and R Schulze (eds), *Information Rights and Obligations* (Aldershot, Ashgate, 2005).

Sale of Goods Act 1979 (as amended) **5.25 (UK)**

Section 14 Implied terms about quality or fitness

(2C) The term implied by subsection (2) above does not extend to any matter making the quality of goods unsatisfactory—

(a) which is specifically drawn to the buyer's attention before the contract is made,

(b) where the buyer examines the goods before the contract is made, which that examination ought to reveal, or

(c) in the case of a contract for sale by sample, which would have been apparent on a reasonable examination of the sample.

The following case raises interesting points for discussion.

Court of Appeal, 2 April 2004[54] **5.26 (UK)**
Bramhill v Edwards

OBLIGATION TO INSPECT GOODS BEFORE SALE

The extra-wide motorhome

A representation made about aspects of the goods can be sufficient to alert the buyer to another aspect that could affect their quality.

Facts: The claimants had purchased a US-manufactured second-hand motorhome. It was not discovered until some time after the sale that the motorhome was slightly wider than permitted by the applicable British regulations regarding road vehicles. Before concluding the contract, the claimants had inspected the interior of the motorhome, but had not measured it on the outside. They claimed that there was a breach of the term implied by section 14(2) of the Sale of Goods Act 1979 that goods must be of satisfactory quality.

Judgment: [Auld LJ] If I am correct in my view that the Judge wrongly found the [motorhome] to be of unsatisfactory quality on the illegality issue, this issue is academic. However, in deference to counsel's submissions, I shall deal with it. ... The question of inspection only became a relevant issue in the event of the Judge finding, as he did, that there had been a representation as to width, albeit as he found, only as to internal width. On such a finding, given Mr and Mrs Bramhill's case that they were aware before the contract that a 102 inches wide vehicle breached the Regulations, the issue arose whether Mr Edwards representation as found by the Judge should have prompted them to measure the width of the vehicle. ... Mr Fletcher sought the permission of the Court to amend the respondents' notice, to uphold the Judge's finding under section 14(2C) under sub-paragraph (a), in addition to sub-paragraph (b), namely that the matter constituting the unsatisfactory quality had been 'specifically drawn to the buyer's attention before the contract ... [was] made'. He submitted that, on the strength of Mr Bramhill's evidence to the Judge that, when he bought the Dolphin, he knew that the maximum permitted width of such a vehicle in this country was 100 inches, coupled with the Judge's finding that Mr Edwards had represented the interior width to be 100 inches, he had specifically drawn to Mr and Mrs Bramhill's attention that the external width must have been greater than permitted. It is clear from the evidence, Mr Fletcher submitted, that Mr and Mrs

[54] [2004] EWCA Civ 403.

Bramhill examined the Dolphin more than once before buying it and, on the Judge's finding as to the nature of Mr Edwards' representation, should have appreciated without measuring the vehicle that it exceeded the maximum permissible width. Given the Judge's finding, which I would uphold, that Mr Edwards made a representation as to the interior width of the Dolphin and that that should have alerted Mr and Mrs Bramhill to the fact that the over-all width was in excess of the permitted limit, this argument merges with that on the primary issue on which, as I have said, Mr Edwards should succeed. It also overlaps with the defence under section 14(2C)(b) of buyer's inspection, on which, as I have said, I would also, if necessary have upheld the Judge's finding.

Notes

(1) The observations by Auld LJ are only obiter dicta, ie they do not form part of the decision in the case. His views have two aspects: the buyers ought to have been alerted about the problem because (i) they inspected the interior of the motorhome and were aware of the requirements of the regulations, and should have examined the motorhome for compliance; and (ii) the information they had been given by the seller ought to have alerted them about the problem.

(2) On the first point, section 14(2C)(b) only applies if the buyer does, in fact, examine the goods, and it is only matters which this particular examination should have revealed that are excluded from the satisfactory quality/conformity requirement. The mere opportunity to examine is not enough to bring that section into play. On the facts, had the buyers measured the outside width of the motorhome, but done so incorrectly, the sellers could have relied on section 14(2C)(b).

(3) On the second point, it was argued that the sellers' representation about the interior width of the motorhome should have made the buyers aware of the fact that its outside width was beyond the permitted range, and that this was sufficient for section 14(2C)(a) to apply. The implication of this argument is that if buyers are given sufficient information to draw the inference that there may be a matter affecting the conformity of the goods, the seller would have done enough to draw a defect specifically to the consumer's attention.

(4) This case therefore raises the interesting question about the information that needs to be given before a particular matter affecting the goods will not result in a finding that the goods are not in conformity with the contract. A number of questions arise. Firstly, at a general level, there it is open to debate just how precise the information identifying a defect should be. Intuitively, one might expect a high degree of precision, although there is room for debate as to how much detail needs to be given. Secondly, if it appears that a consumer should have realised from the information he has that there may be a problem but has not drawn the correct inferences, ought the seller to be able to escape liability? Note that Article 2(3) of the Consumer Sales Directive refers to a lack of conformity of which the consumer 'was aware, or could not have reasonable been unaware', suggesting a fairly low threshold. In contrast, the English provision sets a higher standard, although this may be at the other end of the spectrum and a more nuanced rule may be needed.

(5) A further issue is to what extent consumers can be required to examine goods in order to identify whether they are in conformity with the contract. In the

Consumer Sales Directive, there is no obligation to examine, although there is an optional provision which permits Member States to require the consumer to notify a defect within two months of discovering this.[55] This has been utilised by a majority of the Member States (although ten have decided not to do this). There may be good reasons for having both a duty to examine goods and to notify defects within a certain time, but it may also be argued that this would put unnecessary burdens on consumers, and such a rule may also be difficult to apply in practice.[56]

V. BURDEN OF PROOF

Generally, the burden of establishing a lack of conformity falls on the consumer. In addition, the consumer also has to establish that the lack of conformity existed at the time the goods were delivered. It is, however, often the case that goods have latent defects, ie faults that were not noticeable at the time of delivery, but which may occur at a later point. If such defects did exist at the time of delivery, but did not manifest themselves until later, the consumer still has to show that the non-conformity was present when the seller delivered the goods. A provision introduced in the Consumer Sales Directive assists consumers by putting the onus on the seller to prove that a fault was not present at the time of delivery, provided that this has occurred within six months of delivery.

Consumer Sales Directive (99/44/EC) **5.27 (EU)**

Article 5 (3) Unless proved otherwise, any lack of conformity which becomes apparent within six months of delivery of the goods shall be presumed to have existed at the time of delivery unless this presumption is incompatible with the nature of the goods or the nature of the lack of conformity.

BGH, 29 March 2006[57] **5.28 (DE)**

ANIMAL SALES, REVERSED BURDEN OF PROOF

The allergic horse

The reversed burden of proof is applicable to contracts for the sale of an animal but can be rebutted in the case of certain diseases.

Facts: The defendant is a horse-breeder, who sold a five-year-old horse to the claimant for €7,100 on 18 March 2002. During August, the horse suffered an allergy (summer eczema), and on 17 September 2002, the claimant sought to rescind the contract. The defendant rejected this request.

[55] Art 5(2).

[56] See generally C Jeloschek, *Examination and Notification Duties in Consumer Sales Law—How Far Should We Go in Protecting the Consumer?* (München, Sellier European Law Publishers, 2006).

[57] VIII ZR 173/05 (2006) NJW 2250.

Judgment: (1) At the time of entry into force of the Act modernizing the law of obligations of the 26 November 2001 (BGBl I S 1887), on 1 January 2002, the existing regulations on the purchase of livestock (§§481 to 492 of the German Civil Code), which also applied to horses, were abolished. Compared to §§459ff of the German Civil Code old version, these regulations provided for a limited warranty only, namely for so-called principal defects as defined by the decree of 27 March 1899 (RGBl S 219) regarding the principal defects and warranty period when trading in livestock. The aim of abolishing the particularly well-regulated law on livestock warranty was to apply the general sales law (§§433ff of the German Civil Code) warranties to every type of trade in animals (BT-Drucks 14/6040, p 207). A result of the previous absence of special regulations for warranty when trading in animals is that the legal presumption of §476 of the German Civil Code must also be applied accordingly, under the conditions of §474 of the German Civil Code, to the purchasing of animals (§90 a sentence 3 German Code of Civil Procedure). This is also expressed in the explanation to §474 of the German Civil Code, in which the purchasing of animals in particular is described as a possible case for applying the presumption.

A retrospective presumption as to the condition of the animal at the moment of the transfer of the risk cannot be ruled out either for the mere reason that animals are living creatures which are naturally subject to constant change in their physical condition and health. The earlier law on livestock warranty in §484 of the German Civil Code (old version) already recognised such a presumption, even if only within considerably shorter periods of warranty than the standard period of six months in §476 of the German Civil Code. What is decisive, however, is that consumer protection, which is the aim of §476 of the German Civil Code, taken from Art 5(3) Consumer Sales Directive, militates in favour of also applying this provision to the purchase of animals. The presumption derives its specifically consumer-protective nature from the fact that the consumer is less able to provide proof, and the fact that the seller is in a much better position to know about the condition of the good—in any case in close temporal connection with the delivery—(Official Records of Parliament 14/6040, p 245). This consideration also applies to the purchase of animals between a consumer and a seller. As a rule, the commercially active seller is in a better position to judge the condition of the animal at the time of delivery than a purchaser who is not professionally or commercially involved in buying animals. For this reason, it is in principle justifiable to apply the presumption to the purchasing of animals as well. Whether this is true for all types of animals can remain open; when purchasing a horse, the species of animal does not mean that applying the presumption is excluded from the outset.

In the present case, the presumption is not incompatible with the type of defect either. The Senate has already decided—with regard to the external damage to a motor vehicle—that the presumption that a material defect was already present at he time of passing of the risk, is not then incompatible with the type of defect, if the defect can typically occur at any time and therefore does not permit a sufficient conclusion on whether it was already present on the date of the passing of the risk (judgment of the Senate on 14 September 2005 lc, head note 2). This also applies in principle to the purchase of animals. Even here, there is often uncertainty as to the point in time at which the defect developed, due to its nature. It would not be compatible with the relationship between rule and exception in §476 of the German Civil Code and the consumer-protective nature of the provision, not to apply the presumption merely because the point at which a defect developed typically cannot be established with any reliability;

such a restriction on shifting the burden of proof would largely undermine the consumer protection that was intended with the regulation.

Note

In *Ronald O'Farell v Stephen Moroney*,[58] the Sheriff Court of Lothian and Borders at Edinburgh had to consider the corresponding UK provision in the context of a falcon which had died soon after purchase. The claimant argued that it must have died because of an inherent illness, but the retailer was able to rebut the presumption by showing that the death had most likely been caused by a change in the bird's exercise programme.

The following case illustrates the limitations of the German provision.

BGH, 2 June 2004[59] **5.29 (DE)**

BURDEN OF PROVING NON-CONFORMITY

Torn engine belt

The reversal of the burden of proof only relates to the time at which the defect existed, but not to the existence of the defect itself.

Facts: A belt in a car engine tore. The consumer claimed that the belt had been defective, whereas the trader claimed that a mistake by the consumer—changing into a lower gear at high speed—was responsible for the defect.

Judgment: According to §434(1) s1 and s2 No1 of the German Civil Code, goods are free from material defects if they have the agreed quality upon the passing of the risk. Unless an agreement on quality is made, goods are free from material defects if they are suitable for the use set out in the contract. If the purchaser asserts rights in accordance with §437 of the German Civil Code, as the claimant does here, with reference to the existence of a material defect, after he has received the goods purchased, he is required to state and prove the facts which account for a material defect, according to the new law of obligations ... In the case of a sale of consumer goods, as in the case at hand, §476 of the German Civil Code shifts the burden of proof in favour of the purchaser, but this does not affect the question as to whether a material defect exists at all. In fact, the provision presupposes that a material defect as appeared within six months of the date of the passing of the risk and contains merely a presumption as to the time the defect existed, i.e. that it existed at the at the time of the passing of the risk. ... Accordingly, the appeal court correctly addressed the question as to whether the engine damage, which occurred on 12 July 2002, could be put down to a cause which already existed at the passing of the risk and which had its roots in the quality of the vehicle. The appeal court first established that the engine damage was to be put down to defective material and an excessively high abrasive wear on the engine belt which had been renewed before the conclusion of the contract in November 2001. To the extent that it takes this cause as a

[58] [2008] GWD 35-533.
[59] VIII ZR 329/03 (2004) ZIP 1368.

recognized fact, the appeal court relies on the report of the expert appointed at first instance. ... In his—the expert's—opinion, the causes for this loosening were a material defect and an excessively high abrasive wear on the engine belt. According to the state of technology, one can expect greater durability and longer functional capability from a engine belt than in the present case ... the expert, however, did mention the engagement of a lower gear at higher engine speed as another possible cause for the loosening of the engine belt under the preceding section 'Evaluation'. In accordance with this, when explaining his report at the oral hearing before the regional court on 27 March 2003, the transcript shows that the expert reported that, in retrospect, he could not answer the question as to exactly how the slipping of the engine belt came about. He was still unable to rule out the possibility of damage due to an incorrect gear change. The Court of Appeal, in its further discussion whether or not a material defect was present, did mention the possibility of damage due to a driving mistake in the form of an incorrect gear change, which according to the statements of the expert witness could not be ruled out, but disregarded it. ... Bearing in mind this reversal of the burden of proof, the appeal court ought not to have ruled out the possibility of a driving mistake without further investigation into the evidence. ... As has been shown above, the regional court understood from the expert during the oral hearing that a driving mistake could not be ruled out as the cause of the engine damage. By contrast, however, the appeal court backed up its assumption that a material defect was present by the fact that the expert had put the loosening of the engine belt exclusively down to a material defect and an excessive amount of wear.

Notes

(1) This case illustrates that the reversed burden rule is only of limited assistance. The consumer still has to prove that there is a lack of conformity in the goods. In this case, there was some uncertainty as to whether the defect complained about had been caused by the manner in which the consumer used the goods. As the consumer had not established that there was a lack of conformity, the question of proving its existence at the time of delivery using the benefit of the reversed burden could not arise.

(2) A further difficulty is highlighted by this case: the consumer could not establish that there was a lack of conformity in the goods because the defect could have been caused by the way the goods (ie the car) were used. But would requiring the consumer to prove that the manner of using the goods did not cause the defect not amount to putting the burden back on the consumer in its entirety? Had the reversed burden applied, the seller would have had to prove that the goods were in conformity when delivered, or that the lack of conformity is incompatible with the presumption. Would this have affected the outcome of the case? What does the court's approach suggest about the effectiveness of the reversed burden of proof?

The following case is more favourable to the consumer.

BGH, 22 November 2004[60] **5.30 (DE)**

THIRD PARTY INTERVENTION

Faulty garden pond

The reversed burden of proof applies also where a third party has installed the goods.

Facts: The defendant garden centre sold a fibre-glass garden pond to the claimant, which was delivered to the claimant's home the following day. The pond was installed in the claimant's garden by a third-party specialist contractor. On filling the pond, it was discovered that the pond leaked. The pond was returned to the defendant, who carried out repairs, and it was subsequently collected and reinstalled by the third-party contractor. The leak recurred, and the claimant sought to rescind the contract.

Judgment: According to §476 of the German Civil Code, it is presumed that goods were already defective when risk passed if a material defect appears within six months of this date, unless this presumption is incompatible with the nature of the good or of the defect. The wording of §476 of the German Civil Code offers no evidence in favour of the appeal court's assumption that the provision cannot be applied when the purchaser (the claimant in this case) leaves the intended installation of the good to a third party. In its first clause, §476 of the German Civil Code only requires that a material defect appears within six months after the date of the passing of the risk. According to the conclusions of the local court, to which the appeal court referred, this requirement is fulfilled as the pond was already leaking a few days after its delivery on the 12 July 2002. The appeal court did not reach the conclusion that the legal presumption in the present case is incompatible with the nature of the good or of the defect (§476 of the German Civil Code, 2nd clause). The aim of §476 of the German Civil Code does not justify the legal presumption and accordingly the reversal of the burden of proof to be excluded from the outset if the purchaser has the good installed by a third party. The regulation is aimed at the protection of the consumer. It contains a temporal presumption that a defect which has appeared within six months of the date of the passing of the risk was already present at that point in time (cf Judgment of the Senate of 2 June 2004—VIII ZR 329/03 (2204) NJW 2299 under II 2a). According to the legislative records, the justification for reversing the burden of proof, as the appeal court correctly explained, lies in the fact that the consumer is less able to provide proof and the fact that the seller is in a much better position for knowing about the condition of the good—in close temporal connection with the delivery in any case—(Explanatory Memorandum of the Bill on the Modernization of the Law of Obligations, Bundestag—Drucksachen 14/6040, p 245).The appeal court did not take into account that the consumer who leaves the intended installation of the good to a third party needs to be protected in the same way with regard to the proof of the quality of the good when risk passes as the consumer who installs the good himself.

Notes

(1) In this instance, the court (the same court as in the previous case) focused on the possibility of rebutting the reversed burden. The consumer did not have to prove that the leak was caused by a lack of conformity rather than a mistake made

[60] (2005) DB 1005.

when installing the pool. Is this different from the situation in which a fault in a car could have been caused by the manner in which it was driven?

(2) The decision does seem to cause an additional problem for the seller in seeking to rebut the presumption. Effectively, he will have to establish that a third party was acting negligently when installing the pond in order to rebut the presumption.

In France, Article 5(3) of the Consumer Sales Directive was implemented in Article L 211-7 of the Consumer Code. The presumption of non-conformity during the first six months, however, only applies to consumer contracts and only for the new remedies of the Consumer Code. For the remedies that remain available in the Civil Code, Article 1615 of the Civil Code provides that it is for the buyer to prove the lack of conformity. However, if the latent defects render the good unfit for the use for which it was intended, or impair that use, the lack of conformity will be proved.

Code civil **5.31 (FR)**

Article 1615 A person who claims the performance of an obligation must prove it. Reciprocally, a person who claims to be released must substantiate the payment or the fact which has produced the extinguishment of his obligation.

VI. PERSONS LIABLE

As noted earlier, in the Consumer Sales Directive, liability for delivering goods in conformity with the contract falls on the seller. A consumer has no entitlement to claim against another person, such as the manufacturer (although manufacturers may sometimes accept a degree of responsibility through a consumer guarantee). The obvious justification for this is that the consumer has contracted with the seller. Furthermore, if a problem does occur, the seller will generally be accessible and have staff trained in customer service, which should facilitate the provision of a speedy resolution. However, it may be asked if this holds true in the context of cross-border and online shopping. The distance between consumer and retailer can make it very difficult to obtain a remedy when something has gone wrong with the goods. A system of liability that includes the producer, and perhaps also the members of the producer's authorised distribution network,[61] might offer a better system. Indeed, the idea of direct producer liability has already been accepted in the field of product liability (see chapter 7).

Only a few jurisdictions have developed a system in which the producer can be held directly liable to a consumer. In Belgium and France, case-law has developed which permits buyers to take action against any previous supplier in the distribution chain.

[61] R Bradgate and C Twigg-Flesner, 'Expanding the Boundaries of Liability for Quality defects' (2002) *25 Journal of Consumer Policy* 345–77.

The case below is a leading case about the *action directe* in France. It decided that when a good is defective and if the buyer wants to bring an action against a professional seller of the good, with whom he had not entered into a contract, he must act on the basis of contract law (in this case, the action was grounded on *garantie des vices cachés*). All the remedies dealing with non-conformity (whether the non-conformity stems from the provisions of Articles 1604 or 1641 of the Civil Code) will be transmitted to all the sub-buyers. Sub-buyers are allowed to act against the first sellers on a contractual basis. However, the *action directe* does not apply as far as the provisions issued from the Consumer Sales Directive (99/44/EC) are concerned. This means that the regime of the Directive can only apply between the buyer and the seller with whom he has entered into a contract. However, Article L 211-14 of the Consumer Code provides that

> an action for indemnity may be brought by the final seller against the successive sellers or intermediaries and the producer of tangible movable property, pursuant to the principles of the Civil Code

and thus reflects the requirements of Article 4 of the Directive.

Cass civ 1e, 9 October 1979[62] **5.32 (FR)**

POSSIBILITY FOR SUB-BUYERS TO ACT AGAINST THE FIRST SELLERS ON A CONTRACTUAL BASIS

Defective Lamborghini

A previous supplier can be liable for a defect in the goods.

Facts: Constant bought a second-hand Lamborghini car from Landrau, a car dealer. As a consequence of a defect in the car, an accident occurred. Constant brought a suit against Landrau, Paris-Monceau (the company which sold the car to Landrau), and the Lamborghini Company which had sold the vehicle to Paris-Monceau and knew about the defect in the car having identified it on this particular model. Landrau invoked the liability of Paris-Monceau and the Lamborghini Company. The three were found liable. The two companies contesting their liability appealed the first decision and were found liable again in tort law. They asked the Cour de cassation to review.

Judgment: Considering the first element of the claimant's sole argument in view of Articles 1147 and 1648 of the Civil code: according to the lower instance judges, Constant bought a Lamborghini, model 400 ct, from Landrau, a car dealer, on 5 September 1968. On 15 September of the same year, an accident occurred, which, according to an expert, was caused when the suspension at the back of the car broke because of a manufacturing defect. The manufacturer was aware of the defect and, on 8 May 1967, had written a note on this subject and circulated it amongst the agents with instructions as to how to repair the defect. The company Paris-Monceau, an importer of Lamborghinis in France, had looked after the car on behalf of the previous owner for a certain time, and did not deny having received the letter containing the instructions from the Lamborghini company. Paris-Monceau failed to carry out the repairs suggested by the manufacturer in the letter. Constant and its insurer, l'Uap sought recovery of the damages from Landrau

[62] Bull civ I No 241.

and the car company Paris-Monceau, on the basis of Articles 1147, 1582ff of the Civil Code. Landrau called upon Paris-Monceau in warranty. The court found against the three defendants, ruling that as against one another, their legal responsibility is as follows: the Lamborghini company will bear 3/6 of the responsibility for causing the initial defect, the car dealer Paris-Monceau will bear 2/6 of the responsibility for failing to carry out the repair suggested by the manufacturer, and Landrau, as the professional seller, will bear 1/6 of the responsibility.

In order to substantiate the charge brought against the Lamborghini company and Paris-Monceau and in order to determine that they will bear equal responsibility, the Court of Appeal based its decision upon the liability in tort of both parties. The Court of Appeal held that these two companies are responsible for the damages Constant and its insurer suffered on the basis of Article 1383 of the Civil Code;

In ruling as it did, the Court of Appeal violated the legal provisions previously mentioned. The action direct that the sub-buyer can bring against the producer or the intermediary seller for a guarantee against hidden defects which affects the good as from the moment it is manufactured is necessarily of a contractual nature, and the lower instance judge should therefore have examined, as required by law, whether the action was brought within the short time period specified by law …

Given the above considerations, and without it being necessary to consider neither the second nor the third element of the first argument, the Cour de Cassation overrules and annuls the judgement of 20 December 1977 by the Court of Appeal in Paris.

In Spain, a limited system of producer liability was introduced at the same time as the implementation of the Consumer Sales Directive.

Law 23/2003 concerning warranties in the sale of consumer goods **5.33 (ES)**

Article 10 Claims against the manufacturer

Where it is either impossible for the consumer or it is an unreasonable burden for him to contact the seller in case the goods he has purchased do not match the description of the sales contract, the consumer can directly claim from the manufacturer to have the good repaired or replaced.

In general, and in spite of the fact that the responsibility of the producer will cease when this law takes effect, during the same period of time and under the same conditions as those specified by the seller, the manufacturer will take responsibility for the failure of the goods to meet the description of the sales contract, which relates to the origin and suitability of the goods, as well as to their nature, their purpose and the rules that govern them.

The term 'manufacturer' is defined as the manufacturer of the good or the importer within the European Union or any person who presents him or herself as such when he or she places his or her name, brand or any other distinctive feature on the good.

Whoever answers the consumer's complaint will have a year at his disposal to inform the manufacturer of the good's failure to meet the consumer's expectations. Calculation of the aforementioned time period will begin once the repairs have been completed.

Other countries which have a system of direct producer liability are Finland, Latvia, Lithuania, Portugal and Sweden. In the Green Paper on the Reform of the Acquis,[63] the question is raised whether direct producer liability should be introduced. The case is considered further in the Commission's Report on the implementation of the Consumer Sales Directive,[64] but the conclusion is that there appears to be no sufficient link with the operation of the internal market to justify EU-wide action.[65] This does not, however, mean that a convincing case in favour of introducing direct producer liability cannot be made.

VII. REMEDIES UNDER DIRECTIVE 99/44/EC

When goods are not in conformity with the contract, a consumer has available to him certain remedies which can be exercised against the seller. Following the adoption of the Consumer Sales Directive, these rights are now generally harmonised across the EU, with some exceptions where Member States have not fully or correctly transposed this aspect of the Directive.

Consumer Sales Directive (99/44/EC) **5.34 (EU)**

Article 3 (1) The seller shall be liable to the consumer for any lack of conformity which exists at the time the goods were delivered.

(2) In the case of a lack of conformity, the consumer shall be entitled to have the goods brought into conformity free of charge by repair or replacement, in accordance with paragraph (3), or to have an appropriate reduction made in the price or the contract rescinded with regard to those goods, in accordance with paragraphs (5) and (6).

(3) In the first place, the consumer may require the seller to repair the goods or he may require the seller to replace them, in either case free of charge, unless this is impossible or disproportionate. A remedy shall be deemed to be disproportionate if it imposes costs on the seller which, in comparison with the alternative remedy, are unreasonable, taking into account:

— the value the goods would have if there were no lack of conformity,

—the significance of the lack of conformity, and

—whether the alternative remedy could be completed without significant inconvenience to the consumer.

Any repair or replacement shall be completed within a reasonable time and without any significant inconvenience to the consumer, taking account of the nature of the goods and the purpose for which the consumer required the goods.

(4) The terms 'free of charge' in paragraphs (2) and (3) refer to the necessary costs incurred to bring the goods into conformity, particularly the cost of postage, labour and materials.

[63] COM [2006] 744 final, 30.

[64] Art 12 of the Directive expressly requires the Commission to consider the case for the introduction of direct producer liability.

[65] COM [2007] 210 final, 14.

(5) The consumer may require an appropriate reduction of the price or have the contract rescinded:

—if the consumer is entitled to neither repair nor replacement, or

—if the seller has not completed the remedy within a reasonable time, or

—if the seller has not completed the remedy without significant inconvenience to the consumer.

(6) The consumer is not entitled to have the contract rescinded if the lack of conformity is minor.

Notes

(1) The seller is liable for defects which were present when the goods were delivered (Article 3(1)), but this does not mean that the defect must have been obvious at that time. Some defects are latent and will only manifest themselves once the goods are used. For example, unusually fast wear and tear may be an indication that something was wrong with the goods when they were delivered (and note the reversed burden of proof, discussed above).

(2) The primary remedies under Article 3 are repair and replacement, ie remedies which seek to ensure that the consumer receives the performance contracted for from the seller. This approach was generally already in place in the continental jurisdictions, whereas the remedies for breach of contract in the common law countries were—in limited circumstances—the right to terminate the contract, and a claim for damages. To award repair or replacement would be equivalent to an order for specific performance, and the English courts are very reluctant to award this in the context of normal commercial (and consumer) transactions. There is therefore a fundamental difference in approach. Whilst the United Kingdom has transposed this provision, it has also retained the existing remedies (discussed further below).

VII.A REPAIR AND REPLACEMENT

The initial choice of remedy is to be made between repair and replacement, except where a remedy is impossible, or where it is disproportionate compared to the other remedy. Article 3(3) explains when a remedy is to be regarded as disproportionate. Generally, this will be so when the costs to the seller of providing this remedy would be unreasonable, bearing in mind the loss of value and severity of the non-conformity, and the degree of inconvenience which the alternative remedy might cause to the consumer. For example, if a washing machine needs a new rubber seal around the door because it is leaking, and this seal can be provided and fitted within a day, then replacing the entire washing machine could be regarded as disproportionate. If, however, the machine's motor had failed and obtaining a spare part to repair the washing machine would take six weeks, then replacement would be the appropriate remedy, even if that imposes higher costs on the seller, because of the inconvenience that would be caused to the consumer by having to wait several weeks for the washing machine to be working again.

So, generally, if a non-conformity can easily be repaired, replacement seems likely to be ruled out as an alternative because it would be disproportionate. However, as the following case shows, that may not always be the case.

LG (Court of First Instance) Münster, 7 January 2004[66] **5.35 (DE)**

APPROPRIATE REMEDY FOR MULTIPLE DEFECTS

The car with never-ending problems

The sheer number of defects can tip the balance towards replacement.

Facts: The consumer bought a new car, but it was soon discovered that the car had several defects of varying magnitude. The consumer requested a replacement car, but the car dealer insisted that he be given the opportunity to repair the vehicle instead.

Judgment: The claimant can expect such defects to be absent from a new car. Due to these numerous defects, he has a right to a remedy in accordance with §439(1) of the German Civil Code. Within the scope of this right to a remedy, the buyer has an entirely free choice between having the defect remedied or having the good replaced ... There are no grounds whatsoever for this to be impossible under §275(1) of the German Civil Code. ... In a letter of 22 October 2002, the defendant refused to provide a remedy in the form of a replacement and referred the claimant to the possibility of remedying the defects. ... The objection raised by the defendant to the disproportionality of replacement in accordance with §439(3) of the German Civil Code is not, however, acceptable in this case. The replacement desired by the claimant is neither disproportionate to the value of the vehicle without defects nor disproportionate to the costs of remedying the defects. In particular, the value of the goods when free of defects, the seriousness of the defect and the question as to whether it would be possible to fall back on the other remedies without substantial detriment to the buyer must be taken into account when defining what is unreasonable (§439(3) s 2 of the German Civil Code). It is therefore dependent on the individual case as to when a demand should be deemed unreasonable. ... The maximum amounts established in the precedents up to now and in the literature regarding the question of disproportionality, independent of the question as to whether these are at all sensible, cannot be rigidly adopted. ... On the one hand, the defendant did not bring any arguments with regard to the question of the absolute disproportionality of the replacement. On the other, such absolute disporportionalty would not seem to be present here, since the value of the car in dispute when free of defects must not be below the costs of a replacement. This would be the minimum requirement for the assumption of absolute disproportionality.

VII.A.1 PROPORTIONALITY AS BETWEEN REMEDIES

The application of the proportionality criterion may sound straightforward—a simple balancing exercise between the relative costs to the seller of repairing or replacing the goods. However, this is likely to be much more difficult to apply in practice, particularly with mass-consumption items. Repairing goods will either

[66] (2004) DAR 226.

require the seller to have trained staff, or to send the goods to somebody who can undertake repairs. There will be labour and transport costs that would need to be considered, therefore, and these could be very high, especially if the non-conformity is fairly minor. Providing a replacement may therefore be less costly, especially for goods which do not have a high value. However, if the seller replaces goods, he will have faulty goods which cannot be sold as new to dispose of, and that also creates a cost for him. Under the Directive, the consumer is entitled to ask for repair or replacement intially, and the seller will have to carry the burden of some additional costs. Devising appropriate criteria for assessing the relative costs to the seller can be a difficult undertaking, however.

OLG (Court of Appeal) Braunschweig, 4 February 2003[67] **5.36 (DE)**

REFERENCE PRICE FOR PROPORTIONALITY

Car with missing airbags

The cost of replacement is calculated by deducting the remaining value of the returned good from the value of new goods. In applying the disproportionality test the costs for replacement or repair must be compared not to the actual purchase price, but to the objective value of the goods.

Facts: The consumer bought a pre-registered car (which had 10 km on the odometer) from the defendant car dealer for €11,390. The car had been advertised as having four airbags and ABS, but in fact, there were only two airbags and no ABS. The claimant demanded a replacement which met the description, but the defendant offered either a refund if the car was returned, or a price reduction of €200. The defendant argued that a replacement would be disproportionate because there was no suitable car in stock, nor could one be acquired. Also, the car had depreciated in value after having been used by the consumer. Moreover, the car was sold at a price especially favourable to the consumer. The cost of acquiring a suitable replacement car would be €15,650. The consumer brought an action seeking a replacement car, or—if that was held to be disproportionate—a repair in the form of adding the missing airbags and ABS.

Judgment: It must first of all be pointed out that the defendant did not have the right to refuse to provide follow up performance in the form of replacement on the grounds that it would be impossible (§275 of the German Civil Code), … as the defendant failed to provide any substantial reason as to why the replacement would be impossible. Regardless of this, she did not offer any proof of her corresponding—sweeping—statement in spite of the claimant's challenge. The fact that the defendant might not have another vehicle in stock with the same features stipulated in the contract does not constitute impossibility within the meaning of §275(1) of the German Civil Code as such. … The introduction of the seller's duty to supply the good free from defects (§433(1) s 2 of the German Civil Code) and the right to a remedy following on from that (§439(1) of the German Civil Code) are founded precisely on the idea that the seller must fulfil the interest in performance of the buyer by supplying an (not 'the') item free from defects. This duty to perform can only be deemed impossible if the seller cannot obtain an item, free from defects, of the kind contracted for … Since it is not implicitly clear in the present case that a vehicle of the same type with side airbags and ABS can no longer be

[67] (2003) NJW 1053.

procured on the market, for a demonstration of the requirements of impossibility, a corresponding, isolated declaration on the part of the defendant was needed; this, however, did not occur. As a result, the only thing that is of significance for judging the defendant's right to refuse is whether the replacement would only have been possible at disproportionate expense (§439(3) s 1, 2nd clause of the German Civil Code). Based on the actual statement of the defendant, it is already clear that this is not the case. The reference made in the law to the 'value of the good when free of defects' (§439(3) s 2 of the German Civil Code) makes it clear that the disproportionality of the expense is not determined by comparing the cost of the follow up performance with the purchase price, as the regional court assumed, but by comparing it with the objective value of the goods. This reference to the value of the goods is justified, therefore, as the seller has already sustained the loss of the difference between the purchase price and the value, through what was for him—the seller—a 'bad deal' and for the buyer, what might be called a bargain. This is a loss which arises from the equivalence agreed upon contractually and which therefore must remain entirely out of consideration when applying the disproportionality test, contrary to the view of the regional court ... Based on the market conditions indicated by the defendant herself, this means the following for the present case: the cost of the follow-up performance amounts to €750. This is the amount that, according to the defendant's assertion, should be estimated both for the refit costs and the additional costs associated with delivery and taking the vehicle in question back. With regard to the last-mentioned amount, a possible depreciation in value of the vehicle in question, due to the registration of a further owner as well as its use in the meantime, must remain out of consideration. There has been no substantial evidence presented as to what extent a considerable depreciation in value has occurred. With reference to the value of the good when free from defects, which according to the defendant's statement amounts to €15.651, the cost of the follow up peerformance, which can be estimated as consistent with €750, makes up a share of just 4,7 per cent, such that there was no disproportionality in the sense of §439(3) s 1, 2nd clause of the German Civil Code.

Notes

(1) The court took a simple 'difference in value' approach to determining the cost of replacement, ie the difference between the market value of goods in conformity with the contract and the value of the goods actually delivered, without taking into account the natural depreciation in the value of the car due to it being used by the consumer. This may be an attractive way of determining these costs, but does this fully reflect the costs incurred by the seller?

(2) In considering whether repair would be disproportionate, the court based its conclusions on the cost of the replacement parts and other costs, and concluded that the costs were equivalent to 4.7 per cent of the replacement costs, which meant that repair could not be regarded as disproportionate. The use of a percentage value also seems a sensible yardstick for assessing whether one remedy is disproportionate compared to the other, but is there not a difficulty in establishing where the threshold should be?

It was noted above that one factor that may add to the cost of repair is if the seller does not have its own repair facilities, and the goods have to be sent to the manufacturer, or a third-party, able to undertake this repair. The following case considered whether the costs associated with this could result in repair being deemed disproportionate.

AG (Court of First Instance) Kempen, 18 August 2003[68] **5.37 (DE)**

PROPORTIONALITY WHERE NO OWN REPAIR FACILITIES

Faulty GPS

Repair is not disproportionate merely because the seller does not have his own repair facilities.

Facts: The consumer had bought a GPS (satellite) navigation system, but its CD-ROM drive did not work. The device was sent by the consumer to the manufacturer for repair, and the consumer subsequently claimed the costs of repair from the seller. The seller had not been given an opportunity to repair the device himself, but would, in any event, have had to send it to the manufacturer as the seller did not have repair facilities.

Judgment: Repair is also not disproportionate merely when this can only be undertaken by the manufacturer and the device has already been sent there. This does not absolve the claimant of his obligation to set a deadline for the seller to provide a remedy. The purpose of setting a deadline is to warn the seller that the expiry of this deadline can or will lead to 'serious' consequences. This is so irrespective of who is to provide the repair. Setting a deadline will also enable the defendant to evaluate the claim. In this instance, the defendant did not have the opportunity of assessing the alleged lack of conformity and to contact [the manufacturer] directly, or to offer the claimant an alternative remedy.

Notes

(1) The court's decision firmly closes the door on the argument that the lack of repair facilities and the resulting costs associated with transporting the goods to the manufacturer could rule out this remedy on grounds of disproportionality. However, would this reasoning still hold if the goods were large and the cost of transporting them quite high (eg a freezer)? Would the position be different if the manufacturer sent out staff to repair goods to the consumer's home at the request of the seller?

(2) Note that the court was only concerned with the question of 'proportionality', but did not consider whether repair would be 'impossible' if the seller does not have his own repair facilities. It does seem, however, that an argument by a seller that repair is impossible simply because no facilities are available would not be particularly convincing if the non-conformity is one that could easily be repaired.

(3) Two cases pending before the ECJ at the time of writing may offer further clarification of the proportionality test. In Case C-65/09 *Gebr Weber GmbH v Jürgen Wittmer*, the question is about the degree of disproportionality required before a remedy can be denied. In this case, there is a dispute as to whether a trader who supplied defective floor tiles can be required not only to supply non-defective tiles,

[68] (2003) MDR 1406.

but also to remove the defective tiles which had already been laid in the consumer's home. In Case C-87/09 *Ingrid Putz v Medianess Electronics GmbH*, the question is whether a seller who was not originally required to install an item can be required to do so where the item was installed (correctly) by the consumer but turns out to be faulty. Both cases will provide important clarification about the rights of consumers under the Directive.

VII.A.2 REPLACEMENT AND SECOND-HAND GOODS

If a consumer asks for a replacement, then the seller may attempt to argue that a replacement is not possible because of the unique nature of the goods. Indeed, a very formal approach to sales law would lend some support to this argument. Prior to the modernisation by the *Schuldrechtsreform*, the law in Germany treated many sales transactions as *Stückkauf*, ie the purchase of a specific item. Similarly, English law continues to distinguish between specific and unascertained goods.[69] Where a contract is for the sale of specific goods, then the consumer acquires the particular item he has selected, even if there are many more identical items available from the seller. Thus, a consumer who selects a CD by the Kaiser Chiefs will contract to buy the particular CD he has selected, even though the record store will have many more copies of the same disc in stock. If this—somewhat archaic—analysis is pursued to its logical conclusion, then a replacement would always be impossible where a contract is for the sale of specific goods, but it is clear that such a view would not be in accordance with the requirements of the Consumer Sales Directive. Consequently, an attempt to refuse to provide a replacement merely on the basis of this reasoning should not succeed.

However, the situation may be different where the goods are unique. Some antiques, for example, cannot be replaced because there will not be another such item available. Indeed, it may be argued that second-hand goods are also unique, because their state will depend on the manner in which they have been used and the degree of care taken by a previous owner. This is reflected in Recital 16 of the Consumer Sales Directive, which states that

> the specific nature of second-hand goods makes it generally impossible to replace them … therefore the consumer's right of replacement is generally not available for these goods.

This statement could reflect an intention to exclude the right of replacement from all contracts for the sale of second-hand goods, but as this is not reflected in the operative provisions of the Directive, it would probably go too far to adopt such a view. The position expressed in the recital appears to be that a replacement has to be near-identical to the goods originally supplied. However, as the following case shows, a more nuanced approach is also feasible.

[69] s 61, Sale of Goods Act 1979.

BGH, 7 June 2006[70] **5.38 (DE)**

SECOND-HAND GOODS AND REPLACEMENT

Car with hidden crash damage

The fact that a contract of sale is for specific goods, including second-hand goods, does not preclude the availability of replacement in all circumstances.

Facts: The claimant had bought a used car for €29,000 which had been advertised on the internet by the defendant, a car manufacturer. The claimant had inspected the car at one of the defendant's showrooms. The order form contained a statement to the effect that the vehicle had not previously sustained any damage caused by an accident. During a subsequent service by a garage, it was discovered that the car had, in fact, been damaged significantly in an accident, and that repairs had been carried out inadequately. The claimant sued for the repayment of the purchase price and interest.

Judgment: The appeal court correctly held that the claimant had a right of termination. According to §437(2), 1st old version of the German Civil Code, the buyer of a defective thing can terminate a contract in accordance with §326(5) of the German Civil Code. The vehicle purchased by the claimant was defective because, contrary to its agreed qualities, it had been damaged in an accident ... The appeal court rightly held that the delivery of another, functional used car, of the same value according to the contract, must not be ruled out, not least because it concerns the purchase of specific goods. A restrictive interpretation of §439 para 1 of the German Civil Code as saying that the buyer of an individual good can never demand a replacement, is not supported by the wording of §439 para 1 of the German Civil Code ... This would mean that the priority of the claim for supplementary performance which forms the basis of §§437ff of the German Civil Code ... would not be applicable from the outset when buying specific goods ... Whether or not a replacement is an option should be judged according to the intention of the contract parties when concluding the contract (§§133, 157 of the German Civil Code ...). The replacement will be an option in the view of the parties, if the purchased good, in the event that it is defective, can be replaced by another of the same type and value. In its interpretation of the sales contract, the appeal court concluded that it cannot be assumed that the purchased good was exchangeable according to the intention of the parties concerned, and justified this by explaining that the claimant did not make his decision to buy solely on the basis of objective specifications, but also on the basis of the personal impression of the vehicle he gained when inspecting it. ... In light of the many differences in the degree of wear and tear on used cars—including cars of the same type—caution is demanded before assuming that, in the case of the sale of a used good, the supply of another good will correspond to the intention of the parties. If a replacement is seen as possible, due to the priority of specific performance, this results in the parties first having to tackle the issue of supplying another used good, before termination of the contract or another right from §437(2) and (3) of the German Civil Code can be claimed. In light of the naturally varying states of preservation of used goods and the difficulty, in connection with this, of obtaining a replacement of equal value in every respect, disputes over the equal value of the replacement good offered or to be obtained would occur more frequently if claims for a replacement were regularly asserted when dealing with used goods. This would run counter to the interests of both contract parties to a sales contract.

[70] VIII ZR 209/05 (2006) NJW 2839.

Notes

(1) The Court clarified here that the old distinction in German law between *Stückkauf* (sale of specific goods) and *Gattungskauf* (sale of unascertained goods) has been abandoned in the wake of the Consumer Sales Directive (99/44/EC) and the resulting *Schuldrechtsreform*.

(2) Although in the circumstances of this case, it was indeed held to be impossible to replace the second-hand car, the court made it clear that this could not be ruled out in all circumstances. Crucial factors to be taken into account are the characteristics of the car sought by the consumer—if another second-hand car is available which would satisfy these criteria, then a replacement may be possible.

VII.A.3 ALLOWANCE FOR USE HAD OF THE GOODS

When goods are replaced, the returned goods will be of lower value as a result of the non-conformity. However, if the non-conformity only became apparent several weeks or months after purchase, then the goods will additionally have lost value due to their being used by the consumer—the goods are not new goods with a non-conformity, but effectively second-hand goods with a non-conformity. If the seller has to replace the goods, the returned goods will therefore be worth less not only because of the non-conformity, but also because the consumer has used them. It might be asked whether a consumer should, in such circumstances, pay the seller a sum that would reflect the additional loss in value, because the consumer would otherwise have had free use of the goods. Against this, it can be argued that the consumer has contracted to receive goods in conformity with the contract and that the seller has failed to do so. Consequently, the seller has to absorb the costs associated with replacing the goods.

German law explicitly provides for the possibility that a seller can be reimbursed by a consumer in these circumstances. However, there were serious doubts over the compatibility of this provision with the Consumer Sales Directive, and the first case on the Directive to be referred to the ECJ under the Article 234 EC procedure has considered this point.

ECJ (First Chamber) Case C-404/06, 17 April 2008[71] **5.39 (EU)**
Quelle AG v Bundesverband der Verbraucherzentralen und Verbraucherverbände

PERMISSIBILITY OF A PERIOD-OF-USE ALLOWANCE

The faulty cooker

A consumer may not be required to pay compensation to a retailer for using defective goods until their replacement with goods in conformity with the contract.

Facts: Ms Brüning had purchased a stove-set from a retailer, Quelle, for a cost of €524.90. There was a fault with the oven, and the cooker had to be replaced. On delivering the replacement, the retailer demanded payment of a period-of-use allowance (initially €119.97, later reduced to €69.97), which the consumer paid.

[71] [2008] ECR I-2685.

She then authorised the Bundesverband to take action against Quelle to recover this payment together with interest. Although successful at first instance and on appeal, in the Federal Supreme Court, the view was that German law was clear and that Quelle was entitled to levy this charge. The Federal Court requested a preliminary ruling on the compatibility of German law with the Directive. The Advocate-General delivered her opinion on 15 November 2007, and concluded that Article 3(2), together with (3) first sentence and (4), as well as Article 3(3), 3rd sentence, precludes a rule such as the German one.

Judgment: 25. The German Government observes that the wording of the Directive gives no clear indication whether the seller may, in cases where goods not in conformity are replaced, claim payment for the use of those goods. It points out that, in terms of internal logic, the 15th recital in the preamble to the Directive sets out a very general principle of law, leaving the Member States entirely free to legislate on the question concerning the situations in which the consumer is required to pay compensation for the use of goods.

26. As a preliminary point, it should be borne in mind that, under Article 3(1) of the Directive, the seller is to be liable to the consumer for any lack of conformity in the goods at the time when they are delivered.

27. Article 3(2) of the Directive lists the rights which the consumer may rely on against the seller in cases where the goods delivered are not in conformity. Initially, the consumer has the right to require the goods to be brought into conformity. If that is not possible, he may subsequently require a reduction in the price or rescission of the contract.

28. As regards the bringing into conformity of the goods, Article 3(3) of the Directive states that the consumer is entitled to require the seller to repair the goods or to replace them—in either case free of charge—unless that is impossible or disproportionate. ...

31. The expression 'free of charge' is defined in Article 3(4) of the Directive as referring to 'the necessary costs incurred to bring the goods into conformity, particularly the cost of postage, labour and materials'. It follows from the use by the Community legislature of the adverb 'particularly' that that list is illustrative, not exhaustive. ...

33. Thus it follows from the wording of the Directive, as well as from the related travaux préparatoires, that the Community legislature intended to make the 'free of charge' aspect of the seller's obligation to bring goods into conformity an essential element of the protection afforded to consumers by the Directive.

34. The 'free of charge' requirement attaching to the seller's obligation to bring the goods into conformity, whether by repair or replacement, is intended to protect consumers from the risk of financial burdens which, ... might dissuade them from asserting their rights in the absence of such protection. The certain nature of the 'free of charge' aspect, which was intentional on the part of the Community legislature, means that the seller cannot make any financial claim in connection with the performance of its obligation to bring into conformity the goods to which the contract relates.

35. Support for that interpretation is to be found in the intention, manifested by the Community legislature in the third subparagraph of Article 3(3) of the Directive, to provide effective protection to consumers. That provision states that any repair or replacement is to be completed not only within a reasonable time but also without significant inconvenience to the consumer.

36. That interpretation is also consistent with the purpose of the Directive which, as stated in the first recital in the preamble thereto, is to ensure a high level of consumer protection. As follows from Article 8(2) of the Directive, the protection provided by it is minimal and, although Member States may adopt more stringent provisions, they may not undermine the guarantees laid down by the Community legislature.

37. The other arguments advanced by the German Government against that interpretation are not such as to call it into question.

38. As regards, first, the scope which must be accorded to the 15th recital in the preamble to the Directive, which permits account to be taken of the use the consumer has had of the goods not in conformity, it should be noted that the first part of that recital refers to a 'reimbursement' to be made to the consumer, whereas the second part mentions the 'detailed arrangements whereby rescission of the contract is effected'. ...

39. That terminology makes it clear that the situation envisaged in the 15th recital is restricted to cases where the contract is terminated, as provided for in Article 3(5) of the Directive, and where, pursuant to the principle that the contracting parties must each give up the benefits they have received, the seller must reimburse to the consumer the selling price of the goods. Contrary to the contentions of the German Government, the 15th recital cannot, therefore, be interpreted as a general principle enabling the Member States to take account, in any situation they wish, including that of a mere request for replacement submitted pursuant to Article 3(3) of the Directive, of the use which the consumer has had of goods not in conformity.

40. As regards, secondly, the German Government's assertion that the fact that, by virtue of the replacement of goods not in conformity, the consumer has the benefit of new goods without having to make proper payment constitutes unjust enrichment, it should be borne in mind that Article 3(1) of the Directive makes the seller liable to the consumer for any lack of conformity which exists at the time the goods are delivered.

41. If a seller delivers goods which are not in conformity, it fails correctly to perform the obligation which it accepted in the contract of sale and must therefore bear the consequences of that faulty performance. By receiving new goods to replace the goods not in conformity, the consumer—who, for his part, paid the selling price and therefore correctly performed his contractual obligation—is not unjustly enriched. He merely receives, belatedly, goods in conformity with the specifications of the contract, which he should have received at the outset.

42. The fact remains that the seller's financial interests are protected, on the one hand, by the two-year time-limit laid down in Article 5(1) of the Directive and, on the other, by the fact that, under the second subparagraph of Article 3(3) of the Directive, it may refuse to replace the goods where that remedy would be disproportionate in that it would impose unreasonable costs on the seller.

Notes

(1) This was the first time the ECJ was asked to give a preliminary ruling on the interpretation of a provision of the Consumer Sales Directive, referred seven years after the Directive was adopted.

(2) Compare the German position with Article 46(2) of the UN Convention for the International Sale of Goods 1980 (CSIG) which provides that, in the case of a non-conformity, 'the buyer may require delivery of substitute goods only if the lack of conformity constitutes a fundamental breach of contract'. A fundamental breach under the CISG also entitles the buyer to terminate ('avoid') the contract. Recital 15 of the Directive permits a deduction to be made from a refund where the contract is

rescinded. Do you think the similarities between the Directive and the CISG in some provisions[72] might have influenced the German approach in this regard?

(3) A similar issue has arisen in the context of distance selling: C-489/07 *Messner v Krüger* (see chapter 4.I.C.6.b).

(4) Should the principle from this case also be applied in the context of the remedies of rescission and price reduction? Compare Recital 15 of the Directive.

(5) When the BGH considered the decision, it reinterpreted the provision of German law to apply it only to purely private or business contracts, but not to B2C contracts.[73] German law has since been amended to clarify that in the context of consumer sales, no deductions to reflect the period of use the consumer had of the goods, or any deterioration in value, may be made (see §474(2) sentence 1 BGB).

VII.A.4 CONSUMER ARRANGES REPAIR BY A THIRD PARTY

The Consumer Sales Directive (99/44/EC) imposes liability on the seller to deliver goods which are in conformity with the contract, and requires the seller to provide a remedy where the goods are not in conformity. The onus is therefore on the seller, but, as discussed above, there are circumstances when the seller may not be obliged to provide a particular remedy. A consumer who has discovered a non-conformity would ordinarily contact the seller and ask him to provide an appropriate remedy. However, it may be the case that a consumer finds it easier to ask a third party to repair the goods. In such circumstances, the question arises whether the consumer should be entitled to ask the seller to reimburse him for the costs of having the goods repaired by a third party. The following case considered this issue.

BGH, 23 February 2005[74] **5.40 (DE)**

SELLER TO HAVE OPPORTUNITY TO PROVIDE REMEDY

Faulty car engine

The purchaser does not have the right to remedy defects himself and then seek compensation for expenses incurred afterwards.

Facts: The claimant bought a new car from the defendant car dealer for €6,700, which came with a guarantee. Seven months later, an engine defect occurred. The dealer stated that the guarantee was not applicable as the service requirements appeared not to have been complied with. The engine was replaced by one of the manufacturer's authorised dealers, and the claimant unsuccesfully asked the manufacturer to reimburse him for the cost of replacement. The claimant then demanded that the defendant pay these costs, but this was refused. Legal action to recover damages for the cost of replacing the engine plus interest then commenced.

[72] See S Grundmann, 'Consumer Law, Commercial Law, Private Law—How Can the Sales Directive and the Sales Convention Be so Similar?' (2003) 14 *EBLR* 237–57.

[73] See M Gebauer, 'Der Durchbruch zur richtlinienkonformen Rechtsfortbildung: Anmerkung zu BGH, Urteil vom 26.11.2008, VIII ZR 200/05' [2009] *GPR* 82–86.

[74] III ZR 100/04 (2005) NJW 1348.

Judgment: §§437ff of the German Civil Code contain exhaustive provisions in this respect which also exclude an entitlement to reimbursement of saved expenditure by direct analogy with §326(2) of the German Civil Code. Otherwise, as a result, the buyer would be allowed the right to remedy defects himself at the cost of the seller; a right which the legislator deliberately dispensed with; moreover, the priority of the claim for specific performance, which forms the basis of §§437ff of the German Civil Code, would be circumvented. Reimbursing the saved costs of remedying defects in accordance with §326 para 2, s 2 of the German Civil Code would conflict with the principle of the priority of follow up performance which results from §§437ff of the German Civil Code. §437 of the German Civil Code enumerates the rights and entitlements of the buyer in the event that a good is supplied which is subject to a defect of title or a material defect. A fundamental priority of the right to specific performance over the rights to terminate and to reduce the purchase price (§437(2) of the German Civil Code), as well as over the buyer's entitlement to damages in lieu of performance and to reimbursement of futile expenditure, follows from the fact that these rights of the buyer regularly require the expiry of a deadline set without result for the seller to provide follow up performance. ...

From the seller's point of view, the priority given to specific performance appears to be a right to specific performance or 'right of second delivery' which serves as a safeguard as it can prevent claims of the aforementioned rights of the buyer, by providing specific performance. The seller's opportunity to avoid termination of the contract through remedying defects or providing a replacement in due time is also in the interest of the buyer, since he receives what he may demand under the contract. Specific performance provided by the seller has priority over termination of the contract even if the buyer also has the right to choose between two kinds of specific performance. The appeal court correctly stated that the seller, although ready to render performance, will lose the opportunity to earn the purchase price finally through a 'second delivery' if the buyer repairs the good himself, without previously having given the seller the chance to provide follow up performance. The appeal court rightly took into consideration the fact that the opportunity to provide specific performance, which essentially must be granted by the buyer, enables the seller to check the sold good and that the alleged defect does exist, to check whether it was already present at the passing of the risk, what its cause is, as well as whether or not it can be remedied, and if so how (cf §439(3) of the German Civil Code), and, if necessary, to secure proof of this. The seller loses this opportunity to investigate and secure proof if he is confronted with 'accomplished facts' after a repair is carried out by the buyer as part of the assertion of a claim for reimbursement in accordance with §326 (2) s 2, (4) of the German Civil Code.

Notes

(1) The BGH decided a highly controversial issue. A number of authors had argued that the purchaser should have this right since the consumer would otherwise have to absorb the costs of repair, and the seller would be better off than he deserves as a result of not having incurred any costs despite having delivered non-conforming goods. Among the factors mentioned by the BGH was the intention of the Directive always to give the seller a second chance.

(2) In an earlier case decided by Amtsgericht Kempen,[75] a lower German court had already taken the view that the seller has to be given the opportunity to repair or replace the goods: 'The [seller] has to state unequivocally that he will not carry out his obligations under the contract.' Implicit in this is that if the seller refuses to do so, then the consumer would be entitled to ask a third party to carry out the necessary repairs and then ask the seller to reimburse him for the costs incurred. What is not clear is whether the consumer can do so when all the circumstances indicate that the seller will not perform, although he has not said so explicitly.

(3) Consumers are encouraged to make use of the opportunities offered by the Internal Market, and to shop abroad either by shopping online, or by travelling to another Member State. If goods purchased in this manner turn out to be faulty, persuading a seller located a significant distance away from the consumer could be rather difficult. In such circumstances, getting the goods repaired by a third-party close to the consumer's location may be better for the consumer. However, the seller would still be deprived of the opportunity of examining the goods in order to verify that there is a non-conformity that existed on delivery.

VII.B PRICE REDUCTION AND RESCISSION

In the circumstances set out in Article 3(4), a consumer may be entitled to have the purchase price reduced, or to rescind the contract altogether. In essence, these two remedies are only available if neither repair nor replacement are available (eg if both repair and replacement are impossible), or if the seller cannot provide repair/ replacement without significant inconvenience and/or within a reasonable time. The formulation of these criteria is slightly vague, in that it is not clear if the seller must have attempted to provide repair and replacement and have failed to do so within a reasonable time or without significant inconvienience, or if the mere fact that the seller informs the consumer about this is sufficient. Furthermore, if the seller has completed a repair, but not within a time that would be reasonable, could the consumer still demand a reduction in price or even rescind the contract?

Rescission would have the effect of bringing the contractual relationship to an end, and in light of the Directive's focus on preserving the contractual relationship between seller and consumer, this has to be regarded as a remedy of last resort. The effect of rescission is to bring the contract to an end from the point at which the descision to rescind was taken. Although the consumer should hand back the goods to the retailer and receive a refund, the seller is permitted to make a deduction from this reimbursement to reflect the period of use the consumer has had—as clarified in Recital 15.

Rescission is not available, however, if the lack of conformity is 'minor'. The Directive is silent on the criteria that could be relevant to determining whether a non-conformity is minor, and this is therefore a matter for the national courts. The

[75] Amtsgericht (Court of First Instance) Kempen, 18 August 2003, (2003) MDR 1406 (Faulty GPS) (discussed above at 5.37 (DE) in respect of another matter).

following case considers possible criteria that could be applied in establishing whether a particular lack of conformity is 'minor'.

OLG (Court of Appeal) Düsseldorf, 27 February 2004[76] **5.41 (DE)**

WHEN NON-CONFORMITY IS MINOR

Second-hand car with minor faults

A lack of conformity is minor where the cost of repair constitutes only a small percentage of the purchase price of the goods.

Facts: The consumer had bought a second-hand car which had a number of defects, none of which were particularly serious. The consumer repeatedly demanded that the seller repair these defects, but the seller refused. Eventually, the consumer sought to rescind the contract.

Judgment: In view of the fact that the claimant is merely entitled to a used, but defect-free spare tyre and that the vehicle in question is small, the Senate judges the cost of a replacement to be low. Even including the estimated cost of repair for the muffler and of improving the level of exhaust emissions, the overall costs are likely to remain within limits which do not exceed 2 to 3 per cent of the purchase price. Then defendant's breach of duty can be judged as negligible, however ... and the claimant's right to terminate the contract is excluded. He is free to claim the resulting repair costs as a reduction in the purchase price or as damages.

Note

The approach adopted by the court, ie a percentage-based assessment, has similarities to the criteria developed for establishing whether a remedy is disproportionate. In this case, the cost of repair did not exceed 3 per cent of the price of the goods, and the court concluded that the lack of conformity was therefore minor. This takes a purely cost-based approach to the question of whether a non-conformity is minor. It may be questioned whether this approach is the correct one, because it appears to focus exclusively on the cost of putting right the fault, ie the difference in value between conforming goods and the goods as delivered. However, would it not be possible that a lack of conformity which is not significant in terms of loss of value could nevertheless be more than minor if its implications are quite severe (eg a small problem with a car engine which could have serious safety implications)?[77]

[76] (2004) DAR 392.

[77] Compare the facts in *Bernstein v Pamson Motors (Golders Green)* [1987] 2 All ER 220.

VIII. FURTHER REMEDIES: TERMINATION OF THE CONTRACT AND CLAIMS FOR DAMAGES

Although the remedies introduced by the Directive are extensive, they are not exhaustive and in most legal systems, additional remedies are available (usually because they existed before the Directive was implemented).

As was seen earlier, the position in France is rather complex because provisions from the Civil Code continue to be applicable alongside specific rules for consumer sales, and there are two additional provisions on conformity (Articles 1604 and 1641 of the Civil Code). Consequently, there are also different remedies available for breaches of these provisions.

In case of non-conformity under Article 1604 of the Civil Code, French contract law allows the buyer to sue for specific performance or for the rescission of the contract. It will be granted under Article 1184 of the Civil Code.

Code civil **5.42 (FR)**

Article 1184 A condition subsequent is always implied in synallagmatic contracts, in case one of the two parties does not perform its obligation.

In that case, the contract is not rescinded as of right. The party towards whom the obligation has not been performed has the choice either to compel the other to perform the contract when it is possible, or to request its rescission with damages.

Rescission must be sought in court, and time may be granted to the defendant according to circumstances.

Note

Where this provision applies, a judge will have to assess whether there is a non-conformity. For rescission to be granted, the non-conformity needs to be fundamental. It has been held that a different colour of the wood of furniture from the colour mentioned in the contract offered the possibility for the plaintiff to claim rescission of the contract.[78]

Special remedies are provided for in case of non-conformity under Article 1641. The provisions of the Civil Code are clear.

Code civil **5.43 (FR)**

Article 1643 He [the seller] is liable for latent defects, even though he did not know of them, unless he has excluded liability in that case.

Article 1644 In case of Articles 1641 and 1643, the buyer has the choice either of returning the good and having the price repaid to him or of keeping the good and having part of the price repaid to him, as appraised by experts.

[78] See Cass civ 1e, 1 December 1987, Bull civ I No 324.

Article 1645 In case the seller was aware of the defects of the good, he is liable, in addition to repayment of the price received, for all damages sustained by the buyer.
Art 1646 In case the seller was not aware of the defects of the good, he is only liable for repayment of the price and for reimbursing the buyer for the costs of the sale.

Notes

(1) The Cour de Cassation takes into account the skills of the parties. Non-conformity will be accepted even though the non-professional party checked the goods only superficially.[79]

(2) According to Article 1648 the action resulting from lack of conformity under Article 1641 must be brought by the buyer 'within a period of two years following the discovery of the vice'.

VIII.A DAMAGES

As already discussed, the Consumer Sales Directive (99/44/EC) has introduced a detailed, and rather complex, set of remedies in circumstances where goods are not in conformity with the contract. Nevertheless, the system of remedies is not exhaustive; in particular, there is no provison in the Directive dealing with damages. Member States therefore remain free to determine when a consumer may claim damages when there has been a lack of conformity. Two issues require consideration: (i) a claim for damages instead of pursuing one of the Article 3 remedies, including any restrictions; and (ii) a claim for damages for consequential losses. The following case deals with the first of these issues.

BGH, 23 February 2005[80] **5.44 (DE)**

ENTITLEMENT TO CLAIM DAMAGES

Faulty car engine

The hierarchical structure of the remedies prevents a claim for damages until a reasonable period of time for the seller to repair/replace has elapsed.

Facts: See above, excerpt 4.40 (DE).

Judgment: The right of the buyer to reduce the purchase price, in accordance with §§437(2), 441 of the German Civil Code, as well as the entitlement to damages in lieu of performance because of services not rendered as promised, in accordance with §§437(3), 280(1) and (3), 281 of the German Civil Code, fundamentally require that the buyer set the seller a reasonable period for specific performance (§439 of the German Civil Code) without result. This is expressly regulated for the claim for damages in lieu of performance, in §281(1) s 1 of the German Civil Code. For the right to reduce the purchase

[79] Cass civ 1e, 24 February 1964, Bull civ I No 105.
[80] (2005) NJW 1348.

price, this requirement expresses, in the wording of §441(1) s 1 of the German Civil Code, that the buyer, 'instead' of terminating, can reduce the purchase price by giving notice to the seller. Therefore, in order to be able to reduce the price, the buyer must first fulfil the requirements for terminating the contract in accordance with §§437(2), 323(1) of the German Civil Code, and, as a rule, set a deadline accordingly. This requirement is not fulfilled because the claimant has not set the defendant a period for remedying the engine damage. The appeal court also rightly denied the claimant's claim for payment of the defendant's saved expenses of providing specific performance in accordance with §326(2) s 2 of the German Civil Code (analogously) in connection with §§326(4), 346ff of the German Civil Code. If the buyer remedies a defect of the good purchased, without first setting the seller a necessary period for specific performance, according to §326(2), s 2, (4) of the German Civil Code, he cannot demand that the costs of remedying the defects be (analogously) reimbursed.

Notes

(1) This is an important judgment on the relationship between the Directive and the national rules on damages. The position adopted in German law is therefore that the consumer first has to give the seller an opportunity to repair or replace the goods, and only if this does not happen within a reasonable period can the consumer claim damages instead.

(2) The position is different in English law. The rights from Article 3 of the Directive are contained in Part 5A of the Sale of Goods Act 1979, but these are described as 'additional rights of consumers'. A consumer is always able to bring a claim in damages as an alternative to asking for repair/replacement, and there is no obligation to give the seller an opportunity to repair/replace first. Although section 48(D) of the Sale of Goods Act 1979 prevents a consumer from exercising his right to terminate the contract (see below) if he has asked for repair/replacement before a reasonable time has elapsed, this does not apply with regard to a claim for damages.

(3) Nothing in the Directive, or in domestic law, prevents a consumer from claiming damages for consequential losses incurred as a result of a lack of conformity. Such a claim has to be made in accordance with the normal national law on damages for consequential losses.

VIII.B TERMINATION

As already seen, the Consumer Sales Directive (99/44/EC) provides that a contract may be brought to an end (rescinded) only as a matter of last resort, when no other remedy has provided a satisfactory outcome. The focus is therefore on preserving the contractual relationship and providing the consumer with the performance contracted for. It was noted above that this approach differs significantly from that in the common law countries.

In English law, a consumer (and, indeed, a non-consumer buyer) has always had two remedies open to him in circumstances when goods are not in conformity with the contract: to reject the goods and terminate the contract, and to claim damages. The right to terminate a contract is only available where the breach of contract involves a term that is classified as a condition. If the term is not a condition, it is a warranty only, and a breach of warranty does not permit the termination of the contract.[81] The terms implied by the Sale of Goods Act 1979 which comprise the 'conformity' requirement are deemed to be conditions. However, the right to terminate, whilst a potent right if a non-conformity manifests itself soon after the contract of sale has been concluded, is limited and will be lost once the consumer is deemed, in law, to have accepted the goods. The circumstances in which acceptance can occur are set out in section 35 of the Act.

Sale of Goods Act 1979 **5.45 (UK)**

Section 35 Acceptance

(1) The buyer is deemed to have accepted the goods subject to subsection (2) below—

(a) when he intimates to the seller that he has accepted them, or

(b) when the goods have been delivered to him and he does any act in relation to them which is inconsistent with the ownership of the seller.

(2) Where goods are delivered to the buyer, and he has not previously examined them, he is not deemed to have accepted them under subsection (1) above until he has had a reasonable opportunity of examining them for the purpose–

(a) of ascertaining whether they are in conformity with the contract, and

(b) in the case of a contract for sale by sample, of comparing the bulk with the sample.

(3) Where the buyer deals as consumer or (in Scotland) the contract of sale is a consumer contract, the buyer cannot lose his right to rely on subsection (2) above by agreement, waiver or otherwise.

(4) The buyer is also deemed to have accepted the goods when after the lapse of a reasonable time he retains the goods without intimating to the seller that he has rejected them.

5) The questions that are material in determining for the purposes of subsection (4) above whether a reasonable time has elapsed include whether the buyer has had a reasonable opportunity of examining the goods for the purpose mentioned in subsection (2) above.

(6) The buyer is not by virtue of this section deemed to have accepted the goods merely because—

(a) he asks for, or agrees to, their repair by or under an arrangement with the seller, or

(b) the goods are delivered to another under a sub-sale or other disposition.

Notes

(1) In subsection (2), the phrase 'in conformity with the contract' appears, although the concept is not central to the Sale of Goods Act 1979. As this section is not limited to consumer contracts, the definition of conformity with the contract in section 48(D) of the Act has no application.

[81] Note that English contract law has developed a third category of term, the so-called innominate term. If there has been a breach of such a term, the remedies depend on the seriousness of the consequences of the breach; if serious, a right to terminate exists; if not serious, only damages may be claimed (*Hong Kong Fir Shipping Co Ltd v Kawasaki Kisen Kaisha Ltd* [1962] 2 QB 26). Whether a term is properly classified as a condition, warranty or innominate term depends on the construction of each contract.

(2) Subsection (6) preserves the right of a buyer to reject the goods and terminate the contract even where the seller has been asked to repair the goods. The relationship of this provision with the right to repair in consumer cases is unclear, although the general intention is to facilitate repair whilst preserving the buyer's entitlement to reject (assuming that the right had not been lost previously by virtue of one of the other circumstances listed in this section). Although there may be a general expectation that, once repaired, the buyer would be deemed to have accepted the goods, a recent (non-consumer) House of Lords decision suggests that this will not inevitably be the case; in particular, if the buyer has requested information about the nature of the non-conformity as part of the arrangement for repair, then carrying out the repair without providing this information first does not preclude the consumer from exercising his right of rejection.[82]

The most common situation in which a consumer is likely to lose his right to reject and terminate the contract is by virtue of the lapse of a reasonable time (subsection (4)). In *Bernstein v Pamson Motors (Golders Green)*,[83] the High Court held that this could be the case within a very short time after purchase, although subsequent cases have been more generous. The leading case on this issue is now *Clegg v Andersson*.

Court of Appeal, 11 March 2003[84] **5.46 (UK)**
Clegg v Olle Andersson (t/a Nordic Marine)

REJECTION WHEN FACTS UNCLEAR

Yacht with heavy keel

A buyer can ask the seller to provide further information about the nature of the defect and its implications before having to exercise his right to reject the goods.

Facts: The buyers acquired a yacht worth GBP 236,000. The yacht had a shoal draught keel, ie a lead casting had been bolted to a truncated keel. When the yacht was delivered to the buyer for sea trials, it was noticed that it was lying lower in the water than expected. It transpired that the lead casting, and therefore the yacht, was heavier than specified. Although the buyer tried out the vessel, he asked the seller to consult the manufacturer about how this problem could be rectified. The manufacturer suggested that the excess lead should be shaved off the keel, and engineers were dispatched to do so even though the buyer had not yet accepted this proposal. He did not want to rush into a decision and requested further information about the safety and stability of the yacht both with the keel as delivered and after modification. After several months, during which some information was provided, the buyers rejected the yacht.

Judgment: [The Vice-Chancellor] The terms of s 35 pose three questions, namely (1) did the Cleggs intimate to Mr Andersson that they accepted the Yacht? (2) did the Cleggs do any act in relation to the Yacht which was inconsistent with the ownership of Mr Andersson' and (3) had a reasonable time elapsed by 5 March 2001 in which the Cleggs retained the Yacht without intimating to Mr Andersson that they had rejected it? … [Mr Clegg] refers to the overweight keel as a fundamental point. He asks for a revised

[82] *J & H Ritchie Limited v Lloyd Limited* [2007] UKHL 9.
[83] [1987] 2 All ER 220.
[84] [2003] EWCA Civ 320.

specification and measurements. He questions the effect on EU weight requirements and on a resale and asks for the appointment of an independent surveyor because he does not have the relevant expertise. I do not read this as an intimation of acceptance; rather Mr Clegg was asking for information so that he might then determine whether or not he should accept the Yacht. ... Until at least the information was received Mr Clegg was not in a position to decide whether to accept the Yacht or not. No doubt the Cleggs had left personal effects in the Yacht but, given the outstanding request for further information, that action cannot be regarded as an intimation of acceptance either ... The circumstances existing on 5 September 2000 were that Mr Clegg had sought but had not yet been provided with the information required by him to decide whether or not to accept remedial works to the Yacht. If he had agreed to their repair that would not have amounted to acceptance. In my view Mr Clegg's indication that he did not agree to any remedial works unless and until he had been provided with the information he sought is also incapable of amounting to acceptance of the Yacht. ... I consider that time taken to ascertain what would be required to effect modification or repair is to be taken into account in resolving the question of fact which arises under subsection (4). In the light of the undisputed fact that Mr Clegg did not receive the information he had sought in August and September 2000 until 15 February 2001. ... In my view the reason why the Cleggs rejected the Yacht when they did is irrelevant if, as I consider, they had the right to do so.

[Hale LJ] I agree and would only add that at times the argument before us seemed to lose sight of the real issues in the English law of sale of goods. These are not whether either party has behaved reasonably. The defendant may well feel that he and the manufacturers Malo did their best to put right what had gone wrong and that the claimant purchaser should have taken up one of the options which they advised. If it is established that the seller is in breach of a condition of the contract, however, the choice does not lie with him. ... Seller and buyer often agree to try and put defects right but neither is obliged to do so. The fact that the remedy supplied by English law may be thought disproportionate by some is irrelevant to a consideration of whether the implied term has been broken. ... In English law, however, the customer has a right to reject goods which are not of satisfactory quality. He does not have to act reasonably in choosing rejection rather than damages or cure. He can reject for whatever reason he chooses. The only question is whether he has lost that right by accepting the goods: s 11(4).

Court of Appeal, 13 January 2004[85] **5.47 (UK)**
Jones v Gallagher (t/a Gallery Kitchens and Bathrooms)

IMPACT OF SEEKING INFORMATION ON RIGHT OF REJECTION

No match for existing kitchen units

Not every request for information will preserve the right of rejection.

Facts: New kitchen units were installed in the plaintiff's home but had several shortcomings, notably that the colour of the new units failed to match existing units. Other minor problems arose and the plaintiff repeatedly raised new concerns before attempting to reject the kitchen units.

[85] [2004] EWCA Civ 10.

Judgment: [Thomas LJ] It is clear that when considering … what is a reasonable time, regard must be had to the time taken to effect modifications and repairs. However, in the end, what time is a reasonable time is a question of fact. That must be decided in the circumstances of each particular case. During the course of argument before us counsel for the appellant sought to rely on specific periods of time set out in other cases. In my view that is not the correct approach. It is necessary to consider the facts in each particular case and to decide … what is a reasonable time.

[Buxton LJ] [Counsel for the defendant] argued that the effect of that [section], as understood by Hale LJ, was that, while a period of repair was in progress, or alternatively as in our present case a period of complaint and request for remuneration was in progress, it was not possible for the buyer to have lost his right to reject. That is not a correct construction either of the Act or of what was said by her Ladyship. The Act stresses that the buyer is not deemed to have accepted the goods merely because he asks for or agrees to their repair. The purpose of that subsection was to correct what had previously been thought, rightly or wrongly, to be the law, that the right to reject was lost automatically if one engaged in discussion or activity about repair. That is no longer the law. Such delay is simply a factor to be taken into account in the factual assessment that is placed on the court. … in *Clegg v Andersson* … there was uncertainty as to what was wrong and the buyer was seeking professional information from the seller as to what might be done to put it right. That is a long way from our present case, where there were apparent and easily ascertained defects in the goods … Secondly, I am sure that Hale LJ did not intend to go so far as to say that it was generally impossible to lose the right to reject while a buyer was still seeking information. … There is no absolute rule that a situation in which information was sought cannot involve the loss of a right to reject: because that would be inconsistent with the guiding principle in this Act that assessment of loss of right to reject is a matter of fact to be considered in all the circumstances.

Question

From the two extracts above, how strong a right is an English buyer's entitlement to reject the goods and terminate the contract? Do you think the law is sufficiently clear for consumers?

IX. CONSUMER GUARANTEES

So far, the discussion has centred on the legal rights and remedies of a consumer under a contract of sale. In addition to these rights, a consumer who buys goods, particularly durable goods and domestic electrical goods, will have the benefit of a consumer guarantee.[86] These are usually given by a manufacturer, but they are also increasingly given by retailers. Such a guarantee is provided free of charge, and promises to repair or replace the corresponding goods if there is a defect caused by poor workmanship or materials. It is therefore generally restricted to functional defects, rather than a lack of suitability for the purposes for which a consumer

[86] Generally, C Twigg-Flesner, *Consumer Product Guarantees* (Aldershot, Ashgate, 2003).

requires goods or failure to perform at a level suggested by relevant public statements such as advertising.

Guarantees are essentially regarded as a competitive tool (Recital 21 of the Consumer Sales Directive), and, as such, there is only a limited degree of regulation of such guarantees. The Consumer Sales Directive contains the following provision.

Consumer Sales Directive (99/44/EC) **5.48 (EU)**

Article 6 Guarantees

(1) A guarantee shall be legally binding on the offerer under the conditions laid down in the guarantee statement and the associated advertising.

(2) The guarantee shall:

—state that the consumer has legal rights under applicable national legislation governing the sale of consumer goods and make clear that those rights are not affected by the guarantee,

—set out in plain intelligible language the contents of the guarantee and the essential particulars necessary for making claims under the guarantee, notably the duration and territorial scope of the guarantee as well as the name and address of the guarantor.

(3) On request by the consumer, the guarantee shall be made available in writing or feature in another durable medium available and accessible to him.

(4) Within its own territory, the Member State in which the consumer goods are marketed may, in accordance with the rules of the Treaty, provide that the guarantee be drafted in one or more languages which it shall determine from among the official languages of the Community.

(5) Should a guarantee infringe the requirements of paragraphs 2, 3 or 4, the validity of this guarantee shall in no way be affected, and the consumer can still rely on the guarantee and require that it be honoured.

Notes

(1) This provision is mainly concerned with transparency: the consumer needs to be given sufficient information to evaluate what the guarantee offers and how its benefit can be obtained. Furthermore, it must be made clear to the consumer that a guarantee is an additional route for obtaining a remedy and does not affect the legal rights of the consumer. There is, however, no substantive regulation of the guarantee, and a manufacturer or retailer seeking to offer a guarantee has the freedom to determine the length of the guarantee and the circumstances in which the guarantee is available to the consumer. Such freedom is only restricted by the general legislation on unfair contract terms.

(2) The guarantee statement may specify the conditions on which the guarantee is provided. There is some uncertainty as to whether limitations and exclusions from the guarantee should be treated as defining the core obligation assumed (which might remove this from the control under unfair terms legislation—see chapter 4.II), or merely as related terms, permitting an assessment of their fairness. For example, in the case of a car, the guarantee might state that the consumer has to adhere to the prescribed maintenance schedule, or lose the benefit of the guarantee.

This might be a precondition on the availability of the guarantee, or merely an exclusion. In the latter case, this exclusion has to meet the standard of fairness. The German Federal Supreme Court recently held that a clause in a guarantee which deprived the consumer of its benefit if he failed to undertake maintenance and servicing as required by the car manual was unfair, because it also covered faults which might have been caused by matters unrelated to the failure to comply with the servicing schedule.[87]

(3) A guarantee does not restrict the legal rights of consumers, so a guarantor cannot use it to exclude these rights. However, to what extent can a guarantee influence the assessment of conformity? The following case deals with this issue.

Court of Appeal, 5 November 1986[88] **5.49 (UK)**
Rogers v Parish (Scarborough) Ltd

RELEVANCE OF GUARANTEE TO ASSESSING CONFORMITY

Range Rover with faults

In establishing whether goods are in conformity with the contract, it is irrelevant that goods come with a guarantee, because a guarantee is additional to a consumer's rights.

Facts: See above, 5.21 (UK).

Judgment: [Mustill LJ] … it does not appear from the documents before us whether this [guarantee] was signed or precisely what its contractual status was intended to be, but primarily at least it must have constituted an engagement by the manufacturer collateral to the sale contract itself …

It is however also necessary to deal with an argument based on the fact that the vehicle was sold with the benefit of a manufacturer's [guarantee], a fact which was relied upon to show that the buyer was required to take in his stride to a certain degree at least the type of defects which would otherwise have amounted to a breach of contract. Speaking for myself, I am far from satisfied that this argument is open to the defendants at all, having regard to the express disclaimer in the contract of sale, and also in the [guarantee], of any intention to vary the buyer's rights at common law, and also having regard to section 6 of the Unfair Contract Terms Act 1977. Nor am I convinced that this objection can satisfactorily be answered by saying that the argument founded on the [guarantee] operates not to deprive the buyer of his common law rights but rather as a relevant circumstance for the purposes of section [14(2B)] operating simply to diminish the reasonable expectation of the buyer. Moreover, I am not clear about the logic underlying the argument. Assume that on an accurate balancing of all the relevant circumstances it could be said that the buyer of a new Range Rover could reasonably expect it to have certain qualities and that accordingly he has a contractual right to receive a vehicle possessing those qualities and to recover damages, including damages for any consequential loss, if it does not possess them. Can it really be right to say that the reasonable buyer would expect less of his new Range Rover with a [guarantee] than

[87] BGH, 17 October 2007, VIII ZR 251/06 (2008) NJW 214
[88] [1987] QB 933.

without one? Surely the [guarantee] is an addition to the buyer's rights, not a subtraction from them, and, it may by noted, only a circumscribed addition since it lasts for a limited period and does not compensate the buyer for consequential loss and inconvenience. If the defendants are right a buyer would be well advised to leave his guarantee behind in the showroom. This cannot be what the manufacturers and dealers intend or what their customers reasonably understand.

Notes

(1) For the decision in this case on whether the car met the relevant quality standard, see 5.21 (UK), above.

(2) The decision and reasoning on this point were recently re-examined in Scotland, when Lord Osborne gave the following judgment.

Extra Division, Inner House, Court of Session, **5.50 (UK)**
10 October 2006[89]
Lamarra v Capital Bank plc

GUARANTEES AND LEGAL RIGHTS

Another faulty Range Rover

The availability of a guarantee is not a relevant consideration in assessing conformity with the contract.

Facts: A Range Rover had a string of faults which meant that the car was not of satisfactory quality.The availability of the manufacturer's guarantee to remedy the defects was regarded as irrelevant to the determination of satisfactory quality.

Judgment: A controversial issue, which figured prominently in the debate, was that of the significance of the [guarantee] ... The controversy related to whether the [guarantee] was one of 'the other relevant circumstances' ... The position of the appellants was that it should be so regarded, there being no reason why it should not be seen as relevant. The conclusion which we have reached is that the [guarantee] cannot properly be seen as one of the 'relevant circumstances'. ... While the words 'all the other relevant circumstances' are potentially of wide scope, we consider that, in the context, they must be seen as referring only to circumstances actually bearing upon the quality of the goods in question. ... In our view, a [guarantee] cannot be seen as a matter bearing upon the quality of the goods supplied. In its nature, a [guarantee] can only be seen as an undertaking by the manufacturer of the goods concerned to remedy defects in the goods which emerge and are within the scope of the [guarantee] and that within a specified period of time. Thus the [guarantee] must be seen as a means whereby the defects in existence at the time of delivery, or emerging thereafter within the specified period, may later be remedied by the manufacturer at no cost to the customer. The fact that such defects may be so remedied appears to us not to bear upon the issue of the quality of the goods at the time of their delivery ... In its nature, a [guarantee] is concerned with the provision of remedial action within a limited period after delivery. In short, it seems to us

[89] [2006] CSIH 49.

that, because the issue of whether the quality of the goods is satisfactory requires to be judged as at the time of delivery, the [guarantee] can have no bearing upon that matter.

Note
The existing of a guarantee is treated in much the same way as the possibility of repairing faults with little difficulty—neither affects the determination of whether the goods, as delivered, were of satisfactory quality.

CONCISE BIBLIOGRAPHY

A Bénabent, *Droit civil. Les contrats civils et commerciaux* (Paris, Montchrestien, 2008).
J-S Borghetti, *La responsabilité du fait des produits, étude de droit comparé* (Paris, LGDJ, 2004).
R Bradgate and C Twigg-Flesner, *Blackstone's Guide to Consumer Sales and Associated Guarantees* (Oxford, Oxford University Press, 2003).
J Calais-Auloy and F Steinmetz, *Droit de la consommation* (Paris, Dalloz, 2007).
S Grundman and M Bianca (eds), *EU Sales Directive—Commentary* (Antwerp/Oxford, Intersentia, 2002).
E Poillot, *Droit européen de la consommation et uniformisation du droit des contrats en Europe* (Paris, LGDJ, 2006).
G Raymond, *Droit de la consommation* (Paris, Litec, 2008).
H Schulte-Nölke, C Twigg-Flesner and M Ebers (eds), *EC Consumer Law Compendium* (Munich, Sellier ELP, 2008).
S Whittaker, Liability for Products—English Law, French Law and European Harmonisation (Oxford, Oxford University Press, 2003.

CHAPTER 6
FINANCIAL SERVICES

I. FINANCIAL SERVICES AND CONSUMER PROTECTION

This chapter considers the various methods of consumer protection in the field of financial services, ie credit services, investment services and payment services.[1] Evidently the protection of consumers of financial services builds further upon the protection mechanisms that also exist for consumers of general services and products. However, two elements make the protection of consumers of financial services stand out. First, financial services typically involve complicated products and transactions, often difficult to understand for the 'average' consumer and with important financial consequences—a mortgage loan, for instance, will bind the consumer for a substantial part of his life; a risky investment in securities which goes wrong may have a significant impact on his welfare—resulting in particular means of protection of these consumers. Second, there is a growing awareness that certain financial products and services (eg a bank account, access to electronic payment services or in some cases mortgage loans) enable individuals to participate fully in society and should therefore generally be accessible to everyone. This chapter will be based upon those two themes.

[1] Insurance law will not be considered here.

I.A THE TRADITIONAL INFORMATION PARADIGM VERSUS NEW MEANS OF CONSUMER PROTECTION

Prospectus Directive (2003/71/EC)[2] **6.1 (EU)**

[Preamble] **(18)** The provision of full information concerning securities and issuers of those securities promotes, together with rules on the conduct of business, the protection of investors. Moreover, such information provides an effective means of increasing confidence in securities and thus of contributing to the proper functioning and development of securities markets. The appropriate way to make this information available is to publish a prospectus.
(19) Investment in securities, like any other form of investment, involves risk. Safeguards for the protection of the interests of actual and potential investors are required in all Member States in order to enable them to make an informed assessment of such risks and thus to take investment decisions in full knowledge of the facts.

Notes

(1) According to the preamble to the Prospectus Directive (2003/71/EC), the provision of information protects investors. This idea—which, as we will see, is not restricted to investment services but extends to other financial services as well—is often referred to as the *information paradigm* or the philosophy of *mandatory disclosure*. It is based on the assumption that the compulsory provision of information by the providers of financial services leads to better, more 'informed' decisions of consumers and protects them against 'wrong' decisions resulting from a lack of knowledge. In other words, as Justice Brandeis famously stated

> Publicity is justly commended as a remedy for social and industrial diseases. Sunlight is said to be the best of disinfectants; electric light the most efficient policeman.[3]

Although this intuitive idea dates back a long way, since the 1930s mandatory disclosure has been increasingly used by legislators around the world, and today serves as the basis of the protection of consumers of financial services.

(2) The information paradigm, however, raises several issues (see also, in general, chapter 3.III). In recent years, behavioural finance (the study of the way in which people react—or do not react—in practice to financial law rules) has shown that even if information is readily available, consumers are likely to ignore it. Ignorance, incapability, fear, laziness, lack of interest, social status, press, family, rumours—these all seem to be factors that steer the behaviour of the consumer of financial services and may explain why people do not always optimally use the information provided to them. Although presented as a correction to the 'rational

[2] Directive 2003/71/EC of the European Parliament and of the Council of 4 November 2003 on the prospectus to be published when securities are offered to the public or admitted to trading and amending Directive 2001/34/EC [2003] OJ L 345, 64–89.

[3] L Brandeis, *Other People's Money* (1933) 92.

investor' model, rather than an attack on it, behavioural finance shows the limits of the rationality of retail consumers of financial services.[4] A study conducted by the French Autorité des Marchés Financiers (AMF), for example, came to the staggering conclusion that, with respect to equity investments, only 19 per cent of the respondents regularly consulted company documents—such as the prospectus or company disclosures—and that even only 29 per cent of the respondents regularly consulted the information provided by the banks.[5] Moreover it has been shown that there is a negative correlation between the quantity of the information which is provided and the chances that a consumer will actually read it. A pile of technical information has a discouraging effect and may result in consumers not reading anything, or only the less important parts. Furthermore, compliance with heavy information requirements is not without costs (such as compiling, monitoring, compliance and transmission). Those costs will often be passed on to the recipients of such information.

(3) Information finally also generates responsibility. To a greater or lesser extent, if it can be proven that accurate information has been disclosed, the supposedly informed consumer of financial services can be considered responsible for his or her own acts. The provision of information can therefore lead to a shift in the responsibility risk from the provider of the financial service to the consumer. This is the flip-side of the information paradigm.

In view of the comments made with respect to the information paradigm, there seems to exist a tendency for legislators throughout the European Union to try to complement disclosure rules with alternative ways of—often more substantive—consumer protection. This is very much the case in the context of consumer credit where mandatory disclosure is linked to the concept of 'responsible lending'.

I Ramsay, From Truth in Lending to Responsible Lending[6] **6.2 (EU)**

This [responsible lending] would require a credit supplier to gather information on the likelihood of a consumer being able to repay a credit obligation both at the time of entering an agreement and on any amendment of the agreement. ... The creditor must also choose the most appropriate form of credit for a consumer given the financial situation of the consumer, weighing the advantages and disadvantages associated with the product proposed and the purpose of the credit. Given the limits of consumer decision-making, the concept of responsible lending may be justified as a response to the limits of information disclosure to consumers as a technique for avoiding over-indebtedness.

[4] A Shleifer, *Inefficient Markets—An Introduction to Behavioral Finance* (Oxford, Oxford University Press, 2000) 216 and R Thaler (ed), *Advances in Behavioral Finance*, vol II (New York, Russell Sage Foundation, 2005) 712.

[5] AMF, 'Exploration des processus d'information et de gestion et diagnostic des documents à destination des épargnants (actionnaires, détenteurs d'OPCVM et épargne salariale)—Document de synthèse sur l'ensemble du dispositif (TNS Sofres)' (November 2006) 51, available at www.amf-france.org.

[6] I Ramsay, 'From Truth in Lending to Responsible Lending' in G Howells, A Janssen and R Schulze (eds), *Information Rights and Obligations* (Aldershot, Ashgate, 2004) 57.

Note

In this context, a growing literature on 'financial capability' and 'financial education'—drawing from social science, including consumer behaviour studies—has attracted the attention of many legislators, including the European Commission.[7] In the United Kingdom, the Financial Services Authority (FSA) has set up and leads the National Strategy for Financial Capability.

FSA, Financial Capability in the UK: Delivering Change, March 2006[8] **6.3 (UK)**

Although the responsibilities that individuals face are significant and growing, many people's ability to meet them is weak. This is not surprising: financial education and information has simply failed to keep pace with social and economic developments. But it is a problem: the results of our comprehensive Survey show that, unless action is taken, we may be storing up considerable problems for the future. The Financial Capability Survey results present four main challenges.

—Unless action is taken, the UK population will store up problems for the future. People need to save, both for a rainy day and for the longer-term. Our Survey found that, while most people do not make provision for an unexpected drop in income or major expense, such events are fairly common even in a favourable economic environment, and often push people into difficulties. In addition, adequate pension provision is becoming ever more important: for example, defined benefit ('final salary') schemes are in steep decline.

—Many people could be tipped into financial difficulties by a small change in their circumstances. Two million households are only just managing as it is. Given the general tendency not to plan ahead adequately, many could be pushed into financial difficulties if interest rates or unemployment rise, or simply if their personal circumstances change.

—Many people are taking on inappropriate risks and not shopping around to get a good deal. Many could face problems in the future as a result of risks which they are not protected against, either through poor choices or simply lack of awareness that they face the risk. In addition, most households spend significant amounts on financial services: by shopping around for a good deal, they stand to save themselves substantial sums of money.

—The greatest demands are placed on those least equipped to deal with them. The under-40s face a considerably more demanding environment than their parents did, and consequently can ill afford to make mistakes or ignore the need to take action. There is therefore a particularly pressing need to equip them with greater financial capability.

Overall, our Survey reveals a picture in which many people from all backgrounds and all levels of income lack the ability to manage their finances effectively. This underlines the fact that there is no single 'silver bullet' solution and that a sustained, broadly-based programme is necessary if we are to make progress. It is especially concerning that financial capability is weakest among younger age groups, even allowing for their relative inexperience in dealing with financial institutions. Demographic and other factors place greater demands on them, but they are less able to meet them. In particular, the

[7] Green Paper on Retail Financial Services in the Single Market, COM [2007] 226 final, 15–16.

[8] See www.fsa.gov.uk.

lack of financial capability in planning ahead is storing up potential trouble. In many cases, this is not because people are unaware that they need to do something—rather, they need to know where and how to start addressing the challenges that they see.

Note

The National Strategy for Financial Capability is implemented by the FSA through a series of measures, including (i) requiring schools to provide personal financial education in the classroom, (ii) revamping the FSA's consumer communications and information to make them more targeted, engaging and accessible, (iii) developing and distributing a so-called 'Money Box' containing information for new parents, better equipping them to take on the additional financial responsibilities of parenthood, and (iv) ensuring that consumers have access to financial advice that is relevant, engaging and of good quality.

Questions

(1) 'Financial capability' programmes reflect some degree of optimism that it is possible for legislators or supervisory authorities to improve or rationalise consumers' financial decision making. However, it remains largely unproven whether such measures work effectively. Do you believe that measures such as those proposed by the FSA will gain the attention of the average consumer?

(2) Will these measures gain the attention of vulnerable consumers?

I.B ACCESS TO FINANCIAL SERVICES

Traditionally the initiation of a relationship concerning financial services is perceived as a matter of contract law. Whether a client and a financial institution initiate a relationship depends on whether they both agree to contract with each other. Increasingly, however, this pure contract law approach is being eroded, in at least two different ways. On the one hand, financial institutions are now expected to vet their clients, by checking the origins of their funds (anti-money laundering and anti-terrorism regulations), or their experience and financial capability (consumer credit, investment services). Where those checks reveal that a particular financial service or product may not be suitable for a particular client, the freedom of the financial institution to contract with such a client will be restricted, and sometimes the institution will even have to refrain from contracting with such a client at all.

On the other hand, financial services are increasingly regarded as instruments that enable individuals to participate fully in society. There is a growing awareness that certain financial services are indispensable in a modern society and should therefore be accessible to everyone.

HM Treasury, Financial Inclusion, The Way Forward[9] **6.4 (UK)**

Yet there is growing evidence that the market is not able to meet everyone's needs—and too many families are being left behind. A small but significant minority of people are unable to access even the most basic financial services and instead find themselves trapped outside the financial mainstream. For these people, financial exclusion causes extra costs and real disadvantage in three ways: first, it makes day-to-day money management more difficult and expensive, and can make it harder to find a job; second, financial exclusion makes it harder for families to plan for the future and manage lumpy spending; and third, if things go wrong, financial exclusion makes people more vulnerable to financial distress and a spiral of debt, poverty and hardship.

Note

Consumers who are excluded from certain products or services may find themselves in a position where they are excluded from the opportunities that would otherwise exist. Consequently, the freedom of financial institutions to 'refuse' certain categories of clients has eroded, as in a growing number of jurisdictions initiatives are taken to actively counter the exclusion of groups of consumers from what are considered basic financial services and to guarantee access for everyone to these services.

I.C STRUCTURE OF THE CHAPTER

The further discussion in this chapter attempts to focus on the themes introduced above. The chapter will be divided into three broad sections: credit services, investment services, and banking and payment services. For each of the sections, we consider

- how access is granted to the financial service in question;
- what category of persons is protected; and
- what the mechanisms of consumer protection are—be it information requirements or alternative ways of protection.

It should be noted that provisions that only *indirectly* protect the general public (and thus also consumers of financial services), such as organisational requirements (capital adequacy requirements, quality requirements for management, etc) relating to banks, credit providers, investment firms or collective investment entities, will not be dealt with.

[9] March 2007, see www.hm-treasury.gov.uk.

II. CONSUMER PROTECTION IN THE FIELD OF CREDIT SERVICES

II.A INTRODUCTION

Consumer protection is particularly important in the field of credit services. In most cases, the decision to purchase a house or a car and finance such purchase by way of credit has important financial consequences for consumers (and their families) over a significant period of time. Importantly, this not only concerns 'vulnerable' consumers—including overconfident or irrational consumers—and consumers who are not financially capable, but also 'average' consumers.

The most important types of credit available to consumers are consumer credit and mortgage loans. The first type of credit—consumer credit—is the subject of EC harmonisation, in particular the Consumer Credit Directive (2008/48/EC)[10] which replaced the old Consumer Credit Directive (87/102/EEC).[11] The field of mortgage loans has not yet been harmonised, although a voluntary code of conduct and a Commission Recommendation (2001/193/EC) of 1 March 2001 on pre-contractual information to be given to consumers by lenders offering home loans exist.

II.B ACCESS TO CREDIT SERVICES

Automated credit-scoring processes are increasingly used and bad credit databases are becoming widespread throughout the European Union. This has now also been confirmed in Article 9 of the Consumer Credit Directive (2008/48/EC).

Consumer Credit Directive (2008/48/EC) **6.5 (EU)**

Art 9 (1) Each Member State shall in the case of cross-border credit ensure access for creditors from other Member States to databases used in that Member State for assessing the creditworthiness of consumers. The conditions for access shall be non-discriminatory.

(2) If the credit application is rejected on the basis of consultation of a database, the creditor shall inform the consumer immediately and without charge of the result of such consultation and of the particulars of the database consulted.

(3) The information shall be provided unless the provision of such information is prohibited by other Community legislation or is contrary to objectives of public policy or public security.

[10] Directive 2008/48/EC of 23 April 2008 on credit agreements for consumers and repealing Council Directive 87/102/EEC [2008] OJ L 133, 66–92.

[11] Council Directive 87/102/EEC of 22 December 1986 for the approximation of the laws, regulations and administrative provisions of the Member States concerning consumer credit [1987] OJ L 42, 48–53.

Note

Notwithstanding the practical convenience of such automated systems, a conflict may arise between the protection of financially incapable consumers against over-indebtedness on the one hand, and privacy and their access to affordable financial services (and in particular to consumer credit) on the other hand. Such a conflict cannot be easily resolved.

House of Lords (European Union Committee)[12] **6.6 (UK)**

183. The traditional method of deciding whether credit should be granted to a consumer was by interview of the applicant for credit and appraisal of the application by a loan officer, who would also draw on his or her experience in coming to a decision. That method was shown to be unreliable, in that credit was being granted to consumers who should not have been given it and was being refused to those who were in fact well-qualified to receive it. … So the process of evaluation on an individual basis by a human agency was largely replaced by credit scoring, a computer-based process in which characteristics considered relevant to creditworthiness are assessed electronically in the following way: Income, financial assets, amount of existing indebtedness, length of credit history, payment record, length of residence at current address, occupation, employment pattern, number of accounts and of credit cards held and other relevant data are identified by a statistical analysis of the profiles of a large sample of the creditor's customers and their repayment histories. Each characteristic is weighted according to its relevance to the degree of predictability of the ability to repay or the likelihood of default. The applicant for credit is then measured against the statistical pool of customers and for that purpose is allocated points for each characteristic based on information supplied by the applicant or obtained from other sources, for example, information held on databases maintained by credit reference agencies, and the register of county court judgments. … The total score will determine the applicant's eligibility for credit or alternatively influence the interest rate charged, a feature of the increasingly-used technique of risk-based pricing, in which the rate of interest a consumer is charged varies according to the lender's assessment of the likelihood of default.

Note

Theoretically, those mechanisms are intended to protect vulnerable consumers from over-indebtedness, as lenders may be required to consult the lists and deny credit to bad creditors. As lenders are increasingly required to engage in 'responsible lending' (see below), they should carefully assess the financial ability and capability of borrowers. Such assessment can only viably be made on the basis of available information, and thus it makes sense that all information relating to a borrower and the credit risk can be consulted by the lender. However, a strong reliance on *automated* credit-scoring mechanisms risks creating a dichotomy between good debtors and bad debtors. Whilst the first category can choose the most adequate credit product at the best conditions from the best lender, the latter category may

[12] Session 2005–06, Thirty-Sixth Report, No 183.

become excluded from regular credit, implying that they could end up with higher premiums and annual percentage rates, or even be excluded from credit altogether. Bad credit risk could thus result in a vicious circle, in which credit is being repaid by other credit (which may be packaged in so-called 'roll-over credit cards') with higher annual percentage rates. Even worse, the consumer who, for whatever reason, ends up on such blacklists risks being cut off from normal credit service providers, and is a potential victim for 'loan sharks'—creditors who speculate on defaults on payment in order to charge exaggerated fees and penalties.

Other—even more fundamental—concerns should also be taken into account, as the following excerpt convincingly shows.

F Ferretti, The Regulation of Consumer Credit Information Systems: Is the EU Missing a Chance?[13] **6.7 (EU)**

More important, however, seems the question of how far a consumer should be forced to sacrifice his or her own (not only financial) privacy in the interest of the credit industry (the general interest?), bearing in mind that the 'utilitarian' concerns of the credit industry cannot necessarily prevail over civil liberty and fundamental human rights concerns. To these ends, in fact, it should be taken into account that all privacy rights now benefit from, and should be interpreted in light of, Art 8 of the European Convention for the Protection of Human Rights and Fundamental Freedoms.

Moreover, the profiling and standardisation of the behaviours of individuals not only appear hazardous for the civil rights involved, but also conceited and artificial. Very often, contrary to the very foundations of credit reporting, human behaviours are heterogeneous and unpredictable. As recent research has stressed, in fact, the major factors behind the creditworthiness or over-indebtedness of individuals were found to be unforeseen life events, such as sudden illness, loss of job, death of someone close, etc rather than a mismanagement of resources.

From a different angle, it could be also argued that someone who has had problems in the past does not necessarily have problems at present or in the future. Or, an individual also may have a low profile credit record from failing to make payments, which are either not due or are in conflict with the service provider's claims.

Currently, a tendency seems to exist throughout the European Union that stresses the need for information for lenders, and is designed to make available databases to lenders, within the Member States as well as on a cross-border basis, sacrificing to a certain extent privacy law considerations and potentially provoking exclusion of some categories of consumers.

[13] F Ferretti, 'The Regulation of Consumer Credit Information Systems: Is the EU Missing a Chance?' (2007) 34 *Legal Issues of Economic Integration* 115–31, 124.

Consumer Ombudsman's Newsletter: Data Protection Ombudsman Says No[14] **6.8 (FI)**

A collection agency wanted to expand its operations and start selling information on customers' credit situation that it had collected during collection activities to businesses offering loans. The idea was that businesses offering credit could urge prospective customers to commission the collection agency to supply information, in which case information would only be divulged with the person's consent, according to the agency's interpretation. Such a practice would not be fair, however, since a commission situation is only real if a commission is made voluntarily. A person's right to check his or her own credit information cannot be transferred to another party, even with a commission. The Debt Collection Act also emphasizes the need to protect privacy. The Consumer Ombudsman's guidelines on good practice in consumer debt collection are built on this principle.

Debt collection is a licensed trade in Finland and a collection agency may only include information that is essential for operations in its files. It may not gather other information even with a person's consent. Personal data gathered for debt collection may only be used for this purpose. Consequently the Data Protection Ombudsman has said that information cannot be used for credit decision services.

Note

Questions such as who can gather these data (only public institutions or also private institutions), and who can gain access to these data (can these data be sold as a commercial asset?) have led to interesting discussions on the delicate conflict between privacy issues and economic efficiency.

II.C WHO IS PROTECTED BY THE RULES

It is important to determine who the borrower is that the consumer credit laws intend to protect.

Consumer Credit Directive (2008/48/EC) **6.9 (EU)**

Article 3 (a) 'consumer' means a natural person who, in transactions covered by this Directive, is acting for purposes which are outside his trade, business or profession.

Note

As shown by the excerpt, the Consumer Credit Directive (2008/48/EC) definition of consumer involves two exclusionary aspects: only natural persons are protected and only on the condition that they are not acting on a professional basis. The limitation with respect to the personal scope of the definition of consumer in the Consumer Credit Directive (2008/48/EC)—which is the same as in the old Consumer Credit Directive (87/102/EEC)—has raised various questions, often related to the mixed

[14] Newsletter 9/2006.

personal–business use of a credit or situations where credit is granted to a small business entity. For instance, if the borrower is a small corporate entity, it will fall outside the scope of the harmonised consumer credit laws, even though the borrower may be in a fairly weak position.

The following judgment of the French Cour de Cassation shows that a very careful examination of the circumstances in which the credit was granted is therefore needed.

Cass civ, 18 December 2001[15] **6.10 (FR)**
Vilbert v Crédit Commercial de France

IMPORTANCE OF THE CONTRACTUAL PURPOSE OF THE CREDIT OPERATION

Mixed credit

The contractual purpose of each separate credit transaction must be examined in order to assess whether the consumer credit protection applies.

Facts: The Crédit Commercial de France had granted a renewable credit to Mr Vilbert, which was linked in part to his personal and his professional credit. Mr Vilbert argued that the credit thus became subject to the French consumer credit law.

Judgment: A Court of Appeal violates article L 311-3.3 of the Consumer Code if it fails to apply this provision to the agreed amount of credit on the personal and professional accounts of the borrower and, without examining the contractual purpose of each separate credit transaction, it would hold that the different accounts and credit agreements were all linked to the professional needs of the borrower.

Several jurisdictions, such as Germany, have gone even further and have chosen to broaden the personal scope of application of the consumer credit law.

BGB **6.11 (DE)**

§507 Application to small businesses

§§491–506 also apply to natural persons who are granted a loan, postponement of payment or other financing assistance to commence a trade or start a self-employed professional activity or who enter into an instalment supply contract for this purpose, unless the net loan amount or the cash price exceeds €50.000.

Interestingly, whilst some Member States have tried to expand the consumer notion, others, such as the United Kingdom, have provided the possibility of excluding certain types of consumers, such as "high net worth" individuals.

[15] Bull civ No 9914544.

Consumer Credit Act 2006 **6.12 (UK)**

Section 3 Exemption relating to high net worth debtors and hirers ...

(1) The Secretary of State may by order provide that this Act shall not regulate a consumer credit agreement or a consumer hire agreement where

(a) the debtor or hirer is a natural person;

(b) the agreement includes a declaration made by him to the effect that he agrees to forgo the protection and remedies that would be available to him under this Act if the agreement were a regulated agreement;

(c) a statement of high net worth has been made in relation to him; and

(d) that statement is current in relation to the agreement and a copy of it was provided to the creditor or owner before the agreement was made.

A related question that was considered by the ECJ was whether the scope of the old Consumer Credit Directive (87/102/EEC) also extended to guarantors.

ECJ Case C-208/98, 23 March 2000[16] **6.13 (EU)**
Berliner Kindl Brauerei AG v Andreas Siepert

NON APPLICATION OF THE CONSUMER CREDIT DIRECTIVE TO GUARANTORS

Guarantee for the brewery

The old Consumer Credit Directive 87/102/EEC does not cover a contract of guarantee for repayment of credit where neither the guarantor nor the borrower was acting in the course of his trade or profession.

Facts: Mr Siepert gave a guarantee to Berliner Kindl Brauerei ('the Brewery'), to the value of DEM 90,000, for the repayment of loans granted by the Brewery to a third party for opening a restaurant. In so doing, Mr Siepert was not acting in the course of a trade or profession. Since the principal debtor failed to meet his obligations, the Brewery called in the loans and obtained, by judgment of the Landgericht Rostock, an order directing Mr Siepert to pay the sum of DEM 28,952.43 together with interest. In his capacity as guarantor, Mr Siepert was ordered to pay the same amount, by judgment in default. Subsequently, Mr Siepert made an application to have that judgment set aside.

Judgment: 17. The first point to note is that, under Article 1(2)(c) of the Directive, the only agreements covered are those whereby 'a creditor grants or promises to grant to a consumer a credit in the form of a deferred payment, a loan or other similar financial accommodation'.

18. It is common ground that a contract of guarantee is not a credit agreement within the meaning of Article 1(2)(c). Since the wording of that provision does not accommodate the interpretation that guarantees are covered by the Directive, it must be determined whether they fall within its scope by implication, in the light of its scheme and aims. ...

25. Given the objectives of Directive 87/102, on the other hand, which almost entirely concern the information to be given to the principal debtor regarding the implications of his commitment, and bearing in mind the fact that it is almost devoid of provisions that

[16] [2000] ECR I-01741.

might afford an effective safeguard to the guarantor—whose primary concern is to have knowledge concerning the solvency of the principal debtor in order to assess the likelihood of being called upon to repay the credit granted—that directive must be regarded as not being designed to apply to contracts of guarantee.

26. Furthermore, the scope of the Directive cannot be widened to cover contracts of guarantee solely on the ground that such agreements are ancillary to the principal agreement whose performance they underwrite, since there is no support for such an interpretation in the wording of the Directive, as was pointed out in paragraph 18 above, or in its scheme and aims.

27. In the light of the foregoing, the answer to the question referred for a preliminary ruling must be that, on a proper construction of the Directive, it does not cover a contract of guarantee for the repayment of credit where neither the guarantor nor the borrower was acting in the course of his trade or profession.

Questions

(1) How are similar contracts of guarantee for the repayment of credit treated under the present Consumer Credit Directive (2008/48/EC)?

(2) What is the *rationale* for European legislation to limit the harmonisation to natural persons acting for their private needs only and not to extend certain protection to (small) business owners?

(3) In your opinion, is this a good policy? Consider also that, apart from a 'consumer' protection element, there might be an argument based on the integration of the markets, and the obstacles for a lender to target commercial borrowers in another Member State.

II.D CONSUMER PROTECTION MECHANISMS

II.D.1 INFORMATION REQUIREMENTS

II.D.1.a The harmonisation of the information requirements under the Consumer Credit Directive

The Consumer Credit Directive (2008/48/EC) is aimed at ensuring that the consumer receives 'adequate information' in order to enable him or her to make a decision 'in full knowledge of the facts' (see Preamble 19).

Consumer Credit Directive (2008/48/EC) **6.14 (EU)**

Article 5 (1) In good time before the consumer is bound by any credit agreement or offer, the creditor and, where applicable, the credit intermediary shall, on the basis of the credit terms and conditions offered by the creditor and, if applicable, the preferences expressed and information supplied by the consumer, provide the consumer with the information needed to compare different offers in order to take an informed decision on whether to conclude a credit agreement. Such information, on paper or on another durable medium, shall be provided by means of the Standard European Consumer Credit

Information form set out in Annex II. The creditor shall be deemed to have fulfilled the information requirements in this paragraph and in Article 3, paragraphs (1) and (2) of Directive 2002/65/EC if he has supplied the Standard European Consumer Credit Information. The information in question shall specify:

(a) the type of credit;

(b) the identity and the geographical address of the creditor as well as, if applicable, the identity and geographical address of the credit intermediary involved;

(c) the total amount of credit and the conditions governing the drawdown;

(d) the duration of the credit agreement;

(e) in the case of a credit in the form of deferred payment for a specific good or service and linked credit agreements, that good or service and its cash price;

(f) the borrowing rate, the conditions governing the application of the borrowing rate and, where available, any index or reference rate applicable to the initial borrowing rate, as well as the periods, conditions and procedure for changing the borrowing rate …

(g) the annual percentage rate of charge and the total amount payable by the consumer, illustrated by means of a representative example mentioning all the assumptions used in order to calculate that rate …

(h) the amount, number and frequency of payments to be made by the consumer …

(i) where applicable, the charges for maintaining one or several accounts recording both payment transactions and drawdowns …

(j) where applicable, the existence of costs payable by the consumer to a notary on conclusion of the credit agreement;

(k) the obligation, if any, to enter into an ancillary service contract relating to the credit agreement, in particular an insurance policy, where the conclusion of such a contract is compulsory in order to obtain the credit or to obtain it on the terms and conditions marketed;

(l) the interest rate applicable in the case of late payments and the arrangements for its adjustment, and, where applicable, any charges payable for default;

(m) a warning regarding the consequences of missing payments;

(n) where applicable, the sureties required;

(o) the existence or absence of a right of withdrawal;

(p) the right of early repayment, and, where applicable, information concerning the creditor's right to compensation and the way in which that compensation will be determined in accordance with Article 16;

(q) the consumer's right to be informed immediately and free of charge, pursuant to Article 9(2), of the result of a database consultation carried out for the purposes of assessing his creditworthiness;

(r) the consumer's right to be supplied, on request and free of charge, with a copy of the draft credit agreement. This provision shall not apply if the creditor is at the time of the request unwilling to proceed to the conclusion of the credit agreement with the consumer; and

(s) if applicable, the period of time during which the creditor is bound by the pre-contractual information.

Any additional information which the creditor may provide to the consumer shall be given in a separate document which may be annexed to the Standard European Consumer Credit Information form. …

(6) Member States shall ensure that creditors and, where applicable, credit intermediaries provide adequate explanations to the consumer, in order to place the consumer in a position enabling him to assess whether the proposed credit agreement is adapted

to his needs and to his financial situation, where appropriate by explaining the pre-contractual information to be provided in accordance with paragraph 1, the essential characteristics of the products proposed and the specific effects they may have on the consumer, including the consequences of default in payment by the consumer. Member States may adapt the manner by which and the extent to which such assistance is given, as well as by whom it is given, to the particular circumstances of the situation in which the credit agreement is offered, the person to whom it is offered and the type of credit offered.

Notes

(1) As is clear from the previous excerpts, the Consumer Credit Directive (2008/48/EC) aims at increasing the transparency, comparability and comprehensibility of the information that is given. This is to be achieved by the use of a 'Standard European Consumer Credit Information' form, which (at least in theory) will inform consumers throughout the European Union in an identical manner. Furthermore, Article 5(6) requires creditors and credit intermediaries to provide 'adequate explanations' and where appropriate to explain not only the 'essential characteristics' of the product but also the effects on the consumer.

(2) Taking into account those same goals, Article 4 of the Consumer Credit Directive (2008/48/EC) also regulates the 'standard information' that must be included in advertising (insofar as such advertising indicates an interest rate or any figures relating to the cost of the credit to the consumer). In particular, the standard information must specify 'in a clear, concise and prominent way by means of a representative example': (a) the borrowing rate, together with particulars of any charges included in the total cost of the credit to the consumer; (b) the total amount of credit; (c) the annual percentage rate of charge (in certain circumstances Member States may decide that the annual percentage rate of charge need not be provided); (d) if applicable, the duration of the credit agreement; (e) in the case of a credit in the form of deferred payment for a specific good or service, the cash price and the amount of any advance payment; and (f) if applicable, the total amount payable by the consumer and the amount of the instalments (see Article 4(2)). It is interesting to note that in Article 4(4) it is expressly provided that these advertisement requirements are without prejudice to the Unfair Commercial Practices Directive. Preamble 18 indeed seems to confirm in this regard that the specific provisions of the Consumer Credit Directive (2008/48/EC) are to be read together with the more general provisions of the Unfair Commercial Practices Directive.

(3) Another important information requirement concerns the assignment of the rights of the creditor. Article 17(2) of the Consumer Credit Directive (2008/48/EC) provides that the consumer must be informed of an assignment of the rights of the creditor, except where the original creditor, by agreement with the assignee, continues to service the credit vis-à-vis the consumer. In that context it can be noted that the Directive provides for the rule that the consumer shall be entitled to plead against the assignee any defence which was available to him against the original creditor, including set-off where the latter is permitted in the Member State concerned.

(4) The Consumer Credit Directive (2008/48/EC) does not regulate contract law issues related to the validity of credit agreements. Preamble 30 expressly confirms that the Member States may maintain or introduce national provisions which are in conformity with Community law. Member States may regulate the legal regime governing the offer to conclude the credit agreement, in particular when it is to be given and the period during which it is to be binding on the creditor. However, if such an offer is made at the same time as the pre-contractual information, it should be provided in a separate document which may be annexed to the Standard European Consumer Credit Information.

In contrast to the high degree of harmonisation reached by the Consumer Credit Directive (2008/48/EC), under the old Consumer Credit Directive (87/102/EEC) the information requirements were not harmonised and therefore important divergences continued to exist throughout the European Union. Consider, for instance, the following French case.

Consumer Credit Directive (2008/48/EC)[17] **6.15 (FR)**

[Preamble] **(3)** … reports and consultations revealed substantial differences between the laws of the various Member States in the field of credit for natural persons in general and consumer credit in particular. An analysis of the national laws transposing Directive 87/102/EEC shows that Member States use a variety of consumer protection mechanisms, in addition to Directive 87/102/EEC, on account of differences in the legal or economic situation at national level.

(4) The de facto and de jure situation resulting from those national differences in some cases leads to distortions of competition among creditors in the Community and creates obstacles to the internal market where Member States have adopted different mandatory provisions more stringent than those provided for in Directive 87/102/EEC. It restricts consumers' ability to make direct use of the gradually increasing availability of cross-border credit. Those distortions and restrictions may in turn have consequences in terms of the demand for goods and services.

Note

Diverging national consumer protection rules make little sense in a European market where consumers from one Member State may easily borrow from lenders from another Member State. This seems an obvious case for harmonisation. However, harmonising such a sensitive subject-matter as consumer credit—with a direct impact on the lives of millions of consumers—has proved to be an extremely difficult task for the European legislator. Not surprisingly, the Consumer Credit Directive (2008/48/EC) is a delicate compromise between different— political, ethical and

[17] Directive 2008/48/EC of 23 April 2008 on credit agreements for consumers and repealing Council Directive 87/102/EEC [2008] OJ L 133, 66–92.

ideological—stances on important questions such as: What is the general advantage of consumer credit for society? How to reduce over-indebtedness whilst ensuring access to credit? Should marketing of credit be permitted and how can vulnerable categories of consumers be protected? What benefits to consumers do costly information requirements produce?

Questions

(1) One could also argue that the divergences under the old Consumer Credit Directive (87/102/EEC) do not really matter since this merely results in costs that the lender has to bear to be active in another jurisdiction. Does that counter-argument make sense?

(2) In your opinion, are the divergences existing under the old Consumer Credit Directive (87/102/EEC) obstacles for consumers to borrow in other Member States, or obstacles for lenders to engage in cross-border lending (or both)? Consider, for instance, that a credit product or a credit service that is perfectly legal in one Member State may be illegal in another Member State.

(3) Would the full harmonisation as contemplated by the Consumer Credit Directive (2008/48/EC) be effective enough to create a real single European market in consumer credit? In that respect, consider, for instance, the preamble to the Consumer Credit Directive (2008/48/EC).

Consumer Credit Directive (2008/48/EC) **6.16 (EU)**

[Preamble] **(9)** Full harmonisation is necessary in order to ensure that all consumers in the Community enjoy a high and equivalent level of protection of their interests and to create a genuine internal market. Member States should therefore not be allowed to maintain or introduce national provisions other than those laid down in this Directive. However, such restriction should only apply where there are provisions harmonised in this Directive. Where no such harmonised provisions exist, Member States should remain free to maintain or introduce national legislation. Accordingly, Member States may, for instance, maintain or introduce national provisions on joint and several liability of the seller or the service provider and the creditor. Another example of this possibility for Member States could be the maintenance or introduction of national provisions on the cancellation of a contract for the sale of goods or supply of services if the consumer exercises his right of withdrawal from the credit agreement. In this respect Member States, in the case of open-end credit agreements, should be allowed to fix a minimum period needing to elapse between the time when the creditor asks for reimbursement and the day on which the credit has to be reimbursed.

II.D.1.b Formalities at the core of the consumer credit protection

Credit services disputes relatively often end up before the court. In such cases, the lender typically asks for the credit agreement, or any security taken in the context thereof, to be fully enforced, whilst the borrower—the consumer—pleads that some formality has not been fulfilled.

In its *Rampion* judgment the ECJ decided that the old Consumer Credit Directive (87/102/EEC) was to be interpreted as allowing national courts to apply the consumer credit protection provisions of their own motion.

ECJ Case C-429/05, 4 October 2007[18] **6.17 (EU)**

Max Rampion and Marie-Jeanne Godard v Franfinance SA and K par K SAS

APPLICATION OF CONSUMER PROTECTION PROVISIONS

Windows infested with parasites

Directive 87/102/EEC is to be interpreted as allowing national courts to apply of their own motion the provisions transposing Article 11(2) thereof into national law.

Facts: Following an approach by a door-to-door salesperson, Mr and Mrs Rampion ordered windows from KpK for a total price of €6.150. According to the contract of sale, the windows were to be delivered no later than six to eight weeks after the technician had measured up. The contract of sale furthermore indicated that the purchase was to be financed entirely by means of credit granted by Franfinance. The credit arrangement identified the seller by the reference 'K par K platform account' but did not specify the goods being financed. When the windows ordered were delivered, Mr and Mrs Rampion noticed that the sills and frames were infested with parasites. The work went unfinished and the contract of sale was repudiated.

Judgment: 59. The Court has repeatedly stated that, as is clear from its preamble, Directive 87/102 was adopted with the dual aim of ensuring both the creation of a common consumer credit market (third to fifth recitals) and the protection of consumers who avail themselves of such credit (sixth, seventh and ninth recitals) ...

64. On that point, it should be recalled that while Article 11(2) of Directive 87/102 pursues the dual aim described in paragraph 59 of the present judgment, it seeks to confer on the consumer, in well-defined circumstances, rights vis-à-vis the grantor of credit over and above the consumer's normal contractual rights against the grantor of credit and against the supplier of the goods or services (see paragraph 42 of the present judgment).

65. That aim could not be effectively achieved if the consumer were himself obliged to invoke the right to pursue remedies which he enjoys against the grantor of credit in accordance with the provisions of national law transposing Article 11(2) of Directive 87/102, in particular because of the real risk that the consumer may be unaware of his rights or may encounter difficulties in exercising them. As the Advocate General stated at point 107 of his Opinion, the fact that the main proceedings were brought by Mr and Mrs Rampion and that they are represented in those proceedings by a lawyer does not justify a different conclusion, as the issue must be settled independently of the specific circumstances of the case ...

69. The answer to Question 2 must therefore be that Directive 87/102 is to be interpreted as allowing national courts to apply of their own motion the provisions transposing Article 11(2) thereof into national law.

[18] [2007] ECR I-08017.

Notes

(1) Article 11(2) of the old Consumer Credit Directive (87/102/EEC) provides for the right of the consumer to pursue remedies against the grantor of credit under five—strict—conditions: (a) such right only exists where in order to buy goods or obtain services the consumer has entered into a credit agreement with a person other than the supplier of them; (b) the grantor of the credit and the supplier of the goods or services have a pre-existing agreement under which credit is made available exclusively by that grantor of credit to customers of that supplier for the acquisition of goods or services from that supplier; (c) the consumer has obtained his credit pursuant to that pre-existing agreement; (d) the goods or services covered by the credit agreement are not supplied, or are supplied only in part, or are not in conformity with the contract for supply of them; and (e) the consumer has pursued his remedies against the supplier but has failed to obtain the satisfaction to which he is entitled.

(2) The Consumer Credit Directive (2008/48/EC) reaffirms this right, though it is stated that the directive 'should not deprive consumers of their rights under national provisions attaching joint and several liability to the seller or supplier of services and to the creditor' (see preamble 38 and Article 15(3)). Article 3(n) of the Directive now defines 'linked credit agreement' as a credit agreement where (a) the credit in question serves exclusively to finance an agreement for the supply of specific goods or the provision of a specific service; and (b) those two agreements form, from an objective point of view, a commercial unit; a commercial unit shall be deemed to exist where the supplier or service provider himself finances the credit for the consumer or, if it is financed by a third party, where the creditor uses the services of the supplier or service provider in connection with the conclusion or preparation of the credit agreement, or where the specific goods or the provision of a specific service are explicitly specified in the credit agreement. Article 15(2) of the directive further provides that where the goods or services covered by a linked credit agreement are not supplied, or are supplied only in part, or are not in conformity with the contract for the supply thereof, the consumer shall have the right to pursue remedies against the creditor if the consumer has pursued his remedies against the supplier but has failed to obtain the satisfaction to which he is entitled according to the law or the contract for the supply of goods or services. Member States shall determine to what extent and under what conditions those remedies shall be exercisable.

Questions

(1) How does the new regime of 'linked credit agreements' relate to Article 11(2) of the old Consumer Credit Directive (87/102/EEC)? Do you think the differences will increase the protection of a consumer who is purchasing goods or services on credit?

(2) It is interesting to note Article 15(1) of the Consumer Credit Directive (2008/48/EC) which provides that where the consumer has exercised a right of withdrawal 'based on Community law' concerning a contract for the supply of goods

or services, he shall no longer be bound by a linked credit agreement. In that context also consider the impact of the *Rampion* judgment.

Formalities are really at the core of many national consumer credit laws, as is clear from this excerpt from a judgment of the French Cour de Cassation.

Cass civ 1e, 29 October 2002[19] **6.18 (FR)**
Epoux X v Crédit Foncier de France

FORM IS OF THE ESSENCE OF CREDIT PROTECTION

Crédit foncier de France

Provisions regarding the evidence of a consumer's consent must be strictly complied with.

Facts: Following a credit offer, Mr and Mrs X claimed that they had received a postal offer on 18 August 1992. Under French law, the credit offer must be accepted in writing within ten days of receipt of the offer; in the absence of proof thereof the lender would lose the right to claim interest on the loan. Crédit Foncier de France granted Mr and Mrs X a mortgage, which was recorded in a legal document on 11 September 1992. Mr and Mrs X then argued that the bank failed to show that the ten-day time limit had been respected and that their acceptance had reached the bank by mail. They took legal action against Crédit Foncier in March 1996, attempting to force the bank to be deprived of its right to claim interest.

Judgment: Whereas the contested judgement maintains that ... since Mr and Mrs X signed a declaration that confirmed their acceptance of the offer on 29 August 1992 and acknowledged that they were in possession of a copy of the offer, their acceptance had been proven, even though such acceptance occurred after the time limit of 10 days ...

Whereas, in ruling in this way, since the acceptance had not been presented in the form outlined in article L 312-10 of the Consumer Code, the date of acceptance cannot be evidenced...

Given the above considerations, the judgement is declared null and void.

ECJ Case C-264/02, 4 March 2004[20] **6.19 (EU)**
Cofinoga Mérignac SA v Sylvain Sachithanathan

NO INFORMATION ON APR UPON CREDIT RENEWAL

Cofinoga

The old Consumer Credit Directive does not require, before each renewal, on the existing terms and conditions, of a credit agreement for a specified period entered into in the form of a credit facility that bears an interest rate that is expressed to be variable, that

[19] Bull civ No 1513.
[20] [2004] ECR I-02157.

the lender informs the borrower in writing of the current APR and of the conditions under which the latter may be amended.

Facts: Cofinoga granted a loan to Mr Sachithanathan in the form of a credit facility for a period of one year, with the possibility of renewal, available for drawdown in instalments and linked to a credit card, repayable in monthly instalments at an annual percentage rate (APR) that was expressed to be variable. As sums owing remained unpaid, Cofinoga brought proceedings against Mr Sachithanathan before the Tribunal d'instance de Vienne for payment of the amounts due, together with interest and penalties. The Tribunal d'instance de Vienne asked Cofinoga to provide evidence that the agreement had been properly renewed following the expiry of the initial term of one year, as required by Article L 311-9 of the Consumer Code.

Judgment: 22. In the light of the observations submitted to the Court, the first issue to be considered is whether Article 4 of the Directive should be interpreted as meaning that, where a credit agreement is renewed on the existing terms and conditions, the lender is required to inform the consumer of the APR …

24. As neither the wording of Article 4 of the Directive nor the broad logic of the scheme established by that provision support an interpretation according to which the consumer must be informed of the APR on the renewal of a credit agreement on the existing terms and conditions, the issue arises whether the ends pursued by the Directive require that the consumer be informed at this time.

25. It should be noted in that regard that it is clear from the recitals in the preamble thereto that the Directive was adopted with the dual aim of ensuring both the creation of a common market in consumer credit (third to fifth recitals) and the protection of consumers who avail themselves of such credit (sixth, seventh and ninth recitals) …

26. Informing the consumer of the total cost of credit, in the form of an interest rate calculated according to a single mathematical formula, is of critical importance in this regard. First, this information, which, under Article 3 of the Directive, must be stated in any advertising, contributes to the transparency of the market, as it enables the consumer to compare offers of credit. Secondly, it enables the consumer to assess the extent of his liability.

27. In the light of these aims, and as the Advocate General has noted in point 53 of his Opinion, it appears that the information in question will be particularly useful if it is provided to the consumer at the decisive phase which precedes the entering into of the agreement. Thereafter, for example when the agreement is renewed on its existing terms and conditions, this information, which has already been provided, would appear to be of less importance.

28. It follows that, in the absence of express provision to that effect, and in the absence of factors which, on the basis of the broad logic or the aims of the Directive, might lead to the inference that Article 4 of the Directive should be broadly construed, that provision cannot be interpreted as meaning that it requires the lender to inform the consumer of the APR prior to the renewal of a credit agreement on the existing terms and conditions.

29. The fact that, according to the information provided by the national court, the renewal of a credit agreement is treated in French law not as the extension of the original agreement, but as the entering into of a new agreement, does not affect this analysis. As the Advocate General points out in point 43 of his Opinion, the objective of harmonisation underlying the Directive would be frustrated if the interpretation of the rules laid down under it were to depend on the specific provisions of the national law of a particular Member State.

30. In the light of the interpretation to be given to Article 4 of the Directive, it is then appropriate to consider whether Article 6 of the Directive should be interpreted as meaning that, where a credit agreement is renewed on the existing terms and conditions, the lender is required to inform the consumer of the APR. …

39. In the light of the foregoing, the answer to the first and second questions must be that the Directive does not require, before each renewal, on the existing terms and conditions, of a credit agreement for a specified period entered into in the form of a credit facility that may be drawn down in instalments and is linked to a credit card, that is repayable in monthly instalments and bears an interest rate that is expressed to be variable, that the lender inform the borrower in writing of the current APR and of the conditions under which the latter may be amended.

Notes

(1) The 'annual percentage rate of charge' or APR means the total cost of the credit to the consumer, expressed as an annual percentage of the total amount of credit (see Article 3(i) of the Consumer Credit Directive (2008/48/EC).

(2) The *Cofinoga* case-law of the ECJ is more nuanced than the French Cour de Cassation judgment, interpreting the formal information requirements of the old Consumer Credit Directive (87/102/EEC) in the function of its aims.

(3) The Consumer Credit Directive (2008/48/EC) confirms that in order to enable consumers to make their decisions in full knowledge of the facts, they should receive adequate information, which consumers may take away and consider, prior to the conclusion of the credit agreement, on the conditions and cost of the credit and on their obligations (see Preamble 19). To ensure the fullest possible transparency and comparability of offers, such information should, in particular, include the APR of charge applicable to the credit, determined in the same way throughout the Community.

II.D.2 OTHER SUBSTANTIVE PROTECTION RULES, INCLUDING 'RESPONSIBLE LENDING'

Over-indebtedness is an increasing problem in many jurisdictions; this trend may be seen as an indication that the current consumer credit laws do not prevent consumers from taking out loans which they may not be able to repay. Importantly, intuitive ideas about the categories of consumers that may be subject to the risk of over-indebtedness may prove wrong, as appears from the excerpt below from the report of the Dutch supervisory authority, the Autoriteit Financiële Markten (AFM).

AFM, Report on Consumer Credit[21] **6.20 (NL)**

Among the people who are turning to debt counselling there is … besides the low income group, an increasing number of relatively higher earners who took out a considerable consumer credit together with a significant loan without monthly payments or an

[21] May 2004, at 19–20.

investment mortgage. The number of younger people with debt problems is also increasing. ... Younger people are at a proportionally higher rate getting into financial problems because the credit culture is changing. In general, it is more easy to borrow. ... Younger people not only take out loans from the banks but also from family and friends. ... Youngsters have never learnt to manage their money wisely, also partly due to the fact that parents frequently give in to the wishes of their children. Indebted younger people do not easily free themselves from their debt burden. Their earnings are too low to pay back their lenders. Moreover, they are not often eligible for debt remediation. Financial institutions reason that at a young age there is ample time to solve any debt problem.

Note

Traditionally, there are two main ways in which a legal system can try to deal with problems of over-indebtedness. On the one hand, preventive measures can be imposed on the lender in order to limit the chances that a borrower gets into a situation of over-indebtedness. In this context we refer to the discussion on blacklists and automated systems above. On the other hand, *post factum* curative measures may grant debtors facing over-indebtedness some kind of relief. Many jurisdictions apply a combination of both types of policy measures.

In recent years, however, various jurisdictions have experimented with other means of consumer protection, which, although heterogeneous, can be labelled under the term 'responsible lending'. This concept has now also found its way—albeit, as a result of a political compromise, in a very limited form—into the Consumer Credit Directive (2008/48/EC).

Consumer Credit Directive (2008/48/EC) **6.21 (EU)**

[Preamble] **(26)** Member States should take appropriate measures to promote responsible practices during all phases of the credit relationship, taking into account the specific features of their credit market. Those measures may include, for instance, the provision of information to, and the education of, consumers, including warnings about the risks attaching to default on payment and to over-indebtedness. In the expanding credit market, in particular, it is important that creditors should not engage in irresponsible lending or give out credit without prior assessment of creditworthiness, and the Member States should carry out the necessary supervision to avoid such behaviour and should determine the necessary means to sanction creditors in the event of their doing so. Without prejudice to the credit risk provisions of Directive 2006/48/EC of the European Parliament and of the Council of 14 June 2006 relating to the taking up and pursuit of the business of credit institutions, creditors should bear the responsibility of checking individually the creditworthiness of the consumer. To that end, they should be allowed to use information provided by the consumer not only during the preparation of the credit agreement in question, but also during a long-standing commercial relationship. The Member States' authorities could also give appropriate instructions and guidelines to creditors. Consumers should also act with prudence and respect their contractual obligations.

Note

It follows from the Consumer Credit Directive (2008/48/EC) that Member States have a certain obligation to sanction irresponsible lending practices. However, there is no harmonised concept of 'responsible lending'. This means that what is responsible in one Member State may be considered irresponsible in another. For instance, it has been held by a Belgian court that a lender is not acting responsibly if it grants a roll-over credit when credit is repaid for the fourth time by a new credit line.[22] The effect of such line of court decisions is that it effectively imposes upon the lender due-diligence and client-vetting standards for serial renewal of consumer credit. It is interesting to compare this with other jurisdictions that adhere to the principle that consumers are solely responsible for their decisions. For instance, in Germany it has been held that even if a credit contract openly overburdens the consumer in a way that he will not be able to repay the credit amount, the contract will not be void; the bank is not obliged to assess the borrower's creditworthiness.[23]

In France, the Cour de Cassation has confirmed that lenders are subject to a duty to warn ('obligation de mise en garde') which implies that the bank must give its opinion as to whether the client should consent to a particular loan or not.

Cass civ 1e, 12 July 2006[24] **6.22 (FR)**
Fillol v UCB case

DUTY TO WARN

Excessive mortgage

A lender must warn potential borrowers if the amount borrowed exceeds the repayment possibilities of such borrowers.

Facts: Mr and Ms Fillol had agreed to a mortgage, although the total amount that had to be repaid to the lender exceeded their repayment possibilities.

Judgment: The Court of Appeal has rejected the claim on the basis of the amount of monthly payments of the first year of repayment of the mortgage. These repayments were not manifestly disproportionate to the repayment possibilities … and the plaintiffs did not claim that the [bank] had information, on the basis of their income and reasonable foreseeable repayment possibilities, that they would have ignored themselves.

However, the Court of Appeal has failed to give legal ground to its decision, as the court has not examined…, given the progressive nature of the payments to be made, whether the total debt exceeded the repayment possibilities of the family Fillol, and if not, whether they could be considered as ordinary borrowers, who should have been warned by the [bank].

[22] Rb (Court of First Instance) Antwerpen, 15 November 2002 (2003) DCCR 60.

[23] BGH, 16 March 1989 (1989) NJW 1665.

[24] Juris-Data No 2006-034560.

Notes

(1) Certain authors have argued that *social force majeure* as a doctrinal principle would enable the courts and other decision-makers to take into account unfavourable changes in the consumer's health, work, housing and family situation in cases not regulated by specific legislation, eg by giving the consumer the right of withdrawal from burdensome contracts in such circumstances or to protect his right to retain electricity and telephone connections in spite of his temporary payment difficulties.[25]

(2) Responsible lending reflects some concept of fairness. It should be clear, however, that the general notion of fairness is also limited in its application to such technical rules as mortgages or consumer credits. Consider, for instance, the English mortgage case *Paragon Finance v Staunton*.

Court of Appeal **6.23 (UK)**
Paragon Finance plc v Staunton and Nash[26]

POWER TO SET RATES OF INTEREST

Unfettered interest rates?

The power to set rates of interest is not completely unfettered.

Facts: The claimant mortgage company claimed possession as mortgagee from the defendants in two actions on the ground that the defendants were in arrears with their mortgage interest repayments. Both mortgage agreements contained variable-interest clauses. The defendants admitted the arrears of interest, but asserted that, by reason of the rates of interest that they were required to pay, the mortgage agreements were extortionate credit bargains within the meaning of section 138 of the Consumer Credit Act 1974. The defendants did not complain that the agreements were extortionate credit bargains at the outset, but rather that the agreements had become extortionate at a later date when, by reason of the claimant's failure to adjust the charging rates in line with Bank of England or prevailing market rates, the interest payable so far exceeded those rates as to be exorbitant. The defendants accordingly sought, by counterclaims, orders that the loan agreements be reopened under section 139 of the 1974 Act. The claimant's applications for orders that the defences and counterclaims be struck out on the ground that they had no real prospect of succeeding at trial were granted and applications by the defendants to amend their pleadings were refused. The defendants appealed, and the following issues, inter alia, fell to be determined: (i) whether the discretion given to the claimant in the mortgage agreements to vary the interest rate was subject to an implied term that it was bound to exercise that discretion 'fairly as between both parties to the contract, and not arbitrarily, capriciously or unreasonably'; (ii) whether the mortgage agreements were extortionate credit bargains within the meaning of section 138 of the 1974 Act; and (iii) whether the claimant's reliance on discretion to vary interest rates was contrary to section 3(2)(b)(i) of the Unfair Contract Terms Act 1977. The appeals were dismissed.

Judgment: The power given to the claimant by the mortgage agreements to set interest rates from time to time was not completely unfettered. A construction to the contrary would mean that the claimant would be completely free, in theory at least, to specify interest rates at the most exorbitant level. Neither the existence of the regulatory powers of the Director General of Fair Trading nor the fact that borrowers could redeem their

[25] T Wilhelmson, 'Social Force Majeure—A New Concept in Nordic Consumer Law' [1990] *Journal of Consumer Policy* 1–13.
[26] [2002] 2 All ER 248.

mortgages and seek loans from another source were good reasons for holding that the power to set rates of interest was completely unfettered. Furthermore, commercial considerations were not sufficient to exclude an implied term that the discretion to vary interest rates should not be exercised dishonestly, for an improper purpose, capriciously or arbitrarily. It followed that it was necessary to give effect to the reasonable expectations of the parties that there be implied into both agreements a term that the rates of interest not be set dishonestly, for an improper purpose, capriciously or arbitrarily.

Questions

(1) In your opinion, how much importance should be given to 'fairness' as opposed to the rights and obligations embedded in the credit agreement between lender and borrower? Is it possible that protection rules based on fairness are in conflict with protection rules based on disclosure, or will such rules generally be compatible with each other?

(2) Might concepts such as 'responsible lending' or 'social force majeure' create a moral hazard problem (the borrower wins in every scenario, even if he cannot pay back)?

(3) Should the ultimate decision to grant credit in grey area cases be with the borrower (who may be in desperate need of credit) or with the lender (who would be liable if the credit is given in an irresponsible way)? Consider that a consumer who is cut off from mainstream lenders might easier find his or her way to 'loan sharks' and become subject to abusive lending practices.

III. CONSUMER PROTECTION IN THE FIELD OF INVESTMENT SERVICES

III.A INTRODUCTION

The consumer of investment services—the 'retail investor'—is protected by various harmonised laws, regulating amongst other things the conditions upon which financial instruments can be brought into circulation—mainly the provision of information—and the rules investment firms have to comply with when providing investment services to clients.

Whereas many more traditional consumer products can only be brought into circulation when they meet certain quality requirements, no such quality requirements exist for financial instruments. In principle also 'junk' financial instruments can be issued and brought into circulation, if only the issuer provides sufficient and clear information and sufficient risk warnings, so that the level of risk is apparent. The investor is than deemed able to decide and make an 'informed decision'. The information obligations applicable upon issuance of financial instruments are mainly regulated by the Prospectus Directive (2003/71/EC)[27] and in the UCITS Directive (2009/65/EC).[28]

When a company intends to raise capital from the public, the rules of the Prospectus Directive will be applicable. Pursuant to the Prospectus Directive, a vast information document—the 'prospectus'—should be made available when securities (mainly shares in companies and bonds) are offered to the public or admitted to trading on a regulated market (such as the London Stock Exchange, Euronext NYSE or Deutsche Börse)—unless an exemption applies. The prospectus should provide full information concerning these securities and the issuers of the securities, in order to enable investors to make an informed assessment of the risks involved in investing in those securities. In this sense, the Prospectus Directive is the prototype of the information paradigm.

Small investors will, however, often want to diversify their investments. An increasingly important type of financial instruments are therefore units in collective investment funds. An important type of such collective investment funds are 'undertakings for collective investment in transferable securities' or 'UCITS', regulated by the UCITS Directive. A UCITS is an undertaking (a) with the sole object of collective investment in transferable securities or in other liquid financial assets of capital raised from the public and which operate on the principle of risk-spreading; and (b) with units which are, at the request of holders, repurchased or redeemed, directly or indirectly, out of those undertakings' assets (Article 1(2) UCITS Directive). By investing in units of a collective investment undertaking the investor can thus spread the risk of his or her investment over a whole range of securities without having to invest a large amount of money. Important for purposes of this casebook are again the obligations concerning information to be supplied to unit-holders—in particular the obligation for UCITS to publish a prospectus as well as a key investor information document 'written in a concise manner and in non-technical language … presented in a way that is likely to be understood by retail investors'.[29]

Private investors will, however, usually buy these financial instruments—either upon issuance in the primary market or upon subsequent trade of these securities on the secondary market—through an intermediary. A third important field of securities

[27] Directive 2003/71/EC of the European Parliament and of the Council of 4 November 2003 on the prospectus to be published when securities are offered to the public or admitted to trading and amending Directive 2001/34/EC. This Directive has been implemented by Commission Regulation (EC) 809/2004 of 29 April 2004 implementing Directive 2003/71/EC of the European Parliament and of the Council as regards information contained in prospectuses as well as the format, incorporation by reference and publication of such prospectuses and dissemination of advertisements [2004] OJ L 149, 1–152.

[28] Directive 2009/65/EC of the European Parliament and of the Council of 13 July 2009 on the coordination of laws, regulations and administrative provisions relating to undertakings for collective investment in transferable securities (UCITS) (recast). The previous UCITS Directive 85/611/EEC is repealed with effect from 1 July 2011. It should be noted that only the collective investment undertakings as defined in the UCITS Directive have to comply with the rules of the UCITS Directive. It is possible, within certain boundaries, for Member States to allow for non-harmonised collective investment undertakings, which do not, however, enjoy the European passport.

[29] Art 78(5) UCITS Directive. The UCITS Directive also deals with other important aspects, which more indirectly also benefit investors, such as rules with respect to the authorisation of UCITS, the obligations concerning the management of UCITS and rules regarding the depositary of a unit's trust assets.

legislation is therefore the regulation of the financial institutions (mainly investment firms and credit institutions)[30] providing investment services—such as asset management, investment advice or the execution of client orders—to investors. These financial institutions are subject to the Markets in Financial Instruments Directive (MiFID 2004/39/EC),[31] further implemented by the MiFID Implementing Directive (2006/73/EC).[32] The investor protection mechanisms introduced by the MiFID are much more complex than mere information obligations. Apart from a long list of information and disclosure requirements, financial institutions also have to comply with other and more far-reaching investor protection rules, including a loyalty obligation, rules on how to deal with conflicts of interests, as well as rules requiring investment firms to actively assess the suitability or appropriateness of certain financial instruments or investment decisions for a particular investor and rules requiring investment firms to achieve best execution of client orders.[33]

III.B ACCESS TO INVESTMENT SERVICES

In the area of investment services the access problem can be viewed from two different angles.

Final Report of the Committee of Wise Men on the Regulation of European Securities Markets (Lamfalussy Committee)[34] 6.24 (EU)

The Committee believes that it is of the utmost importance to underline that an integrated European capital market, by raising the real return on capital, will deliver significant direct benefits for citizens. The following indicative figures show why. If a person wants to have benefits that represent 35 per cent of their final salary by investing in a pension scheme over a 40 year career, pension contributions need to be: 5 per cent of salary if the real rate of return of the pension plan is 6 per cent. 10 per cent of salary if the return is 4 per cent. 20 per cent of salary if the return is 2 per cent. As the EU's demographic trends will lead to far more reliance on privately funded pension schemes in the future, these benefits are particularly important.

[30] In the remainder of this chapter, 'investment firm' should be understood as any provider of investment services which are subject to the MiFID (2004/39/EC).

[31] Directive 2004/39/EC of the European Parliament and of the Council of 21 April 2004 on markets in financial instruments amending Council Directives 85/611/EEC and 93/6/EEC and Directive 2000/12/EC of the European Parliament and of the Council and repealing Council Directive 93/22/EEC [2004] OJ L 145, 1–44.

[32] Commission Directive 2006/73/EC of 10 August 2006 implementing Directive 2004/39/EC of the European Parliament and of the Council as regards organisational requirements and operating conditions for investment firms and defined terms for the purposes of that Directive [2006] OJ L 241, 26–58.

[33] The MiFID also provides important sets of rules with respect to other subject matters, such as the authorisation requirements for investment firms (so-called 'prudential requirements', such as initial capital requirements or quality requirements with respect to the persons who effectively manage the business) and the authorisation, management and organisation of regulated markets.

[34] 15 February 2001.

Note

The problem of access to investment services is very different compared to the access problems this Casebook has identified with respect to consumer credit. Whilst consumers borrow to buy consumables or a house, the common view is that investors invest *excess* money in financial products. Intuitively one could therefore argue that access is not an issue here. The argument would be that investment services are for the rich. Such a view would, however, miss the increasing importance of investment services as a tool for members of the general public to plan in the long term, mainly for their pensions (either through direct investments on the stock markets or through investments in private pension funds). Viewed in this way, access to suitable investment services at a competitive cost is an issue that is relevant to a very substantial number of households.

S Choi, Regulating Investors, Not Issuers: Market Based Proposal[35] **6.25 (EU)**

Some investors may lack either the rationality or the capacity to investigate and accurately value protections provided at even the aggregate level. ... In addition, in recognition of the precarious informational state in which unsophisticated investors find themselves, the proposal goes one step further and would limit unsophisticated investors to investments in only passive index mutual funds ...

Note

Access to investment services gives rise to another and even more delicate question: to what extent should access be granted to everyone, regardless of financial capability? Should a high school educated father be allowed to invest all the family savings in a non-diversified, risky company? Or should there be some restrictions, such as an obligation for non-sophisticated investors to invest not directly, but to invest in diversified funds, or through professional advisers? The most complete protection of unsophisticated investors could indeed be to limit access to certain investment products or services. Such an approach would, however, severely restrict the free choice of these investors.

Question

Do you believe that denying access to certain risky investment products for unsophisticated investors is an acceptable means of investor protection? Is this feasible in a globalised, internet society?

[35] S Choi, 'Regulating Investors, Not Issuers: Market Based Proposal' [2000] *California Law Review* 300–01.

III.C WHO IS PROTECTED BY THE RULES

European Commission, White Paper on Enhancing the Single Market Framework for Investment Funds[36] **6.26 (EU)**

There is no common European approach to distinguishing products that are suitable for the retail public from products that should remain the preserve of sophisticated investors. National experience has shown that there is no fully satisfactory basis for making a cast-iron distinction. Views as to what is a safe product for retail investment change over time, as new asset classes mature, risk features are better understood. …

There are no compelling investor protection reasons for national regulators to interfere in financial transactions involving professional investors who understand the risks associated with an investment. …

III.C.1 THE PROSPECTUS DIRECTIVE

The Prospectus Directive does not, as such, distinguish between different types of investors. It stems from the definition of 'public offer' that any offer of securities to be made to the 'public' may entail a prospectus obligation.

Prospectus Directive (2003/71/EC) **6.27 (EU)**

Article 3 (1) Member States shall not allow any offer of securities to be made to the public within their territories without prior publication of a prospectus.

(2) The obligation to publish a prospectus shall not apply to the following types of offer:

(a) an offer of securities addressed solely to qualified investors; and/or

(b) an offer of securities addressed to fewer than 100 natural or legal persons per Member State, other than qualified investors; and/or

(c) an offer of securities addressed to investors who acquire securities for a total consideration of at least €50.000 per investor, for each separate offer; and/or

(d) an offer of securities whose denomination per unit amounts to at least €50.000; and/or

(e) an offer of securities with a total consideration of less than €100.000, which limit shall be calculated over a period of 12 months.However, any subsequent resale of securities which were previously the subject of one or more of the types of offer mentioned in this paragraph shall be regarded as a separate offer …

[The qualified investor mentioned in Article 3(2)(a) is defined in the preceding] **Article 2** (1) …

(e) 'qualified investors' means:

(i) legal entities which are authorised or regulated to operate in the financial markets, including: credit institutions, investment firms, other authorised or regulated financial institutions, insurance companies, collective investment schemes and their management companies, pension funds and their management companies, commodity dealers, as well

[36] COM [2006] 686 final.

as entities not so authorised or regulated whose corporate purpose is solely to invest in securities;

(ii) national and regional governments, central banks, international and supranational institutions such as the International Monetary Fund, the European Central Bank, the European Investment Bank and other similar international organisations;

(iii) other legal entities which do not meet two of the three criteria set out in paragraph (f);

(iv) certain natural persons: subject to mutual recognition, a Member State may choose to authorise natural persons who are resident in the Member State and who expressly ask to be considered as qualified investors if these persons meet at least two of the criteria set out in paragraph 2;

(v) certain SMEs: subject to mutual recognition, a Member State may choose to authorise SMEs which have their registered office in that Member State and who expressly ask to be considered as qualified investors;

(f) 'small and medium-sized enterprises' means:
companies, which, according to their last annual or consolidated accounts, meet at least two of the following three criteria: an average number of employees during the financial year of less than 250, a total balance sheet not exceeding €43.000.000 and an annual net turnover not exceeding €50.000.000.

(2) For the purposes of paragraph 1(e)(iv) the criteria are as follows:

(a) the investor has carried out transactions of a significant size on securities markets at an average frequency of, at least, 10 per quarter over the previous four quarters;

(b) the size of the investor's securities portfolio exceeds €0,5 million;

(c) the investor works or has worked for at least one year in the financial sector in a professional position which requires knowledge of securities investment.

Notes

(1) The Prospectus Directive can be considered to be 'all or nothing'. Either an offering of securities is public and then must comply with the requirement to publish a prospectus, or an offering of securities is private—typically referred to as a 'private placement'—and shall then be exempt altogether from the requirement to publish a prospectus.

(2) One of situations in which the obligation to publish a prospectus does not apply is an offer of securities addressed solely to qualified investors. It is interesting to compare the 'qualified investor' notion of the Prospectus Directive with the 'professional investor' notion of the MiFID (see section III.C.2 below).

(3) Furthermore, a survey of the implementation of the Prospectus Directive (2003/71/EC) in France, Germany, the United Kingdom, Belgium and the Netherlands has shown that, to date, all such Member States have decided to extend the 'qualified investors' notion to small and medium-sized enterprises (SMEs) who ask to be considered as qualified investors (choose to opt-in). Moreover, all such Member States (except for Belgium) have also provided for an opt-in register for natural persons (see Article 2(1)(e)(iv) and (v) of the Prospectus Directive).

III.C.2 THE UCITS DIRECTIVE

Although the UCITS Directive does not distinguish between different types of investors—all of which are referred to as 'unit-holders'—the key investor information document is designed to allow retail investors to make an informed investment decision. The concept of 'retail investor' is not, however, defined in the UCITS Directive.

UCITS Directive (2009/65/EC) **6.28 (EU)**

[Preamble] **(3)** National laws governing collective investment undertakings should be coordinated with a view to approximating the conditions of competition between those undertakings at Community level, while at the same time ensuring more effective and more uniform protection for unit-holders. ...

(59) ... Key investor information should be presented in a short format. A single document of limited length presenting the information in a specified sequence is the most appropriate manner in which to achieve the clarity and simplicity of presentation that is required by retail investors, and should allow for useful comparisons, notably of costs and risk profile, relevant to the investment decision.

III.C.3 MIFID

Unlike the Prospectus Directive or the UCITS Directive, the investor protection system provided by the MiFID is based on a clear delineation between retail investors—which are considered not to have sufficient knowledge of the financial markets, the instruments and the risks involved in securities transactions and therefore need an increased level of protection—and professional investors.[37]

MiFID (2004/39/EC) **6.29 (EU)**

Article 4 Definitions

(1) ... 11. 'Professional client' means a client meeting the criteria laid down in Annex II;

12. 'Retail client' means a client who is not a professional client.

Annex II Professional clients for the purpose of this Directive

Professional client is a client who possesses the experience, knowledge and expertise to make its own investment decisions and properly assess the risks that it incurs ...

I. Categories of client who are considered to be professionals

The following should all be regarded as professionals in all investment services and activities and financial instruments for the purposes of the Directive.

(1) Entities which are required to be authorised or regulated to operate in the financial markets. The list below should be understood as including all authorised entities carrying out the characteristic activities of the entities mentioned: entities authorised by a

[37] Within the group of professional investors a further subgroup of so-called 'eligible counterparties' is distinguished (including amongst others investment firms, credit institutions and insurance companies).

Member State under a Directive, entities authorised or regulated by a Member State without reference to a Directive, and entities authorised or regulated by a non-Member State:

(a) Credit institutions
(b) Investment firms
(c) Other authorised or regulated financial institutions
(d) Insurance companies
(e) Collective investment schemes and management companies of such schemes
(f) Pension funds and management companies of such funds
(g) Commodity and commodity derivatives dealers
(h) Locals
(i) Other institutional investors

(2) Large undertakings meeting two of the following size requirements on a company basis:

—balance sheet total: €20.000.000,
—net turnover: €40.000.000,
—own funds: €2.000.000

(3) National and regional governments, public bodies that manage public debt, Central Banks, international and supranational institutions such as the World Bank, the IMF, the ECB, the EIB and other similar international organisations.

(4) Other institutional investors whose main activity is to invest in financial instruments, including entities dedicated to the securitisation of assets or other financing transactions. …

II. Clients who may be treated as professionals on request …

Clients other than those mentioned in section I, including public sector bodies and private individual investors, may also be allowed to waive some of the protections afforded by the conduct of business rules.

Investment firms should therefore be allowed to treat any of the above clients as professionals provided the relevant criteria and procedure mentioned below are fulfilled. These clients should not, however, be presumed to possess market knowledge and experience comparable to that of the categories listed in section I.

Any such waiver of the protection afforded by the standard conduct of business regime shall be considered valid only if an adequate assessment of the expertise, experience and knowledge of the client, undertaken by the investment firm, gives reasonable assurance, in light of the nature of the transactions or services envisaged, that the client is capable of making his own investment decisions and understanding the risks involved. …

In the course of the above assessment, as a minimum, two of the following criteria should be satisfied:

—the client has carried out transactions, in significant size, on the relevant market at an average frequency of 10 per quarter over the previous four quarters,

—the size of the client's financial instrument portfolio, defined as including cash deposits and financial instruments exceeds €500.000,

—the client works or has worked in the financial sector for at least one year in a professional position, which requires knowledge of the transactions or services envisaged.

Note

Based on the above criteria, each client is automatically categorised as either professional or retail. For that reason this categorisation is referred to as a per se categorisation. Importantly, and contrary to the 'consumer' concept in traditional consumer law, it follows from the definition of 'retail clients' that it is a residual category, including most natural persons. It is, however, also apparent that not only natural persons are considered retail clients, enjoying a higher degree of protection, but also, for example, SMEs.

The originality of the MiFID client categorisation system is that the system is not rigid. Change of category is possible in certain circumstances.

MiFID Implementing Directive (2006/73/EC) **6.30 (EU)**

Article 28 Information concerning client categorisation

(1) Member States shall ensure that investment firms notify new clients, and existing clients that the investment firm has newly categorised as required by Directive 2004/39/EC, of their categorisation as a retail client, a professional client or an eligible counterparty in accordance with that Directive.

(2) Member States shall ensure that investment firms inform clients in a durable medium about any right that client has to request a different categorisation and about any limitations to the level of client protection that it would entail.

Cass comm, 18 February 2004[38] **6.31 (FR)**

CAPACITY OF INFORMED INVESTOR

Losses on futures

The French Supreme Court confirms the criteria upon which the Court of Appeal had determined that an investor was to be considered an informed investor.

Facts: An investor had engaged in speculative operations on the futures market, which resulted in losses on investment. The investment firm claimed payment of these losses, and was put in its right by the Court of Appeal of Toulouse. Before the Supreme Court, the investor argued that the judgment of the Court of Appeal should be nullified as it had not considered that he was not an informed investor and that the investment firm had therefore failed to perform its information duties.

Judgment: Whereas Mr X raises objection against the judgement of the Court of Appeal for having ruled ... that the status of informed investor must be appreciated against three cumulative criteria, namely, the professional competence of the investor, the nature of the performed transactions and the knowledge of the investor with respect to financial instruments and the number of transactions; ... However, given that even before he had opened an account with the company Pinatton, Mr X had already engaged in transactions on the futures market through an account he had opened with BNP and that as soon as he opened the account with Pinatton, Mr X had engaged in speculative

[38] Cass comm, 18 February 2004, No 02-14311.

operations in search of a maximum leverage effect, by carrying out a large number of transactions in several securities, the Court of Appeal was right in concluding that Mr X was an experienced investor, accustomed to transactions on the stock exchange and possessing a good knowledge of the practices and rules with respect to operations of the futures market, with a good grasp of the operations on the stock exchange and could not therefore be considered as a layman; the argument is thus unfounded.

Hoge Raad (Supreme Court), 11 July 2003[39] **6.32 (Nl)**

DIFFERENCE BETWEEN KNOWLEDGE AND COMPETENCE

The stubborn investor

Violation of duty of care in relation to an investor in stock options which did not comply with its margin requirements.

Facts: An investor gives orders to its bank to invest in stock options. As a consequence of the leverage effect inherent in these instruments, investors can face losses greater than their initial investments. Therefore the bank usually asks the client to comply with certain margin requirements, meaning that the client has to provide coverage for losses he or she faces. In this case the bank had regularly warned its client of the risks involved in the transactions which the client asked the bank to execute for him. The bank had even warned the client that his entire portfolio was at risk and that his margins were insufficient to cover the losses suffered. The client was, however, stubborn and difficult to convince. He had explicitly accepted the fact that he had not given sufficient coverage, hoping that by subsequent option trades he would be able to make up for the losses suffered as a result of previous transactions.

Judgment: In the first place the purpose of the duty of care of the bank, as professional and in the risky area of transactions in options competent provider of services, is protection of the individual client against the danger of its own irresponsibility or lack of understanding. In view of this purpose and contrary to what the Court of Appeal had judged, a bank acts in principle contrary to its duty of care if it follows its client in his explicit wish, notwithstanding the fact that he does not comply with the usual margin obligations, to execute his order to sell (write) put-options hoping that the stock market will rise again and his losses will be limited. Competence of the client in the area of option trade can ... admittedly influence the extent of the duty of care, but the mere familiarity with option trade in general and more in particular with the risks involved can, contrary to what the Court of Appeal had held, not lead to the conclusion that the client has relevant competence with respect to the issue at hand.

Notes

(1) Per se categorisation notwithstanding, the MiFID differs from other areas of consumer law in that it allows for some flexibility. Professional investors can request non-professional treatment and retail investors can—subject to certain conditions and a strict procedure—request professional treatment, thereby waiving a large part of the specific rules for the protection of retail investors.

[39] (2003) JOR 199 with note K Frielink; (2005) NJ 103 with note CE Du Perron.

(2) Under the MiFID, financial institutions are required to notify clients at the beginning of their relationship of their categorisation and of their right to request a different categorisation. The advantage of this system is that investors always know from the beginning in which category they have been classified and to what protection they are entitled.

(3) Prior to the MiFID, ex ante classification was not required in many jurisdictions, leading to situations where investment firms ex post tried to convince a court that they did not owe information duties or a specific duty of care to a particular investor, in view of the knowledge, prior experience in investment decisions, profession and/or education of that investor. The investor in such a case would typically argue that he or she did not have that knowledge or experience and that the investment firm was thus liable for the damages he or she had suffered. This kind of case-law was often based on civil law rather than on specific financial law arguments. As is clear from the two cases above, the criteria to consider a person as competent with respect to certain investment products could differ substantially. The criteria laid down in this case-law could still prove relevant for purposes of interpreting the 'knowledge and experience' assessment in the context of the know-your-customer requirements (see section III.D.3.d below).

(4) The judgment of the Dutch Supreme Court is interesting in that it makes a distinction between theoretical knowledge and experience on the one hand, and professional competence on the other hand, thus indicating why even experienced investors cannot always be considered competent.

Questions

(1) How does the 'retail investor' concept compare with more traditional consumer concepts?

(2) How does the MiFID client categorisation system differ from the more traditional consumer law delineation of the persons to be protected? Do you think a MiFID-like system would be useful in a more traditional consumer law context? Why or why not?

III.D CONSUMER PROTECTION MECHANISMS

III.D.1 THE PROSPECTUS DIRECTIVE

The Prospectus Directive is still largely based on the information paradigm. It is, however, interesting to note the growing awareness of the problems raised by behavioural finance scientists in respect of the information paradigm (see section I.A above).

Prospectus Directive (2003/71/EC) **6.33 (EU)**

[Preamble] **(20)** Such information, which needs to be sufficient and as objective as possible as regards the financial circumstances of the issuer and the rights attaching to

the securities, should be provided in an easily analysable and comprehensible form. Harmonisation of the information contained in the prospectus should provide equivalent investor protection at Community level.
(21) Information is a key factor in investor protection; a summary conveying the essential characteristics of, and risks associated with, the issuer, any guarantor and the securities should be included in the prospectus. To ensure easy access to this information, the summary should be written in non-technical language and normally should not exceed 2500 words in the language in which the prospectus was originally drawn up.

Article 5 (1) Without prejudice to Article 8(2), the prospectus shall contain all information which, according to the particular nature of the issuer and of the securities offered to the public or admitted to trading on a regulated market, is necessary to enable investors to make an informed assessment of the assets and liabilities, financial position, profit and losses, and prospects of the issuer and of any guarantor, and of the rights attaching to such securities. This information shall be presented in an easily analysable and comprehensible form. …

(2) The prospectus shall contain information concerning the issuer and the securities to be offered to the public or to be admitted to trading on a regulated market. It shall also include a summary. The summary shall, in a brief manner and in non-technical language, convey the essential characteristics and risks associated with the issuer, any guarantor and the securities, in the language in which the prospectus was originally drawn up. The summary shall also contain a warning that:

(a) it should be read as an introduction to the prospectus;

(b) any decision to invest in the securities should be based on consideration of the prospectus as a whole by the investor; …

Notes

(1) The duty to publish a prospectus is the prototype of the information paradigm. The information contained in the prospectus must enable investors to make an informed investment decision. The specific information requirements are set out in the implementing Prospectus Regulation (809/2004). Whereas the Prospectus Directive (2003/71/EC) lays down principles to be observed when drawing up prospectuses, the Prospectus Regulation specifies the information to be given therein, the format and aspects of publication or dissemination of advertisements.

(2) The reasons mentioned in the Preamble to the Prospectus Directive for including a summary in prospectuses seem to indicate that the European legislator is aware of the difficulty investors have in reading and understanding vast and technical prospectuses. It should, however, be clear that the inclusion of a summary in the prospectus does not mean that the investor should no longer read and understand the entire prospectus. The obligation to include a warning in the summary that it should be read as an introduction to the prospectus and that any decision to invest in the securities should be based on consideration of the prospectus as a whole by the investor, is revealing in this respect.

III.D.2 THE UCITS DIRECTIVE

With respect to the protection measures in the UCITS Directive, the same trend is apparent: it is largely based on the information paradigm, although there is a growing awareness of the problems raised by behavioural finance scientists.

UCITS Directive (2009/65/EC) **6.34 (EU)**

Article 69 (1) The prospectus shall include the information necessary for investors to be able to make an informed judgement of the investment proposed to them, and, in particular, of the risks attached thereto. ...

Article 78 (1) Member States shall require that an investment company and, for each of the common funds it manages, a management company draw up a short document containing key information for investors. That document shall be referred to as 'key investor information' in this Directive. The words 'key investor information' shall be clearly stated in that document ...

(2) Key investor information shall include appropriate information about the essential characteristics of the UCITS concerned, which is to be provided to investors so that they are reasonably able to understand the nature and the risks of the investment product that is being offered to them and, consequently, to take investment decisions on an informed basis.

Committee of European Securities Regulators (CESR), Advice on the Content and Form of Key Information Document disclosures for UCITS[40] **6.35 (EU)**

1. The European Commission has asked CESR to provide advice on the form and contents of Key Investor Information (KII), which it proposes to introduce as a replacement for the Simplified Prospectus (SP). CESR has considered the factors that are likely to make disclosures of product information useful to consumers—in particular, the need for such information to be short, focused, expressed in plain language, and presented in a way that enables comparisons to be easily made between different offerings ...

9. CESR believes that a KID should fundamentally be a tool for helping retail consumers to reach informed investment decisions. Since evidence suggests complicated documents do not inform investment decisions effectively, the KID should contain only the essential elements for making and carrying out those decisions, and should not be encumbered with information serving only legal or regulatory requirements. Nor should it primarily be a marketing or investor education document. Since its use is limited to providing pre-contractual information, it need not address investors information requirements on an ongoing basis after they have invested.

10. A KID should be produced for all UCITS funds, and delivered to all investors in those funds. However, CESR supports examining the possibility of allowing non-retail investors to opt out of receiving a KID if they deem it not relevant to their needs, so as to reduce unnecessary costs. MiFID-regulated distributors are already permitted to tailor the

[40] February 2008.

disclosures they make according to the classification of the investor, though the UCITS Directive currently makes no distinction between different types of investor.

Notes

(1) To date, the mandatory disclosure rules with respect to UCITS require a prospectus together with a key investor information document (which replaces the previously existing simplified prospectus) to be published and approved.

(2) The CESR advice quoted above shows that behavioural finance increasingly influences law-making. The key investor information is indeed considered as a means of overcoming problems of information overload and difficulties with the accessibility and comparability of prospectuses. The introduction of the concept of 'key investor information' could, however, raise new problems. To the extent a fully fledged prospectus will still be required, it can be questioned whether it would be sufficient for a (retail?) investor to take investment decisions on the basis of the key investor information only.

Question

Do you think that making available a prospectus is a good means of investor protection? Have you ever read a prospectus?

III.D.3 MIFID

Interestingly, the MiFID (2004/39/EC) stands in sharp contrast to the almost exclusive focus on the information paradigm in both the Prospectus Directive (2003/71/EC) and the UCITS Directive (2009/65/EC). The most important tools of investor protection in the area of investment services are without a doubt the rules of conduct which investment firms should observe in their relationship with their clients.

In view of the fact that the MiFID entered into force relatively recently, on 1 November 2007, there is as yet hardly any case-law applying the MiFID rules of conduct. The rules of conduct provided by the MiFID are, however, to a certain extent based on the rules of conduct as they were articulated in Article 11 of the previous Investment Services Directive[41] (which has been replaced by the MiFID). The pre-MiFID case-law in the different Member States will therefore (i) to a certain extent still be useful for interpreting the new MiFID rules of conduct, and (ii) provide interesting examples of why certain new rules introduced by the MiFID are indeed useful.

III.D.3.a Duty of care

The first MiFID rule of conduct is a general duty of care.

[41] Directive 93/22/EEC of 10 May 1993 on investment services in the securities field [1993] OJ L 141, 27–46.

MiFID (2004/39/EC) **6.36 (EU)**

Article 19 (1) Member States shall require that, when providing investment services and/or, where appropriate, ancillary services to clients, an investment firm act honestly, fairly and professionally in accordance with the best interests of its clients and comply, in particular, with the principles set out in paragraphs 2 to 8.

Gerechtshof (Court of Appeal) 's-Hertogenbosch, 6 November 2007[42] **6.37 (NL)**

REACH OF DUTY OF CARE WITH RESPECT OF INVESTMENT SERVICES

Dexia Legiolease

The bank, as a professional and with respect to lease of securities particularly competent provider of services, has a particular duty of care towards its private, non-professional clients. The extent of the duty of care will vary depending on the circumstances, taking into account the complexity of the product, the risks involved in the product, the competence of the client and his or her financial capacity. Insufficient risk warnings and insufficient awareness of the financial capacity of the client constitute violations by the bank of this duty of care.

Facts: Non-professional, private clients were approached by the bank to engage in a contract of lease of securities, a high-risk financial product whereby the client leases securities which he or she will have to buy at the end of the contract term.

Judgment: 4.13.4. In its assessment of the bank's obligations in its legal relationship with [claimant 1], the starting point should be that the bank—as a professional and in the area of lease of securities deemed particularly competent service provider—has a particular duty of care towards individual non professional clients in view of the great risks which can be involved in a contract of lease of securities as the one in the case at hand. The purpose of this duty of care is to protect the client against the risk of his own irresponsibility or lack of understanding. If the risk materialises and such can be (partly) attributed to a breach of duty of care of the bank ... the fault of the client resulting from his irresponsibility or lack of understanding will in principle weigh less than the breach of duty of care of the bank. The extent of the duty of care will vary depending on the circumstances, taking into account the complexity of the product, the specific risks involved, if the case may be, the (level of) competence of the client and his or her financial position (income and wealth). ...

4.13.7 As has been explained ... the risks of the ... construction are considerable. For a combination of investment products as the one in the case at hand, the complexity of which is not easy to grasp for retail clients, an instruction as complete as possible and in unambiguous terms, is required. This instruction should at least have included a warning against the non negligible chance that, depending on the evolution of the securities market, the original investment could be entirely lost and that in case of termination of the contract before the end of term the investor could be indebted towards the bank. ... The contract of lease of securities mentions that in case of termination before the end of

[42] LJN: BB7875, Case No C0501437 (2007) JOR 309.

term, the client will have to pay the remainder of the principal sum. This information alone, which is not further substantiated by other documents, cannot be seen as an explicit and unambiguous warning against the possibility of a debt in case of termination of the contract before the end of term, also in view of the 'good weather scenario' that was given to [claimant 1] by Spaar Select, and especially since at the end of term of the contract there would in any event be no debt left to the bank. Such general warnings neglect that the protection of individual investors against their own irresponsibility or lack of understanding particularly requires that such investors be made aware of the risks of these complex products in an explicit and unambiguous manner.

4.13.8 Second, the bank has breached its duty of care in not gathering sufficient information concerning the income and wealth position of [claimants] before the conclusion of the agreements. …

4.13.8.2 From the data known to the bank, it was clear that the claimants' income, taking into account their fixed costs, was insufficient at the time of the conclusion of the contract to live up to the obligation resulting from the contract to pay a monthly sum of €885,01 on top of these fixed costs. …

4.13.8.4. The income position of [claimants] should have withheld the bank from engaging in the contracts, as this income would not allow [claimant 1] to bear a possible decline of the exchange rates. The bank did moreover not request information with respect to the wealth position of the client, which could have altered this decision. The bank could only have avoided liability if it had made sure that [claimant 1] was aware of the dangers that he would face in concluding the contracts and still insisted to engage in the contracts. …

4.13.11. The bank has not, as has been considered above, complied with its specific duty of care, since it did not or not sufficiently warn [claimant 1] against the great and extra risks in the financial construction it offered. Afterwards it is no longer possible to establish whether [claimant 1] would have neglected such warning. One therefore has to assume that, if he would have been aware of these risks, he would not have engaged in the contracts, which … had such far-reaching consequences, in the same form. There are no indications to accept the contrary, being that [claimant 1], if he had been sufficiently warned, would have accepted these risks. The bank did not argue that a warning would not have mattered.

This uncertainty therefore has to come to the bank's account. The conclusion is therefore that a causal link should be accepted between the breach of duty of care and the damages suffered by [claimant 1]. …

Notes

(1) The duty of care works as an umbrella rule of conduct. On the one hand, the other rules of conduct are specific applications of this first general rule of conduct, meaning that compliance with the MiFID duty of care at least requires compliance with the other rules of conduct. The MiFID duty of care is, on the other hand, also broader than that, and can be seen as a specific articulation in the area of investment services of the general duty of care, existing in different formulations in the contract and/or tort law of the EU Member States.

(2) The judgment of the Dutch Court of Appeal of 's-Hertogenbosch is one of the many concerning the infamous Dexia Legiolease products. The facts date back from long before the MiFID. The judgment, however, shows that in the pre-existing

Dutch law the duty of care was also seen as an umbrella principle on the basis of which other duties of the bank, such as information obligations and know-your-customer obligations, were put into play.

(3) It should be noted that the exact extent of the MiFID duty of care may be delineated differently from the civil or common law duties of care pre-existing in the various Member States.

Question

Do you think that it was useful or even necessary to explicitly articulate a harmonised duty of care in view of the fact that the pre-existing civil/common law duty of care in many Member States has achieved similar results?

III.D.4.b Conflict-of-interest situations

In Europe and in the rest of the world, large financial institutions provide a whole range of services to both retail clients and large companies. The size of those financial institutions and the array of services they offer increase the risk of conflicts of interests, which may, amongst other things, induce investment firms to serve interests other than the client's best interest. An important aspect of investor protection are therefore the rules with respect to the avoidance and management of conflicts of interests.

MiFID (2004/39/EC) **6.38 (EU)**

Article 13 Organisational requirements

(3) An investment firm shall maintain and operate effective organisational and administrative arrangements with a view to taking all reasonable steps designed to prevent conflicts of interest as defined in Article 18 from adversely affecting the interests of its clients. …

Article 18 Conflicts of interest

(1) Member States shall require investment firms to take all reasonable steps to identify conflicts of interest between themselves, including their managers, employees and tied agents, or any person directly or indirectly linked to them by control and their clients or between one client and another that arise in the course of providing any investment and ancillary services or combinations thereof.

(2) Where organisational or administrative arrangements made by the investment firm in accordance with Article 13(3) to manage conflicts of interest are not sufficient to ensure, with reasonable confidence, that risks of damage to client interest will be prevented, the investment firm shall clearly disclose the general nature and/or sources of conflicts of interest to the client before undertaking business on its behalf.

Hof van Beroep (Court of Appeal) Antwerpen, 16 September 1997[43] **6.39 (BE)**

CONFLICT OF INTEREST BETWEEN BANK-CREDITOR AND CLIENT-INVESTOR

The bankrupt company director

A bank giving priority to its own interests as a creditor over its duty of loyalty towards its client-investor breaches its duty of care towards that client.

Facts: A client of the bank considered an investment in a company to which the bank had granted a loan (a fact of which the client was unaware).

Judgment: If the bank omits to warn its client that the company director had been declared personally bankrupt and if the bank has given priority to its own interests as a creditor over its duty of loyalty towards its client investor, the bank does not comply with its duty of care as a professional banker, and therefore the bank may face tort liability.

Notes

(1) The MiFID deals with conflict-of-interest situations in three stages, providing for a mix of organisational requirements and disclosure requirements. The MiFID first provides that financial intermediaries should identify conflicts of interests. In the second stage financial intermediaries are required to take all reasonable steps to prevent conflicts of interest adversely affecting the interests of their clients, meaning that they should maintain and operate effective organisational and administrative arrangements. It is, however—in the third stage—not forbidden for investment firms to do business when the existence of conflict-of-interest situations which could damage clients' interests cannot be excluded, notwithstanding these measures. In that case the investment firm must inform the client of these situations. The client is deemed able to decide for himself whether he still wants to deal with the investment firm.

(2) To the extent that compliance with these MiFID rules cannot fully prevent the existence of a conflict of interest, the duty of care should guarantee that the investment firm nevertheless acts in the best interest of the client. The judgement of the court of Appeal of Antwerp (decided pre-MiFID) exemplifies the close relationship between the conflicts-of-interest rules and the duty of care.

Numerous sources of conflicts of interests exist, as is shown in the illustrative list of Article 21 of the MiFID Implementing Directive below.

[43] (1998) RDC/TBH 843.

MiFID Implementing Directive (2006/73/EC) **6.40 (EU)**

Article 21 Member States shall ensure that, for the purposes of identifying the types of conflict of interest that arise in the course of providing investment and ancillary services or a combination thereof and whose existence may damage the interests of a client, investment firms take into account, by way of minimum criteria, the question of whether the investment firm or a relevant person, or a person directly or indirectly linked by control to the firm, is in any of the following situations, whether as a result of providing investment or ancillary services or investment activities or otherwise:

(a) the firm or that person is likely to make a financial gain, or avoid a financial loss, at the expense of the client;

(b) the firm or that person has an interest in the outcome of a service provided to the client or of a transaction carried out on behalf of the client, which is distinct from the client's interest in that outcome;

(c) the firm or that person has a financial or other incentive to favour the interest of another client or group of clients over the interests of the client;

(d) the firm or that person carries on the same business as the client;

(e) the firm or that person receives or will receive from a person other than the client an inducement in relation to a service provided to the client, in the form of monies, goods or services, other than the standard commission or fee for that service.

Corte di Cassazione (Supreme Court), 19 December 2007[44] **6.41 (IT)**

DUTY TO REDUCE THE CONFLICTS OF INTERESTS AND THE INFORMATION DUTIES REGARDING THE EXISTENCE OF CONFLICT OF INTERESTS

Parmalat—Cirio

The failure to comply with information duties when the intermediary acts in a conflict-of-interest situation gives rise to a contractual liability. Violation of rules of conduct results in pre-contractual or contractual liability; it does not lead to the nullity of the contract of intermediation.

Facts: Parmalat SpA was in a precarious financial condition, burdened by heavy debts owed to the banking industry. The creditor banks of Parmalat therefore organised bond issues of Parmalat (both of the Italian company and of the Luxemburg holding, so as to circumvent the capital/debt ratio prescribed in the Italian Civil Code) which were placed with retail investors. The capital raised by the bond issues was used to reimburse the creditor banks, which equally obtained a commission for organising the bond issues. Shortly after the bond issues, the insolvency of Parmalat SpA became suddenly apparent. Parmalat was subjected to an insolvency procedure and did not reimburse the bonds.

Judgment: The numerous judgments on the behaviour of financial institutions in conflict of interest situations in relation to the placement of the Parmalat … bonds, dealt with (a) the question whether preventive disclosure of the conflict of interests was sufficient to render it understandable to the retail clients so as to allow them to make an informed

[44] Cassazione civile, Sez SS UU, 19 December 2007, No 26724 and 26725.

decision and (b) the civil effects of the infringement of the provision of article 21 of the Consolidated Law on Finance.

Jurisprudence on the information duties as to the conflict of interests was not univocal: in certain cases a general pre-contractual declaration was deemed sufficient (v ex multis Tribunal of Turin 21 March 2005), while in other cases a specific and circumstantial declaration was required to reasonably allow the investor to evaluate whether the specific interest of the bank was in conflict with its own (v ex multis Tribunal of Venice 29 September 2005).

The Supreme Court (sezioni unite No 26724/2007) has solved the jurisdictional conflict on the civil effects of the breach of information duties relating to the existence of conflicts of interests, stating, amongst other things, that: …

II. Regarding the possible effects of a breach of rules of conduct: the violation of the information duties of the client and the violation of the correct execution of the acts that are legally imposed on the entities that are authorized to perform financial investments can give rise to pre-contractual liability, and thus a duty to pay damages, in case such violations occur either in the phase preceding or coincide with the contract of intermediation that is aimed at specifying the subsequent relations between the parties; it can however give rise to contractual liabilities, and possibly lead to the dissolution of the contract in question, if the violations concern the investment or disinvestment by executing the contract of financial intermediation. In none of the cases, in the absence of a normative expectation, will the violation of the rules of conduct lead to the nullity of the contract of intermediation, or of the acts as a result thereof …

Notes

(1) The MiFID Implementing Directive provides a non-exhaustive list of sources of conflicts of interests.

(2) The infamous *Parmalat* case in Italy (under the pre-MiFID regime) provides an example of the possible consequences of conflicts of interests: it emerged that on the eve of the company's insolvency, creditor banks were still selling bonds to their customers.

(3) There are of course numerous other kinds of conflict of interests. 'Switching and churning', for example, is a conflict of interest situation whereby financial institutions—often remunerated on an executed transaction basis—advise a client to engage in transactions or to switch an investment or an investment portfolio when that is not in its interest or in line with its investment strategy.

Question

Do you think that retail investors are able to assess the consequences of a conflict-of-interests situation when it is disclosed to them? Consider in this respect that it is probable that investment firms will provide a standardised list of possible sources of conflict of interests.

III.D.3.c Information requirements

An important, and in any event the most elaborated, category of rules of conduct are the various information obligations of the investment firm. The MiFID thus embodies the information paradigm. The MiFID information obligations are long and detailed, including rules on the quality, the presentation and the minimum content of the information.

(i) Quality of the information

In general, as in most other domains of consumer law, all information—including marketing communications—given to investors should be fair, clear and not misleading. An example of what these abstract rules may mean in concrete cases is provided in the judgement of the German Bundesgerichtshof of 9 June 1998.

MiFID (2004/39/EC) **6.42 (EU)**

Article 19 (2) All information, including marketing communications, addressed by the investment firm to clients or potential clients shall be fair, clear and not misleading. Marketing communications shall be clearly identifiable as such.

MiFID Implementing Directive (2006/73/EC)[45] **6.43 (EU)**

Article 27 (2) It shall be accurate and in particular shall not emphasize any potential benefits of an investment service or financial instrument without also giving a fair and prominent indication of any relevant risks.

It shall be sufficient for, and presented in a way that is likely to be understood by, the average member of the group to whom it is directed, or by whom it is likely to be received.

It shall not disguise, diminish or obscure important items, statements or warnings.

BGH, 9 June 1998[46] **6.44 (DE)**

INFORMATION ON RISKS OF LOSS TO BE PROVIDED IN UNAMBIGUOUS TERMS AND IN EYE-CATCHING FORM

Insufficient risk warnings

The risks that clients can suffer losses and the fact that the chances of profit might be lower should also be clear to the hasty reader, by using unambiguous terms and an eye-catching form and by avoiding any extenuation.

[45] Art 25 of the MiFID Implementing Directive further prohibits certain important examples of misleading information (eg the use of the name of any competent authority in such a way that would indicate or suggest endorsement or approval by that authority of the products or services of the investment firm) and puts forward conditions which should be fulfilled when certain types of information are given (eg when financial products are compared to one another; when an indication of past performance is given; when reference is made to simulated past performance; when information is provided on future performance; or when information on a particular tax treatment is provided).

[46] XI ZR 220/97, BGH (1998) WM 1527–29.

Facts: Inexperienced investors bought units in a futures fund with capital guarantee. After having suffered losses they claimed that they were insufficiently informed of the risks involved in the transaction.

Judgment: 12. The content and scope of the information that should be provided to investors depend on the nature of the investment, as the Court of Appeal rightly noted. According to the case law of the federal court, commercial agents selling futures are obliged to inform clients in writing and before the conclusion of the contract of the fundamental aspects, the economic functioning, the risks involved and any reduction in the chances of making profits, even without being asked. The hasty reader should be clearly informed of the extent of the risk of loss imposed on him, as well as of the decrease in the likelihood of making profits; this should be done in an unambiguous manner and in eye-catching form without any extenuation.

13. These principles should not be applied indiscriminately, as the Court of Appeal recognised, but in accordance with the particulars of the investment at hand. ... Of fundamental importance for the investors, for whom their decision to invest in the speculative fund depended on the possibility of achieving the highest profits, were the profit prospects. Information should have been given on this and in particular on circumstances likely to reduce profits.

14. This did not happen. Rather, the prospectus, which the defendant used to explain the investment, presents the profit prospects far too positively.

15. aa) The investors' chances of making profits overall from their participation in the investment fund were considerably reduced by several factors which are only mentioned incidentally in the prospectus and without establishing any practical consequences. ...

19. bb) The prospectus, which the defendant had used to promote the investment to the claimant, in fact gives the impression that an investment in the futures fund is far superior to a conservative investment in terms of return. On page 7 of the prospectus, in a sample calculation, a profit of 9 per cent before tax on a conservative investment is contrasted with a profit of 35.5 per cent on the futures fund. Furthermore it was claimed that returns of 15–20 per cent a year were achievable in view of previous experiences with the fund. These details were false. There had been no comparable previous experiences. ...

21. a) According to the Senate's established case law, on which the Court of Appeal based its judgment, anyone who violates a contractual or pre-contractual information obligation when dealing in futures, will bear the burden of proof that the client would have suffered the damages even if proper information had been given. The only exception to this is the event that proper information to the client would have solved a problem in the decision making process, when there was not just one but several possibilities for explanatory procedures. [references omitted]

Notes

(1) Although the MiFID disclosure requirements are vast, they still allow a certain degree of flexibility, resulting from the use of vague words such as 'accurate', 'sufficient' and 'comprehensible'. Precisely what these concepts cover will depend on the specific situation, such as the level of sophistication of the members of the group to whom the information is directed, but also the complexity and riskiness of the products or services involved. Case-law will therefore continue to

play an important role in determining how these concepts should be interpreted in different situations.

(2) The judgment of the German Bundesgerichtshof of 9 June 1998, quoted above, dates back from before the MiFID entered into force. Although it therefore cannot be seen as an interpretation of the relevant MiFID provisions, it does give a good indication of what it may mean for information to be 'not misleading', to give 'a fair and prominent indication of any relevant risks'; to present information 'in a way that is likely to be understood by, the average member of the group to whom it is directed, or by whom it is likely to be received' and to 'not disguise, diminish or obscure important items, statements or warnings'.

(3) See also Gerechtshof (Court of Appeal) 's-Hertogenbosch, 6 November 2007 discussed under 6.37(NL) and especially paragraph 4.13.7 of the judgment.

(ii) Minimum information and presentation of the information

Next to quality rules, there are also long lists of minimum information to be provided to (retail) investors.

MiFID (2004/39/EC) **6.45 (EU)**

Article 19 (3) Appropriate information shall be provided in a comprehensible form to clients or potential clients about:

—the investment firm and its services,

—financial instruments and proposed investment strategies; this should include appropriate guidance on and warnings of the risks associated with investments in those instruments or in respect of particular investment strategies,

—execution venues, and

—costs and associated charges

so that they are reasonably able to understand the nature and risks of the investment service and of the specific type of financial instrument that is being offered and, consequently, to take investment decisions on an informed basis. This information may be provided in a standardised format.

Notes

(1) Article 19(3) MiFID is implemented by Articles 28–34 of the MiFID Implementing Directive (2006/73/EC), representing a four-page list of specifications on the information to be given to (retail) investors. It is beyond the scope of this case book to discuss these rules in detail.

(2) It should be noted that flexibility is built into these rules also with respect to the minimum information to be provided to clients of investment services. *Appropriate* information should be provided *in order to fulfil the specific aim* of the provision of information: enabling clients to take investment decisions on an informed basis.

(3) The presentation and format of information can be as important to investors as its content. Article 19(3) of the MiFID therefore specifies that the minimum information (i) should be provided in a *comprehensible* form and (ii) *may* be provided in a *standardised* format.

Question
Do you think that providing information in a standardised format is as effective as tailor-made information? What would be the reason for explicitly allowing the provision of information in a standardised format?

(iii) Harmonised information requirements and non-harmonised rules of civil procedure

Although the substantive information requirements are now to a large extent harmonised by the MiFID, contract and tort law and rules of civil procedure vary widely from Member State to Member State, which may de facto still result in very different levels of investor protection.

Hof van Beroep (Court of Appeal) Brussel, 23 January 2004[47] **6.46 (BE)**

CAUSAL LINK BETWEEN VIOLATION OF INFORMATION REQUIREMENTS AND DAMAGES—BURDEN OF PROOF

Disastrous investment in futures

It is not sufficient for an investor to prove that an investment firm has breached its information obligations, in order to obtain damages. The investor also has to prove that if he had been sufficiently informed, he would have changed his investment strategy.

Facts: Y DM, the administrator of a luxury food company, who was explicitly held to be an inexperienced investor, invested in futures on the advice of the company's investment firm, Sinn. Y DM subsequently suffered great losses on this investment and claimed damages from the investment firm.

Judgement: Irrespective of the question of the annual delivery of the extracts of his account, which Y DM claimed not having received, it is clear that no additional warning drawing the client's attention to the disastrous nature of his investment strategy and to the high risk he faced, was sent to the client;

This absence of risk warnings constitutes a breach of contract in respect of Sin's duty to advise;

In the same circumstances (that is to say, a speculative transaction in a security which had been globally stable for nearly three years), any other investment firm, acting with the usual level of care, would have drawn its client's attention to the existence of other

[47] (2006) RDC/TBH 112.

financial products as well as to the danger of investing all of his financial assets in one financial instrument within the context of one speculative transaction;

Y DM can however not prove and it is by no means evident that if it had been duly warned about the risks he faced in carrying out this speculative transaction, he would have ... altered his investment strategy:

It is common with respect to transactions on the stock exchange to wait for the situation to improve before selling an investment and reorientating the investment strategy, hoping to reduce or even recover the losses, which indeed frequently happens.

Notes

(1) Even if an investor succeeds in proving that an investment firm has violated its information obligations, this does not mean that he will be entitled to damages. Whether an investor will be able to recover damages suffered as a result of a failure of a financial institution to comply with its information obligations will also depend on the applicable rules of civil law and the law of civil procedure, which still vary widely from Member State to Member State.

(2) The above case shows how the answer to the question of who has to bear the burden of proof with respect to the causal link between a fault of the investment firm and damages suffered by the investor influences the chances of recovery of the investor. Under Belgian law the *plaintiff* has to prove this causal link, which is often very difficult. Other jurisdictions have, however, under certain circumstances allowed a shift in the burden of proof in this respect. In these jurisdictions it may therefore be easier for investors to obtain damages. Compare the above case in this respect with BGH, 9 June 1998 (see 6.44 (DE)), especially number 21 and Gerechtshof (Court of Appeal) 's-Hertogenbosch, 6 November 2007 (see 6.37 (NL)), especially number 4.13.11.

Questions

(1) Do you see other differences in national law systems which may result in different levels of investor protection in the different Member States, notwithstanding the fact that the substantive information requirements are harmonised?

(2) Do you think that the burden of proof of the causal link should be on the investor or on the financial institution? In answering this question, consider that the financial institution could in certain circumstances 'get away' with a violation of the law and that in other circumstances an investor could receive damages although in fact compliance by the financial institution would not have altered his investment decision.

III.D.3.d 'Know your customer'—principles of suitability and appropriateness

As was explained in the introduction to this chapter, it has become clear that individuals do not always optimally absorb the available information. Especially in the area of investment services the available information is vast and often difficult to understand. A second, and equally important pillar of investor protection has therefore emerged in this field. The 'know your customer' obligations require financial institutions in certain circumstances to request relevant information from their client in order to assess his investment decision, taking into account his particular circumstances.

These 'know your customer' requirements are different for providers of investment advice and portfolio management, on the one hand, and providers of other investment services in which the investment firm has a less active role to play (eg order execution), on the other hand.

(i) Investment advice and portfolio management—suitability test

In respect of investment services which require the investment firm to be actively involved in the decision-taking process, the 'know your customer' obligations require the investment firm to assess three aspects of its client's personal situation.

MiFID (2004/39/EC) **6.47 (EU)**

Article 19 (4) When providing investment advice or portfolio management the investment firm shall obtain the necessary information regarding the client's or potential client's knowledge and experience in the investment field relevant to the specific type of product or service, his financial situation and his investment objectives so as to enable the firm to recommend to the client or potential client the investment services and financial instruments that are suitable for him.

When providing investment advice and portfolio management, financial institutions are subject to the so-called 'suitability test'. A recent study by the UK Financial Services Authority (FSA) has shown that this 'know your customer' requirement is frequently violated in practice.

UK FSA, Quality of advice process in firms offering financial advice: findings of mystery shopping research[48] **6.48 (EU)**

Where firms in our sample are offering advice on only specific customer objectives, they are neither explaining the implications of this to their customers nor gathering sufficient KYC [know your customer] information to make a suitable recommendation even in those areas.

In almost half of the mystery shops (23 out of 50) there was evidence that advisers gave advice before any relevant or in-depth fact-finding. There is a considerable risk that this advice will be unsuitable.

Just over a quarter of firms in the sample (13 out of 50) established customers' attitude to risk ambiguously and some (4 out of 50) did not establish it at all.

[48] August 2006, available at: www.fsa.gov.uk/pubs/consumer-research/crpr52.pdf, 12.

Where customers were investing for income or growth, the purpose and amount of income or the target growth and timeframe were rarely established.

In a few cases, there was also evidence to suggest that firms were inadequately assessing income and expenditure. This was thrown into sharp relief due to some customers having recently made redundant and others investing for additional income. This could impact both on assessing affordability of the recommendation and its suitability.

The following examples may help giving a sense of what exactly is aimed at with the 'know your customer' and 'suitability' rules.

Examples of good practice

Adviser J explained attitude to risk on-screen with the assistance of an numbered scale, a description of how various products might fit within this scale and also explained the impact of the length of time an investment is held. This provided the customers with a clear understanding of not only their personal risk profile but also the risk profile of the products and how the timescale of an investment could impact on the risk. The adviser established that the customer was cautious following detailed discussions and easy-to-understand descriptions of the various risk profiles. The adviser also took the time to ascertain the future risk appetite of the customer as their circumstances and priorities could change over time. The adviser's subsequent recommendation was in line with this risk profile (which had been clearly established to ensure suitability) and the customer had been given sufficient information and clear explanations in order to make an informed decision.

Adviser L asked the customer to explain his requirements, which were to invest a lump sum of money for retirement planning. The adviser proceeded to obtain KYC information on all areas of financial planning. After completion of the KYC process the adviser recommended that income protection should be a priority for this customer. The adviser confirmed the customer's objectives prior to making the recommendation enabling the customer to reconsider his priorities and come to an informed decision as to how to proceed. The adviser was able to identify pother areas of need (deemed to be a higher priority) which may otherwise have been overlooked if the advice process was limited to one particular objective. …

Examples of poor practice

The customer approached adviser N seeking advice as to whether to invest an inheritance of GBP 50,000. The fact-find did cover other areas including protection and pensions provision but in no depth. The suitability letter stated that the firm gave 'comprehensive advice' based on complete financial needs. The customer had no pension provision but did have mortgage life cover. This did not prompt the adviser into any kind of discussion regarding the adequacy of protection, although the customer was a single man with no dependants, and he had life cover but no critical illness cover or income protection. The lack of pension provision and income protection was not investigated nor addressed. The fact-finding and KYC process were inadequately conducted as the adviser appeared only to want to investigate what he could do with the shopper's GBP 50,000 in investment terms. The weak fact-finding process meant that KYC information was limited to the areas that the adviser wished to discuss. And although the adviser was purporting to offer this service to the customer, the lack of holistic financial planning appeared to leave the customer with an inaccurate picture of this financial status and needs.

Notes

(1) Investment advice is the investment service where the financial institution provides personal recommendations to a client, either upon his or her request or at the initiative of the investment firm, in respect of one or more transactions relating to financial instruments. The client subsequently takes the investment decision. Portfolio management means that the investment firm manages the client's portfolio on a discretionary basis in accordance with the mandate given by the client. The portfolio manager—and not the client—thus takes the investment decisions with respect to the client's portfolio.

(2) Investment advice and portfolio management are investment services in which the investment firm has an active role to play with respect to the client's investment decision. The 'know your customer' requirements are therefore elaborated.

(3) The MiFID 'know your customer' requirements are rather abstractly formulated. In the UK, as in certain other Member States (see for the Netherlands Gerechtshof (Court of Appeal) 's-Hertogenbosch, 6 November 2007, under 6.37 (NL), especially paragraph number 4.13.8), there is a longer tradition with 'know your customer' requirements. The examples given in the report of the UK FSA may be helpful in giving a more concrete meaning to the aim of these 'know your customer' obligations. It should, however, again be noted that what is described in the FSA report as examples of good and bad practices is pre-MiFID UK law. It is not (yet) certain that the MiFID 'know your customer' obligations should be construed in exactly the same manner.

(ii) Other investment services—Appropriateness test

In respect of investment services in which the investment firm is in principle not actively involved in the investment decision of the client, the investment firm will only have to comply with lighter 'know your customer' obligations. The most typical investment service in this respect is order execution, whereby the investment firm acts to conclude agreements to buy or sell one or more financial instruments on behalf of the client.

MiFID (2004/39/EC) **6.49 (EU)**

Article 19 (5) Member States shall ensure that investment firms, when providing investment services other than those referred to in paragraph 4 [ie investment advice or portfolio management], ask the client or potential client to provide information regarding his knowledge and experience in the investment field relevant to the specific type of product or service offered or demanded so as to enable the investment firm to assess whether the investment service or product envisaged is appropriate for the client.

In case the investment firm considers, on the basis of the information received under the previous subparagraph, that the product or service is not appropriate to the client or potential client, the investment firm shall warn the client or potential client. This warning may be provided in a standardised format. ...

Notes

(1) With respect to investment services other than portfolio management and investment advice, such as order execution, the investment firm has only to perform an appropriateness test, which implies that the financial institution when assessing the client's investment decision only has to consider the knowledge and experience of the client, and not his financial situation or investment objectives.

(2) Article 19(6) MiFID provides for an exception to the obligation for investment firms to perform a suitability or appropriateness test, when the investment firm provides so-called 'execution-only' services (execution and/or the reception and transmission of client orders) and when a series of conditions are met (amongst other things, the order should concern a non-complex financial instrument,[49] the services should be provided at the initiative of the client and the client should be informed of the fact that no 'know your customer' obligations apply).

Questions

(1) What is the rationale for the stricter suitability test that applies in relation to portfolio management and investment advice than in relation to other investment services, such as order execution?

(2) Do you think that the 'know your customer' obligations are a necessary means of investor protection, or a paternalistic interference with individuals' investment decisions? Is your opinion different for the different investment services discussed above?

(iii) Insufficient information—consequences

If an investor refuses to co-operate and give the necessary information to the investment firm so that it can assess whether the envisaged investment is suitable or appropriate for that client, the consequences of such a refusal differ in the context of portfolio management and investment advice from those in the context of other investment services, such as order execution.

MiFID Implementing Directive (2006/73/EC) **6.50 (EU)**

Article 35 (5) Where, when providing the investment service of investment advice or portfolio management, an investment firm does not obtain the information required under Article 19(4) of Directive 2004/39/EC, the firm shall not recommend investment services or financial instruments to the client or potential client.

MiFID (2004/39/EC) **6.51 (EU)**

Article 19 (5) ... In cases where the client or potential client elects not to provide the information referred to under the first subparagraph, or where he provides insufficient

[49] Such as shares, bonds or units in collective investment undertakings. Complex instruments are, for example, options and other derivative contracts related to securities.

information regarding his knowledge and experience, the investment firm shall warn the client or potential client that such a decision will not allow the firm to determine whether the service or product envisaged is appropriate for him. This warning may be provided in a standardised format.

Note
If a client does not give sufficient information for the investment firm to perform a suitability test in the context of portfolio management or investment advice, it may not provide these services. If a client of other investment services does not, however, provide sufficient information for the investment firm to perform the appropriateness test, the investment firm should warn the client, but can still perform the service.

Question
What would be the rationale for this difference?

III.D.3.e Best execution

In a globalised world there are numerous trading venues where a client order can be executed. There are not only the traditional stock exchanges in the different Member States and countries world wide, but also other regulated markets, such as multilateral trading facilities (MTFs)[50] and possibilities for investment firms to match orders internally. It would to too much to go into detail here on these different possibilities. It is, however, apparent that execution of the same order in a different venue is not irrelevant: transaction costs or the speed of execution may differ for example. It is extremely difficult for investors to assess such elements or even to gather the necessary information on these issues for the different trading venues. The MiFID therefore requires investment firms to achieve the optimal execution of client orders.

MiFID (2004/39/EC) **6.52 (EU)**

Article 21 (1) Member States shall require that investment firms take all reasonable steps to obtain, when executing orders, the best possible result for their clients taking into account price, costs, speed, likelihood of execution and settlement, size, nature or any other consideration relevant to the execution of the order. Nevertheless, whenever there is a specific instruction from the client the investment firm shall execute the order following the specific instruction.

(2) Member States shall require investment firms to establish and implement effective arrangements for complying with paragraph 1. In particular Member States shall require investment firms to establish and implement an order execution policy to allow them to obtain, for their client orders, the best possible result in accordance with paragraph 1.

[50] Multilateral trading facility (MTF) means a multilateral system, operated by an investment firm or a market operator, which brings together multiple third-party buying and selling interests in financial instruments—in the system and in accordance with non-discretionary rules—in a way that results in a contract in accordance with the MiFID provisions (Art 4(15) MiFID).

Notes

(1) Before the MiFID entered into force, many jurisdictions (including Belgium, France, Italy and Spain) set out a relatively easy way to best execution, by providing that the best-execution requirement was deemed to be satisfied if an order was executed on a regulated market. This led in practice, however, to a concentration of trade on regulated markets—which was indeed one of the initial reasons for what is often referred to as 'the concentration rule'—to the detriment of other trading systems. In times when securities trade was much more national and—in certain Member States—less developed, the concentration rule had to ensure that there would be sufficient liquidity on these regulated markets.

(2) The new MiFID best-execution rule undoubtedly reflects a more economic approach to the best-execution principle, in that it requires the taking into account of all relevant aspects of order execution, but makes it also more difficult to decide what the best execution is in a particular case.

(3) The MiFID therefore does not require that a financial institution should actually obtain the best possible result for each individual order, but that financial institutions should take 'all reasonable steps' to reach this goal. This means that financial institutions should establish and maintain an order execution policy, which should be regularly monitored in order to verify that it indeed allows the financial institution to consistently achieve best execution. If the financial institution lives up to its correctly established and maintained order execution policy, it will in principle have complied with its best-execution obligation.

IV. CONSUMER PROTECTION IN THE FIELD OF BANKING AND PAYMENT SERVICES

IV.A INTRODUCTION

In contrast to most other financial services, which are to a greater or lesser extent harmonised at the EU-level, the protection of consumers of banking services largely depends on the Member State and the activity concerned. The exact position of a consumer will differ significantly from Member State to Member State. One important exception to this is the important area of payment services. In 2002 the European Commission, the European Central Bank and the banking industry took up a project to achieve a Single Euro Payments Area (SEPA).

Charlie McCreevy, SEPA: An Opportunity for Europe—Role of the Public Sector[51] **6.53 (EU)**

If some in this audience today still have doubts, I think today's conference should help dispel any worries. No one doubts the current market structure is highly inefficient, and

[51] SEPA Conference (Conference for Public Administrations), 8 May 2007 (Mr McCreevy was the European Commissioner for Internal Market and Services).

there are enormous potential economies of scale. For example: Why does Europe need 24 clearing houses? Does the market really need separate infrastructures for high and low value payments, and yet another system for cards? Do banks really need to maintain different systems for domestic, cross-border, euro and non-euro payments? Do we wish to accept the cost of maintaining 27 different national payment systems?

And what about the users of payment systems? Should they continue to bear the cost of connecting to 27 proprietary banking and hundreds of individual payment systems? Couldn't corporates make better use of their working capital if it were not tied up in expensive cash-collection and payment processes?

So the potential for savings really is large. And as a former Finance Minister, I believe in this project as it is a way of freeing up capital in the economy. Of course, I do not deny that that there will be some cost for banks to bear at the outset. But I would encourage them to think of it as like getting an injection: mildly painful and inconvenient at the time, but highly beneficial over the longer term.

Note

One of the main aims of the SEPA is to allow customers to make non-cash euro payments to any beneficiary located anywhere in the eurozone using a single bank account and a single set of payment instruments, so that all retail payments in euros become 'domestic', and there will no longer be any differentiation between national and cross-border payments within the euro area. The most important achievement of the SEPA project at present is the Payment Services Directive,[52] which must be implemented in the Member States by 1 November 2009. As a consequence of the Payment Services Directive (2007/64/EC) the area of payment services will be—after transposition and subject to a few exceptions—fully harmonised.

IV.B ACCESS TO BANKING AND PAYMENT SERVICES

Certain Member States, eg France and Belgium, have developed a doctrine of 'fundamental banking rights', in which basic banking services, such as opening an account are considered to be (quasi-) fundamental rights. Belgium, for instance, has enacted a law that guarantees access to banking services to all consumers with their principal residence in Belgium. In France a similar law has been adopted, which goes even further, providing for banking services at no charge to the consumer.

Act of 24 March 2003 concerning the basic banking service[53] **6.54 (FR)**

Article 3 §1. All financial institutions must offer the basic banking service as defined in §2. All consumers are entitled to a basic banking service.

[52] Directive 2007/64/EC of the European Parliament and of the Council of 13 November2007 on payment services in the internal market amending Directives 97/7/EC, 2002/65/EC, 2005/60/EC and 2006/48/EC and repealing Directive 97/5/EC [2007] OJ L 319, 1–36.

[53] Loi du 24 mars 2003 instaurant un service bancaire de base, MB 15 May 2003.

§2. The basic banking service is defined as a current account, consisting of: 1° the opening, management and closing of a current account; 2° the availability of manual payments as well as electronic payments depending on the financial institution; 3° the possibility to execute standing payment orders and to domicile invoices; 4° the facility to execute deposits in Belgium. Deposits include: cash deposits, current account crediting of cheques and circular cheques; excluded are deposits of more than 100 coins; 5° the facility in Belgium of cash withdrawal from the teller as well as electronic withdrawal depending on the financial institution; 6° availability in Belgium of periodic bank statements ...

§3. The maximum contribution for the service may not exceed €12 per year.

Decree no 2001-45 of 17 January 2001 implementing article L 312-1 of the monetary and financial code[54] **6.55 (FR)**

Article 1 The basic banking services mentioned in the third and fourth paragraphs of art L 312-1 of the monetary and financial code consist of: account opening, maintenance and closing; one address change per year; remittance upon request of the postal or banking particulars; domiciliation of banking and postal transfers; monthly remittance of a statement of all account transactions; execution of cash transactions; the payout of cheques and bank or postal transfers; deposits and cash withdrawal at the teller of the account holding institution; payments through withdrawal in the bank; interbank payments title or bank or postal tranfers; the availability of remote access to the account balance; a payment card with systematic authorisation, if the financial institution is able to deliver this or, by default, a card with a weekly withdrawal facility from the ATMs of the financial institution; two monthly bank cheque options or equivalent payout methods offering the same services.

Every natural or legal person domiciled in France having opened a deposit account at an institution designated according to the proceedings defined in para 2 of article L 312-1 of the monetary and financial code is entitled to the banking services mentioned in article 1 without contribution on his behalf.

This regulatory choice is in sharp contrast to other countries, such as Germany. Consider the judgment of the OLG Bremen that overruled the judgment of the LG Bremen.

LG (Court of first instance) Bremen, 16 June 2005[55] **6.56 (DE)**
X v Bank

THE LEGAL NATURE OF THE 'CURRENT ACCOUNT FOR EVERYONE' RECOMMENDATION BY THE ZENTRALEN KREDITAUSSCHUSSES

A current account for everyone?

The 'Current Account for Everyone' recommendation by the Zentralen Kreditausschusses is binding for all credit institutions which are therefore obliged to set up a current account for their customers.

[54] JORF No 15, 18 January 2001, 938.
[55] No 2 O 408/05.

Facts: Due to overdrafts of a credit line, the bank decided to terminate the current account of its client. The client argued in turn that the bank was obliged to make available a current account as the bank was a member of the Zentralen Kreditausschusses. That organisation had recommended a 'Current Account for Everyone' plan.

Judgment: 1. The recommendation by the *Zentralen Kreditausschusses* for a 'Current Account for Everyone' constitutes a voluntary commitment on the part of the credit services sector aimed at avoiding the enactment of a legal obligation to contract. The recommendation is an abstract recognition of liability for the benefit of a third party.

2. The recommendation by the *Zentralen Kreditausschusses* is binding for all credit institutions that are member of this umbrella organisation. They are therefore obliged to set up a current account for their customers.

3. The fact that the credit institution advertises the introduction of the 'Current Account for Everyone' on its website can only mean that it is expressly subscribing to the *Zentralen Kreditausschusses'* voluntary commitment.

OLG (Court of Appeal) Bremen, 22 December 2005[56] **6.57 (DE)**
X v Bank

THE LEGAL NATURE OF THE 'CURRENT ACCOUNT FOR EVERYONE' RECOMMENDATION BY THE ZENTRALEN KREDITAUSSCHUSSES

A current account for everyone? (Appeal)

Clients have no enforceable claim to a current account on the basis of the 'Current Account for Everyone' recommendation.

Facts: See 6.56 (DE) above.

Judgment: 1. The 'Current Account for Everyone' recommendation by the *Zentralen Kreditausschusses* merely constitutes a request to its members to comply with this recommendation in the future.

2. Even if a credit institution affiliated to the *Zentralen Kreditausschusses* advertises the introduction of 'Current Accounts for Everyone' on its website, this does not mean that an interested party has an enforceable claim to a current account to be made available to him by the credit institution. With its statement on the website the bank is advertising. In particular, the bank is not making its potential customers an offer, that could be be accepted, to set up an account according to the guidelines of the recommendation by the *Zentralen Kreditausschusses*.

Questions

(1) Do you agree with the policy of certain Member States to provide certain banking services for free, even if that would mean that the prices of other services provided by these banks might be higher to compensate for this?

(2) Does it make sense to distinguish, as the OLG Bremen seems to do, between advertisements referring to a 'Current Account for Everyone' and the existence of a right on behalf of the bank's customers to claim such a current account?

[56] 2 U 67/05.

IV.C THE CONSUMER OF BANKING AND PAYMENT SERVICES

Access to banking services, as well as access to the underlying protection, is not just a theoretical issue. Millions of consumers are confronted with banking services everyday. Protection rules in this area of the law, however, protect varying categories of persons according to specific interests (eg the interest of an account holder, the interest of a consumer who uses online banking, the interest of a consumer who engages in cross-border banking, etc), without explicitly distinguishing between 'consumers' and 'traders'. An important exception to this is again the Payment Services Directive (2007/64/EC).

Payment Services Directive (2007/64/EC) **6.58 (EU)**

[Preamble] **(20)** As consumers and enterprises are not in the same position, they do not need the same level of protection. While it is important to guarantee consumers' rights by provisions which cannot be derogated from by contract, it is reasonable to let enterprises and organisations agree otherwise. However, Member States should have the possibility to provide that micro-enterprises, as defined by Commission Recommendation 2003/361/EC of 6 May 2003 concerning the definition of micro, small and medium-sized enterprises [15], should be treated in the same way as consumers. In any case, certain core provisions of this Directive should always be applicable irrespective of the status of the user.

Payment Services Directive (2007/64/EC) **6.59 (EU)**

Article 4 (7) 'payer' means a natural or legal person who holds a payment account and allows a payment order from that payment account, or, where there is no payment account, a natural or legal person who gives a payment order;

(8) 'payee' means a natural or legal person who is the intended recipient of funds which have been the subject of a payment transaction; …

(10) 'payment service user' means a natural or legal person making use of a payment service in the capacity of either payer or payee, or both;

(11) 'consumer' means a natural person who, in payment service contracts covered by this Directive, is acting for purposes other than his trade, business or profession

Title III. Transparency of conditions and information requirements for payment services …

Article 30 Scope

(1) This Title shall apply to single payment transactions, framework contracts and payment transactions covered by them. The parties may agree that it shall not apply in whole or in part when the payment service user is not a consumer.

(2) Member States may provide that the provisions in this Title shall be applied to micro enterprises in the same way as to consumers.

Note
The typical consumer protection measures included in this Directive are applicable to all 'payment service users'. There is, however, an opt-out mechanism, allowing for payment service users that are not consumers to agree not to enjoy these protective measures. On the other hand, Member States may provide that these protective measures apply to micro-enterprises in the same way as to consumers.

IV.D CONSUMER PROTECTION MECHANISMS

IV.D.1 INFORMATION REQUIREMENTS

The Payment Services Directive (2007/64/EC) is obviously also to a large extent based on the Information Paradigm. The list of minimum information and conditions to be included in the draft framework contract is again very long. It is therefore beyond the scope of this Casebook to discuss these in detail.

Payment Services Directive (2007/64/EC) **6.60 (EU)**

[Preamble] **(23)** The information required should be proportionate to the needs of users and communicated in a standard manner. However, the information requirements for a single payment transaction should be different from those of a framework contract which provides for the series of payment transactions.

Article 36 Prior general information

(1) Member States shall require that before the payment service user is bound by any single payment service contract or offer, the payment service provider, in an easily accessible manner, makes available to the payment service user the information and conditions specified in Article 37. At the payment service user's request, the payment service provider shall provide the information and conditions on paper or on another durable medium. The information and conditions shall be given in easily understandable words and in a clear and comprehensible form, in an official language of the Member State where the payment service is offered or in any other language agreed between the parties.

(2) If the single payment service contract has been concluded at the request of the payment service user using a means of distance communication which does not enable the payment service provider to comply with paragraph 1, the payment service provider shall fulfill its obligations under that paragraph immediately after the execution of the payment transaction.

(3) The obligations under paragraph 1 may also be discharged by supplying a copy of the draft single payment service contract or the draft payment order including the information and conditions specified in Article 37.

Article 37 Information and conditions

(1) Member States shall ensure that the following information and conditions are provided or made available to the payment service user:

(a) a specification of the information or unique identifier that has to be provided by the payment service user in order for a payment order to be properly executed;

(b) the maximum execution time for the payment service to be provided;

(c) all charges payable by the payment service user to his payment service provider and, where applicable, the breakdown of the amounts of any charges;

(d) where applicable, the actual or reference exchange rate to be applied to the payment transaction.

(2) Where applicable, any other relevant information and conditions specified in Article 42 shall be made available to the payment service user in an easily accessible manner.

Note

Interestingly—and in contrast to the other areas of financial law in which information obligations also play an important role—Article 33 of the Payment Services Directive (2007/64/EC) includes a provision on the burden of proof on information requirements: 'Member States may stipulate that the burden of proof shall lie with the payment service provider to prove that it has complied with the information requirements set out in this Title.' As this Article only includes a possibility and not a firm obligation for the Member States, this will probably not lead to harmonisation of this issue.

Question

Do you think that it is useful to harmonise issues such as the burden of proof on information requirements? Can you think of other non-harmonised issues that may prevent the creation of a level playing field?

IV.D.2 OTHER SUBSTANTIVE PROTECTION RULES

One of the most important forms of protection in the domain of the banking and payment services are the deposit guarantee schemes that are organised in each EU Member State. In 1994, Directive 94/19/EC on Deposit-Guarantee Schemes (DGSs) was adopted, achieving minimum harmonisation of deposit protection policies across Member States. As stated in the Directive, 'deposit protection is an essential element in the completion of the internal market and an indispensable supplement to the system of supervision of credit institutions'. Deposit protection is achieved by requiring every credit institution to join a deposit guarantee scheme, which in turn guarantees any depositor up to an amount the minimum level of which is currently set at €50,000.

Directive 94/19/EC of the European Parliament and of the Council of 30 May 1994 on deposit-guarantee schemes **6.61 (EU)**

[Preamble] Whereas harmonization must be confined to the main elements of deposit-guarantee schemes and, within a very short period, ensure payments under a guarantee calculated on the basis of a harmonized minimum level;

Whereas deposit-guarantee schemes must intervene as soon as deposits become unavailable; ...

Whereas the harmonization of deposit-guarantee schemes within the Community does not of itself call into question the existence of systems in operation designed to protect credit institutions, in particular by ensuring their solvency and liquidity, so that deposits with such credit institutions, including their branches established in other Member States, will not become unavailable; whereas such alternative systems serving a different protective purpose may, subject to certain conditions, be deemed by the competent authorities to satisfy the objectives of this Directive; whereas it will be for those competent authorities to verify compliance with those conditions;

Whereas several Member States have deposit-protection schemes under the responsibility of professional organizations, other Member States have schemes set up and regulated on a statutory basis and some schemes, although set up on a contractual basis, are partly regulated by statute; whereas that variety of status poses a problem only with regard to compulsory membership of and exclusion from schemes; whereas it is therefore necessary to take steps to limit the powers of schemes in this area;

Whereas the retention in the Community of schemes providing cover for deposits which is higher than the harmonized minimum may, within the same territory, lead to disparities in compensation and unequal conditions of competition between national institutions and branches of institutions from other Member States; whereas, in order to counteract those disadvantages, branches should be authorized to join their host countries' schemes so that they can offer their depositors the same guarantees as are offered by the schemes of the countries in which they are located; whereas it is appropriate that after a number of years the Commission should report on the extent to which branches have made use of this option and on the difficulties which they or the guarantee schemes may have encountered in implementing these provisions; whereas it is not ruled out that home Member State schemes should themselves offer such complementary cover, subject to the conditions such schemes may lay down

Article 7(1) Deposit-guarantee schemes shall stipulate that the aggregate deposits of each depositor must be covered up to [€] 20.000 in the event of deposits' being unavailable. ...

(3) This Article shall not preclude the retention or adoption of provisions which offer a higher or more comprehensive cover for deposits. In particular, deposit-guarantee schemes may, on social considerations, cover certain kinds of deposits in full.

In 2005 the European Commission launched a review of the Deposit-Guarantee Schemes Directive. It held a public consultation (with the majority of the 43 contributions from trade associations at national or European level, national public administrations, trade unions and credit institutions; replies from consumer associations and the schemes accounted for approximately only 10 per cent each)[57] followed by a report and a Communication. In the conclusions of the Communication, the European Commission took the following view:

[57] European Commission, *Synthesis of the Results of the Public Stakeholder Consultation on Deposit Guarantee Schemes (DGS)*, H1/TB D(2006), available at the website of DG Internal Market.

Communication from the Commission concerning the review of Directive 94/19/EC on Deposit Guarantee Schemes[58] **6.62 (EU)**

The Commission takes the view that many improvements to DGS can best be achieved in the shorter term without the need to change the existing Directive and proposes to address those issues without delay. …

A convincing case has still to be established as to whether a more fundamental change to the existing regulatory framework will be necessary in a longer term perspective and whether or not the expected benefits of such change outweigh the costs. The Commission recognises that there is insufficient evidence of tangible progress on the broader safety net issues at the present stage to be able to undertake those changes aimed at addressing some of the more specific and fundamental shortcomings in the Directive. Addressing these shortcomings would require an important legislative effort to harmonise the funding of national schemes with significant financial consequences for a number of Member States' banking sectors but with few apparent immediate benefits. Any further legislative change will depend on ongoing work in other connected areas … as well as on sufficient support from Member States and stakeholders and will be preceded by appropriate impact assessments. In particular a clearer picture is needed of the division of supervisory responsibilities and, if necessary, more consistency in 'burden-sharing' approaches (ie who foots the bill) in the event of a cross-border EU banking crisis.

Notes

(1) The proposed actions that were included in Annex IIA—and that would be dealt with 'without delay'—concerned, amongst other things, the following: (i) survey on savings products covered under national DGSs; (ii) development of a non-binding model agreement on exchange of information; (iii) development of common voluntary approaches to inclusion of risk-based elements for DGSs; (iv) improvement of comprehensible information about the extent of coverage of DGSs to consumers; and (v) improvement of payment delays to depositors.

(2) The financial turmoil of 2008 and the bankruptcy or near-insolvency of various banks made clear that the systems of DGS did not offer the safety net that such banks' clients were expecting. As a result—and in contrast with the cautious approach of the European Commission—Directive 94/19/EC has been profoundly modified on short term, amongst other things raising the minimum level of deposit guarantee protection from €20,000 to €50,000, to be further raised to €100,000 by 31 December 2010 (Directive 2009/14/EC).

Questions

(1) With the benefit of hindsight it appears that the Commission's assertion in 2005 that 'addressing these shortcomings would require an important legislative effort … with significant financial consequences for a number of Member States'

[58] Available at the website of DG Internal Market.

banking sectors but with few apparent immediate benefits' may have been fundamentally flawed. Do you think the European Commission may have been biased in favour of the banking sector without duly taking into account the externalities of inaction in this respect?

(2) In your opinion, should DGSs be 'totally' harmonised? What are the arguments in favour and against such harmonisation?

DGSs, of course, are not the only ways of protecting the consumer of banking and paying services. Other, more typical ways, involve the allocation of liability for the bank and the consumer. Consider, for instance, the following provisions of the Payment Services Directive.

Payment Services Directive (2007/64/EC) **6.63 (EU)**

Article 56 Obligations of the payment service user in relation to payment instruments

(1) The payment service user entitled to use a payment instrument shall have the following obligations:

(a) to use the payment instrument in accordance with the terms governing the issue and use of the payment instrument; and

(b) to notify the payment service provider, or the entity specified by the latter, without undue delay on becoming aware of loss, theft or misappropriation of the payment instrument or of its unauthorised use.

(2) For the purposes of paragraph 1(a), the payment service user shall, in particular, as soon as he receives a payment instrument, take all reasonable steps to keep its personalised security features safe.

Article 60 Payment service provider's liability for unauthorised payment transactions

(1) Member States shall ensure that … in the case of an unauthorised payment transaction, the payer's payment service provider refunds to the payer immediately the amount of the unauthorised payment transaction and, where applicable, restores the debited payment account to the state in which it would have been had the unauthorised payment transaction not taken place.

(2) Further financial compensation may be determined in accordance with the law applicable to the contract concluded between the payer and his payment service provider.

Article 61 Payer's liability for unauthorised payment transactions

(1) By way of derogation from Article 60 the payer shall bear the losses relating to any unauthorised payment transactions, up to a maximum of 150, resulting from the use of a lost or stolen payment instrument or, if the payer has failed to keep the personalised security features safe, from the misappropriation of a payment instrument.

(2) The payer shall bear all the losses relating to any unauthorised payment transactions if he incurred them by acting fraudulently or by failing to fulfil one or more of his obligations under Article 56 with intent or gross negligence. In such cases, the maximum amount referred to in paragraph 1 of this Article shall not apply.

Note

The question whether the payer has incurred losses as a result of his or her fraudulent action or as a consequence of not fulfilling one of his or her obligations with intent or gross negligence, is quite important. The answer to this question determines who should bear the losses. Similar provisions already existed in various Member States prior to the enactment of the Payment Services Directive and mostly attributed liability to the consumer in the event such consumer behaved in a 'grossly' negligent manner. Courts have been asked to decide, for instance, whether a consumer keeping a Visa card in a wallet, hidden in a locked car, was grossly negligent (it was not considered gross negligence)[59] or whether a consumer was liable for fraud during online transactions (he was not).[60] In Germany, the BGH confirmed that, whilst it is legally valid to contractually allocate the risk of fraud with a credit card, it is not possible to shift all the risk away from the credit card company.[61] As it appears from the following judgment of the BGH, the protection in this field largely depends on the factual circumstances.

BGH, 5 October 2004[62] **6.64 (DE)**

EVIDENCE IN RELATION TO BANK CARD MISUSE

Stolen PIN

Under certain circumstances a rebuttable presumption exists that the consumer kept his secret PIN together with his bank card in his wallet.

Facts: The consumer requested the disbursement of funds that were withdrawn at an ATM. The bank card in question was stolen on 23 September 2000 between 15:00 and 17:00 in a wallet. The Personal Identification Number (PIN) was not stolen. The thief must have decoded the PIN in some other way.

Judgment: If promptly after the theft of a bank card cash is withdrawn through the use of this card and by entering the correct PIN at cash machines, then the *prima facie* evidence essentially implies that the card holder noted the PIN on the bank card or kept it together with it, unless other reasons for misuse of the card can be shown. The possibility of an unknown third party having watched in secret as the PIN was entered is essentially only taken into consideration as another reason if the cash card was stolen close to a time when the PIN was entered by the card holder at a cash terminal.

CONCISE BIBLIOGRAPHY

C Duve and M Keller, 'MiFID: Die neue Welt des Wertpapiergeschäfts. Lernen Sie Ihre Kunden kennen—Kundenklassification und -information' (2006) *BetriebsBerater* 2425–32.

[59] Hof van Beroep (Court of Appeal) Brussel, 13 September 2005 (2006) NjW 708.

[60] Audiencia Provincial (Court of Appeal) Barcelona, Sección 1ª, No 906/2004, 22 December 2004, Recurso No 704/2003.

[61] BGH, 16 April 2002, XI ZR 375/00.

[62] XI ZR 210/03.

F Easterbrook and D Fischel, 'Mandatory Disclosure and the Protection of Investors' (1984) 70 *Vanderbilt Law Review* 669.

H Eidenmüller and W Schön (eds), *The Law and Economics of Creditor Protection* (The Hague, Asser, 2008).

J Ekkenga and H Maas, *Das Recht der Wertpapieremissionen* (Berlin, Erich Schmidt Verlag GmbH & Co, 2006).

M Elderfield (ed), *A Practitioner's Guide to MiFID* (Londen, City & Financial Publishing, 2007).

E Ferran, *Building an EU Securities Market* (Cambridge, Cambridge University Press, 2004).

G Ferrarini, K Hopt and P Giudici, 'Financial Scandals and the Role of Private Enforcement: The Parmalat Case' (2005) *ECGI Working Paper Series*, available at SSRN: http://ssrn.com/abstract=730403.

F Ferretti, 'The Regulation of Consumer Credit Information Systems: Is the EU Missing a Chance?' (2007) 34(2) *Legal Issues of Economic Integration*, 115–131.

CM Grundmann-Van De Krol, *Koersen door de Wet op het financieel toezicht—Regelgeving voor uitgevende instellingen, beleggingsinstellingen en beleggingsondernemingen* (The Hague, Boom Juridische Uitgevers, 2007).

K Hopt and H-C Voigt, *Prospekt- und Kapitalmarktinformationshaftung—Recht und Reform in der Europäischen Union, der Schweiz und den USA* (Tübingen, Mohr Siebeck, 2005).

A Hudson, *Securities Law* (Londen, Sweet & Maxwell, 2008).

D Mavromati, *The Law of Payment Services in the EU: The EC Directive on Payment Services in the Internal Market* (Dordrecht, Kluwer Law International, 2008).

N Moloney, *EC Securities Regulation* (Oxford, Oxford University Press, 2002).

N Moloney, 'The Lamfalussy Legislative Model: A New Era For the EC Securities And Investment Services Regime' (2003) 52 *International and Comparative Law Quarterly* 509.

I Ramsay, 'From Truth in Lending to Responsible Lending' in G Howells, A Janssen and R Schulze (eds), *Information Rights and Obligations* (Aldershot, Ashgate, 2004) 47–65.

P Rott, 'Consumer Credit' in H-W Micklitz, N Reich and P Rott, *Understanding EU Consumer Law* (Anwerpen, Intersentia, 2009) 177–212.

A Shleifer, *Inefficient Markets—An Introduction to Behavioral Finance* (Oxford, Oxford University Press, 2000).

Ph Wood, *Regulation of International Finance* (Londen, Sweet & Maxwell, 2007).

E Wymeersch, 'CESR, A Building Block in Europe's Future Financial Regulatory System' [2007] *Euredia* 1, 15.

CHAPTER SEVEN
PRODUCT LIABILITY

Product liability can be defined as the liability of manufacturers and other suppliers for damage caused by their products. As such, it is not only a matter of consumer law, as damage caused by products can be inflicted on persons who do not act as consumers at the time of the accident, such as workers harmed by poorly designed or maintained machinery. However, it is the development of a consumer society and the increase in the number of accidents caused by consumer goods, such as cars, pharmaceuticals, beauty products or domestic appliances, which led to the emergence of product liability as a distinct branch of law, first of all in the United States, as early as the 1940s, and after World War II in Western Europe.

The European Community intended to harmonise the law of product liability in the Member States through a 1985 Directive. More than twenty years after the adoption of this Directive, the regime of product liability that the Directive has created is not yet totally settled, as consideration of the different elements of this regime will show. This field of law thus testifies to the difficulty of harmonising different legal systems and traditions.

I. THE ORIGINS AND JUSTIFICATIONS OF HARMONISATION

Before the 1980s, no European country had adopted a comprehensive product liability regime and it was left to the courts to deal with the compensation of damage caused by products. They did so using traditional legal devices, mainly negligence liability. Even though the courts tried to bend the rules so as to ease the path to compensation, it was widely felt during the 1970s across Europe that an adequate legal answer was still to be found for the social problem raised by harmful consumer products. Notorious tragedies caused by products such as Thalidomide in Britain, Germany and Scandinavia strengthened the call for legal reform.

It was in this context that the European Community chose to take action in the field of product liability and to harmonise this field of law, as part of a consumer protection programme initiated in 1975. In fact the negotiations which finally resulted in the adoption of a European Directive on the subject lasted from 1974 to 1985. The length of the process bears witness to the bitter debates that took place among the Member States. Whereas some states and stakeholders, such as consumer associations, wanted to achieve as high a level of consumer protection as possible, other states and business organisations were very insistent on the need not to impose too heavy a burden of liability on businesses.

There was therefore a fundamental tension between the ambition to increase consumer protection and the necessity to create a liability regime which could be applicable across Europe and acceptable to all Member States. In other words, there was a conflict between internal market harmonisation and consumer protection.[1] A compromise was finally struck, which resulted in the adoption of the Product Liability Directive.[2]

This Directive created a new product liability regime and was to be implemented by 31 July 1988 in all Member States.[3] Most of them, however, were late in complying with their obligations. France was last, among the then Member States, to implement the Directive, through a 1998 statute. One of the reasons for this delay was that the various French governments were reluctant to implement a regime that proved to be less protective of consumers than pre-existing French case-law on product liability. In order to avoid a reduction in the level of consumer protection, the French implementing statute departed on certain points from the Directive. However, these provisions have been struck down by the ECJ, which affirmed that the Product Liability Directive (85/374/EEC) is a maximum harmonisation measure.[4] This interpretation of the Directive as requiring maximum harmonisation appears to be technically correct, but nevertheless stresses the paradox which exists between the two aims of the text: harmonising legislation and improving consumer protection. Given that the

[1] See above ch 1.I.C.

[2] Council Directive 85/374/EEC of 25 July 1985 on the approximation of the laws, regulations and administrative provisions of the Member States concerning liability for defective products [1985] OJ L 210, 2933.

[3] On some specific points, the 1985 Directive left options open to the Member States. One of these options concerned the inclusion of primary agricultural products and game within the field of the new regime. Several Member States had chosen not to include these products, but the 'mad cow crisis' at the end of the 1990s led to the adoption of Directive 1999/34/EC of 10 May 1999 amending Council Directive 85/374/EEC on the approximation of the laws, regulations and administrative provisions of the Member States concerning liability for defective products which suppressed this option and made it compulsory to include primary agricultural products and game among the products to which the 1985 Directive applies. Others options concerned the admission of the development risk defence and the setting of a financial cap on producers' liability (see below).

[4] Case C-52/00 *Commission of the European Communities v French Republic* [2002] ECR I-3827, paras 12–24. See also Case C-154/00 *Commission v Greece* [2002] ECR I-3879, paras 10–20.

Directive's solutions are, on certain points, less favourable to consumers than the solutions previously reached by some national courts, interpreting the Directive as a maximum harmonisation one and forbidding the Member States to improve on it in their implementation statutes necessarily entails that these statutes are, on certain points, less protective of consumers than previous case-law. This raises the question whether national courts can still apply the rules that they had developed before the adoption of the Directive, or whether these rules have been entirely superseded by the new regime created by the Directive. This needs to be looked at before turning to the various aspects of the product liability regime created by the Directive.

II. THE CONTINUED EXISTENCE OF NATIONAL PRODUCT LIABILITY REGIMES

Article 13 of the Product Liability Directive (85/374/EEC) provides:

> This Directive shall not affect any rights which an injured person may have according to the rules of the law of contractual or non-contractual liability or a special liability system existing at the moment when this Directive is notified.

There have been some discussions on the extent to which this provision enables the upholding of the various product liability regimes which existed in the various Member States at the time the Directive was adopted. This question was addressed by the European Court of Justice in the following case.

ECJ Case C-183/00, 25 April 2002[5] **7.1 (EU)**
María Victoria González Sánchez v Medicina Asturiana SA

EXCLUSIVENESS OF THE EC PRODUCT LIABILITY REGIME

Contaminated blood

A system of producer liability founded on the same basis as that put in place by the Directive and not limited to a given sector of production is not compatible with the Directive.

Facts: María Victoria González Sánchez had received a blood transfusion in a medical establishment belonging to Medicina Asturiana. She maintained that in the course of that transfusion she had been infected by the Hepatitis C virus. She sought compensation from Medicina Asturiana for the damage suffered under the general provisions of the Spanish Civil Code and Articles 25–28 of Law No 26/84 for the Protection of Consumers and Users (LGDCU), which provide for a system of strict liability enabling consumers and users to obtain compensation for damage caused by the use of a thing, product or service. Medicina Asturiana challenged the applicability of those articles of Law No 26/84 in the light of the first final provision of Law No 22/94 which transposed the 1985 Directive into Spanish law and which provides that Articles 25–28 of Law No 26/84 do not apply to civil liability for damage caused by the defective products mentioned by Law No 22/94. The Spanish court regarded it as established that the facts underlying the dispute came within the scope *ratione materiae* and *ratione temporis* of both Law No 26/84 and Law No

[5] [2002] ECR I-3901.

22/94. Following an analysis of those two laws, the court concluded that the rights which consumers and users may rely on under Law No 26/84 are more extensive than those which the victims of damage may rely on under Law No 22/94 and that, consequently, the transposition of the Directive into internal law under Law No 22/94 operated to curtail the rights enjoyed by the persons concerned at the time when the Directive was notified. Taking the view that the dispute thus raised a question concerning the interpretation of Article 13 of the Directive, the Spanish court decided to stay the proceedings and to refer the following question to the ECJ for a preliminary ruling on the question:

> Must Article 13 of Council Directive 85/374/EEC of 25 July 1985 on the approximation of the laws, regulations and administrative provisions of the Member States concerning liability for defective products be interpreted as precluding the restriction or limitation, as a result of transposition of the Directive, of rights granted to consumers under the legislation of the Member State?

Judgment: 30. In those circumstances Article 13 of the Directive cannot be interpreted as giving the Member States the possibility of maintaining a general system of product liability different from that provided for in the Directive.

31. The reference in Article 13 of the Directive to the rights which an injured person may rely on under the rules of the law of contractual or non-contractual liability must be interpreted as meaning that the system of rules put in place by the Directive, which in Article 4 enables the victim to seek compensation where he proves damage, the defect in the product and the causal link between that defect and the damage, does not preclude the application of other systems of contractual or non-contractual liability based on other grounds, such as fault or a warranty in respect of latent defects.

32. Likewise the reference in Article 13 to the rights which an injured person may rely on under a special liability system existing at the time when the Directive was notified must be construed, as is clear from the third clause of the 13th recital thereto, as referring to a specific scheme limited to a given sector of production (see judgments of today in Case C-52/00 *Commission v France* [2002] ECR I-0, paras 13 to 23, and Case C-154/00 *Commission v Greece* [2002] ECR I-0, paras 9 to 19).

33. Conversely, a system of producer liability founded on the same basis as that put in place by the Directive and not limited to a given sector of production does not come within any of the systems of liability referred to in Article 13 of the Directive. That provision cannot therefore be relied on in such a case in order to justify the maintenance in force of national provisions affording greater protection than those of the Directive.

34. The reply to the question raised must therefore be that Article 13 of the Directive must be interpreted as meaning that the rights conferred under the legislation of a Member State on the victims of damage caused by a defective product under a general system of liability having the same basis as that put in place by the Directive may be limited or restricted as a result of the Directive's transposition into the domestic law of that State.

Notes

(1) This decision confirms that harmonisation of national laws is more important than consumer protection as far as the Product Liability Directive (85/374/EEC) is concerned. See also *Commission v France*,[6] and *Commission v Greece*.[7]

[6] Case C-52/00 [2002] ECR I-3827.

[7] Case C-154/00 [2002] ECR I-3879.

(2) The ECJ gives a rather restrictive interpretation of the 'contractual or non-contractual liability or special liability system existing at the time of the notification of the Directive, mentioned by Article 13 thereof, and which can remain in force after the implementation of the Directive. According to the Court, apart from the system put in place by the Directive, there can be no other general system of liability having the same basis, ie the defectiveness of the product. This solution was reaffirmed in the case C-402/03 *Skov Æg v Bilka Lavprisvarehus A/S*.[8]

Such an interpretation makes it impossible to apply in matters of product liability the strict liability regime resulting from Articles 25–28 of Law No 26/84 in Spain, but also the product liability regime which had been developed by French courts before the implementation of the Directive and which was grounded on the notions of defectiveness, as the following case shows.

Cass civ 1e, 15 May 2007[9] **7.2 (FR)**

ANCIENT AND NEW PRODUCT LIABILITY LAW

Defective television set

A national product liability regime which makes the supplier liable for damage caused by the product's defect cannot apply after the date by which the Directive should have been implemented.

Facts: The claimant had bought a television set from a famous distance-selling company. The television set caused the claimant's flat to be set on fire. The claimant brought a suit against the seller of the television set, which had not manufactured the product. Such an action against the seller is not possible under the Directive-based product liability regime (see infra), but used to be possible under Article 1147 of the French Civil Code (pertaining to contractual liability). On the basis of this Article, French courts had ruled that professional sellers were bound to deliver products free from any defect which might prove dangerous for persons or goods. In this case, however, the Court of Appeal rejected the claim. It argued that the supplier could no longer be made liable for damage caused by the product's defect on the basis of Article 1147 Civil Code, after the date on which the Directive should have been translated into French law, since the Directive-based product liability regime excluded sellers' liability for defective products. The claimant brought the case before the Cour de Cassation.

Judgment: The appellate court found that the company 'La Redoute' was only the supplier of the TV set in question and not the manufacturer. In employing methods recognised under national law, the Court did no more than interpret, as is its duty, article 1147 of the Civil Code in light of Directive 85/374/EEC of the Council of 25 July 1985 on the approximation of the laws, regulations and administrative provisions of the Member States concerning liability for defective products with a view to obtaining the result desired by EU regulations, in a dispute that falls under the scope of application of the aforementioned directive, that had not been transposed yet, and born out of facts subsequent to the expiry date of the period prescribed for transposing the directive. The

[8] [2006] ECR I-00199 para 47. This case is discussed in ch 1.IV and below 7.8 (EU).

[9] No 05-17947; (2007) D 1593, note I Gallmeister; (2007) JCP(G) I, 125, No 7, note Ph Stoffel-Munck; (2007) RDC 1147, note J-S Borghetti; (2007) RTD civ 580, note P Jourdain.

appellate court thus rightly decided that the claim in contractual liability against the manufacturer, based upon domestic law and thus interpreted, was inadmissible

Notes

(1) This judgment settled a much-discussed question in French law. It decided that the existence of the Directive-based regime precluded the application of the previous judge-made regime. This solution stands in conformity with the ECJ's position, since the regime that French courts had built out of Article 1147 Civil Code was based on the product's defectiveness, ie was founded on the same basis as that put in place by the Directive (see Case 153/00 above).

(2) The pre-eminence of the Directive-based regime applies as of the date by which it should have been transposed into French law, ie 30 July 1988. It is therefore not relevant that France only translated the directive in 1998.

(3) If liability had been fault-based instead of being defect-based, the solution should have been different. In Case 183/00 *María Victoria González Sánchez v Medicina Asturiana SA*,[10] the ECJ expressly stated that Article 13 of the Directive does not preclude the application of other systems of contractual or non-contractual liability based on other grounds, such as fault or a warranty in respect of latent defects. This is very important, as it means that most judge-made national product liability regimes, which except for France are usually negligence-based, may remain in force. This has actually been the case and up to the present day many claimants in the Member States prefer to act on the basis of these regimes rather than on the basis of the system which has been put in place by the Directive. This tends to confirm that the Directive has not substantially improved the level of consumer protection.

III. PRODUCTS

According to Article 1 of the Product Liability Directive (85/374/EEC), the producer shall be liable for damage caused by a defect in his product. Article 2, as modified by Directive 99/34/EC,[11] goes on to define the notion of 'product'. It provides:

> For the purpose of this Directive, 'product' means all movables even if incorporated into another movable or into an immovable. 'Product' includes electricity.

The main questions raised by this provision concern the application of the liability regime put in place by the Directive to blood and body parts on the one hand, and to intellectual products on the other hand.

[10] [2002] ECR I-3901.

[11] The 1985 Directive had left an option open to the Member States concerning the inclusion of primary agricultural products and game within the field of the new regime. Several Member States had chosen not to include these products, but the 'mad cow crisis' at the end of the 1990s led to the adoption of Directive 1999/34/EC of 10 May 1999 which suppressed this option and made it compulsory to include primary agricultural products and game among the products to which the 1985 Directive applies.

III.A BLOOD AND BODY PARTS

Contaminated blood has been a major subject of concern in many European countries and has given rise to significant product liability litigation. Article 2 of the Product Liability Directive does not expressly mention blood as a product, but there is little doubt that blood can be a product in the sense of the Directive. The issue has not even been taken in the English case *A v National Blood Authority*,[12] which applied the Directive's liability regime to transfusions of contaminated blood. However, for the regime set up by the Directive to apply, it is not enough that blood be considered as a product. It must also have been put into circulation by someone whom the Directive considers as a producer (see below).

As far as body parts are concerned, no further details are provided by the Directive. However, the French legislator, when implementing the Directive into the Civil Code, implicitly included elements of the human body or products thereof into the 'products' category.

Code civil **7.3 (FR)**

Article 1386 (12) A producer may not invoke the exoneration ground provided for in Article 1386 (11) (4) [development risk defence], where damage was caused by an element of the human body or by products thereof.

Note

This provision was not challenged by the European Commission in front of the ECJ, even though the Commission did challenge what was then the second sentence of Article 1386(12) of the French Civil Code. This tends to indicate that the Commission deems that elements of the human body or byproducts thereof can be considered as products in the sense of the Directive. As with blood, however, the regime set up by the Directive is liable to apply to damage caused by such products only if these have been put into circulation by someone whom the Directives considers as a producer (see below).

III.B INTELLECTUAL PRODUCTS

Article 2 of the Directive does not make any distinction between corporeal and incorporeal movables. It could therefore be assumed that the Directive must apply to corporeal and incorporeal movables alike. The Belgian legislator, however, took a different view when transposing the directive.

[12] [2001] 3 All ER 289.

Product Liability Act[13] **7.4 (BE)**

Article 2 Under the present law, the term 'product' is understood as any tangible product. This includes products that are incorporated into other movable or immovable products or any property deemed immovable.

Most authors agree that the Directive was not designed to apply to incorporeal products.

J-S Borghetti, La responsabilité du fait des produits. Etude de droit comparé [Product Liability for Defective Goods. A Comparative Legal Study] **7.5 (EU)**

The Product Liability Directive does not specify whether or not the products under discussion in article 2 are necessarily tangible. As the old saying goes ubi lex non distinguit, non debemus distinguere ('where the Law does not distinguish, neither ought we to distinguish'). The silence that surrounds this issue could thus indicate that non-tangible products are covered under the Directive. However, it would appear that the question of non-tangible products was not addressed when the text was drafted, and that in the legislator's intent, the sole aim of the Directive is to cover tangible products. Whatever the truth of the matter may be, the European Commission upholds this interpretation today and in its recent Green Paper on liability for defective products, it always talks about tangible products when tackling the question of products covered under the directive (*Green Paper on liability for defective products*, COM(1999)396 final). A majority of authors also agree that the Directive does not apply to damages caused by non-tangible products.

The author of this text believes that this position should be endorsed, not because the 'manufacturers' of non-tangible products should receive preferential treatment, but rather because the concepts employed in the Directive are hardly appropriate for the intangible universe. Many of the notions covered in the European Directive have little meaning if one attempts to apply them to a non-tangible item, such as information contained in a book, for example. What is the raw material of a non-tangible item, or its component part? Who is the 'manufacturer' and who is the 'importer'? And how can its 'presentation' or 'putting into circulation' be pinned down? Attempting to apply the rules of the Directive to non-tangible products would likely provoke a number of queries regarding interpretation. And the benefits, even if one looks at the situation from the victim's point of view, remain to be seen. Up until now, it does not appear that the absence of a strict liability regime for damages caused by non-tangible items has been seen as a problem. If non-tangible products (notably, information) were to be covered by the Directive, this could furthermore cause additional problems vis-à-vis freedom of expression.

The non-tangible products that pose a real problem are IT and software programmes. Following recent developments in the field of IT and advanced systems, there is an increased risk that they will cause material damage and even bodily injuries. However, it

[13] Act 25 February 1991, MB 22 March 1991.

could be that it is not necessary to include non-tangible property amongst the products covered by the Directive in order that the responsibility stated in the Directive apply to damage caused by software programmes. Some believe that software is effectively a material good since it cannot exist without material support and it could not have material effects if it were truly immaterial. This way of viewing software as a tangible good could explain why the European Commission believes that the Directive applies to software programmes (Parliamentary response given by the Commission on 15 November 1988, OJ C 114, 8 May 1989, 42), while holding that only tangible goods are covered by the text.

If we accept that the Directive is applicable to damage caused by software programmes, either because they are tangible items or because non-tangible property is already covered by the European text, a number of problems still need to be resolved. Notably, the question of what constitutes a defect in a software programme arises. The presence of a virus or a bug that alters the normal functioning of the software programme constitutes undoubtedly such a defect. It can be likened to a manufacturing defect since it arises from a discrepancy between the normal characteristics of the product and those sought by the manufacturer. However, if a software programme is affected by a virus, the manufacturer will only be held responsible if he cannot prove that the 'contamination' occurred after its 'putting into circulation'. But if a software programme has been designed so that it is unable to fulfil the functions it is supposed to perform, this will rather fall under the design defect category. ... As is the case with ordinary products, it is likely that proof of a defect will then frequently amount to proof of negligence on the manufacturer's part.

Questions

(1) Do you think the Product Liability Directive should apply to intellectual products? Why? In such a case, would the content of a book be considered as a product? In France, a court of first instance once made a publisher liable for damage caused by the content of a book.[14] The book dealt with fruits and plants and described a certain one as being edible, without warning against that this plant was similar in appearence to another, toxic plant. A child who had read the book picked the toxic plant, thinking it was the edible one, and brought it back home, where it was served at the family dinner. This resulted in a lethal intoxication. A successful action was later brought against the publisher. But the publisher was made liable on the basis that it had been negligent, and not because of the book's defectiveness.

(2) If the Directive were to apply to intellectual products, under what guise could a defect appear? A virus in a computer program would certainly be considered as a defect. But could a computer game which incites violence be regarded as defective?[15]

[14] TGI Paris, 28 May 1986 (1986) RTD civ 552, note J Huet.

[15] See also S Whittaker, 'European Product Liability and Intellectual Products' (1989) 105 *LQR* 125.

IV. LIABLE PERSONS

IV.A CHANNELLING LIABILITY TO PRODUCERS

The Directive made the choice of channelling liability for defective products to producers. It is only in limited circumstances, provided for by Article 3, that liability can be imposed on other professionals.

Product Liability Directive (85/374/EEC) **7.6 (EU)**

Article 1 The producer shall be liable for damage caused by a defect in his product.

Article 3 (1) 'Producer' means the manufacturer of a finished product, the producer of any raw material or the manufacturer of a component part and any person who, by putting his name, trade mark or other distinguishing feature on the product presents himself as its producer.

(2) Without prejudice to the liability of the producer, any person who imports into the Community a product for sale, hire, leasing or any form of distribution in the course of his business shall be deemed to be a producer within the meaning of this Directive and shall be responsible as a producer.

(3) Where the producer of the product cannot be identified, each supplier of the product shall be treated as its producer unless he informs the injured person, within a reasonable time, of the identity of the producer or of the person who supplied him with the product. The same shall apply, in the case of an imported product, if this product does not indicate the identity of the importer referred to in para 2, even if the name of the producer is indicated.

The choice of channelling product liability on the producer is not self-evident. In the United States, the Restatement of the Law, Third, Torts: Product Liability, following US case-law, assigns liability to all persons 'engaged in the business of selling or otherwise distributing products' (section 1). In addition, as outlined below, the Restatement gives a wide definition of those persons.

Restatement of the Law, Third, Torts: Products Liability **7.7 (US)**

§20 Definition of 'One Who Sells or Otherwise Distributes'

For purposes of this Restatement:

(a) One sells a product when, in a commercial context, one transfers ownership thereto either for use or consumption or for resale leading to ultimate use or consumption. Commercial product sellers include, but are not limited to, manufacturers, wholesalers, and retailers.

(b) One otherwise distributes a product when, in a commercial transaction other than a sale, one provides the product to another either for use or consumption as a preliminary step leading to ultimate use or consumption. Commercial nonsale product distributors include, but are not limited to, lessors, bailors, and those who provide products to others as a means of promoting either the use or consumption of such products or some other commercial activity.

(c) One also sells or otherwise distributes a product when, in a commercial transaction, one provides a combination of products and services and either the transaction taken as a whole, or the product component thereof, satisfies the criteria in Subsection (a) or (b).

Notes

(1) The reason why US law imposes product liability on producers and sellers alike is that product liability in the United States developed out of the law of sales and therefore rested from the outset on sellers, regardless of whether they are producers. In those European countries where product liability also developed out of the law of sales before the adoption of the Product Liability Directive, the channelling of product liability to producers by the Directive has not been well accepted. This has been the case especially in France and Denmark.

(2) This actually led the French legislator, when it first transposed the Directive, to provide at Article 1386(7) of the Civil Code that 'A seller, a hirer, with the exception of a finance lessor or a hirer similar to a finance lessor, or any other professional supplier is liable for the lack of safety of a product in the same conditions as a producer.' But this provision led to France's condemnation by the ECJ in Case C-52/00, which asserted that the Product Liability Directive is a maximum harmonisation one.[16] This led to a new version of Article 1386(7) of the Civil Code, which was again struck down by the ECJ (Case C-177/04).[17] Article 1386(7) was therefore again modified and now hopefully stands in conformity with Article 3(3) of the Product Liability Directive. It only departs from the latter inasmuch it specifies the 'reasonable time' within which the supplier must inform the claimant of the identity of the producer. The French legislator, like his Italian[18] and Spanish[19] counterparts, has given the supplier a three-month period in which to disclose the producer's identity. In Germany, this period is only one month.[20]

(3) Likewise in Denmark, when translating the Directive through Law No 371 of 7 June 1989 on product liability, the legislator chose to make suppliers liable for defective products in the same way as producers. Paragraph 10 of the statute provided that:

[16] 25 April 2002, *Commission of the European Communities v French Republic* [2002] ECR I-3827.

[17] 14 March 2006, *Commission of the European Communities v French Republic* [2006] ECR I-02461.

[18] Art 4 Decreto del Presidente della Repubblica No 224 of 24 May 1988, Attuazione della direttiva CEE 85/374 relativa al ravvicinamento delle disposizioni legislative, regolamentari e amministrative degli Stati membri in materia di responsabilità per danno da prodotti difettosi, *Gazzetta Ufficiale* No 146 of 23 June 1988.

[19] Art 4(3) Law 22/1994 on Product Liability (de responsabilidad civil, por los daños causados por productos defectuosos (LRP)), *Boletín Oficial del Estado* of 7 July 1994.

[20] §4(3) Act on Product Liability (Gesetz über die Haftung für fehlerhafte Produkte (ProdHaftG)), 15 December 1989 (1989) *Bundesgesetzblatt* I 2198.

An intermediary (defined as a person who in the course of business puts a product into circulation without being regarded as a producer) shall be directly liable for product liability to injured persons and subsequent intermediaries in the distribution chain.

This provision was questioned by a Danish court in a reference to the ECJ. The case *Skov Æg v Bilka Lavprisvarehus A/S* gave the Court of Justice an occasion to reassert its position on the extent of the harmonisation brought about by the Directive and to restate the reasons which led the European legislator to channel product liability to producers.

ECJ Case C-402/03, 10 January 2006[21]
Skov Æg v Bilka Lavprisvarehus A/S **7.8 (EU)**

LIABILITY OF SUPPPLIERS IS ALSO REGULATED BY DIRECTIVE 85/374

Toxic eggs

The Directive precludes a national rule under which the supplier is answerable for the no-fault liability which the Directive establishes and imposes on the producer.

Facts: After eating eggs they had bought at a shop belonging to Bilka, which had in turn obtained them from the producer Skov, two persons fell ill with Salmonella poisoning. They brought proceedings against the supplier Bilka, which joined the producer Skov in the proceedings. A Danish District Court found that the eggs had been defective, there was a causal link between the defect and the damage suffered, and no fault on the part of the injured parties had been shown. Bilka was ordered to pay compensation to the injured persons, and Skov was ordered to reimburse Bilka for that compensation. The Regional Court referred the matter to the ECJ for a preliminary ruling. The first question was, in substance, whether the Directive precludes a Member State from regulating the liability of the supplier by laying down that he is to be answerable for the liability of the producer.

Judgment: Extent of the harmonisation brought about by the Directive

24. In the context of the present proceedings, the injured persons and the Danish Government submit that the Directive does not operate a complete harmonisation of liability for defective products but only of the producer's liability for defective products. Relying on the wording of Articles 1 and 3 of the Directive, they argue that it does not regulate the supplier's liability and leaves the Member States a margin of discretion as regards the definition of the class of persons liable. …

27. The reasons why it appeared appropriate to hold the producer liable are explained in Article 1(e) of the statement of reasons in the proposal for a directive (document COM(76) 372 final; OJ 1976 C 241, p 9), to which the Danish Government refers. Those reasons, which refer to Articles 1 and 2 of the proposal, which without substantive changes became Articles 1 and 3 of the Directive, may be summarised as follows.

28. While acknowledging that the possibility of holding the supplier of a defective product liable in accordance with the provisions of the Directive would make it simpler for an injured person to bring proceedings, there would—it was observed—be a high price to pay for that simplicity, inasmuch as, by obliging all suppliers to insure against such liability, it would result in products becoming significantly more expensive. Moreover, it would lead to a multiplicity of actions, with the supplier seeking recourse in

[21] [2006] ECR I-00199.

turn against his own supplier, back up the chain as far as the producer. Since, in the great majority of cases, the supplier does no more than sell the product in the state in which he bought it and only the producer is able to influence its quality, it was thought appropriate to concentrate liability for defective products on the producer.

29. It follows that it was after weighing up the parts played by the various economic operators involved in the production and distribution chain that the choice was made to allocate liability for damage caused by defective products in principle to producers, and only in certain defined cases to importers and suppliers, in the legal system established by the Directive.

30. Contrary to the view put forward by the injured persons and the Danish Government, Articles 1 and 3 of the Directive are not thus confined to regulating the liability of the producer of a defective product, but determine which of the operators who have taken part in the manufacture and marketing processes will have to assume the liability established by the Directive.

Transfer to the supplier of the producer's no-fault liability under the Directive

31. By its first group of questions, the national court asks whether the Directive is to be interpreted as precluding a national rule under which the supplier is answerable without restriction for the no-fault liability which the Directive establishes and imposes on the producer. …

33. Since the Directive, as pointed out in para 23 above, seeks to achieve complete harmonisation in the matters regulated by it, its determination in Articles 1 and 3 of the class of persons liable must be regarded as exhaustive.

34. Article 3(3) of the Directive provides for the supplier to be liable only in the case where the producer cannot be identified. By laying down in Paragraph 10 of Law No 371 that the supplier is to be answerable directly to injured persons for defects in a product, the Danish legislature therefore extended the class of persons liable against whom the injured person is entitled to bring proceedings under the system of liability laid down by the Directive beyond the limits fixed by the Directive.

35. The Danish Government submits that the national legislation does not impose an autonomous liability on the supplier, because he is liable to the injured persons only to the extent that the producer, against whom he has a right of recourse, may be liable. It argues that the position of the supplier is thus similar to that of a surety with joint and several liability.

36. That factor is not decisive. Beside the fact that the system established by the national legislation imposes on the supplier a burden considered by the Community legislature to be unjustified (see para 28 above), it entails a multiplicity of actions, which is precisely what the direct action against the producer available to the injured person under the conditions laid down in Article 3 of the Directive is intended to avoid (see *Commission v France*, para 40, and para 28 above).

37. It follows that the Directive must be interpreted as precluding a national rule under which the supplier is answerable without restriction for the liability of the producer under the Directive.

Notes

(1) Given the position already taken by the ECJ in Cases C-52/00 and C-183/00, it was clear that it would not accept the Danish provision making the

supplier answerable for the no-fault liability which the Directive establishes and imposes on the producer.

(2) Danish legislation has been amended to comply with the judgement (see Law No 261 of 20 March 2007). Under the new legislation an intermediary can still be liable instead of the producer for damage or injury caused by a product where the producer or other intermediary has acted negligently or the producer is located outside the EU.

(3) The reasons underlying the channelling of liability to producers, which the ECJ restates at paragraph 28, are not very convincing. It is true that acknowledging that the possibility of holding the supplier of a defective product liable in accordance with the provisions of the Directive might lead to a multiplicity of actions, with the supplier seeking recourse in turn against his own supplier, back up the chain as far as the producer. However, most national laws would enable the first supplier to join his own supplier in the proceedings and so on, which would greatly limit the number of actions. Note that this is just what happened in the *Skov* case in front of the Danish District Court. The idea according to which holding suppliers of defective products liable would oblige them to insure against such liability and would result in products becoming significantly more expensive also appears to be questionable. As a matter of fact, nothing indicates that products were more expensive in countries which used to impose liability for defective products on suppliers, eg France, than in countries which have always channelled product liability on producers, eg Germany or the Netherlands.

Cour de Cassation, 6 April 2006[22] **7.9 (BE)**

THE FAILED PRODUCER IS STILL A PRODUCER

Excessive electric voltage

The producer who fails to carry out a normal step in the production process and delivers an untransformed product does not for this reason cease to be a producer.

Facts: The defendant was an association responsible for the distribution of electricity. Part of its task consisted in transforming high-voltage electricity into electricity of a voltage that can be used by consumers. This appears to be a two-step process. In the case at hand, the second step of the process (further reduction of the voltage of the electricity through the use of a specific technical device in the cable) was not carried out because of the malfunctioning of that specific technical device. It was argued that the association could not be considered to be a producer of electricity, since a producer would cease to be a producer if a step that is a normal step in the production process is not carried out.

Judgment: The producer of a product who fails to carry out a normal step in the production process and for this reason delivers an untransformed product, does not for this reason cease to be a producer.

[22] (2007) NjW 460, note I Boone; (2006) Pas 802.

Note

Considering the person responsible for the distribution of electricity as a producer can be seen as a way of circumventing the *Skov* decision, since this person could rather more convincingly be described as a supplier.

IV.B LIABILITY OF NON-PRODUCERS

IV.B.1 LIABILITY OF IMPORTERS

In the current era of globalisation, it will very often happen that the producer of a defective product operates outside Europe, eg in China. In such a case, even though the claimant may in theory bring an action against the producer whose product caused damage, in practice such an action is likely to prove impossible. It is therefore most welcome that the Product Liability Directive provides at Article 3(2) that

> without prejudice to the liability of the producer, any person who imports into the Community a product for sale, hire, leasing or any form of distribution in the course of his business shall be deemed to be a producer within the meaning of this Directive and shall be responsible as a producer.

The aim of this provision is that the claimant should always find a defendant whom he can sue within the European Union.

IV.B.2 LIABILITY OF FRANCHISORS AND OWN-BRANDERS

Article 3 of the Directive provides that 'any person who, by putting his name, trade mark or other distinguishing feature on the product presents himself as its producer' shall be considered as a producer in the sense of the Directive. This rule is also most welcome, as claimants would face a formidable obstacle if they could not rely on the information written on products or on their packaging in order to identify the person they must sue. This provision is likely to apply especially to big retail companies which market an increasing number of products which they have not manufactured under their own name or trade mark.

It can happen that both the identity of the company that puts its name or trade mark on the product and the identity of the company that manufactures the product appear on it. In such a case, both companies might be considered as producers in the sense of the Directive. Article 5 of the Directive should then apply, which provides:

> Where, as a result of the provisions of this Directive, two or more persons are liable for the same damage, they shall be liable jointly and severally, without prejudice to the provisions of national law concerning the rights of contribution or recourse.

However, it could equally be argued that in some cases the brander does not present himself as the producer, especially if he uses wording like 'goods selected for him'.

IV.B.3 LIABILITY OF SUPPLIERS

As is made clear by Article 3(3) of the Directive and by the ECJ's decisions, supplier liability can only be of a subsidiary nature as far as the system set up by the Directive is concerned. However, the Directive does not prevent the imposition on suppliers of liability for damage or harm caused by their products, as long as this liability is based on other grounds than the product's defectiveness, such as fault or a warranty in respect of latent defects. For example, in France, contractual liability makes it fairly easy for the claimant to bring a claim against the supplier of the product. In the *Skov* case, the ECJ validated the Danish case-law according to which the supplier bears unlimited responsibility for the producer's fault-based liability established in case-law in respect of liability for defective products resulting in personal injury or damage to consumers' property.

V. SUPPLY/PUTTING INTO CIRCULATION

According to the Directive, the producer is only liable for damage caused by a defect in a product that *he put into circulation*. This is made clear by Article 7(a) of the Directive which provides that the producer shall not be liable if he proves that he did not put the product into circulation. This notion of putting into circulation is all the more important as other provisions of the Directive also refer to it. Article 6(1) provides that, in order to assess the product's defectiveness, all circumstances must be taken into account, including, amongst others, the time at which the product was put into circulation. Article 6(2) adds that a product shall not be considered defective for the sole reason that a better product is subsequently put into circulation. According to Article 7(b), the producer shall not be liable as a result of this Directive if he proves that, having regard to the circumstances, it is probable that the defect which caused the damage did not exist at the time when the product was put into circulation by him. The producer can also escape liability under Article 7(e) if he proves that the state of scientific and technical knowledge at the time when he put the product into circulation was not such as to enable the existence of the defect to be discovered. Article 11 provides that the rights conferred upon the injured person pursuant to the Directive shall be extinguished upon the expiry of a period of ten years from the date on which the producer put into circulation the actual product which caused the damage, unless the injured person has in the meantime instituted proceedings against the producer.

The notion of putting into circulation is therefore a crucial one in the system established by the Directive. However, the latter gives no definition of it and the Commission seems to have been too casual when in the Explanatory Memorandum to the first Proposal it said 'it was not considered necessary to define the term put into circulation since this is self-explanatory in the ordinary meaning of the words'.[23] The lack of a definition is problematic and has led several national legislators to

[23] Bulletin of the European Communities Supplement 11/76.

chose to provide a definition of putting into circulation. Unfortunately, and as could be expected, these definitions vary.

Product Liability Act[24] **7.10 (BE)**

Article 6 The present law understands the term 'putting into circulation' to refer to the initial act whereby the manufacturer manifests his product's intended purpose either through its transfer to a third party or its profitable use by a third party.

Code civil **7.11 (FR)**

Article 1386 (5) A product is put into circulation when the producer has voluntarily parted with it. A product is put into circulation only once.

Decree No 224 implementing the Product Liability Directive[25] **7.12 (IT)**

Article 7 The putting into circulation of the product.

1. The product is considered into circulation when it is delivered to the purchaser, the user or to an assistant of the latter, also if for inspection or to test.

2. The putting into circulation also occurs through the delivery to the forwarder or to the dispatcher who will send the product to the purchaser or the user.

3. The liability is not excluded if the putting into circulation depends on a forced acquisition, except where the debtor has specifically signalized the defect with a judicial act of levy of execution or an act notified to the precedent creditor and deposited at the office of the court competent for execution within fifteen days from the levy of execution itself.

Consumer Protection Act 1987 **7.13 (UK)**

Section 46 (1) Subject to the following provisions of this section, references in this Act to supplying goods shall be construed as references to doing any of the following, whether as principal or agent, that is to say—

(a) selling, hiring out or lending the goods;

(b) entering into a hire-purchase agreement to furnish the goods;

(c) the performance of any contract for work and materials to furnish the goods;

(d) providing the goods in exchange for any consideration (including trading stamps) other than money;

(e) providing the goods in or in connection with the performance of any statutory function; or

(f) giving the goods as a prize or otherwise making a gift of the goods;

[24] Act 25 February 1991, MB 22 March 1991.

[25] 24 May 1988, No 224, *Gazzetta Ufficiale* No 146 of 23 June 1988.

and, in relation to -as or water, those references shall be construed as including references to providing the service by which the gas or water is made available for use.[26]

It is hard to reconcile these definitions of putting into circulation. But the question now appears to be to what extent each one of these can be reconciled with the definition of putting into circulation which is emerging from the ECJ's case-law.

ECJ Case C-203/99, 10 May 2001[27] **7.14 (EU)**
Henning Veedfald v Århus Amtskommune

PUTTING INTO CIRCULATION AND PROVISION OF A SERVICE

Danish kidney

A product is put into circulation when it is put to the use for which it was intended.

Facts: Mr Veedfald was due to undergo a kidney transplant operation at a Danish hospital. After a kidney had been removed from the donor, Mr Veedfald's brother, it was prepared for transplantation through flushing with a perfusion fluid designed for that purpose. This fluid proved to be defective and a kidney artery became blocked during the flushing process, making the kidney unusable for any transplant. The fluid had been manufactured in the laboratories of the dispensary of another hospital and prepared with a view to its use in the hospital where the transplant was to take place. The Amtskommune is the owner and manager of both hospitals. Relying on Law No 371 (transposing Directive (85/374/EEC) into Danish law), Mr Veedfald claimed damages from the Amtskommune. The latter denied liability on the ground, amongst others, that it had not put the product into circulation. The action came before the Højesteret, the highest Danish court. Being unsure as to the proper interpretation of Danish law in the light of the provisions of the Directive, the Højesteret decided to stay proceedings and to refer the following question to the ECJ for a preliminary ruling:

> Must Article 7(a) of Council Directive (85/374/EEC) of 25 July 1985 be construed as meaning that a defective product is not put into circulation if the producer of the defective product, in the course of providing a specific medical service, produces and uses the product on a human organ which, at the time when the damage occurred, had been removed from a donor's body in order to be prepared for transplant into another person's body, with resulting damage to the organ?

Judgment: 11. By its first question, the national court asks essentially whether Article 7(a) of the Directive is to be interpreted as meaning that a defective product is not put into circulation when the manufacturer of the product makes it and uses it in the course of providing a specific medical service, consisting in preparing a human organ for transplantation, and when the damage caused to the organ results from that preparatory treatment.

12. First, as regards the argument raised by the Amtskommune and the Danish Government that use of a product in the course of providing a service cannot in principle be covered by the Directive in the absence of any Community legislation on services, it is sufficient to observe that the present case involves the defectiveness of a product used in the course of providing a service and not any defect in the service as such.

13. According to the Amtskommune, in a situation such as the present, no product has been put into circulation within the meaning of Article 7(a) of the Directive. In the

[26] The Consumer Protection Act 1987 uses the notion of 'supply' instead of that of 'putting into circulation'.

[27] [2001] ECR I-03569.

present situation, the patient had no intention to buy the product, and that product, intended for strictly internal use by the manufacturer himself, never left the sphere of control of the unit consisting of the hospital dispensary and the doctors undertaking the treatment.

14. In response to that argument it is to be observed that the Directive provides no definition of the expression put into circulation. This concept must therefore be interpreted in accordance with the purpose and aim pursued by the Directive.

15. Article 1 of the Directive, read in the light of the second recital to its preamble, lays down the principle that a producer is to be liable without fault for a defect in his product where it causes damage. However, according to Article 7 of the Directive, a producer may be exempt from liability in a certain number of cases, exhaustively listed by that provision, if he proves that the circumstances of his case fall within their ambit. In those circumstances, such cases must, in accordance with established case-law, be interpreted strictly.

16. As Mr Veedfald, the Austrian, French and United Kingdom Governments and the Commission have rightly pointed out, the exemption from liability provided for in Article 7(a) of the Directive where the product has not been put into circulation is intended primarily to cover cases in which a person other than the producer has caused the product to leave the process of manufacture. Moreover, as the Austrian and French Governments and the Commission point out, uses of the product contrary to the producer's intention, for example where the manufacturing process is not yet complete, and use for private purposes or in similar situations are excluded from the scope of the Directive. However, the facts of the case as presented to this Court do not appear to fall within one of those situations.

17. As regards the Amtskommune's argument that the product was never put into circulation since it never left the medical sphere of control of the dispensary which made the fluid and the hospital where it was used, such circumstances are not decisive where, as in the present case, the use of the product is characterised by the fact that the person for whom it is intended must bring himself within that sphere of control. Where a patient is admitted to hospital, it cannot matter whether the product used in the course of medical treatment was made in the hospital establishment or was acquired from a third party, as it might have been in this instance, as the United Kingdom Government has pointed out. Whether a product used in the provision of a service was made by a third party, by the service provider himself or by an entity linked to the service provider cannot of itself alter the fact that the product was put into circulation.

18. The answer to be given to the first question must accordingly be that Article 7(a) of the Directive is to be interpreted as meaning that a defective product is put into circulation when it is used during the provision of a specific medical service, consisting in preparing a human organ for transplantation, and the damage caused to the organ results from that preparatory treatment.

Notes

(1) It could be argued that this case is in fact a case on services that has been treated by the ECJ as a product liability issue. The fact remains, however, that *Veedfald* does provide some assistance on defining what putting into circulation can mean.

(2) The decision, in fact, does not give a definition of putting into circulation. However, it is apparent from it that the ECJ favours a substantive, rather than formal,

approach to the concept. What is decisive is not the transfer of the product from one person to the other, but the fact that the product has been put to the use which it was meant for. The consequence is that a service provider can be liable under the system established by the Directive, in so far as it produces and uses a product in the course of its activity.

The ECJ has gone a step further in defining the notion of putting into circulation in Case C-127/04.

ECJ Case C-127/04, 9 February 2006[28] **7.15 (EU)**
Declan O'Byrne v Sanofi Pasteur MSD Ltd and Sanofi Pasteur SA

DEFINITION OF PUTTING INTO CIRCULATION

Vaccine alleged to be defective

A product is put into circulation when it is taken out of the manufacturing process and enters a marketing process.

Facts: A child, Declan O'Byrne, was vaccinated on 3 November 1992 with an anti-Haemophilus vaccine in the United Kingdom. Following that vaccination the child suffered severe harm. He claimed that his injuries had been caused by the fact that the vaccine that had been administered to him was defective. The producer of the vaccine was APSA, a company incorporated under French law. On 18 September 1992 APSA had sent a consignment of units of the vaccine, including that which was administered to Declan O'Byrne, to APMSD, a company incorporated under the law of England and Wales. That latter company, which was a wholly owned subsidiary of APSA and acted as a distributor of their products in the United Kingdom, received the consignment at issue on the following 22 September. On delivery APSA sent an invoice which was duly paid by APMSD. At a later date, which remains unknown, part of the consignment was sold by APMSD to the Department of Health of the United Kingdom and delivered by APMSD directly to a hospital nominated by the Department of Health. The hospital in turn supplied it to the surgery where the child was vaccinated on 3 November 1992. On 2 November 2000, the claimant in the main proceedings brought a first action for damages against APMSD, claiming that the latter was the producer of the product. On 7 October 2002, proceedings were lodged in a second action against APSA. Those advisers indicated that it was not until during the summer of 2002 that it became clear to them for the first time that the producer of the product was in fact APSA and not APMSD. In those second proceedings, APSA maintained that the action against it was statute-barred, since the product had been put into circulation by its delivery of 18 September 1992 to APMSD and the action was only brought on 7 October 2002, after the expiry of the period of ten years for bringing an action provided for by section 11A(3) of the Consumer Protection Act 1987. According to the claimant in the main proceedings, the action was not statute-barred. The putting into circulation of the product did not take place until the moment when it was supplied by APMSD to the hospital nominated by the Department of Health. That delivery was effected on a date less than ten years prior to the bringing of the second action. It was in those circumstances that the High Court decided to stay the proceedings and to refer the following question to the ECJ for a preliminary ruling:

> On a true interpretation of Article 11 of the … Directive, when a product is supplied pursuant to a contract of sale by a French manufacturer to its wholly-owned English subsidiary, and then by the English company to another entity, is the product put into circulation: (a) when it leaves the French company; or (b) when it reaches the English company; or (c) when it leaves the English company; or (d) when it reaches the entity receiving the product from the English company?

[28] [2006] ECR I-01313.

Judgment: 20. By its first question the referring court asks essentially whether, in the case where a product is transferred by a producer company to a distribution subsidiary and sold by that subsidiary to a third party, Article 11 of the Directive is to be interpreted as meaning that the putting into circulation of the product occurs at the time of the transfer of the product from the production company to the subsidiary, or instead when that product is transferred by the subsidiary to the third party.

21. The claimant in the main proceedings, the Italian Government and the Commission of the European Communities consider that the putting into circulation of a product depends on the producer's loss of control over that product or that it occurs when the product was transferred to a person over whom the producer does not have any authority. It is the entry of the product into the chain of distribution by delivery to a third party which is important. According to them, it is possible for a wholly-owned subsidiary of the producer, such as that involved in the main proceedings, not to be regarded as a third party.

22. The defendants in the main proceedings consider, on the contrary, that the fact that the product leaves its actual place of production is relevant to the definition of being put into circulation, and the fact of its being sent to a subsidiary cannot have a determining role in that regard.

23. At the outset, it should be stated that the Directive does not define the concept of 'put into circulation', which is referred to, in particular, in Article 7(a) of the Directive, dealing with the circumstances where the producer will be exempt from liability and Article 11, which lays down the rights conferred on the injured person pursuant to the Directive. …

25. … The Court decided, at para 15 of *Veedfald*, that the cases exhaustively listed by Article 7 of the Directive by which a producer may exempt himself from liability, are to be interpreted strictly. Such an interpretation seeks to protect the interests of the victims of damage caused by a defective product.

26. Article 11 of the Directive, the purpose of which is to place a time-limit on the exercise of the rights conferred by the Directive on the victim is, on the other hand, of a neutral character. As is clear from the 10th recital in the preamble to the Directive, the aim of that provision is to satisfy the requirements of legal certainty in the interests of the parties involved. The establishment of the time-limits within which the victim's action must be brought must therefore satisfy objective criteria.

27. In light of those considerations, a product must be considered as having been put into circulation, within the meaning of Article 11 of the Directive, when it leaves the production process operated by the producer and enters a marketing process in the form in which it is offered to the public in order to be used or consumed.

28. Generally, it is not important in that regard that the product is sold directly by the producer to the user or to the consumer or that that sale is carried out as part of a distribution process involving one or more operators, such as that envisaged in Article 3(3) of the Directive.

29. When one of the links in the distribution chain is closely connected to the producer, for example, in the case of a wholly-owned subsidiary of the latter, it is necessary to establish whether it is a consequence of that link that that entity is in reality involved in the manufacturing process of the product concerned.

30. The examination of such a close relationship must not be influenced by the question whether or not distinct legal persons are involved. On the other hand it is of relevance whether those are companies carrying out different production activities or are, on the contrary, companies one of which, i.e. the subsidiary company, acts simply as

a distributor or depository for the product manufactured by the parent company. It is for the national courts to establish, having regard to the circumstances of each case and the factual situation of the matter before them, whether the links between the producer and another entity are so close that the concept of producer within the meaning of Articles 7 and 11 of the Directive also includes that latter entity and that the transfer of the product from one to the other of those entities does not amount to putting it into circulation within the meaning of those provisions.

31. In any case, contrary to what is maintained by the defendants in the main proceedings, the fact that the products are invoiced to a subsidiary company and that the latter, like any purchaser, pays the price, is not conclusive. The same applies to the question of knowing which entity is to be considered as owner of the products.

32. Therefore the reply to the first question must be that Article 11 of the Directive is to be interpreted as meaning that a product is put into circulation when it is taken out of the manufacturing process operated by the producer and enters a marketing process in the form in which it is offered to the public in order to be used or consumed.

Notes

(1) In this decision, the ECJ confirms its substantive approach of 'putting into circulation'. Putting into circulation does not happen when a precise legal operation takes place, but when the product:

> is taken out of the manufacturing process operated by the producer and enters a marketing process in the form in which it is offered to the public in order to be used or consumed.

This definition can seem quite convincing, as it tries to stick to the economic operations that underlie product liability. However, since the manufacturing and marketing processes can be very opaque, assessing the exact moment when the product was put into circulation might prove difficult.

(2) It is therefore crucial to know who bears the burden of proof. In France, for example, it is the defendant, ie the producer, who must demonstrate that the claim has been made too late.[29] If he is unable to demonstrate the exact time at which the product was put into circulation, he might have to fall back on a date on which he can demonstrate that the product had necessarily already been put into circulation (at the latest, the date when the product was used by the claimant). In the UK, however, it may be the claimant who will have to prove that the case falls within the limitation period.

(3) In those countries in which the legislators give a definition of 'putting into circulation', it must now be assessed whether this definition can be reconciled with the definition adopted by the ECJ. If not, the principles of EC law make it an obligation for national courts to disregard the former in order to comply with the latter.

Question

If one takes the example of French law, it appears that the definition found in Article 1386(5) Civil Code is quite different from that given by the ECJ. But could the two be

[29] See eg Ph le Tourneau, *Droit de la responsabilité et des contrats*, 6th edn (Paris, Dalloz, 2006) No 8462.

reconciled if one interprets the Civil Code not as giving a definition, but as creating a rebuttable presumption that the putting into circulation of the product, as defined by the ECJ, takes place 'when the producer has voluntarily parted with it'?

VI. DEFECT

VI.A DISTINCTION BETWEEN MANUFACTURING AND DESIGN DEFECTS

It has been customary to distinguish between different types of defect. Manufacturing defects arise from something going wrong in the production process, possibly because of poor-quality raw materials, an error of a production line worker or product contamination. Design defects, by contrast, concern the underlying design of the product. Defects based on failure to warn or instruction defects can be viewed as subsets of design defects, if the product is broadly construed so as to include the labelling, packaging and accompanying material.

In the US this distinction has been written into the face of the Third Restatement of Torts: Product Liability.

Restatement of the Law, Third, Torts: Products Liability **7.16 (US)**

§2 Categories of Product Defect

A product is defective when, at the time of sale or distribution, it contains a manufacturing defect, is defective in design, or defective because of inadequate instructions or warnings. A product:

(a) contains a manufacturing defect when the product departs from its intended design even though all possible care was exercised in the preparation and marketing of the product;

(b) is defective in design when the foreseeable risks of harm posed by the product could have been reduced or avoided by the adoption of a reasonable alternative design by the seller or other distributor, or a predecessor in the commercial chain of distribution, and the omission of the alternative design renders the product not reasonably safe;

(c) is defective because of inadequate instructions or warnings when the foreseeable risks of harm posed by the product could not have been reduced or avoided by the provision of reasonable instructions or warnings by the seller or other distributor, or a predecessor in the commercial chain of distribution, and the omission of the instructions or warnings renders the product not reasonably safe.

Note

This approach by the Third Restatement has politicised the categorisation of defects as it applies different standards to the categories, reserving strict liability for manufacturing defects. The Directive does not formally distinguish between the different types of defects. This distinction is, however, familiar to the academic literature. Some national laws have drawn the distinction. Article 5(3) of the Italian Decree 224 of 24 May 1988 provides that: 'A product shall be considered defective if it does not provide for the safety which is usually provided for by other models of the same type.'[30] Article 3(2) of Spanish Law 22/94 of 6 July 1994 provides that: 'In any case a product is defective if it does not offer the safety normally offered by models in the same line.' It has also been used by the courts, for instance by the German Supreme Court which decided that the development risks defence did not apply to manufacturing defects in *German Mineral Water Bottle*.[31]

However, the manufacturing/design defect distinction was rejected in the important UK High Court case of *A v National Blood Authority* by Burton J in favour of his own distinction between non-standard and standard products.

High Court, 26 March 2001[32] **7.17 (UK)**
A v National Blood Authority

TYPES OF DEFECT

National blood case

There is no need to use the US distinctions of manufacturing and design defects; instead a more useful terminology is standard and non-standard products.

Facts: Blood infected with the Hepatitis C virus was supplied at a time when the National Blood Authority, which was under a legal duty to supply blood, knew of the risk of infection, but there was no means of identifying which blood supplied was defective. It had informed the medical community, but not the general public, of the risk.

Judgment: Non-Standard Products. ... the Claimants make a separate case in relation to the blood products here in issue: namely that they are what is called in the United States 'rogue products' or 'lemons', and in Germany '*Ausreisser*'—escapees or 'off the road' products. These are products which are isolated or rare specimens which are different from the other products of a similar series, different from the products as intended or desired by the producer. In the course of Mr Forrester QC's submissions, other more attractive or suitable descriptions were canvassed, and I have firmly settled on what I clearly prefer, namely the 'non-standard' product. Thus a *standard* product is one which is and performs as the producer intends. A *non-standard* product is one which is different, obviously because it is deficient or inferior in terms of safety, from the standard product: and where it is the harmful characteristic or characteristics present in the non-standard product, but not in the standard product, which has or have caused the material injury or damage. Some Community jurisdictions in implementing the Directive have specifically provided that there will be liability for 'non-standard' products, i.e., that such will automatically be defective within Article 6: Italy and Spain have done so by express legislation, and Dr Weber, in *Produkthaftung im Belgischen Recht* 1988 at 219-20, considers that that is now the position in Belgium also as a result of the implementation of the Directive.

[30] Translation by C Hodges, *Product Liability* (London, Sweet & Maxwell, 1993) 442
[31] See below s VII.B.
[32] [2001] 3 All ER 289.

41. If the distinction is between a standard and non-standard product, the critique of a non-standard product will be the same, namely by virtue of its difference from a standard product, whether it is treated as a one-off manufacturing defect or as a design defect resulting from a way in which the producer's system was designed, which led to all the producer's product being subject to the same risk. The approach to whether non-standard and standard products are defective may however be different, primarily because non-standard products fall to be compared principally with the standard product, while standard products, if compared at all, will be compared with other products on the market..

Questions

(1) Given Burton J himself noted the Directive does not contain any categorisation of different types of defects, was the judge guilty of falling into the trap he sought to avoid when rejecting the manufacturing/design defect distinction and merely used different language when he distinguishes non-standard and standard products?

(2) Is it inevitable that different types of defect have to be treated in different ways? Whereas a product that fails to comply with the intended design may be easily said to fail to fulfil legitimate expectations, is a more careful balancing of the risks and benefits called for when the basic design in challenged?

VI.B CONSUMER EXPECTATIONS AND RISK: UTILITY

A key debate surrounding the defectiveness standard is whether it should be based on consumer expectations (sometimes the phrase 'legitimate expectations' is preferred)[33] or risk–utility analysis. The consumer expectations standard has its heritage in contract law, whereas risk–utility smacks of tort law analysis. Strict product liability is a tort that also has in many jurisdictions origins in contract law, especially sales law. The introduction of 'risk–utility considerations' is controversial because these can easily be seen to slide into a negligence-type analysis. This need not be the case. It all depends on how risk–utility is viewed and in particular whether it is only foreseeable risks and benefits that are considered and whether it is the sole test or part of a composite test establishing what the consumers are entitled to expect. The language of the Product Liability Directive seems to favour the consumer expectation approach. In contrast, the General Product Safety Directive,[34] which provides for the public regulation of safety, might be read as favouring risk–utility analysis.

Product Liability Directive (85/374/EEC) **7.18 (EU)**

Article 6 (1) A product is defective when it does not provide the safety which a person is entitled to expect, taking all circumstances into account, including:

[33] See Burton J in *A v National Blood Authority* [2001] 3 All ER 289 para 31.

[34] Directive 2001/95/EC of the European Parliament and of the Council of 3 December 2001 on General Product Safety [2002] OJ L 11, 4–17.

(a) the presentation of the product;
(b) the use to which it could reasonably be expected that the product would be put;
(c) the time when the product was put into circulation.

(2) A product shall not be considered defective for the sole reason that a better product is subsequently put into circulation.

General Product Safety Directive (2001/95/EC) **7.19 (EU)**

Article 2(b) 'safe product' shall mean any product which, under normal or reasonably foreseeable conditions of use including duration and, where applicable, putting into service, installation and maintenance requirements, does not present any risk or only the minimum risks compatible with the product's use, considered to be acceptable and consistent with a high level of protection for the safety and health of persons, taking into account the following points in particular:

(i) the characteristics of the product, including its composition, packaging, instructions for assembly and, where applicable, for installation and maintenance;

(ii) the effect on other products, where it is reasonably foreseeable that it will be used with other products;

(iii) the presentation of the product, the labelling, any warnings and instructions for its use and disposal and any other indication or information regarding the product;

(iv) the categories of consumers at risk when using the product, in particular children and the elderly.

The feasibility of obtaining higher levels of safety or the availability of other products presenting a lesser degree of risk shall not constitute grounds for considering a product to be 'dangerous';

It is often assumed, based on US experiences, that the consumer expectation standard is a more consumer-friendly approach, although there was some doubt as to whether in the hands of the judge it would be as advantageously applied as it has been by US juries. The English judge Lord Griffiths, writing extra-judicially, signalled that risk–benefit analysis might continue to play a role, suggesting that whilst not overtly adopting a cost–benefit approach, English judges 'would as an educated response to the facts of a particular case undertake a balancing exercise of an analogous kind'.[35]

However, in the hands of Mr Justice Burton in the English High Court in *A v National Blood Authority* it was certainly applied in a pro-claimant manner. His judgment was bold and has provoked much debate. Perhaps the most interesting part is the process by which he considers how expectations ought to be assessed.

[35] Lord Griffiths, de Val and Dorner 'Developments in English Product Liability Law: A Comparison with the American System' (1988) 62 *Tulane LR* 353, 381.

High Court, 26 March 2001[36] **7.20 (UK)**
A v National Blood Authority

DEFECTIVENESS

National blood case

'All circumstances' in Article 6 means 'all relevant circumstances'.

Facts: see above 7.17 (UK).

Judgment: 31. … v. In the assessment of that question the expectation is that of persons generally, or the public at large.

vi. The safety is not what is actually expected by the public at large, but what they are entitled to expect. …

vii. The Court decides what the public is entitled to expect: Dr Harald Bartl in *Produkthaftung nach neuem EG-Recht* described the Judge (as translated from the German) as 'an informed representative of the public at large'. … Such objectively assessed legitimate expectation may accord with actual expectation; but it may be more than the public actually expects, thus imposing a higher standard of safety, or it may be less than the public actually expects. Alternatively the public may have no actual expectation—eg, in relation to a new product …

57. In this context I turn to consider what is intended to be included within '*all circumstances*' in Article 6. I am satisfied that this means all relevant circumstances. It is quite plain to me that … the Directive was intended to eliminate proof of fault or negligence … it was also intended to make it easier for claimants to prove their case, such that not only would a consumer not have to prove that the producer did not take reasonable steps, or all reasonable steps, to comply with his duty of care, but also that the producer did not take all legitimately expectable steps either.

58. … even without the full panoply of allegations of negligence, the adoption of tests of avoidability or of legitimately expectable safety precautions must inevitably involve a substantial investigation. What safety precautions or tests were available or reasonably available? Were they tests that would have been excessively expensive? Tests which would have been more expensive than justified the extra safety achieved? Are economic or political circumstances or restrictions to be taken into account in legitimate expectability? Once it is asserted that it is legitimately expectable that a certain safety precaution should have been taken, then the producer must surely be able to explain why such was not possible or why he did not do it; in which case it will then be explored as to whether such tests would or could have been carried out, or were or would have been too expensive or impracticable to carry out. If risk and benefit should be considered, then it might be said that, the more beneficial the product, the lower the tolerable level of safety; but this could not be arrived at without consideration as to whether, beneficial or not, there would have nevertheless been a safer way of setting about production or design. …

68. The circumstances specified in Article 6 may obviously be relevant—the product may be a second hand product—as well as the circumstances of the supply. But it seems to me that the primary issue in relation to a non-standard product may be whether the public at large accepted the non-standard nature of the product—ie, they accept that a

[36] [2001] 3 All ER 289.

proportion of the products is defective (as I have concluded they do not in this case). That, as discussed, is not of course the end of it, because the question is of legitimate expectation, and the Court may conclude that the expectation of the public is too high or too low. But manifestly questions such as warnings and presentations will be in the forefront. However I conclude that the following are not relevant:

i. Avoidability of the harmful characteristic—ie impossibility or unavoidability in relation to precautionary measures.

ii. The impracticality, cost or difficulty of taking such measures.

iii. The benefit to society or utility of the product: (except in the context of whether—with full information and proper knowledge—the public does and ought to accept the risk).

Notes and Questions

(1) Was the judge right to read *all* circumstances as being limited to *all relevant* circumstances? The judge was keen to point to the policy objective of keeping costs down so that justice could be in the reach of consumers. However, is this possible where the design of a product is being called into question?

(2) Although the judge found the infected blood was a non-standard product, he also felt that a similar analysis could be applied to standard products. Most commentators, however, consider that risk–utility analysis has to have some role to play in the context of design defects. Miller and Goldberg, *Product Liability*, talking in the context of discussing *A v National Blood Authority* state 'it cannot be right to prevent risk–utility considerations being reflected in the level of safety which persons generally are entitled to expect'.[37] Howells, *The Law of Product Liability*,[38] tries to find a way of incorporating risk/utility within a test based on expectations:

> However, in arguing that risk:utility is a relevant factor this does not mean that the test is solely determined by these factors, merely that they are factors to be taken into consideration. The test remains what 'persons generally are entitled to expect' and Burton J's approach of asking whether the harmful characteristic is socially acceptable remains a sensible way of framing that question. Part of the answer as to what is socially acceptable in relation to design defects should include elements of risk and utility as is indeed reflected in the judge's own inclusion of comparable products and price as relevant factors. Of course just how those factors are to be applied remains to some extent elusive because of the inherent ambiguity about the underlying rationale for the strict liability regime. The answer must lie partly in determining what was intended by reference to 'the risks inherent in modern technological production' mentioned in recital 2 to the Directive.

(3) Is this approach a helpful means of reconciling the tension between the two approaches to defectiveness? Burton J in the context of non-standard products had considered as not relevant: 'The benefit to society or utility of the product: except in the context of whether—with full information and proper knowledge—the public does and ought to accept the risk.' Is this transparency requirement also a valid precondition for risk–utility being relevant to design defects?

[37] CJ Miller and RS Goldberg, *Product Liability* (Oxford, Oxford University Press, 2004) 417.

[38] G Howells, *The Law of Product Liability*, 2nd edn (London, Butterworths, 2007) 366.

VI.C FAULT

The move to strict liability was intended to remove the need to prove fault. Proof of defect is enough without having to prove how the defect arose. Sometimes judgments find it hard to avoid adopting traditional approaches. Thus in the United Kingdom in *Foster v Biosil*[39] (a case involving a breast implant that leaked, where surgical error was excluded) the judge said 'the claimant must establish on the balance of probabilities that there was a defect in the product', adding that it was not enough to show 'merely that the product failed in circumstances which were unsafe and contrary to what persons generally might expect'. A good example of the contrary approach is a decision of the Court of Appeal of Paris in a toy safety case that noted that the defectiveness standard was based on what could be legitimately expected and did not necessarily require a design or manufacturing defect.[40]

Again English case-law has at times flirted with reading negligence values into strict liability. In *Bogle v McDonald's Restaurants*[41] (a case alleging McDonald's coffee was defective because it was too hot) the judge seemed implicitly to introduce the issue of fault by citing the conduct of the defendant company as a reason for not finding defect. Similar dalliances with fault type issues can be seen throughout the European Union as courts unfamiliar with strict liability can easily be tempted back into the more familiar language of negligence. Mr Justice Gray in *Ide v ATB Sales Ltd*,[42] a case concerning defective bicycle handlebars, seems to have the right approach when he said:

> [I]t is not necessary, in order for Mr Ide to succeed on the issue of liability, for him to establish how the accident happened, that is, what was the cause of the weakness which lead to the fracture of the handlebar of the accident.

Fault should certainly not be a requirement under the Product Liability Directive. This is different from the argument that the concept of defect may implicitly raise similar issues to a fault type analysis, albeit that they are handled in a different context. The position has not been helped by some comments in the Commission's Third Report on Product Liability,[43] which gives the impression of confusing fault and defectiveness:

> In a number of Member States, national courts have been prepared to infer the existence of fault from the fact that the product is defective. Examples of this practice have been reported in cases in the Netherlands and Ireland. In such cases, there is effectively a reversal of the burden of proof, with a requirement for the defendant to present evidence to convince the court that he was not at fault, notwithstanding the defective condition of the product. This is also seen in Denmark. Similarly, the Supreme Court in Spain has established in many judgments that the claimant has only to prove the damage and the causal link between the defendant's activity and the damage; fault is presumed unless the

[39] Decision of Cherie Booth QC in London County Court [2001] 59 BMLR 178.
[40] Decision of 10 December 2007.
[41] Decision of J Field, 25 March 2002 [2002] EWHC 490.
[42] [2007] EWHC 1667.
[43] COM [2006] 496 final, 9-10.

defendant can prove a high level of due diligence. In many cases the defendant will only be exonerated if he can prove the intervention of a fortuitous event or *force majeure*, or the exclusive fault of the claimant or a third party. In Italy, in the case of injury caused by 'hazardous' products, the burden rests on the defendant to prove that all suitable measures had been taken to prevent the damage if the defendant wishes to avoid liability.

Fault should not be an issue in an action under the Directive. However, there is a separate matter concerning the extent to which courts are willing to infer defectiveness. Several courts have been very flexible in this regard. The Commission in its Third Report cited decisions finding liability in this regard of the Tribunal de Grande Instance in Aix en Provence[44] involving a glass window in a fireplace and the Belgian courts[45] concerning a soft drinks bottle both of which exploded.[46] Similar examples have also been cited involving in Austria concerning a coffee machine.[47] Below is a good example of this approach from France.

Cour d'appel (Court of Appeal) Poitiers, 8 March 2005[48] **7.21 (FR)**
SA Automobile Citroën v Duchene

ESTABLISHING DEFECT

Car spontaneously catches fire

The court can find a defect because the product behaved in a manner that did not provide the expected safety.

Facts: A car was destroyed by a fire which started in the engine, but could not be explained.

Judgment: Article 1386(1) of the Civil Code deems that the manufacturer of a defective product bears responsibility for his product, regardless of whether or not he is bound by a contract with the victim. Article 1386(4) states that a product is defective when it does not provide the safety which a person is entitled to expect. And in assessing this safety account must be taken of all circumstances, particularly the use to which it could reasonably be expected that the product would be put and the time when the product was put into circulation.

In this way, the law deems that the manufacturer is subject to strict liability whilst requiring that the victim provide the proof of the defect in the product, damage and the causal link. The victim does not have to prove the origin of the lack of safety. Damage whose cause is unknown remains the manufacturer's responsibility.

In this case, it is not disputed that M Jean-Luc Duchene provided proof that the vehicle spontaneously combusted. Given the above considerations, it can be concluded that the vehicle did not demonstrate the safety that can be legitimately expected.

[44] Decision of 2 October 2001 (2001) D inf rap 3092

[45] Rb (Court of First Instance) Namur, 21 November 1996, *Riboux v SA Schweppes Belgium* (1997) JMLB 104.

[46] COM [2006] 496 final, 10.

[47] OGH, 22 October 2002, 10 Ob 98/02.

[48] *Jurisdata* 2005-274233.

Notes

(1) In contrast to this willingness by several continental courts to infer defect, UK judicial practice requires courts there to give a more detailed explanation for why a defect exists. The different role of French judges is nicely explained in the context of product liability by Simon Whittaker, *Liability for Products*:[49]

> In their discussion of defects, many jurists point out the key role of the *juges du fond* on the clear understanding that this issue is for their 'sovereign power of assessment' … While of course the Cour de Cassation could intervene in their assessment of 'defect' under the *loi* of 1998, for example, if a lower court 'denatured' the evidence of an *expertise* or contradicted itself, it is unlikely that it will interfere so as to control *which* circumstances are relevant, let alone in their overall balancing of considerations. As Viney and Jourdain conclude the test of defect gives 'to the *juge* rather a large discretion' ('une assez grande liberté') or as Jamin more critically puts it, it allows the *juges du fond* to 'do what they want according to their perception, very largely subjective, of the sociology of the time'.

(2) It has been suggested that if it was recognised that defeating expectations of safety was the ground for finding a defect and there was no need to find a physical defect, this might help bridge the gap between UK and continental court practice.[50] However, not all continental decisions go in the same direction. For instance, the Italian Supreme Court in case involving a hair colourant has stressed that defect must be proven and cannot simply be inferred from the existence of causation between the damage and use of the product.[51]

VI.D INHERENT RISKS

There are some products that carry inherent risks. Obviously a knife might cause hurt, but unless it was defective in the sense of posing an additional unjustified risk other than that which is inherent in the product, there will be no liability simply because it is the cause of the harm. Similarly alcohol, fatty foods and even tobacco will most likely not be found to be defective per se under the Directive. This is well illustrated by the following German case.

[49] S Whittaker, *Liability for Products* (Oxford, Oxford University Press, 2005) 484.

[50] G Howells, 'Defect in English Law—Lessons for the Harmonisation of European Product Liability' in D Fairgrieve (ed), *Product Liability in Comparative Perspective* (Cambridge, Cambridge University Press, 2005) 138.

[51] Case noted in Rolla, 'Italian Supreme Court rules on Burden of Proof in Product Liability Claims' (2007) 27 *European Product Liability Review* 18.

OLG (Court of Appeal) Düsseldorf, 20 December 2002[52] **7.22 (DE)**
Brinkman v Masterfoods

LIABILITY FOR INHERENT DEFECTS

Chocolate bars

No liability for inherent and well-known dangers of products.

Facts: A consumer complained that eating chocolate bars had caused illness and argued that they were defective in composition and because of lack of warnings. The consumer had been eating at least two chocolate bars per day since 1994 and claimed damages because of diabetes and tooth decay. The bars of this chocolate producer contained almost 50 per cent refined sugar.

Judgment: 44. A manufacturer must take necessary and reasonable measures to avoid dangers that, in concrete cases, result from the use of his product. If one classifies typical producer's duties in categories, design, constructional and instructional errors fall for consideration. From neither of these perspectives can a dereliction of duty be imputed to the defendant. …

46. The defendant has committed no design error. There is clearly nothing wrong from a food stuffs law perspective, with the ingredients used to make the chocolate bar, in particular refined sugar and cocoa. Now, a producer will not necessarily be able to resist challenges by having fulfilled safety regulations or other legal standards obtaining at the time… The use of refined sugar and cocoa in the producer's bars cannot be objected to on the basis of the dangers of these products as argued by the claimant either. Refined sugar and cocoa are used in a plethora of foodstuffs …

In any case, several of the dangers of cocoa and in particular refined sugar are well-known with respect to obesity and dental damage, especially when frequently consumed It is therefore principally the responsibility of the individual to tailor his nutrition according to his needs and desires and to decide on the respective importance of his health and his pleasure. The producers of foodstuffs are not obliged to produce food so that it maximises the health of consumers,… A legal order which in the general interest of the individual takes it upon itself pre-emptively to eliminate the possibility of endangerment, reduces freedom and agency in an indefensible way …

47. … b) The defendant is also not liable for a violation of any duty to instruct.

51. According to the principles of product liability, the producer must not only assume liability for damage stemming from poor design or construction of products. More fundamentally, he is also obliged to redress a consumer for damage where he has failed to alert the consumer to dangers of using the product, notwithstanding its flawless construction. It is also the case, in the context of instructional duties, that the manufacturer's observance of the existing legal requirements will not necessarily suffice. If a producer can perceive that use of his product might be dangerous, in spite of it meeting technical regulations and the observance of official standards, he must warn consumers. The duty to warn typically consists of giving the user of the goods the possibility to protect himself from certain dangers he would not foresee. …

53. Instructional duties obtain exclusively in the context of reasonable consumer expectations. That which lies in the realm of general knowledge of the relevant group of buyers need not be included in a product's instructions or in a warning. In this vein, the

[52] 14 U 99/02.

average knowledge and expectations of the consumer for whom the product is intended are decisive.

54. Given these principles, the defendant was not obliged to warn consumers on the packaging of its bars of the health dangers of consumption. ...

59 Whether the consumption of refined sugar can directly or indirectly cause Diabetes Type IIb is insignificant for the present question of an instructional duty of the defendant. As noted above, the central problem is that the dangers of excessive consumption of very sugary foods are generally well-known. Besides, an explanation by the defendant about medical details is neither necessary, nor, in the present case, could such an explanation be seriously communicated in a warning in the fabrication of the product. In this respect, it should also be considered that an excess of warnings is more likely to increase the danger, because the attention paid by the consumer to such warnings would diminish corresponding to the frequency of the warnings and the more they seem to be a mere formality. The individual's responsibility to protect himself against the generally known and easily recognisable dangers, the responsibility for running one's own life can disappear from view. [references omitted]

Notes

(1) The product was thus held not to be defective. Consumers should be taken to know that excessive consumption of chocolate bars could lead to health problems. Very often, however, these cases are not as laughable as they might appear. Everyone knows of the liability imposed in the US for damage caused by hot coffee that spilled whilst driving.[53] The similar English case against McDonald's failed.[54] However, whilst no one can doubt that coffee has to be hot, the case was really about whether it needed to be as hot as it was, although the English judge did not seem to want to engage with this point. Similarly claims against fatty foods, alcohol or tobacco products are likely to be based on claims the products pose more risks than necessary. For instance, with regards to light cigarettes it is sometimes claimed the descriptor lulled consumers into a false belief that they were safer than ordinary cigarettes.

(2) Very often there is dispute as to whether the inherent risk was something that was so obvious that there was no need expressly to warn against it or whether a warning was needed to ensure the product was not defective: the warning on tobacco products, for instance, makes it less likely that the products will be held defective and there is dispute as to the extent to which this was common knowledge before warnings were required: see Scottish case of *McTear v Imperial Tobacco Ltd* 2005 2 SC 1.

It is instructive to contrast the decision in *Brinkman v Masterfoods*[55] with regard to warnings with the approach of an earlier German case decided under negligence principles.

[53] *Liebeck v McDonald's Restaurants, PTS, Inc*, No D-202 CV-93-02419 (1995) WL 360309 (Bernalillo County, NM Dist Ct 18 August 1994).

[54] *Bogle v McDonald's Restaurants Ltd* [2002] EWHC 490.

[55] 7.22 (DE).

BGH, 12 November 1991[56] **7.23 (DE)**

LIABILITY FOR FAILING TO WARN OF INHERENT DEFECTS

Sweetened tea

There is liability in negligence for failing to warn of risks, which although inherent might not be recognised by all consumers.

Facts: Sweetened tea was sold for babies, but caused tooth decay when given in bottles that were left with the babies.

Judgment: The claimant is entitled to damages for the caries on the incisors of his upper jaw. The defendant, as manufacturer, neglected her obligation to instruct on and monitor the product. According to the undisputed facts of the case it can be assumed that when administering the sugary tea products for children from the feeding bottle through the modern orthodontically formed teat to babies and infants, the stream of the drink flows to the rear of the front teeth of the upper jaw where there is barely any saliva to protect the teeth with its rinsing effect. With longer exposure, caries develop on these teeth in particular, when children use this drink as a long-term comforter before being put to bed or even during the night. Once this danger had become apparent, the defendant did indeed print a notice on the packaging. However, what was printed on the packaging did not satisfy the requirements of an adequate warning in form or content. The warning was not highlighted clearly enough because it was given within the instructions for preparation and not made as a warning specially. The defendant must have expected that users familiar with her product, such as the mother of the claimant, would already have known how to prepare the tea. They had no reason, therefore, to read the instructions again and consequently take notice of the warning. Thus the defendant can be blamed in particular for the fact that the packaging, at least for the consumer familiar with the product, showed no changes so significant that the consumer would be prompted to check the text on the packaging again. The insufficient warning constitutes a failure to warn on the part of the defendant, because she did not prove the opposite.

Note

Liability can be imposed on this basis also under the Product Liability Directive.

OGH (Supreme Court), 8 April 1997[57] **7.24 (AT)**

LIABILITY FOR FAILING TO WARN OF INHERENT DEFECTS

Austrian mineral bottle

A company needs to warn of risks that are not obvious to the public.

Facts: On a hot and sunny day in August 1992 the claimant and his wife set off on a trip. They took some bottles of water with them. The bottles were kept unrefrigerated for more than 20 hours. The claimant took

[56] VI ZR 7/91 (1992) NJW 560.

[57] 4 Ob 87/97s.

a bottle from the boot of the car to drink from it. As the claimant opened the lid of the bottle, it popped like a champagne bottle though no mineral water came out. The bottletop struck the claimant in his right eye, causing him an injury. In both first instance and on appeal the producer was held liable.

Judgment: According to §5(1) of the Product Liability Act, a product is defective if it is not safe considering all reasonably foreseeable circumstances, in particular in light of i) the presentation of a product, ii) the use of the product which one can justifiably expect, iii) the time at which the product was brought into circulation …

With respect to defective products, a distinction must be made between design errors, manufacturing errors and instructional errors. As to design errors, the disappointment of safety expectations is grounded in a technical idea; in the 'design of the product'. With manufacturing errors or errors in fabrication, expectations correspond to the 'ideal product', not to individual wares, and entail a failure to meet standards of production. With instructional errors, only a failure properly to present a product renders it defective. …

In the present case, there is no design error, but an error of production must be acknowledged. That the bottletop exploded like a projectile on opening, can only result from an isolated fault—from foreign bodies invisible to the naked eye and also to electronic inspection machines, slight imperfections or inconsistencies on the inside of the bottle which upset the balance in a single bottle—because accidents of this type with mineral water bottles in general and those of the defendant in particular obviously occur only very rarely (SV-Gutachten, S 81 f). Whether the defendant is nevertheless guilty of a failure to instruct, by neglecting to insert a warning about possible dangers of opening the bottle under certain conditions, depends on whether the defendant ought to reckon with accidents like the one in question here. That remains to be discussed.

The defendant asserts in its appeal that the claimant was careless opening the bottle and that it was incumbent on him to open the bottle in such a manner as to avoid injury in the case of the explosion of the bottletop. This cannot be accepted:

It is the case that the safety obligations in the §5 Product Liability Act are only helpful to the consumer if the latter conducts himself in a responsible manner—§5 (1) Z 2 Product Liability Act refers to uses of the product that can reasonably be anticipated (Fitz/Purtscheller aaO Rz 13). It must be examined whether the consumer's behaviour was foreseeable for the producer, since the producer will not be liable for unforeseeable or absurd uses. However, a socially normal use, eg, the habit of putting pens in the mouth or to use stools as steps is clearly, without more, foreseeable for the producer. Also included underneath the umbrella of socially normal behaviour is conduct amounting to an abuse which suggests itself, as long as it is not merely a theoretically conceivable abuse (Fitz/Purtscheller aaO Rz; Welser aaO Rz 14).

The public, excepting certain experts, are not aware that the mineral water bottletops can, under certain conditions, behave like the corks of champagne bottles. Therefore no one takes particular care in opening a bottle of mineral water. There is no generally acknowledged rule that one should hold the bottle away from oneself. The defendant has no reason to assert that a purchaser would, if bottles have been stored uncooled on hot days, take particular care when opening them.

The claimant has not neglected any duty to take care by opening a mineral water bottle (that had not been cooled for over 20 hours) on a hot day. He had not acted according to the common understanding of the term under 'extreme conditions' and did not behave in a risky manner. No contributory negligence can therefore be imputed to the claimant. Since the defendant obviously, based on special knowledge, was aware of the risks of mineral water bottles, this danger should have been clearly marked on the bottles to warn the claimant. The defendant must have been aware that even where all due care was used in the production process and in subsequent tests, faults cannot be excluded that can, in specific circumstances, cause considerable damage … [These conclusions led to the confirmation of the contested judgment.]

Questions

(1) If a drug has side-effects that are random so that the consumers are in effect playing a game of Russian roulette, should the luckless victims be compensated even if the drug is generally beneficial? Would they be compensated under the Directive's defectiveness standard? Does this accord with the intentions behind those who promoted the Directive?

(2) Although many people would think such unfortunate victims should be compensated, it is debatable whether they would be under the Directive. This may seem strange given that the Directive was a response to such a tragedy in the case of Thalidomide. This might cause us to question whether the Directive really has achieved its purpose or whether alternatives, such as those from the Nordic states, need to be investigated.

In the excerpt below C Hodges comments on the origin of the Nordic schemes and notes the interest in the Nordic schemes in law reform around Europe.

C Hodges, Nordic Compensation Schemes for Drug Injuries[58] **7.25 (EU)**

The Nordic schemes can be viewed as manifestations of a general philosophical Nordic approach towards social solidarity and 'risk protection', which might be linked with a European policy of increased consumer protection in the second half of the 20th century. The Nordic approach now covers an unusually wide range of risks, including injuries resulting from medical, pharmaceutical, and traffic accidents, as well as other events including unemployment, sickness and enforcement of legal rights. The development of Nordic schemes has been traced in particular to developments in the 1970s that encompassed all relevant sectors in a comprehensive network of social and collective insurance-based arrangements providing compensation for injury. …

In Europe, there is interest in whether a Nordic model might be replicable in other States or even as a European Community mechanism. For example, there is renewed interest in a no fault, or alternative, approach to medical accidents. France introduced in 2002 a statutory compensation approach for medical accidents, which includes accidents caused by medicines and medical devices, and England is working on introducing two schemes, one for brain-damaged babies and the other for general medical accidents. There is also renewed interest in the New Zealand Accident Compensation Scheme. In addition, the possibility of a pan-European compensation scheme for unforeseeable injuries caused by defective products has been proposed.

[58] C Hodges, 'Nordic Compensation Schemes for Drug Injuries' (2006) 29 *Journal of Consumer Policy* 143.

Notes

(1) Four Nordic states operate indemnity compensation arrangements for those injured by drugs. In Sweden and Finland these are voluntary; in Denmark and Norway they are statutory. The basic principle is that liability is based on causation rather than fault, and an aspect of the schemes that seems most helpful to claimants relates to the tests of causation and standard of proof. Each scheme varies somewhat, but the Swedish scheme, for instance, requires a 'preponderant probability' that the injury was caused by a drug, which is deliberately intended to be lower than the normal tort law standard. Hodges in 'Nordic Compensation Schemes for Drug Injuries' notes that this generous attitude was supported by Swedish Supreme Court, where it was held that the requirements for evidence regarding the causal relationship between defect and injury could be relieved when the course of events were 'hard to grasp' and the events relating to difficult technical or scientific questions were complicated such that experts could have different opinions.[59] A good discussion of the Swedish voluntary scheme can be found in C Oldertz, 'The Patient, Pharmaceutical and Security Insurance'.[60]

(2) These schemes have much to commend them and it is worth noting that the Fonazione Rosselli study for the Commission, 'Analysis of the Economic Impact of the Development Risks Clause as Provided by Directive 85/374/EEC on Liability for Defective Products' (2004)[61] recommended the consideration for such schemes to cover difficult risks. However, many commentators wonder whether the viability of the Nordic schemes lies in the fact that they award modest levels of damages as they simply top up existing generous social security schemes.

VI.E WARNINGS AND INSTRUCTIONS

Warnings and instructions play an important role. Indeed it is necessary to understand the different functions of instructions and warnings. Instructions provide the means to use a product safely, whereas warnings allow consumers to avoid or at least be aware of the inevitable risk a product might pose. Importantly warnings provide the producer with the opportunity to avoid liability for harm caused by his product that is unavoidable. Of course there is always the danger that a producer might seek to evade all liability by providing blanket warnings and it was judicially noted by Burton J in *A v National Blood Authority* that this might conflict with the no right to exclude principle of Article 12 of the Product Liability Directive. Do you think a warning can ever be treated as an exclusion clause and hence not be valid and so not prevent liability arising?

Warnings may not be sufficient if the risks could easily be avoided by choosing an alternative design. In an Austrian case a garden chopper that cut off four fingers of

[59] (1982) NJA 421, *Leo Pharmaceuticals*.

[60] In Oldertz and Tidefelt (eds), *Compensation for Personal Injury in Sweden and other Countries* (Stockholm, Juristforlagert, 1988).

[61] Available at the website of DG Enterprise.

the user's right hand was held to be defective despite the risk being warned of since the device could easily have been designed with a security guard.[62]

In practice it is a difficult decision for a responsible producer to decide which risks to warn against. The more severe and more frequent the risks, the more appropriate it is to warn against them. There can be a tendency for courts to consider warnings as easily given, and hence be quick to impose liability where warning of a risk was not given.

Cour d'appel (Court of Appeal) Paris, 23 September 2004[63] **7.26 (FR)**

WARNINGS OF EXCEPTIONAL RISKS

Pentasa

The state of scientific and technical knowledge might depend upon the international consensus of opinion.[64]

Facts: A drug was marketed without warning of the risk that it might cause interstitial nephritis. This risk was known of as a possibility, but had not been confirmed by a consensus of the scientific community.

Judgment: Considering that the report carried out by the expert shows that interstitial nephritis immunoallergy, from which Christophe M suffered, is a direct and certain result of taking Pentasa®, a medicine produced or at least marketed in France by the company F; it is not disputed that the instructions and medical information on the packet did not warn the user of this medicine (or the prescribing physician) about the existence of possible side-effects, even very rare ones, such as renal failure, from which Christophe M suffered; this lack of information can be likened to a product defect and thus constitutes the breach of the safety obligation which company F could be charged with; Considering that at the time the incident occurred, the state of knowledge about the damaging side-effects of Pentasa® was in fact limited: The expert report, which was not seriously challenged, shows that in the various other countries in which Pentasa® is marketed, the instructions (with varying degrees of detail) recommended that the drug be used with caution if being taken by a person who has a known history of renal problems (which is not the case with Christophe M) since the potentially toxic effect of the tablets on the renal tubules was known at the time (p 34–37–38);

However, little was known about immunological complications—such as interstitial nephritis, as was the case with Christophe M or nephritic syndrome—which are completely unforeseeable consequences, occurring after different periods of treatment and different doses depending on the patient, and affecting kidneys which had been entirely healthy up until that point in time (p 34–35);

No international consensus existed at the time on the necessity to warn the members of the medical profession on the subject of the immuno-allergic risk presented by Mesalazine; given the small number of articles published on this subject at the time (p 38), even if the Japanese laboratory Yamanouchi had recommended in March 1996 that

[62] OGH, 11 May 2000, 8 Ob 192/99i (2000) RdW 644.

[63] No 02/16712 (2005) D 1012.

[64] Point not held relevant on appeal to Cour de Cassation.

the effects of a prolonged treatment on the kidneys be monitored, as Christophe M indicates;

A pharmacovigilence report carried out by company F which was handed to the Agence du médicament (the French drugs supervision agency) on 17 April 1996, shows that 5 cases of damaging side-effects (involving renal toxicity) had been reported; a further case of serious side-effect involving Pentasa® was reported on 14 May 1997 to the Agence by company F;

On 17 April 1996, Company F asked Professor Girard for an expert's report; after analysing the 8 known cases involving renal problems following use of Mesalazine between 1986 and 1996 (2 of which were similar to Christophe M's case), this expert concluded that patients that suffered from chronic inflammation of the intestines (including ulcerative colitis, as was Christophe M's case), could not do without this. He also stated that kidney monitoring was necessary, and especially a measure of plasmatic creatinine, first before six months of treatment, then after six months of treatment and finally on a yearly basis (p 20-23). It was the responsibility of the health authorities both to decide whether or not such a level of risk should be indicated on the packet of the medicine and to evaluate to what extent the cost of including additional precautions is justified given that the risk is only hypothetical (that is to say, possible not definite) as regards its amplitude (the number of accidents) and its gravity (mortality and reversibility) (p 25).

The other sources support these conclusions (p 23–24);

Eventually, on 5 November 1996 company F presented a request to the Agence du médicament that the instructions and medical information contained on the packet be modified. However, at the date the damage occurred Agence du médicament had not made a decision on the matter. Given the absence of a decision, company F could not legally alter the instructions and medical information contained on the packets (p 35). The decision was not made until 24th November 1998 (p 38–39);

Considering that, given the state of scientific knowledge and the legal factors that regulated the pharmaceutical information, company F can be exonerated from its responsibility. Company F cannot be criticised for failing to fulfil its safety obligations; Indeed, as evidenced by the statement of Christophe M there is no doubt that Christophe M was the object of a renal investigation (dosage of serous creatinine between 1994–5 and urine analyses in 1997, which eliminated the possibility that he was suffering from serious renal problems (p 11–14) during the period September 1995 to March 1997. In this way, even if the instructions and medical information contained on the Pentasa® packets had recommended regular checks following a prolonged period of treatment, the unforeseeable damage, which was of an immuno-nature and could have arisen at any moment, as has been noted by the experts (p 34–35), could have occurred nonetheless.

Note and Questions

Is it right that the producer should be liable for failure to warn of unlikely and/or insignificant risks? In any event, will there be no liability because of causation problems, ie if a risk is rare and insignificant it is unlikely that a consumer would have changed their behaviour and not used the product or used it differently because of such a warning? This is often a problem with a case based on defective warnings as the injured person has to show that an appropriate warning would have caused them to behave differently so as to avoid the harm; otherwise there is no causal link between the defect and the injury.

Warnings and instructions must be fit for purpose. Thus in *Palmer v Palmer*[65] instructions accompanying the 'Klump Klick' seatbelt device were inadequate as they failed to indicate what amounted to excessive slack. It is worth remembering, however, that the warning need only be an appropriate one. Strict liability does not require that products be of the highest standard, merely that they meet the minimum expectations of safety. This is exemplified by the following case.

High Court, 3 December 1999[66] **7.27 (UK)**
Worsley v Tambrands

WARNINGS

Tampons

Warnings have only to be adequate; it is irrelevant that better warnings could be given (and may even have been given in other jurisdictions).

Facts: A woman suffered 'toxic shock syndrome' from the use of tampons and claimed that the warnings were inadequate.

Judgment: The claimant's main complaint is that the leaflet was designed in such a way that it did not have a sufficient impact upon her, whereas the United States warnings current in 1994 were more prominent, fuller and would have had an impact. It is true that the 1994 United States leaflet is a single-language document with the warning in larger type than the contemporary United Kingdom leaflet. It also contains advice on how to reduce the risk of TSS by alternating tampon and towel use, or by not using tampons at all. As a design, I accept that the United States model is better than the United Kingdom one. But that is not the point. The issue is not whether the United Kingdom pattern could have replicated the United States one (I am prepared to accept that it could, in the absence of evidence to the contrary), but whether in the United kingdom one falls below the statutory or common law standard by reason of its design and/or contents, and, if it did, whether a different design would have caused the claimant to have acted differently.

The United Kingdom leaflet is, because it is multilingual, set out in the columns of relatively small print in blue type on white. There are four columns on the page which contains the English language warning. The symptoms of TSS are in bold type. I consider the original to be legible without undue effort. There is no evidence before me to suggest that multilingual documents are less likely to be read than single language ones. I would have thought that we are all used to them by now. I reject the argument that they fall below the standard which persons might generally be entitled to expect.

Because the claimant lost the relevant leaflet, she is driven to argue that either the full warning should have been on the box, which I have rejected, or that over a period of

[65] [2006] EWHC 1284, [2006] All ER (D) 86 (Jun).
[66] [2000] PIQR P95.

years the warnings on the leaflet should have been designed to make a greater impact on her memory. On her own evidence, she had possibly read the leaflet which would have been current in July 1994, so she was not dissuaded from doing so by its layout of style. She had read the symptoms and the very specific warnings as to how to react to them. She decided her symptoms were not TSS and sadly did not react to them until it was too late a stage.

If the claimant had had the leaflet available to her, as I say, I accept she may have reacted differently. That is the purpose of the leaflet in every pack. Whilst I accept that reading leaflets repeatedly over the years may have a cumulative effect upon the reader, I do not consider that they should be designed so to do. The impact needs to be fully present in each one. A different design or content in earlier leaflets would not have altered the claimant's reaction. In July 1994 she knew what they said. Had a leaflet been before her, it would have been sufficient to direct her attention to the need to remove her tampon and see her doctor and tell him, had she chosen to do so.

The additional United States advice in relation to alternating tampon and towels or not using them at all was not material to this claimant. Indeed, her evidence that it would have affected her conduct was unconvincing, and I reject it. Mrs Worsley had been using Tampax Regular for many years, and doing so in accordance with the health and hygiene warnings supplied with them. She knew from the packet and from the earlier leaflets of the risk of TSS and of the need to keep the leaflets referred to when necessary.

...

The reality of this case is that the claimant had lost the relevant leaflet and, for some inexplicable reason, misremembered its contents as to the onset of the illness. That does not render the box or the leaflet defective, and the claim must fail. The defendant had done what a menstruating woman was, in all the circumstances, entitled to expect: (1) they had a clearly legible warning on the outside of the box directing the user to the leaflet; (2) the leaflet was legible, literate, and unambiguous and contained all the material necessary to convey both the warning signs and the action required if any of them were present; and (3) they cannot cater for lost leaflets or for those who choose not to replace them, as the claimant could have done after the Tuesday when she discovered the loss.

In those circumstances, whilst it is a sad fact that the claimant suffered a frightening and near fatal illness, there must be judgment for the defendant on its submission of no case to answer.

Notes

(1) See also the County Court Zwolle, 24 April 2002.[67] That case found the instructions were satisfactory and the producers not liable when a 16-year-old girl placed a mini-tampon in her urethra by mistake.

(2) Is it expecting too much for consumers to read in detail information provided with regular everyday products, and in particular to notice when the warnings change over time? Note that in the sweetened tea case[68] the issue of highlighting changes to regular users of the product was raised. The woman concerned in the tampon case had been to her doctor, who had not been alerted to the risk of toxic

[67] (2002) Prg 5921.

[68] See above excerpt 7.23 (DE).

shock syndrome although he knew she was menstruating. Is a consumer supposed to be more astute than their doctor? On the other hand, how can producers protect themselves from an inherent risk associated with the product?

(3) Does multilingualism justify reduced protection? The court in the tampon case was content for the packaging merely to refer to more detailed instructions. In Germany a court has held a warning on a delivery note adequate without the need for a separate instruction sheet.[69]

VI.F LOCATION OF SALE

In an interesting decision the Higher Regional Court of Munich[70] discussed whether the place of usage was a relevant factor. It considered it was, and so justified German cars not having automatic central locking, which was standard in the US. Are Germany and the US really that different? Another example used in that case was of cars being used in developing countries having to have better suspension. Is that a sounder distinction?

VI.G AGE OF USER

The age of the user can also be relevant. Age was considered a relevant factor by the Belgian Court of Cassation in finding defective a dental face mask that had to be untied using elastic bands.[71]

VI.H MARKETING

The way in which a product is marketed can affect whether it is defective. In a decision of the Court of Appeal of Athens it was held that an airbag that failed to activate in a crash was not defective as according to the marketing literature it was only supposed to activate in the case of a head-on collision at more than 25 km/h and this collision was less than 25 km/h.[72] The marketing can, however, also help establish liability, as in the following Austrian case.

[69] See OLG (Court of Appeal) Celle, 29 January 2003, 9 U 176/01 (2004) VersR 86.

[70] OLG (Court of Appeal) München, 5 August 2002, 17 U 2297/02, (2004) VersR 886.

[71] See Hof van Cassatie (Court of Cassation), 26 September 2003 (2003) Arr Cass 1765; (2003) Pas 1494.

[72] Decision No 7827/20000.

OGH (Supreme Court), 28 April 1998[73] **7.28 (AT)**

EFFECT OF MARKETING ON DEFECTIVENESS

Racing handlebars

Marketing can affect the question of defectiveness.

Facts: The producer of bicycle handlebars had not explicitly advertised their use in extreme conditions, but had been informed that top Austrian sportspeople were using their products in bicycle races. The producer had not warned they were unsuitable for racing conditions.

Judgment: It is the case that the product in question was not expressly created for the extreme burdens of cycle sport but the defendant was aware that top Austrian mountain bike riders were using the handle-bars for racing. Further, it can be assumed that there was neither a set of instructions for mounting the handle-bars in the form of "instructions for use" nor that the defendant had indicated whether the handle-bars were or were not suitable for competitive sport. In every competitive sport, in which the achievement of best times is in the foreground, the general concern is to use the lightest possible equipment. That the defendant did not expressly create or promote the product for racing, does not alone mean that it ought not to be used by competitive sportsmen. It is a matter of common sense that not only amateur but also competitive sportsmen might purchase such products. The statements also show that many top Austrian mountain bikers had used this sort of lightweight handle-bars. The defendant must therefore be aware that the legitimate safety expectations are not only those of the average consumer, but also those of more specialised consumers, namely competitive sportsmen. It would therefore have been necessary, to include a warning in instructions for mounting or using the handle-bars that the same were not suitable for competitive sport or that they had not been tested for their resistance to the burdens of such use. The defendant had refrained from including such notices and had clearly taken account of the fact that the handle-bars would also be used in competition by top Austrian sportsmen. The defendant has also not produced evidence that it carried out any performance tests, nor has it argued in these proceedings that the breaking of the handle-bars had not resulted from faulty material but specifically and solely from the complainant's incorrect mounting of the product. If the producer does not manage to fashion the product so that it is fault-free for all conceivable uses and for all possible consumer dangers, the remaining area of danger can be covered by the duty of instruction and warning of the particular consumers. With those products whose usage in particular areas is known to the producer, but cannot be recommended by him, he is obliged either to warn against the use of the product in that area or to point out the products limited suitability with reference to necessary safety precautions.

The producer or seller of a product which in itself is fault-free, whose usage in specific ways or fields could lead to damage, has the additional duties of instruction and clarification: The liability for generally, abstractly fault-free products, whose use in individual concrete situations could lead to damage and which are as a result dangerous, is to be affirmed when the producer or distributor should have taken such a use into account; correspondingly he is obliged properly to label the products. [References omitted]

VI.I COMPLIANCE WITH STANDARDS

There is no pre-emption defence in Europe so that compliance with regulations or standards does not provide an automatic defence. The compliance with mandatory regulations defence in Article 7(d) of the Product Liability Directive is very limited and only applies when there is no way in which regulations could be complied with and the product not be defective. Nevertheless compliance with a standard is likely to be persuasive evidence and this seems to be especially the case in Germany. However, even there mere compliance with standards may not be enough.

OLG (Court of Appeal) Düsseldorf, 20 December 2002[74] **7.29 (DE)**
Brinkman v Masterfoods

COMPLIANCE WITH REGULATIONS OR STANDARDS

Chocolate bars

One may have to warn of dangers even if such warnings are not prescribed in regulations or standards

Facts: See above 7.22 (DE).

Judgment: 46. ... Now, a producer will not necessarily be able to resist challenges by having fulfilled safety regulations or other legal standards obtaining at the time.

OLG (Court of Appeal) Schleswig-Holstein, 19 October 2002[75] **7.30 (DE)**

DEFECT AND COMPLIANCE WITH STANDARDS

Overheating washing machine

A product can be defective despite complying with technical standards.

Facts: Unusual amounts of chloride aggregation caused a washing machine to overheat and cause damage to the contents and surrounding kitchen.

Judgment: The expert witness Dr B explained comprehensibly in his supplementary report of the 11 October 2005 that no special technical component diagrams, detailed information on construction, calculations etc, according to which manufacturers had to exactly recreate, check or produce their appliances and component parts, are published in the standard specifications and regulations for 'white goods'. Rather, general effective safety objectives that the manufacturer had an obligation to fulfil were generally defined and described. The manner in which he did this was left up to him. In the present case the defendant adhered to these requirements; the pitting corrosion on the heating

[73] 10 Ob 399/97t.
[74] 14 U 99/02.
[75] 17 U 43/07.

element is not part of the range of hazard controls according to the standards and regulations. Similarly, placing thermostats in separate cases is not demanded anywhere in the standard specifications and regulations.

41. (3) In as far as technical standards contain no requirements, the defendant was also obliged as a manufacturer of dishwashers, however, to ensure, within the bounds of the technically possible and as far as is economically reasonable, that its products did not bring about any damage to other property belonging to the customer, within the limits of normal use. The defendant did not meet these requirements to a satisfactory extent.

42. (a) The standard for what an average user objectively expects or can expect in terms of the safety of a dishwasher is that, on the one hand, the danger must not be purely of a theoretical nature and, on the other, it must not be a matter of dangers which are typically connected with the usage of the product and which are recognised and fundamentally accepted by the users.

43. With a dishwasher comes a legitimate expectation that as far as is possible it exhibits no defects which will lead to a malfunction or destruction of the appliance; but this defect—in view of the serious danger to property and even health or life, produced by the combination of electricity and water—should at least remain restricted to the defective part and not spread to further property belonging to the user through heat, fire or similar.

44. (b) This expectation has to be balanced with the measures that the manufacturer must take in order to guarantee protection defined in this way. [References omitted]

Note

The above cases concerned whether compliance with a technical standard could be a defence. On the other hand, failure to comply with standards is likely to lead to a finding that the product is defective, unless the producer can point to special reasons why the standard should not be followed. *Pollard v Tesco*[76] concerned a washing powder that contained a child-resistant closure that did not comply with British Standards. The judge held that these standards were not relevant as they were not mandatory for that product. Was the judge right or are consumers entitled to expect that any closure used complies with relevant standards?

VI.J DEFENCES

VI.J.1 GENERAL

One of the differences between strict liability and absolute liability is the availability of defences under strict liability regimes. The Product Liability Directive provides for certain specific defences. The burden of proof lies on the defendant to establish the defence.

[76] [2006] EWCA Civ 393; [2006] All ER (D) 86.

Product Liability Directive (85/374/EEC) **7.31 (EU)**

Article 7 The producer shall not be liable as a result of this Directive if he proves:

(a) that he did not put the product into circulation; or

(b) that, having regard to the circumstances, it is probable that the defect which caused the damage did not exist at the time when the product was put into circulation by him or that this defect came into being afterwards; or

(c) that the product was neither manufactured by him for sale or any form of distribution for economic purpose nor manufactured or distributed by him in the course of his business; or

(d) that the defect is due to compliance of the product with mandatory regulations issued by the public authorities; or

(e) that the state of scientific and technical knowledge at the time when he put the product into circulation was not such as to enable the existence of the defect to be discovered; or

(f) in the case of a manufacturer of a component, that the defect is attributable to the design of the product in which the component has been fitted or to the instructions given by the manufacturer of the product.

Note

Two of these defences (Article 7(a) and (c)) have been before the ECJ in the same case. The question of whether the product in this case was supplied has already been considered above (see above 7.14 (EU)).

ECJ Case C-203/99, 10 May 2001[77] **7.32 (EU)**
Henning Veedfald v Århus Amtskommune

WHETHER A PRODUCT IS SUPPLIED AND WHETHER A PRODUCT IS SUPPLIED FOR AN ECONOMIC PURPOSE

Danish kidney

There is a supply since the product is produced by a service provider and the user has to bring himself under the control of the service provider. Public hospitals are acting for an economic purpose.

Facts: See 7.14 (EU).

Judgment: 21. As to that point, the fact that products are manufactured for a specific medical service for which the patient does not pay directly but which is financed from public funds maintained out of taxpayers' contributions cannot detract from the economic and business character of that manufacture. The activity in question is not a charitable one which could therefore be covered by the exemption from liability provided for in Article 7(c) of the Directive. Besides, the Amtskommune itself admitted at the hearing that, in similar circumstances, a private hospital would undoubtedly be liable for the defectiveness of the product pursuant to the provisions of the Directive.

77 [2001] ECR I-3569.

One of the defences most likely to be invoked in practice is Article 7(b), which provides a defence where the defect did not exist at the time of supply. Here the burden of proof may be crucial. Simply relying on evidence of quality assurance systems to establish that the product was unlikely to have been defective when supplied will rarely be sufficient. *Piper v JRI Manufacturing Ltd*[78] may be the exception that proves this rule as the manufacturer's quality assurance system was accepted as evidence that the product was not defective when supplied. The Court of Appeal was clearly influenced by the nature of the product—an artificial hip—for which there was convincing evidence that the workers inspected each individually and extremely carefully.

VI.J.2 DEVELOPMENT RISKS

Undoubtedly the development risks defence is the most controversial defence. Some view its inclusion as undermining the whole rationale of strict liability by reintroducing elements of fault and foreseeability. For others it is a necessary safeguard, especially for innovative industries. The Commission was resistant to the inclusion of the defence, but some Member States, particularly the United Kingdom, would only agree to the Directive if it was included. It was therefore made optional, but only Luxemburg and Finland have chosen to exclude it, whilst Spain excludes it for high-risk products, France for products derived from human body parts and in Germany pharmaceuticals are governed by the Medicines Act which does not offer an identical defence. There is much debate about the scope of the defence. Some argue it is a very narrow defence whose burden is on the defendant, whereas others suggest it has to be interpreted in a way that a reasonable producer can make use of. This latter approach lies behind the wording of section 4(1)(e) of the United Kingdom's Consumer Protection Act 1987, which provides:

> that the state of scientific and technical knowledge at the relevant time was not such that a producer of products of the same description as the product in question might be expected to have discovered the defect if it had existed in his products while they were under his control.

This has been subject to an infringement action in the ECJ where the Commission contended that the United Kingdom's implementation was too generous to the producers. The Commission lost the case on a technical issue relating to the burden of proof, with the ECJ being (perhaps unfairly) critical of the Commission for bringing the case before English case-law had established whether the defence was in practice different from that required by the Directive. However, the Court seemed to have had some sympathy with the United Kingdom's desire to ensure the defence was one that was practically available to producers. Mildred captures the essence of the debate nicely when he suggests it is about whether the defence required 'absolute undiscoverability' or 'undiscoverability by reasonable means'.[79]

[78] [2006] EWCA Civ 1344; All ER (D) 181; 92 BMLR 141.

[79] M Mildred, 'The Development Risks Defence' in D Fairgrieve (ed), *Product Liability in Comparative Perspective* (Cambridge, Cambridge University Press, 2005) 170.

ECJ Case C-300/95, 29 May 1997[80] **7.33 (EU)**
Commission v United Kingdom

DEVELOPMENT RISKS DEFENCE

Commission challenge to UK

It is not proven that section 4(1)(e) of the Consumer Protection Act 1987 does not correctly implement Article 7(e) of the Product Liability Directive.

Facts: The implementation of the development risks defence by the United Kingdom was challenged by the European Commission as it was considered too subjective.

Opinion of AG Tesauro: 20. It should first be observed that, since that provision refers solely to the 'scientific and technical knowledge' at the time when the product was marketed, it is not concerned with the practices and safety standards in use in the industrial sector in which the producer is operating. In other words, it has no bearing on the exclusion of the manufacturer from liability that no-one in that particular class of manufacturer takes the measures necessary to eliminate the defect or prevent it from arising if such measures are capable of being adopted on the basis of the available knowledge.

Other matters which likewise are to be regarded as falling outside the scope of Article 7(e) are aspects relating to the practicability and expense of measures suitable for eliminating the defect from the product. Neither, from this point of view, can the fact that the producer did not appraise himself of the state of scientific and technical knowledge or does not keep up to date with developments in this area as disclosed in the specialist literature, be posited as having any relevance for the purposes of excluding liability on his part. I consider, in fact, that the producer's conduct should be assessed using the yardstick of the knowledge of an expert in the sector. [For example, if a chemist or a pharmacologist has to keep up to date with the characteristics of a given substance, similar knowledge will be required for present purposes of an industrialist producing pharmaceuticals containing the same substance.]

Judgment: 25. Certain general observations can be made as to the wording of Article 7(e) of the Directive.

26. First, as the Advocate General rightly observes in para 20 of his Opinion, since that provision refers to 'scientific and technical knowledge at the time when [the producer] put the product into circulation', Article 7(e) is not specifically directed at the practices and safety standards in use in the industrial sector in which the producer is operating, but, unreservedly, at the state of scientific and technical knowledge, including the most advanced level of such knowledge, at the time when the product in question was put into circulation.

27. Second, the clause providing for the defence in question does not contemplate the state of knowledge of which the producer in question actually or subjectively was or could have been apprised, but the objective state of scientific and technical knowledge of which the producer is presumed to have been informed.

[80] [1997] ECR-I02649. Opinion of Advocate General Tesauro delivered on 23 January 1997.

28. However, it is implicit in the wording of Article 7(e) that the relevant scientific and technical knowledge must have been accessible at the time when the product in question was put into circulation.

29. It follows that, in order to have a defence under Article 7(e) of the Directive, the producer of a defective product must prove that the objective state of scientific and technical knowledge, including the most advanced level of such knowledge, at the time when the product in question was put into circulation was not such as to enable the existence of the defect to be discovered. Further, in order for the relevant scientific and technical knowledge to be successfully pleaded against the producer, that knowledge must have been accessible at the time when the product in question was put into circulation. On this last point, contrary to what the Commission seems to consider, Article 7(e) of the Directive raises difficulties of interpretation which, in the event of litigation, the national courts will have to resolve having recourse, if necessary, to Article 177 EC (now, after amendment Article 234 EC).

30. For the present, it is the heads of claim raised by the Commission in support of its application that have to be considered.

Notes and Questions

(1) Is the requirement of accessibility justified? Does the Manchuria example work? Are computers nowadays sufficiently advanced to track down articles in Manchurian? What about articles written in Greek or Bulgarian?[81] Does the introduction of the requirement for accessibility of knowledge undermine the widely accepted principle that the standard is objective and a defendant cannot use lack of resources or compliance with industry standards as a defence.

(2) Is the concept of the most advanced knowledge helpful? Would it cover 'the random guess of a discredited mystic'[82] or does the person making the statement have to have some expertise. What amounts to the state of scientific and technical knowledge can be difficult to discern. Scientific knowledge is not fixed and changes as new consensuses emerge. However, it seems that the most advanced state of knowledge is taken as the benchmark, even if it is not accepted as true when first advanced.

(2) The German Supreme Court in *Mineral Water Bottle*[83] decided (without considering it necessary to refer to the ECJ) that the defence was not available for manufacturing defects. Is this so obvious given that there may be scientific and technical constraints on the quality control systems?

Differing views have been taken on whether the development risk defence should be available if the generic risk is known, but it is impossible to detect in individual products. The Amsterdam County Court held the defence was available in such circumstances, but the English High Court disagreed.

[81] See M Mildred and G Howells, 'Infected Blood: Defect and Discoverability: A First Exposition of the EC Product Liability Directive' (2002) 65 *Modern Law Review* 95–105.

[82] See J Stapleton, 'Products Liability in the United Kingdom: the Myths of Reform' (1998) 34 *Texas International Law Journal* 45.

[83] (1995) NJW 2162.

Gerechtshof (Court of Appeal) Amsterdam, 3 February 1999[84] **7.34 (NL)**
Schollten v Foundation Sanquin of Blood Supply

AVAILABILITY OF DEVELOPMENT RISKS DEFENCE WHEN RISK NOT IDENTIFIABLE IN PARTICULAR PRODUCTS

HIV-infected blood

The development risk defence applies where there is no way of knowing that a product contains a risk.

Facts: Blood was supplied containing HIV at a time when there was no test to detect such contamination.

Judgment: 10. The foundation further argues that it is not responsible for the damages caused by the blood product concerned, as in the state of science and technology at the time the blood product was brought into circulation, it was impossible to detect the contamination of the blood with HIV in the window phase just after taking the blood on 29 May 1996 and before the delivery of the blood on 5 June 1996 …

11. It is clear that the foundation has tested the blood product concerned through the regular, specific HIV-1/2 screening test. The result of this test as well as the result of the HIV p24-anti gene test that was carried out afterwards on the second sample was negative. It was only the result of HIV-1 RNA test that was also carried out afterwards on the second sample that was suspect. It is not disputed that the HIV-1 RNA test is a laborious test that is hard to run even in a laboratory.

It is further undoubted that this test is still in an experimental phase and has not been approved or validated as a screening test

It also stems from the report that was submitted by the German Paul Ehrlich Institut, the content of which was not disputed by S, that the HIV-1 RNA test has not been thus developed yet that its use can be recommended. This leads to the conclusion that, in the state of science and technology at the time the blood was given and delivered to S, it was impossible for the foundation from a practical point of view and could not be demanded to use the HIV-1 RNA test as a screening test to detect HIV in blood products.

S did further not sufficiently contest that it is unpracticable to detect HIV-infection by using the quarantine method in the window phase.

The foundation has therefore acted in accordance with the state of science of technology by using the regular HIV-1/2 screening test. The defence of the foundation is therefore effective

[84] (1999) NJ 621.

High Court, 26 March 2001[85] **7.35 (UK)**
A v National Blood Authority

DEVELOPMENT RISKS

National blood case

The development risks defence does not apply where the generic risk is known even if not discoverable in individual products.

Facts: See above 7.17 (UK).

Judgment: 74. ... (i) I note (without resolving the question) the force of the argument that the *defect* in Article 7(b) falls to be construed as the defect in the particular product; but I do not consider that to be determinative of the construction of Article 7(e), and indeed I am firmly of the view that such is not the case in Article 7(e).

(ii) The analysis of Article 7(e), with the guidance of *Commission v UK*, seems to me to be entirely clear. If there is a known risk, i.e., the existence of the defect is known or should have been known in the light of non-Manchurianly accessible information, then the producer continues to produce and supply at his own risk. It would, in my judgment, be inconsistent with the purpose of the Directive if a producer, in the case of a known risk, continues to supply products simply because, and despite the fact that, he is unable to identify in which if any of his products that defect will occur or recur, or, more relevantly in a case such as this, where the producer is obliged to supply, continues to supply without accepting the responsibility for any injuries resulting, by insurance or otherwise.

(iii) The *existence of the defect* is in my judgment clearly generic. Once the *existence of the defect* is known, then there is then the *risk* of that defect materialising in any particular product.

75. The purpose of the Directive, from which Article 7(e) should obviously not derogate more than is necessary (see Recital 16) is to prevent injury, and facilitate compensation for injury. The Defendants submit that this means that Article 7(e) must be construed so as to give the opportunity to the producer to do all he can in order to avoid injury: thus concentrating on what can be done in relation to the particular product. The Claimants submit that this will rather be achieved by imposing obligation in respect of a known risk irrespective of the chances of finding the defect in the particular product, and I agree.

76. The purpose of Article 7(e) was plainly not to discourage innovation, and to exclude development risks from the Directive, and it succeeds in its objective, subject to the very considerable restrictions that are clarified by *Commission v UK*: namely that the risk ceases to be a development risk and becomes a known risk not if and when the producer in question (or, as the CPA inappropriately sought to enact in Section 4(1)(e) '*a producer of products of the same description as the product in question*') had the requisite knowledge, but if and when such knowledge were accessible anywhere in the world outside Manchuria. Hence it protects the producer in respect of the unknown (*inconnu*). But the consequence of acceptance of the Defendants' submissions would be that protection would also be given in respect of the known.

[85] [2001] 3 All ER 289.

77. The effect is, it seems to me, not, as the BGH [here the judge was referring to the German *Mineral Water Bottle* case] has been interpreted as concluding (or perhaps as it did conclude, but if it did then I would respectfully differ) that non-standard products are incapable of coming within Article 7(e). Non-standard products may qualify once—ie if the problem which leads to an occasional defective product is (unlike the present case) not known: this may perhaps be more unusual than in relation to a problem with a standard product, but does not seem to me to be an impossible scenario. However once the problem is known by virtue of accessible information, then the non-standard product can no longer qualify for protection under Article 7(e).

Note

In the Australian case of *Graham Barclay Oysters Pty v Ryan*[86] the defect was required to be discoverable in the particular product (oysters), but this case was distinguished by Burton J in *A v National Blood Authority* on the basis of the different wording of the Australian law.

It seems clear that where knowledge was available, but simply not applied, the defence will not be available.

High Court, 21 December 2000[87] **7.36 (UK)**
Abouzaid v Mothercare

DEVELOPMENT RISKS

Cosytoes

The development risk defence does not apply where a risk was known about but had not yet materialized in that context.

Facts: A 'Cosytoes' fleeceliner for a pram was supplied with an elasticated strap tied by metal buckles. These injured the eye of a sibling who was trying to tie the liner to a pram.

Judgment: 46. [explaining why the development risks defence provides no assistance] ... the question whether the producer might have been expected to have discovered the defect in 1990—before the accident to the claimant had occurred—has nothing to do with the state of scientific or technical knowledge at that time. There was no difficulty in discovering the defect by a simple practical test—as Dr Hayward's evidence makes clear. No advance in scientific or technical knowledge since 1990 was required to enable that test to be carried out. The only reason that it was not carried out before 1990 was that manufacturers (it seems) had not thought of doing so. The defence under section 4(1)(e) of the Act is simply not engaged in the present case.

[86] 102 FCR 307.
[87] [2000] All ER (D) 243.

In France only one case has considered the development risks defence and it seems to have applied it very generously in favour of a producer of a defective drug; although ultimately on appeal the defence was not found to be applicable.

Cour d'appel (Court of Appeal) Paris, 23 September 2004[88] **7.37 (FR)**

DEVELOPMENT RISK DEFENCE

Pentasa

The development risk defence can be available when the medical evidence is not sufficiently advanced to justify a warning.

Facts: See 7.26 (FR).

Judgment: On the question of the failure to fulfil the safety obligation, article 1386(1) and so on, following law number 98-389 of 19 May 1998, do not apply in this case since the putting into circulation of the drug Pentasa® dates back to 1987 or 1988; however, following articles 1147 and 1384, para one, of the Civil Code, interpreted in the light of Directive 85/374/EEC of 24 July 1985, any manufacturer is liable for damage caused by a defect in his product, both to direct and indirect victims, without there being any need to distinguish between contracting parties and third parties; the manufacturer has an obligation to deliver a product that does not contain any defect that could endanger people or goods, that is to say, a product that provides the safety which a person is entitled to expect; equally, in light of Directive 85/374/EEC of 24 July 1985, the manufacturer may however be able to exonerate himself due to the state of scientific knowledge at the time when he put the product into circulation; [There then follows a discussion of the state of scientific knowledge that has already been produced at 7.26 (FR).]

Note

These considerations seem to reflect fault-based thinking rather than an interpretation of a defence that was deliberately drafted narrowly and has been so interpreted by the ECJ. For example, how does this judgment fit with the ECJ's statement in C-300/95 *EC Commission v United Kingdom*[89] at paragraph 26 that the state of scientific and technical knowledge included the most advanced level of such knowledge? This decision was overturned by the Cour de Cassation[90] because the defence did not apply as the Directive had not been implemented in France at the relevant time. Nevertheless this judgment may be cited as it is the only opinion of a French appellate court on this controversial aspect of the Directive. It is to be hoped that higher courts will be unenthusiastic about adopting this approach, which seems out of line with the spirit of the Directive and other judicial pronouncements on the interpretation of the defence.

[88] No 02/16713 (2005) D 1012.

[89] 29 May 1997 [1997] ECR I-02649.

[90] Cass civ 1e, 15 May 2007, No 05-10.234 (2007) D 1592, note Ph Stoffel-Munck; (2007) RDC 1147, note J-S Borghetti.

VII. DAMAGES

VII.A HEADS OF DAMAGE

Product Liability Directive (85/374/EEC) **7.38 (EU)**

Article 1 The producer shall be liable for damage caused by a defect in his product.

Article 9 For the purpose of Article 1, 'damage' means:

(a) damage caused by death or by personal injuries;

(b) damage to, or destruction of, any item of property other than the defective product itself, with a lower threshold of 500 ECU, provided that the item of property:

(i) is of a type ordinarily intended for private use or consumption, and

(ii) was used by the injured person mainly for his own private use or consumption.

This Article shall be without prejudice to national provisions relating to non-material damage.

The expression 'national provisions relating to non-material damage' can be interpreted as referring to 'préjudice moral' and pure economic loss. According to the ECJ, any damage caused by a defective product necessarily falls within one of the types of damage mentioned by the Directive.

ECJ Case C-203/99, 10 May 2001[91]
Henning Veedfald v Århus Amtskommune **7.39 (EU)**

HOW TO CLASSIFY DAMAGE

Danish kidney

The Directive contains an exhaustive list of heads of damage which qualify for compensation under its regime.

Facts: See 7.14 (EU). In this case, the Højesteret referred another question to the ECJ and asked whether damage to a human organ, which, at the time when the damage occurred, had been removed from a donor's body for immediate transplant into a certain other person's body, is covered by the expression 'damage caused by … personal injuries' (Article 9(a) of the Directive) or the expression 'damage to, or destruction of, any [other] item of property' (Article 9(b)) in relation to the intended recipient of the organ?

Judgment: 30. The national court asks for guidance on the application of the term damage to the circumstances of the case before it.

31. It must be borne in mind at the outset that under Article 234 EC the Court has no power to apply rules of Community law to a particular case, but only to rule on the interpretation of the Treaty and of acts adopted by Community institutions (see, in particular, the judgment in Joined Cases C-9/97 and C-118/97 *Jokela and Pitkäranta* [1998] ECR I-6267, para 30).

[91] [2001] ECR I-03569.

32. As regards the aspects of the Directive which call for an interpretation by the Court, it should be observed that Article 1 of the Directive provides that the producer is to be liable for damage caused by a defect in his product. Article 9 indicates the various heads of damage covered by the Directive, namely damage caused by death or personal injuries and damage to, or destruction of, an item of property, other than that caused to the defective product itself, whilst leaving it to the Member States applying their own national laws to provide for compensation for non-material damage. Articles 1 and 9 therefore set out exhaustively the heads of damage that may be possible.

33. It follows that the national court is required, under the Directive, to examine under which head the circumstances of the case are to be categorised, namely whether the case concerns damage covered either by point (a) or by point (b) of the first paragraph of Article 9 or non-material damage which may possibly be covered by national law. The national court may, however, not decline to award any damages at all under the Directive on the ground that, where the other conditions of liability are fulfilled, the damage incurred is not such as to fall under any of the foregoing heads.

Notes

(1) According to the ECJ, damage caused by a product that is defective in the sense of the Directive necessarily falls within one of the heads of damage mentioned by Article 9, ie (i) damage caused by death or by personal injuries; or (ii) damage to, or destruction of, any item of property other than the defective product itself. Non-material damage is left to national law. In other terms, the Directive provides potentially for any possible type of damage.

(2) It may, however, prove difficult to integrate certain types of damage within the Directive's framework. One can wonder, for example, if pure economic loss, which even a consumer can incur due to a defect in a product intended for private use, must be considered as non-material damage in the sense of Article 9. The ninth recital of the Directive's preamble suggests that this head of damage was first and foremost intended to include pain and suffering. However, these are not exclusive of other types of non-material damage, and pure economic loss probably should fall within this category—if only because it can hardly be considered as damage caused by death or by personal injuries or as damage to an item of property. Loss of chance, which many European laws recognise as a recoverable head of damage, is also difficult to fit within the Directive's typology.

Questions

(1) Under what head of damage should the loss of a chance not to suffer personal injury be classified?

(2) In the *Veedfald Case*, the ECJ ruled that damage caused to a human organ awaiting transplantation necessarily fell under one of the heads of damage mentioned by the Directive, but did not say which. Had you been the Danish court faced with this problem, how would you have categorised this damage?

Code civil **7.40 (FR)**

Article 1386 (2) The provisions of this Title shall apply to compensation for damage caused by personal injury.

They shall also apply to compensation for damage above an amount fixed by decree to an item of property other than the defective product itself.

Note

Although France has been condemned twice for failure to comply with the Directive, this French provision meant to implement the Directive seems to have gone unnoticed by the European Commission. Yet, in apparent contradiction with Article 9(b) of the Directive, it does not restrict the compensation of damage to property to cases where the item of property (i) is of a type ordinarily intended for private use or consumption, and (ii) was used by the injured person mainly for his own private use or consumption. This discrepancy can be explained by the fact that French law is not used to distinguishing between different kinds of damage and restricting compensation to certain kinds of damage.

The ECJ was given an occasion to address this issue in the following case.

ECJ Case C-258/08, 4 June 2009[92] **7.41 (EU)**
Moteurs Leroy Somer v Dalkia France

PROPERTY INTENDED FOR A PROFESSIONAL USE

The exploding alternator

Compensation for damage to an item of property intended for professional use does not fall within the scope of application of the Directive.

Facts: A generator installed in 1995 in a hospital in Lyon caught fire due to the fact that the alternator manufactured and put into circulation in 1994 by Moteurs Leroy Somer overheated. Dalkia France, which was responsible for the maintenance of this installation, paid compensation for the material damage caused to the hospital by that accident and then brought an action against Moteurs Leroy Somer so as to obtain reimbursement of the sums Dalkia had paid. Moteurs Leroy Somer was ordered to pay those sums by a French appellate court and challenged that decision before the French Cour de Cassation. The latter referred a question to the ECJ and asked whether Articles 9 and 13 of Directive 85/374 preclude the interpretation of domestic law or settled domestic case-law such that it enables an injured person to seek compensation for damage to an item of property intended for professional use and employed for that purpose, where that person simply proves damage, the defect in the product and the causal link between that defect and the damage

Judgment: 24. However, the fact remains that Directive 85/374 can preclude a system of liability such as that at issue in the main proceedings only on condition that that system is covered by the scope of application of that directive.

25. Although Directive 85/374, as was pointed out in para 21 of the present judgment, seeks to achieve, in the matters regulated by it, complete harmonisation of

[92] [2009] ECR I-0000.

the laws, regulations and administrative provisions of the Member States, it does not, however, as is apparent from the 18th recital in the preamble thereto, seek exhaustively to harmonise the field of liability for defective products beyond those matters.

26. As Dalkia France, Ace Europe, the French and Austrian Governments and the Commission contend in their respective observations submitted to the Court, a system of liability such as that at issue in the main proceedings is not covered by the scope of application of Directive 85/374.

27. It is apparent both from the wording and from the structure of Directive 85/374, and in particular from Article 1, Article 9 and the ninth recital in the preamble thereto, that compensation for damage to an item of property intended for professional use and employed for that purpose is not one of the matters regulated by that directive, such damage not being covered, as was pointed out in para 17 of the present judgment, by the term 'damage' for the purposes of Article 1 of Directive 85/374, as defined in Article 9 thereof.

28. It must therefore be held that compensation for damage to an item of property intended for professional use and employed for that use is not covered by the scope of application of Directive 85/374.

29. That interpretation is not invalidated by the fact that Directive 85/374, as is clear from the first recital in the preamble thereto and from the case-law of the Court (Case C-52/00 *Commission v France* [2002] ECR I-3827, para 17; Case C-154/00 *Commission v Greece* [2002] ECR I-3879, para 13; and Case C-183/00 *González Sánchez* [2002] ECR I-3901, para 26), aims not only to avoid differences in levels of consumer protection, but also to ensure undistorted competition between traders and to facilitate the free movement of goods.

30. Nothing in the wording of Directive 85/374 leads to the conclusion that the Community legislature, by limiting compensation for damage to goods under that directive to items of property intended for private use or consumption, intended, so as to ensure undistorted competition and to facilitate the free movement of goods, to deprive the Member States of the power, concerning compensation for damage to an item of property intended for professional use and employed for that purpose, to provide for a system of liability which corresponds to that established by that directive.

31. Therefore, as the harmonisation brought about by Directive 85/374 does not cover compensation for damage to an item of property intended for professional use and employed for that purpose, that directive does not prevent a Member State from providing in that respect for a system of liability corresponding to that established by that directive.

32. In view of all the foregoing considerations, the answer to the question referred is that Directive 85/374 must be interpreted to mean that it does not preclude the interpretation of domestic law or the application of settled domestic case-law according to which an injured person can seek compensation for damage to an item of property intended for professional use and employed for that purpose, where the injured person simply proves the damage, the defect in the product and the causal link between that defect and the damage.

Notes

(1) Moteurs Leroy Somer had been ordered to pay damages not on the basis of Article 1386(2) of the French Civil Code, but on the basis of the French judge-made

product liability regime.[93] As far as damage to property is concerned, however, the legislative and the judge-made regimes are similar. They both depart from the Directive in that they allow for compensation of damage to property without making any distinction based on the type of property or the use to which it is put. Although the question referred to the Court of Justice did not explicitly concern Article 1386(2) of the Civil Code, the compatibility of this provision with EU law was also at stake in this case.

(2) Given the extensive conception of the harmonisation of laws in the field of product liability that the ECJ had previously adopted, most authors expected it to answer the referred question negatively and to decide that a liability regime based on the product's defect could not depart from the Directive and allow for the compensation of damage to an item of property intended for professional use and employed for that purpose. But the ECJ has taken a different position, taking into account the scope of application of the Directive. According to it, Article 9 not only defines part of the regime set up by the Directive, but also delineates its scope of application. Heads of damage whose compensation is excluded by this provision fall outside the scope of application of the Directive. They are therefore not concerned by the harmonisation process and the Member States remain free to organise their compensation as they wish.

(3) In the French context, this solution leads to a paradox. Within the scope of application of the Directive, French law has not been able to retain some of the solutions which had been developed by case-law, with the result that the Directive has in effect led to a decrease in the level of consumer protection. But outside the scope of application, rules which are more favourable to claimants than those of the Directive may remain in force or even be introduced. In the case of damage caused to an item of property intended for professional use and employed for that purpose, and on the basis of judge-made rules, the owner may therefore bring a claim against a professional who sold the defective product without having manufactured it, whereas a consumer is not allowed to do so under the Directive if he suffers physical damage to himself or to any item of property intended for private use. Professional interests are thus better protected than consumer interests, because they escape the 'protection' which the Directive allegedly intended to offer.

Questions

How can the main aim of the Directive, ie the suppression of divergences between product liability rules in the Member States which may distort competition and affect the movement of goods within the common market (cf 1st recital of the Directive), be reconciled with the limitation of its scope of application and the exclusion of damage caused to goods intended for professional use and employed for that purpose? From an economic point of view, is not such a type of damage likely to be more important than damage caused to goods intended for private use, or even bodily injuries?

[93] On which see above s II.

VII.B MAXIMUM LIABILITY

Article 16(1) of the Directive provides that 'any Member State may provide that a producer's total liability for damage resulting from a death or personal injury and caused by identical items with the same defect shall be limited to an amount which may not be less than [€] 70 million'. Only Germany and Spain chose to set a maximum amount to the liability incurred by producers. Greece had originally included a limit, but repealed it when it amended its law. By that time the level in drachma had fallen below the prescribed level, indicating the problem of harmonising financial limits—of course this problem no longer exists within the eurozone.

It is noteworthy that this potential limitation of liability only applies to 'damage resulting from a death or personal injury', but not to damage to property. This means that property is potentially better protected than physical integrity.

VII.C €500 THRESHOLD

According to Article 9 of the Directive, a lower threshold of €500 applies to the compensation of damage to property. France and Greece were condemned by the ECJ for not having mentioned this threshold when they first translated the Directive (Cases C-52/00[94] and C-154/00[95]). It might also be suggested that, given the different standards of living in the various Member States, €500 can be a lot of money in some countries, but appear as a rather moderate sum in others. This shows that full harmonisation is hard to reach in practice.

National legislators have interpreted the €500 threshold differently. Most consider it is only the damage to property in excess of €500 that is ever recoverable, treating it like an insurance excess. The United Kingdom and Netherlands, however, allow the full amount to be recovered so long as the threshold of €500 is exceeded.

Product Liability Act[96] **7.42 (BE)**

Article 11 §2 Damage to goods does only entitle to compensation if those goods are usually intended for use or consumption in the private sphere and if the victim did mainly apply them for use or consumption in its private sphere.

Damage to the defective product itself shall not be compensated.

Compensation for damage to goods is only due over and above a threshold of €500.

Consumer Protection Act 1987 **7.43 (UK)**

Section 5 (4) No damages shall be awarded to any person by virtue of this Part in respect of any loss of or damage to any property if the amount which would fall to be so awarded to that person, apart from this subsection and any liability for interest, does not exceed £275.

[94] [2002] ECR I-03827.
[95] [2002] ECR I-03879.
[96] Act 25 February 1991, MB 22 March 1991.

CONCISE BIBLIOGRAPHY

J-S Borghetti, *La responsabilité du fait des produits. Étude de droit comparé* (Paris, LGDJ, 2004).

A Clark, *Product Liability* (London, Sweet & Maxwell, 1989).

D Fairgrieve (ed), *Product Liability in Comparative Perspective* (Cambridge, Cambridge University Press, 2005).

C Hodges, *Product Liability: European Laws and Practice* (London, Sweet & Maxwell, 1993).

G Howells, *Comparative Product Liability* (Aldershot, Dartmouth, 1993).

G Howells (ed), *The Law of Product Liability*, 2nd edn (London, Butterworths, 2007).

HJ Kullmann, *Produkthaftungsgesetz* (Berlin, Erich Schmidt Verlag, 2004).

CJ Miller and RS Goldberg, *Product Liability*, 2nd edn (Oxford, Oxford University Press, 2004).

J Stapleton, *Product Liability* (London, Butterworths, 1994).

S Taylor, *L'Harmonisation Communautaire de la Responsabilité du Fait des Produits Défectueux* (Paris, LGDJ, 1999).

G Wagner, in *Münchner Kommentar zum Bürgerlichen Gesetzbuch*, vol 5 (München, Beck, 2004).

S Whittaker, *Liability for Products: English Law, French Law and European Harmonisation* (Oxford, Oxford University Press, 2005).

CHAPTER EIGHT
LITIGATION, REDRESS AND ENFORCEMENT

This chapter addresses the following question: how can consumers ensure that the rights conferred on them pursuant to the rules described in the preceding chapters are enforced?

It is often said that there are no rights without remedies. Designing adequate remedies and procedures is particularly important in consumer law. Consumers' claims are often small claims, claims of a relatively low monetary value. Existing procedures are generally too costly. Where appropriate procedures exist, consumers typically do not have sufficient knowledge and expertise as to how they can exercise their rights. This chapter reviews existing rules on the enforcement of consumer rights, or in the contemporary terminology: the law of consumer redress.

Not all procedures and rules discussed in this chapter are consumer specific. Increasingly, however, legislatures have enacted special provisions for B2C disputes, eg in the field of jurisdiction, the law applicable, small claims and so on. These laws will be discussed in this chapter.

Consumer redress is still mainly a question of national law. So far few rules on consumer redress exist at EU level; those that do are basically limited to cross-border situations. This can (partly) be explained by the existing doubts about the competence of the EU to harmonise the rules on domestic procedures.

Article 95 EC enables the EU legislature to adopt measures for the approximation of the provisions laid down by law, regulation or administrative action in Member States which have as their object the establishment and functioning of the internal market. However, in a certain number of judgments, in particular *Tobacco advertising I*, the ECJ has drawn some important limits on the use of Article 95 EC (see chapter 1).

Another legal basis in the Treaty for rules in the field of civil procedure is Article 65 EC. Article 65 EC states that measures in the field of judicial co-operation in civil matters 'having cross-border implications' are to be taken in accordance with Article

67 EC and in so far as necessary for the proper functioning of the internal market. These measures 'shall include … eliminating obstacles to the good functioning of civil proceedings, if necessary by promoting the compatibility of the rules on civil procedure applicable in the Member States'. Article 67 EC contains the rules for decision-making pursuant to Article 65.

Regulation 861/2007/EC on small claims procedures (not limited to consumer claims) is restricted to cross-border disputes. The original proposal also concerned domestic situations but the scope of the Regulation has since been narrowed down.

The general instruments in the field of civil procedure such as the 'Brussels' I Regulation (containing specific rules for consumer contracts) as well as in private international law (Rome I and Rome II Regulation) are also limited to cross-border situations.

Finally, Article 153(3)(b) EC should be mentioned. This Article allows the European Parliament and the Council to adopt measures which support, complement and monitor the policy pursued by the Member Sates in the field of consumer protection.

This provision has been little used. Indeed only Directive 98/6/EC on consumer protection in the indication of the prices of products offered to consumers has been adopted on this basis, all other consumer law directives having been adopted on the basis of Article 95 EC. The application of this Article in the field of consumer redress has not yet been tested.

In all EU Member States consumer rights are enforced by a mix of public and private law. The mix differs from Member State to Member State: criminal law, administrative law and the law of civil procedure play a role that varies according to the Member State concerned and the consumer interest at issue.

Although enforcement of consumer rights remains mainly an issue for the Member States, the ECJ has laid down some requirements with regard to the applicable rules for enforcement when these rights stem from Community law. There is no room to reiterate all relevant cases here.[1] In a recent judgment of the ECJ these principles and the role of the national courts in this respect are stated powerfully.

ECJ Case C-432/05, 13 March 2007[2] **8.1 (EU)**
Unibet v Justitiekanslerrn

EFFECTIVE REMEDIES FOR VIOLATION OF EC LAW

Unibet

National law must guarantee the effective application of the rights that individuals derive from Community law.

[1] For an overview of the relevant cases, see eg P Craig and G De búrca, *EU Law. Text, Cases and Materials* (Oxford, Oxford University Press, 2008) 230ff (ch 9).

[2] [2007] ECR I-2271.

Facts: Unibet, a UK company, purchased advertising space in Swedish media to promote its gaming services on the internet. In accordance with Swedish law on lotteries, the Swedish state took a number of measures, including obtaining injunctions and commencing criminal proceedings against media which had agreed to provide Unibet with advertising space. Unibet, which was not sued, brought several actions in a Swedish court, in order to obtain a declaration that its activity was legal in the light of Article 49 EC (free provision of services). Eventually the Supreme Court (Högstadomstolen) referred several questions to the ECJ. One question was whether Community law requires that individuals have a free-standing action for an examination of the compatibility of national provisions with Article 49 EC. The ECJ ruled that there is no such requirement under Community law when there are other legal remedies under national law according to which such compatibility can be determined as a preliminary issue provided these remedies are not less favourable than those governing similar domestic actions.

Judgment: 42. Thus, while it is, in principle, for national law to determine an individual's standing and legal interest in bringing proceedings, Community law nevertheless requires that the national legislation does not undermine the right to effective judicial protection (see, inter alia, Joined Cases C-87/90 to C-89/90 *Verholen and Others* [1991] ECR I-3757, paragraph 24, and *Safalero*, paragraph 50). It is for the Member States to establish a system of legal remedies and procedures which ensure respect for that right (*Unión de Pequeños Agricultores v Council*, paragraph 41).

43. In that regard, the detailed procedural rules governing actions for safeguarding an individual's rights under Community law must be no less favourable than those governing similar domestic actions (principle of equivalence) and must not render practically impossible or excessively difficult the exercise of rights conferred by Community law (principle of effectiveness) (see, inter alia, Case 33/76 *Rewe*, paragraph 5; *Comet*, paragraphs 13 to 16; *Peterbroeck*, paragraph 12; *Courage and Crehan*, paragraph 29; *Eribrand*, paragraph 62; and *Safalero*, paragraph 49).

44. Moreover, it is for the national courts to interpret the procedural rules governing actions brought before them, such as the requirement for there to be a specific legal relationship between the applicant and the State, in such a way as to enable those rules, wherever possible, to be implemented in such a manner as to contribute to the attainment of the objective, referred to at paragraph 37 above, of ensuring effective judicial protection of an individual's rights under Community law.

Note

Although neither the EC Treaty nor the case-law of the ECJ requires in general that Member States develop 'new remedies' for breach of EC law, several judgments require that a particular kind of remedy be made available in specific situations, with a view to the effective application of Community law. This has notably been the case with regard to state liability for breach of EC law (see below, section VI) and claims for damages for breach of certain directly effective Community law provisions by individuals (see chapter 1.I.B (*Courage* and *Manfredi*).

I. ADMINISTRATIVE ENFORCEMENT AND SELF-REGULATION

The basic methods of enforcement differ from each other with regard to their objective, their effect and the instruments used. Administrative and criminal law enforcement does not lead to immediate satisfaction of consumers' claims although it helps to enforce businesses' obligations. Differences also exist with respect to consumer participation in this enforcement.

W van Boom and M Loos, Private, Public, and Collective Mechanisms[3] **8.2 (EU)**

How can collective consumer interests be served best? A number of instruments of enforcement are relevant here. In this section, we will make some remarks on self-regulation on the one hand, and supervision by public authorities on the other. They seem to be on two opposite ends of the spectrum, but in practice they may well converge.

At a European level, self-regulation through so-called codes of conduct seems very popular: in EU private law, policy trade associations and professional associations are encouraged to develop such codes. This instrument may not only help to empower interest groups, but can also facilitate concrete rulemaking on the basis of vague private law standards such as 'good faith' and 'unfair' terms or 'unfair' commercial practices. As Viitanen, Hodges, and Van den Bergh rightly emphasize, the use of self-regulation may add to private and public enforcement. Under specific conditions self-regulation, either on a fully voluntary basis or stimulated by state intervention or committal, can be a very effective instrument of both standard-setting and reaching compliance by business. For this reason, voluntary arrangements such as codes of conduct are stimulated in, eg, the Unfair Commercial Practices Directive. State supported negotiations concerning standard contract terms are a good example of such self-regulation.

Contrastingly, public authorities may step in where self-regulation fails. Remember the case of unfair contract terms: consumer may enforce their rights ex post, namely by avoiding the unfair term from the contract as soon as the professional counterpart using the term invokes it. This does not seem to be the most effective way of stamping out unfair contract terms. In such cases a more direct instrument of enforcement of the underlying private law values—although not necessarily a perfect one—would be an ex ante evaluation of standard terms of trade either by a government agency or private interest group or a procedure facilitating forced erasure of the clauses altogether. Indeed, Article 7 of the Unfair Contract Terms Directive provides that the Member States must ensure that 'adequate and effective means exist to prevent the continued use'of unfair general clauses. Moreover, in Commission/Italy (Case C-372/99 ECR 2002 I-819), the ECJ emphasised that under this article, the Member States are required to facilitate the possibility of a procedure against unfair terms even before they are used in practice. This leads public authorities such as the OFT (Office of Fair Trading) and the recently instated Dutch Consumer Authority to actively pursue enforcement against businesses that continue to use unfair contract terms.

[3] W van Boom and M Loos, 'Private, Public, and Collective Mechanisms' in W Van Boom and M Loos (eds), *Effective Enforcement of Consumer Law in Europe* (Groningen, Europa Law Publishing, 2007) 243ff.

Notes

(1) The extent to which Member States rely on administrative enforcement/self-regulation differs substantially. In some Member States public bodies play an important, and even a dominant, role in protecting consumers' interests. Such public bodies exist in, inter alia, the Scandinavian countries with the consumer ombudsmen, in Ireland with the National Consumer Agency, in the Netherlands with the Consumer Authority, in the UK with the OFT. In many newly acceded Member States (eg Cyprus, Latvia, Lithuania, Poland, Slovakia, Malta, Hungary), public bodies and administrative enforcement also play an important role. This is certainly the case in the former socialist-communist countries where private consumer organisations are still rare, which explains the need for administrative control.

(2) The powers of and procedures used by such public bodies vary considerably. A procedure of negotiation and guidelines to induce business to act in accordance with good marketing practices is typical for the Scandinavian countries, but also for the UK (OFT). The Nordic consumer ombudsmen focus on prevention through negotiation and recommendations. In a number of Member States, public bodies not only have the right to bring an action in court (these actions are dealt with below), they also have the power to issue a compliance order. Thus, the Danish Consumer Ombudsman can issue orders in respect of conduct that cannot be changed by negotiation and which is in clear contravention of the Marketing Practice Act. When a prohibition or injunction imposed by a court/Ombudsman is not observed, this may be punished by a fine or imprisonment. In Sweden, where negotiations fail in cases of lesser significance, the Ombudsman may also make a prohibitory order. If a prohibition is not observed or if the case is one of significant public interest, then the Ombudsman can apply for an injunction before the Market Court. Similar to this, in Finland, the Consumer Ombudsman may impose an injunction in cases that are not of significant importance. The injunction becomes void if the addressee objects to the injunction within eight days. The Consumer Ombudsman may also impose a conditional fine, but the Market Court decides whether or not it is payable.[4]

(3) However, in Austria and Germany, enforcement of unfair commercial practices law lies in the hands of private business and consumer associations.

II. 'TRADITIONAL' INDIVIDUAL REDRESS

The legal position of a consumer as a plaintiff is generally similar to that of any other individual plaintiff. Ordinary court proceedings are also open to consumers whose rights have been infringed, but the number of consumers that actually find their way to the ordinary courts is very limited. According to the 'Special Eurobarometer' Report of the European Commission on 'European Union Citizens and Access to

[4] H Schulte-Nölke, C Twigg Flesner and M Ebers, *Consumer Law Compendium* (München, Sellier, 2008) 423–26.

Justice',[5] 18 per cent of European Union citizens are prepared to go to court for amounts higher than €500 and another 18 per cent for amounts higher than €1,000. Only 29 per cent of European citizens would be prepared to bring a claim of less than €500 to court. This may be because of the length of proceedings, expenses involved (court fees and/or lawyers' fees), formalities, etc. Furthermore, application of the 'loser pays' principle may have a deterrent effect. In a similar way as arbitration and mediation proceedings try to provide an alternative (see section III below), in many jurisdictions small claims procedures and/or courts have therefore been developed. The aim of these procedures is usually formulated as providing a cheaper, faster and less formal alternative to traditional civil court procedures, giving individuals better access to justice to resolve commonplace disputes as well as the possibility of obtaining redress at a cost and burden not disproportionate to the amount of their claim.[6] Small claims procedures are specific court procedures for the resolution of claims below a certain threshold value, which are different from (and simplified in comparison to) ordinary court procedures. These procedures may take place in ordinary courts or in small claims courts, ie courts the competence of which is determined on the basis of the value of the claim. Small claims procedures are not necessarily limited to consumer claims.

Study Centre for Consumer Law, Alternative Means of Consumer Redress other than Redress through Ordinary Judicial Proceedings[7] **8.3 (EU)**

Most small claims procedures were initially introduced in order to provide a more efficient and accessible dispute resolution for small claims, regardless of the identity of the plaintiff and the nature of the subject matter of the claim. The recovery of small debts was accordingly considered to be a valid use of the small claims procedure. In the 1960s and 1970s, the consumer justice movement brought a new emphasis to small claims procedures, whereby the focus shifted towards a particular class of disputants—that is, consumer plaintiffs. From this perspective, small claim procedures were criticised on the basis that collection used by large businesses and corporations had overtaken the use of small claims procedures by wage earners and small business owners, for whom these courts had originally been developed.

[5] Special Eurobarometer, European Union citizens and access to justice, October 2004.

[6] OECD, *Consumer Dispute Resolution and Redress in the Global Marketplace* (2006) 24; CJ Whelan, 'Small Claims Courts: Heritage and Adjustment', in CJ Whelan, *Small Claims Courts. A Comparative Study* (Oxford, Clarendon Press, 1990) 5 and 8; Centre National de la Recherche Scientifique IDHE, ENS-CAHAN, *Des Procedures de Traitement Judiciaire des Demandes de Faible Importance ou non contestées dans les droits des Etats-Membres de L'Union Européenne*, 26; Explanatory memorandum to the Proposal for a Regulation of the European Parliament and the Council establishing a European Small Claims Procedure, COM [2005] 87 final, 2.

[7] J Stuyck, E Terryn, V Colaert, T Van Dyck, N Peretz, N Hoekx and P Tereszkiewicz, Study Centre for Consumer Law, *Alternative Means of Consumer Redress other than Redress through Ordinary Judicial Proceedings* (Leuven, 2007) 193.

In several jurisdictions proposals were made, therefore, to narrow the scope of application of the small claims procedures, either by barring collection agencies as plaintiffs or by introducing consumer claims tribunals with a consumer specific scope of application. In most jurisdictions, however, this problem was attempted to be resolved by the establishment of a small claims procedure with a general scope of application, next to an efficient separate order for payment procedure, so that debt collection cases should not overly burden the small claims procedure (although it could, in theory, still be used for these purposes). The European Commission has also taken this approach, by issuing both a Proposal for a Regulation establishing a European Small Claims Procedure with a general scope of application, and a Proposal for a Regulation creating a European order for payment procedure.

Note

These proposals have been adopted in the mean time. Another European instrument that purports to improve access to justice in cross-border cases is also discussed below.

Regulation (EC) 861/2007 Establishing a European Small Claims Procedure[8] **8.4 (EU)**

Article 1 Subject matter

This Regulation establishes a European procedure for small claims (hereinafter referred to as the 'European Small Claims Procedure'), intended to simplify and speed up litigation concerning small claims in cross-border cases, and to reduce costs. The European Small Claims Procedure shall be available to litigants as an alternative to the procedures existing under the laws of the Member States.

This Regulation also eliminates the intermediate proceedings necessary to enable recognition and enforcement, in other Member States, of judgments given in one Member State in the European Small Claims Procedure.

Article 2 Scope

(1) This Regulation shall apply, in cross-border cases, to civil and commercial matters, whatever the nature of the court or tribunal, where the value of a claim does not exceed 2000 at the time when the claim form is received by the court or tribunal with jurisdiction, excluding all interest, expenses and disbursements. It shall not extend, in particular, to revenue customs or administrative matters or to the liability of the State for acts and omissions in the exercise of State authority (acta jure imperii).

(2) This Regulation shall not apply to matters concerning …

Article 4 Commencement of the Procedure

(1) The claimant shall commence the European Small Claims Procedure by filling in standard claim Form A, as set out in Annex I, and lodging it with the court or tribunal with jurisdiction directly, by post or by any other means of communication, such as fax or e-mail, acceptable to the Member State in which the procedure is commenced. The claim

[8] Regulation (EC) 861/2007 of the European Parliament and of the Council of 11 July 2007 establishing a European Small Claims Procedure [2007] OJ L 199, 1–22.

form shall include a description of evidence supporting the claim and be accompanied, where appropriate, by any relevant supporting documents. …

Article 5 Conduct of the Procedure

(1)The European Small Claims Procedure shall be a written procedure. The court or tribunal shall hold an oral hearing if it considers this to be necessary or if a party so requests. The court or tribunal may refuse such a request if it considers that with regard to the circumstances of the case, an oral hearing is obviously not necessary for the fair conduct of the proceedings. The reasons for refusal shall be given in writing. The refusal may not be contested separately.

(2) After receiving the property filled in claim form, the court or tribunal shall fill in Part I of the standard answer Form C, as set out in Annex III. …

Article 15 Enforceability of the judgment

(1)The judgment shall be enforceable notwithstanding any possible appeal. The provision of a security shall not be required.

(2) Article 23 shall also apply in the event that the judgment is to be enforced in the Member State where the judgment was given. …

Article 20 Recognition and enforcement

A judgment given in a Member State in the European Small Claims Procedure shall be recognised and enforced in another Member State without the need for a declaration of enforceability and without any possibility of opposing its recognition. …

Regulation (EC) 1896/2006 Creating a European Order for Payment Procedure[9] 8.5 (EU)

Article 1 Subject matter

(1) The purpose of this Regulation is:

(a) to simplify, speed up and reduce the costs of litigation in cross-border cases concerning uncontested pecuniary claims by creating a European order for payment procedure; and

(b) to permit the free circulation of European orders for payment throughout the Member States by laying down minimum standards, compliance with which renders unnecessary any intermediate proceedings in the Member State of enforcement prior to recognition and enforcement.

(2) This Regulation shall not prevent a claimant from pursuing a claim within the meaning of Article 4 by making use of another procedure available under the law of a Member State or under Community law.

Article 2 Scope

(1) This Regulation shall apply to civil and commercial matters in cross-border cases, whatever the nature of the court or tribunal. It shall not extend, in particular, to revenue, customs or administrative matters or the liability of the State for acts and omissions in the exercise of State authority ('acta iure imperii').

(2) This Regulation shall not apply to:

(a) rights in property arising out of a matrimonial relationship, wills and succession;

[9] [2006] OJ L 399, 1-32.

(b) bankruptcy, proceedings relating to the winding-up of insolvent companies or other legal persons, judicial arrangements, compositions and analogous proceedings;

(c) social security;

(d) claims arising from non-contractual obligations, unless:

(i) they have been the subject of an agreement between the parties or there has been an admission of debt, or

(ii) they relate to liquidated debts arising from joint ownership of property.

(3) In this Regulation, the term 'Member State' shall mean Member States with the exception of Denmark.

Article 3 Cross-border cases

(1) For the purposes of this Regulation, a cross-border case is one in which at least one of the parties is domiciled or habitually resident in a Member State other than the Member State of the court seised.

(2) Domicile shall be determined in accordance with Articles 59 and 60 of Council Regulation (EC) 44/2001 of 22 December 2000 on jurisdiction and the recognition and enforcement of judgments in civil and commercial matters.

(3) The relevant moment for determining whether there is a cross-border case shall be the time when the application for a European order for payment is submitted in accordance with this Regulation.

Notes

(1) The European Small Claims Procedure is meant to significantly simplify and speed up litigation and enforcement regarding small claims, defined as monetary or non-monetary claims of a total value not exceeding €2.000. This procedure applies in civil and commercial matters with a number of exclusions similar to those in Article 1 of the Brussels I Regulation (on jurisdiction). The procedure is based on a wide use of standard forms and is normally in writing only. Representation by a lawyer is not mandatory. The judgment must be rendered within six months. The national procedural law of the Member State of the forum decides on the availability of appeal.

(2) Although the initial consideration was that the European Small Claims Procedure should exist as an alternative to existing national small claims procedures, the scope of application has finally been limited to cross-border small claims (because doubts have been raised as to the Community's competence—under Article 65 EC—to harmonise rules of procedure applicable to non-cross border disputes). It remains to be seen the ease with which people will become familiar with a procedure that is applicable only in the still rather exceptional circumstances of cross-border small claims disputes.

(3) The procedure based on Regulation 1896/2006 creating a European Order for Payment Procedure is intended to be used for uncontested pecuniary claims in cross-border cases. The scope of the Regulation is partly similar to the scope of the Brussels I Regulation. The principal features of the Regulation are that the court seized of the application for a European Order for Payment issues, after a summary examination of the application's admissibility, an Order calling upon the defendant to pay or to oppose the claim. The Order is served on the defendant in accordance with

specific and detailed rules, mostly inspired by the minimum standards set in Regulation 805/2004 creating a European Enforcement Order for Uncontested Claims. The Order becomes enforceable unless the defendant lodges a statement of opposition within 30 days. If the defendant lodges such a statement, proceedings will continue in accordance with the rules of ordinary civil procedure, unless the claimant explicitly requests the termination of the proceedings. The European Order for Payment procedure is substantially simplified by the use of standard forms and representation by a lawyer is not mandatory. It serves as an additional and optional means for the claimant, who remains free to resort to any other procedure available under domestic or Community law. It is not particularly intended to protect consumers and will probably be mostly used against them, but it may also give the consumer an instrument that enables him to enforce cross-border claims without substantial costs.[10]

Regulation (EC) 805/2004 Creating a European Enforcement Order for Uncontested Claims[11] **8.6 (EU)**

Article 1 Subject matter

The purpose of this Regulation is to create a European Enforcement Order for uncontested claims to permit, by laying down minimum standards, the free circulation of judgments, court settlements and authentic instruments throughout all Member States without any intermediate proceedings needing to be brought in the Member State of enforcement prior to recognition and enforcement.

Article 2 Scope

(1) This Regulation shall apply in civil and commercial matters, whatever the nature of the court or tribunal. It shall not extend, in particular, to revenue, customs or administrative matters or the liability of the State for acts and omissions in the exercise of State authority ('acta iure imperii').

(2) This Regulation shall not apply to:

(a) the status or legal capacity of natural persons, rights in property arising out of a matrimonial relationship, wills and succession;

(b) bankruptcy, proceedings relating to the winding-up of insolvent companies or other legal persons, judicial arrangements, compositions and analogous proceedings;

(c) social security;

(d) arbitration.

(3) In this Regulation, the term 'Member State' shall mean Member States with the exception of Denmark.

Note

EC Regulation 805/2004 of 21 April 2004 creating a European Enforcement Order for Uncontested Claims, which applies from 21 October 2005 to judgments given

[10] N Reich, 'Cross-border Consumer Protection' in H Micklitz, N Reich and P Rott, *Understanding EU Consumer Law* (Antwerp/Oxford, Intersentia, 2009) 308.

[11] Regulation (EC) 805/2004 of the European Parliament and of the Council of 21 April 2004 creating a European Enforcement Order for uncontested claims [2004] OJ L 143, 15–39.

after its entry into force on 21 January 2005, is an independent legal instrument of EC law. However, it is obviously intended to function as a complement to the Brussels I Regulation, mainly by introducing an alternative, simplified enforcement procedure with regard to uncontested claims irrespective of the amount. It does not limit itself to enforcement though, as it also simplifies the recognition of judgments regarding such claims.

In view of the mutual trust in the administration of justice in the Member States, the regulation authorises the court making the judgment regarding an uncontested claim to issue, in addition to the judgment itself, a standardised certificate showing that all conditions imposed by the Regulation are fulfilled. Such certificate enables the judgment, thus certified as a European Enforcement Order, to be enforced in the other Member States without the need for any declaration of enforceability and to be recognised there without any possibility of opposing the recognition (Article 5).

The scope of application of the regulation is practically the same as that of the Brussels I Regulation, as far as the subject matter of the dispute is concerned. This follows from Article 2 of the Regulation creating an European Enforcement Order, which corresponds to Article 1 of the Brussels I Regulation.

The regulation applies only to claims for payment of a specific sum of money that has fallen due or for which the due date is indicated in the judgment (Article 4(2)). Demands regarding a specific performance, even if uncontested, are thus not included. On the other hand, the certification applies also to the costs related to the court proceedings, unless the debtor, during the proceedings, has specifically objected to the obligation to bear those costs (Article 7). The certification may be partial if only a part of the judgment fulfils the conditions imposed by the Regulation (Article 8). Just like the European Order for Payment procedure, the European Enforcement Order has not been designed for consumer protection purposes.

Council Directive 2003/8/EC to Improve Access to Justice in Cross-border Disputes by Establishing Minimum Common Rules Relating to Legal Aid for such Disputes[12] **8.7 (EU)**

Article 1 Aims and scope

(1) The purpose of this Directive is to improve access to justice in cross-border disputes by establishing minimum common rules relating to legal aid in such disputes.

(2) It shall apply, in cross-border disputes, to civil and commercial matters whatever the nature of the court or tribunal. It shall not extend, in particular, to revenue, customs or administrative matters.

(3) In this Directive, 'Member State' shall mean Member States with the exception of Denmark.

Article 2 Cross-border disputes

(1) For the purposes of this Directive, a cross-border dispute is one where the party applying for legal aid in the context of this Directive is domiciled or habitually resident in

[12] Council Directive 2003/8/EC of 27 January 2003 to improve access to justice in cross-border disputes by establishing minimum common rules relating to legal aid for such disputes [2003] OJ L 26, 41–47.

a Member State other than the Member State where the court is sitting or where the decision is to be enforced.

(2) The Member State in which a party is domiciled shall be determined in accordance with Article 59 of Council Regulation (EC) 44/2001 of 22 December 2000 on jurisdiction and the recognition and enforcement of judgments in civil and commercial matters.

(3) The relevant moment to determine if there is a cross-border dispute is the time when the application is submitted, in accordance with this Directive.

Article 3 Right to legal aid

(1) Natural persons involved in a dispute covered by this Directive shall be entitled to receive appropriate legal aid in order to ensure their effective access to justice in accordance with the conditions laid down in this Directive.

(2) Legal aid is considered to be appropriate when it guarantees:

(a) pre-litigation advice with a view to reaching a settlement prior to bringing legal proceedings;

(b) legal assistance and representation in court, and exemption from, or assistance with, the cost of proceedings of the recipient, including the costs referred to in Article 7 and the fees to persons mandated by the court to perform acts during the proceedings.

In Member States in which a losing party is liable for the costs of the opposing party, if the recipient loses the case, the legal aid shall cover the costs incurred by the opposing party, if it would have covered such costs had the recipient been domiciled or habitually resident in the Member State in which the court is sitting.

(3) Member States need not provide legal assistance or representation in the courts or tribunals in proceedings especially designed to enable litigants to make their case in person, except when the courts or any other competent authority otherwise decide in order to ensure equality of parties or in view of the complexity of the case.

(4) Member States may request that legal aid recipients pay reasonable contributions towards the costs of proceedings taking into account the conditions referred to in Article 5.

(5) Member States may provide that the competent authority may decide that recipients of legal aid must refund it in whole or in part if their financial situation has substantially improved or if the decision to grant legal aid had been taken on the basis of inaccurate information given by the recipient.

Note

Legal treatment of the rights of the poor is an expression of access to justice, ie a fundamental right of citizens. In addition to the instruments mentioned above, action has also been taken at EC level with regard to legal aid. Council Directive 2003/8/EC of 27 January 2003 tries to improve access to justice in cross-border disputes by establishing minimum common rules relating to legal aid. The scope of the directive is, however, limited as it only concerns cross-border disputes, but it does apply to extrajudicial procedures, if the law requires the parties to use them, or if the parties to the dispute are ordered by the court to have recourse to them.[13] National systems of legal aid vary widely.

[13] Art 10 Directive 2003/8/EC.

III. ARBITRATION AND MEDIATION

III.A INTRODUCTION

Alternative dispute resolution (ADR) has seen gradual development in Europe, including in the field of consumer protection. ADR refers to structured methods of resolving disputes other than formal court-based adjudication. It includes arbitration, mediation as well as schemes that combine elements of both.[14] Although most countries have developed mediation and arbitration schemes to some extent, the differences are huge.

Study Centre for Consumer Law, Alternative Means of Consumer Redress other than Redress through Ordinary Judicial Proceedings[15] **8.8 (EU)**

Different legal traditions, judicial delay, costs involved in ordinary judicial procedures, the role of judges, the availability of an efficient small claims procedure and procedural particularities all influence the development of alternative dispute resolution schemes such as arbitration and mediation. For example, the possibility of discovery or cross-examination, identified as a burden on procedures in certain common law jurisdictions, was highlighted as an important impetus for the development of out-of-court ADR procedures in certain common law countries. Further, the greater flexibility to adapt court rules that exists in most common law jurisdictions contributed to the earlier development of ADR in the context of judicial proceedings in common law jurisdictions. In addition, many divergent factors determine or at least influence the ADR landscape for resolving consumer disputes such as:

—the organizational structure of the industry;

—the enforceability of arbitration clauses in consumer contracts;

—(statutory) requirements that oblige companies to adhere to sector specific industry based private dispute resolution schemes in order to obtain a license.

Notwithstanding these particularities and occasional arbitrary features of legal and economic systems, and keeping in mind that there are exceptions, it is nevertheless possible to outline some general trends.

It is fair to say that the Scandinavian countries have been at the forefront with regard to developing alternatives to litigation specifically for the resolution of consumer conflicts. The consumer ombudsman has the important task of supervising marketing practices in these countries. In addition, Scandinavian countries all have municipal consumer advisers at the local level (providing mediation services) and consumer complaint boards at a centralised level. The idea of an ombudsman has been copied in many of the reviewed jurisdictions but rarely with the same broad and consumer specific competence. ... The common law jurisdictions were at the forefront with regard to the

[14] The concept of ADR used in this book is thus broader than the definition of ADR adopted in the Commission's 2002 Green Paper on alternative dispute resolution in civil and commercial law, COM [2002] 196 final (hereinafter 'Green Paper').

[15] Stuyck et al, above n 7.

development of (non consumer specific) mediation. Current mediation in most common law countries can be traced back to the establishment of Community Justice Centres in the 1970s and 1980s: meanwhile, mediation is also practiced in the private sector in a wide range of court related programs. In civil law countries mediation has only recently been recognised as a valuable alternative to litigation. There are, however, exceptions such as the Netherlands. Such general schemes for mediation are, however, not always the most popular ADR schemes to resolve consumer disputes. Sector specific (binding and non binding) arbitration schemes exist in all of the aforementioned jurisdictions, some of them very popular, but the wide variety of schemes has not always contributed to the coherency and transparency of the dispute resolutions mechanisms available.

At the other end of the spectrum, the development of ADR mechanisms is a very recent development in most of the Central and Eastern European countries that acceded to the EU in 2004. ADR initiatives for consumer disputes are not very widespread in some of these countries and most initiatives date from the 1990s or even more recently, which often means that evaluation would be premature. Many schemes have been adopted in view of the accession to the EU and as a consequence of the implementation of the acquis communautaire.

It is interesting to see that some of these new Member States have opted for a more general approach towards the enforcement of consumer law and have chosen to combine the function of market surveillance with complaint handling functions. … Such general systems, combining market surveillance with a general competence to settle individual claims seem to present important advantages. The individual claims provide important indications of problems that might need to be tackled by a market surveillance authority. The market surveillance tasks of this body can increase the visibility with consumers who might more easily find their way to the appropriate dispute resolution mechanism. …

The rationale behind these out of court ADR procedures is the same. Where efforts to resolve disputes directly with businesses fail, out of court ADR can offer consumers a quick, effective and cheap way to obtain a remedy without the burden and expense of formal legal action. ADR offers parties the possibility to come to a win-win situation, which could be especially useful in relationships between consumers and businesses where consumer confidence is an important issue. Out of court ADR moreover improves access to justice as it enables consumers to obtain redress in disputes that would otherwise never come to court.

Note

ADR schemes—like small claims procedures—try to cure the perceived deficiencies of 'traditional' in-court litigation, which is often considered as too expensive, formalistic and slow. Although ADR schemes are not necessarily consumer specific—indeed arbitration is quite often used in commercial disputes—for consumer disputes, these schemes often present a way to obtain redress in disputes for which a court procedure is not a realistic alternative.

ADR schemes, however, do not only intend to cure the perceived deficiencies of traditional in-court litigation. Their flexibility also allows for the development of true alternatives to in-court litigation, with more room for specialisation (eg according to the sector) and more room for a different, more consensus-based, approach, allowing parties to resume a dialogue instead of being each other's opponents. It is possible to distinguish between truly voluntary schemes which increase consumer rights and minimise costs on the one hand and those schemes—such as some arbitration schemes (especially in the US)—that rather limit consumer rights.

III.B DEFINITIONS AND TERMINOLOGY

There is no consensus on the terminology describing the different forms of ADR. The position and role of third persons relative to the parties in dispute are crucial in the various attempts to categorise these schemes.

Consumer Law Enforcement Forum, Glossary[16] **8.9 (EU)**

Arbitration: Where a neutral third party that has been agreed upon by the parties decides on a claim and the decision is binding for the parties. Arbitration is most commonly used for commercial disputes, but not for consumer disputes.

Arbitration-type ADR: The European Commission with recommendation 98/257/EC on arbitration-type ADR has defined this type of ADR as the settling of a dispute through the active intervention of a third party, who proposes or imposes a solution.

Mediation: Any process, however named or referred to, where two or more parties to a dispute are assisted by a third party to reach an agreement on the settlement of the dispute, and regardless of whether the process is initiated by the parties, suggested or ordered by a court or prescribed by the national law of a Member State.

Mediation-type ADR: The European Commission in recommendation 2001/310/EC on mediation-type ADR has defined this type of ADR as a third party attempt to resolve a dispute by bringing the parties together to convince them to find a solution by common consent.

Ombudsman: A unique definition of Ombudsman across Europe does not exist. Its role and functions will vary from one country to another. In the United Kingdom, it is used to identify an independent third party who offers a (usually) free service and whose decisions usually bind the business but not the consumer. These may be established on a private industry basis or be established by the state (eg Financial Services Ombudsman). ... In central Europe, it is often used by industry and commerce to designate an independent person, often a former judge who is in charge of dealing with consumer complaints addressed to the respective industry sector (banking or insurances). ... In the Nordic countries, the Ombudsman is an enforcement body for marketing practices and contractual terms. The Ombudsman is appointed by the government and does not deal with individual consumer complaints.

[16] Consumer Law Enforcement Forum, www.clef-project.eu.

Notes

(1) This excerpt is taken from the Consumer Law Enforcement Forum Glossary (CLEF), where it was drafted as a pragmatic attempt to set common standards for discussion. Different definitions and categorisations may be found.

(2) Many schemes cannot be easily fitted into the dichotomy arbitration and mediation and combine elements of both (sometimes referred to as 'med-arb').

(3) See also the definition of mediation in Directive 2008/52/EC on certain aspects of mediation in civil and commercial matters[17] that broadly coincides with the CLEF definition.

III.C REGULATION OF ADR

III.C.1 INTRODUCTION

The regulation of ADR schemes represents a tension between the need for flexibility and innovation on the one hand and the need for legal certainty as to the outcome, procedure and quality and impartiality of the third party involved on the other. A general legal framework is currently absent both at European and national level, although there is a tendency to proceed to increased regulation and institutionalisation. A number of instruments on arbitration and mediation have been issued by the Council of Europe,[18] but the EU institutions are also trying to foster ADR by both initiatives of a general nature and consumer-specific initiatives.

III.C.2 GENERAL EU INITIATIVES

As part of the follow-up to the 2002 Green Paper on ADR in civil and commercial matters,[19] which initiated a broad consultation on the primary legal feature of ADR processes, a European Code of Conduct on mediation was adopted that sets out a series of norms that can be applied to mediation.

European Code of Conduct for Mediators **8.10 (EU)**

This code of conduct sets out a number of principles to which individual mediators can voluntarily decide to commit, under their own responsibility. It is intended to be applicable to all kinds of mediation in civil and commercial matters.

Organisations providing mediation services can also make such a commitment, by asking mediators acting under the auspices of their organisation to respect the code.

Organisations have the opportunity to make available information on the measures they are taking to support the respect of the code by individual mediators through, for example, training, evaluation and monitoring.

[17] [2008] OJ L 136, 3.

[18] See eg the 1966 Convention providing for a uniform law on arbitration; the Council of Europe Recommendation (1998) 1 on mediation in family matters of 21 January 1998; the Council of Europe Recommendation (2002) 10 on mediation in civil matters of 18 September 2002.

[19] COM [2002] 196 final.

For the purposes of the code mediation is defined as any process where two or more parties agree to the appointment of a third-party—hereinafter 'the mediator'—to help the parties to solve a dispute by reaching an agreement without adjudication and regardless of how that process may be called or commonly referred to in each Member State.

Adherence to the code is without prejudice to national legislation or rules regulating individual professions.

Organisations providing mediation services may wish to develop more detailed codes adapted to their specific context or the types of mediation services they offer, as well as with regard to specific areas such as family mediation or consumer mediation.

Note

The Code of Conduct sets out a series of norms which can be applied to the practice of mediation and which can be adhered to by mediation organisations. The norms relate to the competence and appointment of mediator, his independence and impartiality, the mediation agreement, process, settlement and fees, and also to confidentiality.

In addition to the Code of Conduct, a directive on mediation was recently adopted.

Directive 2008/52/EC on Mediation in Civil and Commercial Matters[20] **8.11 (EU)**

Article 1 Objective and scope

(1) The objective of this Directive is to facilitate access to alternative dispute resolution and to promote the amicable settlement of disputes by encouraging the use of mediation and by ensuring a balanced relationship between mediation and judicial proceedings.

(2) This Directive shall apply, in cross-border disputes, to civil and commercial matters except as regards rights and obligations which are not at the parties' disposal under the relevant applicable law. It shall not extend, in particular, to revenue, customs or administrative matters or to the liability of the State for acts and omissions in the exercise of State authority ('acta iure imperii').

Notes

(1) The Directive wishes to encourage the use of mediation by making certain legal rules available within the legal systems of the Member States. These rules cover, inter alia, the confidentiality of the mediation process, the enforceability of agreements resulting from mediation the effect of mediation on limitation and prescription periods. The directive is limited in scope as it only applies to cross-border disputes.

(2) In addition to these instruments, a number of important instruments facilitate the cross-border enforcement of arbitral awards and even of settlement agreements that may be the outcome of mediation processes (subject to certain

[20] [2008] OJ L 136, 3.

conditions), such as the Regulation establishing a European Enforcement Order (see above section II) and the Brussels I Regulation (see below section III.G).

(3) It remains to be seen whether this Directive will be important for consumers.

III.C.3 CONSUMER SPECIFIC EU INITIATIVES

Commission Recommendation 98/257/EC on the Principles Applicable to the Bodies Responsible for Out-of-Court Settlement of Consumer Disputes[21] **8.12 (EU)**

Whereas this recommendation must be limited to procedures which, no matter what they are called, lead to the settling of a dispute through the active intervention of a third party, who proposes or imposes a solution; whereas, therefore, it does not concern procedures that merely involve an attempt to bring the parties together to convince them to find a solution by common consent;

Whereas the decisions taken by out-of-court bodies may be binding on the parties, may be mere recommendations or may constitute settlement proposals which have to be accepted by the parties; whereas for the purposes of this recommendation these various cases are covered by the term 'decision'; …

Recommends that all existing bodies and bodies to be created with responsibility for the out-of-court settlement of consumer disputes respect the following principles:

I Principle of independence

The independence of the decision-making body is ensured in order to guarantee the impartiality of its actions. …

II Principle of transparency

Appropriate measures are taken to ensure the transparency of the procedure. These include:

(1) provision of the following information, in writing or any other suitable form, to any persons requesting it:

—a precise description of the types of dispute which may be referred to the body concerned …

—the rules governing the referral of the matter to the body, …

—the possible cost of the procedure for the parties, including rules on the award of costs at the end of the procedure,

—the type of rules serving as the basis for the body's decisions…

—the decision-making arrangements within the body,

—the legal force of the decision taken, …

(2) Publication by the competent body of an annual report setting out the decisions taken, enabling the results obtained to be assessed and the nature of the disputes referred to it to be identified.

[21] [1998] OJ L 155, 31–34.

III Adversarial principle

The procedure to be followed allows all the parties concerned to present their viewpoint before the competent body and to hear the arguments and facts put forward by the other party, and any experts' statements.

IV Principle of effectiveness

The effectiveness of the procedure is ensured through measures guaranteeing:

—that the consumer has access to the procedure without being obliged to use a legal representative,

—that the procedure is free of charges or of moderate costs,

—that only short periods elapse between the referral of a matter and the decision,

—that the competent body is given an active role, thus enabling it to take into consideration any factors conducive to a settlement of the dispute.

V Principle of legality

The decision taken by the body may not result in the consumer being deprived of the protection afforded by the mandatory provisions of the law of the State in whose territory the body is established. In the case of cross-border disputes, the decision taken by the body may not result in the consumer being deprived of the protection afforded by the mandatory provisions applying under the law of the Member State in which he is normally resident in the instances provided for under Article 5 of the Rome Convention of 19 June 1980 on the law applicable to contractual obligations. All decisions are communicated to the parties concerned as soon as possible, in writing or any other suitable form, stating the grounds on which they are based.

VI Principle of liberty

The decision taken by the body concerned may be binding on the parties only if they were informed of its binding nature in advance and specifically accepted this. The consumer's recourse to the out-of-court procedure may not be the result of a commitment prior to the materialisation of the dispute, where such commitment has the effect of depriving the consumer of his right to bring an action before the courts for the settlement of the dispute.

VII Principle of representation

The procedure does not deprive the parties of the right to be represented or assisted by a third party at all stages of the procedure.

Commission Recommendation 2001/310/EC on the Principles for Out-of-Court Bodies Involved in the Consensual Resolution of Consumer Disputes[22] **8.13 (EU)**

The Commission of the European Communities … hereby recommends:

That the principles set out in Part II are respected by all existing and future bodies providing out-of-court consumer dispute resolution procedures falling within the scope of this recommendation as defined in Part I:

[22] [2001] OJ L109, 56–61.

I Scope:

(1) This recommendation applies to third party bodies responsible for out-of-court consumer dispute resolution procedures that, no matter what they are called, attempt to resolve a dispute by bringing the parties together to convince them to find a solution by common consent.

(2) It does not apply to customer complaint mechanisms operated by a business and concluded directly with the consumer or to such mechanisms carrying out such services operated by or on behalf of a business.

II Principles:

A. Impartiality...
B. Transparency...
C. Effectiveness...
D. Fairness...

Notes

(1) Whereas the 1998 Recommendation covers 'arbitration type ADR', the 2001 Recommendation covers 'mediation-type ADR'.

(2) Both the 1998 and 2001 recommendations play a central role in the functioning of the European Consumer Centres Network (ECC-Net) and FIN-NET (see the next section for more information on these networks). ADR schemes which can be considered to respect the principles set out in the recommendations are notified to the European Commission by Member States for inclusion in a database. The ECC and FIN-NET contact points provide consumers with information on the bodies that Member States consider to meet the demands of the Commission recommendations. There is not much knowledge available as to how these systems work in practice.

III.D VARIETY AND AVAILABILITY

There is an enormous variety in ADR bodies, their structure and the procedures they conduct. Several hundreds of different schemes exist throughout the EU, ranging from public ADR schemes (with general[23] or sector-specific[24] scopes of application) to private ADR schemes (mainly sector-specific).[25] Nevertheless, the availability of an ADR scheme for a specific dispute is not always guaranteed.

[23] eg the Danish and Finnish consumer complaint board.

[24] eg the Ombudsman for Pensions in Ireland.

[25] eg the 41 Dutch sector-specific schemes that are grouped in an umbrella organisation (the Stichting Geschillencommissie Consumenten).

DTI and National Consumer Council, Seeking Resolution. Availability and Usage of Consumer-to-business Alternative Dispute Resolution in the UK[26] **8.14 (UK)**

The provision of ADR for consumer problems remains ad hoc and presents a lottery for the consumer. Whether ADR is available depends on the type of problem faced, on where the problem arises and sometimes on the ability of the consumer to afford the fee.

Notes

(1) This statement in a report on ADR provision in the UK also holds good for many other EU jurisdictions. The availability of ADR schemes varies widely throughout the EU. Not all goods/services are covered and national coverage is not guaranteed.

(2) The enormous variety in ADR schemes is an advantage, as it ensures diversity and flexibility. Nevertheless, it can be hard for consumers to find their way to the right scheme—if it exists. The importance of bodies facilitating the use of ADR schemes should not therefore be underestimated. ECC-Net plays an important role in this regard. It is an EU-wide network designed to promote consumer confidence by advising citizens on their rights as consumers and providing easy access to redress, particularly in cases where the consumer has made a cross-border purchase. It was created by merging two previously existing networks: the European Consumer Centres or 'Euroguichets', which provided information and assistance on cross-border issues; and the European Extra-Judicial Network (EEJ-Net) which helped consumers to resolve their disputes through ADR schemes using mediators or arbitrators.

(3) In addition to ECC-Net, the European Commission launched an out-of-court complaints network for financial services in 2001. This network, called FIN-NET, has been designed particularly to facilitate the out-of-court resolution of consumer disputes when the service provider is established in an EU Member State other than that where the consumer lives. These European initiatives mainly deal with cross-border issues, but similar initiatives exist in certain national jurisdiction (eg Malta and France), where 'clearing-houses' for consumer complaints exist. These are institutions which perform the function of one-stop shops for consumers who wish to obtain information about a specific consumer matter. After a consumer's petition (or complaint) lodged with such a body is processed, the body can either take legal action on its own initiative or refer a consumer to the competent body. How FIN-NET is working in practice is by and large not clear.

III.E ARBITRATION CLAUSES IN CONSUMER CONTRACTS

In the US, consumers are generally free to consent to be bound by the jurisdiction of ADR bodies (although there are many instances where contractual arbitration

[26] DTI and National Consumer Council 2004, 1.

clauses may be found by the court to be inapplicable depending on which state's law is applied). In Europe, most jurisdictions have a rather restrictive approach towards arbitration clauses in consumer contracts. EC law itself also regards arbitration clauses in consumer contracts with suspicion.

Unfair Contract Terms Directive 93/13/EEC[27] **8.15 (EU)**

Annex Terms referred to in Article 3(3)

(1) Terms which have the object or effect of: ...

q) excluding or hindering the consumer's right to take legal action or exercise any other legal remedy, particularly by requiring the consumer to take disputes exclusively to arbitration not covered by legal provisions, unduly restricting the evidence available to him or imposing on him a burden of proof which, according to the applicable law, should lie with another party to the contract.

Notes

(1) The rules on unfair terms apply to arbitration (and mediation) clauses in consumer contracts, meaning that a contractual term that has not been individually negotiated may not cause, contrary to the requirement of good faith, a significant imbalance in the parties' rights and obligations arising under the contract, to the detriment of the consumer.[28] The indicative list annexed to the Directive moreover mentions certain arbitration clauses as examples of unfair terms. Where a clause refers to an arbitration scheme that is covered by legal provision, the clause may still fall foul of the Directive, but the onus rests on the consumer to demonstrate that it is unfair in that it imbalances the rights of the parties to the detriment of the consumer and is contrary to the principles of good faith. It could, however, be argued on the basis of the *Mostaza Claro* judgment of the ECJ, mentioned in the next paragraph, that the onus of proof no longer rests on the consumer but on the national court, which has to examine, on its own initiative, whether the clause is unfair. In the Proposal for a Directive on Consumer Rights, a clause requiring the consumer to take disputes exclusively to arbitration not covered by legal provisions is considered a 'black' clause, implying that it is considered unfair in all circumstances.[29]

(2) One arbitration clause even reached the ECJ, in the case of *Mostaza Claro*, but the ECJ did not need to rule on its validity because the Spanish court had asked a different question. Several Spanish courts have recently declared null and void a standard term that imposes non-official and private arbitration by the European Association of Law and Equity Arbitration (AEADE) in the case of disputes on mobile telephones. The reason was that the arbitration court was linked to the professional and the consumer had to pay the costs.

[27] [1993] OJ L 95, 29–34.

[28] See Art 3 Council Directive 93/13/EEC of 5 April 1993 on unfair terms in consumer contracts [1993] OJ L 95, 29–34.

[29] Annex II COM [2008] 614.

(3) In addition to the Unfair Contract Terms Directive 93/13/EEC, Article 6 ECHR should be taken into account in a European context. Allowing arbitration or mediation clauses, including in consumer contracts, does not in itself breach the fundamental principle of access to court. The right of Article 6 §1 ECHR is not absolute, and restrictions are possible if they pursue a legitimate aim. The ECtHR has confirmed the validity of arbitration clauses, although they are 'a partial renunciation of the exercise of the rights defined in Article 6 §1'. An arbitration clause, 'which has undeniable advantages for the individual concerned as well as for the administration of justice, does not in principle offend against the Convention'. The arbitration clause, as it limits a fundamental right, must, however be consented to in an unequivocal manner and out of free will.

Whether or not the consumer is well aware of the renunciation is a major concern of the European Commission. The 1998 Commission Recommendations provides that out-of-court 'procedures may not deprive consumers of their right to bring the matter before the courts unless they expressly agree to do so, in full awareness of the facts and only after the dispute has materialised'. Furthermore, according to the Commission recommendation of 2001, the freedom of participation is regarded as an aspect of procedural fairness ('The parties should be informed of their right to refuse to participate or to withdraw from the procedure at any time…').

(4) In several national jurisdictions, the limitations on arbitration (and sometimes also mediation) clauses go beyond the unfair contract terms control or the inclusion in an indicative list of unfair terms.[30]

UK Arbitration Act **8.16 (UK)**

Section 91 Arbitration agreement unfair where modest amount sought.

(1) A term which constitutes an arbitration agreement is unfair for the purposes of the Regulations so far as it relates to a claim for a pecuniary remedy which does not exceed the amount specified by order for the purposes of this section. …

Code civil **8.17 (FR)**

Article 2061 Except where there are specific statutory provisions, an arbitration clause is valid in contracts concluded for professional purposes.

Note

This Code civil Article is usually interpreted as meaning that arbitration clauses are prohibited in consumer contracts. This prohibition is, however, limited in two respects:

— It only applies to arbitration clauses. Once the dispute is born, the consumer and the professional can agree to use arbitration to resolve it. The French

[30] On the different laws in the Member States, see N Reich, 'More Clarity after "Claro"?' [2007] *ECRL* 4.

Supreme Court (Cour de Cassation) has also allowed contractual mediation clauses, so long as they do not impede a contracting party from bringing an action before the courts when mediation fails.[31]

— The prohibition only applies to internal contracts. Arbitration clauses are not prohibited in international contracts, even if a consumer is a party to the contract.[32] In an international consumer contract, an arbitration clause is therefore not illegal per se. Both arbitration and mediation clauses can fall under the prohibition of unfair contract terms. As a matter of fact, the third sentence of Article L 132-1 Code de la consommation provides that

> an annex to this code includes an illustrative and non-exhaustive list of clauses that may be regarded as unfair if they satisfy the conditions posed in the first paragraph. In the event of dispute concerning a contract that includes one such clause, the applicant is not exempt from submitting proof of the unfair nature of this clause.

In the said annex, which constitutes a greylist of potentially unfair contract terms, point (q) mentions that the terms with the aim or effect of

> cancelling or impeding the institution of legal proceedings or means of redress by the consumer, in particular, obliging the consumer to *exclusively* refer the case to arbitration not covered by legal provisions, by unduly limiting the means of giving evidence available to the consumer or by making the latter responsible for providing proof which, by virtue of applicable law, should normally lie with another party to the contract.

This is borrowed from the indicative list of unfair terms in the Annex to Directive 93/13/EEC (see also 8.15 (EU)). German law is also relatively strict on arbitration agreements. Such an agreement is only valid if signed separately by the parties. Nevertheless, the agreement may still come under the control of unfair terms. It is not necessarily unfair but unfairness may stem from the place of the arbitration, from the selection of arbiters, or from the particularities of the proceedings. However, the German Federal Court[33] refused to review an arbitration clause as unfair either under German or (not mentioned) EU legislation. If the consumer's right to name an arbitrator is unduly restricted, he can ask a state court to take care of the fair balancing of the arbitration panel. Even stricter are the Nordic countries. In Sweden and Finland, arbitration clauses in consumer relations are void.[34] In the UK an arbitration agreement or clause where one of the parties is a consumer is considered to be unfair insofar as it relates to a claim for an amount which does not exceed a figure specified by statutory instrument.

[31] Cass civ 1e, 1 February 2005, No 03-19.692 (2005) JCP (G) IV, 1532; C Pelletier, 'Les clauses de conciliation et de médiation dans les contrats de consommation' [2005] *JCP* 479–80.

[32] Cass civ 1e, 30 March 2004, Bull civ I, No 97.

[33] BGH (2008) JZ 359 with a critical comment of G Mäsch.

[34] s 6 of the Swedish Arbitration Act (1999:116); ch 12, s 1 d of the Finnish Consumer Protection Act, as amended 1994 (1994/16).

IV. COLLECTIVE REDRESS

IV.A INTRODUCTION

The traditional legal position in the various Member States of the Community—whether they be civil law or common law jurisdictions, used to be that a natural or legal person may not institute legal proceedings unless he establishes a direct personal interest, ie is qualified to act. This is particularly problematic when the interest of a number of consumers or of consumers generally is affected—either actually or potentially—by, for example, an unfair trade practice or a dangerous product.[35] In all countries and also at EU level, procedures have been developed that depart from this position and that allow individuals, public bodies or private organisations to bring actions either in the collective interest or to defend individual interests other than their own.

The variety of procedures is enormous and various classifications are possible, depending on, inter alia, who may institute proceedings, on the remedies that may be obtained, on the interests that are defended or represented (either the collective interest or a bundle of individual interests), etc. In what follows, we will discuss some types of collective redress according to the main remedies that can be obtained: injunctions and damages.

IV.B ACTIONS FOR INJUNCTION

In the last couple of years the debate on collective enforcement of consumer rights in Europe has gained momentum since the European Commission has shown a keen interest in the phenomenon. This interest is, however, not completely new: the possibilities of introducing collective actions to improve consumer access to justice were being discussed as long ago as 1984, but a binding solution at EU level was then judged premature, and the decision was taken to support national initiatives for the time being.[36] This nothwithstanding, quite a number of Directives have been adopted that triggered many Member States to adopt procedures in the collective interest and to recognise a category of interests whose scope is:

- wider than that of individual interests (which are traditionally defended via the right of individual action), but
- more limited than that of the general interest (whose defence usually lies with the ministry responsible for public order).[37]

[35] See Memorandum for the Commission. Discussion paper: consumer redress, COM [1984] 629 final, 12 December 1984.

[36] Memorandum for the Commission. Discussion paper: consumer redress, COM [1984] 629 final.

[37] Green Paper: Access of consumers to justice and the settlement of consumer disputes in the internal market, COM [1993] 576, 64.

UCPD 2005/29/EC[38] **8.18 (EU)**

Article 11 (1) Member States shall ensure that adequate and effective means exist to combat unfair commercial practices in order to enforce compliance with the provisions of this Directive in the interest of consumers.

Such means shall include legal provisions under which persons or organisations regarded under national law as having a legitimate interest in combating unfair commercial practices, including competitors, may:

(a) take legal action against such unfair commercial practices;

and/or

(b) bring such unfair commercial practices before an administrative authority competent either to decide on complaints or to initiate appropriate legal proceedings.

It shall be for each Member State to decide which of these facilities shall be available and whether to enable the courts or administrative authorities to require prior recourse to other established means of dealing with complaints, including those referred to in Article 10.

These facilities shall be available regardless of whether the consumers affected are in the territory of the Member State where the trader is located or in another Member State.

It shall be for each Member State to decide:

(a) whether these legal facilities may be directed separately or jointly against a number of traders from the same economic sector; and

(b) whether these legal facilities may be directed against a code owner where the relevant code promotes non-compliance with legal requirements.

Unfair Contract Terms Directive 93/13/EEC[39] **8.19 (EU)**

Article 7 (1) Member States shall ensure that, in the interests of consumers and of competitors, adequate and effective means exist to prevent the continued use of unfair terms in contracts concluded with consumers by sellers or suppliers.

(2) The means referred to in paragraph 1 shall include provisions whereby persons or organizations, having a legitimate interest under national law in protecting consumers, may take action according to the national law concerned before the courts or before competent administrative bodies for a decision as to whether contractual terms drawn up for general use are unfair, so that they can apply appropriate and effective means to prevent the continued use of such terms.

(3) With due regard for national laws, the legal remedies referred to in paragraph 2 may be directed separately or jointly against a number of sellers or suppliers from the same economic sector or their associations which use or recommend the use of the same general contractual terms or similar terms.

[38] [2005] OJ L 149, 22.

[39] Council Directive 93/13/EEC of 5 April 1993 on unfair terms in consumer contracts OJ L [1993] 95, 29–34.

Notes

(1) An injunction generally aims to ensure that businesses cease the infringement and do not engage in similar conduct in the future. Often, national procedures also provide for all or part of the relevant court decision or a corrective announcement to be published.

(2) The provision in the Unfair Commercial Practices Directive, which derives from the former Misleading Advertising Directive 84/450/EEC, has provided the opportunity for many Member States to give standing to consumer organisations to bring actions for an injunction in the collective interest of consumers, all be it with considerable procedural variations and from their own national perspectives.[40]

(3) Many subsequent Directives contain similar provisions, eg the Unfair Contract Terms Directive 1993/13/EEC cited above. All Member States now provide for collective court procedures, by which the use or recommendation of unfair terms in legal agreements shall be prohibited. In a number of Member States, the emphasis is on administrative proceedings, in almost all Member States it is furthermore possible to pursue collective court actions against unfair clauses.[41] In most Member States consumer associations are entitled to seek injunctions,[42] and in some Member States the initiative can also be taken by a regulator responsible for defending the public interest or consumer interests, eg the OFT in the UK, the Director of Consumer Affairs in Ireland, the consumer ombudsmen in the Nordic states, and the relevant ministries in Spain and Portugal.

(4) Directive 98/27/EC on injunctions for the protection of consumers' interests[43] finally took a more horizontal approach and obliged Member States—which had already introduced procedures for some aspects of consumer law—to make it possible for qualified entities to take action before national courts to protect the various specific rights given to consumers by legislation implementing the consumer protection Directives. These actions may be taken purely domestically, ie a body from a Member State can bring an action in that Member State to prevent infringements of the legislation by a trader from the same Member State. In addition, Directive 98/27/EC also introduced specific provisions on the cross-border action for injunction by allowing entities from one Member State to take action against traders from another Member State in the courts of that trader's jurisdiction (the cross-border aspects are dealt with in section VII.C).

[40] See Green Paper, above n 37, 65.

[41] Schulte-Nölke, Twigg Flesner and Ebers, above n 4, 422.

[42] Only in Lithuania and Malta do consumer associations not have standing.

[43] Directive 98/27/EC of the European Parliament and of the Council of 19 May 1998 on injunctions for the protection of consumers' interests [1998] OJ L 166, 51, now repealed by Directive 2009/22/EC see below section VII.C.

IV.C ACTIONS FOR DAMAGES

IV.C.1 DIFFERENT APPROACHES IN THE MEMBER STATES

Policymakers and scholars in Europe have shown an increasing interest in resolving the following question: how can consumers effectively join claims for damages that they are unable to bring in court individually, in view of the complexity or costs of procedure. For very small claims, neither small claims procedures, nor arbitration or mediation is a solution. If many consumers with a small claim could therefore act together, they can share the costs.[44] The following broad categorisation can be made:

- —joint actions, where individual claims are merely bundled in a single trial and the outcome only binds parties;
- —representative actions, where rights are assigned to one entity that acts on behalf of the individual plaintiffs;
- —test cases, where a judgment on one individual claim serves as a model for similar cases;
- —real group actions, where a plaintiff acts on behalf of a group of individuals who will be bound by the outcome of the procedure if they have 'opted-in' ('European' type of group action) or unless they have 'opted-out' (US type of class action).

Class actions (opt-out actions for damages to the benefit of a 'class' of persons) are very common in the United States and in other non-European common law countries, eg Australia and Canada. In Europe they do not (yet) or hardly exist (see the few exceptions mentioned hereafter). Although it might be said that there is a kind of creeping evolution towards class actions in Europe, there is still a general reluctance to use the term, because of some of the features of US-type class actions that are very broadly disliked or unknown in Europe: the discovery process, contingency fees and even the opt-out character that is felt to be contrary to the due process of law principle. Industry is generally (and sometimes fiercely) opposed to class actions because it fears that such actions will expose it to heavy costs. The dilemma is obvious: how to ensure that consumers are compensated and businesses deterred from harming consumers while bona fide businesses are not exposed to unmeritorious claims and disproportionate costs.[45]

[44] S Issacharoff, 'Group Litigation of Consumer Claims: Lessons from the US Experience' (1999) 34 *Texas International LJ* 135.

[45] About regulatory enforcement, see A Ogus, 'Better Regulation—Better Enforcement' in S Weatherill (ed), *Better Regulation* (Oxford, Hart Publishing, 2007) 109: 'The costs for traders arising from infringements are significantly broader than the penalties imposed by the law. They include also the "hassle" and personal inconvenience arising from encounters with the victims of regulatory infringements and with public officials, legal and other defence expenditures, as well as any loss of market reputation resulting from the infringement being detected. The same can be said of claims for damages, especially when they involve a large number of plaintiffs, such as in class actions.'

J Stuyck, Class Actions in Europe—Opt-In or Opt-Out. That's the Question[46] **8.20 (EU)**

Opt-in Group Actions

Opt-in group actions exist in Denmark, Sweden, Finland and Italy (and the UK if the GLO is qualified that way).

The Swedish Group Proceedings Act of 2002 was adopted after a report of a Government Commission on Group Actions from 1995. The starting point was the US system of class actions. The conclusions of the Report and the Swedish Act however did not follow the US example.[47] The Act applies to all areas of civil law. Group actions are brought in district courts designated by the Government. The law distinguishes private group actions which can be brought by a member of a group, organization group actions which can be brought in the consumer and environmental area's only, by non-profit organizations and, finally, public group actions which can be brought by the Consumer Ombudsman and the Environmental Protection Agency only.

In all the three forms of group actions the plaintiff can petition for injunctions as well as for damages. Normal rules on causation in tort law and calculation of damages apply.

There is no certification process but class actions are only admissible if they fulfil conditions comparable to those of Rule 23 of the US Federal Rules of Procedure: numerousity, communality, superiority, suitability.

The big difference with US type of class actions is that the Swedish group action is based on opting in. Group representatives are empowered to settle on behalf of the group. However group members are not bound by the settlement unless it is approved by the court. The loser pays principle applies. Contingent fees are not allowed but plaintiffs can conclude a 'risk agreement' with the lawyer.

An association is sometimes established with the aim to present the claims of the members in a particular case. A well known example is the Skandia case. This case concerned the illegal transfer of money between the parent company Skandia AB and other subsidiaries to the detriment of 1.2 million private insurance policy holders of the subsidiary Skandia Liv. To make the procedure more manageable the association Föreningen Grupptalan mot Skandia was founded. The group action was financed by the membership fees and a risk contract with the lawyers.

In the period 2002–2007 nine cases have been brought under this Act.

In Finland, though initially considering to adopt the Swedish model, it was decided to limit the opt in collective action by the Ombudsman. This 'Act on Class Action' came into force in October 2007.

Opt-out group actions or class actions

As such opt-out class actions do not exist in Europe, with the exception of Portugal, in the Dutch procedure on the collective settlement of mass damage 2005 and to a limited extent, since 1 January 2008, in Denmark (ie where a public authority, such as the Consumer Ombudsman, acts).

In *Portugal* a general law on 'people's actions' (acçao popular) has been adopted in 1995. Such action is an action in the collective interest of those harmed. Individual victims as well as the Public Prosecutor and the Instituto do Consumidores (Consumer

[46] J Stuyck, 'Class Actions in Europe—Opt-In or Opt-Out. That's the Question' [2009] *EBLR* 488–89.

[47] See PH Lindblom, *National Report: Group Litigation in Sweden, Paper for 'The Globalization of Class Actions'*, Oxford Conference, 12–14 December 2007.

Protection Agency) can initiate proceedings. The Agency does not seem to use this power, preferring to refer matters to arbitration. There is little information on this procedure, but apparently some Portugese law firms claim to be experts in this field.

As the title of the Dutch law indicates this law does not establish a group action in court but provides for the possibility of a collective settlement, a settlement between a group of plaintiffs, represented by an association, on the one hand, an the defendant on the other. The settlement is then confirmed by the court. The judgment is binding on al members of the class that have not opted out.

In Denmark, as indicated here above, the Consumer Ombudsman (and some other public bodies) can now bring op-out actions for damages.

Notes

(1) In Italy a new Article 140bis was introduced in the Consumer Code, introducing a collective action for damages. The action can be brought by consumer associations and councils and by every member of the class having standing. The procedure is based on an 'opt-in' and is available for damages arising from specific circumstances. The rules should become effective on 1 January 2010.

In Denmark the Act No 181 of 28 February 2007 on group actions entered into force on 1 January 2008. Group actions can be brought by a member of the group, a private organization or a public authority, such as the Consumer Ombudsman. The model is based on an opt-in. However for individual claims not exceeding DKK 2,000 (€270) a public authority can bring an action under an opt out model. The fees are based on an hourly rate with the provision that the rate will be doubled or trebled if the action is successful, and reduced to half if it is not.

(2) An excellent overview of existing class and representative actions in Europe and a discussion of all major issues is given by Christopher Hodges in his book *The Reform of Class and Representative*.[48]

Group Proceedings Act[49] **8.21 (SW)**

Introductory provisions. Group action

Section 1 In this Act, group action means an action that a plaintiff brings as the representative of several persons with legal effects for them, although they are not parties to the case. A group action may be instituted as a private group action, an organisation action or a public group action. Group means the persons for whom the plaintiff brings the action.

Group proceedings

Section 2 Proceedings where a group action is brought are referred to as group proceedings. Group proceedings can relate to claims that can be dealt with by a general court in accordance with the rules contained in the Code of Judicial Procedure on civil

[48] C Hodges, *The Reform of Class and Representative Actions in European Legal Systems. A New Framework for Collective Redress in Europe* (Oxford and Portland, Hart Publishing 2008).

[49] Issued on 30 May 2002.

cases. The provisions of the Code of Judicial Procedure on civil cases apply to group proceedings, except for Chapter 1, Section 3d, unless otherwise stated in this Act. Group proceedings may also be brought in accordance with special provisions contained in the Environmental Code.

How a group action is instituted, etc. ...

Right to bring an action

Section 4 A private group action may be instituted by a natural person who, or legal entity that, himself, herself or itself has a claim that is subject to the action.

Section 5 An organisation action may be instituted by a not-for-profit association that, in accordance with its rules, protects consumer or wage-earner interests in disputes between consumers and a business operator regarding any goods, services or other utility that the business operator offers to consumers. ...

An organisation action referred to in the first paragraph may also include a dispute of another kind, provided there are significant advantages with the disputes being jointly adjudicated taking into consideration the investigation and other circumstances.

Section 6 A public group action may be instituted by an authority that, taking into consideration the subject of dispute, is suitable to represent the members of the group. The Government decides which authorities are allowed to institute public group actions. ...

Special preconditions for proceedings

Section 8 A group action may only be considered if

1. the action is founded on circumstances that are common or of a similar nature for the claims of the members of the group,
2. group proceedings do not appear to be inappropriate owing to some claims of the members of the group, as regards grounds, differing substantially from other claims,
3. the larger part of the claims to which the action relates cannot equally well be pursued by personal actions by the members of the group,
4. the group, taking into consideration its size, ambit and otherwise is appropriately defined, and
5. the plaintiff, taking into consideration the plaintiff's interest in the substantive matter, the plaintiff's financial capacity to bring a group action and the circumstances generally, is appropriate to represent the members of the group in the case. ...

Notifications to the members that group proceedings have been instituted

Section 13 If the plaintiff's application to commence group proceedings is not dismissed, the members of the group shall be notified of the proceedings.

The notification shall, to the extent considered appropriate by the court, contain

1. a brief description of the application
2. information about

a) group proceedings as a form for processing,
b) the opportunity for the members to personally participate in the proceedings,
c) the legal effect of a judgment in group proceedings, and
d) the rules applicable to litigation costs,

3. details of the names and addresses of the plaintiff and attorney,

4. notice of the date determined by the court for notices in accordance with Section 14, and

5. information about other circumstances that are important for the rights of the members of the group.

Definition of the group

Section 14 A member of the group who does not give notice to the court in writing, within the period determined by the court, that he or she wishes to be included in the group action shall be deemed to have withdrawn from the group.

Status of the member of the group

Section 15 A member of the group shall be equated with a party when applying the rules of the Code of Judicial Procedure on disqualification situations, pending proceedings, joinder of cases, examination during the proceedings and other issues relating to evidence. …

Subsequent processing …

Obligations of the plaintiff

Section 17 When conducting the action, the plaintiff shall protect the interests of the members of the group.

On important issues, the plaintiff shall afford the members of the group an opportunity to express their views, if this can be done without great inconvenience. If a member of the group so requests, the plaintiff shall provide such information as is of importance for the rights of the member. …

Settlement

Section 26 A settlement that the plaintiff concludes on behalf of a group is valid, provided the court confirms it by judgment. The settlement shall at the request of the parties be confirmed, provided it is not discriminatory against particular members of the group or in another way manifestly unfair. …

Content of the determination

Section 28 The court shall specify in a judgment the members of the group to which the judgment refers. This also applies to a decision, if this is necessary having regard to the nature of the issue.

Legal force

Section 29 The determination of the court in group proceedings has legal force in relation to all members of the group who are subject to the determination. …

Notes

(1) The Swedish Act has set standards for the European debate on how to deal with collective actions. Contrary to what was originally envisaged, the finally adopted version establishes an opt-in mechanism. The Act provides for private group actions as well as actions brought by organisations and public group actions (sections 4, 5 and 6). Both actions for injunctions and for monetary compensation for group

members can be brought. The Act is not restricted to consumer law or environmental law. It applies in all cases normally brought before ordinary courts of first instance. The group action should only be used when it is practical, manageable and the best procedural alternative ('superiority') (see section 8). This comes very close to the respective provisions in the famous Rule 23 of the US Class Action. If the claim does not meet these demands in practice, it is not accepted as a group action. Finally, the Act is purely procedural. It provides for rules on the notification to the members that group proceedings have been instituted (section 13) and on the obligations of plaintiffs on the conditions under which the members of the group need to be consulted. The court is given a managerial role. It has the task of making sure that the leading plaintiff is taking the interests of the other members into consideration and it has to approve a possible settlement (section 26A). The Swedish Act does not affect the content of substantive law. There are no new rules on causation, calculation and distribution of damages, etc.[50]

(2) The Act entered into force on 1 January 2003. As of November 2008, Lindblom reported that 12 group actions had been initiated before the ordinary courts. There have also been media reports concerning about a dozen cases that have not gone to trial, sometimes because the parties have settled.[51] This remains far behind what has been expected after the new law was enacted.

Gerechtshof (Court of Appeal) Amsterdam, 1 June 2006[52] **8.22 (NL)**
The Companies, The Insurers, Stichting DES Centrum and Stichting BD v W, X, Y and Z

COURT APPROVAL OF COLLECTIVE SETTLEMENT

DES

The exclusion of certain persons from an collective settlement is no obstacle to declare the agreement binding.

Facts: Since 1947 preparations with the synthetic hormone diethylstilbestrol (DES) have been marketed in the Netherlands and prescribed to pregnant women to prevent early birth and miscarriage. Since the 1970s a relationship has been established between the intake of DES and physical harm both to pregnant women themselves and their children. Since 1976 the prescription of DES for pregnant women is no longer allowed. In 1986 Stichting DES Centre brought claims for damages on behalf of women affected by DES before the Dutch courts against ten established pharmaceutical companies that had marketed the hormone. The Hoge Raad (the Dutch Supreme Court) found that the companies were liable (judgment of 9 October 1992). The procedure was suspended because the companies and their insurers on the one hand and the Stichting on the other had started negotiations with a view to a settlement. The settlement was reached in 2000. A DES Fund was established. In 2005 the parties reached an agreement on the compensation of the DES victims. The application in this present case was aimed at obtaining a judicial declaration that the agreement is binding on the beneficiaries mentioned in the agreement. The defendants in this case were

[50] PH Lindblom, 'Class Actions, Group Litigation, Swedish Report'.
[51] Ibid.
[52] AX6440, R05/1743.

persons who were not included in the list. They asked the court to reject the application or to modify the agreement.

Judgment: 5.8. The question arises whether Stichting DES Centre is representative. …

5.9. For many years Stichting DES Center has taken care of the interests of DES-victims. Therefore it has gained national notoriety. Since 1992 it has given DES victims the possibility to register. At the moment of the application 17.000 persons were registered with the Stichting. It is not contested that as far as the number of represented DES victims is concerned the Stichting is representative.

5.10. The agreement is the result of negotiations.
The result of the negotiations, including the amount of the compensation, has to be based on the good and bad chances of the various claims for damages of persons that have been harmed by DES. Possibly the result of those negotiations are short of what some might have hoped or expected, but there is insufficient evidence that a significant group of DES victims that were represented by the Stichting would reject that result. Insofar there is no reason to hold the Stichting not (anymore) representative. Furthermore, the circumstance that other persons have remained outside the settlement does not mean that the Stichting would cease to be representative for the purpose of seeking compensation. …

5.25. The request for a declaration of binding force complies with the legal conditions therefore and there are grounds for a rejection of the request or for supplementing or modifying the agreement. Therefore the Court grants the declaration.

5.26. The Court fixes the time limit of Article 7:908(2) of the Civil Code for a beneficiary to opt out, by a written declaration at three months from the announcement of this declaration according to Article 117(2)(f) Code of Civil Procedure.

5.27. As soon as possible after the moment when this declaration has become definitive the applicants have to make an announcement of:

—the declaration of the binding force of the agreement;

—a short description thereof;

—the way in which payment can be obtained;

—the time limits to claim payment;

—the consequences of the declaration of binding force;

—the time limits for and the way in which the beneficiaries can be freed from the consequences of this Order and the agreement in the website of this Court (www.rechtspraak.nl) and, at their request at the registry of the Court;

—the possibility to consult the same on the website of the Stichting (www.desfonds.nl);

—the possibility to receive, on request, a copy of the Order and the agreement at the Stichting DES Centrum …;

5.28 The announcement referred to in 5.27 has to be made, in compliance with Article 1017(3) Code of Civil Procedure:

—by ordinary mail to the beneficiaries that are known by the Stichting;

—in the national newspapers De Volkskrant and De Telegraaf;

—on the websites of the Stichting DB and Stichting DES Centrum;

5.29. The text of the Order and the Agreement has to be placed on the website of Stichting DB. …

Note

The DES case was the first court-approved opt-out class settlement ever both in the Netherlands and in Europe. The Dutch provisions on collective settlement of mass damages (Article 7:907-910 of the Civil Code and Article 1013-1018 of the Code of Civil Procedure CCP) came into force on 1 August 2005. They make court approval of an (opt-out) collective settlement possible. When parties agree to settle a dispute (out of court), they can ask the court to declare the settlement fair and binding even on non-parties to the agreement (on an opt-out basis). A second court-approved collective settlement was the Dexia settlement relating to retail investment products.[53] A third such settlement is the Royal Dutch Shell reserves recategorisation settlement that was submitted for court approval on 11 April 2007. This may be a landmark settlement as it aims to achieve a world-wide settlement (with the exception of US shareholders).[54]

Question

Are the rights of non-parties who are also bound by the settlement sufficiently guaranteed by an opt-out procedure?

Oberster Gerichtshof (Supreme Court), 12 July 2005[55] **8.23 (AT)**
BAK v VKI

ASSIGNMENT OF RIGHTS TO CONSUMER ORGANISATIONS

BAK

One representative can bring several claims provided there is sufficient communality.

Facts: In this procedure a group action 'according to Austrian law' was brought by an association to which 684 consumers had assigned their claim. The consumers had taken out credit for private purposes from the defendant and considered that they were prejudiced by the revision of the interest rate by the defendant. The total amount of the claims was €1.95 million. The defendant argued that the form in which the action had been brought was inadmissible.

Judgment: The Senat finds the solution proposed by Kodek and Kals convincing. According to these authors the articulation of several claims through one representative is admissible, when the facts on which the claims are based are not identical but when there is sufficient communality between the different clams, ie when the content of the claims is largely similar. In addition the factual and legal questions which may arise under the main issue or as a preliminary question, must be significantly of the same nature.

Notes

(1) Although test cases are used in many Member States, only a few of these countries have introduced provisions that give a judgment in a test case effect over

[53] Gerechtshof (County Court) Amsterdam, 25 January 2007, AZ7033, 1783/05.

[54] See I Tzankova and D Lunsingh, 'Class Actions, Group Litigation, Dutch Report'.

[55] 4 Ob 116/05w.

and above the parties to the test case itself. If anything, the legal effects are binding on those parties who have joined the test case or who have assigned their rights to an association which files action on their behalf. Austria has set standards for the role and function of this particular form of group actions.

(2) In Austria two different forms have been made available: (a) §29 of the Consumer Protection Act, which lists certain institutions competent to bring cases. Among these institutions, the Verein für Konsumenteninformation (VKI) is the one of most practical relevance. The VKI can represent a consumer who assigns his claims to the VKI. If such a procedure is brought by one of these institutions (eg a representative test case procedure according to §502(5) Civil Procedural Act in connection with §29 KSchG) the consumer does not participate in the court proceedings. The final judgment has no legal effect beyond the consumer who assigned his rights and suffered the respective damage. (b) Through a combination of §227, §502(5) of the Civil Procedural Act, the VKI, inter alia, can also act as a representative for more than one consumer and therefore bring a traditional representative action. The action aims at obtaining damages in one single court procedure, which are then distributed among the consumers who have assigned their claims. The consumers themselves do not participate in the court proceedings. The judgment has no legal effect beyond those consumer(s) who have transferred their rights to the consumer organisations.

(3) The judgment of the OGH concerned the second variant. It must be regarded as a breakthrough in the Austrian history of collective action. With its decision the court paved the way for Austrian consumer organisations to engage and professionalise in representative actions. More than 20 cases have been filed with the help and support of process insurers. If the consumer organisation succeeds in obtaining a judgment on the common facts and common legal questions which unite all consumers who have assigned their rights, the consumer organisation often manages to settle the conflict to the benefit of the consumers. The representative action turns out to be a useful tool which pushes the defendants to recognise the legal effect of a judgment beyond its formal boundaries.[56]

(4) Using the Austrian law and the Austrian experience as a blueprint, the German legislator has introduced a similar legal mechanism in §8 Rechtsdienstleistungsgesetz (Act on Legal Services).[57] Consumer organisations are entitled to bring an action on behalf of a consumer before the court provided the consumer has transferred his or her right to the consumer organisation. A claim before the German court is based on a cause of action which a consumer had transferred to the German Consumer Organisation. On this basis the Federal German Consumer Organisation initiated the *Quelle* case in the ECJ[58] (see chapter 5.VII.A.3). The German Act has not yet acquired an importance similar to the Austrian experience. This might be

[56] See for a full account of the results, A Klauser, 'Massenschäden erfordern Sammelklagen—Praxisprobleme aus der Sicht von Verbraucher/innen' in T Gabriel and B Priker-Hörmann (eds), *Massenverfahren Reformbedarf für die ZPO? Verbraucherrecht, Verbraucherpolitik* (Verlag Österreich, Band 33, 2005) 79.

[57] 12 December 2007, BGBl I, 2840.

[58] ECJ, Case C-404/06 [2008] ECR I-2685.

partly due to the fact that Austrian litigation is financed by process insurers, which claim 30 per cent of the gains in the case of success. However, the first cases financed by process insurers are now pending before the German courts.

IV.C.2 RECENT EC INITIATIVES ON COLLECTIVE ACTIONS FOR DAMAGES

In parallel with the initiatives that are being taken in the field of collective actions for damages for breaches of competition law (described in chapter 1), the European Commission (DG Sanco) is investigating the possibilities of introducing collective consumer redress with a more general scope of application. Further studies were carried out in 2008 and a public consultation launched on benchmarks that should be respected by effective and efficient collective redress systems in order to ensure satisfactory redress for consumers. The draft benchmarks were published on the Commission's website.

European Commission, Benchmarks for Collective Redress **8.24 (EU)**

1. The mechanism should enable consumers to obtain satisfactory redress in cases which they could not otherwise adequately pursue on an individual basis.

2. It should be possible to finance the actions in a way that allows either the consumers themselves to proceed with a collective action, or to be effectively represented by a third party. Plaintiffs' costs for bringing an action should not be disproportionate to the amount in dispute.

3. The costs of proceedings for defendants should not be disproportionate to the amount in dispute. On the one hand, this would ensure that defendants will not be unreasonably burdened. On the other hand, defendants should not for instance artificially and unreasonably increase their legal costs. Consumers would therefore not be deterred from bringing an action in Member States which apply the 'loser-pays' principle.

4. The compensation to be provided by traders/service providers against whom actions have been successfully brought should be at least equal to the harm caused by the incriminated conduct, but should not be excessive as for instance to amount to punitive damages.

5. One outcome should be the reduction of future harm to all consumers. Therefore a preventive effect for potential future wrongful conduct by traders or service providers concerned is desirable—for instance by skimming off the profit gained from the incriminated conduct.

6. The introduction of unmeritorious claims should be discouraged.

7. Sufficient opportunity for adequate out-of-court settlement should be foreseen.

8. The information networking preparing and managing possible collective redress actions should allow for effective 'bundling' of individual actions.

9. The length of proceedings leading to the solution of the problem in question should be reasonable for the parties.

10. Collective redress actions should aim at distributing the proceeds in an appropriate manner amongst plaintiffs, their representatives and possibly other related entities.

Note

As explained above, in recent years the European Commission has paid a great deal of attention to improving the effectuation of consumer rights through mechanisms of collective redress. The Commission has recently published the results of two empirical studies in this field,[59] as well as its first policy paper in this regard: the Green Paper, of which we include a short extract, describing the four options it is exploring.

Green Paper on Consumer Collective Redress[60] **8.25 (EU)**

The options are:

—taking no immediate action while continuing to monitor the impact of the national and EU systems which are already in place or are about to be implemented;

—setting up a cooperation scheme between Member States which would extend the protection of national collective redress systems to consumers from other EU countries and recommend to Member States which do not have a collective redress system to establish one;

—putting in place a policy mix of tools which can be either non-binding or binding. The option combines: promoting collective mediation or arbitration, recommending to Member States that they allow consumers to bring small mass claims under their small claims procedure, enabling consumer public authorities who are members of the EU enforcement network to require traders to compensate consumers or to skim off the profit of the traders (this would involve amendments to the Consumer Protection Cooperation Regulation), encouraging business to improve complaint handling schemes and raising consumers' awareness of existing means of redress;

—proposing a non-binding or binding EU measure to ensure that a judicial collective redress procedure exists in all Member States. This would mean that every consumer throughout the EU would be able to obtain adequate redress in mass cases. The issues to be considered for this option include: how the procedure would be financed, the conditions under which consumer organisations or public authorities could bring a mass claim to court, how unfounded claims could be prevented and whether an opt-in procedure (consumers have to take action to join a court action) or an opt-out procedure (consumers are covered by a court action unless they decide to step out) is chosen.

These options as well as a combination of elements from different options could also be considered.

Notes

(1) The European approach to collective actions is rather cautious. It seems as if the European Commission will leave the floor to the Member States. Thus there is room in the Member States for experimenting with quite different solutions.

[59] Study on the Evaluation of the effectiveness and efficiency of CR mechanisms in the European Union (Evaluation Study) and Study regarding the problems faced by consumers in obtaining redress for infringements of consumer protection legislation, and the economic consequences of such problems (Problem Study), 42 on the website of DG Sanco.

[60] Press release of the European Commission MEMO/08/741; for further details see the full text of the Green Paper COM [2008] 794 final; see also Commentation Paper of DG Sanco for the hearing of 29 May 2009 on the website of DG Sanco.

Experience so far remains scarce. It will take time and many more cases will have to be decided before a solid basis might be available for deciding on the feasibility of a European solution.

(2) However, the variety of national solutions will lead to problems in cross-border litigation. It is here where Community action is most urgently needed as neither the Brussels I Regulation nor the Rome I and II Regulations deal properly with cross-border collective litigation (see section VII).

V. CRIMINAL LAW SANCTIONS

Some Member States (eg France) have a long tradition of criminal sanctions in consumer law. Other Member States have introduced such sanctions more recently. Sometimes criminal sanctions are a (seldom applied) alternative to civil sanctions (as in Belgium); sometimes they only apply in the case of serious infringements of certain rules (as in German trade practices law). The sanctions are generally fines only. Imprisonment is exceptional. A recent British law provides for the possibility of imprisonment of directors of companies violating antitrust laws. Fines can apply both to natural persons and to legal persons. In certain Member States, eg the Czech Republic, only natural persons can be criminally prosecuted for infringement of consumer laws.

Czech Penal Code **8.26 (CZ)**

§121 Injuring a consumer

(1) Whosoever causes another's property to suffer damage of no negligible extent by injuring a consumer in a manner including, without limitation, by defrauding such consumer in regard to the quality, amount or weight of goods, or by introducing to the market a relatively large quantity of products, works or services while concealing material defects therein, shall be punished by lawful imprisonment for a term of between six months and three years or by prohibition of its activities or by a pecuniary punishment.

(2) An offender shall be punished by lawful imprisonment for a term of between two and eight years in the event that:

a) it commits a crime according to subsection above as a member of an organized group,

b) it obtains significant benefit from such crime, or

c) it has been lawfully convicted for such a crime in the preceding five years or has been given a suspended sentence of lawful imprisonment for such a crime.

Note

The Czech provision relates to protection of a consumer's property (health is protected in a special, stricter form under different case merits). It is in a way paradigmatic for a policy whereby penal sanctions are regarded as an effective means of consumer law enforcement. Traditionally penal sanctions play a more important role in Roman law countries where they have been used beyond health and safety issues in the field of unfair commercial practices and unfair contract terms. The Germanic law countries, on the contrary, rely on private collective judicial enforcement mainly via injunctions. The European Commission has never developed a policy on the degree to which penal sanctions should be used as a means of consumer law enforcement. It has left the choice to the Member States which goes along with the procedural autonomy of the Member States which the ECJ constantly stresses when it comes down to giving shape to the principle of equivalence and the principle of effectiveness (see the introduction to this chapter).

VI. STATE LIABILITY

The ECJ has recognised that consumers are entitled to compensation vis-à-vis a Member State where they suffer from a violation by that Member State of a Community law duty, such as the failure to implement in a timely fashion and correctly a Directive creating consumer rights. This right to compensation is important because—as was discussed in chapter 1—consumers cannot directly rely on a Directive if this amounts to imposing obligations, not provided for by national law, on other private parties, such as private businesses. The principle was established in *Dillenkofer*. Here consumers were successful. The Federal Republic of Germany was liable for the loss incurred by consumers by the failure of that Member State to provide for a guarantee fund in the case of insolvency of tour operators. The *Paul* case shows certain limits of the *Dillenkofer* doctrine, in particular with regard to state liability for improper supervision.

ECJ Joined cases C-178/94, C-179/94, C-188/94, C-189/94 and C-190/94, 8 October 1996[61]
Dillenkofer ea v Bundesrepublik Deutschland **8.27 (EU)**

STATE LIABILITY FOR FAILURE TO TRANSPOSE CORRECTLY A CONSUMER LAW DIRECTIVE

The insolvent tour operator

A Member State is liable to pay damages to consumers who lost money as a result of the bankruptcy of a tour operator when it has failed to protect consumers against insolvency of tour operators by correctly implementing the Package Holiday Directive.

Facts: Germany had failed to implement Article 7 of Directive 90/314/EEC on package travel, which provides that the organiser and/or retailer party to the contract shall provide sufficient evidence of security for the refund of money paid over and for the repatriation of the consumer in the event of insolvency. Dillenkofer and others, having lost money as a result of the insolvency of a tour operator, claimed damages from the German state. The court found the German state liable for violation of its obligations under the Directive.

[61] [1996] ECR I-4845.

Judgment: 34. According to the actual wording of Article 7, this provision prescribes, as the result of its implementation, an obligation for the organizer to have sufficient security for the refund of money paid over and for the repatriation of the consumer in the event of insolvency.

35. Since the purpose of such security is to protect consumers against the financial risks arising from the insolvency of package travel organizers, the Community legislature has placed operators under an obligation to offer sufficient evidence of such security in order to protect consumers against those risks.

36. The purpose of Article 7 is accordingly to protect consumers, who thus have the right to be reimbursed or repatriated in the event of the insolvency of the organizer from whom they purchased the package travel. Any other interpretation would be illogical, since the purpose of the security which organizers must offer under Article 7 of the Directive is to enable consumers to obtain a refund of money paid over or to be repatriated.

37. That result is, moreover, confirmed by the penultimate recital in the preamble to the Directive, according to which both the consumer and the package travel industry would benefit if organizers were placed under an obligation to provide sufficient evidence of security in the event of insolvency.

38. In that connection, the German and United Kingdom Governments' argument that the Directive, which is based on Article 100a [now, after amendment, Article 95] of the Treaty, is aimed essentially at ensuring freedom to provide services and, more generally, freedom of competition cannot be valid.

39. First, the recitals in the preamble to the Directive repeatedly refer to the purpose of protecting consumers. Secondly, the fact that the Directive is intended to assure other objectives cannot preclude its provisions from also having the aim of protecting consumers. Indeed, according to Article 100a(3) [now, after amendment, Article 95] of the Treaty, the Commission, in its proposals submitted pursuant to that article, concerning inter alia consumer protection, must take as a base a high level of protection.

40. Similarly, the German and United Kingdom Governments' argument that the actual wording of Article 7 shows that this provision simply requires package travel organizers to provide sufficient evidence of security and that its lack of reference to any right of consumers to such security indicates that such a right is only an indirect and derived right must be rejected.

41. In this regard, it suffices to point out that the obligation to offer sufficient evidence of security necessarily implies that those having that obligation must actually take out such security. Indeed, the obligation laid down in Article 7 would be pointless in the absence of security actually enabling money paid over to be refunded or the consumer to be repatriated, should occasion arise.

42. Consequently, it must be concluded that the result prescribed by Article 7 of the Directive entails the grant to package travellers of rights guaranteeing the refund of money that they have paid over and their repatriation in the event of the organizer's insolvency.

43. The next point to be examined is whether the content of the rights in question are identifiable on the basis of the provisions of the Directive alone.

44. The persons having rights under Article 7 are sufficiently identified as consumers, as defined by Article 2 of the Directive. The same holds true of the content of those rights. As explained above, those rights consist in a guarantee that money paid over by purchasers of package travel will be refunded and a guarantee that they will be repatriated in the event of the insolvency of the organizer. In those circumstances, the

purpose of Article 7 of the Directive must be to grant to individuals rights whose content is determinable with sufficient precision.

45. That conclusion is not affected by the fact that, as the German Government points out, the Directive leaves the Member States considerable latitude as regards the choice of means for achieving the result it seeks. The fact that States may choose between a wide varieties of means for achieving the result prescribed by a directive is of no importance if the purpose of the directive is to grant to individuals rights whose content is determinable with sufficient precision.

46. The reply to the first two questions must therefore be that the result prescribed by Article 7 of the Directive entails the grant to package travellers of rights guaranteeing a refund of money paid over and their repatriation in the event of the organizer's insolvency; the content of those rights is sufficiently identifiable.

ECJ Case C-222/02, 12 October 2004[62] **8.28 (EU)**
Peter Paul ea v Bundesrepublik Deutschland

NATIONAL RULES LIMITING STATE LIABILITY

Compensation for lost deposits

National provisions precluding individuals from claiming compensation for damage resulting from defective supervision can be in accordance with EC law.

Facts: Mr Paul et al were customers of the BVH Bank für Vermögensanlagen und Handel AG ('BVH Bank'). In 1987, that bank had received authorisation from the Bundesaufsichtsamt (the banking watchdog) to engage in banking transactions, but it was not a member of a deposit-guarantee scheme. From 1987 to 1992, the bank applied unsuccessfully for admission to the deposit-guarantee fund of the Bundesverband deutscher Banken eV (the German banking association), but it withdrew from the admission process since it did not fulfil the necessary conditions. In 1991, 1995 and 1997, BVH Bank's difficult financial situation prompted the Bundesaufsichtsamt to carry out examinations of its affairs. Following the third such examination, on 14 November 1997 the Bundesaufsichtsamt filed a bankruptcy petition and revoked the bank's authorisation to engage in banking transactions. Mr Paul et al had opened term deposit accounts with the BVH Bank between 1993 and 1995. In the context of the bankruptcy proceedings opened in December 1997, they declared claims in the sums of DEM 131,455.80, DEM 101,662.51 and DEM 66,976.20. In this situation Mr Paul et al brought proceedings before the Landgericht Bonn (Regional Court) against the Bundesrepublik Deutschland for compensation in respect of the losses of their deposits. They claimed that they would not have lost those deposits if Directive 94/19 had been transposed within the period prescribed in Article 14(1) thereof, ie before 1 July 1995. The Bundesaufsichtsamt would then have taken supervisory measures vis-à-vis the BVH Bank before the applicants made payments to that bank. At first instance, the Landgericht Bonn held that the belated transposition of Directive 94/19 constituted a serious breach of Community law by the Bundesrepublik Deutschland and ordered the defendant to pay to each of the applicants the equivalent of €20,000, ie the amount prescribed in Article 7(1) of Directive 94/19, plus interest. According to appellate courts, liability for breach of official duty was precluded in the case of the Bundesaufsichtsamt, which exercises the functions assigned to it only in the public interest. Paul et al thus brought an appeal on a point of law ('Revision') before the Bundesgerichtshof (Federal Court of Justice) and sought an order against the Bundesrepublik Deutschland for payment of damages for breach of Community law. The BHG referred questions to the ECJ.

Judgment: 39. Furthermore, Directives 77/780, 89/299 and 89/646 impose on the national authorities a number of supervisory obligations vis-à-vis credit institutions.

[62] [2002] ECR I-09425.

40. However, contrary to the claims of Paul and others, it does not necessarily follow either from the existence of such obligations or from the fact that the objectives pursued by those directives also include the protection of depositors that those directives seek to confer rights on depositors in the event that their deposits are unavailable as a result of defective supervision on the part of the competent national authorities.

41. In that regard, it should first be observed that Directives 77/780, 89/299 and 89/646 do not contain any express rule granting such rights to depositors.

44. Moreover, as under German law, it is not possible in a number of Member States for the national authorities responsible for supervising credit institutions to be liable in respect of individuals in the event of defective supervision. It has been submitted in particular that those rules are based on considerations related to the complexity of banking supervision, in the context of which the authorities are under an obligation to protect a plurality of interests, including more specifically the stability of the financial system.

45. Finally, in adopting Directive 94/19 the Community legislature introduced minimal protection of depositors in the event that their deposits are unavailable, which is also guaranteed where the unavailability of the deposits might be the result of defective supervision on the part of the competent authorities.

46. Under those conditions, as pointed out by the Commission and the Member States which submitted observations to the Court, Directives 77/780, 89/299 and 89/646 cannot be interpreted as meaning that they confer rights on depositors in the event that their deposits are unavailable as a result of defective supervision on the part of the competent national authorities.

47. In the light of the foregoing, the answer to the second question must be that Directives 77/780, 89/299 and 89/646 do not preclude a national rule to the effect that the functions of the national authority responsible for supervising credit institutions are to be fulfilled only in the public interest, which under national law precludes individuals from claiming compensation for damage resulting from defective supervision on the part of that authority.

Note

The *Peter Paul* judgment made clear that not all Directives that aim to protect certain groups of citizens or consumers confer rights on individuals capable of giving rise to liability on the part of the state on the basis of Community law. According to the ECJ, the Directives at issue could not be considered to confer rights on depositors in the event that their deposits were unavailable as a result of defective supervision on the part of the competent national authorities. Neither were the Directives found to preclude a national rule to the effect that the functions of the national authority responsible for supervising credit institutions are to be fulfilled only in the public interest, which under national law precludes individuals from claiming compensation for damage resulting from defective supervision on the part of that authority. As a consequence of this judgment, the depositors could not claim compensation from the state for damage caused by the national authorities' supervision, which was defective and not in conformity with EU law.[63] In *Dillenkofer*, on the other hand, the ECJ

[63] H van Rijswijck and R Widdershoven, 'Doorwerking van het EG-recht, in het bijzonder in het waterbeheer' (2005) 2 *Tijdschrift voor Milieu Aansprakelijkheid* 54.

granted protection to consumers who had suffered a loss as a result of the insolvency of a private company. That protection was granted by recognising the consumers' right to compensation against the state, which had failed to require tour operators to provide sufficient evidence of security for the refund of money paid over and for the repatriation of the consumer in the event of insolvency.

VII. INDIVIDUAL CROSS-BORDER ENFORCEMENT

VII.A INTRODUCTION

Cross-border litigation raises two important sets of questions: jurisdiction (What court is competent? How is a writ of summons served? How can judgments be enforced outside the territory of the court that has rendered the judgment?, etc) and the applicable law (chosen by the parties? The law of the country of the plaintiff or the defendant?).

The questions in case of consumer claims against businesses are not different, but the solutions may differ. Lawmakers will consider that in many situations consumers are in an inferior position to their counterparty. Hence the court or the law chosen 'by the parties' may not be the expression of the consumer's free will (party autonomy). Being sued abroad or having to sue abroad may also be inadequate for an inexperienced consumer.

Questions of jurisdiction and enforcement have been dealt with in the EU since the entry into force in 1973 of the Brussels Convention of 1968 on jurisdiction in civil and commercial matters. Recently this Convention has been replaced by an EC Regulation, the so-called Brussels I Regulation (Regulation 44/2001 on jurisdiction and the recognition and enforcement of judgments in civil and commercial matters).[64] Specific regulations have been adopted on questions relating to jurisdiction or jurisdiction in specific areas. They will not be discussed here because they are not relevant for consumer law. The Brussels I Regulation contains specific rules on jurisdiction in consumer matters.

EU rules on the applicable law are more recent. The first such instrument was the Rome Convention of 1980 on the law applicable to contractual obligations. Recently this Convention was replaced by a regulation, the Rome I Regulation 593/2008 on the law applicable to contractual obligations,[65] which is more consumer-friendly than the Rome Convention. Finally the, also recent, Rome II Regulation 864/2007 on the law applicable to non-contractual obligations[66] contains, as its name suggest, rules on the law applicable to extra-contractual obligations.

[64] [2001] OJ L 12, 1–23.
[65] [2008] OJ L 176, 6.
[66] [2007] OJ L 199, 1.

VII.B JURISDICTION

VII.B.1 SCOPE OF APPLICATION BRUSSELS I REGULATION

Brussels I Regulation 44/2001 **8.29 (EU)**

Article 1 (1) This Regulation shall apply in civil and commercial matters whatever the nature of the court or tribunal. It shall not extend, in particular, to revenue, customs or administrative matters.

(2) The Regulation shall not apply to:

(a) The status or legal capacity of natural persons, rights in property arising out of a matrimonial relationship, wills and succession;

(b) Bankruptcy, proceedings relating to the winding-up of insolvent companies or other legal persons, judicial arrangements, compositions and analogous proceedings;

(c) Social security;

(d) Arbitration.

(3) In this Regulation, the term 'Member State' shall mean Member States with the exception of Denmark.

Notes

(1) The predecessor to the Brussels I Regulation, the Brussels Convention on jurisdiction and enforcement of judgments in civil and commercials matters, has been enacted as an international treaty though only open to the Member States of the European Community. Adoption through an international convention was the only possibility until the Amsterdam Treaty introduced Article 65(b) EC (cf the introduction to this chapter). New Member States had to accept the Convention as part of the *acquis communautaire* and to ratify it, though an exception was made for the two last enlargement rounds when 12 new members (Bulgaria, Cyprus, Czech Republic, Estonia, Hungary, Latvia, Lithuania, Malta, Poland, Romania, Slovakia and Slovenia) acceded. By that time (1 May 2004 and 1 January 2007), the private international law and jurisdiction rules in the European Union had been brought within the remit of the EC Treaty, and Regulation 44/2001 (Brussels I Regulation) had already replaced the Convention without these 12 ratifications. Therefore, with respect to the Brussels Convention there are now two groups of Member States: the old 15 Member States which have ratified this Convention and the 12 new Member States which have not.

(2) Until 1 July 2007, the Regulation did not apply if the defendant was domiciled in Denmark. An Agreement was, however, concluded between Denmark and the Community concerning the extension of the provisions of the Brussels I Regulation to Denmark that entered into force on that date.[67]

[67] Council Decision 2006/325/EC of 27 April 2006 concerning the conclusion of the Agreement between the European Community and the Kingdom of Denmark on jurisdiction and the recognition and enforcement of judgments in civil and commercial matters [2006] OJ L 120, 22.

(3) The Convention has now ceased to govern the relations between most Member States, but it remains important for the purpose of uniform interpretation and application of the Brussels I Regulation, as the Regulation itself stresses the continuity between the Convention and the Regulation (recital 19). This is the reason why case-law under the Convention remains important and is referred to below.[68]

(4) The Brussels I Regulation only applies where a European element is involved. This element can be the place of the parties' domiciles, the place of delivery, the place of payment, the place where the events occurred, and any choice of another court. It has been suggested that a case that involved the branch office of a defendant not domiciled in the European Community and a consumer domiciled in the same state as the branch office would not bring the Regulation into play as the situation lacks the necessary European character.

VII.B.2 SPECIFIC RULES FOR CONSUMER CONTRACTS

The general rule of jurisdiction under the Brussels I Regulation is that a defendant domiciled in a Member State is to be sued in the courts of that Member State.[69] For consumers, that would mean that they would have to bring proceedings in the supplier's Member State, which may be far from home. Certain disputes, where one of the parties is deemed to be in a substantially weaker position and therefore in need of enhanced procedural protection, are subject to separate jurisdictional provisions in the Regulation. This is the case for consumer disputes inter alia (Articles 15–17). The main idea behind these provisions is to protect the weaker party against being sued in a Member State other than his own, while at the same time giving that party the option to sue in his own country even when the defendant is domiciled in another Member State. The privileged treatment given to consumers, defined in Article 15(1), is described in Article 16.

Brussels I Regulation 44/2001 **8.30 (EU)**

Article 15 (1) In matters relating to a contract concluded by a person, the consumer, for a purpose which can be regarded as being outside his trade or profession, jurisdiction shall be determined by this Section, without prejudice to Article 4 and point 5 of Article 5, if:

(a) it is a contract for the sale of goods on instalment credit terms;

(b) it is a contract for a loan repayable by instalments, or for any other form of credit, made to finance the sale of goods; or

(c) in all other cases, the contract has been concluded with a person who pursues commercial or professional activities in the Member State of the consumer's domicile or, by any means, directs such activities to that Member State or to several States including that Member State, and the contract falls within the scope of such activities.

[68] Reich, above n 10, 299.

[69] Art 2 Brussels I Regulation. In addition, there are 'special jurisdictions' rules, allowing parties to derogate from the general rule, such as Art 5, allowing to sue in the courts of the state where the contract obligation was performed.

(2) Where a consumer enters into a contract with a party who is not domiciled in [a][70] Member State but has a branch, agency or other establishment in one of the Member States, that party shall, in disputes arising out of the operations of the branch, agency or establishment, be deemed to be domiciled in that State.

(3) This Section shall not apply to a contract of transport other than a contract which, for an inclusive price, provides for a combination of travel and accommodation.

Article 16 (1) A consumer may bring proceedings against the other party to a contract either in the courts of the Member State in which that party is domiciled or in the courts for the place where the consumer is domiciled.

(2) Proceedings may be brought against a consumer by the other party to the contract only in the courts of the Member State where the consumer is domiciled."

(3) This Article shall not affect the right to bring a counter-claim in the court in which, in accordance with this Section, the original claim is pending.

Notes

(1) The effect of Article 16 is that the consumer can choose to bring an action either before the courts of the domicile of the business or before the courts of the Member State of his own domicile. By contrast a professional can only sue in the courts of the Member State of the domicile of the consumer. In principle the provisions in Articles 15 and 16 are mandatory. Derogations from these principles are only possible in one of the three situations described in Article 17 (see section VII.B.5).

(2) As these specific provisions only apply to consumer contracts, there is a considerable amount of case-law on the scope of application of these provisions and the similar provisions of the Brussels Convention. The ECJ has consistently stressed the exceptional character of the rules and has adhered to a strict interpretation of the notion of consumer. See in this regard, especially the *Gruber* case, included in chapter 1 (1.30 (EU), at paragraphs 36ff). Mixed contracts were thus held only to fall under the specific provisions when the professional purpose is so limited as to be negligible. In *Shearman*, the ECJ decided that only the consumer himself benefits from these rules, not his assignee.[71] In *Benincasa*, the ECJ decided that persons starting up a business do not fall under the scope of these rules either.[72] Finally, when a consumer by his own behaviour creates the impression that he enters into the contract within the framework of his trade or profession (eg by using a business letterhead or by claiming the right to restitution of value added tax), he may be considered to have validly renounced the protection of Articles 15 and 16, provided that his counterpart has acted in good faith.[73]

(3) Section 4 (Articles 15–17) of the Brussels I Regulation does not apply to all consumer contracts, but only the contracts expressly listed in Article 15(1). Article 15

[70] The official English version says 'in the Member State' but this cannot be correct as the other language versions demonstrate.

[71] ECJ, 19 January 1993, Case C-89/91 *Shearson* [1993] ECR I-139.

[72] ECJ, 3 July 1997, Case C-269/95 *Benincasa* [1997] ECR I-3767.

[73] Cf Reich, above n 10, 299.

presupposes that a *contract* in the sense of a reciprocal agreement has been concluded by the consumer. According to Article 15(1) the protection granted by Article 16 only applies to disputes concerning instalment sales of goods, instalment loans or other credits made to finance a sale of goods, and—and this is certainly the most important category of cases—any other contract concluded by the consumer with a person who pursues commercial or professional activities in the Member State of the consumer's domicile or directs by any means such activities to that Member State (or several countries including that Member State), an additional condition being that the contract falls within the scope of such activities.

(4) Section 4 applies regardless of the value of the goods or services provided under the contract since no upper or lower limit in terms of money has been prescribed by section 4. Consequently, the provisions can be invoked with respect to both small and large claims. Furthermore, section 4 does not require that the goods concerned are of a kind that consumers usually buy.

VII.B.3 THE CONCEPT OF CONSUMER CONTRACT

The scope of Article 13 of the Brussels Convention (Article 15 of the Brussels I Regulation) has given rise to extensive case-law with regard to the question as to whether and to what extent sending sweepstakes to consumers can be regarded as a 'contract', allowing him to sue the company at his domicile. The issue went several times to the ECJ.

ECJ Case C-96/00, 11 July 2002[74] **8.31 (EU)**
Rudolf Gabriel v Schlank & Schick

CAN SENDING SWEEPSTAKES BE REGARDED AS A CONTRACT?

Sweepstakes I

Winning a prize and ordering goods means that a contract is concluded.

Facts: Schlank & Schick GmbH, a company established under German law and having its registered office in Lindau (Germany), sells goods by mail order in, inter alia, Germany, Austria, France, Belgium and Switzerland. In October 1999 Mr Gabriel, an Austrian consumer, received at his private address and in a sealed envelope several personalised letters from Schlank & Schick which he claims were of such a kind as to lead him to believe that, following a draw, he was the lucky winner of ATS 49,700 and that he was entitled to receive that amount simply on demand, subject only to the condition that he ordered at the same time from that company goods for a minimum value of ATS 200, to be selected in a catalogue and entered on an order form attached to those letters. Mr Gabriel duly filled out and returned to Schlank & Schick the relevant documents to claim payment of the financial benefit promised and placed an order for goods in that company's catalogue for an amount in excess of ATS 200. Schlank & Schick subsequently delivered to him the goods which he had ordered but did not send him the sum of ATS 49,700 which he claimed to have won. Mr Gabriel sued Schlank & Sclick in an Austrian Court. Questions were referred to the ECJ by the Oberster Gerichtshof (Supreme Court of Austria).

[74] [2002] ECR I-6367.

Judgment: 38. It follows from the actual wording of Article 13 that it is applicable only in so far as the action relates generally to a contract concluded by a consumer for a purpose outside his trade or profession. …

40. With regard, more specifically, to a contract for the supply of services—other than a contract of transport, which is excluded from the scope of Section 4 of Title II of the Brussels Convention pursuant to the third paragraph of Article 13 thereof—or a contract for the supply of goods, as referred to in Article 13, first paragraph, point 3, that provision sets out two additional conditions of application, namely that the conclusion of the contract was preceded in the State of the consumer's domicile by a specific invitation addressed to him or by advertising, and that the consumer took in that State the steps necessary for the conclusion of that contract. …

44. The concepts of 'advertising' and 'specific invitation addressed' featuring in the first of those conditions common to the Brussels and Rome Conventions cover all forms of advertising carried out in the Contracting State in which the consumer is domiciled, whether disseminated generally by the press, radio, television, cinema or any other medium, or addressed directly, for example by means of catalogues sent specifically to that State, as well as commercial offers made to the consumer in person, in particular by an agent or door-to-door salesman.

45. With regard to the second of those conditions, the expression 'steps necessary for the conclusion' of the contract refers to any document written or any other step whatever taken by the consumer in the State in which he is domiciled and which expresses his wish to take up the invitation made by the professional.

46. It must be concluded that all of those conditions are satisfied in a case such as that in the main proceedings.

47. First, it is common ground that Mr Gabriel has in this case the capacity of a private final consumer covered by the first paragraph of Article 13 of the Brussels Convention inasmuch as it is clear from the case-file that he ordered goods offered by Schlank & Schick for his personal use, without that transaction having any connection whatever with his trade or profession.

48. Second, in a situation such as that in point in the main proceedings, the consumer and the professional vendor were indubitably linked contractually once Mr Gabriel had ordered goods offered by Schlank & Schick, thereby demonstrating his acceptance of the offer—including all conditions attaching thereto—which that company had sent to him in person.

49. Furthermore, that concordance of intention between the two parties gave rise to reciprocal and interdependent obligations within the framework of a contract which has specifically one of the objects described in Article 13, first paragraph, point 3, of the Brussels Convention.

50. Thus, in regard to a case such as that in the main proceedings, that contract relates more specifically to the supply, through a mail-order sale, of goods ordered by a consumer on the basis of a proposal made and at a price specified by the vendor.

ECJ Case C-27/02, 20 January 2005[75] **8.32 (EU)**
Petra Engler v Janus Versand GmbH

CAN SWEEPSTAKES BE REGARDED AS A CONTRACT?

Sweepstakes II

Winning a prize without ordering goods means that no contract is concluded.

Facts: Ms Engler brought an action before Landesgericht Feldkirch (Austria) against Janus Versand GmbH, a mail order company established in Germany, which she said had awarded her a prize. Ms Engler claimed that Janus Versand had given the impression that she had won a prize in a letter personally addressed to her. The Landesgericht Feldkirch dismissed Ms Engler's action for lack of jurisdiction, since it held that she had not shown the connection between Janus Versand and the sender of the prize notification. Ms Engler appealed against that judgment to the Oberlandesgericht (OLG) Innsbruck. The OLG Innsbruck took the view that in order to decide the question of jurisdiction, regard must be had to the Brussels Convention. In that connection, it is necessary to establish whether the action brought by Ms Engler must be regarded as being founded on a contractual right for the purpose of Article 5(1) of the Brussels Convention, whether the action is in tort, delict or quasi-delict for the purpose of Article 5(3), or whether it is covered by Article 13 first paragraph, point 3, of that Convention (corresponding to Article 15 of the Brussels I Regulation). The OLG Innsbruck referred the matter to the ECJ.

Judgment: 34. As regards, more specifically, Article 13, first paragraph, point 3, of the Brussels Convention, the Court has already held, on the basis of the criteria set out in the previous paragraph, that point 3 of that provision is applicable only in so far as, first, the claimant is a private final consumer not engaged in trade or professional activities, second, the legal proceedings relate to a contract between that consumer and the professional vendor for the sale of goods or services which has given rise to reciprocal and interdependent obligations between the two parties and, third, that the two conditions specifically set out in Article 13, first paragraph, point 3(a) and (b) are fulfilled (see the judgment in *Gabriel*, paragraphs 38 to 40 and 47 to 51).

35. However, it must be concluded that those conditions are not all satisfied in a case such as that in the main proceedings.

36. Although it is indisputable that in a situation of that kind the claimant in the main proceedings is a consumer covered by the first paragraph of Article 13 of the Brussels Convention and that the vendor made contact with the consumer in the manner provided for in point 3(a) of that provision, by sending her a personalised letter containing a prize notification together with a catalogue and an order form for the sale of its goods in the Contracting State where she resides in order to induce her to take up the vendor's offer, the fact remains that in this case the vendor's initiative was not followed by the conclusion of a contract between the consumer and the vendor for one of the purposes referred to in that provision and in the course of which the parties assumed reciprocal obligations.

37. It is common ground that, in the case in the main proceedings, the award of the prize allegedly won by the consumer was not subject to the condition that she order goods from Janus Versand and no order was in fact placed by Ms Engler. Furthermore, it does not appear anywhere in the file that, by claiming the award of the promised 'prize', Ms Engler assumed any obligation towards that company, even by incurring an expense in order to obtain the award of the prize.

[75] [2005] ECR I-481.

38. In those circumstances, an action such as that brought by Ms Engler in the case in the main proceedings cannot be regarded as being contractual in nature for the purposes of Article 13, first paragraph, point 3, of the Brussels Convention.

39. Contrary to the submissions of Ms Engler and the Austrian Government, that finding is not invalidated by the objective underlying that provision, namely to ensure adequate protection for the consumer as the party deemed to be economically weaker, or by the fact that, in this case, the letter was sent by Janus Versand to the consumer in person accompanied by a claim form entitled 'request for trial without obligation' and clearly intended to induce her to place an order for goods sold by that company.

Note

At first sight the ECJ takes a clear stand: if the consumer has filled out the coupon and ordered the products, a contract is concluded and Article 13 Brussels Convention/Article 15 Brussels I Regulation applies. If the consumer has received the sweepstake but has not responded to the offer to order products or if the trader has not made such an offer to place an order, Article 13 does not apply due to the lack of reciprocal obligation. From a marketing point of view the situation is relatively similar in both situations. The consumer has to react: either to order the product or to order the prize. The distinction of the ECJ seems artificial as the applicability of Article 13 depends on the prior sales of goods. The ECJ had to respond a third time to a similar question, this time in relation to the Brussels I Regulation.

ECJ Case C-180/06, 14 May 2009, nyr **8.33 (EU)**
Renate Ilsinger v Martin Dreschers

SWEEPSTAKES CAN BE REGARDED AS A CONTRACT EVEN INDEPENDENT FROM THE SALE OF GOODS

Sweepstakes III

Even when a prize is offered and accepted without a sale of goods there can be a contract

Facts: Ms Ilsinger received, at her home address and in a sealed envelope, a letter addressed to her personally from Schlank & Schick. The envelope, on which the words 'Important documents!', 'Please open immediately' and 'Private' were written, contained, inter alia, a message addressed to Ms Ilsinger personally which gave the impression that she had won a prize of €20,000. The next day, in order to obtain payment of the financial benefit promised, Ms Ilsinger tore off a coupon containing an identification number attached to an envelope included in the letter, attached the coupon, as requested to do in the letter, to the 'prize claim certificate' and returned it to Schlank & Schick. Ms Ilsinger states that at the same time she placed a trial order. That assertion is challenged by Schlank & Schick, which submits to the contrary that no goods were ordered by the applicant. However, the award of the prize supposedly won by Ms Ilsinger did not depend on such an order. Four months later, as she had still not obtained payment of the financial benefit claimed, Ms Ilsinger brought an action for that purpose before the Landesgericht (Regional Court) St Pölten as she was domiciled within the territorial jurisdiction of that court. Her action brought against Schlank & Schick was based on national procedural law in conjunction with Article 16(1) of Regulation 44/2001. Schlank & Schick then raised an objection that the Landesgericht St Pölten lacked jurisdiction, arguing essentially that the provisions of Articles 15 and 16 of Regulation 44/2001 were not applicable since they presupposed the existence of a contract for valuable consideration, which was, however, lacking in this case. Participation in the promotional game was not subject to the placing of an order, even on a trial basis without obligation and with the right to return the goods. Furthermore, Ms Ilsinger had not ordered goods and was not therefore entitled to protection as a consumer. Schlank & Schick added that, even assuming that a right of a contractual nature existed under Article 5(1) of Regulation 44/2001, the Austrian courts would not have jurisdiction on the ground that the place of performance of the alleged obligation was in Germany. Mr Dreschers, in his capacity as administrator in the insolvency of that company, approved that line of argument and requested the continuation of the proceedings. The case came before the Oberlandesgericht Wien (Court of Appeal of Vienna), which referred questions to the ECJ.

Judgment: 43. First, in paragraphs 48 to 52 of the judgment in *Gabriel*, the Court found that the condition for application of point 3 of the first paragraph of Article 13 of the Brussels Convention, relating to the existence of a 'contract concluded by' a consumer with a professional vendor, within the meaning of that provision, was satisfied in that case on the basis of the fact that the concordance of intention between the two parties, manifesting itself in the offer of goods made by the mail-order company and the acceptance of that offer by the consumer when he placed an order for such goods as a result, had given rise to a contract concluded between those parties, characterised by reciprocal and interdependent obligations between them and concerning one of the purposes set out in that provision, namely, in that case, the supply of goods.

44. Second, in paragraphs 38 and 54 to 58 of the judgment in *Gabriel*, the Court held that the prize notification was intimately linked to the order for goods and, therefore, to the conclusion of a contract for valuable consideration, with the result that the legal proceedings by which the consumer sought an order requiring a professional vendor to send him a prize which he had apparently won had to be capable of being brought before the same court as that which had jurisdiction to deal with the contract concluded by that consumer in order to avoid, in so far as possible, creating a situation in which a number of courts had jurisdiction in respect of one and the same contract.

45. On the other hand, it must also be recalled that, in paragraphs 37, 38 and 44 of the judgment in Case C-27/02 *Engler* [2005] ECR I-481, the Court excluded the application of point 3 of the first paragraph of Article 13 of the Brussels Convention in a case where the consumer had claimed the payment of the financial benefit promised, even though the payment of the prize apparently won was not subject to the condition that the consumer order goods from the mail-order company and that, in fact, no order had been placed by that consumer.

46. The Court based that solution on the fact that, in such a case, the sending of a letter containing a misleading promise to award a prize had not been followed by the conclusion of a contract by the consumer with the mail-order company, because no order of goods offered for sale had been made, whereas it was clear from its very wording that the application of point 3 of the first paragraph of Article 13 of the Brussels Convention was subject to a number of conditions, among which the condition relating to the conclusion of such a contract by the consumer is specifically mentioned (*Engler*, paragraphs 36 to 38 and 40).

47. The Court takes the view that such an approach is supported by the position of the rules on jurisdiction set out in Articles 13 to 15 of the Brussels Convention over consumer contracts in the scheme of that convention, which give rise to a strict interpretation of those articles which cannot go beyond the cases envisaged by that convention. Thus, the objective underlying those provisions, namely to ensure adequate protection for the consumer as the party deemed to be economically weaker, does not permit a different outcome (*Engler*, paragraphs 39 and 41 to 43).

48. However, it must be held that the wording of Article 15(1) of Regulation 44/2001, the interpretation of which is sought by the national court in the present reference for a

preliminary ruling, is not identical in every respect to that of the first paragraph of Article 13 of the Brussels Convention.

49. More specifically, while the first paragraph of Article 13 of the Brussels Convention limited the field of application of point 3 thereof to 'any other contract for the supply of goods or a contract for the supply of services', Article 15(1)(c) of Regulation 44/2001 is drafted in more general and broader terms.

50. Thus, apart from certain transport contracts excluded from the scope of the rules on jurisdiction over consumer contracts by Article 15(3) of Regulation 44/2001, Article 15(1)(c) covers all contracts, whatever their purpose, if they have been concluded by a consumer with a professional and fall within the latter's commercial or professional activities. Furthermore, the specific conditions for application that those contracts must fulfil, which were set out in detail in headings (a) and (b) of point 3 of the first paragraph of Article 13 of the Brussels Convention, are now worded more generally in Article 15(1)(c) of Regulation 44/2001 in order to ensure better protection for consumers with regard to new means of communication and the development of electronic commerce.

51. It follows that, although the Court has held that the application of the first paragraph of Article 13 of the Brussels Convention is limited to contracts which give rise to reciprocal and interdependent obligations between the parties, basing itself, moreover, expressly on the wording of that provision referring to a 'contract for the supply of goods or a contract for the supply of services' (see *Gabriel*, paragraphs 48 to 50, and *Engler*, paragraphs 34 and 36), the scope of Article 15(1)(c) of Regulation 44/2001 appears, by contrast, to be no longer being limited to those situations in which the parties have assumed reciprocal obligations.

52. It must be stated, however, that Article 15 of Regulation 44/2001 is applicable only if the legal proceedings concerned relate to a contract which has been concluded between a consumer and a professional.

53. By virtue of the actual wording of both the introductory paragraph of Article 15(1) of Regulation 44/2001 and Article 15(1)(c), that article requires a 'contract' to have been 'concluded' by a consumer with a person who pursues commercial or professional activities. That finding is also supported by the heading of Section 4 of Chapter II of that regulation, in which Article 15 appears, which refers to '[j]urisdiction over consumer contracts'. It must also be pointed out that, with respect to the condition relating to the conclusion of a contract, the wording of Article 15 is essentially identical to that of Article 13 of the Brussels Convention.

54. As regards that condition, it is, of course, conceivable, in the context of Article 15(1)(c) of Regulation 44/2001, that one of the parties merely indicates its acceptance, without assuming itself any legal obligation to the other party to the contract (see paragraph 51 of the present judgment). However, it is necessary, for a contract to exist within the meaning of that provision, that the latter party should assume such a legal obligation by submitting a firm offer which is sufficiently clear and precise with regard to its object and scope as to give rise to a link of a contractual nature as referred to by that provision.

55. That latter requirement may be regarded as being satisfied only where, in the context of a prize notification, such as that at issue in the main proceedings, there has been a legal commitment contracted by the mail-order company. In other words, the latter must have expressed clearly its intention to be bound by such a commitment, if it is accepted by the other party, by declaring itself to be unconditionally willing to pay the prize at issue to consumers who so request. It is for the national court to determine whether that requirement is fulfilled in the dispute before it.

56. If that were not the situation in this case, a commercial practice of the kind which has given rise to this dispute could not, without more, be regarded as assuming a contractual nature or as relating to a contract within the meaning of Article 15 of Regulation 44/2001 in its current version.

57. In that latter case, such a situation would at most be liable to be classified as pre-contractual or quasi contractual and might therefore, where appropriate, be covered solely by Article 5(1) of that regulation, a provision which must be acknowledged as having, on account of its wording and its position in the scheme of that regulation, a broader scope than that of Article 15 thereof (see, by analogy, with regard to the Brussels Convention, Engler, paragraphs 44 and 49).

58. In the light of those factors, and in the absence of a substantial difference in drafting between Article 15 of Regulation 44/2001 and Article 13 of the Brussels Convention as regards the requirement of the conclusion of a contract between the parties, it must therefore be held that the case-law resulting from the judgments in Gabriel and Engler, relating to the second of those provisions, must be transposed to Article 15 of Regulation 44/2001 for the purposes of resolving a case such as that at issue in the main proceedings. If there is such similarity between the drafting of a provision of the Brussels Convention and a provision of Regulation 44/2001 it is necessary to ensure, in accordance with Recital 19 in the preamble to the latter, continuity in the interpretation of those two instruments, as such continuity is also the means to ensure observance of the principle of legal certainty, which constitutes one of the corner stones of those instruments.

59. Therefore, it must be held that, in the light of the present wording of Article 15 of Regulation 44/2001, Article 15(1)(c) cannot apply to legal proceedings such as those at issue in the main proceedings if the professional did not undertake contractually to pay the prize promised to the consumer who requests its payment. In that case, Article 15(1)(c) is applicable to such legal proceedings only on condition that the misleading prize notification was followed by the conclusion of a contract by the consumer with the mail-order company evidenced by an order placed with the latter.

60. Consequently, the answer to the questions referred is that, in a situation such as that at issue in the main proceedings, in which a consumer seeks, in accordance with the legislation of the Member State in which he is domiciled and before the court for the place in which he resides, an order requiring a mail-order company established in another Member State to pay a prize which that consumer has apparently won, and

—where that company, with the aim of encouraging that consumer to conclude a contract, sent a letter addressed to him personally of such a kind as to give him the impression that he would be awarded a prize if he requested payment by returning the 'prize claim certificate' attached to that letter,

—but without the award of that prize depending on an order for goods offered for sale by that company or on a trial order,

the rules on jurisdiction laid down by Regulation 44/2001 must be interpreted as follows:

—such legal proceedings brought by the consumer are covered by Article 15(1)(c) of that regulation, on condition that the professional vendor has undertaken in law to pay that prize to the consumer;

where that condition has not been fulfilled, such proceedings are covered by Article 15(1)(c) of Regulation 44/2001 only if the consumer has in fact placed an order with that professional vendor.

Note
The ECJ observed that Article 15(1) Regulation 44/2001 is not identical to Article 13 Brussels Convention: Article 15(1) is drafted in more general terms. However, as to the requirement that a 'contract' exists between vendor and consumer, Article 15 of the Regulation has to be interpreted like Article 13 of the Convention. The ECJ first looked at its *Gabriel* and *Engler* case-law and then made an important differentiation. There can indeed be a contract when the vendor has declared to be unconditionally willing to pay the prize at issue to consumers who so request. It is for the national court to determine whether that requirement is fulfilled in the dispute before it.

VII.B.4 THE CONCEPT OF ACTIVE TRADER

The Brussels Convention only protected the 'passive' consumers as Article 13(1)(c) only covered consumer contracts where the conclusion of the contract was 'preceded by a specific invitation addressed to him or by advertising'. Under the new wording of Article 15(1)(c) of the Brussels I Regulation, it suffices that the trader is active in the sense that he 'directs' his activities to the Member State where the consumer is domiciled. The new wording was subject to a controversial debate between the Member States and the European Commission and has also triggered extensive litigation with regard to the question as to whether marketing activities on the internet, which can be accessed anywhere in the world, are actually 'directed' to the consumer's country or not.

BGH, 17 September 2008[76] **8.34 (DE)**

DIRECTING ACTIVITIES TO ANOTHER MEMBER STATE

Sales advertising via the website of the German embassy in Athens

A passive website which provides for information only does not suffice to constitute jurisdiction under Article 15(1)(c).

Facts: The applicant, a German resident, intended to purchase two freehold flats on the island of K. While visiting the flats he agreed with the flat owner that the defendant, a German-speaking local Greek attorney, should assist with the transaction procedure. The contract was not concluded, as the owner was no longer willing to sell her flats. The defendant therefore refused to use his mandate to sell the respective objects on behalf of the owner. The applicant claimed for compensation through the defendant as the defendant refused to use his mandate contrary to his duty. He found that his claim fell under the jurisdiction of German courts as it was a consumer matter according to Article 15(1)(c) of the Brussels I Regulation; the defendant focused his business on the Federal Republic of Germany as he was listed on the website of the German embassy in Athens, the website of 'Immobilien-K' and on the website of three German defence insurances as an attorney working in Greece.

Judgment: The accessibility of a passive website alone and the fact that consumers may only be aware of such service or possibilities to purchase products through the advertisement of such service or products are admittedly insufficient to fulfil the requirements of the competence norm ... The Council's and Commission's joint declaration on Article

[76] JurPC Web-Dok 182/2008.

15 of Regulation 44/2001 … therefore explicitly reads: '… the mere fact that an Internet site is accessible is not sufficient for Article 15 to be applicable, although a factor will be that this Internet site solicits the conclusion of distance contracts and that a contract has actually been concluded at a distance, by whatever means …'

The defendant did not operate his own website in casu; his contact details were rather distributed through a third party as a service for their own clients respectively nationals. Even if he was listed on the website of the German embassy in Athens as an attorney resident in the district of the embassy, on the website of 'Immobilien-K', and on the website of three German defence insurances and one may assume that these listings, at least the one of the website of the German embassy, were not issued without his knowledge and consent, these facts are not comparable to the operation of an (own) passive website.

Furthermore, the commercial or professional activities have to be 'directed' to the Member State of the consumer's domicile, so that he was at least motivated there to conclude the contract, even if the contract was not necessarily concluded in the domicile state … The norm is therefore, especially if one takes into account its character as exception and the need to autonomous and narrow interpretation of its requirements …, not applicable, when a consumer 'coincidently' concludes contracts with an 'entrepreneur' on a trip outside its domicile state …

Accordingly, one may not assume a direction in the sense of Art 15(1)(c) Brussels I as the applicant's attention on the defendant was undisputedly not raised in Germany or via the internet; he did not even know the websites he made come into fore, on which the defendant is listed. The alleged contract with the defendant was moreover concluded, because he was recommended as attorney through the owner living on K, the applicant thereby found out about the defendant only on occasion of his visit to Greece and met him in situ directly after a flat viewing. If one would affirm a 'direction' even under these circumstances the norm would completely lose its exceptionary character.

The lacked fulfilment of the element 'direction' is so obvious that neither the admittance of a revision in order to clarify legal questions nor a reference to the European Court of Justice is necessary …

Notes

(1) National courts had difficulties in finding out whether under specific circumstances the activity of the other party was directed to the country where the consumer had his residence. The English judges have found the conspicuous formula that the co-contracting party must have 'solicited business' in the consumer's country. This problem arose in particular with regard to internet homepages and other forms of internet advertising. For the Oberlandesgericht Dresden,[77] a website in the German language accessible in Germany is already directed to Germany within the meaning of Article 15(1)(c). The distinction between passive websites and active websites is widespread. It goes back as to a common declaration of the Council and the Commission.[78] Like the OLG Dresden, Austrian courts are rather generous in applying Article 15(1)(c). For them cross-border advertising accessible via a website

[77] (2006) IPrax 44.
[78] Reprinted in (2001) IPrax 259.

is sufficient. The German Supreme Court now took a different and less consumer-friendly position. What is really striking is that the German Supreme Court did not recognise the need to refer the case to Luxemburg. The ECJ will have to decide on the matter soon anyway as the Austrian Supreme Court has recently asked for a preliminary reference on that exact question:

> Is the fact that a website of the party with whom a consumer has concluded a contract can be consulted on the internet sufficient to justify a finding that an activity is being 'directed', within the terms of Article 15(1)(c) of the Brussels I Regulation?[79]

Related to this problem is the question of whether, if a consumer moves to another Member State after the contract has been concluded, he can bring proceedings in either Member State. Under the Brussels Convention it was held that this choice existed with respect to Article 15(1) and (2), but not (3), since the steps necessary for the conclusion of the contract would have been taken in the old Member State. Since Articles 15(1) and (2) of the Brussels I Regulation correspond to the relevant provisions of the Brussels Convention, the consumer clearly has the right to choose the forum in the situations of Article 15(1)(a) and (b) of the Brussels I Regulation, ie for contracts for the sale of goods on instalment and contracts for a loan repayable by instalment. As to the third—and more important—kind of consumer contracts referred to in Article 15(1)(c), ie other contracts where the other party pursues a commercial or professional activity in the Member State of the consumer or directs such activities to that Member State, the decisive factor is no longer the place where the consumer took the steps necessary for the conclusion of the contract, but whether the other party pursues an economic activity in the consumer's Member State. Consequently the consumer should have the right to choose in this case as well.

VII.B.5 JURISDICTION CLAUSES

Brussels I Regulation 44/2001 **8.35 (EU)**

Article 17 The provisions of this Section may be departed from only by an agreement:

(1) which is entered into after the dispute has arisen; or

(2) which allows the consumer to bring proceedings in courts other than those indicated in this Section; or

(3) which is entered into by the consumer and the other party to the contract, both of whom are at the time of conclusion of the contract domiciled or habitually resident in the same Member State, and which confers jurisdiction on the courts of that Member State, provided that such an agreement is not contrary to the law of that Member State.

Notes

(1) Articles 15 and 16 Brussels I Regulation are mandatory. Derogations from these principles are only possible in one of the three situations described in Article 17. The last-mentioned exception in Article 17 presupposes that the agreement is valid according to the law of the Member State in question.

(2) Jurisdiction clauses are of great importance. The Regulation (paragraph 13 of the preamble) puts emphasis on consumer protection, whilst stressing contractual freedom (paragraph 14 of the preamble). Under Article 17, jurisdiction clauses arranged for individually are admissible in passive proceedings, provided that the consumer is granted the choice of additional courts exercisable after the dispute arises, or provided that the consumer may choose the court(s) of the Member State wherein both parties had their permanent or usual residences when the relevant clause was concluded.

(3) Jurisdiction clauses are the true problem in standard contract terms. In *Océano*, the ECJ held that jurisdiction clauses may impair the exercise of the consumer's rights and hold the term unfair.[80] One might argue that the Unfair Contract Terms Directive 93/13/EEC constitutes a *lex specialis* and takes precedence over the Regulation.[81] Although the Regulation affects all types of jurisdiction clauses, the Directive expressly provides for jurisdiction clauses in standard clauses only. In a number of Member States, jurisdiction clauses that do not allow the consumer to bring the claim before the court that would normally be competent have been blacklisted—see, for example, Article 6:236 sub n of the Dutch Civil Code:

> In an agreement between a user of standard terms, and a counterparty, natural person, acting for non-professional purposes, the following standard terms are considered to cause a significant imbalance: a clause that provides for the adjudication of a dispute by a judge, other than the judge competent according to the law, or by one or more arbitrators, unless the counterparty has a period of at least one month, from the moment the user invokes the clause in writing, to choose for the judge that would be normally competent to adjudicate the dispute.

(4) Jurisdiction agreements outside 'consumer matters' as defined in Article 15, are allowed according to Article 23, but only under strict conditions. The strict conditions that were developed by the ECJ mainly with regard to agreements between businessmen cannot be but reinforced in contracts with consumers. The agreement must, above all, include a clear expression of the consent with a foreign forum (Case C-313/85 *Iveco Fiat*).[82] Article 23 requires a written agreement or a verbal agreement which has been confirmed in writing. Article 23 of the Regulation fixes strict conditions as to form, allowing a national court to readily decide whether it has jurisdiction. Considerations about the links between the court designated and the relationship at issue, and about the validity of the clause, are unconnected with those requirements (Case C-159/97 *Transporti Castelletti*).[83]

[79] Reference for a preliminary ruling from the Oberster Gerichtshof (Austria) lodged on 24 April 2009, Case C-144/09 *Hotel Alpenhof GesmbH v Oliver Heller* [2009] OJ C153, 26.

[80] Joined Cases C-240/98 to C-244/98 [2000] ECR I-4941. See ch 4.II.B.3.

[81] H Micklitz, Reich and Rott, above n 10, 7.5 and 7.40.

[82] [1986] ECR 03337.

[83] [1999] ECR I-01597.

VII.B.6 APPLICABLE LAW

In the private international law of most EU Member States, the most important conflict rules regarding contracts were to be found in the Convention on the Law Applicable to Contractual Obligations, opened for signature in Rome on 19 June 1980 and commonly called the Rome Convention or Rome I Convention. The Convention entered into force in 1991 after having been ratified by seven Member States (in this context denoted Contracting States). Since then, it was joined by all of the remaining pre-2004 Member States. A convention on the accession of the ten new (2004) Member States to the Rome Convention was signed in April 2005. The Rome Convention has been converted after long discussions into Regulation 593/2008 on 17 June 2008 on the law applicable to contractual obligations (Rome I).[84] The Rome I Regulation entered into force on 17 December 2009. The Rome Convention did not provide for rules on the choice of law in non-contractual obligations. On the 22 July 2003 the European Commission presented a first draft of the so-called Rome II Regulation and on 21 February 2006 a revised version taking into account numerous suggestions made during proceedings in the European Parliament and the Council. Eventually a new Regulation 864/2007 of 11 July 2007 on the law applicable to non-contractual obligations (Rome II) was adopted.[85] The Rome II Regulation entered into force on 11 January 2009.

VII.B.6.a Contracts—the Rome Convention and the Rome I Regulation

Rome Convention **8.36 (EU)**

Article 3 Freedom of choice

(1) A contract shall be governed by the law chosen by the parties. The choice must be expressed or demonstrated with reasonable certainty by the terms of the contract or the circumstances of the case. By their choice the parties can select the law applicable to the whole or a part only of the contract.

(2) The parties may at any time agree to subject the contract to a law other than that which previously governed it, whether as a result of an earlier choice under this Article or of other provisions of this Convention. Any variation by the parties of the law to be applied made after the conclusion of the contract shall not prejudice its formal validity under Article 9 or adversely affect the rights of third parties.

(3) The fact that the parties have chosen a foreign law, whether or not accompanied by the choice of a foreign tribunal, shall not, where all the other elements relevant to the situation at the time of the choice are connected with one country only, prejudice the application of rules of the law at the country which cannot be derogated from by contract, hereinafter called 'mandatory rules.

(4) The existence and validity of the consent of the parties as to the choice of the applicable law shall be determined in accordance with the provisions of Articles 8, 9 and 11.

[84] [2008] OJ L 177, 6.
[85] [2007] OJ L 199, 40.

Article 5 Certain consumer contracts

(1) This Article applies to a contract the object of which is the supply of goods or services to a person ('the consumer`) for a purpose which can be regarded as being outside his trade or profession, or a contract for the provision of credit for that object.

(2) Notwithstanding the provisions of Article 3, a choice of law made by the parties shall not have the result of depriving the consumer of the protection afforded to him by the mandatory rules of the law of the country in which he has his habitual residence:

—if in that country the conclusion of the contract was preceded by a specific invitation addressed to him or by advertising, and he had taken in that country all the steps necessary on his part for the conclusion of the contract, or

—if the other party or his agent received the consumer's order in that country, or

—if the contract is for the sale of goods and the consumer travelled from that country to another country and there gave his order, provided that the consumer's journey was arranged by the seller for the purpose of inducing the consumer to buy.

(3) Notwithstanding the provisions of Article 4, a contract to which this Article applies shall, in the absence of choice in accordance with Article 3, be governed by the law of the country in which the consumer has his habitual residence if it is entered into in the circumstances described in paragraph 2 of this Article.

(4) This Article shall not apply to:

(a) a contract of carriage;

(b) a contract for the supply of services where the services are to be supplied to the consumer exclusively in a country other than that in which he has his habitual residence.

(5) Notwithstanding the provisions of paragraph 4, this Article shall apply to a contract which, for an inclusive price, provides for a combination of travel and accommodation.

Article 7 Mandatory rules

(1) When applying under this Convention the law of a country, effect may be given to the mandatory rules of the law of another country with which the situation has a close connection, if and in so far as, under the law of the latter country, those rules must be applied whatever the law applicable to the contract. In considering whether to give effect to these mandatory rules, regard shall be had to their nature and purpose and to the consequences of their application or non-application.

(2) Nothing in this Convention shall restrict the application of the rules of the law of the forum in a situation where they are mandatory irrespective of the law otherwise applicable to the contract.

Article 8 Material validity

(1) The existence and validity of a contract, or of any term of a contract, shall be determined by the law which would govern it under this Convention if the contract or term were valid.

(2) Nevertheless a party may rely upon the law of the country in which he has his habitual residence to establish that he did not consent if it appears from the circumstances that it would not be reasonable to determine the effect of his conduct in accordance with the law specified in the preceding paragraph.

Notes

(1) The Rome Convention is in essence based on the overriding idea of putting both contracting parties in a position to make autonomous and responsible decisions.

At the heart of the Convention lies the free choice of law, Article 3. The choice may be implicit or explicit but is crucial for the application of Article 3. From a consumer point of view, the biggest problem is standard terms on choice of laws. There is a great degree of uncertainty concerning the rules applicable to choice-of-law clauses in standard terms, which results from the fact that the Rome Convention allows such choice in consumer contracts in principle and fails to provide for a review mechanism.[86] Maack[87] has convincingly established that a justified need for protection of the consumer can only be derived from Article 8(2) of the Rome Convention if the consequences of the foreign statutory provision have not been recognisable to him. This would mainly concern cases of silence where silence cannot be implied as consent to the choice-of-law clause in the standard terms, as well as cases where the standard terms have not been provided in the correct language. This is supported by the requirement of transparency which is derived from Article 8 of the Convention. The main argument of the approach taken here lies within the interrelation of the principle of transparency as derived from Article 8 of the Rome Convention with the similar principle as contained in Directive 93/13/EEC (see chapter 4). Article 7 of the Rome Convention allows making the protective provisions which are derived from EC Law internationally mandatory and would therefore need to be applied by the courts irrespective of the *lex causae*.[88]

(2) If the applicable law has not been chosen, Article 4 of the Rome Convention applies. The contract shall then be governed by the law of the country with which it is most closely connected. For consumer contracts this will normally be the place of business, or the branch of the seller or party providing the service, and not the domicile or habitual residence of the consumer. The Rome Convention thereby established a 'country-of-origin principle', which can, however, be waived by agreement of the parties.[89] The Rome Convention can thus easily lead to the application of foreign law in cross-border consumer contracts, unless Article 5 applies or the contract is more closely connected to another country.

(3) Article 5 of the Rome Convention regulates consumer contracts without defining them. Here similar problems with regard to the concept of contract arise as under the Brussels Convention and the Regulation (see section VII.B.3). The German Supreme Court has taken a narrow approach, thereby narrowing down the scope of the Convention. Unilateral promises of prizes are therefore excluded.[90] The concept of the consumer is a narrow one. In this respect the standards in the Brussels and the Rome Convention are the same.

(4) Article 5 does not cover every sort of consumer contract. A consumer contract presupposes that movable goods are delivered (ie transactions concerning immovable property, securities, assignment of claims and other rights are excluded) or services are provided or services are financed. The sale of a property or the

[86] Reich, above n 10, 272.

[87] A Maack, *Die Durchsetzung des AGB-rechtlichen Transparenzgebotes in internationalen Verbraucherverträgen* (Baden Baden, Nomos, 2001) 239–40.

[88] Ibid, 207.

[89] Reich, above n 10, 273.

[90] BGH (2006) NJW 230.

purchase of a share in a business will not be subject to Article 5 of the Rome Convention; the financing of the service, however, which is a prerequisite for the purchase, constitutes a consumer contract in terms of the Convention.[91] According to the wording of Article 5 of the Rome Convention, simple consumer credit contracts not attached to the financing of goods or services will not come under the definition of a consumer contract. Such an exemption is clearly inappropriate and can only be explained by referring to the origin of the Convention.

(5) The key problem for the application of Article 5 results from the concept of the passive consumer which the wording of para 2 makes clear. The three variations are all united in the idea that there is a very substantial connection of the contract to the domestic country of the consumer—the contract was preceded by a specific invitation addressed to him or by advertising from a country different from his domicile, the other party or his agent received the consumer's order in a different country, or the contract results from an excursion of the consumer to that other country. The narrow wording has raised concern as to whether Article 5 is applicable beyond its strict wording. The problem could be avoided by considering the consumer protection rules of the consumer's home country as mandatory rules in the sense of Article 7(2) of the Rome Convention. The consumer could thus be protected even in cases where the strict requirements of Article 5 would not be met. The *Ingmar* case[92] seems to indicate that the consumer is protected via mandatory EC contract rules. The case concerned a choice-of-law clause in a contract with a commercial agent doing business in the UK and a US principal, according to which Californian law was to apply. The ECJ relied on protection of the commercial agent by mandatory harmonised EC rules. The judgment could be read so as to imply that Article 7 of the Rome Convention could be a provision having both a theoretical and also practical impact on consumer protection.[93] However, the ECJ has no chance so far to confirm this interpretation of its own case-law.

Regulation 593/2008 on the Law Applicable to Contractual Obligations (Rome I)[94] **8.37 (EU)**

Article 6 Consumer contracts

(1) Without prejudice to Articles 5 and 7, a contract concluded by a natural person for a purpose which can be regarded as being outside his trade or profession ('the consumer') with another person acting in the exercise of his trade or profession ('the professional') shall be governed by the law of the country where the consumer has his habitual residence, provided that the professional:

[91] Reich, above n 10, 275.

[92] ECJ, 9 November 2000, Case C-381/98, *Ingmar GB Ltd/Eaton Leonard Technologies Inc* [2000] ECR I-9305.

[93] For a more detailed view on the topic, see H Micklitz, 'Der Vertragsbegriff in den Übereinkommen von Brüssel und Rom' in R Schulze and H Schulte-Nölke (eds), *Europäisches Vertragsrecht in den EG-Richtlinien* (Trier, ERA, 2002) 71.

[94] The Regulation applies to contracts concluded after 17 December 2009.

(a) Pursues his commercial or professional activities in the country where the consumer has his habitual residence, or

(b) by any means, directs such activities to that country or to several countries including that country,

and the contract falls within the scope of such activities.

(2) Notwithstanding paragraph 1, the parties may choose the law applicable to a contract which fulfils the requirements of paragraph 1, in accordance with Article 3. Such a choice may not, however, have the result of depriving the consumer of the protection afforded to him by such provisions that cannot be derogated from by contract by virtue of the law which, in the absence of choice, would have been applicable on the basis of paragraph 1.

(3) If the requirements in points (a) or (b) of paragraph 1 are not fulfilled, the law applicable to a contract between a consumer and a professional shall be determined pursuant to Article 3 and 4.

(4) Paragraph 1 and 2 shall not apply to:

(a) A contract for the supply of services where the services are to be supplied to the consumer exclusively in a country other than that in which he has his habitual residence;

(b) A contract of carriage other than a contract relating to package travel within the meaning of Council Directive 90/314/EEC of 13 June 1990 on package travel, package holidays and package tours;

(c) A contract relating to a right in rem in immovable property or a tenancy of immovable property other than a contract relating to the right to use immovable properties on a timeshare basis within the meaning of Directive 94/47/EC;

(d) Rights and obligations which constitute a financial instrument and rights and obligations constituting the terms and conditions governing the issuance or offer to the public and public take-over bids of transferable securities, and the subscription and redemption of units in collective investment undertakings in so far as these activities do not constitute provision of a financial service;

(e) A contract concluded within the type of system falling within the scope of Article 4 (1)(h).

N Reich, Cross Border Contracts[95] **8.38 (EU)**

1. Issues for reform of PIL

7.14 The PIL of consumer contract law has been in urgent need of reform. Concerning the proposed reform, the following issues have arisen:

—whether the protective provisions, as opposed to Article 5 of the Rome Convention, should differentiate between contracts concluded within the EU and those concluded outside it;

—whether goods and services are covered uniformly;

—how to deal with the individual situations in which Article 5 of the Convention imposes a special connection, and with contracts concluded on the internet;

—how to ensure the harmonization of the reform with the new provision of Article 15 of Regulation (EC) No 41/2001 which contains a paradigm change from the 'passive consumer' to the 'active trader'. ...

[95] Micklitz, Reich and Rott, above n 10, 279–83.

3. Rome I-Regulation—relation to the Convention

7.16 After long and controversial debates in the European Parliament, it adopted a modified proposal for a Rome I regulation on 29 November 2007. Articles 3 and 5 in the Commission proposal which met strong opposition both from stakeholders and from governments had been redrafted. The critique was concerned with a reference to the choice of 'soft law' in Article 3 and to the 'consumer country principle' in Article 5. The European Parliament to a great extent went back to the formulations in the original Rome Convention, in particular Article 3. Recital 13 of the Regulation clarified that the parties are always allowed to incorporate by reference in their contract a non-State body of laws or an international agreement as 'lex contractus', but within the limits of mandatory law of the State law applicable to the contract. The aspects of the choice-of-law clauses related to the existence and validity of the consent of the parties shall be determined by national law designated by Articles 10, 11 and 13 of the Regulation (Article 3.5).

The default rules of Article 4 had been extended to cover a catalogue of types of contract; usually the law of the seller or provider of services will apply. A contract to a right in rem in immovable property or to a tenancy of immovable property shall be governed by the law of the country where the property is located, with an exception to a tenancy of less than 6 months.

Special rules had been inserted for contracts of carriage (Article 5) and insurance contracts (Article 7). The general norm for consumer contracts will be a new Article 6 ...

4. Reformulation of consumer contracts

7.17 ... Article 6 on consumer contracts as defined by the European parliament has universal application, that is it applies whether consumers reside in the EU or not. It had been modified in two important directions by closely following Article 15 of the Brussels Regulation 44/2001; recital (7) of the Rome I Regulation requires consistent interpretation: it applies now to any consumer contract, thus replacing the narrow formulation in Article 5 of the Rome Convention which was limited to the sale of goods and the provision of services and their financing, but not to simple consumer credit; there are exceptions for certain types of financial instruments which need to be governed by 'a single law' according to recital 29 (Article 6(4), (d) and (e); contracts relating to rights in rem including lease and tenancy (lit c); it is sufficient that the 'professional' directs his marketing activities to the country of the consumer's habitual residence.

On the other hand, the balancing test of the Rome Convention in the case of choice of law has been maintained. The main reason is not to impede the trader from doing cross-border business on the internet and submit him to all the provisions of the consumer's country of residence; this was regarded as an unnecessary impediment to cross-border marketing. This rule applies notwithstanding whether the professional is doing business from 'inside' or 'outside' the EU since the Regulation enjoys universal application according to Article 2.

The concept of 'directing' activities which was left unclear in the Brussels Regulation particularly with regard to e-commerce ... was defined in recital 24 by reference to a joint declaration of the Council and the Commission to the prior Article 15: '... for Art 15 (1) to be applicable it is not sufficient for an undertaking to target its activities at the Member State of the consumer's residence, or a number of Member States including that Member State; a contract must also be concluded within the framework of its activities ... the mere fact that an Internet site is accessible is not sufficient for Art 15 to be applicable, although a factor will be that this Internet site solicits the conclusion of a distance contracts and that a contract has actually been concluded at a distance, by whatever means. In this respect, the language or currency which a website uses does not constitute a relevant factor.'

This declaration is by no means clear and needs interpretation. Problematic is the case of the so-called 'active consumer' who travels abroad and should at least be protected by the mandatory provisions of the law of the country of his temporary stay; this seems to be excluded by Article 6, according to Garcímartin a 'loophole of the text' which would allow unlimited free choice under Article 3(1).

Article 9(2) contains the provision on the application of the mandatory provisions of the law of the forum which are now reformulated to 'overriding mandatory provisions', thus taking up the case law of the ECJ in Arblade [Joined Cases C-369 and C-376/96], referring to such provisions which are regarded 'as crucial by a country for safeguarding its political, social or economic organisation, to such an extent that they are applicable to any situation falling within their scope, irrespective of the law otherwise applicable to the contract under his Regulation'. This is quite a narrow definition which must be interpreted strictly according to recital 37, thus excluding most consumer protection norms of Member States beyond EC law. Para (3) of Article 9 allows the application of 'overriding mandatory provisions' of the law of the country where the obligations arising out of the contract have to be or have been performed' ... The application is however not imposed on Member countries, but is only optional. [references omitted]

Note

Article 6 of the Rome I Regulation provides that the law of the consumer's habitual residence shall govern a contract under three conditions: (i) the contract must be a contract concluded by a consumer and a professional; (ii) the professional must direct business activities to the consumer's habitual place of residence; (iii) the contract must fall within the scope of such activities. Here similar issues arise as with regard to Article 15(1)(c) of the Brussels I Regulation 44/2001.

Article 6 departs from the Rome Convention in several respects. Firstly, it mainly provides for the application of the law of the Member State in which the consumer has his habitual residence and does not start from the principle of free choice of law applied under the Convention. Secondly, it defines consumer contracts with exclusive reference to the persons involved and thus does not follow the Convention's approach of defining consumer contracts with additional reference to the object of the contract.[96] Thirdly, it restricts the application of the consumer's law with the help of the targeted activity criterion and thus replaces the long and complex, yet incomplete, list of conditions applied under the Convention to limit the principle of free party choice of law.

However—and contrary to the original proposal[97]—even under the Rome I Regulation the contracting parties may determine the governing law by choice. Like the Rome Convention, such a choice of law must not deprive the consumer of the protection granted to him by mandatory provisions of the law of the country of his

[96] There are, however, a number of express exclusions, see J Hill, *Cross Border Consumer Contracts* (Oxford, Oxford University Press, 2008) 12.55–68.

[97] COM (2005) 650, and Hill, above n 98, 12.16.

habitual residence (Article 6(2) Rome I Regulation). This makes it necessary to compare the level of protection guaranteed under the relevant national legal orders.

In addition, and especially relevant for contracts that do not fall within the scope of application, Article 9(2) of the Rome I Regulation provides that the Regulation does not restrict the application of 'overriding mandatory provisions' of the forum. The standard set seems, however, tighter than in Article 7(2) of the Rome Convention.[98]

VII.B.6.b Contracts—secondary Community Law

The Rome I Regulation does not fully harmonise the applicable law in consumer contracts. There are rules on the applicable law in a number of Directives varying in scope and outlook, though to a diminishing degree. Article 9 of Directive 94/47/EC on time-sharing still stated:

> The Member States shall take the measures necessary to ensure that, whatever the law applicable may be, the purchaser is not deprived of the protection afforded by this Directive, if the immovable property concerned is situated within the territory of a Member State.

The revised Directive 2008/122/EC contains rules on the applicable law only with regard to non-EU Member States.[99]

Unfair Terms Directive 93/13/EEC **8.39 (EU)**

Article 6 (2) Member States shall take the necessary measures to ensure that the consumer does not lose the protection granted by this Directive by virtue of the choice of the law of a non-Member country as the law applicable to the contract if the latter has a close connection with the territory of the Member States.

Electronic Commerce Directive 2000/31/EC **8.40 (EU)**

Article 3 Internal market

(1) Each Member State shall ensure that the information society services provided by a service provider established on its territory comply with the national provisions applicable in the Member State in question which fall within the coordinated field.

(2) Member States may not, for reasons falling within the coordinated field, restrict the freedom to provide information society services from another Member State.

(3) Paragraphs 1 and 2 shall not apply to the fields referred to in the Annex.

Annex Derogations from Article 3

As provided for in Article 3(3), Article 3(1) and (2) do not apply to: ...

—the freedom of the parties to choose the law applicable to their contract,

[98] Cf Recital (37).

[99] See Art 12(2) Directive 2008/122/EC [2009] OJ L 33, 10.

—contractual obligations concerning consumer contacts,
—formal validity of contracts creating or transferring rights in real estate where such contracts are subject to mandatory formal requirements of the law of the Member State where the real estate is situated,
—the permissibility of unsolicited commercial communications by electronic mail.

Credit Agreements for Consumers Directive 2008/48/EC **8.41 (EU)**

Article 22 (2) Member States shall ensure that consumers may not waive the rights conferred on them by the provisions of national law implementing or corresponding to this Directive.

Note

The European Community has not taken a consistent approach so far. There are Directives which do not contain rules on the applicable law at all, such as Directive 85/577/EEC on doorstep selling and Directive 90/314/EEC on package tours. Here the Rome Convention, respectively the Rome I Regulation, will prevail. On the other hand there are Directives which contain particular rules on the applicable law, thereby setting somewhat different standards.

Article 6(2) of the Unfair Contract Terms Directive 93/13/EEC is of practical importance mainly with regard to those consumer contracts that are not covered by Article 6 of the Rome I Regulation (eg because the professional did not direct his activities to the country of the consumer) but, in the absence of choice of law by the parties, would be governed by the law of a Member State. Some of the Member States have implemented Article 6(2) in a more far-reaching and consumer-friendly manner than is warranted by its wording. This is permitted by the Directive's Article 8, which allows the Member States to adopt or retain more stringent provisions to ensure a maximum degree of protection for the consumer, but it is doubtful whether such extensive implementation, going beyond what the Directive requires and varying from Member State to Member State, is compatible with Article 20 of the Rome Convention, as that Article gives precedence to national laws merely to the extent they are harmonised in implementation of EC instruments. The provision giving rise to Community conflict-of-law rules was maintained in Article 23 of the Rome I Regulation. Be that as it may, the recent Proposal for a Directive on Consumer Rights no longer contains any rules on private international law at all.[100]

Directive 2000/31/EC on electronic commerce establishes a country-of-origin principle, which could be seen to be in conflict with the primacy the Rome Convention and the Rome I Regulation give to the law of the country in which the consumer is habitually resident. The most important exceptions from the country-of-origin principle follow from Article 3(3) of Directive 2000/31/EC on electronic commerce, which stipulates that the first two paragraphs of Article 3 do not apply in

[100] See COM [2008] 614 final.

the fields referred to in an Annex. In view of the general exclusion of private international law from the scope of the Directive (see its Article 1(4)), it is surprising and confusing to find the freedom of the parties to choose the law applicable to their contract among the exclusions in the Annex, which in addition refers to certain other typical matters of private law, such as contractual obligations concerning consumer contracts and formal validity of certain contracts concerning real property. Other authors see no possible conflict or room for confusion as Article 3 of Directive 2000/31/EC should be interpreted as only dealing with the legal regulation of information society service providers and not with the law applicable to transactions that take place via the internet.[101]

It remains to be seen whether the European Commission will at least be successful in the ongoing revision of the *consumer acquis*[102] to do away with these differences and to establish one coherent approach. The Rome I Convention, respectively the Rome I Regulation, would then set the standard for all sorts of consumer contracts. However, the Electronic Commerce Directive would remain the exception to the rule.

VII.B.6.c Torts and other non-contractual obligations

Regulation 864/2007 on the Law Applicable to Non-Contractual Obligations (Rome II Regulation) **8.42 (EU)**

Article 1 Scope

(1) This Regulation shall apply, in situations involving a conflict of laws, to non-contractual obligations in civil and commercial matters. It shall not apply, in particular, to revenue, customs or administrative matters or to the liability of the State for acts and omissions in the exercise of State authority (acta iure imperii).

(2) The following shall be excluded from the scope of this Regulation:

(a) Non-contractual obligations arising out of family relationships and relationships deemed by the law applicable to such relationships to have comparable effects including maintenance obligations;

(b) Non-contractual obligations arising out of matrimonial property regimes, property regimes of relationships deemed by the law applicable to such relationships to have comparable effects to marriage, and wills and succession;

(c) Non-contractual obligations arising under bills of exchange, cheques and promissory notes and other negotiable instruments to the extent that the obligations under such other negotiable instruments arise out of their negotiable character;

(d) Non-contractual obligations arising out of the law of companies and other bodies corporate or unincorporated regarding matters such as the creation, by registration or otherwise, legal capacity, internal organisation or winding-up of companies and other bodies corporate or unincorporated, the personal liability of officers and members as such for the obligations of the company or body and the personal liability of auditors to a company or to its members in the statutory audits of accounting documents;

[101] Hill, above n 98, 12.27.

[102] See COM [2006] 744 final.

(e) Non-contractual obligations arising out of the relations between the settlers, trustees and beneficiaries of a trust created voluntarily;

(f) Non-contractual obligations arising out of nuclear damage;

(g) Non-contractual obligations arising out of violations of privacy and rights relating to personality, including defamation.

Article 14 Freedom of choice

(1) The parties may agree to submit non-contractual obligations to the law of their choice:

(a) By an agreement entered into after the event giving rise to the damage occurred; or

(b) Where all the parties are pursuing a commercial activity, also by an agreement freely negotiated before the event giving rise to the damage occurred.

The choice shall be expressed or demonstrated with reasonable certainty by the circumstances of the case and shall not prejudice the rights of third parties.

(2) Where all the elements relevant to the situation at the time when the event giving rise to the damage occurs are located in a country other than the country whose law has been chosen, the choice of the parties shall not prejudice the application of provisions of the law of that other country which cannot be derogated from by agreement.

(3) Where all the elements relevant to the situation at the time when the event giving rise to the damage occurs are located in one or more of the Member States, the parties' choice of the law applicable other than that of a Member State shall not prejudice the application of provisions of Community law, where appropriate as implemented in the Member State of the forum, which cannot be derogated from by agreement.

Note

(1) This Regulation applies from 11 January 2009 (see Article 32). Non-contractual obligations comprise both obligations arising out of a tort/delict and obligations resulting from unjust enrichment and *negotiorum gestio* (agency without authority). Furthermore, the Regulation will apply not only to compensation for damage that has already arisen but also to actions to prevent future damage (Article 2). The Regulation's conflict rules do not require reciprocity, and any law specified by the Regulation will be applied regardless of whether or not it is the law of a Member State (Article 3).

(2) Pursuant to its Article 1, the Regulation applies to conflicts of law regarding non-contractual obligations in civil and commercial matters, excluding matters of revenue, customs or administrative law.

(3) Article 15 of the Regulation contains a non-exhaustive list of issues that are governed by the law applicable to a non-contractual obligation: inter alia, the basis and extent of liability, the grounds for exemption from liability, any limitation of liability and any division of liability, the existence and kinds of injury or damage for which compensation may be due, the assessment of the damage, the question of whether a right to compensation may be assigned or inherited, the liability for the acts of another person and the manner in which an obligation may be extinguished including time limitation. The law applicable to non-contractual obligations also governs the measures which a court has the power to exercise in order to prevent or

terminate injury or damage (eg the power to issue an injunction prohibiting certain harmful behaviour), but only within the limits of the court's powers under its own procedural law. Procedure and evidence are otherwise in principle excluded from the Regulation (Article 1), but Article 22 provides that the law governing the non-contractual obligation will apply to presumptions of law and the burden of proof pertaining to such obligations.

(4) Some general problems of tort law are dealt with by separate conflict rules, eg direct action against the wrongdoer's insurer (Article 18), subrogation (Article 19) and multiple liability (Article 20). A number of other Articles deal with some general questions of private international law, such as overriding mandatory rules (Articles 16), exclusion of *renvoi* (Article 24), states with more than one legal system (Article 25) and public policy (Article 26). In particular, with respect to US law, it should be noted that Recital 32 declares that the application of rules awarding excessive non-compensatory damages (eg exemplary or punitive damages) may be considered incompatible with the public policy of the forum. The practical value of this declaration seems to be merely that the ECJ cannot find the use of the public policy exception in such cases to be abusive.

(5) In contrast to contractual obligations, parties to a non-contractual liability dispute do not normally have the opportunity to agree on applicable law in advance. The parties, however, may wish to agree on a law of their choice after their dispute has arisen, eg in order to avoid the high costs of procuring information about the otherwise applicable foreign law. According to Article 14 of the Regulation, such choice will be respected provided that the choice is expressed or demonstrated with reasonable certainty by the circumstances of the case. Except in relations between businessmen, such choice can be made only after the dispute has arisen.

Regulation 864/2007 on the Law Applicable to Non-Contractual Obligations (Rome II Regulation) **8.43 (EU)**

Article 4 General rule

(1) Unless otherwise provided for in this Regulation, the law applicable to a non-contractual obligation arising out of a tort/delict shall be the law of the country in which the damage occurs irrespective of the country in which the event giving rise to the damage occurred and irrespective of the country or countries in which the indirect consequences of that event occur.

(2) However, where the person claimed to be liable and the person sustaining damage both have their habitual residence in the same country at the time when the damage occurs, the law of that country shall apply.

(3) Where it is clear from all the circumstances of the case that the tort/delict is manifestly more closely connected with a country other than that indicated in paragraphs 1 or 2, the law of that other country shall apply. A manifestly closer connection with another country might be based in particular on a pre-existing relationship between the parties, such as a contract, that is closely connected with the tort/delict in question.

Notes

(1) With respect to situations where the parties have not agreed on the law to be applied to a non-contractual obligation, Article 4(1) prescribes that the law applicable is the law of the country in which the direct damage arose, irrespective of the country in which the event giving rise to the damage occurred or the indirect consequences of that event arose.

(2) Article 4 contains two exceptions to the application of the law of the country of the damage. The first exception in Article 4(2) stipulates that if both the person claimed to be liable (the alleged wrongdoer) and the person suffering direct damage (the alleged victim) have their habitual residence in the same country at the time of the damage, the law of that country will be applied. Habitual residence of companies and other legal persons is defined in Article 23 as the place of the central administration, unless the event giving rise to the damage occurs or the damage arises in the course of operation of a subsidiary, branch or another establishment (in which case the place where the branch, agency or any other establishment is located is treated as the place of habitual residence). If the damage has arisen in the course of the business activity of a natural person, the principal place of business of that person will be treated as his habitual residence.

(3) The second exception to the application of the law of the country of the damage is found in Article 4(3) and pertains to those cases where it is clear from all the circumstances that the tort/delict is manifestly more closely connected with some other country. The law of that country then applies.

Regulation 864/2007 on the Law Applicable to Non-Contractual Obligations (Rome II Regulation) **8.44 (EU)**

Article 5 Product liability

(1) Without prejudice to Article 4(2), the law applicable to a non-contractual obligation arising out of damage caused by a product shall be:

(a) The law of the country in which the person sustaining the damage had his or her habitual residence when the damage occurred, if the product was marketed in that country; or, failing that,

(b) The law of the country in which the product was acquired, if the product was marketed in that country; or, failing that,

(c) The law of the country in which the damage occurred, if the product was marketed in that country.

However, the law applicable shall be the law of the country in which the person claimed to be liable is habitually resident if he or she could not reasonably foresee the marketing of the product, or a product of the same type, in the country the law of which is applicable under (a),(b) or(c).

(2) Where it is clear from all the circumstances of the case that the tort/delict is manifestly more closely connected with a country other than that indicated in paragraph 1, the law of that other country shall apply. A manifestly closer connection with another country might be based in particular on a pre-existing relationship between the parties, such as a contract, that is closely connected with the tort/delict in question.

Note

A conflict rule on liability arising out of a damage or risk of damage caused by a defective product (product liability) is found in Article 5, which stipulates the application of the law of the country where the victim is habitually resident at the time of the damage, unless the person alleged to be liable can show that he could not reasonably foresee the product being marketed in that country. In the last-mentioned situation, the law of the country of the habitual residence of the person claimed to be liable will be applied instead.

Regulation 864/2007 on the Law Applicable to Non-Contractual Obligations (Rome II Regulation) **8.45 (EU)**

Article 6 Unfair competition and acts restricting free competition

(1) The law applicable to a non-contractual obligation arising out of an act of unfair competition shall be the law of the country where competitive relations or the collective interests of consumers are, or are likely to be, affected.

Note

Non-contractual obligations arising out of unfair commercial practices are governed pursuant to Article 7 by the law of the country (countries) of the directly and substantially affected market(s). However, if the act merely affects the interests of a specific competitor, Article 4 will apply (Article 6(2)). This means, for example, that if both competitors reside in the same country, the law of that country will apply, unless the obligation is manifestly more closely connected with another country. The new rule brings an end to the protracted conflict fought in various Member States over the question of the applicable law in cross-border unfair commercial practices.[103]

VII.C COLLECTIVE CROSS-BORDER ENFORCEMENT VIA ACTIONS FOR INJUNCTIONS

The European Community adopted two pieces of legislation for cross-border enforcement, each with a different approach. Directive 98/27/EC[104] relies heavily on consumer harmonisation playing a prominent role in trans-border enforcement. Regulation 2006/2004,[105] on the contrary, relies on the co-operation of public agencies in the handling of trans-border litigation. A codified version of Directive 98/27/EC, which had been amended substantially several times, was recently adopted:

[103] With regard to the German debate in particular in transborder enforcement via injunctions, see H-W Micklitz at §31.17–25 in N Reich and H-W Micklitz, *Europäisches Verbraucherrecht* (Baden Baden, Nomos, 2003). See also below 8.48 (BE).

[104] Directive 98/27/EC of the European Parliament and the Council of 19 May 1998 on injunctions for the protection of consumers' interests, [1998] OJ L 166, 51.

[105] [2004] OJ L 364, 1.

Directive 2009/22/EC,[106] which repeals Directive 98/27/EC but that does not involve substantial changes. References to the repealed directive are to be construed as references to the codified directive (Article 9 Directive 2009/22/EC).

Directive 2009/22/EC on injunctions for the protection of consumers' interests **8.46 (EU)**

Article 1 Scope

(1) The purpose of this Directive is to approximate the laws, regulations and administrative provisions of the Member States relating to actions for an injunction referred to in Article 2 aimed at the protection of the collective interests of consumers included in the Directives listed in Annex I, with a view to ensuring the smooth functioning of the internal market.

(2) For the purposes of this Directive, an infringement means any act contrary to the Directives listed in Annex I as transposed into the internal legal order of the Member States which harms the collective interests referred to in paragraph 1.

Article 2 Actions for an injunction

(1) Member States shall designate the courts or administrative authorities competent to rule on proceedings commenced by qualified entities within the meaning of Article 3 seeking:

(a) an order with all due expediency, where appropriate by way of summary procedure, requiring the cessation or prohibition of any infringement;

(b) where appropriate, measures such as the publication of the decision, in full or in part, in such form as deemed adequate and/or the publication of a corrective statement with a view to eliminating the continuing effects of the infringement;

(c) in so far as the legal system of the Member State concerned so permits, an order against the losing defendant for payments into the public purse or to any beneficiary designated in or under national legislation, in the event of failure to comply with the decision within a time limit specified by the courts or administrative authorities, of a fixed amount for each day's delay or any other amount provided for in national legislation, with a view to ensuring compliance with the decisions.

(2) This Directive shall be without prejudice to the rules of private international law with respect to the applicable law, that is, normally, either the law of the Member State where the infringement originated or the law of the Member State where the infringement has its effects.

Article 3 Entities qualified to bring an action

For the purposes of this Directive, a 'qualified entity' means any body or organisation which, being properly constituted according to the law of a Member State, has a legitimate interest in ensuring that the provisions referred to in Article 1 are complied with, in particular:

(a) one or more independent public bodies, specifically responsible for protecting the interests referred to in Article 1, in Member States in which such bodies exist; and/or

[106] Directive 2009/29/EC of the European Parliament and the Council of 23 April 2009 on injunctions for the protection of consumers' interests [2009] OJ L 110, 30.

(b) organisations whose purpose is to protect the interests referred to in Article 1, in accordance with the criteria laid down by the national law.

Article 4 Intra-Community infringements

(1) Each Member State shall take the measures necessary to ensure that, in the event of an infringement originating in that Member State, any qualified entity from another Member State where the interests protected by that qualified entity are affected by the infringement, may apply to the court or administrative authority referred to in Article 2, on presentation of the list provided for in paragraph 3 of this Article. The courts or administrative authorities shall accept this list as proof of the legal capacity of the qualified entity without prejudice to their right to examine whether the purpose of the qualified entity justifies its taking action in a specific case.

(2) For the purposes of intra-Community infringements, and without prejudice to the rights granted to other entities under national legislation, the Member States shall, at the request of their qualified entities, communicate to the Commission that these entities are qualified to bring an action under Article 2. The Member States shall inform the Commission of the name and purpose of these qualified entities.

(3) The Commission shall draw up a list of the qualified entities referred to in paragraph 2, with the specification of their purpose. This list shall be published in the Official Journal of the European Union; changes to this list shall be published without delay and the updated list shall be published every six months.

C Twigg-Flesner, Comparative Analysis[107] **8.47 (EU)**

The Directive 98/27 requires that all member states make it possible for qualified entities to take action before domestic courts to protect the various specific rights given to consumers under the measures implementing the EC directives on consumer law into the domestic legal system. Such action may be taken for purely domestic problems, ie, an entity from member state A can taken action before the courts in that state to prevent infringements of the relevant legislation by a trader from that state. In addition, the Directive 98/27 introduces specific provisions on the cross-border enforcement of such rights by allowing qualified entities from one member state to take action against a trader from another member state in the courts of that trader's jurisdiction.

The Directive 98/27 therefore differs from all of the other directives under consideration in this study, because it does not confer any specific rights on individual consumers. Rather, this measure is concerned with the enforcement of consumer law by „qualified entities'. Such entities are empowered to seek an injunction to protect the 'collective interests' of consumers. It is not dealing with class actions by consumers against traders.

The structure of this particular analysis therefore adopts a different format from the analyses of the directives covered so far, concentrating on the procedural rules specified in the Directive 98/27, and the use of the minimum harmonization clause in Art 7 of the Directive. It should be noted that even that clause is not a minimum harmonization clause as they appear in the other consumer directives, because Art 7 of the Directive is not concerned with granting consumers a higher degree of protection, but rather permits the adoption/maintenance of more extensive rights to take action at the national level. …

[107] In Schulte-Nölke, Ebers and Twigg-Flesner, above n 4, 579.

Article 1(2) of the Directive 98/27 sets out the definition of 'infringement' for the purposes of the Directive. There has to be an „act contrary to the Directives listed in the Annex as transposed in the internal legal order of the member states', and this act has to harm the 'collective interests of consumers'. Such 'collective interests' do not, however, include the culmination of the interests of individual consumers harmed by an infringement. An action for an injunction to protect the collective interests of consumers is therefore not the same as a 'class action', representing a group of consumers harmed by an infringement.

Article 2 requires that the member states designate a court or administrative authority which has the competence to deal with applications for an injunction. The powers of the court/authority concerned must include: (i) to issue an order to stop the continuation, or prohibit, an infringement; (ii) to initiate the publication of the decision in an appropriate format and/or of a corrective statement to deal with the continuing effects of the infringement; and (iii) to make an order for penalty payments for non-compliance, but only if the domestic legal system of the member state would already permit this.

Note

Only three relevant cases have been reported in the last 20 years, one came to the courts before the adoption of Directive 98/27/EC,[108] the others involved cross-border actions by the Office of Fair Trading (OFT) against a Belgian company (*OFT v Duchèsne*) and a Dutch company (*OFT v Best Sales BV*)[109] engaging in sweepstakes.

Cour d'Appel (Court of Appeal) Bruxelles, 8 December 2005[110] **8.48 (BE)**
Duchèsne v Office of Fair Trading

CROSS-BORDER ADVERTISING

Cross-border sweepstakes

Mutual recognition of standing in cross-border litigation.

Facts: The applicant, a Belgian company, operated in the sale-by-correspondence sector. Its main operating zone was France, and it also entered the UK and the Netherlands markets, in 2001 and 2002, respectively. In the UK, the applicant traded under the names TV Direct Distribution and Just 4 You. The applicant carried out no business involving Belgian consumers. The applicant approached its customers by sending out catalogues advertising households, decoration, leisure and DIY articles. These articles were generally promoted by means of sweepstake. This was a promotional game organised in the form of a lottery, by means of which a preliminary prize draw took place, following which all the tickets were distributed with the catalogues and each recipient was asked to contact the game organiser by means of an application form to take part, to find out whether the ticket received was a winning one, prior to the closing date for the game. In the terms of the ruling challenged, the OFT was an independent administrative authority, or Statutory Corporation, under the terms of the Establishment Act of 1 April 2003, whose mission was to ensure correct trading practices on behalf of consumers. Following the distribution of advertising materials accompanied by a sweepstake to certain UK consumers, the defendant summoned the applicant before the Commercial Court of Brussels. The OFT asked the chairman of the Court to rule that sending a sales

[108] H-W Micklitz, 'Cross-Border Consumer Conflicts—A French–German Experience' (1993) *Journal of Consumer Policy* (Special Issue, European Consumer Policy After Maastricht) 411–34.

[109] Rb (Court of first instance) Breda, 9 July 2008 (2009) 2 TvC 66-71, note M Van Campen.

[110] (2005) *Jaarboek Handelspraktijken & Mededinging* 243, (2006) RDC/TBH 990, note P Wautelet.

catalogue accompanied by a sweepstake to UK consumers is a violation of the terms of Articles 23.1, 23.2, 23.4, 23.10, 23.14 and 94 (old numbering) of the 14 July 1991 Trade Practices Act and of the terms of the English law of 23 May 1988 on consumer protection, entitled Control of Misleading Advertising Regulations 1988—Statutory Instrument No 915.

Judgment: 7. By a judgment of 6 December 2004, the first judge has:

—held that (the applicant) distributes advertising messages in the UK addressed to individually named consumers, in which (the applicant) informs them that they have won a significant cash prize, and encourages them to claim this prize by returning a claim slip with an order for a product contained in the catalogue which accompanies the advertising message...

—held that the consumer who receives this message is encouraged to place an order with a view to claiming the prize.

—held that the mailing operations in question misled the consumer, or could do so, by leading him to believe that he has won a prize in a draw which has already taken place, and that the sum won is definitely and immediately available, where in fact this prize has not been allocated.

—held that the advertising message in question damages or could damage the collective interests of consumers in the UK.

—stated in law that the practices in question are violations of the English Control of Misleading Advertising Regulations.

—ordered the cessation of the action and the advertising materials in which the action is contained, on pain of a fine of twenty five thousand Euros per violation confirmed as from the date of notification of this ruling. ...

We confirm the judgement challenged with the sole amendment that the fine be reduced to €2.500 per brochure sent out in violation of the cessation order and the total amount of the fine cannot exceed €1.000.000.

H-W Micklitz, Transborder Law Enforcement: Does it Exist?[111] **8.49 (EU)**

On 4 March, Duchesne was summoned to appear before the President of the Commercial Court of Brussels hearing an urgent application. In his judgment of 6 December 2004, the first judge held that the sales promotion measure violated the Control of Misleading Advertising Regulations 1988 and ordered cessation of the acts thus recorded and the advertising material in which those were contained, on pain of a fine of €25.000 per contravention ascertained as from the date when the judgment was reported. On 9 December 2005, the Chamber of the Appeal Court of Brussels upheld the first decision. There are a number of points to be underlined:

(1) The plaintiff is a public agency and not a private organisation. Distant Shopping demonstrated that substantial resources are needed to prepare and to execute a transborder injunctive action. Consumer organisations are generally short of money. Distant Shopping[112] was made possible through additional funds granted from the European Commission. The OFT acted on its own. However, it seems even a public agency is unable systematically to pursue transborder violations of consumer law due to scarce resources.

[111] U Bernitz and S Weatherill (eds), *The Regulation of Unfair Commercial Practices under Directive 2005/29. New Rules and New Techniques* (Oxford, Hart Publishing, 2006) 235–54.

[112] Micklitz, above n 108.

(2) The OFT filed an action in Belgium and not in the UK, so it circumvented the problems faced by the German and French consumer organisations in Distant Shopping which both intended to protect French consumers from their national home base. The French consumers' organisations wanted to protect French consumers against German-based unfair commercial practices. They did not consider filling an action for an injunction in Germany. German consumer organisations were trying to strike down unfair commercial practices at their origin, ie in Germany. They argued in favour of a source responsibility (Quelleverantwortung) of the Member State in which the company was based and from which the commercial practices originated.

(3) The Belgian courts did not call into question the standing of the OFT to sue a Belgian company. This might underline the need mutually to recognise standing as provided for under Directive 98/27/EC. However, one might wonder whether the Belgian courts would have confirmed the standing of a registered national consumer organisation in the same way or whether they would have challenged the competence of the consumers' organisation to deal with transborder unfair commercial practices under Article 4(1)(3) of Directive 98/27/EC.

(4) The Belgian courts regarded commercial practices as extra-contractual obligations, which is in line with the Rome II project. According to Article 5, claims arising from unfair competition or other harmful marketing practices are assessed under the law of the country in which the unfair competition or other practice affects competitive relations or the collective interests of consumers. Rome II will therefore codify the so called 'market rule' (Marktwirkungsregel), eg applicability of the law of the market where the competitive relations or collective consumer interests are affected. Article 5 is very much in line with the general policy of Rome II as laid down in Article 3, which acknowledges the lex loci delicti commissi, ie where the damage arises or is likely to arise (usually the place of residence of the victim). Hitherto the Belgian courts would have had to apply UK law. Surprisingly the Court of Appeal decided to apply Belgian law instead. Contrary to the first instance, it did not consider the country where the effects of the advertising are felt as the one which defined the applicable law, but instead chose the country of origin where the advertising measures come from. The judgment might be read as a late confirmation of efforts in legal doctrine to stop unfair commercial practices at their point of origin.

(5) The Belgian courts did not differentiate between the average British and the average Belgian consumer. Duchesne argued British consumers are more robust than continental consumers, which may not be factually correct but which is very much in line with predominant cultural prejudices. At the same time the Court of Appeal rejected the OFT´s argument that the advertising measures were particularly dangerous to vulnerable consumers as the OFT did not manage to provide evidence of that. It is common ground that the distinction between the average and the vulnerable consumer as inserted in the Directive 2005/29/EC, though politically sound, will produce uncertainties on the concrete yardstick to apply. In the case at issue, the Belgian courts carefully analysed the sales promotion material and came to the conclusion that the general presentation was designed to convince consumers that they had definitely won the amount of the cheque mentioned. That means it went beyond mere attraction.

(6) The amount of the periodic penalty payment to be imposed on Duchesne remains a subject of controversy. The first instance court foresaw rather draconic measures where the company went on to send out folders in contravention of the cessation order. A penalty of €25.000 per folder sent out would be due. The Court of Appeal found such a penalty excessive and reduced it to €2.500 per folder sent out, thereby limiting the

penalty to a maximum of €1.000.000 so as to avoid the possibility of its producing undesired effects, that is to say 'imperilling' Duchesne. EC law is not of much help here as it requires only sanctions that are 'effective, proportionate and deterrent'. Member States retain discretion in fixing the fine. EC law may step in only if the fine remains symbolic, which does not seem to be the case at issue.

(7) In practical terms, it is very important who bears the preparatory costs of the litigation. The OFT spent substantial resources in the investigation, ie to find out who the correct plaintiff was and to translate the necessary documents. It wanted to be reimbursed of the translation costs by the defendant. However, the Court of Appeal rejected the OFTs claim for reimbursement of the translation costs and those incurred in obtaining a sworn translation of some of its documents without further discussion. The court simply stated that translation costs were 'not expenses essential to the proceedings'. Whether or not the Court of Appeal correctly applied Belgian law might be a subject for discussion. However, the reasoning demonstrates that the judges are far away from reality. Translation of the necessary documents is an indispensable prerequisite in transborder enforcement. The denial of reimbursement is indeed 'deterrent', but rather to the qualified entities which intend to pursue transborder violations of consumer law than to the wrongdoers!'

Notes

(1) The aim of Directive 98/27/EC (now Directive 2009/22/EC) is to provide for the principle of mutual recognition of authorities authorised to sue in cross-border disputes. Therefore, the Member States have designated their national authorities authorised, under the Directive, to file actions. However, the Directive does not specifically provide for the right to sue; it does not prescribe any specified requirements for the right to sue, and it does not stipulate the applicable rules through the governing law. Therefore, the solution must be sought in the national laws. The starting point is the legal nature of the *actio negatoria* (action to compel someone to refrain from doing something), which, based on Community law, may be qualified as delictual or quasi-delictual.[113] The governing law shall be set in compliance with the Rome II Regulation (see section VII.B.6.c).

(2) It needs to be reiterated that the *locus standi* of the OFT was never the subject of controversy. The Cour de Cassation rejected the appeal and confirmed the judgment of the Court of Appeal on the 2 November 2007. The only point of discussion was whether the advertising measures had to be judged on the basis of UK or Belgian law. The advertising company had opted for the application of the UK law which it believed to be more liberal than the respective Belgian rules. Throughout the litigation Duchèsne wanted the case to be referred to the ECJ in order to find out whether the seemingly stricter Belgian rules on sweepstakes are compatible with primary Community law. The Court de Cassation applied Belgian law, upheld the decision of the Court of Appeal and refuted the need to refer the litigation to Luxemburg.

[113] N Reich, 'Legal Protection of Individual and Collective Consumer Interests' in Micklitz, Reich and Rott, above n 10, 357.

VII.D ADMINISTRATIVE CO-OPERATION

The most important piece in the field of administrative co-operation is Regulation 2006/2004, which sets up an entirely new system of rules intended to foster and to strengthen co-operation in cross-border conflict resolution.

Regulation (EC) 2006/2004 on cooperation between national authorities responsible for the enforcement of consumer protection laws[114] **8.50 (EU)**

Article 1 Objective

This Regulation lays down the conditions under which the competent authorities in the Member States designated as responsible for the enforcement of the laws that protect consumers' interests shall cooperate with each other and with the Commission in order to ensure compliance with those laws and the smooth functioning of the internal market and in order to enhance the protection of consumers' economic interests.

Article 2 Scope

(1) The provisions on mutual assistance set out in Chapters II and III shall cover intra-Community infringements.

Article 4 Competent authorities

(1) Each Member State shall designate the competent authorities and a single liaison office responsible for the application of this Regulation.

(2) Each Member State may, if necessary in order to fulfil its obligations under this Regulation, designate other public authorities. They may also designate bodies having a legitimate interest in the cessation or prohibition of intra-Community infringements in accordance with Article 8(3).

(3) Each competent authority shall, without prejudice to paragraph 4 have the investigation and enforcement powers necessary for the application of this Regulation and shall exercise them in conformity with national law.

(4) The competent authorities may exercise the powers referred to in paragraph 3 in conformity with national law either:

(a) directly under their own authority or under the supervision of the judicial authorities; or

(b) by application to courts competent to grant the necessary decision, including, where appropriate, by appeal, if the application to grant the necessary decision is not successful.

(5) Insofar as competent authorities exercise their powers by application to the courts in accordance with paragraph 4(b), those courts shall be competent to grant the necessary decisions.

(6) The powers referred to in paragraph 3 shall only be exercised where there is a reasonable suspicion of an intra-Community infringement and shall include, at least, the right:

(a) to have access to any relevant document, in any form, related to the intra-Community infringement;

[114] [2004] OJ L 364, 1–11.

(b) to require the supply by any person of relevant information related to the intra-Community infringement;

(c) to carry out necessary on-site inspections;

(d) to request in writing that the seller or supplier concerned cease the intra-Community infringement;

(e) to obtain from the seller or supplier responsible for intra-Community infringements an undertaking to cease the intra-Community infringement; and, where appropriate, to publish the resulting undertaking;

(f) to require the cessation or prohibition of any intra-Community infringement and, where appropriate, to publish resulting decisions;

(g) to require the losing defendant to make payments into the public purse or to any beneficiary designated in or under national legislation, in the event of failure to comply with the decision.

(7) Member States shall ensure that competent authorities have adequate resources necessary for the application of this Regulation. The competent officials shall observe professional standards and be subject to appropriate internal procedures or rules of conduct that ensure, in particular, the protection of individuals with regard to the processing of personal data, procedural fairness and the proper observance of the confidentiality and professional secrecy provisions established in Article 13.

(8) Each competent authority shall make known to the general public the rights and responsibilities it has been granted under this Regulation and shall designate the competent officials.

G Betlem, Public and Private Transnational Enforcement of EU Consumer Law[115] **8.51 (EU)**

The most extensive piece of Community law legislation focusing on the enforcement of consumer law is the 2004 Cooperation Regulation. Its purpose is to create a network of national authorities responsible for enforcing EC consumer law and to oblige them to work together (mutual assistance) and with the Commission (Article I). The mischief the Regulation seeks to address is the lack of effectiveness of enforcement in cross-border case. Its solution is to require Member States to set up enforcement authorities—where they do not yet exist—and to lay down a minimum of common investigation and enforcement powers for these 'watchdogs' (preamble, recital 6). Like its sister act, the 1998 Consumer Injunctions Directive, the 2004 Regulation is solely concerned with cross-border situations. The Directive does not make this clear at all in its title, but the Regulation states it deals with cooperation between national authorities, which implies transnational scenarios. Although not mentioned as such, the Regulation must be seen as complementary to the Injunctions Directive in that it adds to the remedies made available under the Directive. The Regulation indicates it does not contain any rules of private international law, in particular on jurisdiction and choice of law, nor does it seek to impact on them. This is comparable to the Injunctions Directive and eg the Services Directive Proposal. It is clear that the Regulation on Consumer Protection Cooperation only deals with public/private enforcement in transnational scenarios; leaving it up to each Member State how to deal with purely internal situations. This is no surprise as the

[115] In W Van Boom and M Loos (eds), *Effective Enforcement of Consumer Law in Europe* (Groningen, Europa Law Publishing, 2007) 39–41, 44–45.

core provisions of the Regulation concern mutual assistance between the various national watchdogs and cooperation with the European Commission. There is no harmonisation of enforcement powers and administrative, civil and criminal causes of action as such, albeit that the watchdogs will have to posses certain powers in order to combat the transnational infringements. The Regulation also makes it clear that any other form of cooperation between authorities of the Member States remains fully available, notably judicial cooperation in both civil and criminal matters.

The obligation of the watchdogs to engage in mutual assistance, including the possible exercise of investigative and/or enforcement powers, applies when there are intra-Community infringements of the national laws transposing the EC consumer acquis communautaire and as listed in the Annex of the Regulation (cumulative requirements). This acquis includes fourteen Directives and one Regulation, including the 1985 Doorstep Selling Directive and the 2004 Air Passengers Regulation. As with any list-based system, it must be constantly updated as new legislation is adopted. The 16th instrument has already been added: the important Unfair Commercial Practices Directive. The scope of the Cooperation Regulation ratione materiae does not extend to national consumer law that goes beyond the norms of EC law as transposed into Member State law and must affect the collective interest of consumers. In borderline cases it may be difficult to assess which is which. These matters will not be further explored here as this paper focuses on transnational issues.

A final point as an introduction to the Consumer Protection Cooperation Regulation is that it is not the first consumer law act requiring the setting up of a network of national authorities who are to cooperate with the European Commission. A separate European enforcement network to remain in place even after the 2004 Regulation was created by the General Product Safety Directive. Its Article 10 speaks of 'administrative cooperation' rather than use the terms 'mutual assistance' as does the 2004 Regulation, although the forms of administrative assistance listed in this provision do amount to similar mechanisms as covered by the Consumer Protection Cooperation Regulation. But the provisions of the 2004 Regulation are far more detailed and more extensive powers for the watchdogs are required. Since this General Product Safety Directive is not one of those listed by the 2004 Regulation, the networks are apparently envisaged to carry on their own separate lives.

So far we spoke of watchdogs as the bodies empowered (and obliged) to take action against traders committing intra-Community infringements. But who precisely are potential enforcers under the Regulation? In addition to public authorities, Member States are empowered, not obliged, to designate non-governmental bodies as enforcers (Article 4). New for a number of Member States (Germany, the Netherlands) is that they must now designate a specific public body responsible for the enforcement of EC consumer law; in others they already exist such as the Office of Fair Trading (UK) or the Konsumentenverket (Sweden). But in addition to what was called the watchdog above, other public authorities may be designated as equally empowered (coming within the notion of 'watchdog' then) and, mutatis mutandis, 'bodies having a legitimate interest in the cessation or prohibition of intra-Community infringements in accordance with Article 8(3).

Normally these would be non-governmental consumer associations or the like, including business/trade organisations as well as self-regulatory bodies such as those supervising advertising standards or providers of alternative dispute resolution services. Importantly, where they are so designated by a Member State, the cited Article 8(3) of the Regulation contemplates that they may be entrusted with the task of taking action against a trader on behalf of a watchdog, who, in turn, was requested to act by a watchdog of another Member State; the Regulation talks about the requested and the applicant authorities. But they are a kind of second class enforcer as the Regulation makes the exercise of its powers, where the watchdog of, say State A, is the requested authority, subject to approval by the applicant authority of State B. This position of secondary rather than primary enforcer is not the view taken by the Dutch government. On the contrary, it only sees a role for the public enforcers (notably the newly to be established principal watchdog: the Consumentenautoriteit (Consumer Authority) as a subsidiary enforcer where self-regulation and civil actions are incapable of thwarting unfair practices by rogue traders.

What sort of powers are we talking about here? Article 4 spells out what enforcers must be able to do. Under the Regulation, all watchdogs, ie each 'competent authority', 'shall' have all necessary investigation and enforcement powers to apply its provisions properly (Article 4(3)). However, it is up to each Member State to decide whether the watchdog will be able to exercise these powers directly (possibly subject to judicial supervision) or indirectly by applying to competent courts to seek the necessary judicial orders (Article 4(4)). Parenthetically it may be noted that, strictly speaking, this provision could be read as requiring Member States to opt for an either/or system: the watchdogs exercise their powers either directly or via the courts. However, should it not be up to the watchdog to decide which powers to use once so empowered by the national law implementing the Regulation? The norm does not seem to be addressed to the legislature but to the watchdogs who must be given a choice under national law.

A non-exhaustive list of specific powers which the competent authorities (the watchdogs) must be able to exercise is given in Article 4(6) and includes seizure of documents, entry to premises and the right:

'(e) to obtain from the seller or supplier responsible for intra-Community infringements an undertaking to cease the intra-Community infringement; and, where appropriate, to publish the resulting undertaking:

(f) to require the cessation or prohibition of any intra-Community infringement and, where appropriate, to publish resulting decisions;

(g) to require the losing defendant to make payments into the public purse or to any beneficiary designated in or under national legislation, in the event of failure to comply with the decision'.

Note

The European Commission set up the co-operation network on the 27 November 2007.[116] So far little experience on the operation of the network is available. That is why it is hard to say whether Regulation 2006/2004 can be regarded as a success story. In researching the impact of EU law generally it is an endemic problem that much practice becomes buried within national and local judicial and administrative networks, and it is consequently very difficult to evaluate the true effects of an intervention by the EU.

What remains to be discussed is the relationship of this Regulation with Directive 2009/22/EC. Austria and Germany have integrated consumer and trader organisations into the co-operation network. Both governments have concluded agreements

[116] [2007] OJ C 286, 1.

with the respective organisations to take over the obligations under the regulation. One might wonder whether and to what extent Regulation 2006/2004 will lead to the establishment of even more and even stronger national enforcement authorities, thereby weakening the established set of consumer and trader organisations. The European Commission seems to favour consumer law enforcement via public agencies across Europe.

CONCISE BIBLIOGRAPHY

G Betlem, 'Public and Private Transnational Enforcement of EU Consumer Law' (2007) *European Business Law Review* 638.

P Cachia, 'Consumer Contracts in European Private Law: the Sphere of Operation of the Consumer Contract Rules in the Brussels I and Rome I Regulations' (2009) 34 *European Law Review* 476–90.

F Cafaggi and H-W Micklitz, *New Frontiers of Consumer Protection, the Interplay between Private and Public Enforcement* (Antwerp, Intersentia, 2009).

H-W Micklitz, N Reich and P Rott, *Understanding EU Consumer Law* (Antwerp/Oxford, Intersentia, 2009).

J Hill, *Cross-Border Consumer Contracts* (Oxford, Oxford University Press, 2008).

E Hondius, 'Towards a European Small Claims Procedure' in L Thévenoz and N Reich (eds), *Liber Amicorum Bernd Stauder* (Nomos-Schultess, 2006).

C Hodges, *The Reform of Class and Representative Actions in European Legal Systems* (Oxford, Hart, 2008).

A Maack, *Die Durchsetzung des AGB-rechtlichen Transparenzgebotes in internationalen Verbraucherverträgen* (Bremen, Schriftenreihe des Zentrums für Europäische Rechtspolitil and der Universität Bremen, 2001).

W Van Boom and M Loos, *Collective Enforcement of Consumer Law* (Groningen, Europa Law Publishing, 2007).

INDEX